Preface

On behalf of the PROFES Organizing Committee, we are proud to present the proceedings of the 20th International Conference on Product-Focused Software Process Improvement (PROFES 2019) held in Barcelona. The hosting institution was the Universitat Politècnica de Catalunya - BarcelonaTech in Spain. Since 1999, PROFES has established itself as one of the top recognized international process improvement conferences. In the spirit of the PROFES conference series, the main theme of PROFES 2019 was professional software process improvement (SPI) motivated by product, process, and service quality needs.

PROFES 2019 provided a premier forum for practitioners, researchers, and educators to present and discuss experiences, ideas, innovations, as well as concerns related to professional software development and process improvement driven by product and service quality needs. At PROFES 2019, solutions found in practice and relevant research results from academia were presented.

A committee of leading experts in software process improvement, software process modeling, and empirical software engineering selected the technical program. This year, 65 full research papers were submitted. At least three independent experts reviewed each paper. After thorough evaluation, 24 technical full papers were finally selected (37% acceptance rate). In addition, four out of nine industrial papers were selected to the program.

Furthermore, we received 30 short paper submissions. Each submission was reviewed by three members from the PROFES Program Committee. Based on the reviews and overall assessments, 11 short papers were accepted for presentation at the conference and for inclusion in the proceedings (37% acceptance ratio).

Continuing the open science policy in the previous PROFES 2017 and PROFES 2018, we encouraged and supported the authors of all accepted submissions to make their papers and research publicly available.

The topics addressed in this year's papers indicate that SPI is still a vibrant research discipline, but is also of high interest for industry. Several papers report on case studies or SPI-related experience gained in industry. The accepted papers of PROFES 2019 addressed, for example, the following topics:

- Continuous Delivery and Experimentation
- Software Testing
- Software Development
- Technical Debt
- Estimations
- Microservices

Since the beginning of the PROFES conference series, the purpose has been to highlight the most recent findings and novel results in the area of process improvement. We were proud to have Professor Neil Maiden (City, University of London) and

Jennifer Nerlich (Vogella), two renowned keynote speakers from research and industry, at the 2019 edition of PROFES.

Further relevant topics were added by the events co-located with PROFES 2019: the Third International Workshop on Managing Quality in Agile and Rapid Software Development Processes, the 4th International Workshop on Human Factors in Software Processes, and four tutorials addressing themes relevant to industry. The role of two European space co-chairs was added to the Organizing Committee. Responsibilities included providing an opportunity for researchers involved in ongoing and/or recently completed research projects (national, European, and international) related to the topics of the conference to present their projects and disseminate the objectives, deliverables, or outcome. Complementing the main scientific program, these events were included in the program to bring together researchers and representatives from industry by providing researchers with the opportunity to attend industry tutorials and providing practitioners with the latest research.

We are thankful for the opportunity to have served as chairs for this conference. The Program Committee members and reviewers provided excellent support in reviewing the papers. We are also grateful to all authors of submitted manuscripts, presenters, and session chairs for their time and effort in making PROFES 2019 a success. We would also like to thank the PROFES Steering Committee members for the guidance and support in the organization process. Furthermore, we thank everyone in the organization team as well as the student volunteers for making PROFES 2019 an experience that will live on in the participants' memory for years to come.

November 2019   Xavier Franch
                                                                  Tomi Männistö
                                                      Silverio Martínez-Fernández

Organization

Organizing Committee

General Chair

Xavier Franch — Technical University of Catalunya, Spain

Program Co-chairs

Tomi Männistö — University of Helsinki, Finland
Silverio Martínez-Fernández — Fraunhofer IESE, Germany

Short Paper Co-chairs

Oscar Dieste — Universidad Politécnica de Madrid, Spain
Pilar Rodríguez — University of Oulu, Finland

Industry Paper Chair

Danilo Caivano — SER & Practices, Italy

Workshop Co-chairs

Casper Lassenius — Aalto University, Finland
Andreas Vogelsang — Technical University of Berlin, Germany

Tutorial Co-chairs

Matthias Galster — University of Canterbury, New Zealand
Dietmar Pfahl — University of Tartu, Estonia

Journal-First Track Chair

Daniel Méndez Fernández — Blekinge Institute of Technology, Sweden, and fortiss GmbH, Germany

European Project Space Co-chairs

Alessandra Bagnato — Softeam, France
Davide Fucci — HITeC – University of Hamburg, Germany

Organization Chair

Carme Quer — Technical University of Catalunya, Spain

Proceedings Co-chairs

Claudia Ayala	Technical University of Catalunya, Spain
Jordi Marco	Technical University of Catalunya, Spain

Social Media and Publicity Co-chairs

Marc Oriol	Technical University of Catalunya, Spain
Anna Maria Vollmer	Fraunhofer IESE, Germany

Webmaster

Carles Farré	Technical University of Catalunya, Spain
Maria José Salamea	Technical University of Catalunya, Spain

Contact Person

Dolors Costal	Technical University of Catalunya, Spain

Local Organization Team

Katarzyna Biesialska	Technical University of Catalunya, Spain
Xavier Burgués	Technical University of Catalunya, Spain
Cristina Gómez	Technical University of Catalunya, Spain
Lidia López	Technical University of Catalunya, Spain
Martí Manzano	Technical University of Catalunya, Spain
Cristina Palomares	Technical University of Catalunya, Spain

Program Committee

Full Research and Industry Papers Program Committee

Silvia Abrahao	Universitat Politècnica de València, Spain
Sousuke Amasaki	Okayama Prefectural University, Japan
Maria Teresa Baldassarre	University of Bari, Italy
Vita Santa Barletta	University of Bari, Italy
Stefan Biffl	Vienna University of Technology, Austria
Andreas Birk	SWPM, Germany
Luigi Buglione	Engineering Technology Services (ETS), Italy
Gerardo Canfora	University of Sannio, Italy
Bruno da Silva	California Polytechnic State University, USA
Maya Daneva	University of Twente, The Netherlands
Michal Dolezel	University of Economics – Prague, Czech Republic
Christof Ebert	Vector, Germany
Fabian Fagerholm	University of Helsinki, Finland
Davide Falessi	California Polytechnic State University, USA
Masud Fazal-Baqaie	Fraunhofer, Germany
Michael Felderer	University of Innsbruck, Austria
Davide Fucci	HITeC – University of Hamburg, Germany
Lina Garcés	University of São Paulo, Brazil

Carmine Gravino	University of Salerno, Italy
Daniel Graziotin	University of Stuttgart, Germany
Noriko Hanakawa	Hannan University, Japan
Frank Houdek	Daimler AG, Germany
Andrea Janes	Free University of Bolzano, Italy
Petar Jovanovic	Universitat Politècnica De Catalunya – Barcelona Tech, Spain
Oliver Karras	Leibniz Universität Hannover, Germany
Petri Kettunen	University of Helsinki, Finland
Jil Klünder	Leibniz Universität Hannover, Germany
Jingyue Li	Norwegian University of Science and Technology, Norway
Lidia López	Universitat Politècnica De Catalunya – Barcelona Tech, Spain
Stephen MacDonell	University of Otago, New Zealand
Kenichi Matsumoto	Nara Institute of Science and Technology (NAIST), Japan
Maurizio Morisio	Politecnico di Torino, Italy
Maleknaz Nayebi	Ecole Polytechnique de Montréal, Canada
Risto Nevalainen	Spinet Oy, Finland
Edson Oliveira Jr.	State University of Maringá, Brazil
Paolo Panaroni	INTECS, Italy
Dietmar Pfahl	University of Tartu, Estonia
Rudolf Ramler	Software Competence Center Hagenberg, Austria
Daniel Rodriguez	The University of Alcalá, Spain
Simone Romano	University of Basilicata, Italy
Bruno Rossi	Masaryk University, Czech Republic
Gleison Santos	Federal University of the State of Rio de Janeiro, Brazil
Giuseppe Scanniello	University of Basilicata, Italy
Klaus Schmid	University of Hildesheim, Germany
Kari Smolander	Lappeenranta University of Technology, Finland
Martin Solari	Universidad ORT, Uruguay
Michael Stupperich	Daimler AG, Germany
Guilherme Travassos	Federal University of Rio de Janeiro, Brazil
Rini Van Solingen	Delft University of Technology, The Netherlands
Antonio Vetrò	Politecnico di Torino, Italy
Stefan Wagner	University of Stuttgart, Germany
Hironori Washizaki	Waseda University, Japan
Dietmar Winkler	Vienna University of Technology, Austria

Short Papers Program Committee

Muhammad Ovais Ahmad	Karlstad University, Sweden
Elina Annanperä	University of Oulu, Finland
Beatriz Bernárdez Jiménez	Universidad de Sevilla, Spain
Dante Carrizo	University of Atacama, Chile

Jessica Díaz	Universidad Politécnica de Madrid, Spain
Efraín R. Fonseca C.	Universidad de las Fuerzas Armadas ESPE, Ecuador
Davide Fucci	HITeC — University of Hamburg, Germany
Vahid Garousi	Queen's University Belfast, UK
Itir Karac	University of Oulu, Finland
Kati Kuusinen	Technical University of Denmark, Denmark
Lucy Ellen Lwakatare	Chalmers University of Technology, Sweden
Marc Oriol	Universitat Politècnica de Catalunya, Spain
Simone Romano	University of Basilicata, Italy
Norsaremah Salleh	International Islamic University Malaysia, Malaysia
Davide Taibi	Tampere University of Technology, Finland
Xiaofeng Wang	Free University of Bozen–Bolzano, Italy

Additional Reviewers

Corrado Aaron Visaggio
Monica Anastassiu
Justus Bogner
Eliezer Dutra
Jonas Fritzsch

Hong Guo
Nektaria Kaloudi
Vasileios Theodorou
Eugenio Zimeo

Intertwining Creative and Design Thinking Processes for Software Products (Keynote Abstract)

Neil Maiden

Cass Business School, City, University of London, 106 Bunhill Row, London EC1Y 8TZ, UK
N.A.M.Maiden@city.ac.uk

Abstract. Most software development processes still pay little attention to creativity and creative thinking, even though creative outcomes are pre-requisites for innovation. The recent interest in design thinking methods places shifts the focus to both software products and processes, but still does not address the creativity deficit of most design thinking practices. This keynote presentation and paper proposes an alternative and more effective framing of design thinking – as situated uses of creativity techniques and design artefacts, opportunistically, in agile development processes. It will introduce the role of design thinking as creative thinking for specific ends. It will summarize common characteristics of high-performance design behaviours – behaviours that are often impeded by software development methods. It will then demonstrate, with multiple examples, how coupling creativity techniques with playful artefacts for design thinking can lead to original design outcomes, often more productively, than with existing software development processes and models.

Keywords: Software development · Software product · Creativity

1 Creativity, Design Thinking and Innovation

Creativity and creative thinking have emerged as essential capabilities of most businesses. It has become a strategic, macro-economic activity, replacing the focus on information at the end of the last century. The World Economic Forum identified it to be a top-three need for economic growth in the next decade, alongside complex problem solving and critical thinking. It is identified as a precondition for business success – for example an IBM survey of 1500 CEOs identified creativity as the leading need and differentiator in their businesses [3]. It is also recognized as a critical pre-condition to effective innovation, generating new forms of creative capitalism based on knowledge and talent. And as digital technologies have become critical to the functioning of many organizations, creativity assumes a more important role in the specification and design of these technologies. Unfortunately, few methods and techniques for software product development explicitly support creative thinking by developers or stakeholders.

Outside of software product development, creative thinking is core to early design activities. For example, the United Kingdom's Design Council defines design as shaping ideas to become practical and attractive propositions for users or customers, and it can be described as creativity deployed to a specific end. Design is both a creative and user-centred approach to problem solving that cuts across different professions, from art and design to engineering and architecture. As such, creativity is needed to generate new ideas that design can shape to become the practical and attractive propositions for users or customers [2].

To deliver more creative design processes over the last decade, design thinking has become accepted practice for many forms of product and service. Design thinking is a human-centred innovation process that involves observation, collaboration, fast learning, the visualization of ideas and rapid prototyping, all of which run concurrent to business analysis activities [4]. It has been successfully used in projects to design new workplaces, consumer products and even brands.

However, one criticism that can be leveled at most design thinking processes is the lack of explicit use of creativity techniques from creative problem solving communities. Indeed, we observe an increasing disconnect between design thinking and creative problem solving, and believe that new techniques and tools that bridge the outputs of these communities are needed. More connected creative problem solving and design thinking methods and techniques can impact on the development of many forms of service and product, including software products.

This keynote proposes an alternative and more effective framing of design thinking – as situated uses of creativity techniques and design artefacts, opportunistically, in agile and other software development processes. It will introduce the role of design thinking as creative thinking for specific ends. It will summarize common characteristics of high-performance design behaviours – behaviours that are often impeded by software development methods. It will then demonstrate, with multiple examples, how coupling creativity techniques such as constraint removal [5] and creativity triggers [1] with playful artefacts for design thinking such as storyboards and desktop walkthroughs [6] can lead to original design outcomes, often more productively, than with existing software development processes.

References

1. Burnay, C., Horkoff, J., Maiden, N.: Stimulating stakeholders' imagination: new creativity triggers for eliciting novel requirements. In: Proceedings of IEEE International Requirements Engineering Conference, 12–16 September 2016, Beijing, China (2016)
2. Design Council, Design for Innovation (2011). https://www.designcouncil.org.uk/sites/default/files/asset/document/DesignForInnovation_Dec2011.pdf
3. IBM, IBM Global CEO Study: Capitalizing on Complexity (2010)
4. Lockwood, T.: Design Thinking, Allworth Press, New York (2010)
5. Maiden, N.A.M., Robertson, S.: Integrated creativity into requirements processes: experiences with an air traffic management system. In: Proceedings of 13th IEEE International Conference on Requirements Engineering, 105–114. IEEE Computer Society Press (2015)
6. Stickdorn, M., Schneider, J.: This is Service Design Thinking, BIS Publishers (2010)

Contents

Technical Debt

Estimations

Continuous Delivery

Agile

Project Management

Microservices

Continuous Experimentation

European Project Space

**3rd International Workshop on Managing Quality in Agile
and Rapid Software Development Processes (QuASD)**

4th International Workshop on Human Factors in Software Development Processes (HuFo)

Short Tutorials

Testing

An Empirical Assessment on Affective Reactions of Novice Developers When Applying Test-Driven Development

Simone Romano[1]([✉])[iD], Davide Fucci[2][iD], Maria Teresa Baldassarre[1][iD], Danilo Caivano[1][iD], and Giuseppe Scanniello[3][iD]

[1] University of Bari, Bari, Italy
{simone.romano,mariateresa.baldassarre,danilo.caivano}@uniba.it
[2] University of Hamburg, Hamburg, Germany
fucci@informatik.uni-hamburg.de
[3] University of Basilicata, Potenza, Italy
giuseppe.scanniello@unibas.it

Abstract. We study whether and in which phase Test-Driven Development (TDD) influences affective states of novice developers in terms of pleasure, arousal, dominance, and liking. We performed a controlled experiment with 29 novice developers. Developers in the treatment group performed a development task using TDD, whereas those in the control group used a non-TDD development approach. We compared the affective reactions to the development approaches, as well as to the implementation and testing phases, exploiting a lightweight, powerful, and widely used tool, *i.e.,* Self-Assessment Manikin. We observed that there is a difference between the two development approaches in terms of affective reactions. Therefore, it seems that affective reactions play an important role when applying TDD and their investigation could help researchers to better understand such a development approach.

Keywords: Test-Driven Development · TDD · Affective state · SAM

1 Introduction

Test-Driven Development (TDD) is an Agile software development approach in which a developer first writes a unit test to frame a chunk of functionality and then writes production code to make the test pass and applies refactorings to improve the internal quality of production and test code. This iterative process happens in fast-paced iterations of five to ten minutes [2].

TDD promises to increase external quality of software (*i.e.,* less functional bugs) and developers' productivity as: *(i)* writing test first forces developers to break a problem into simpler ones; *(ii)* the tests provide initial software quality assurance; and *(iii)* the regression test suite resulting after several iterations allows the developer to catch breaking changes early. The safety net provided by the regression tests boosts developers' confidence to the extent that TDD

© Springer Nature Switzerland AG 2019
X. Franch et al. (Eds.): PROFES 2019, LNCS 11915, pp. 3–19, 2019.
https://doi.org/10.1007/978-3-030-35333-9_1

is referred to as "The art of fearless programming" [22]. However, empirical research on the effects of TDD has so far shown inconclusive results [29,32,39]. Some research relates these results to the negative affective states that developers experience when initially exposed to TDD—*e.g.,* frustration due to the counter-intuitive behavior of designing test cases rather than immediately working on a solution [39].

Recent studies have leveraged affective states of developers to improve requirements engineering [8], software development [17], and software evolution [31]. Further, sentiment analysis has been applied to study the collaborative facets of software development [15]. These previous studies are based on the analysis of artifacts, mostly in textual form, produced during the software development life-cycle. Graziotin *et al.* [17] showed that unhappiness (*i.e.,* experiencing a sequence of negative affective states) impacts developers' productivity.

Although there is a growing interest in studying the affective states of developers and previous research hypothesizes that TDD elicits negative and positive affects (*e.g.,* counter-intuitive order and regression tests), no work has investigated whether and in which phase TDD influences affective states of (novice) developers. To fill this gap, we conducted a controlled experiment with 29 novice developers. Our experimental design allowed us to isolate the affective reactions to TDD from a baseline—*i.e.,* "Your Way development" (YW)—, in the short run, in terms of four dimensions: pleasure, arousal, dominance, and liking. To measure these dimensions, we relied on a lightweight yet powerful tool, namely Self-Assessment Manikin (SAM) [4].

The results of our study provide initial evidence that novice developers like TDD less than YW. Moreover, developers following TDD seem to like the implementation phase less than the others, and the testing phase seems to make developers using TDD less happy. To foster replications of our study so increasing the confidence in this initial evidence, we make our laboratory package public.[1]

Paper Structure. Sect. 2 discusses background and related work. Section 3 details the planning of our experiment. The results from the experiment are presented in Sect. 4 and discussed in Sect. 5. Possible limitations are reported in Sect. 6. Section 7 concludes the paper.

2   Background and Related Work

In this section, we report background information and work investigating developers' affective states. We also provide evidence on the effects of TDD.

2.1   Affective States and Studies About Developers' Affective States

In psychology, affective states are due to a set of stimuli and directed toward such stimuli. They can be characterized according to two theories, discrete and dimensional [37]. The former states that there is a fixed set that can be firmly

---

[1] https://doi.org/10.6084/m9.figshare.9778019.v1.

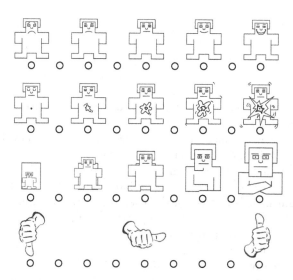

Fig. 1. From top down, the pleasure, arousal, dominance, and liking dimensions visualized by means of the extended version of SAM by Koelstra *et al.* with nine-point rating scales to self-assess each dimension [26].

distinguished (*e.g.,* resulting in joy, fear, or disgust). The latter characterizes affective states over three orthogonal dimensions: pleasure, arousal, and dominance. Pleasure varies from unpleasant (*e.g.,* sad/unhappy) to pleasant (*e.g.,* joyful/happy). Arousal varies from inactive (*e.g.,* calm/bored) to active (*e.g.,* stimulated/excited). Finally, dominance ranges from a helpless and weak feeling (*i.e., "without control"*) to an empowered one (*i.e., "in control"*) [26].

SAM is a non-verbal self-assessment method for a person's affective reaction based on the dimensional theory and it is used to measure pleasure, arousal, and dominance associated with a stimulus [4]. Each dimension is described graphically and evaluated thanks to a rating scale—usually a nine-point rating scale—placed below the graphical representation of that dimension (Fig. 1). For example, pleasure is visualized by means of figures ranging from an unhappy figure to a happy one. SAM was extended by Koelstra *et al.* [26], who added the liking dimension. This dimension ranges from dislike to like and is visualized through thumb-down, -middle, and -up symbols with the rating scale placed below these symbols (Fig. 1). SAM is used in Human-Computer Interaction (HCI) and affective computing studies [19,26,36]; lately Software Engineering (SE) work has used this method to study developers' affective states [16,18].

Graziotin *et al.* [18] showed that happier developers are more productive. They studied eight developers working on individual projects. Every ten minutes, they measured the developers' affective states using SAM and their productivity using a self-assessment questionnaire. The results of a mixed-effect model show that pleasure, arousal, and dominance explained 25% of the variance in productivity. A follow-up multi-method study with 317 professional developers [17] showed that both happiness and unhappiness are experienced in relation to increased and decreased productivity and quality of the development process. A survey of 49 developers provides further evidence that affective states influence the productivity of software developers [41]. In particular, positive ones enhance development productivity, whereas negative ones—particularly frustration—are associated with decreased productivity. In an interview with 45 professional developers, Ford and Parnin [11] showed that frustration can occur due to the difficulty of constructing a mental model of the code, learning new tools, dealing with too large task sizes, on boarding a new project, accurate effort estimation, dealing with teammates. Mueller and Fritz [28] investigated frustration—and its counterpart, progress or flow [9]—using biometrics. Physiological signals are suited to distinguish the affective states experienced by software developers. The authors studied 17 novice developers, equipped with three biometric sensors, performing software evolution. Their results show that different affective states are correlated with the perceived (*i.e.,* self-assessed) progress.

Developers' affective states can be identified in the textual artifact produced during software development (*e.g.,* commit messages). Murgia *et al.* [30] analyzed 17 open-source projects to investigate whether and to what extent issue reports contain information that can be related to specific affective conditions. They showed that developers express mostly positive affects. Mantyla *et al.* [27] investigated the association between developers' affective states and productivity by applying sentiment analysis to 700,000 Jira issue reports. The authors showed that different pleasure is associated with different types of issues (*e.g.,* enhancement vs. bug fix request).

Only a few studies assessed affective reactions of developers while performing a task in a controlled fashion. An example is the work of Khan *et al.* [25]. The authors linked the effect of mood on debugging in two experiments. In the first, they elicited specific affective states of 72 developers, who then performed debugging. The results show a significant difference in performance between the developers exposed to a stimulus eliciting low arousal and the ones exposed to a stimulus eliciting high arousal. In the second, 19 developers worked on a debugging task for 16 min, then performed physical exercise, and finally continued working on that task. After the physical exercise, the authors reported increased arousal and pleasure correlated with better task performance.

2.2 Effects of TDD

The effects of TDD on a number of outcomes (*e.g.,* developers' productivity) is the subject of several empirical studies, summarized in Systematic Reviews (SR) and Meta-Analysis (MA). Turhan *et al.*'s SR [39] includes 32 primary studies (*e.g.,* case studies) investigating TDD in different settings (*e.g.,* industry and academia). The results are inconsistent, as they show a positive effect on quality, but not regarding productivity. Rafique and Misic [32] conducted an MA of 25 controlled experiments published between 2000 and 2011. Overall, the results are mixed. However, TDD seems to improve quality to the cost of a loss in productivity when considering subjects from academia. Finally, Munir *et al.*'s

SR [29] took into account 41 primary studies. The results show, for both student and professional developers, that TDD increases quality but not productivity.

3 Experiment Planning

To conduct our experiment, we followed Wohlin *et al.*'s guidelines [40]. We report the planning of this experiment based on Jedlitschka *et al.*'s template [21].

3.1 Goals

We studied the following Research Question (RQ):

RQ1. Is there a difference in the affective reactions of novice developers to a development approach (*i.e.*, TDD vs. a non-TDD one)?

With RQ1, we aimed to understand the affective reactions of novice developers due to the use of TDD in terms of pleasure, arousal, dominance, and liking. A positive (or negative) effect of TDD with respect to these four dimensions might imply that TDD developers are more (or less) effective when performing development tasks. We deepened our investigation by focusing on two central phases of the process underlying TDD: testing and implementation.[2] To this end, we considered the effect of TDD in terms of the four above-mentioned dimensions when testing and implementing code. Accordingly, we devised two further RQs:

RQ2. Is there a difference in the affective reactions of novice developers to the implementation phase when comparing TDD to a non-TDD development approach?

RQ3. Is there a difference in the affective reactions of novice developers to the testing phase when comparing TDD to a non-TDD development approach?

3.2 Experimental Units

The participants of the experiment were 29 final-year undergraduate students in Computer Science (CS) at the University of Basilicata. In particular, the students were enrolled in the SE course, which represents the context of our experiment. To encourage participation in the study, we informed the students that, regardless of the outcomes they would achieve in the experiment, they would be rewarded with two bonus points on the course final mark. We can consider final-year undergraduates in CS as a proxy of novice software developers [20,38].

Before the SE course, the participants had passed exams related to Procedural and Object Oriented Programming. During these courses, all students had acquired programming experience in C and Java. According to the curricula,

---

[2] Although refactoring is part of the process underlying TDD, we did not consider this phase because refactoring could not be performed when following a non-TDD development approach (and some participants who used a non-TDD approach did not refactor their code).

the students did not have a notion of TDD. We also verified that they had never practiced TDD. We trained the participants with a series of both frontal and laboratory lessons after which they performed three homework assignments (*i.e.,* development tasks) in preparation for the experiment. The lessons covered unit testing, JUnit, Test-Last (TL) development,[3] Incremental Test-Last (ITL) development,[4] and TDD. Initially, 47 students accepted to take part in the experiment; 29 completed the training. This sample is homogeneous in terms of skills because of the training process the students underwent (Sect. 3.7) and their similar academic background.

3.3   Experimental Material

The experimental objects consisted of the specifications of two development tasks to be implemented in the Java programming language: Bowling Score Keeper (BSK)—an API for calculating the score of a bowling game including bonus— and Mars Rover API (MRA)—an API for controlling the movements of a rover on a 2D planet on which obstacles are present. Regardless of the experimental object, we provided the students with the following experimental material: *(i)* a brief description of the program (*i.e.,* a problem statement); *(ii)* a series of features to implement reported as a set of user stories; *(iii)* a template project for the Eclipse IDE containing stubs of the expected API signatures and an example JUnit test class; and *(iv)* an acceptance test suite, developed by the authors, to simulate customers' acceptance of the user stories. The acceptance tests were executed using the Concordion framework.[5] We opted for BSK and MRA as experimental objects because they are often adopted to learn/practice TDD and were used in past empirical studies on TDD [10,13,14,38].

   To gather the affective reactions, we relied on the extended version of SAM by Koelstra *et al.* [26], which includes four dimensions: pleasure, arousal, dominance, and liking. Each dimension was thus measured through a nine-point rating scale.

3.4   Tasks

We asked the participants to carry out one development task each, in which they tackled either BSK or MRA. That is, we asked them to implement the user stories associated with these programs—MRA had 11 user stories, while BSK had 13 user stories—by following TDD or an alternative approach. The participants were asked to take into account one user story at a time (starting from the first one). The participant could implement the next user story only when the current one passed its related acceptance test suite. The total time allotted to accomplish the task was three hours. Right after the development task, we asked the participants to self-assess their affective reactions—in terms

---

[3] In TL development, a developer first implements a feature entirely and then tests it.

[4] In ITL development, a developer alternates implementing a code increment with testing that increment until the entire feature is implemented.

[5] https://concordion.org/.

of pleasure, arousal, dominance, and liking—of the development approach using SAM. Similarly, they self-assessed their affective reactions to the testing and implementation phases.

Table 1. Summary of the dependent variables.

Name	Values	Description
APP_{PLS}	1–9	Affective reaction to the development approach in terms of pleasure
APP_{ARS}	1–9	Affective reaction to the development approach in terms of arousal
APP_{DOM}	1–9	Affective reaction to the development approach in terms of dominance
APP_{LIK}	1–9	Affective reaction to the development approach in terms of liking
IMP_{PLS}	1–9	Affective reaction to the implementation phase in terms of pleasure
IMP_{ARS}	1–9	Affective reaction to the implementation phase in terms of arousal
IMP_{DOM}	1–9	Affective reaction to the implementation phase in terms of dominance
IMP_{LIK}	1–9	Affective reaction to the implementation phase in terms of liking
TES_{PLS}	1–9	Affective reaction to the testing phase in terms of pleasure
TES_{ARS}	1–9	Affective reaction to the testing phase in terms of arousal
TES_{DOM}	1–9	Affective reaction to the testing phase in terms of dominance
TES_{LIK}	1–9	Affective reaction to the testing phase in terms of liking

3.5 Hypotheses, Parameters, and Variables

We manipulated two independent variables: *Approach* and *Object*. The former represents the development approach the participants had to follow to carry out the development task, namely TDD or the approach they preferred (*i.e.,* YW). Therefore, Approach is a categorical variable with two values, TDD and YW. The Object variable indicates the experimental object the participants dealt with (*i.e.,* BSK or MRA) in the experiment. Similarly to Approach, Object is a categorical variable. It can assume the following two values: BSK and MRA.

Table 2. Number of participants assigned to each studied approach and object.

		Approach	
		TDD	YW
Object	MRA	7	7
	BSK	8	7

To measure PLeaSure (PLS), ARouSal (ARS), DOMinance (DOM), and LIKing (LIK) associated with the development APProach (APP), we used the following ordinal dependent variables: APP_{PLS}, APP_{ARS}, APP_{DOM}, and APP_{LIK}. Similarly, we quantified pleasure, arousal, dominance, and liking for the IMPlementation (IMP) and TESting (TES) phases by means of the following ordinal dependent variables: IMP_{PLS}, IMP_{ARS}, IMP_{DOM}, IMP_{LIK}, TES_{PLS}, TES_{ARS}, TES_{DOM}, and TES_{LIK}. In Table 1, we summarize the dependent variables of our experiment.

We formulated and tested the following null hypotheses:

$H0_X$. There is no difference between TDD and YW with respect to the dependent variable $X \in \{APP_{PLS}, APP_{ARS}, APP_{DOM}, APP_{LIK}, IMP_{PLS}, IMP_{ARS}, IMP_{DOM}, IMP_{LIK}, TES_{PLS}, TES_{ARS}, TES_{DOM}, TES_{LIK}\}$.

3.6 Experiment Design

The design of our experiment was 2×2 factorial—a type of between-subjects design [40]. In particular, each participant used only one development approach (*i.e.,* either TDD or YW). Within each development approach, each participant tackled only one experimental object—*i.e.,* either BSK or MRA. Those who used TDD (either tackling BSK or MRA) form the treatment group, while those who experimented YW (either tackling BSK or MRA) form the control group.

In Table 2, we show the number of participants assigned to each of four groups constituted by the combination of development approaches and experimental objects. The assignment was randomly performed. By looking at Table 2, we can notice that the number of participants distributed among development approaches, experimental objects, and their combination was almost uniform.

3.7 Procedure

The experimental procedure included the following steps.

1. We gathered the availability of the students to participate in the experiment through a questionnaire (also used to gather demographic information).
2. The participants attended the frontal lessons on unit testing, JUnit, TL development, and ITL development. They also took part in a laboratory session (of two hours) on unit testing with JUnit.
3. We (randomly) split the participants into two groups: TDD and YW. The participants in the YW and TDD groups were 14 and 15, respectively (Table 2). Based on the group, the participants underwent two different training:

- The students in the TDD group attended a face-to-face lesson on TDD and experimented this approach through two laboratory sessions (of two hours each) and three homework assignments. Handing in the assignments was mandatory to participate in the experimental session.
- The students in the YW group did not attend lessons on TDD nor used the approach in the laboratory sessions and assignments. However, the students in the YW group took part in two laboratory sessions (of two hours each) and performed the same homework assignments as the TDD group, but to practice TL and ITL. Similarly to the TDD group, homework assignments were mandatory.

4. The experimental session took place under controlled conditions in a research laboratory at the University of Basilicata. All the laboratory computers were equipped with the same hardware and software. Furthermore, they contained all the material necessary to complete the tasks, *i.e.,* the template project (of Eclipse) corresponding to the assigned experimental object. During the experimental session, the participates performed the development tasks and then they self-assessed their affective reactions (Sect. 3.4). We avoided interactions among participants by monitoring them during the task execution.

3.8 Analysis Procedure

We relied on diverging stacked bar plots to summarize the distributions of the values of the dependent variables. To test the null hypotheses (one for each dependent variable), we used a non-parametric version of ANOVA, namely ANOVA Type Statistic (ATS) [5]. We opted for ATS because this method is frequently used in the medical field and recommend, in place of ANOVA, in the HCI field to analyze data from rating scales in factorial designs like ours [23]. For each dependent variable X, we built ATS models as follows: $X \sim Approach + Object + Approach : Object$.

Approach and Object are the variables we manipulated, while Approach:Object represents their interaction. That is, this model allows determining if Approach, Object, and Approach:Object had statistically significant effects on a given dependent variable. To judge whether an effect is statistically significant, we used $\alpha = 0.05$ as the threshold value. It indicates 5% chance that a Type-I-error occurs (*i.e.,* rejecting the null hypothesis when it is true) [40]. If a p-value is less than α, it is deemed statistically significant. In case of a statistically significant effect of Approach, we quantified the magnitude of that effect through the Cliff's δ effect size. We opted for such a kind of effect size since it was originally developed for use with ordinal variables (like ours) [7]. The effect size is considered: *negligible* if $|\delta| < 0.147$, *small* if $0.147 \leq |\delta| < 0.33$, *medium* if $0.33 \leq |\delta| < 0.474$, or *large* if $|\delta| \geq 0.474$ [33].

Further Analysis. To better contextualize our experiment, we also assessed participants' performance. We counted the number of user stories each participant implemented in the allotted time. We normalized them in the [0, 1] interval to obtain a fair comparison between participants tackling tasks with a different number of user stories. We named this additional dependent variable STR. The strategy we followed to quantify participants' performance is *time-fixed*—the number of successful steps within a fixed time span defines performance [3]. The higher the value of STR, the better the developer's performance.

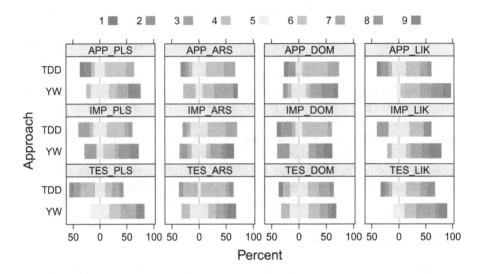

Fig. 2. Diverging stacked bar plots for the dependent variables. (Color figure online)

4   Results

In Fig. 2, we show the diverging stacked bar plots summarizing the distributions of the values of the twelve dependent variables. The x-axes report the frequencies of the dependent variable values, which range from one—the most negative value—to nine—the most positive value. Therefore, the neutral value is five. The diverging stacked bar plots display positive values in shades of blue, while those negative in shades of red. The neutral value is displayed in grey. The y-axes allow grouping the values based on the Approach variable. As for the results from ATS, they are summarized in Table 3.

RQ1—Affective Reactions to Development Approach. By looking at Fig. 2, there is no noticeable difference between TDD and YW regarding pleasure (APP$_{\text{PLS}}$), arousal (APP$_{\text{ARS}}$), and dominance (APP$_{\text{DOM}}$). As for liking (APP$_{\text{LIK}}$), Fig. 2 suggests that participants in the YW group liked this approach more, compared to the participants in the TDD group.

The ATS results (Table 3) indicate that there is no statistically significant difference between TDD and YW regarding pleasure, arousal, and dominance. Accordingly, we cannot reject the corresponding null hypotheses. The test results allow us to reject $H0_{\text{APP}_{\text{LIK}}}$, showing an effect of the development approach on

Table 3. Results from ATS—F-statistic (in parentheses) and p-values (in bold those less than $\alpha = 0.05$) for the dimensions associated with the development approach, and implementation and testing phases.

Dep. Var.	Indep. Var.		
	Approach	Object	Approach:Object
APP_{PLS}	0.1615 (2.1094)	0.7721 (0.0861)	0.8998 (0.0162)
APP_{ARS}	0.2774 (1.2378)	0.7794 (0.0803)	0.1816 (1.8985)
APP_{DOM}	0.2796 (1.2313)	0.8569 (0.0333)	0.4296 (0.6487)
APP_{LIK}	**0.0024** (11.4580)	0.1650 (2.0467)	0.6368 (0.2285)
IMP_{PLS}	0.2008 (1.7454)	0.6663 (0.1914)	0.9793 (0.0007)
IMP_{ARS}	0.6799 (0.1755)	0.6881 (0.1661)	0.5752 (0.3249)
IMP_{DOM}	0.3449 (0.9330)	0.5614 (0.3480)	0.4672 (0.5481)
IMP_{LIK}	**0.0396** (4.7562)	0.1862 (1.8557)	0.2703 (1.2752)
TES_{PLS}	**0.0178** (6.5782)	0.6500 (0.2118)	0.7652 (0.0915)
TES_{ARS}	0.4147 (0.6887)	0.4765 (0.5230)	0.3406 (0.9451)
TES_{DOM}	0.6341 (0.2324)	0.2564 (1.3508)	0.4738 (0.5293)
TES_{LIK}	0.0504 (4.2785)	0.1194 (2.6224)	0.0547 (4.1112)

APP_{LIK}. The frequencies displayed in Fig. 2 suggest that such an effect is in favor of YW. The effect size is *large* ($\delta = 0.6048$, CI95% $= [0.2018, 0.8326]$).

Based on these results, we can answer RQ1 as follows: *developers using TDD seem to like their development approach less than those using a non-TDD one.*

RQ2—Affective Reactions to Implementation Phase. Figure 2 does not highlight remarkable difference between TDD and YW for pleasure (IMP_{PLS}), arousal (IMP_{ARS}), and dominance (IMP_{DOM}) during the implementation phase. However, for these dimensions, we can observe a slight trend in favor of YW since the percentages of very positive scores (*i.e.*, >6) appear to be higher for YW. With respect to the liking dimension (IMP_{LIK}), Fig. 2 suggests that participants who followed YW liked the implementation phase more, compared to the ones following TDD.

The results in Table 3 do not show a statistically significant difference between TDD and YW regarding pleasure, arousal, and dominance. Accordingly, we cannot reject the null hypotheses corresponding to these dimensions. We reject $H0_{IMP_{LIK}}$ as there is a statistically significant effect of Approach on IMP_{LIK}. The effect is in favor of YW as the plot in Fig. 2 suggest. The size of the effect of Approach is *medium* ($\delta = 0.4286$, CI95% $= [0.0209, 0.714]$).

According to the obtained results, we can answer RQ2 as follows: *developers using TDD seem to like the implementation phase less than those using a non-TDD development approach.*

RQ3—Affective Reactions to Testing Phase. Figure 2 suggests that there is a difference between TDD and YW in terms of pleasure (TES_{PLS}) during the testing phase. In particular, the participants using TDD reported negative scores with some frequency while those using YW never reported negative scores. When considering the arousal (TES_{ARS}) and dominance (TES_{DOM}) dimensions, we cannot observe any substantial difference between the two development approaches (Fig. 2). On the contrary, when considering liking (TES_{LIK}), we can notice a difference between TDD and YW in favor of the latter as YW tends to have more very positive scores (*i.e.*, > 6) than TDD.

The results of ATS (Table 3) reveal a statistically significant difference for the pleasure dimension, which allows us to reject the $H0_{TES_{PLS}}$ hypothesis. Such a difference is in favor of YW (Fig. 2). The effect size is *large* ($\delta = 0.5$, CI95% = [0.0796, 0.7694]). As for arousal and dominance, the effect of the development approach is not statistically significant during the testing phase. Regarding liking, the observed difference in TES_{LIK} between YW and TDD is not significant.

The obtained results allowed us to answer RQ3 as follows: *the testing phase seems to make developers using TDD less happy compared to those using a non-TDD development approach.*

Further Analysis Results. We also studied participants' performance by running ATS using STR as dependent variable.[6] The results indicates that Approach (p−value = 0.4765), Object (p−value = 0.2596) and their interaction (p-value = 0.0604) have no statistically significant effect on STR.

5   Discussion

The results from this experiment present initial evidence about aspects that are not investigated by the empirical TDD research. Current research on the effects of TDD shows inconclusive results [29,32,39], which can be attributed to the disliking the developers experience when using TDD, at least in the experiment time frame. We show initial evidence—supported by a large effect size—that, although participants' performance do not vary significantly (Sect. 4) due to the development approach, TDD seems to negatively impact affective reactions (*i.e.*, liking) of novice developers. Researchers need to be aware of the effect that disliking TDD can have (*e.g.*, low motivation to perform a task) when designing experiments involving such an approach.

We observed a difference between TDD and YW regarding the liking dimension for the implementation phase. The medium effect size shows initial evidence that implementing production code when performing TDD seems to be disliked by developers. Writing production code during TDD is trivial, at least in the first few iterations, and usually consists in taking shortcuts (*e.g.*, returning hard-coded values) to make the test pass. In our study, developers did not like such an activity. We conjecture this may be the case because they did not base their implementation on creative activities requiring challenging decisions. Conversely,

---

[6] STR does not meet the normality assumption (Shapiro-Wilk normality test p−value = 0.0114); this is why we run ATS (rather than ANOVA).

this should have resulted in different levels of arousal (*i.e.*, low for TDD) compared to non-TDD developers which we did not observe. Our explanation for the lack of such an observation lies in the task complexity which could have not been enough to elicit stronger arousal responses. The lack of significant effect due to the Object in our ATS models partially supports this explanation.

The liking dimension could change over time. Longitudinal studies could be necessary to validate such hypothesis and qualitative studies are required to pinpoint the reason for the observed results. In particular, the latter is necessary to explain the contrasting results presented in Romano *et al.* [34,35] in which a preference for the implementation phase among TDD developers emerged due to its rewarding feeling (*i.e.*, observing the JUnit red bar turn green).

The testing phase seems to make developers using TDD less happy than those using a non-TDD approach. Previous work [34,35] shows that TDD developers create a mental model of their solution to a task which is then translated into unit tests. Novice developers can be uncomfortable with such an activity due to the counter-intuitiveness of this step, but also due to the difficulty of writing tests of good granularity in the absence of the underlying production code [12,24]. Conversely, developers following the non-TDD approach can decide when and what to test without (mindlessly) following a process. Such freedom of action— *e.g.*, testing what is worth according to the developer's own understanding—can explain the higher pleasure score of non-TDD developers. Although this can be the case in the short term, longitudinal studies of TDD developers' affective states are also necessary in this case.

In general, our observations are supported by the results of a survey among professional developers, who are new to TDD [1]. They expressed concerns that worrying about writing unit tests and working in small increments distracts them from achieving their implementation goals while the extra effort necessary to perform TDD is perceived as waste [1]. Practitioners should take into account the results of this study when introducing TDD. The disliking attitude towards this development approach can (negatively) impact developers' performance in the long run (which we did not observe in the short term). Considering the results regarding the (negative) affective reactions to the implementation and testing phases, we suggest that, for greenfield development tasks, developers could skip TDD for few initial iterations and rely on their preferred development approach. This should not have an impact on performance but could reduce their negative affect which, in turn, could impact motivation and job satisfaction [17,39].

6   Threats to Validity

We discuss the threats that could affect the validity of the results according to the guidelines presented by Wohlin *et al.* [40]. We ranked these threats from the most to the least sensible for the goal of our study. In particular, being this the first investigation of developers' effective states when using TDD, we prioritize threats to internal validity. That is, we were more interested in studying that cause-effect relationships were correctly identified.

Internal Validity. A possible threat is the voluntary participation in the study (*i.e., selection threat*) by students particularly willing to be assessed. However, we limited this threat by embedding the experiment in the SE course and did not consider its outcome when grading. To deal with a *threat of diffusion or treatments imitations*, two authors of this paper monitored participants to prevent them from exchanging information during the experiment. Another threat might be *resentful demoralization*—participants assigned to a less desirable treatment might not perform as good as they normally would.

Construct Validity. Each dependent variable was measured by means of a single self-assessment at the end of the task. If there was a measurement bias, the results would be misleading (*i.e., mono-method bias threat*). Although the participants were not informed about the research goals of our experiment, they might guess them and change their behavior accordingly (*i.e., threat of hypotheses guessing*). To deal with an *evaluation apprehension threat*, we did not evaluate the participants in the experiment on the basis of their performances. We acknowledge the presence of a *threat of restricted generalizability across constructs*. That is, while influencing the affective states, the approach might affect other non-measured constructs (*e.g.,* cognitive load).

Conclusion Validity. To mitigate a *threat of random heterogeneity of participants*, our sample included students who followed the same course at the same university, underwent a similar training, and had similar background, skills and experience. A *threat of reliability of treatment implementation* might occur (*e.g.,* some participants might follow TDD more strictly than others so influencing their affective reactions). In several occasions, during the task execution, we reminded the participants to follow the treatment they were assigned to. Finally, our sample was limited because of the difficulty of recruiting participants available for all the period of the experiment including training.

External Validity. The participants in our study were undergraduate students. This could pose some threats to the generalizability of the results to the population of professional developers (*i.e., threat of interaction of selection and treatment*). However, the use of students has the advantage that they have homogeneous background and are particularly suitable to obtain preliminary evidence from empirical studies [6]. Therefore, the use of students could be considered appropriate, as suggested in the literature [6,20]. The used experimental objects might pose a *threat of interaction of setting and treatment*. BSK and MRA can be completed in a single exercise session of three hours [13,14] so allowing a better control over the participants. This was our preferred trade-off due to the theory-testing nature of our experiment.

7   Conclusions

We presented a controlled experiment to study whether and in what phase TDD influences affective states of novice developers in terms of pleasure, arousal, dominance, and liking. Developers in the treatment group implemented a task using TDD whereas the control group used a non-TDD development approach (*i.e.,* YW). We compared the affective reactions of developers with respect to the development approach they used, further focusing on the implementation and the testing phases. The results indicate a significant difference between the two development approaches in terms of affective reactions. Developers seem to like YW more than TDD. Moreover, developers like the implementation phase in YW more than that in TDD and the testing phase makes developers using TDD less happy. The findings from our study can help explain the inconclusive results of experiments focusing on the claimed effect of TDD. As future work, we plan to conduct replications, investigations focusing on settings closer to the real world, and longitudinal studies to measure affective states in the long run.

References

1. Aniche, M.F., Ferreira, T.M., Gerosa, M.A.: What concerns beginner test-driven development practitioners: a qualitative analysis of opinions in an agile conference. In: Proceedings of Brazilian Workshop on Agile Methods. Springer (2011)
2. Beck, K.: Test-Driven Development: By Example. Addison-Wesley (2003)
3. Bergersen, G.R., Sjøberg, D.I.K., Dybå, T.: Construction and validation of an instrument for measuring programming skill. IEEE Trans. Softw. Eng. **40**(12), 1163–1184 (2014)
4. Bradley, M.M., Lang, P.J.: Measuring emotion: the self-assessment manikin and the semantic differential. J. Behav. Ther. Exp. Psychiatry **25**(1), 49–59 (1994)
5. Brunner, E., Dette, H., Munk, A.: Box-type approximations in nonparametric factorial designs. J. Am. Stat. Assoc. **92**(440), 1494–1502 (1997)
6. Carver, J., Jaccheri, L., Morasca, S., Shull, F.: Issues in using students in empirical studies in software engineering education. In: Proceedings of International Symposium on Software Metrics, pp. 239–249. IEEE (2003)
7. Cliff, N.: Ordinal Methods for Behavioral Data Analysis. Psychology Press (1996)
8. Colomo-Palacios, R., Hernández-López, A., García-Crespo, Á., Soto-Acosta, P.: A study of emotions in requirements engineering. In: Lytras, M.D., Ordonez de Pablos, P., Ziderman, A., Roulstone, A., Maurer, H., Imber, J.B. (eds.) WSKS 2010. CCIS, vol. 112, pp. 1–7. Springer, Heidelberg (2010). https://doi.org/10.1007/978-3-642-16324-1_1
9. Csikszentmihalyi, M.: Finding Flow: The Psychology of Engagement with Everydaylife. Basic Books (1997)
10. Erdogmus, H., Morisio, M., Torchiano, M.: On the effectiveness of the test-first approach to programming. IEEE Trans. Softw. Eng. **31**(3), 226–237 (2005)
11. Ford, D., Parnin, C.: Exploring causes of frustration for software developers. In: Proceedings of International Workshop on Cooperative and Human Aspects of Software Engineering, pp. 115–116. IEEE (2015)
12. Fucci, D., Erdogmus, H., Turhan, B., Oivo, M., Juristo, N.: A dissection of the test-driven development process: does it really matter to test-first or to test-last? IEEE Trans. Softw. Eng. **43**(7), 597–614 (2017)
13. Fucci, D., et al.: A longitudinal cohort study on the retainment of test-driven development. In: Proceedings of International Symposium on Empirical Software Engineering and Measurement, pp. 18:1–18:10. ACM (2018)

14. Fucci, D., et al.: An external replication on the effects of test-driven development using a multi-site blind analysis approach. In: Proceedings of International Symposium on Empirical Software Engineering and Measurement, pp. 3:1–3:10. ACM (2016)
15. Gachechiladze, D., Lanubile, F., Novielli, N., Serebrenik, A.: Anger and its direction in collaborative software development. In: Proceedings of International Conference on Software Engineering: New Ideas and Emerging Technologies Results Track, pp. 11–14. IEEE (2017)
16. Girardi, D., Lanubile, F., Novielli, N., Fucci, D.: Sensing developers' emotions: the design of a replicated experiment. In: Proceedings of International Workshop on Emotion Awareness in Software Engineering, pp. 51–54. IEEE (2018)
17. Graziotin, D., Fagerholm, F., Wang, X., Abrahamsson, P.: What happens when software developers are (un)happy. J. Syst. Softw. **140**, 32–47 (2018)
18. Graziotin, D., Wang, X., Abrahamsson, P.: Are happy developers more productive? In: Heidrich, J., Oivo, M., Jedlitschka, A., Baldassarre, M.T. (eds.) PROFES 2013. LNCS, vol. 7983, pp. 50–64. Springer, Heidelberg (2013). https://doi.org/10.1007/978-3-642-39259-7_7
19. Herbon, A., Peter, C., Markert, L., Van Der Meer, E., Voskamp, J.: Emotion studies in HCI-a new approach. In: Proceedings of International Conference on Human-Computer Interaction (2005)
20. Höst, M., Regnell, B., Wohlin, C.: Using students as subjects-a comparative study of students and professionals in lead-time impact assessment. Empirical Softw. Eng. **5**(3), 201–214 (2000)
21. Jedlitschka, A., Ciolkowski, M., Pfahl, D.: Guide to advanced empirical software engineering. In: Shull, F., Singer, J., Sjoberg, D.I.K. (eds.) Guide to Advanced Empirical Software Engineering, pp. 201–228. Springer, London (2008). https://doi.org/10.1007/978-1-84800-044-5_8
22. Jeffries, R., Melnik, G.: Guest editors' introduction: TDD-the art of fearless programming. IEEE Softw. **24**(3), 24–30 (2007)
23. Kaptein, M.C., Nass, C., Markopoulos, P.: Powerful and consistent analysis of likert-type ratingscales. In: Proceedings of International Conference on Human Factors in Computing Systems, pp. 2391–2394. ACM (2010)
24. Karac, I., Turhan, B.: What do we (really) know about test-driven development? IEEE Softw. **35**(4), 81–85 (2018)
25. Khan, I.A., Brinkman, W.P., Hierons, R.M.: Do moods affect programmers' debug performance? Cogn. Technol. Work **13**(4), 245–258 (2011)
26. Koelstra, S., et al.: Deap: a database for emotion analysis using physiological signals. IEEE Trans. Affect. Comput. **3**(1), 18–31 (2012)
27. Mäntylä, M., Adams, B., Destefanis, G., Graziotin, D., Ortu, M.: Mining valence, arousal, and dominance: possibilities for detecting burnout and productivity? In: Proceedings of International Conference on Mining Software Repositories, pp. 247–258. ACM (2016)
28. Müller, S.C., Fritz, T.: Stuck and frustrated or in flow and happy: sensing developers' emotions and progress. In: International Conference on Software Engineering, vol. 1, pp. 688–699. IEEE (2015)
29. Munir, H., Moayyed, M., Petersen, K.: Considering rigor and relevance when evaluating test driven development: a systematic review. Inf. Softw. Technol. **56**(4), 375–394 (2014)
30. Murgia, A., Tourani, P., Adams, B., Ortu, M.: Do developers feel emotions? an exploratory analysis of emotions in software artifacts. In: Proceedings of Working Conference on Mining Software Repositories, pp. 262–271. ACM (2014)

31. Ortu, M., et al.: The emotional side of software developers in JIRA. In: Proceedings of International Conference on Mining Software Repositories, pp. 480–483. ACM (2016)
32. Rafique, Y., Mišić, V.B.: The effects of test-driven development on external quality and productivity: a meta-analysis. IEEE Trans. Softw. Eng. **39**(6), 835–856 (2013)
33. Romano, J., Kromrey, J., Coraggio, J., Skowronek, J.: Appropriate statistics for ordinal level data: should we really be using t-test and Cohen'sd for evaluating group differences on the NSSE and other surveys? In: Annual Meeting of the Florida Association of Institutional Research, pp. 1–3 (2006)
34. Romano, S., Fucci, D., Scanniello, G., Turhan, B., Juristo, N.: Results from an ethnographically-informed study in the context of test driven development. In: Proceedings of the International Conference on Evaluation and Assessment in Software Engineering, pp. 10:1–10:10. ACM (2016)
35. Romano, S., Fucci, D., Scanniello, G., Turhan, B., Juristo, N.: Findings from a multi-method study on test-driven development. Inf. Softw. Technol. **89**, 64–77 (2017)
36. Rudmann, D.S., McConkie, G.W., Zheng, X.S.: Eyetracking in cognitive state detection for HCI. In: Proceedings of international conference on Multimodal interfaces, pp. 159–163. ACM (2003)
37. Russell, J.A.: Core affect and the psychological construction of emotion. Psychol. Rev. **110**(1), 145–172 (2003)
38. Salman, I., Misirli, A.T., Juristo, N.: Are students representatives of professionals in software engineering experiments? In: International Conference on Software Engineering, vol. 1, pp. 666–676. IEEE (2015)
39. Turhan, B., Layman, L., Diep, M., Erdogmus, H., Shull, F.: How effective is test-driven development. In: Making Software: What Really Works, and Why We Believe It, pp. 207–217. O'Reilly Media (2010)
40. Wohlin, C., Runeson, P., Hst, M., Ohlsson, M.C., Regnell, B., Wessln, A.: Experimentation in Software Engineering. Springer, New York (2012). https://doi.org/10.1007/978-1-4615-4625-2
41. Wrobel, M.R.: Emotions in the software development process. In: Proceedings of International Conference on Human System Interactions, pp. 518–523. IEEE (2013)

Applying Surveys and Interviews in Software Test Tool Evaluation

Päivi Raulamo-Jurvanen[1]([⊠]), Simo Hosio[2], and Mika V. Mäntylä[1]

[1] ITEE, M3S, University of Oulu, Oulu, Finland
{paivi.raulamo-jurvanen,mika.mantyla}@oulu.fi
[2] ITEE, UBICOMP, University of Oulu, Oulu, Finland
simo.hosio@oulu.fi

Abstract. Despite the multitude of available software testing tools, literature lists lack of right tools and costs as problems for adopting a tool. We conducted a case study to analyze how a group of practitioners, familiar with Robot Framework (an open source, generic test automation framework), evaluate the tool. We based the case and the unit of analysis on our academia-industry relations, i.e., availability. We used a survey ($n = 68$) and interviews ($n = 6$) with convenience sampling to develop a comprehensive view of the phenomena. The study reveals the importance of understanding the interconnection of different criteria and the potency of the context on those. Our results show that unconfirmed or unfocused opinions about criteria, e.g., about *Costs* or *Programming Skills*, can lead to misinterpretations or hamper strategic decisions if overlooking required technical competence. We conclude surveys can serve as a useful instrument for collecting empirical knowledge about tool evaluation, but experiential reasoning collected with a complementary method is required to develop into comprehensive understanding about it.

Keywords: Test automation · Software testing tool · Tool support · Tool evaluation · Case study · Survey · Interviewing

1 Introduction

Testing and test automation are expected to have potential combining quality with speed and reducing costs. Nevertheless, those tasks are reported to be under-exploited activities in Quality Assurance (QA) [2]. It seems rather easy to search for types of software testing tools, but practically hard to evaluate and select the most suitable one from the plethora of tools. Despite the volume of software testing tools available, practitioners tend to find lack of right tools as an obstacle [2,18]. Marketing material or promotional tool comparisons tend to focus on desirable benefits, but seem to fail in providing realistic details about prerequisites or related challenges. In software engineering (SE), practitioners tend to find beliefs of their peers more credible than empirical evidence [15,19].

In this paper, we report a case study [23,29], a common case of a tool evaluation in the context of software testing. We find it relevant to ask, whether expert

X. Franch et al. (Eds.): PROFES 2019, LNCS 11915, pp. 20–36, 2019.
https://doi.org/10.1007/978-3-030-35333-9_2

advice is accurate and appropriate for tool selection. Case studies are suitable to settings where *how* and *why* questions are favorable, researchers do not have control over variables and the focus is on some contemporary events [16,29]. The use of multiple sources of evidence is a major strength of case study data collection [29]. We study the different criteria of the tool and its potential, as evaluated by software practitioners in the field, in the form of a survey. To provide a broader view on the concept, we complement the survey with interviews and assess quantitative results of the survey in the light of qualitative data from the interviews. We formulated the following research questions:

- RQ1. *How do practitioners ground their tool evaluations?*
- RQ2. *How to identify possible false expectations from tool surveys?*

To answer our research questions, we will compare the results of both methods for supportive and conflicting perceptions. By triangulation, we intend to capture rich dimensions on the characteristics of the tool [23].

2   Related Work

Evaluating software testing techniques and tools is time-consuming, expensive and difficult [17,28]. According to Fenton et al. [4], a single tool evaluation trial, even with a realistic project having realistic subjects, is not adequate, and claims by analytical advocacy are considered insupportable. In academia, publication bias of positive research results may be a problem, especially in stronger sources of evidence [18]. Dybå et al. [3] promoted evidence-based SE (EBSE) as a mechanism to aid adoption of technology related decisions. The research should seek evidence of realization of expected outcomes, potential side effects and causes of those, that can be integrated from both research and practical experience [3]. Sjøberg et al. [25] consider the viewpoint of practitioners as means to explore, describe, predict and explain phenomena.

Murphy-Hill et al. [13] focused on events where a need for a tool arises on its discovery. They reported tool encountering to be the most frequent discovery mode [13]. A widely used tool is likely found useful upon tool discovery [13]. In software projects, the need for a software testing tool is often perceived, but it is problematic to discover and select the most suitable tool(s). Comprehensive understanding of usage habits of software practitioners in a community is seen more reliable than an opinion of just one individual [13]. It is important to understand the experiences, both positive and negative, related to those habits.

Practitioners seem to have common but not systematically applied consensus about important criteria for selecting software testing tools [20,21]. For example, costs, in general is one frequently mentioned factor for the adoption and use of software testing tools [1,5,14,20,27]. Cost is an important factor, but not considered to be a characteristic of product quality[1]. Rather, costs are categorized as a tool external factor [21]. In our prior research on tool evaluations [22], we

---

[1] http://iso25000.com/index.php/en/iso-25000-standards/iso-25010.

found that practitioner evaluations for a tool, in a survey, may be dispersed. To improve understanding and robustness of the results, we analyze the topic using a complementary method.

3   Case Study Design

We apply a case study as an empirical research method for studying the evaluation of the selected software testing tool, in the context of shared open source software (OSS) ecosystem. For a case study, both the case and the unit of analysis should be selected intentionally [23]. We based the tool selection on our existing academia-industry relations, i.e., availability [23]. The case tool is Robot Framework, an open source (OS), *"generic test automation framework for acceptance testing and acceptance test-driven development (ATDD)"*[2]. The tool is utilized by a set of collaborating companies in our research project, EUREKA ITEA3 TESTOMAT [3]. We could reach practitioners familiar with the tool via the companies, representing an example case of shared OSS ecosystem. See Fig. 1 for the design of the case study.

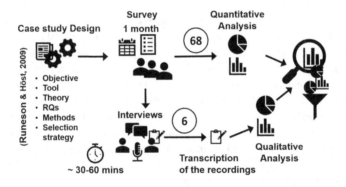

Fig. 1. Case study design, complementing a survey with interviews

The primary objective of our study is of exploratory nature. Perry et al. [16] find case studies to be useful for exploratory studies that *"attempt to understand and explain phenomenon or construct a theory"*. Kitcheham et al. [8] emphasize that although case studies are not scientifically as rigor as formal experiments, those are useful in judging whether some technologies will be of advantage in a setting. To evaluate software testing tools, we need collective information, knowledge from people who have invested in choosing and using tools [20]. For our study, we considered two methods for collecting data, a survey and interviews. Kitchenham et al. [9] outline a survey as *"comprehensive system for collecting information to describe, compare or explain knowledge, attitudes and behavior"*.

---

[2] https://robotframework.org/.
[3] https://itea3.org/project/testomatproject.html.

Complementing a survey with interviews allows us to increase the amount and diversity of the data, to develop a more comprehensive understanding about the phenomena and possibly to confirm the validity of conclusions [11,23,24].

3.1 Tool Evaluation Survey

The questionnaire[4] included 15 questions. The questions are based on our prior work [20] and on the ISO/IEC 25010 quality model. The approach for the survey tool was adopted from the studies of Hosio et al. [7] and Goncalves et al. [6]. The survey tool was validated by the authors and an industry partner. As a result, we added the options to indicate the basis of the answers (i.e., hands-on experience or generic opinion) and any experience in the development of the tool to the questionnaire. The survey was sent to seven software professionals collaborating in the research project (March 1st, 2018). We requested them to distribute the survey to their colleagues experienced with Robot Framework. To reach users of the tool, the survey was also promoted in Robot Framework Slack and in Twitter (with hashtag *robotframework*). The survey was open for a month.

Background information was given in 80 unique responses. We excluded the responses known to be for testing purposes, and those having only default values. 68 respondents completed the survey (998 unique questionnaire answers for the 15 criteria, in total). The response rate among those having started the survey was 85%. We could not calculate the overall response rate as the number of practitioners having received the link was not known. As the survey was anonymous, we could not ask for reasons not completing or not responding the survey. We used MS Excel and R/RStudio for analyzing the data. We analyzed the numeric data using descriptive statistics and graphical visualization (boxplots).

3.2 Interviews

While the purpose of the survey was to collect quantitative data, the interviews were designed to collect rich descriptions, i.e., qualitative data. The interview questions were based on the questionnaire, to have the experts elaborate on their personal experiences. We recruited six volunteering practitioners, using convenience sampling [10] for interviews, from our contacts via the TESTOMAT project and Robot Framework Slack.

The objective of the interviews was descriptive and explanatory. The interviews were semi-structured, the questions open and the content and order of the questions the same for all interviewees although the questions could be answered freely. The interviews were conducted via Skype (March–April 2018). To mitigate the risks of misunderstandings and loss of information, we requested each interviewee the permission to record the interview. To minimize the bias related to different interviewers, the interviews were conducted by one of the authors. The recordings were analyzed in NVivo 11. The data were coded against the survey criteria, to find explanations in the descriptions, i.e., to *"illuminate the quantitative findings"* [24].

---

[4] https://drive.google.com/open?id=1xzXG5ypANvOCbMdRyAyUnmYd0N24VCr4.

4   Results

First, we present the demographics of the survey respondents and interviewees in Sect. 4.1. Thereafter, we present the overview of the results from both the survey and the interviews in Sect. 4.2. To build a comprehensive picture of the phenomena under study, we will triangulate the results from both methods, in detail in Sect. 4.3 and answer our research questions in Sect. 5.

4.1   Background Information

Unsurprisingly, most of the survey respondents (54%) work in Finland (the tool originated in Finland, and the survey was initially promoted via Finnish collaboration companies). Most questionnaire answers (97%) were based on hands-on experience using the tool. Of the respondents, nearly 6% had contributed to the development of *either* the core of the tool *or* both the core of the tool and related libraries, about 21% to the development of related libraries, while majority (63%) had not contributed at all. About 85% of the respondents had used Python in their work and 50% Java. Six respondents had not used either of those while two had not reported (or used) any programming languages.

The interviewees represented different companies, in different domains (from consulting to cyber security). Regarding the experience *in the industry*, the interviewees were more experienced than the survey respondents in areas other than the maximum number of years, see Table 1. Three interviewees had not contributed to the development of the tool, two had contributed to the development of libraries, and one to both the core of the tool and libraries. Five interviewees had been using Python and two Java in their work while one had not been using either of those.

Table 1. Experience in years

Source	Experience in	Min	Max	Mean	Median	Mode
Survey (68)	Industry	3.0	33.0	12.4	10.0	5.0
	Current role	0.0	14.0	3.5	2.0	1.0
Interviews (6)	Industry	11.0	18.0	14.2	13.5	11.0
	Current role	0.0	6.0	2.2	1.5	0.0

4.2   Overview of Data from Tool Surveys and Interviews

In the boxplots[5] of questionnaire answers, see Fig. 2, the median is shown as a horizontal line and the arithmetic mean as a dot. The interquartile range

---

[5] https://www.rdocumentation.org/packages/graphics/versions/3.5.3/topics/boxplot.

(IQR) describes the middle 50% of the data. By default, in R, the formula for calculating the upper whisker is $min(max(x), Q3 + 1.5 * IQR)$, and for the lower whisker $max(min(x), Q1 - 1.5 * IQR)$.

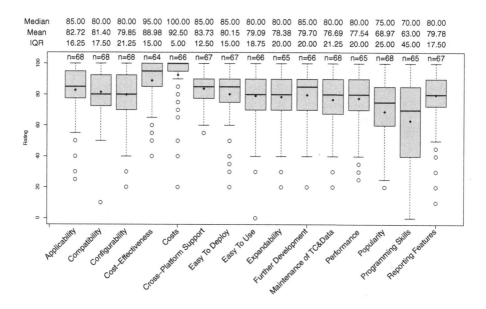

Fig. 2. Variability of questionnaire answers for the criteria in the survey

The interview transcripts were coded according to the criteria (related sentences were coded accordingly) as the questions were based on those. We classified the thoughts for the criteria from the interviews as positive, negative and neutral, based on the sentiment, see Table 2. The column *"Rank"* in Table 2 indicates the order of the column *"n"*, the total number of coded items for each criterion. The columns *"Positive"*, *"Negative"* and *"Neutral"* items include the number of coded items and the number of associated interviewees. Most of the coded items were either positive or neutral (roughly about 40% both), see example statements in Table 3. The quantity of coded items provides an overview of the topics of interest or familiarity, those the interviewees felt easy, comfortable or important to discuss. A high positive rank may indicate favorable attitude towards the criterion while a high negative rank may reveal concerns or problems. Next, we will discuss the criteria in the light of the thoughts from the interviews.

4.3   Analysis of the Criteria

Applicability. The participants evaluated the applicability of the tool to their tasks, methods and processes. The interviewees highlighted that the tool is applicable for various different purposes, provided the users have relevant technical

Table 2. Interview data coded as Positive, Negative & Neutral items

Rank	n	Criterion	Positive items		Negative items		Neutral items	
			#	Interviewees	#	Interviewees	#	Interviewees
4	33	Applicability	16	6	7	3	10	4
9	26	Compatibility	15	6	1	1	10	4
15	17	Configurability	11	6	0	0	6	4
10	25	Cost-effectiveness	13	4	2	2	10	5
10	25	Costs	4	3	4	3	17	5
13	18	Cross-platform support	8	4	0	0	10	5
12	20	Easy to deploy	8	5	11	6	1	1
2	44	Easy to use	18	6	7	2	19	5
3	36	Expandability	23	6	3	2	10	3
1	52	Further development	16	5	12	4	24	4
6	31	Maintenance	7	3	11	5	13	6
13	18	Performance	4	4	7	5	7	3
6	31	Popularity	11	5	6	4	14	6
5	32	Programming skills	4	3	10	4	18	6
8	28	Reporting features	17	4	3	2	8	4
Total	436		175		84		177	

\# = Number of coded items, Interviewees = Number of unique respondents

skills. However, applicability was seen as a dilemma. A multitude of possible contexts and ways of utilizing the tool prevents generalizing, e.g., providing detailed guidelines and best practices. *"The fact that the tool is desinged to be a command line tool enables its use in many contexts, in many operating systems. So, I would say rather well."* (#2)[6]. *"In terms of tools, it is very applicable and then, in terms of the language, the structure of writing tests in Robot Framework, that is also very applicable, because the group that I am working in, this is mostly manual testers."* (#4).

Compatibility. Compatibility of Robot Framework with the existing tools was not considered to be a problem threshold by the interviewees. In the survey, it was the only criterion for which the arithmetic mean was greater than median. The interviewees pointed out that there are always issues that could be simply improved, in general. For example, there were needs to have the tool started via REST-API, or to integrate it with other tools. *"And then, whenever there is not*

---

[6] #n = ID of the interviewee.

Table 3. Example statements from the interviews

Criterion	ID	Type	Statement
Applicab.	2	-	"Many times people try to use Robot Framework for many other purposes for which it is not the best tool"
	1	+/-	"It is good for mature cases, where the lifespan of the product or system is long"
Compatib.	4	+	"It is very compatible. The community has created a large number of libraries for integrating with other tools"
	2	-	"In my opinion the problem is that people expect it to work out-of-the box and that is not how it always work"
Configurab.	3	+	"It is an advantage that we can easily do configurations from files and we can avoid hard-coded items"
	4	+	"I think it is highly configurable, meaning there are several ways in which to override settings, several ways in which to specify settings"
Cost-Effect.	3	+	"Cost-effectiveness and re-use are developed along with the experience and know-how of the tool and its usage"
	6	-	"It (test automation) may not even be any cheaper than manual work"
Costs	4	+	"They are, I mean the only cost is training, so they are very low"
	6	-	"Deployment costs, a lot, to gain benefits"
Cross-Pl.S.	1	+	"You can run the tool basically for any platform where needed"
	4	+/-	"Depending on the environment you are running in, you can specify the configuration for that, at run-time"
Easy to Dep.	2	-	"You don't have to have in-depth know-how but for a non-technical person deployment may be quite difficult"
	1	+/-	"Building the test environment is many times the biggest challenge in every project. But it not necessarily due to the selected tool but more about the characteristics of the underlying system"
Easy to Use	2	-	"To use the tool efficiently, you need to have technical competence. That is not always clear"
	6	+/-	"There are many libraries, developed in many ways for different purposes and it's more of a question which libraries you use and how easy that is"
Expandab.	5	-	"For developing libraries you will need programming skills and more understanding about the system"
	6	+/-	"It is open source and if you want to touch the core system, that is doable. And the libraries, those are, as a general rule, open source and you may expand those, too"
Further Dev.	3	+	"There is the Foundation developing the tool and it convinces again, end customers or other customers, that there is sustainable development for the tool"
	5	-	"It was some web-automation demo I found, and I tried to use it... it did not quite work and the instructions would require small elaboration and the links updating... then it would be easier for the people to get started"
Maintainab.	1	+	"Another good feature is the tool is keyword-based, at the core of the maintainability, how you can create layers of keywords and how you can create meaningful abstractions for the test cases"
	4	+/-	"The way in which you write your tests and your keywords... will essentially determine how easy or how difficult it is, for maintenance and re-use in the future"
Performance	2	+	"The tool itself is good, or has always been adequate, so I have not had such problems"
	1	+/-	"At the end of the day, it is up to the user of the tool"

(continued)

Table 1. (*continued*)

Criterion	ID	Type	Statement
Popularity	6	+	"In Finland, the tool is well-known and you would have to have good reasons for selecting another tool"
	3	-	"A community-type tool like this has not had credibility in all branches of industry"
Progr. Skills	5	+	"I have heard that people without any programming skills can create test-automation scripts with the tool, and that is based on the keywords"
	6	-	"If you have a misconception about Robot Framework, library or any other framework, that you do not have to write any code, that is a terrible misconception"
Reporting F.	4	+	"As long as the tests were written well, anybody without programming skills should be able to read the log and understand what happened"
	5	-	"There is not much visualization. If you want something more, you have to build it yourself, that is my opinion"

ID=Interviewee ID, Type: (+)=Positive, (-)=Negative & (+/-)=Neutral

a particular library for integrating with a tool, it is often to make a tool available via an API, so that Robot simply then just calls the tool's API." (#4).

Configurability. Our participants evaluated the possibilities for configuring the tool for their needs. The interviewees found configuration of both the run time environment and reporting for a test set very practical. None of the interviewees came up with negative coded items, but *Configurability* had the least coded items. Thus, it could be seen as an issue having no use for emphasis. For those having experience with configurations, the tool seems configurable. "*There are moderately a lot of different options to configure the handlig of the tests, the kind of tests you want, how you want to view the report, format and all that.*"(#6).

Cost-Effectiveness. Surprisingly, there were not very many coded items, and most of those were positive or neutral. A tool, as test automation in general, is cost-effective if applied the right way, at the right time alongside the development work. What is the right way and the right time are volatile and contexts specific concepts. Amount of money was seen as a likely issue for consultants and clients to discuss, but difficult to verify in real life. One of the interviewees pointed out cost-effectiveness as a way to prioritize the work load. They emphasized the fact that test automation helps to become faster, i.e., in the best case it helps to deliver software more often, in smaller batches and with better quality. "*If one starts from the scratch, it takes some time and some studying. Like everything else, from scratch, so I do not see that as a problem .*"(#3).

Costs. The tool was evaluated for expected costs (for acquisition and use). In survey responses, the median was the highest. We expect the main reason for that to be the fact the tool is free. *Costs* was the criterion with the most outliers (given by 10 respondents having been in the software industry on average

12.9 years). In the interviews, there were 25 coded items, most of which were neutral (17). The interviewees highlighted the importance of understanding the inevitable costs related to the tool. The required resources for setting up and maintaining a system (e.g., people, training or time) depend on the context, and have direct effect on *Costs* and *Cost-Effectiveness*. *"The problem is, how you organize the use in the company... where the costs come from, that holds true how much you have available resources, people, how technically competent they are."* (#2). *"And its [test automation] maintenance costs, a lot."* (#6).

Cross-Platform Support. The participants evaluated their view on cross-platoform support of the tool. In the interviews, there were no negative coded items. The tool was considered to have good support for different platforms. *"The support for SUTs comes via the libraries and the support is broad. We have tested all kinds of systems, from elevators to insurance systems... and network protocols, and dynamic web-applications, so it is very, very versatile, in that sense."* (#1). *"You may run Robot anywhere where you can run Python, which means from mainframes to Raspberry Pi's and small micro controllers."* (#6).

Easy to Deploy. The participants considered the initial efforts to take the tool into use. In the interviews, there were the 2nd most negative items (of all criteria). All interviewees had stated one or more negatively coded items. Although the interviewees found the deployment to be rather easy, they emphasized the need for technical know-how, preferably with Python. The interviewees highlighted the fact that the difficulties may not only be related the tool but also to test automation, in general, and to the underlying system itself as well. *"When considering the easiness of the deployment, it is difficult to disassociate the tool, the system and all that is around it."* (#1). *"In a way, it is easy to deploy, but the difficulty lies in that it truly requires planning."* (#3).

Easy to Use. We requested the participants to consider their perceptions of *Easy to Use*. In the interviews, the criterion had the 2nd most coded items. Those were mainly positive (18) and neutral (19). Thus, we assume interviewees felt easy to talk about their experiences using the tool. The interviewees pointed out the need for technical know-how. They thought that the concept of test automation in general, in the given context, may be difficult to comprehend. Possible wrong choices or mistakes in the setup may require unexpected changes to the test sets (or even to the system) later on. Effective use of the tool requires careful planning. *"Planning must be done the right way, meaning, that you can also make bad choices that may backfire on you later."* (#3). *"The people on my teams have really seen the effectiveness of it, and have enjoyed working in it."* (#4). *"Writing the actual tests is easy and clear, of course."* (#5).

Expandability. For *Expandability*, the participants could share their views on the possibility to remold or expand the tool. An OSS tool has its benefits and its downsides when considering expandability. There may be an active community of software practitioners developing the features of the tool. Nevertheless, one needs programming skills and understanding of the problem area and/or the architecture to make changes. *"With Robot Framework, you need to be careful whether to talk about the tool itself or the ecosystem, as many issues that have been discussed over the years, that would be good to have in a tool in one way or another, are such that could already be done as an extension (library) and in that sense there is necessarily no need to modify the tool itself."* (#2). *"There are true programming languages to use, and the sky is the limit, so, expandability can be achieved with those."* (#1).

Further Development. The participants could evaluate whether they find the *Further Development* of the tool (by the OS community) active or not. The criterion was the most discussed among the interviewees and the coded items were mainly neutral (24). What could not be understood from the survey was the dualistic nature of the tool. The tool consists of two fundamental entities, the core tool and related ecosystem (libraries and tooling type of development). The core tool is a framework using the functionality provided by the ecosystem. The two concepts are distinct, developed and maintained separately. The core tool itself is rather stable. It is the ecosystem that needs to change according to the conditions around the tool, in the industry, in general. The interviewees emphasized that the core tool is well designed for adding new functionality via libraries. The documentation must be up-to-date to provide value to the users.

The Robot Framework Foundation supports the resourcing for the development of the core tool. *"We have this foundation, which will support development, collect membership fees from member companies to finance basic updates to Robot [Framework] to keep it compatible and to work in all platforms in the future, too. And of course, there is the open source community that contributes a lot to the libraries."* (#1). *"The fact that the foundation supports the development, it is a good thing."* (#3). It was noted that if the difference between the core tool and the ecosystem is not understood, a low quality library may invite unfounded criticism for the core tool. *"What I hope is that the discussions, in general, would move from the core tool to the libraries and testing... and there would be the common understanding that if something goes wrong, it is not necessarily Robot Framework but some library, instead. And even though Robot Framework has a public site for reporting bugs, many of those are closed because those are not related to the core tool but to some specific library."* (#2). *"You should develop all libraries and other type of development following the good software development practices, but what those really are, that is a good question."* (#2).

Maintenance of Test Cases and Data. The participants could evaluate maintenance and re-use of test cases and data. In the interviews, the coded items were mainly neutral (13) and negative (11). It became clear the practitioners find maintenance of test cases and data laborious and costly, if not planned carefully. Furthermore, practitioners maintaining the test system must need competence for the tasks. The help of possible external consultants must meet the needs and competence level of the clients. *"I think that you have to be very careful in setting up your library of tests, and it can be very simple to create a maintenance headache for yourself."* (#4). *"Development of libraries may be challenging, development of keywords, what I have heard, may easily explode."* (#5).

Performance. We queried about the *Performance* of the tool for its purpose. In the survey, based on the boxplots, *Performance* was evaluated as many other criteria. In the interviews, there were not many coded items. The interviewees considered the tool itself to be fine, performance-wise, although they found performance to be a difficult concept to measure. The problems with performance can be related to the system under test (SUT), set up of the overall test system and its users, not just the tool. So, this is not a self-contained criterion. *"So, as you are using the tool, the tool itself performs just fine, but... there are things like parsing files, for example, that is probably done faster outside of the tool."* (#4).

Popularity. In the survey, *Popularity* had the 2nd lowest arithmetic mean. The interviewees noted that the tool is rather well-known in Finland and in the Nordic countries, but not globally. According to the interviewees, practitioners seem to rely on positive hearsay and meet-ups, as well as testimonials from reference companies. Companies may be reluctant to change an invested tool, even if the tool was not found as the best option in the task. *"Testing as a field suffers a bit from the fact that information is not shared the similar way as in software development."* (#2). *"I'm not actively involved in the community but I have been following the Slack channel, the Slack work space, which I think is great... I think the most important enablers for future development are the community itself, the fact that the community is welcoming, that the community is helpful."* (#4).

Programming Skills. The participants assessed the level of required *Programming Skills*. In the survey, the criterion had the lowest arithmetic mean. In the interviews, it was the 5th most coded criterion. Programming skills and technical skills are issues of importance for the use of the tool. A high variance in questionnaire answers and a negative nuance in the coded items from the interviews, suggests that technical competence, in general, is of importance. Building and maintenance of the test environment, and development of needed functionalities are linked to performance and cost-effectiveness of the tool yet tool cost itself is not the issue. *"Would be good to understand the basic concepts of programming for creating test cases in the right abstraction level, which impacts maintainability."* (#1). At the time of the study, the testing capabilities of the tool could be extended by test libraries implemented with Python or Java[7]. So, it is not only about programming skills, but also about specific programming languages.

---

[7] https://robotframework.org/.

Reporting Features. The participants assessed the set of reporting features in the tool to be limited or rich. In the interviews, the coded items in the interviews were mainly positive (17). The interviewees emphasized *Reporting Features* as a tool not only for the developers, testers and managers but also for the clients. The tool provides logs for finding bugs and understanding the behaviour of the system, and rich data for visualization. Programming skills are not needed for reading the logs or reports, but for creating rich reports with charts and graphs (for connecting external tools). *"An example of tasks where you don't need programming skills, I would say, reading the logs and reading the reports."* (#4).

5 Discussion

Tool evaluations depend on the interpretation of a construct under study, i.e., have a degree of subjectivity [26] but also validity as measures [12]. The questionnaire answers are results from plain realism acquired from personal experiential knowledge for reasoning about each criterion as such. We conducted interviews to grasp detailed understanding about the findings.

For **RQ1**. *"How do practitioners ground their tool evaluations?"* we assessed the foundation for the responses of the interviews. One emphasized testable requirements and realistic benefits for the test system to be built. Another noted that test automation is expensive in the short term, but may be very economical, in the long run. Importantly, test automation is efficient and prudent use of resources in the development process. *"It (test automation) helps you to be faster... helps you to achieve the goals and to release faster, more often, in small batches. It helps you to achieve better quality, if you have done it the right way."* (#6).

The different criteria are interconnected. The interviewees connected criteria like *Costs*, *Cost-Effectiveness* and *Expandability* not only to the to technical competence, but also to the level of *Programming skills*. Evaluation of a tool criteria may be related to the level of knowledge of the system, in general. *"Building the test environment is the biggest challenge, in general, in every project."* (#1). *"Sometimes, it is really difficult to find the right way to apply your solution... efficient use of the tool requires some level of technical competence."* (#2). *"Test automation is always a programming issue, and if you want to have test automation, you need to be able to program."* (#6).

The issues regarding *Costs* and *Programming skills* are interconnected to the main characteristics of OSS[8]: free to use and source code accessible to all. An OS tool is free and expandable, and there may be an active OS community developing it. Yet, tool related tasks require investments (e.g., competent people, time and money), within contexts of the organizations utilizing the tool and the community developing the tool. Lack of technical competence or programming skills seem disadvantageous for tool usage and evaluations. Practitioners seem

---

[8] https://opensource.org/osd.

to ground their evaluations on conscious understanding of encountered or envisioned issues. The interviewees reflected on their insights with rich, informative examples from real life, verbalizing their reasoning.

With *RQ2. "How to identify possible false expectations from tool surveys?"*, we focused on finding possible potentially misleading or restrictive perceptions. From the boxplots (see Fig. 2), we could observe many of the criteria, for example, *Easy to Use*, *Expandability* and *Performance*, to be of similar shape, and to have both the median and the length of the whiskers roughly the same. However, *Costs* and *Programming Skills* were the criteria having the lowest and the highest variance in the questionnaire answers, respectively. Furthermore, the findings for those criteria from the two methods were contradictory.

The respondents agreed the most on *Costs*, majority finding costs for acquisition and usage of the tool to be very low. The finding suggests they considered the licensing fee, not costs of required training or using the tool. Thus, it seems we missed to cover different aspects of *Costs* in the survey. However, it is possible they had not faced costs (as *extra costs* but *work*) or needs for training. *"If you have enough of technical competence, at that stage, costs will be trivially small, because you just re-prioritize the tasks of those people for Robot Framework"* (#2). The interviewees, highlighted that software test automation costs, a lot, no matter the tool. *"Test automation is always a big investment for a company. It costs, always. Costs is not about just getting the software, it is about using it, setting up the infrastructure, learning to use it, creating, maintaining, all that. It includes a lot of costs and Robot Framework is not an exception."* (#6).

Programming skills had the lowest arithmetic mean and median of the criteria. Role and tasks of a practitioner using the tool impact the level of required programming skills. The interviews revealed the dualistic nature of the tool. The Robot Framework foundation is resourcing the development of the core tool, but has no control over resourcing or quality of the ecosystem around it. *"If some of the libraries does not support your thing, you are basically on your own, you need to build the library yourself."* (#6).

To summarize our findings, we consider that well-argued experiences from expert practitioners allow to reveal unexpected problems, clarify common misconceptions or confirm understanding about tool criteria. Neither single criterion nor grounded reasoning by a peer should be decisive. *"It is the accumulation of that information, not the ratings themselves, that is decisive [12]"*.

6 Threats to Validity

As our target population for the use case was very specific, i.e., software practitioners experienced with Robot Framework, we could not rely on random samples. We used non-probabilistic sampling methods: convenience sampling complemented with snowball sampling [10]. We expected to have representative samples of the target population, i.e., software practitioners experienced on using the tool (in their contexts). While the survey respondents (n = 68) were expected to be experienced in using Robot Framework, we could not assess their experiences of each criterion. In a survey, the likelihood of participation may be related to negative experiences [10]. To mitigate deficiencies in collecting data and to understand the phenomena better, we used a complementary method, interviewing $(n = 6)$, and triangulated the results with those from the survey.

As the participants of the study were mainly from Finland, the results may be biased by confounding factors e.g., knowledge of the tool or contexts. However, the survey participants came from 13 countries, 10 participants from other European countries and 21 from outside Europe. Experience in the development of the tool was seen as in depth view of the tool. The cohesion and consistency of the results from the survey are impacted by the facts that tool evaluations are highly subjective, and we could not control the contexts or the constructs. Thus, our results are not generalizable as such, but provide a snapshot of opinions, in a given time, and are presented to be useful for analyzing dissenting opinions.

7 Conclusions and Future Work

We complemented a survey with interviews for analyzing differing opinions about characteristics of an OSS testing tool. Our survey revealed *Costs* and *Programming Skills* to be quite different from the other criteria. The interviews clarified a tool may be free, but investments carry costs which, in turn, are always context specific. While cost is not a quality characteristic of a tool, tool related costs are restrictive and can hamper strategic decisions. Technical competence is vital for efficient tool adoption and usage, and development of the tool. A tool is no silver bullet but a facility for re-prioritizing tasks in the software development work.

We conclude that complementary methods can dispel common misconceptions about characteristics or usage of a tool, or about software test automation as a whole. Contradictions should merit further studies and reasoning, in the context. There is a need for more, in depth research on software testing tool evaluations. In the future, we plan to study viewpoints of the practitioners, in more detail. Academic research on software test tool criteria can help the practitioners to view the forest from the trees, and focus on achievable goals.

Acknowledgments. The work was supported partially by research Grants No.: 3192/31/2017 from Business Finland for the EUREKA ITEA3 TESTOMAT project (16032), and No.: 286386-CPDSS from the Academy of Finland for the CPDSS project.

References

1. Bhargava, S., Guleria, S., Gaurang, A.: A study on the current trends in software testing tools. Int. J. Adv. Res. Comput. Sci. **8**(5), 129–131 (2017)
2. Capgemini, Micro Focus and Sogeti: World quality report 2017–2018 (2017). https://www.sogeti.com/globalassets/global/downloads/testing/wqr-2017-2018/wqr_2017_v9_secure.pdf. Accessed 5 June 2019
3. Dybå, T., Kitchenham, B.A., Jørgensen, M.: Evidence-based software engineering for practitioners. IEEE Softw. **22**(1), 58–65 (2005). https://doi.org/10.1109/MS.2005.6

4. Fenton, N., Pfleeger, S.L., Glass, R.L.: Science and substance: a challenge to software engineers. IEEE Softw. **11**(4), 86–95 (1994). https://doi.org/10.1109/52. 300094

5. Garousi, V., Zhi, J.: A survey of software testing practices in canada. J. Syst. Softw. **86**(5), 1354–1376 (2013). https://doi.org/10.1016/j.jss.2012.12.051

6. Goncalves, J., Hosio, S., Kostakos, V.: Eliciting structured knowledge from situated crowd markets. ACM Trans. Internet Technol. **17**(2), 1–21 (2017). https://doi.org/ 10.1145/3007900

7. Hosio, S., Goncalves, J., Anagnostopoulos, T., Kostakos, V.: Leveraging wisdom of the crowd for decision support. In: Proceedings of the 30th International BCS Human Computer Interaction, pp. 1–12. BCS Learning & Development Ltd., Swindon (2016). https://doi.org/10.14236/ewic/HCI2016.38

8. Kitchenham, B., Pickard, L., Pfleeger, S.L.: Case studies for method and tool evaluation. IEEE Softw. **12**(4), 52–62 (1995). https://doi.org/10.1109/52.391832

9. Kitchenham, B.A., Pfleeger, S.L., Pickard, L.M., Jones, P.W., Hoaglin, D.C., Emam, K.E., Rosenberg, J.: Preliminary guidelines for empirical research in software engineering. IEEE Trans. Softw. Eng. **28**(8), 721–734 (2002). https://doi.org/ 10.1109/TSE.2002.1027796

10. Kitchenham, B.A., Pfleeger, S.L.: Personal opinion surveys. In: Shull, F., Singer, J., Sjøberg, D.I.K. (eds.) Guide to Advanced Empirical Software Engineering, pp. 63–92. Springer, London (2008). https://doi.org/10.1007/978-1-84800-044-5_3

11. Lethbridge, T.C., Sim, S.E., Singer, J.: Studying software engineers: data collection techniques for software field studies. Empirical Softw. Eng. **10**(3), 311–341 (2005). https://doi.org/10.1007/s10664-005-1290-x

12. Linacre, J.M.: Judge ratings with forced agreement. Trans. Rasch Meas. SIG Am. Educ. Res. Assoc. **16**(1), 857–858 (2002)

13. Murphy-Hill, E., Lee, D.Y., Murphy, G.C., McGrenere, J.: How do users discover new tools in software development and beyond? Comput. Support. Coop. Work (CSCW) **24**(5), 389–422 (2015). https://doi.org/10.1007/s10606-015-9230-9

14. Ng, S.P., Murnane, T., Reed, K., Grant, D., Chen, T.Y.: A preliminary survey on software testing practices in Australia. In: Proceedings of the 2004 Australian Software Engineering Conference, pp. 116–125. IEEE, NJ, USA (2004). https:// doi.org/10.1109/ASWEC.2004.1290464

15. Pano, A., Graziotin, D., Abrahamsson, P.: Factors and actors leading to the adoption of a Javascript framework. Empirical Softw. Eng. **23**(6), 3503–3534 (2018). https://doi.org/10.1007/s10664-018-9613-x

16. Perry, D.E., Sim, S.E., Easterbrook, S.M.: Case studies for software engineers. In: Proceedings. 26th International Conference on Software Engineering, pp. 736–738 (2004). https://doi.org/10.1109/ICSE.2004.1317512

17. Poston, R.M., Sexton, M.P.: Evaluating and selecting testing tools. In: Proceedings of the Second Symposium on Assessment of Quality Software Development Tools, pp. 55–64 (1992). https://doi.org/10.1109/AQSDT.1992.205836

18. Rafi, D.M., Moses, K.R.K., Petersen, K., Mäntylä, M.V.: Benefits and limitations of automated software testing: systematic literature review and practitioner survey. In: 7th International Workshop on Automation of Software Test (AST), pp. 36–42 (2012). https://doi.org/10.1109/IWAST.2012.6228988

19. Rainer, A., Hall, T., Baddoo, N.: Persuading developers to "buy into" software process improvement: a local opinion and empirical evidence. In: Proceedings of the 2003 International Symposium on Empirical Software Engineering, 2003, ISESE 2003, pp. 326–335. IEEE, Rome, September 2003. https://doi.org/10.1109/ISESE. 2003.1237993

20. Raulamo-Jurvanen, P., Kakkonen, K., Mäntylä, M.: Using surveys and web-scraping to select tools for software testing consultancy. In: Abrahamsson, P., Jedlitschka, A., Nguyen Duc, A., Felderer, M., Amasaki, S., Mikkonen, T. (eds.) PROFES 2016. LNCS, vol. 10027, pp. 285–300. Springer, Cham (2016). https://doi.org/10.1007/978-3-319-49094-6_18

21. Raulamo-Jurvanen, P., Mäntylä, M.V., Garousi, V.: Choosing the right test automation tool: a grey literature review of practitioner sources. In: Proceedings of the 21st International Conference on Evaluation and Assessment in Software Engineering, EASE 2017, pp. 21–30. ACM, New York (2017). https://doi.org/10.1145/3084226.3084252

22. Raulamo-Jurvanen, P., Hosio, S., Mäntylä, M.V.: Practitioner evaluations on software testing tools. In: Proceedings of the Evaluation and Assessment on Software Engineering, EASE 2019, pp. 57–66. ACM, New York (2019). https://doi.org/10.1145/3319008.3319018

23. Runeson, P., Höst, M.: Guidelines for conducting and reporting case study research in software engineering. Empirical Softw. Eng. 14(2), 131–164 (2009). https://doi.org/10.1007/s10664-008-9102-8

24. Seaman, C.B.: Qualitative methods in empirical studies of software engineering. IEEE Trans. Softw. Eng. 25(4), 557–572 (1999). https://doi.org/10.1109/32.799955

25. Sjøberg, D.I.K., Dybå, T., Jørgensen, M.: The future of empirical methods in software engineering research. In: Future of Software Engineering, FOSE 2007, pp. 358–378. IEEE (2007). https://doi.org/10.1109/FOSE.2007.30

26. Stemler, S.E.: A comparison of consensus, consistency, and measurement approaches to estimating interrater reliability. Pract. Assess. Res. Eval. 9(4), 1–11 (2004). https://www.ingentaconnect.com/content/doaj/15317714/2004/00000009/00000004/art00001

27. Taipale, O., Smolander, K., Kälviäinen, H.: Cost reduction and quality improvement in software testing. In: Software Quality Management Conference (2006)

28. Vos, T.E.J., Marin, B., Escalona, M.J., Marchetto, A.: A methodological framework for evaluating software testing techniques and tools. In: 12th International Conference on Quality Software, pp. 230–239. IEEE (2012). https://doi.org/10.1109/QSIC.2012.16

29. Yin, R.K.: Case Study Research: Design and Methods. SAGE Publications, Inc. (2014)

Test-Case Quality – Understanding Practitioners' Perspectives

Huynh Khanh Vi Tran[(✉)], Nauman Bin Ali, Jürgen Börstler,
and Michael Unterkalmsteiner

SERL Sweden, Blekinge Institute of Technology, 371 79 Karlskrona, Sweden
{huynh.khanh.vi.tran,nauman.ali,jurgen.borstler,
michael.unterkalmsteiner}@bth.se

Abstract. Background: Test-case quality has always been one of the major concerns in software testing. To improve test-case quality, it is important to better understand how practitioners perceive the quality of test-cases.

Objective: Motivated by that need, we investigated how practitioners define test-case quality and which aspects of test-cases are important for quality assessment.

Method: We conducted semi-structured interviews with professional developers, testers and test architects from a multinational software company in Sweden. Before the interviews, we asked participants for actual test cases (written in natural language) that they perceive as good, normal, and bad respectively together with rationales for their assessment. We also compared their opinions on shared test cases and contrasted their views with the relevant literature.

Results: We present a quality model which consists of 11 test-case quality attributes. We also identify a misalignment in defining test-case quality among practitioners and between academia and industry, along with suggestions for improving test-case quality in industry.

Conclusion: The results show that practitioners' background, including roles and working experience, are critical dimensions of how test-case quality is defined and assessed.

Keywords: Software testing · Natural-language test case · Test-case quality

1 Introduction

Testing plays an important role in software quality assurance, which has been one of the main concerns in the software development life cycle. The fundamental artefacts in testing are test cases. Grano et al. have shown in their study that good test cases in terms of being simple and readable make it easier for developers to maintain them and to keep up with fast software development life cycle [11]. A study by Athanasiou et al. also showed that high quality of test code could also increase the performance of development teams in fixing bugs and implementing

© Springer Nature Switzerland AG 2019
X. Franch et al. (Eds.): PROFES 2019, LNCS 11915, pp. 37–52, 2019.
https://doi.org/10.1007/978-3-030-35333-9_3

new features [1]. Therefore, good test cases increase the confidence in testing, and thereby assist product release decisions. Hence, assuring the quality of test cases is an important task in quality assuring software-intensive products.

There have been studies which focused on different test-case quality attributes such as performance, readability, and effectiveness [3, 7, 10, 11, 13, 17, 19, 20, 24]. Some studies adapted the ISO standard for software quality to define test-case quality [18, 23]. Those studies provided researchers' perceptions of test-case quality. Though the contributions from academia are important, it is necessary to verify how knowledge could be transferred between academia and industry. The first step would be to investigate how test-case quality is understood by practitioners. However, there is currently a lack of empirical studies on the topic.

To reduce this gap, we conducted an exploratory study to investigate how test-case quality is defined and assessed in practice. Our focus was manual test cases written in natural language. This type of test cases is still required for testing levels such as system testing, acceptance testing, and for a testing approach such as exploratory test. Hence, studying how the quality of natural-language tests is perceived in practice is as important as of code-based test cases. The contributions of the study are as follows:

- Descriptions of test-case quality attributes identified by practitioners.
- Reasons for the difference in defining and assessing test-case quality among practitioners with different roles, and between academia and practice.
- Context factors to consider when defining test-case quality.
- Suggestions to improve test-case quality by practitioners.
- Sources of information for understanding and assessing test-case quality suggested by practitioners.

The remainder of the paper is structured as follows: Sect. 2 describes related work. Section 3 describes the study design, followed by Sect. 4 which discusses threats to validity. Section 5 discusses our findings. Our conclusions and future work are summarised in Sect. 5.

2   Related Work

We identified nine studies which involved practitioners in their work focusing on test-case quality [1, 2, 4, 6, 8, 9, 12, 15, 22]. We organised them into three groups.

The first group includes two studies which integrated practitioners' knowledge into the studies' results regarding test-case quality [2, 22]. Adlemo et al. [22] introduced 15 criteria for good test cases. There was no specific focus on types of test cases. Of those criteria, ten were inspired by the literature while five came from practitioners' suggestions. The criteria were ranked by 13 Swedish practitioners with experience in software testing and software development. *Repeatability*, meaning that a test case should produce the same result whenever it receives the same input, had the highest votes from practitioners. Bowes et al. [2], focused on test code in unit testing. The authors identified 15 testing principles collected from three sources: a workshop with industrial partners, their software testing teaching materials, and practitioners' books. *Simplicity* in terms of test-code size, number of assertions and conditional test logic, is considered as the most important principle, and is the foundation for the other ones.

The second group contains four studies which had practitioners evaluate their hypotheses relating to some test-case quality attributes [1,4,6,15]. Jovanovikj et al. [15] introduced an approach and a tool to evaluate and monitor test-case quality. They presented eight quality characteristics based on Zeiss et al.'s work [23], which relied on the ISO/IEC 25010 (ISO/IEC, 2011) software quality models. To verify their approach's applicability, they conducted a case study in the context of natural-language tests, and had interviews with two quality managers and some testers. Similarly, Athanasiou et al. [1] proposed a model to assess three test-code quality attributes, namely Completeness, Effectiveness, and Maintainability with associated metrics. To verify if the model was aligned with practitioners' opinions, they compared its results from two software systems with the evaluations of two experts via focused interviews. They concluded that there is a strong correlation between test code quality, throughput, and productivity of issue handling. In another study, Daka et al. [6] introduced a model of unit test readability which could help to generate test suites with high coverage and high readability. Their model involved human judgement, but there was no clear indication on their selection criteria. Focusing on only test-case effectiveness, Chernak [4] proposed an evaluation and improvement process for test cases in general. The process was used by one project team, including three testers and 10 developers who worked on a banking system.

The third group includes three studies which discussed test smells [8,9,12]. Hauptman et al. [12] presented seven test smells in natural-language tests, which were collected based on their experiences with evaluating natural-language system tests. Their study was claimed as the first work on test smells in the context of natural-language tests. For smells in test code, Garousi et al. [9] conducted a systematic 'multivocal' literature mapping and developed a classification for 196 test smells. The authors included their descriptions of top 11 most discussed test smells in a subsequent study [8].

The related works show that practitioners' perceptions of test-case quality have not been well studied. Particularly, we have not identified any study focusing on eliciting first-hand data from practitioners on their perceptions of test-case quality in the context of natural language tests.

3   Research Method

The objective of the study is to gain a better understanding of practitioners' perceptions towards test-case quality. We conducted an exploratory study with a multinational telecommunication company in Sweden. This type of study was chosen since the research focus on eliciting practitioners' genuine perspective on test-case quality has not been well studied. The exploratory study helped us to get more familiar with the research topic, to determine what the study design(s) should be for our subsequent studies on the same topic.

In this study, we used semi-structured interviews to explore the practitioners' perspectives on the topic. According to Robson and McCartan [21], this interview approach allows researchers to flexibly modify the interview questions depending on the interviewees' answers. Since the interviews were about discussing test-case quality, the same strict questionnaire would not be applicable to all interviewees. Also, the interviews were based on real test cases provided by the interviewees. Thanks to the explicit test cases, our approach makes it easier for interviewees to refer to instances of quality aspects instead of vague, generic or abstract ideas.

3.1   Research Questions

- *RQ1. How do practitioners describe test-case quality?* The research question directly connects to our study's objective. Without defining quality criteria upfront, we first want to elicit information on how practitioners perceive test-case quality.
- *RQ2. How well is the understanding of test-case quality aligned among practitioners in a company?* Test-case quality might be assessed differently depending on how it is perceived by the assessors. That could affect testing-related activities such as test-case design, and test-case maintenance. Therefore, we want to understand whether practitioners perceive test-case quality differently; if so, then we want to identify the potential reasons.
- *RQ3. What context factors do practitioners consider when assessing test-case quality?* The context factors could be testing level, testing purpose, characteristics of the software system under test, etc. Test-case quality might be context-dependent. Hence, we want to identify the potential context factors or aspects which could influence how test-case quality is assessed.
- *RQ4. What are potential improvements suggested by practitioners for improving test-case quality?* Answers to this research question would help us to understand practitioners' needs regarding test-case quality, which could give us and researchers potential research directions.
- *RQ5. What information sources guide practitioners' opinions of test-case quality?* Identifying such information sources could helps us to understand why practitioners perceive test-case quality in certain ways.

3.2   Data Collection

The data was collected from the interviews which included test cases provided by the interviewees. Before conducting the study, we had a meeting with the company's representatives to present our study's design and to obtain basic understanding of the company's structure, and potential interviewees.

Interview Design. Before conducting the interviews, we asked each participant to provide us three test cases with their quality classification (good, bad or normal). They could choose any test case from the company's test suites that they are familiar with. We also asked for a written rationale for the classification, since we not only wanted to see whether other interviewees would rate them similarly, but also whether they would provide similar reasons. We intentionally did not define quality criteria upfront in order to elicit the genuine perceptions of the interviewees. We swapped the test cases between two participants who work in the same team. Before the interviews, we informed the interviewees which test cases they had to review extra. Hence, in the interviews, the swapped test cases were also judged by the interviewees so that we could gauge their alignment.

We used the pyramid model [21] for our interview session. Hence, each interview starts with specific questions followed by more open questions. More specifically, the interview session is divided into three phases.

- Part 1: Background Information: we focused on obtaining information about the interviewee's testing experience.
- Part 2: Test Case Classification: we asked the interviewee to clarify his reasons for his test-case quality classification and to discuss some test cases given by another participant.
- Part 3: General Perception of Test-Case Quality: we had a more generic discussion with the interviewee about his or her perception of test-case quality.

To mitigate flaws in our interview design, we conducted a pilot interview with a colleague whose research interest includes software testing and has been working with test cases for years. The interview questionnaire could be found at https://tinyurl.com/y6qakcjc.

Participants Selection. Our selection criteria were that (1) a participant should be a tester and/or a developer; (2) the participant has at least one year of working experience relating to software testing. Our selection is convenience sampling [16] as we involved those who meet our criteria and are willing to participate in the interviews. At the end, we had six participants from three different teams working in different projects. Their information is described in Table 1. Even though four of them are test architects, their responsibilities still involve working with test cases. Hence, having them participate in the study did not affect our study design.

Interview Execution. The interviews were conducted by two researchers each. One researcher asked questions while the other took notes and added extra questions for clarification if needed. Each interview took around one hour, and was audio-recorded with the participant's consent.

Test Cases. In total, we collected 17 manual natural-language test cases as not all practitioners followed the instruction of providing three test cases each. They were extracted from the company's test suites for functional testing. We focused on the following information of a test case in our analysis: ID, name, description, and steps. Even though there is no strict format for the test case's description, it often includes, but does not require, the following information:

Table 1. Participants' experience, roles, tasks and test cases provided

ID	Role	Exp[a]	Make TP[b]	Design TCs[c]	Review TCs	Report TR[d]	Maintain TCs	Execute TCs	TC ID
P1	Test architect	6	✓	✓	✓	✓	✓		P1.1-3
P2	Tester	14					✓	✓	P2.1-4
P3	Test architect	6	✓	✓	✓	✓	✓		P3.1-2
P4	Tester, test architect, consultant	20	✓	✓	✓	✓		✓	P4.1-3
P5	Developer	5		✓				✓	P5.1-2
P6	Test architect	15	✓	✓	✓	✓	✓		P6.1-3

[a] Exp: number of years of working experience in testing
[b] TP: test plan
[c] TC: test case
[d] TR: test results

purpose, preconditions, additional information, references, and revision history. Additionally, we also received the quality classification (Good/Bad/Normal) and the written explanations before the interviews. Nonetheless, we could not report the actual test cases' content due to confidentiality reasons.

3.3   Data Analysis

Interview Data. Before analysing the data, the first author transcribed and anonymised all audio recordings of the interviews. The transcribed data were coded using a thematic coding approach [5]. More specifically, we applied an integrated approach, which allows codes to be developed both inductively from the transcribed data and deductively from the research questions and researchers' understanding of test-case quality in general. The main themes which were inspired by the research questions are as follows:

- Practitioners' Background Information: contains information such as roles, testing experience;
- Test-Case Quality Description: contains information about how practitioners described test-case quality and their selection of the top three quality indicators or attributes of a good test case and of a bad one;
- Test-Case Quality Assessment: contains information about practitioners' classification of test-case quality and their reasoning;
- Test-Case Quality Alignment: contains information about differences and similarities in practitioners' perceptions of test cases and their reasoning;
- Test-Case Quality Improvement: contains information about practitioners' suggestions to improve test-case quality;
- Source of Information: contains information about sources that practitioners refer to when they need to assess or get a better understanding of test-case quality.

For each interview, we followed the following steps:

Step 1: Starting from the beginning of the interview, mark a segment of text which is relevant to the pre-defined themes with a code and assign it to a corresponding theme. For the Test-Case Quality Description theme, relevant codes could be test-case quality attributes such as *understandability, effectiveness, traceability*, etc. Some of those attributes were named and explained explicitly by the practitioners while the others were generated based on their discussions during the interviews.

Step 2: Find the next relevant segment of text. Mark it with an existing code or with a new code and assign it to a relevant main theme. If the information is related to test-case quality but does not belong to any main theme then a new theme is created for that new information. It helps us to capture emerging concepts related to our study's focus.

Step 3: Repeat Step 2 until no relevant information is found.

Step 4: Create sub-themes under every main theme to cluster related codes together.

During the process, codes, themes, and their descriptions were continuously refined to fit the data. We used a commercial tool to complete this coding process, which allows us to maintain traceability between the transcribed data and the related codes and themes. To mitigate bias and increase the reliability of the coding, the first set of codes and themes were discussed by two researchers, and the coding scheme was refined. Furthermore, the final set was reviewed by all researchers. All disagreements regarding the coding were resolved in a meeting by discussion.

To obtain an overall ranking of the top quality indicators and attributes of a good test case and of a bad one, each of them gets three points if it was ranked first by a practitioner, two points if it was ranked second, and one point otherwise. We wanted to get a general picture of which quality attributes or indicators are normally considered more important than the other by practitioners. Hence, we did not consider the contextual factors identified by RQ3 in the ranking.

Test Case Data. To analyse the collected test cases, we extracted the quality classifications and reasons from practitioners' written notes. The information was coded in the same manner as the interview data (see previous section). To compare practitioners' opinions with the literature, before the interviews, we searched for test smells in those test cases based on test smells' descriptions from two studies [8,12]. This step did not only give us another assessment angle but also helped us to better understand the test cases' quality. We selected those studies for reference for two reasons. The first study [12] is the most recent work on test smells of natural-language tests. The second study [8] provides us descriptions of the top 11 most discussed smells of test code. There are common characteristics between natural language test cases and unit test cases such as testing logic, issues in test steps, dependencies between test cases, test behaviour when executing, etc. Hence, the study of Garousi et al. [8] is a relevant reference.

Even though that study was based on a former work of Garousi et al. [9], the former one did not provide definitions of test smells, hence not chosen as a reference.

4 Threats to Validity

Construct Validity. Construct validity is concerned with the reliability of operational measures to answer the research questions. Our interviews were semi-structured with follow-up questions which gave us opportunities to clarify practitioners' answers and reduce misunderstandings during the interview. Their written explanations for the test cases' quality assessment reduced the risk of misinterpreting their answers. The test cases were selected subjectively by the practitioners to demonstrate their perspective of good/bad/normal test cases in terms of their perceived quality. Since our study's type is exploratory and attempts to capture practitioners perspective, this selection method is not considered a threat to the validity of our results. Additional information about practitioners such as whether they were ISTQB[1]-certified might influence their perspective on test-case quality. Since we did not collect this information, it is a limitation of the study. Nevertheless, we collected important information (their testing experience, roles, and working tasks relating to test cases) which would be still sufficient to describe the participants' background information.

Internal Validity. Internal validity is about causal relations examined in the study. Even though we identified possible aspects which should be considered when defining and assessing test-case quality, our focus was not to generate a complete list of such aspects. By not eliminating one aspect or another, this type of threat is not of concern.

External Validity. External validity is concerned with the generalisability of the study's findings. In general, with the "convenience sampling" [16], the sample might not represent the population, which could potentially affect the findings' generalisability. However, as our study is exploratory, not confirmatory, this sampling method is not considered as a validity threat. Our study's context is characterised by the type of the company, which is a global company working on embedded software systems, the practitioners' documented working background and the nature of the natural-language tests. That is the context to which the findings can be potentially applied.

Reliability. Reliability is about the reliability of the results. Our study's design was discussed among all authors of the paper. The interviews were conducted by two researchers and the findings were discussed by all researchers to mitigate the bias from one researcher. The data collection process and interview questions were clearly documented to increase the reliability.

---

[1] https://www.istqb.org/.

5   Results and Discussion

In this section, we present and discuss our findings in relation to each of the research questions stated in Sect. 3.1.

5.1   Test-Case Quality Definition (RQ1)

To answer the first research question, we asked practitioners to define test-case quality and explain how they would assess such quality (the interview question Q7–11). Table 2 contains a list of 11 test-case quality attributes that we collected. It also includes the practitioners' authentic terms and phrases used to describe the attributes. It is worth mentioning that the use of specific test cases, chosen by the participants from the organization's test suites, triggered more in-depth reflections. The insights from practitioners regarding these test cases identified as many unique test-case quality attributes as a discussion in abstract of what constitutes test-case quality.

Overall, we could see that the quality attributes could be placed into two groups. The first group, including *understandability, step cohesion, completeness, efficiency*, and *flexibility*, is oriented around quality attributes of a test case which could be relevant for practitioners when executing it. The second group includes *understandability, simplicity, completeness, homogeneity, issue-identifying capability, repeatability, traceability, effectiveness*, and *reasonable size*. The latter group of attributes relates to general concerns, namely the design, the maintenance, and the objective of testing in general.

Understandability is the most common attribute, and discussed by all practitioners. A reason for this could be the nature of the discussed test cases, which were written in natural language. Hence, it makes sense that ambiguity in test cases is considered as a major concern. We could also see an alignment between practitioners' perceptions and the literature. *Understandability* is directly connected to three test smells, namely *ambiguous tests* in natural-language tests [12], *long/complex/verbose/obscure test*, and *bad naming* in test code [8]. Even though the last two smells are for test code, according to their definitions, which are "It is difficult to understand the test at a glance. The test usually has excessive lines of code" and "The test method name is not meaningful and thus leads to low understandability" respectively, those smells could also occur in natural-language tests. The other connection is between the quality attribute *simplicity* and the test smell *eager test*, which is described as "The test is verifying too much functionality in a single test method" [8].

Apart from identifying test-case quality attributes, practitioners also listed the top characteristics and indicators of a good test case and of a bad one. The outcome is a mixture of specific quality indicators: *clear objective* (the purpose of a test case), *clear precondition* (how to set up the testing environment), *clear steps with clear expected results*, and general quality attributes: *understandability, completeness, effectiveness*. According to our ranking scheme, *understandability* is rated as the most important attribute. This is consistent with the most commonly discussed quality attributes in the general discussion. The second place goes to the quality indicator *clear objective*. One of the reasons given by one practitioner was that "the objective of each test case or of each component of the test scope is the most important thing because those are combined to make sure that all the requirements of each of the projects are met."

Table 2. Test-case quality attributes

Quality attribute	Description	Practitioners' phrases	N[a]
Understand-ability	The information of a test case (name, objective, precondition, steps, terms) should be easy to understand by both testers, and developers	Straightforward, understandable description, how and what to test, clear steps, clear objective, clear precondition	6
Simplicity	A test case should not combine different test cases together nor contain so many steps	A big story for many test, not so many steps cases	4
Step cohesion	Steps in a test case should be well connected. The test case should not contain redundant steps or miss necessary steps	Unnecessary step, mandatory steps	3
Completeness	A test case should contain all relevant information for its execution	All information needed to perform the test, all kind of information that developers and testers need	2
Homogeneity	Test-case design should follow the same rules	Homogeneous, unity with the same rules, harmony	2
Issue-identifying capability	A test case should help to identify issues, weakness of features/functions	Find bug, mitigate possible issues	2
Repeatability	A test case returns the same results every time it is executed	Run any time, tested repeatedly	2
Traceability	There should be traces between a test case and other related artefacts such as issues, ISO quality attributes, functionality	Mentioned issue, function category, ISO attributes category	2
Effectiveness	A test case covers the expected requirements	Meets the requirement	1
Efficiency	A test case should be easy to run so that it does not waste time	Efficient, easy to run, not complicated, save time	1
Flexibility	A test case should have flexibility in how to execute it	Flexible, loosely written test, freedom, run differently	1

[a]N: Number of practitioners discussed the quality attribute

5.2 Alignment in Understanding of Test-Case Quality (RQ2)

We asked practitioners to classify test cases given by the others into *good, bad* or *normal* in terms of their quality (Sect. 2 of the interview questionnaire). Due to the interviews' time constraint, only seven out of 17 test cases, were analysed by more than one practitioners as shown in Table 3. Half of them, P1.3, P2.4, P3.1, and P3.2, had the same quality classification while the other half, P1.2, P3.1, P4.1, and P5.2, received a mixed assessment.

In general, we could see that test-case *understandability* was always the first concern. For the test cases having the same quality assessment (P1.3, P2.4, P3.1, P3.2), a test case's quality is considered as absolutely bad if the practitioners could not understand what they are supposed to do, especially when both the test objective and other details like steps, precondition, expected results of steps are unclear. If the test case's objective is sufficiently clear enough that the practitioners could get some idea about its purpose, they would consider its quality as acceptable or normal, though other details like preconditions are missing.

By analysing test cases which had different quality classification results (P1.2, P3.1, P4.1, and P5.2), we could see that the difference is strongly associated with the practitioners' responsibilities relating to test cases. If one of their responsibilities is to execute test cases, then they are more concerned about whether they have all relevant information to run the test cases. If they are responsible for broader tasks, in this case mainly about test-case maintenance and test results analysis such as what faults to fix, then they would have other concerns such as the test cases' complexity or their traceability to issues, bugs.

Our observation aligns with the perceptions of practitioners as they explained that they might have different concerns regarding test cases depending on their responsibilities. Those responsible for executing test cases prioritise *understandability* and *completeness* of test cases, that is, whether they have all relevant and clear information for executing the test cases. Those responsible for broader tasks like test architects do not only care about how test cases execute but also about the outcome of the test cases and the test suites in general. Hence, they have extra expectations such as whether the test cases cover the requirements, or whether it is easy to maintain the test cases. They also explained that the difference in working styles might have an impact on the test-case quality assessment. If they have different approaches in designing test cases, they would have different requirements on how to assure the test-case quality.

To provide a different perspective on the test-case quality assessment, the lead author used the list of test smells from the literature (see Sect. 3.3) to identify test smells in those seven test cases. As a result, there is a considerable overlap between the practitioners' concerns and the identified test smells (*ambiguous test* [12], *conditional tests* [12], *long/complex/verbose/obscure test* [8], and *eager test* [8]) (shown in Table 3). It is shown that the concerns about *understandability, ambiguity, cohesion* of test cases match with the test smells *ambiguous test* and *long/complex/verbose/obscure test*. Likewise, the concerns about the *complexity* of test cases directly relate to the test smells *eager test*.

However, the concerns about two quality attributes, *traceability* and *repeatability*, have no corresponding smells according to our list of test smells. One potential reason is that those quality concerns could be the consequences of some other test smells. *Traceability* could be affected by the test smells *eager test, ambiguous test* and *long/complex/verbose/obscure test*. As pointed out by

Table 3. Test-Case (TC) quality classification

TC ID	Concerns from Assessor 1	Classification (G/B/N)	Concerns from Assessor 2	Literature [8, 12]
P1.2	-Understandability: explained objective, links to specs/requirements, unclear precondition -Complexity: combination of multiple TCs -Traceability to bugs: not clear due to the complexity	Assessor1 [P1]: N Assessor2 [P4]: G	-Ambiguity: not well written pre-conditions -Complexity: combination of multiple TCs	-Ambiguous test [12] -VOLC test [8] -Eager test [8]
P4.1	-Ambiguity: unclear terms, missing expected results of steps, missing pre-conditions	Assessor 1 [P4]: B Assessor 2 [P1]: N	-Ambiguity: unclear terms -Repeatability: can be run anytime	-Ambiguous test [12] -VOLC test [8]
P5.2	-Ambiguity: unclear terms -Complexity: combination of multiple TCs -Traceability to bugs: not clear due to the complexity	Assessor 1 [P5]: B Assessor 2 [P2]: N	-Ambiguity: unclear terms	-Ambiguous test [12] VOLC test [8] -Eager test [8]
P3.1	-Understandability: sufficient description	Assessor 1 [P3]: N Assessor 2 [P2]: B	-Ambiguity: unclear terms due to poor English	-Conditional test [12] -Ambiguous test [12] -VOLC test [8]
P3.1	-Understandability: sufficient description	Assessor1 [P3]: N Assessor2 [P5]: N	-Understandability: explained objective -Ambiguity: missing pre-conditions -Traceability to bugs: established	-Conditional test [12] -Ambiguous test [12] -VOLC test [8]
P1.3	-Ambiguity: unclear objective -Complexity: combination of multiple TCs -Traceability to bugs: not clear due to the complexity	Assessor1 [P1]: B Assessor2 [P6]: B	-Ambiguity: unclear objective, unclear terms, unclear expected results for multiple steps -Complexity: combining several TCs	-Conditional test [12] -Ambiguous test [12] -VOLC test [8] - Eager test [8]
P2.4	-Ambiguity: missing pre-conditions	Assessor1 [P2]: B Assessor2 [P5]: B	-Ambiguity: unclear objective, missing pre-conditions	-Ambiguous test [12] -VOLC test [8]
P3.2	-Ambiguity: missing objective -Cohesion: missing steps	Assessor1 [P3]: B Assessor2 [P5]: B	-Ambiguity: unclear step	Ambiguous test [12] -VOLC test [8]

[1]VOLC: Long/complex/verbose/obscure [8]

practitioners, if a test case contains multiple test cases, it becomes complex. Hence, it is harder to understand which part the test case leads to found issue(s). Ambiguity in a test case's description could also make the test execution non-deterministic [12], which potentially affects the traceability to found issue(s). Likewise, *repeatability* might not be possible if there are dependencies among the test cases. Indeed, there are test smells due to dependencies in testing [8]. However, they were not in our list as they were not the top discussed smells [8].

5.3   Quality-Related Factors (RQ3)

By answering our interview questions (Q4–9), the practitioners described factors which could influence how they assess test-case quality. In general, practitioners believe that the test-case quality depends on the test case's context. For example, the assessment could depend on whether the practitioner knows how the code was written. He or she might have a different opinion on how to design test cases for testing that code compared with those who do not know the code. Another context factor is the maturity level of the software system under test (SUT). According to three practitioners, to save their time, they could combine multiple test cases into one when the SUT is more or less working properly as those test cases hardly fail at that state. Hence, in that case, a test case is not considered as bad even though it contains different test cases. Two practitioners mentioned that the testing level also has an impact on how test-case quality is defined. For example, for exploratory tests, practitioners whose responsible is execute test cases prefer to have flexibility in executing test cases. They would rather not to follow steps so closely as that might not help them to identify new issues. Therefore, if an exploratory test case's execution instructions are restrictive, that test case could be perceived as bad. Hence, practitioners' pre-knowledge of the test-case context has a strong influence on their test-case quality perceptions.

5.4   Improvement (RQ4)

With the interview question Q14, we identify several suggestions for improving test-case quality. In general, a homogeneous directive or procedure for test-case design could improve the quality as it could guarantee test cases are designed systematically. A uniform quality policy could also help to ensure the quality is met and aligned among practitioners. More specifically, to enhance test-case understandability in the test-case design phase, it was suggested that each test case should contain all necessary information. Importantly, the information should be relevant to both testers and developers. That will help to avoid a situation in which testers or developers have to look for information of related test cases in order to understand their assigned test cases. For test-case maintenance, the most common suggestion was that test cases should be reviewed regularly as they could become obsolete due to the evolution of the SUT. Updating test cases so that they contain all relevant information for execution and removing no-longer-needed test cases are important steps in this phase. Apart from improvements in test-case design and maintenance, practitioners also suggested that developers and testers should have active communication in order to mitigate misunderstanding in executing and analysing test results.

5.5 Source of Information (RQ5)

With the interview question Q15, we collected information sources that practitioners refer to for a better understanding of test-case quality. The most common source is from colleagues like testers and developers working on the same projects, especially seniors who have experience in similar tasks. It is consistent with the previous research on information sources consulted by practitioners [14].

Regarding test-case design, product specifications are considered the most relevant internal source of information. Other types of internal sources include software architect documents, test cases in previous projects, guidelines and templates for writing test cases, rules and policies from test architects, and test plans. The practitioners also refer to external sources such as guidelines provided by the ISTQB and ISO standards. Apart from those common sources, one practitioner also mentioned that he or she learns about test-case quality by attending industrial seminars and workshops on related topics. Some practitioners also said that they rely on their own experience when assessing test-case quality.

6 Conclusions and Future Work

We conducted an interview-based exploratory study involving six practitioners, working in three different teams in a company to understand practitioners' perceptions of test-case quality. We identified 11 quality attributes for test cases, of which *understandability* was perceived as most important. That could be due to the nature of the studied test cases, which were written in natural language. Nevertheless, the study of Garousi et al. [8] also reported the related test smell *long/complex/verbose/obscure test* as the main concern in test code, which means that *understandability* is also important in test code.

We also found that there is a misalignment in practitioners' perceptions of test-case quality. The explanation is that, depending on the practitioners' responsibilities, they have different quality requirements. For practitioners whose responsibility is to run test cases, the focus is more on acquiring relevant information for test-case execution. Hence, their priority is the *understandability* of test cases. For those who need to design and maintain test cases like test architects and developers, their concerns are more about test-case maintenance and outcomes of test suites. Therefore, they require other quality attributes such as *traceability* to other artefacts, *efficiency, effectiveness, repeatability*, etc. The context factors of test cases, such as code-related knowledge, the maturity level of software under test, testing types such as exploratory test potentially also impact how practitioners define test-case quality.

We also identified suggestions for improving test-case quality. The most common suggestion is a homogeneous procedure for test-case design, with focus on completeness of test cases, meaning that a test case should contain all relevant information for execution by any involved party. Reviewing test cases and regular communication between developers and testers were also highly recommended by practitioners. Practitioners also discussed different sources of information they refer for a better understanding of test-case quality. In general, their information comes from external sources such as ISTQB and ISO standards. For specific test cases, they rely on the internal sources, such as product specifications, and discussion with other colleagues.

Even though our findings were based on a few data points, we had a sound, repeatable strategy to identify them. They are not generic, but for a specific context. For more general findings, we plan to interview more practitioners in different contexts. We will also compare our findings of the quality attributes and quality definition(s) with other existing studies. Another planned future work is to have a broader investigation on differences and similarities between the industry and the literature on defining and assessing test-case quality.

Acknowledgment. This work has been supported by ELLIIT, a Strategic Area within IT and Mobile Communications, funded by the Swedish Government, and by the VITS project from the Knowledge Foundation Sweden (20180127).

References

1. Athanasiou, D., Nugroho, A., Visser, J., Zaidman, A.: Test code quality and its relation to issue handling performance. IEEE Trans. Softw. Eng. **40**(11), 1100–1125 (2014)
2. Bowes, D., Hall, T., Petric, J., Shippey, T., Turhan, B.: How good are my tests? In: 2017 IEEE/ACM 8th Workshop on Emerging Trends in Software Metrics (WET-SoM), pp. 9–14, May 2017
3. Čaušević, A., Sundmark, D., Punnekkat, S.: Test case quality in test driven development: a study design and a pilot experiment. In: 16th International Conference on Evaluation Assessment in Software Engineering (EASE 2012), pp. 223–227, May 2012
4. Chernak, Y.: Validating and improving test-case effectiveness. IEEE Softw. **18**(1), 81–86 (2001)
5. Cruzes, D.S., Dyba, T.: Recommended steps for thematic synthesis in software engineering. In: 2011 International Symposium on Empirical Software Engineering and Measurement, pp. 275–284, September 2011
6. Daka, E., Campos, J., Fraser, G., Dorn, J., Weimer, W.: Modeling readability to improve unit tests. In: Proceedings of the 2015 10th Joint Meeting on Foundations of Software Engineering, ESEC/FSE 2015, pp. 107–118. ACM, New York (2015)
7. Garousi, V., Felderer, M.: Developing, verifying, and maintaining high-quality automated test scripts. IEEE Softw. **33**(3), 68–75 (2016)
8. Garousi, V., Kucuk, B., Felderer, M.: What we know about smells in software test code. IEEE Softw. **36**(3), 61–73 (2019)
9. Garousi, V., Küçük, B.: Smells in software test code: a survey of knowledge in industry and academia. J. Syst. Softw. **138**, 52–81 (2018)
10. Gopinath, R., Jensen, C., Groce, A.: Code coverage for suite evaluation by developers. In: Proceedings of the 36th International Conference on Software Engineering, ICSE 2014, pp. 72–82. ACM, New York (2014)

11. Grano, G., Scalabrino, S., Gall, H.C., Oliveto, R.: An empirical investigation on the readability of manual and generated test cases. In: Proceedings of the 26th Conference on Program Comprehension, ICPC 2018, pp. 348–351. ACM, New York (2018)

12. Hauptmann, B., Junker, M., Eder, S., Heinemann, L., Vaas, R., Braun, P.: Hunting for smells in natural language tests. In: 2013 35th International Conference on Software Engineering (ICSE), pp. 1217–1220, May 2013

13. Inozemtseva, L., Holmes, R.: Coverage is not strongly correlated with test suite effectiveness. In: Proceedings of the 36th International Conference on Software Engineering, ICSE 2014, pp. 435–445. ACM, New York (2014)

14. Josyula, J., Panamgipalli, S., Usman, M., Britto, R., Ali, N.B.: Software practitioners' information needs and sources: a survey study. In: Proceedings of the 9th International Workshop on Empirical Software Engineering in Practice (IWESEP), pp. 1–6, December 2018

15. Jovanovikj, I., Narasimhan, V., Engels, G., Sauer, S.: Context-specific quality evaluation of test cases. In: Proceedings of the 6th International Conference on Model-Driven Engineering and Software Development - Volume 1: MODELSWARD, pp. 594–601. INSTICC, SciTePress (2018)

16. Kitchenham, B., Pfleeger, S.L.: Principles of survey research: part 5: populations and samples. SIGSOFT Softw. Eng. Notes **27**(5), 17–20 (2002)

17. Nagappan, N., Williams, L., Osborne, J., Vouk, M., Abrahamsson, P.: Providing test quality feedback using static source code and automatic test suite metrics. In: 16th IEEE International Symposium on Software Reliability Engineering (ISSRE 2005), pp. 10–94, November 2005

18. Neukirchen, H., Zeiss, B., Grabowski, J.: An approach to quality engineering of TTCN-3 test specifications. Int. J. Softw. Tools Technol. Transf. **10**(4), 309 (2008)

19. Pfaller, C., Wagner, S., Gericke, J., Wiemann, M.: Multi-dimensional measures for test case quality. In: 2008 IEEE International Conference on Software Testing Verification and Validation Workshop, pp. 364–368, April 2008

20. Reichhart, S., Gîrba, T., Ducasse, S.: Rule-based assessment of test quality. J. Object Technol. **6**(9), 231–251 (2007)

21. Robson, C., McCartan, K.: Real World Research: A Resource for Users of Social Research Methods in Applied Settings, 4th edn. Wiley, Hoboken (2016)

22. Tan, H., Tarasov, V.: Test case quality as perceived in Sweden. In: 2018 IEEE/ACM 5th International Workshop on Requirements Engineering and Testing (RET), pp. 9–12, June 2018

23. Zeiss, B., Vega, D., Schieferdecker, I., Neukirchen, H., Grabowski, J.: Applying the ISO 9126 quality model to test specifications - exemplified for TTCN-3 test specifications. In: Bleek, W.G., Raasch, J., Züllighoven, H. (eds.) Software Engineering 2007 - Fachtagung des GI-Fachbereichs Softwaretechnik, pp. 231–242. Gesellschaft für Informatik e. V, Bonn (2007)

24. Zhu, H., Hall, P.A.V., May, J.H.R.: Software unit test coverage and adequacy. ACM Comput. Surv. **29**(4), 366–427 (1997)

Test Reporting at a Large-Scale Austrian Logistics Organization: Lessons Learned and Improvement

Dietmar Winkler[1,2]([⊠]) , Kristof Meixner[1,2], Daniel Lehner[2], and Stefan Biffl[2]

[1] Christian Doppler Laboratory for "Security and Quality Improvement in the Production System Lifecycle", Institute of Information Systems Engineering, Vienna University of Technology, Favoritenstrasse 9-11, 1040 Vienna, Austria
{Dietmar.Winkler,Kristof.Meixner}@tuwien.ac.at
[2] Institute of Information Systems Engineering, Vienna University of Technology, Favoritenstrasse 9-11, 1040 Vienna, Austria
{Daniel.Lehner,Stefan.Biffl}@tuwien.ac.at

Abstract. *Context and Background.* Software testing and test automation are important activities in software development where frequent requirements changes and the fast delivery of software increments are supported by traditional and agile development processes. Test reports are often used as "proof of evidence" for executed software tests. However, the practical impact of test reports, such as decision making and quality assessment, requires structured information which might not be available in sufficient quality. *Goal.* In this paper we (a) report on needs of test reports of different stakeholders at a large-scale Austrian logistics organization, (b) develop candidate improvement actions based on the state of the practice, and (c) conceptually evaluate selected improvement actions. *Method.* We used surveys and interviews to elicit needs and expected capabilities for test reporting and developed candidate improvement. We used expert discussions prioritize improvement actions in the organization context for further implementation. *Results.* Based on 23 recommended improvement actions, 14 were initially selected for implementation. Most of these accepted improvement action focus on regular test status reports and visualization aspects of test reports. *Conclusion.* Although test reporting is systematically applied in development processes, there is still some potential to improve test reports to gain (additional) benefits for related stakeholder.

Keywords: Software testing · Test reporting · Engineering process improvement · Case study

1 Introduction

Delivering high-quality software products is the most important objective in software development projects [9]. Static quality assurance approaches, such as reviews and inspections can help to identify defects early in the software development life cycle [6].

© Springer Nature Switzerland AG 2019
X. Franch et al. (Eds.): PROFES 2019, LNCS 11915, pp. 53–69, 2019.
https://doi.org/10.1007/978-3-030-35333-9_4

Because no executable software code is required, reviews and inspection can focus on various types of software artifacts, e.g., requirements specifications, architecture diagrams, or code. Dynamic quality assurance approaches, such as software tests, require executable code and can help identifying defects in the software system or sub-systems based on defined test scenarios and test cases [8]. In context of continuous integration and test strategies [2], test runs are typically embedded within a software build process and, thus, represents the foundation for test automation. Figure 1 presents a typical and simplified continuous integration and test process: (1) *Developers* commit newly constructed software code into a code repository; (2) *Release Managers* initiate a build process (on purpose or on a regular basis, e.g., daily/nightly builds) including test runs and reporting; (3) *Test managers* and *Testers* prepare test scenarios, test cases and test data for test execution; (4) *Developers* receive feedback, e.g., by using test reports, on the test runs with focus on of their committed piece of code; (5) finally, a test report is generated, used by different stakeholders for analysis and decision making. For instance, *test managers* and *testers* can use test reports for providing evidence on the results of executed test runs, *project managers can* use test reports for analyzing the quality of the software code and for assessing the status of the project and *business managers* can use test reports to assess the overall progress of the project, e.g., based on coverage analysis.

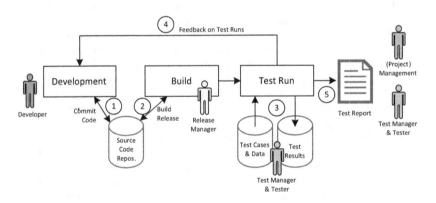

Fig. 1. Simplified continuous integration and test process.

However, an important question focus on the impact of test reports usage, i.e., to derive what is most beneficial in a test report for all involved stakeholders. Although there exist standards for test reporting, e.g., by ISO/IEC/IEEE 29119-3:2013 [4] a remaining question is to what extent required (and standardized) test documentation can help development teams or test/project managers to better control software engineering projects.

In this paper we focus on (a) the identification of stakeholder needs in context of test reporting at a large-scale Austrian Logistics Organization, (b) identifying improvement candidates based on test report best-practices as foundation for improvement action implementation, and (c) on a conceptual analysis of selected improvement actions in the study context. For identifying stakeholder needs we conducted a survey and a set of interviews at the logistics organization. Based on the results we developed a set of candidate improvements as foundation for improvement and discussed benefits and limitations with the related stakeholders in the organization. Finally, we conceptually evaluated selected improvement actions in the study context. Note that the implementation and further investigations remain for future work.

The remainder of this paper is structured as follows: Sect. 2 summarizes related work on software testing and test automation, test reporting, and engineering process improvement. We present the research issues in Sect. 3 and describe the study process in Sect. 4. Section 5 summarize results and Sect. 6 focuses on the discussion of the results. Finally, Sect. 7 summarizes and concludes.

2   Background and Related Work

This section summarizes background and related work on Software Tests and Test Automation (2.1) Test Reporting (2.2), and Engineering Process Improvement (2.3).

2.1   Software Test Automation

Software tests aim at identifying defects in executable software engineering artefacts, i.e., in software code [8, 10]. Manual testing approaches and the creation of manual test reports require (high) human effort for test case and test data definition and test execution. However, frequent test runs, common in agile software development, make it hard to manage manual tests because of effort and cost considerations. In addition, testing of non-functional requirements, such as performance and load tests, require appropriate tool support because such type of tests cannot be conducted efficiently by human experts [7]. Thus, automated tests embedded within continuous delivery strategies need to be implemented to overcome limitations of manual activities and/or enable defined types of tests, such as performance or load testing [3].

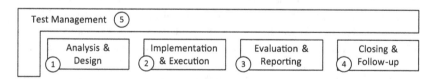

Fig. 2. Basic software test process according to Spillner *et al.* [10].

Although application context and customer requirements have a strong impact on selection appropriate test types, test processes follow a defined sequence of steps (see Fig. 2):

1. Test *Analysis and Design* focuses on the specification of test levels and types. Test levels focus on different levels/scopes of the software/system under test, such as units, components, sub-systems, or systems. Test types refer approaches how to test these system parts, e.g., functions, performance, or load.

2. *Implementation & Execution* includes the setup of the test infrastructure, generation/construction of test cases, test data and the (automated) execution of software tests.
3. *Evaluation & Reporting* include test results analysis for feedback (e.g., within a continuous integration and test strategy) and for test report generation.
4. *Closing & Follow-up* focuses on test run and environment archiving and preparing decision support for test and/or project management.
5. *Test management* includes test planning, decision of test strategies, and control of test runs based on analysis results and test reports.

In this paper we focus on test reports and the impact of test reports on a defined set of stakeholders, e.g., developers, release managers, test managers, test experts, and (project) management – key stakeholders as depicted in Fig. 1. Often test reports are used to provide some evidence on executed test runs and for decision making. However, based on observations in industry, we see the need to investigate test reports to improve the acceptance and usability of test reports.

2.2   Test Reporting

The ISO/IEC/IEEE 29119-3 standard [4] focuses on general *software test documentation templates* and how they map to the several levels/scopes of software testing. Furthermore, the standard defines the *Organizational Test Documentation* including the *Test Policy* and *Organizational Test Strategies* derived from this policy as general guidelines from the organization to be used for test processes in specific projects. The *Test Management Documentation* contains *Test Plans* for defining particular testing strategies beforehand as well as a *Test Completion Report* available after a particular testing effort. The *Dynamic Test Documentation* which is produced during actual testing efforts including the *Test Specification, Test Environment Readiness Report*, and *Test Data Readiness Report* (prerequisites for executing the tests). When executing test cases, *Test Execution Documentation* holds related information. *Incident Reports* include defects, deviations, and incidents identified during test execution.

Although this standard provides some guidance for implementing test reporting in an organization, one should also consider more general factors to satisfy a wider range of stakeholders. Kelley [5] defines a set of guidelines and recommendations for reporting in a medical context: (a) *Quality before quantity*, i.e., focus on data that is needed by readers of the reports in order to do their job; (b) *Focus on patterns*, rather than on isolated occurrences; (c) Apply *benchmarks* for comparing current results to similar institutions; (d) Include *Data Analysis and Interpretation*, i.e., never use raw or unexplained data; and (e) Include a *Management Summary*, i.e., highlight actions and options for board consideration. In this work, we want to find out to which degree these recommendations are relevant in the context of test reporting. For example, a test report, e.g., embedded within a continuous integration and test strategy (see Fig. 1), holds test individual case definitions and test results that can be aggregated to test scenarios, and related (summarized) results. Furthermore, individual test results represent the foundation for deriving quality metrics, such as test coverage or quality estimations for decision-making.

2.3   Engineering Process Improvement

Industry organization often follow a pre-defined set of test report items (e.g., recommended by standards, such as [4]) without carefully analyzing strength and limitations of test reports in their individual context. Thus, we see the need to analyse the current state of the practice in organizations, identify strength and limitations in context of best practices, and initiate a process improvement initiative to improve test reporting and tests processes. For initiating and executing engineering process improvement strategies, there is the need to follow a systematic process approach, such as the *Quality Improvement Paradigm* (QIP) [1]. In context of this paper we applied the *Quality Assurance Tradeoff Analysis Method* (QATAM) [11], an engineering process improvement approach that helps identifying strengths and limitations and suggests candidate improvements in a defined context (see Fig. 3 for a conceptual overview). Main building blocks of the QATAM approach includes (1) *Context and Scope* definition of the planned improvement initiative, e.g., improving test reporting; (2) *Method Repositories* as a pool of mechanisms, methods and tools available from best practice recommendations; (3) *Candidate Improvement Options* as possible improvement strategies; and (4) *Evaluation of Candidate Improvements* as a foundation from implementation in the organization context.

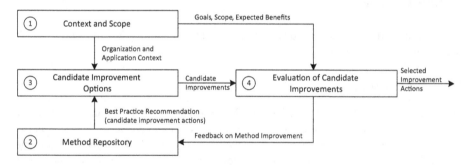

Fig. 3. Quality Assurance Tradeoff Analysis Method (QATAM) according to [11].

In context of this paper, we focus on test reporting *(Context and Scope)* based on best practice recommendations *(Method Repository)*, e.g., in [4] to derive an initial set *Candidate Improvement Options* to be evaluated in collaboration with the organization to elicit appropriate improvement action *(Strategy Evaluation and Selection)*.

3   Research Issues

Based on the related work on test automation and test reporting, we identified a set of research issues as part of the process improvement initiative at a large-scale Austrian logistics organization.

RQ.1: What are critical stakeholder requirements for test reporting in context of the case study organization? Although there are some further goals of reports, like documenting the work that has been done, we want to focus on reports for transmitting information with a clear purpose, to a specific audience, i.e., to relevant stakeholders like developers, testers, test managers, release managers, project management, and business management. The first research question focusses on eliciting requirements from best practice recommendations and defined stakeholder groups at the industry partner.

RQ.2: What are the best-practices implemented in the organization, i.e., a large-scale Austrian logistics organization? Up to now, test reports have been established within the organization. A *specific test department* offers testing as a service to developer groups. However, it remains unclear how individual reports are implemented and used and what are the conclusions drawn out of the reports. In context of this work, we used a survey to identify he current use of test reports. Thus, the second research questions focuses on identifying best practices implemented in the organization.

RQ.3: What is the impact of improved reporting in context of a logistics organization? Following the QATAM approach, we analysed strength and limitations of current approaches, derived improvement actions, and discussed selected improvement actions in the organization as foundation for implementation. The third research question focuses on investigating the impact of improved test reports.

4   Study Process

This section introduces to the study company (4.1) and summarizes the study design and process steps (4.2).

4.1   Case Study Company

The case study organization is a large-scale Austrian logistics organization with an integrated IT department with around 250 people, including dedicated departments for *testing* and *architecture and project management*. These two departments represent important core producers and consumers of test reports. The main business goal of the logistics organization focuses on worldwide shipping of items (and related processes and applications). The software developed and maintained by the IT department aims at supporting and optimizing relevant processes, e.g., passing metadata of items through barcodes as well as improving customer experience, e.g., tracking of items.

4.2   Study Process

Main objective of this work focus on (a) identifying test reporting needs and requirements, (b) analyzing the state of the practice in the case study organization, and (c) eliciting and evaluating improvement candidates. Figure 4 illustrates the study design and the study process steps.

Step 1. Test Report Requirements Identification. We used *surveys* to capture specific test report needs of external stakeholders (i.e., stakeholders that are outside the testing department, e.g., project managers) in the organization. The second part of the requirements elicitation process focuses on interviewing test managers to identify their expectation on test reporting.

Step 2. State of the Practice Analysis. Test processes and related artifacts are standardized in the case study company, we selected a typical project to analyze the state of the practice on test report usage in the study context. The analysis process focuses on whether or not identified requirements are captured in the selected project.

Step 3. Identification of Improvement Candidate. We identified gaps between the state of the practice (step 2), requirements (step 1), and the state of the art derived from the literature. Based on the results of this analysis process step we came up with a set of 25 concrete improvement suggestions (i.e., improvement candidates) for optimizing test reporting to close these gaps.

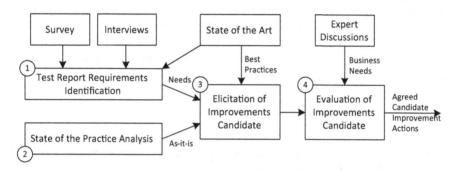

Fig. 4. Study process overview.

Step 4. Evaluation of Improvement Candidates. We evaluated improvement candidates (Step 3) to assess their relevance in the case study organization and whether or not they can be accepted by key stakeholders in the organization, i.e., test managers. The assessment was based on informal interviews and discussions with test managers in the case study company. The study was executed in 2017 by process improvement and testing experts, i.e., the authors. One of the authors was responsible for conducting the study at the case study organization, supervised by the other authors. Several feedback rounds were implemented to ensure the quality of the study design.

4.3   Survey and Interview Structure

For the assessment of requirements, we separated internal and external stakeholders. We created a survey with focus on team members of the *Architecture and Project Management Office*, involving 30 people. The department consists of *project managers*, i.e., users of test reports, as well as roles whose work is indirectly influenced by test reports, e.g., *requirements engineers* and *enterprise architects*. Additionally, we included *team leads* who are responsible for a group of project managers, requirement engineers and enterprise architects. As line managers, they need to have an overall view on the projects of their team members. Therefore, they are mainly interested in the current quality status of the individual projects. Additionally, they want to improve the working conditions of their staff, so they are highly interested in improving test reports to improve the engineering process and support project management. These employees were all considered external stakeholders of the testing department.

The survey is structured into seven sections: (a) Demographics and Background; (b) General Question on test reporting; (c) Current Usage of Regular Test Reports; (d) Test Automation; and (e) Current Usage of Final Test Status Reports. The detailed questionnaires are available online[1]. We used an online tool for executing the survey[2].

In addition, we interviewed the *test managers* within the testing department (i.e., internal stakeholders). Main tasks of test managers is to plan and control the execution of testing, to solve problems that occur during testing and to communicate the work of the testing department by sending out reports. The four test managers that were employed by the testing department had a different view on the work and especially on the reporting of the testing department. The goal of the interviews was to capture insights and get a broader and more un-biased view on test reports. We used open questions (see footnote 1) to get qualitative information on the state of the practice and to complement quantitative data collected during the surveys.

5   Results

This section summarizes the results of the improvement initiative in context of test reporting at the case study organization.

5.1   Stakeholder Needs for Test Reporting

We derived general stakeholder needs (requirements) from the literature for identifying general factors of "well-designed" reports (see [5] Section 2.2) and extended requirements derived from [4] as the test reporting framework at the case study organization was initially set up using this standard. Note that the organization decided to apply all reports (recommended by the standard [4]).

Additionally, we identified some further needs of stakeholders during the case study. Note that the mapping between identified requirements and stakeholders was based on a discussion with test center managers. Table 1 summarizes identified requirements and shows the relevant and related stakeholders. Note that requirements (R07–R12) were identified during the case study (see Sects. 5.2 and 5.3 for details).

5.2   Survey Results

The survey has been sent to 30 external stakeholders of the testing department (see Sect. 4.3 for details). We received an overall number of 15 responses, i.e., a response

---

[1] Complementary study material: qse.ifs.tuwien.ac.at/profes-2019-test-reporting

[2] Online Survey: www.umfrageonline.com/

Table 1. Identified requirement and related stakeholders.

Req.ID	Requirement	Stakeholder			
		PM	TM	BM	Others
R01	Quality before quantity	x		x	x
R02	Patterns instead of isolated occurrences	x		x	x
R03	No raw or unexplained data	x		x	x
R04	Highlight actions and options	x			
R05	Use benchmarks	x		x	
R06	Fulfill standard, e.g., ISO/IEC/IEEE 29119-3:2013 [4]		x	x	
R07	*Use graphics instead of metrics for visualization*	x		x	x
R08	*Modular reports*	x			
R09	*Support decision making*	x	x	x	
R10	*Status of software development*	x		x	
R11	*Status of software testing*		x		
R12	*Minimum time effort for reporting*		x		

PM = Project Management, TM = Test Management, BM = Business Management, Others = developers, testers, etc.)

rate of 50%. We divided the responses into three groups: (a) Project Managers (PM), (b) Team Leads (TL), and (c) ENGineers (ENG), including requirements engineers and enterprise architects, as their work is indirectly influenced by test reports.

The survey results were exported as raw .csv data and then analyzed by using descriptive statistics supported by a spreadsheet solution. Table 2 presents *background and demographics* of participant roles of collected responses. The majority of survey respondents were project managers (PM), i.e., 8 participants (53%), followed by technical experts and engineers (ENG) including 5 participants (33%) and team leads (TL) with 2 participants (14%).

Table 2. Distribution of participant roles of collected responses.

Role Distribution	PM	TL	ENG*	ALL
Number of responses	8	2	5	15
Share of Responses	53%	14%	33%	100%

*Engineer includes 2 Requirements Engineers, 2 Enterprise Architects and 1 Developer

The first section batch of questions focuses on *general questions regarding test reports*, i.e., how test reports are perceived by the participants. Figure 5 summarizes the goals of stakeholders related to test reports they receive from the testing center. Note that in the case study company a dedicated testing support supports various projects. We used a Likert-Scale for collecting different ratings (1 refers to disagreement and 6 indicates a high agreement to a given statement). Figure 5 presents mean values of responses related to test report aspects and roles.

What is your goal when using test reports you receive from the testing department?

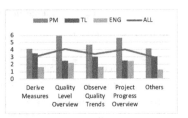

	PM	TL	ENG	ALL
Derive Measures	4,1	**3,5**	1,6	3,1
Quality Level Overview	**5,9**	2,5	2,2	4,1
Observe Quality Trends	4,7	3,0	1,6	3,4
Project Progress Overview	**5,6**	2,5	**2,4**	4,0
Others	4,1	**3,0**	1,2	2,9

*mean value based on Likert Scale 1 (disagree) to 6 (agree)

Fig. 5. Goals of test report usage from different perspectives.

The main goal of PMs is to get an *overview of the quality level* based to executed tests and some indication on the *project progress*. For TL it is more important to receive *concrete measures*, provided by the test center, to improve the product. Engineering roles focus on a *project progress overview* and some *decision support* (i.e., classified as "others" in Fig. 5) It is notable that PM are more interested in test reports, i.e., all aspects has been rated above average, while for TL and ENG test reports seem to be less important.

Results on the question regarding stakeholder expectations on the content of test reports are summarized in Fig. 6. For PM *trend graphics* (mean value: 3.5) are most important to assess the project progress and to have a quality level overview. TL expect *textual summaries* (4.0) and *quality metrics* (3.0) as foundation for decision support and to derive measures, while ENG are most interesting in a textual summary including measures and improvement suggests from the test center.

What do you expect from a test report?

	PM	TL	ENG	ALL
Textual Summary	2,3	**4,0**	**3,2**	2,8
Quality Metrics	2,5	**3,0**	2,0	2,4
Trend Graphics	**3,5**	1,0	2,3	2,7
Status Graphics	1,5	2,0	2,2	1,8

*mean value based on Likert Scale 1 (disagree) to 6 (agree)

Fig. 6. Expectations of test report content.

In the case study company, the test center provides *testing as a service* for individual projects. Typically, there is an order for the test center to execute a set of tests related to a test plan, e.g., a sequence of manual tests that could be relevant for acceptance testing. Another option is an order for implementing a continuous integration and test strategy as testing infrastructure that can be maintained by project members. However, an interesting question focuses on the expectation when to place which type of testing orders in the test center. Figure 7 summarize the findings.

Based on the results, PM expect *highlighted issues and defect reports* (5.7) based on the test runs to *ensure the quality* (5.6) of the product under test. For TL, in addition to *ensuring the quality*, where all participants agreed (6.0), they also expect suggestion

What do you expect when placing an order in the testing department?

	PM	TL	ENG	ALL
Highlight Issues	**5,7**	4,0	**4,6**	5,1
Ensure Quality	**5,6**	**6,0**	**5,0**	5,4
Suggest QA Activities	5,1	4,5	4,0	4,6
Improve Communic.	4,0	4,0	3,6	3,9

*mean value based on Likert Scale 1 (disagree) to 6 (agree)

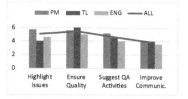

Fig. 7. Expectations when placing an order in the testing department.

for *QA and testing activities* to further improve the product. ENG focus on similar goals compared to PM but with a lower rate of agreement.

In test automation, reports are typically generated on a regular basis, e.g., based on iterations or based on a defined schedule, e.g., once a week or month. Therefore, we asked for the *current usage of regular test reports* with focus on *content* and *frequency*. Figure 8 presents typical content elements of (regular) test reports and the estimations on their stakeholder value. It is notable that highlighted test report elements seem to be of limited interest (maximum mean value 3.0 on a Likert-Scale from 1 to 6). This is quite surprising as common test reports are often based on a standard configurations. However, another question is, how well are test report content elements understood by test report consumers. Figure 9 summarizes the results on the *understandability* of test reports components. The results show on average that test report elements are well-understood by PM and TL but of limited value for ENG. Thus, there seem to be an improvement option to increase the usefulness of test reports.

Which parts of a regular test status report has most value for your own work?

	PM	TL	ENG	ALL
"Traffic Light Status"	1,0	2,0	1,7	1,3
Management Summary	1,4	2,0	2,0	1,7
Next Steps	1,1	2,0	2,3	1,6
Defect Trend	1,3	2,0	2,3	1,7
Requirements Coverage	1,4	3,0	1,7	1,7
Test Case Evolution	1,6	3,0	2,3	1,9
Defect Evolution	1,3	3,0	2,3	1,7
Metrics	1,5	3,0	2,3	1,9

*mean value based on Likert Scale 1 (disagree) to 6 (agree)

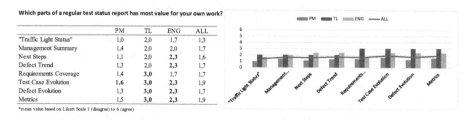

Fig. 8. Perceived importance of test report components.

How well understandable are the following parts of a regular test status report?

	PM	TL	ENG	ALL
"Traffic Light Status"	**3,7**	**4,0**	2,5	3,5
Management Summary	**3,7**	2,0	2,0	3,1
Next Steps	**3,7**	**4,0**	2,5	3,5
Defect Trend	**3,1**	2,0	1,0	2,8
Requirements Coverage	**4,0**	3,0	2,5	3,4
Test Case Evolution	**3,8**	3,0	1,0	3,3
Defect Evolution	**3,8**	3,0	1,0	3,4
Metrics	**3,0**	-	1,0	2,7

*mean value based on Likert Scale 1 (disagree) to 6 (agree)

Fig. 9. Understandability of test reports components.

64   D. Winkler et al.

Often, test reports are generated and distributed on a regular and timely basis. This could lead to effects that test reports do not receive much attention. The results on the frequency of test reports showed that PM would like to receive test reports on a *weekly basis* (72%) while TL want to receive test reports *weekly* (50%) and *depending on the project context* and project state (50%). In contrast to PM and TL, ENG support *longer time-interval* (e.g., bi-weekly or monthly) but would also prefer to configure test report frequency *depending on the project context* (similar to TL) and *on request*.

Independent on test report frequency, Fig. 10 presents the value of regular status reports per stakeholder group. PM are mainly interesting in the *quality status* and *suggestions for QA activities*, TL are interested in the *testing progress* and *quality trends* and ENG stakeholders focus on the *quality status* and *quality trend*. The result seem to be in conflict to goals and expectations of test reports in general (see Figs. 5 and 6).

Where do you see the value of regular test status reports?

	PM	TL	ENG	ALL
Testing Progress	5,0	5,5	4,5	5,0
Quality Trends	5,0	5,5	5,0	5,1
Quality Status	6,0	5,0	5,0	5,6
Propose QA Activities	5,3	4,5	3,0	4,7

*mean value based on Likert Scale 1 (disagree) to 6 (agree)

Fig. 10. Perceived value of regular test reports.

In context of *Test Automation*, were test reports are typically generated as part of the testing tool chain automatically, we wanted to know to what extent test automation has been applied by the stakeholders. While 86% of PM and 100% of TL have already applied test automation at least in one project, 75% of ENG did not apply test automation in their projects. Note that ENG include requirements engineers and architects. Similar results have been derived when asking whether or not test automation should be strengthened in their projects. Although there is some agreement to include test automation results in the test report, an interesting question focuses on the perceived value of a final test report. Figure 11 summarizes these results. PM participants see the *summary of issues* as most valuable part of test reports (5.7). TL are more interested in *final test results* and *detailed defect detection results* (5.5 each) all ENG participant see final test status report as most beneficial for a *summary of issues* (6.0).

What is the perceived value of a final test status report?

	PM	TL	ENG	ALL
Summary of Issues	5,7	5,0	6,0	5,6
Test Effort Review	4,3	5,0	2,5	4,1
Final Test Results	5,0	5,5	5,5	5,2
Deviation Detection	4,7	5,5	5,0	4,9
Improvement Options	5,0	3,0	4,0	4,5

*mean value based on Likert Scale 1 (disagree) to 6 (agree)

Fig. 11. Perceived value of final test report.

To improve test reporting and test automation, we included as set of candidate improvements in the survey. Figure 12 summarize the survey results. All stakeholder groups support and *expect recommendations from the test center* based as core part of a test report. The management roles PM and TL would prefer to adapt test activities (based on current test results and their needs) instead of sticking to a standardized test report. This adaption also include the definition of the frequency of test reports, which is especially interesting for TL. For ENG, capabilities for test report configuration is critical as size and complexity seem to be too large for this stakeholder group.

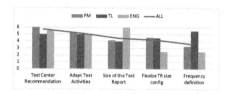

How do you rate the following improvement suggestions in context of test reports and test automation?				
	PM	TL	ENG	ALL
Test Center Recommendation	6,0	5,0	5,5	5,7
Adapt Test Activities	5,3	5,0	5,0	5,2
Size of the Test Report	4,1	4,0	6,0	4,5
Flexibe TR size config	4,6	4,5	2,5	4,2
Frequency definition	3,3	5,5	2,5	3,5

*mean value based on Likert Scale 1 (disagree) to 6 (agree)

Fig. 12. Suggested improvements for test reports and test automation.

Based on these survey, we conducted *three interviews* with test managers to discuss the results and derive additional requirements (see Table 1). Stakeholders use reports to support decision making (R09) and get an overview of the status of software development (R10) and software testing (R11). Additionally, they found some parts of the reports unnecessary and wanted modular reports where they could define for each project separately which parts should be included into a specific test report (R08). More generally, they stated to prefer graphics for visualizing data instead of raw numbers in the form of metrics (R07). Finally, the effort for reporting should be minimized (R12) as data visualization currently takes much effort and involves a couple of manual human steps to produce test reports. Finally, each of the test managers stated that they would like to establish a cross-project learning process. The idea came up to implement an internal report only used within the testing department that summarizes and documents key learnings with a more general project summary.

5.3 Candidate Improvements and Assessment

Following the QATAM approach (see Fig. 3) and the study process (see Fig. 4), we collected a set of candidate improvements based on survey results, complemented with interview results, and industry best practices.

Table 3 summarizes 23 candidate improvement action (I01-I23) to be considered for improving the usage (and acceptance) of test reporting at our industry partner. Note that we classified these candidate improvements according to the survey structure and assigned them to identified requirements (see Table 1). Note that Table 1 consists of best practices recommended by standards (R01–R06) such as [4] complemented by additional requirements coming from survey results and interviews (R07–R12).

Some of the candidate improvements (i.e., I02 and I12) are not directly linked to requirements but were elicited from interviews to improve internal testing processes.

Table 3. Candidate improvements and stakeholder assessment results.

ID	Suggested Improvement	Requirement	Category	Assessment	Decision
I01	Provide modular and configurable reports	R01, R06, R08	General	yes	Selected
I02	Establish a cross-project learning process	-	General	yes	Selected
I03	Include recommendations/suggestions from test center for QA- Actions	R04	Test Status Report	yes	Selected
I04	Report current testing progress according to target measures (defined at	R10, R11	Test Status Report	yes	Selected
I05	Focus on a management summary explaining the "traffic-light" status	R04, R07	Test Status Report	yes	Selected
I06	State-Gate-Model following QATAM	-	Test Status Report	yes	Selected
I07	Make "Defect Trends" and "Indicators and Metrics" more	R04, R05	Test Status Report	yes	Selected
I08	Clarify "Requirements coverage"	R01, R03	Test Status Report	no	not now
I09	Dynamic Interval for sending the report	-	Test Status Report	no	not now
I10	Focus on trends instead of the current status	R02, R03, R07	Test Status Report	no	Not planned
I11	Define target goals for specific measures at the beginning of the project	R05, R09	Test concept	yes	Selected
I12	Send test concept only in project with external partners	-	Test concept	yes	Selected
I13	Define specific Test End Criteria	R05, R09	Test concept	no	Not planned
I14	Generate reports according to stated stakeholder needs	R06, R08	Final Test Status report	no	not now
I15	Overview on identified Issues in the Final Test Status Report	R01, R04, R12	Final Test Status report	no	not now
I16	Include lessons learned in the Final Test Status Report	F04	Final Test Status report	no	not now
I17	Create Cross-Project Learning Backlog for internal use	-	Final Test Status report	no	not now
I18	Suggest possible application of Test Automation at the project start	R01, R08	Test automation	yes	Selected
I19	Explicitly highlight Test automation results in the Test status report	R01, R08, R12	Test automation	yes	Selected
I20	Visualize Data instead of presenting statistical metrics	R07	Test automation	yes	Selected
I21	Present a general trend in the specific test (overview) followed by	R10, R11	Test automation	yes	Selected
I22	Use Graphs instead of tables to support understandability	R01, R07	Test automation	yes	Selected
I23	Create standard report templates	R12	Test automation	no	not now

Candidate improvements were informally discussed with testing experts at our industry partner, i.e., test managers, which were stakeholders similar to the interview partners. Because they represent key stakeholders in the testing center, they are also responsible for implementation. We have discussed all candidate improvements with these testing experts, elicited benefits and limitations based on the current state of the practice. Based on the discussion results we classified every candidate improvement with a yes/no decision. "Yes" means that this candidate improvement is important and promising to be implemented at the industry partner. "No" refers to candidate improvements that (a) are less important for implementation in the near future; (b) has been considered as less useful in the given company context; or (c) needs further investigations on the expected benefits. Finally, based on the assessment (see Table 3) 14 suggested candidate improvements (61%) have been selected for implementation in the near future. Those candidate improvements which have not been selected in the near future were separated in (a) promising approaches that need to be considered for future improvement initiatives (i.e., 7 improvement actions (30%)) and (b) improvement actions that are not planned yet (i.e., 2 improvement actions (9%)).

Based on these evaluation results, 14 improvement actions have been selected for implementation. Note that implementing these improvement actions and the evaluation are out of scope of this paper.

6   Discussion and Limitations

The goal of this paper was to analyse the usage, benefits, expectations and acceptance of test reporting at our industry partner, a large-scale Austrian logistics organization with focus on improving test reports to increase the benefits, provided by test reports on the quality of projects. Therefore, we set up a case study to collect requirements (based on survey and interviews), developed candidate improvements based on the state-of-the-practice and industry best practices, given by standards (such as [4]), evaluated candidate improvements in informal interviews with test experts at the industry partner as foundation for establishing an improvement strategy in the company.

RQ.1: What are critical stakeholder requirements for test reporting in context of the case study organization? We derived basic stakeholder needs and requirements based on literature as the case study organization follows the suggestions given by the standard [4]. Based on a survey, where we received 15 qualified responses from different stakeholder groups, we complemented the list of requirements by stakeholder needs from the organization. In total we derived 12 requirements, where 7 requirements have been derived from literature and 6 additional requirements have been derived from survey and interviews in the case study organization. Table 1 presents the summarized results of retrieved requirements.

RQ.2: What are the best-practices implemented in the organization, i.e., a large-scale Austrian logistics organization? We applied the survey approach to identify the state of the practice at our industry partner in context of test reporting, test status reports, and test automation (see Sect. 5.2 for the results). As the case study organization typically follow test reporting standards, we identified a set of limitations regarding the usage and acceptance of the current practice. The most important finding focus on the structure and complexity of test reporting which have to be improved and modularized to improve acceptance. Therefore, there is a need for a configuration capability according to the project context which needs to be considered in the improvement initiative.

RQ.3: What is the impact of improved reporting in context of a logistics organization? We used the QATAM approach [11] for driving the improvement initiative. Based on identified requirements (derived from RQ.1), survey results and interviews we came up with a set of 23 candidate improvements where 14 improvement actions have been found useful for implementation and 7 remain for future work, and 2 have been rejected (for now). Note that the candidate improvement actions have been assessed by testing experts from the organization, supported by the authors by using informal interviews and discussions. However, 14 improvement actions have been finally selected for implementation in the organization.

Limitations: In context of the study we have identified a set of threats to validity and tried to address them. The most critical limitation focuses the selection of survey and interview participants because of the low number of participants. Survey participants include 15 experts (including 8 project managers (PM), 2 team leads (TL), and 5 engineers (ENG) including requirements engineers and software architects). The low number of participants may not be representative enough for generalization. However, in the case study organization and the study context the selection of participants is representative. Similar arguments apply for the selection of interview partners (3 test managers of the case study organization). The setup of the questionnaire and the interview guideline was designed to initiate an improvement strategy at the case study organization. However, the questionnaire can be used in different contexts as foundation for eliciting the state of the practice in context of test reporting. In addition these guidelines have been extensively reviewed by testing experts (i.e., the authors, where one author designed the questionnaire and the others provide feedback on the content) to ensure the correctness and completeness in the stud context.

7 Conclusion and Future Work

Test reporting us usually used to provide some evidence on the quality of a software product or to report on the quality status of a project/product at a defined time within the project course. However, a well-defined test report can also be used to support project teams in better monitoring and supporting the project progress. An agreed test report structure, the content and the level of detail of a test report (within a project team or an organization or) represent the foundation for acceptance and for application in the project context. Therefore, we initiated an improvement initiative at our industry partner as starting point for establishing test reports and vehicle for project and quality improvement. We used surveys, interviews, and industry best-practices as foundation for providing a set of candidate improvement that are evaluated by testing experts at the case study organization. 14 improvement action have been selected for evaluation. Based on the case study results we believe that the case study approach (in general) and the identified improvement actions can support organizations in improving test reports and, as a consequence, improving engineering projects.

Future work will include two aspects: (a) we are planning to support the case study organization in the implementation of the suggested and selected candidate improvements. Furthermore, an empirical study is planned to investigate the impact of improvements of test reporting in context to the state of the practice; (b) with focus on the questionnaire we are planning to re-visit the survey questionnaire and interview guidelines with respect to improving and re-using the material in other contexts, such as organizations with testing and test report needs. Future work will also include replication of the improvement approach in larger contexts to collect a higher number of responses and interviews.

Acknowledgement. The financial support by the Austrian Federal Ministry for Digital, Business and Enterprise and the National Foundation for Research, Technology and Development is gratefully acknowledged.

References

1. Basili, V.R.: The experience factory and its relationship to other improvement paradigms. In: Sommerville, I., Paul, M. (eds.) ESEC 1993. LNCS, vol. 717, pp. 68–83. Springer, Heidelberg (1993). https://doi.org/10.1007/3-540-57209-0_6
2. Duvall, P.M., Matyas, S., Glover, A.: Continuous Integration: Improving Software Quality and Reducing Risk. Addison-Wesley, Boston (2007)
3. Humble, J., Farley, D.: Continuous Delivery: Reliable Software Releases Through Build, Test, and Deployment Automation. Pearson Professional, Gurugram (2010)
4. ISO/IEC/IEEE 29119-3:2013: Software and Systems Engineering. Software Testing. Part 3: Test Documentation. International Standard, ISO/IEC/IEEE (2013)

5. Kelley, J.J.: Quality assurance reporting to the governing board. Trustee: J. Hospital Governing Boards **43**(5), 10–12 (1990)
6. Laitenberger, O., DeBaud, J.-M.: An encompassing life cycle centric survey of software inspection. J. Syst. Softw. **50**(1), 5–31 (2000)
7. Molyneaux, I.: The Art of Application Performance Testing: From Strategy to Tools, 2nd edn. O'Reilly and Associates, Sebastopol (2014)
8. Myers, G.J., Sandler, C., Badgett, T.: The Art of Software Testing, 3rd edn. Wiley, Hoboken (2011)
9. Sommerville, I.: Software Engineering. Global Edition, 10th edn. Pearson Education Limited, Bengaluru (2015)
10. Spillner, A., Linz, T., Schaefer, H.: Software Testing Foundations: A Study Guide for the Certified Tester Exam, 4th edn. Rocky Nook, San Rafael (2014)
11. Winkler, D., Elberzhager, F., Biffl, S., Eschbach, R.: Software process improvement initiatives based on quality assurance strategies: a QATAM pilot application. In: Riel, A., O'Connor, R., Tichkiewitch, S., Messnarz, R. (eds.) EuroSPI 2010. CCIS, vol. 99, pp. 71–82. Springer, Heidelberg (2010). https://doi.org/10.1007/978-3-642-15666-3_7

Software Development

Embracing Software Process Improvement in Automotive Through PISA Model

Fabio Falcini and Giuseppe Lami[(✉)]

Consiglio Nazionale delle Ricerche, Istituto di Scienza e Tecnologie
dell'Informazione, via G. Moruzzi, 1, 56124 Pisa, Italy
giuseppe.lami@isti.cnr.it

Abstract. Vehicles innovation is principally driven by electronics components and software that play today a predominant role for the vehicle's functions. Because the quality of on-board automotive electronic systems is strongly dependent on the quality of their development practices, car-makers and suppliers proactively focused on improvement of technical and organizational processes. In this setting, several reference standards for the assessment and improvement of automotive electronics processes and projects have been conceived and used in the last decade. Although the effects of the application of them in automotive industry have been generally positive, getting compliance in the short period may represent, in some contexts, a target hardly achievable, or even a chimera. In this context, a novel scheme addressing both project evaluation and process improvement and targeting a hand-on approach for the practitioners has been recently developed starting from the analysis of practitioners needs and success factors in the software process improvement. This scheme is named Process Improvement Scheme for Automotive (PISA Model). The structure and contents of the PISA Model is described in this paper.

1 Introduction

The last two decades witnessed a deep change in the vehicle manufacturing, car OEMs (Original Equipment Manufacturer) reshaped their vehicles from mechanical devices into elaborated digitally controlled systems. As a result, the software (with increasing demand in terms of size and complexity and cybersecurity) is a crucial component since it is part of embedded systems called Electronic Control Units (ECU) that control electronically a large number of the vehicle functions. The number of ECUs, from economic to luxury vehicle models, is remarkably increased during the last fifteen/twenty years. Electronics is so pervasive in today's cars that almost all the main features and functionalities are controlled by software; not to mention the innovation driven by the deep-learning-based systems that are becoming pervasive in automobiles [8]. But technological innovation still run on the fast lane, today's trend towards connected and autonomous cars is presenting new and very complex challenges.

In this setting, the quality of on-board automotive electronic systems is the key issue OEMs shall face. Because the quality of products strongly dependent on the quality of their development practice, car-makers and suppliers are proactively and increasingly focusing on the improvement of technical and organizational processes.

X. Franch et al. (Eds.): PROFES 2019, LNCS 11915, pp. 73–88, 2019.
https://doi.org/10.1007/978-3-030-35333-9_5

Several models and standards addressing both automotive system and software development are available for the automotive market. These models and standards have typically a strong focus on processes; among them the most relevant and influencing are Automotive SPICE [1], ISO 26262 [4], and IATF 16949 [15]. Moreover, it is worth mentioning the ISO 21434 [14] that is on the way to be published.

The application of such standards, in particular Automotive SPICE, produced undoubted positive effects on the automotive industry in the last years. Advancements have been achieved in terms process awareness, possibility of benchmarking, development discipline, and incitement to improvement [7].

Nevertheless, the specifics and the complexities reached by today's automotive software-intensive systems have shown that current models and standards have some drawbacks in responding to the needs of the automotive industry [5, 6]. In particular, the automotive players are in need of the following aspects: more focus on projects rather than a pure process-centred approach, improved technical guidance, and explicit links to already established automotive quality frameworks. Several initiatives and studies have been conducted with the aim of finding out solutions to such problems [9–11].

In this context, a novel scheme addressing both project evaluation and process improvement and targeting a hand-on approach for the practitioners has been developed. This scheme is named Process Improvement Scheme for Automotive (PISA Model). The PISA Model [12] is being applied in practice by means of trials on real projects with the aim of getting feedbacks and identifying improvement indications for the next releases. In this paper the PISA Model Rating System is addressed. Starting from the definition of the quality characteristic the PISA Model addresses (i.e. Adequacy), the mechanism to determine the rating will be presented and discussed.

This paper is structured as follows: in Sect. 2 the overview of relevant existing standards in automotive is provided. In Sect. 3 a discussion on the motivations for a new scheme for process assessment and improvement in automotive is provided. In Sect. 4 the Adequacy quality characteristic is defined. The structure of the PISA Model is described in Sect. 5 and the PISA Model rating system in Sect. 6. Finally, in Sect. 7 conclusions are provided and on-going activities are described.

2   Reference Standards in Automotive Software-Intensive Components Development

In automotive, similarly to the other transportation domains (e.g. aerospace and railways), exist several technical standards that are often used as reference for evaluation or qualification of software-intensive components.

In this Section an overview of the existing automotive-specific reference models for evaluating or qualifying software-intensive development projects and processes is provided. In the last years standards addressing software development have been released and applied in automotive, the most relevant and impacting are:

Automotive SPICE (SPICE stands for Software Process Improvement and Capability Determination) [1]: it provides a process framework that disciplines, at high level of abstraction, the software development activities and allows their capability assessment in matching pre-defined sets of numerous process requirements. Automotive SPICE, as a de-facto process standard, is used by car manufacturers to push software process improvement among suppliers of software-intensive systems [2]. The purpose of the standard is to provide both a scheme for evaluating the capability of software processes and a path for their improvement. Process capability is defined as a characterization of the ability of a process to meet current or projected business goals. Many car makers are using also this standard to qualify suppliers by requiring to them the achievement of specific rating [3]. Automotive SPICE standard provides a Process Reference Model and a Process Assessment Model including a Measurement Framework to assign ratings to processes.

ISO 26262 [4]: it is a Functional Safety standard titled Road vehicles – Functional safety released in late 2011. Similarly to its parent standard IEC61508, ISO 26262 is a risk based safety standard, where the risk of hazardous operational situations are qualitatively assessed and safety measures are defined to avoid or control systematic failures and to detect or control random hardware failures, or mitigate their effects. The ISO 26262 standard:

Provides an automotive safety lifecycle (management, development, production, operation, service, decommissioning) and supports tailoring the necessary activities during these lifecycle phases.

Covers functional safety aspects of the entire development process (including such activities as requirements specification, design, implementation, integration, verification, validation, and configuration).

Provides an automotive-specific risk-based approach for determining risk classes (Automotive Safety Integrity Levels, ASILs).

Uses ASILs for specifying the item's necessary safety requirements for achieving an acceptable residual risk.

Provides requirements for validation and confirmation measures to ensure a sufficient and acceptable level of safety is being achieved.

The ISO 26262 scope embraces the whole system life cycle and addresses specifically the hardware and the software development lifecycles.

The application of the ISO 26262 standard in industry represents a real challenge for many automotive software-intensive systems. In fact, the 687 requirements, 100 work products and 62 decisional tables in the standard require a significant effort (both from a technical and managerial point of view) to adapt existing (hopefully sound and mature) processes and to acquire possible additional technical competencies and tools as well.

ISO/PAS 21448 [13] - Safety of the Intended Functionality (SoTIF). This standard, recently published, aims at overcome a limitation of the ISO 26262 standard. In fact, what it is not always recognized is that ISO 26262 only covers fault failures and not the so-called Safety of the Intended Functionality (SOTIF). This ISO document addresses the fact that for some automotive applications there can be safety violations with a system free from faults - for example a false-positive detection by a radar of an obstacle for the vehicle – because it is extremely problematic to develop systems able to address every possible scenario. The ISO/PAS 21448 aims at providing guidance to the design, verification and validation measures applicable to avoid malfunctioning behaviour in the system in absence of faults, resulting from system definition shortcomings. It is intended to be applied to systems for which a proper situational awareness by the item is critical for safety, and is derived from complex sensors and processing algorithms, especially.

ISO/SAE CD 21434 [14]: This standard is still under development (it reached the status of CD on September 2018). Its focus is on defining common terminology and the key aspects of cybersecurity in automotive. The application of the standard aims to help companies demonstrate responsible and careful handling of vehicle development and cyber-threat prevention. The activities in the product development according to standard are controlled on the basis of a risk assessment, for this purpose measures for the organizational anchoring are demanded. Although processes are required, the standard only describes the task of a process, but leaves the design of the process to the user. Special technologies or solutions are not proposed and autonomous vehicles are not given special status in the recommendations of the standard.

IATF 16949: it is a standard for the Quality Management System (QMS) in automotive [15]. It is based on the requirements of the ISO9001 standard with the addition of specific requirements for automotive. The definition of such a special version of the ISO 9001 for automotive, has been supported by major international car manufacturers with the aim of providing a mean to increase the confidence in the automotive suppliers. The IATF 16949 promotes a process-oriented approach in the development, enactment, and improvement of the QMS.

3   Motivations for a New Process Assessment and Improvement Model in Automotive

In this section we discuss, on the basis of our wide experience as Automotive SPICE Principal Assessors (qualification obtained by the IntACS [18]), some objective motivations for the definition of a new model for process assessment and improvement in automotive.

1. *Automotive-native Assessment and Improvement Schemes:*
   Automotive electronics is an application domain having its own peculiarities and specific characteristics both in terms of product and process. Automotive software-intensive components are principally ECUs, inter-connected via the vehicle network, with specific demands in terms of interoperability, modularity, calibration, and time-to-market. The platform-based approach to the design and development of automotive software-intensive systems, as well as the wide deployment of model-driven software development and the application of agile methods make the picture even more complex. In such a context, generic process assessment and improvement schemes are not able fit at all for such a kind of products. In particular, Automotive SPICE is a model derived from the generic SPICE model (former ISO/IEC 15504, today moved in the ISO 33000 series). For this reason, though Automotive SPICE contains automotive-specific elements, nevertheless it is still affected by the original approach. In particular, some process elements to be addressed to achieve compliance (e.g. Base Practices) are both hard to be applied in real development project contexts and at the same time can provide little added

value from a process improvement perspective. Moreover, the terminology used in Automotive SPICE is sometimes far from the technical lexicon and then difficult to understand by practitioners.

2. *Technology readiness:*

If we consider the main success factors for software process improvement according to the existing literature [18, 19] [20], we can understand that some of them are not sufficiently addressed by current reference standards, in particular by Automotive SPICE. In particular, the resource availability as suitable technology for deploying and supporting development projects (identified as a relevant success factor) is a success factor that is not sufficiently addressed by the existing standards. Technology is not explicitly addressed by reference standards principally because the need of being general (i.e. applicable in several contexts) as well as the need of being updated (i.e. the technology evolves in a fast way and the standard should be maintained updated with a high frequency). Nevertheless, technology factor cannot be omitted, because in such a context, in which innovation runs in a very fast way, the technological readiness is a fundamental requirement.

3. *Unique Rating*:

As in automotive process assessment results are used to qualify E/E suppliers (mainly on the basis of Automotive SPICE), the availability of reference assessment models providing a unique final rating is desirable. Unfortunately, Automotive SPICE doesn't provide a unique rating but it is able to provide a rating for each single process under assessment, and for this reason it not suitable at all for this purpose. To cope with this gap OEMs defined assessment scopes (composed of processes and related target ratings) for supplier qualification purposes. Such a situation presents some drawbacks as, for instance, the heterogeneity of target assessment scopes due to different requirements from different OEMs. Having a qualification scheme providing a unique rating for qualification purposes would be an advantage.

4. *Availability of application guidelines:*

Standard should be a proper balance between general clauses and precise guidelines for their implementation. Automotive SPICE, for instance, lacks of guidelines for a correct interpretation and an easier implementation of clauses. For this reason, a book has been recently released by VDA with the aim of filling this gap [19]. Anyway, having a standard inclusive of application guidelines would give benefits in order to facilitate the application of and the achievement of compliance with respect standards as well as increase the uniformity.

5. *Cross references among different standards*:

The reference standards presented in Sect. 2 have some commonalities in terms of technical and managerial areas addressed. Moreover, an organization may need to achieve compliance with several standards on the same development project. For these reasons, it is important standards have cross references each other in order to optimize achievement of compliance with respect different standards. Currently such a kind of mutual reference among automotive standards is poor.

4 Adequacy Quality Characteristic

The authors, in order to overtake the drawbacks discussed in Sect. 2, defined a new approach to face the challenge of providing an effective model for quantitatively evaluate quality of automotive software-intensive developments from a process perspective. As initial step a new quality characteristic has been defined, such a characteristic has been named *Adequacy*.

Definition: *Adequacy* is the responsiveness of process deployed in development projects to automotive demands from technical and organizational perspectives.

A new framework able to allow the rating of a development project in terms of Adequacy has been developed by the authors. Such a framework has been named PISA (Process Improvement Scheme for Automotive) Model [12]. The PISA Model will be described in detail in Sect. 4.

A project is then said being Adequate (i.e. it fulfils the quality characteristic of Adequacy) when the project performance includes the deployment of a core set of technical and managerial practices and when state-of-the-art technology is used.

Adequacy has been defined in order to integrate the concepts of: process capability, organizational maturity and technological readiness. In the following, the way these concepts have been addressed in the definition of the quality characteristics of Adequacy is described:

1. Process capability: the achievement of project Adequacy is based on the performance of a precise set of technical and managerial practices. Performing a predefined set of practices is the basis of the achievement of process capability (as, for instance, in the case of Automotive SPICE). The combination of the PISA Model-provided practices allows to define the processes and addresses their capability as well.
2. Organizational maturity is defined as "the extent to which an organizational unit consistently implements processes within a defined scope that contributes to the achievement of its business needs" [16]. It's about the derivation of a unique rating valid for the whole organization calculated starting from ratings of single processes. The approach of the PISA Model is the same. As it will be described later in this paper, the Adequacy characteristic is derived by combination of the ratings of single processes.
3. Technological readiness is a novel element in existing automotive process models. Technology is a key element to achieve high quality process and to improve them as well. The PISA Model addresses this element by including among the Adequacy indicators a set of requirements addressing the use of state-of-the-art technology in development projects.

The PISA Model is composed of the three pillars:

- Process Scope and Augmented Framework
- Process Structure and Requirements
- Evaluation and Rating System

In Sect. 4 Process Scope and Augmented Framework, and the Process Structure and Requirements are presented. Evaluation and Rating System is presented and discussed in Sect. 5.

5 Process Improvement Scheme for Automotive (PISA Model)

The purpose of the PISA (Process Improvement Scheme for Automotive) Model is to provide the automotive community with a quality model with innovative features that targets the specific needs of the automotive industry in the context of the development of electronic systems.

Explicitly, the peculiar needs for an effective quality model in the context of automotive electronics developments are:

- Ability to evaluate the project performance in the context of automotive in order to provide usable feedbacks on the project risk level;
- Ability to evaluate process capability in the context of automotive, as a means to identify risks associated to development processes.

The PISA model addresses both project evaluation and process improvement in a balanced fashion and targets a hand-on approach for the practitioners.

The PISA model, in the context of electronic automotive systems, addresses:

1. System-level development
2. Electronic and mechanics hardware-level development
3. Software-level development.

The PISA Model fits the characteristics of automotive developments by incorporating automotive technical and procedural requirements as well as a more project-centered perspective into a standard process framework. Conceptually, the PISA Model can be defined as an automotive-specific "augmentation" of a process model, conceived to better serve the needs of automotive electronics developments.

5.1 Processes Scope and Augmented Framework

The PISA Model encompasses processes at technical and managerial levels that incorporate the backbone of a typical automotive project structure. The processes belonging to the PISA Model are twenty-two (22) in total (as shown in Fig. 1).

They are divided into five (5) Process Segments:

- Three (3) Technical Segments: System Engineering, Hardware Engineering, and Software Engineering
- Two (2) Coordination Segments: Management, and Sustenance.

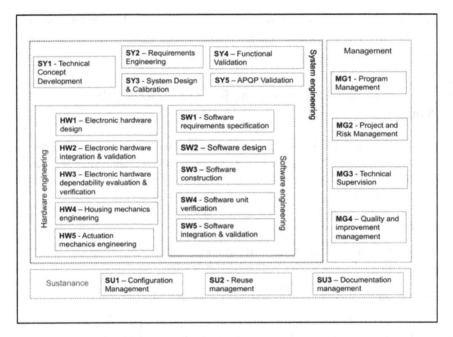

Fig. 1. PISA model processes

In the following, the PISA Model processes are grouped by segment and shortly described. System Engineering Segment processes address the product view – the processes belonging to this segment are described in Table 1.

Table 1.

Process Id. and Name	Pertinence
SY1 - Technical concept development	Early setup of the overall system architecture; this process acknowledges the fact that in the automotive market crucial design decisions are often taken during the commercial phases of the project
SY2 – Requirements engineering	Definition, documentation and maintenance of requirements for development at system level
SY3 – System design and calibration	Definition of a detailed system design with strong focus on hardware-software interfaces and system calibration aspects. Such a level of design takes into account typical automotive design drivers such as "design for manufacturing"
SY4 – Functional validation	Verification of the conformance of the developed system to its functional specification
SY5 – Advanced product quality planning (APQP) validation	Confirmation that the organization can produce products that meet customer requirements in a cost-effective and repeatable way

Hardware Engineering Segment processes address the product view – the processes belonging to this segment are described in Table 2.

Table 2.

Process Id. and Name	Pertinence
HW1 – Electronic hardware design	Definition of electronics design, including the preparation of the physical layout
HW2 – Electronic hardware integration and validation	Validation of electronic sub-system(s) from a functional and electrical point of views
HW3 – Electronic hardware verification and dependability evaluation	Performance of in-depth design verification as well as the performance of dependability analysis
HW4 – Housing mechanics engineering	Deployment of both the design and the verification of mechanical housing
HW5 – Actuation mechanics engineering	Deployment of both the design and the verification of actuation mechanical hardware

Software Engineering Segment processes address the product view – the processes belonging to this segment are described in Table 3.

Table 3.

Process Id. and Name	Pertinence
SW1 – Software requirements specification	Definition, documentation and maintenance of requirements for software development
SW2 – Software design	Definition of the software architectural design following a multi-level and multi-perspective approach
SW3 – Software construction	Deployment of consolidated best practices for the implementation of the software design
SW4- Software units verification	Deployment of verification activities to ensure correctness of software units. The robustness verification of software units is pivotal for this process
SW5 – Software integration and validation	Verification and validation of software sub-system(s) from a functional and performance point of views

Management Segment processes address the product view – the processes belonging to this segment are described in Table 4.

Table 4.

Process Id. and Name	Pertinence
MG1 – Program management	High-level management of projects within the program umbrella and related customer interfacing
MG2 – Project and risk management	Management of projects according to automotive industry best practices
MG3 – Technical supervision	Management of technical operative aspects of project activities

Sustenance Segment processes address the product view – the processes belonging to this segment are described in Table 5.

Table 5.

Process Id. and Name	Pertinence
SU1 – Configuration management	Deployment of configuration management at system, hardware and software levels
SU2 – Reuse management	Management of the reuse of hardware and software elements
SU3 – Documentation management	Deployment of a rigorous and lean documentation management

5.2   Process Structure and Requirements

The PISA Model process definition structure is composed of the following fields:

1. Process Name
2. Context of the Process: general information on the process and on its context of use.
3. Entry Criteria: pre-conditions that are expected to be satisfied when the process starts.
4. Input Work products
5. Requirements: definition of practices to be performed by the process.
6. Output Work Products and related content outline
7. Exit Criteria: conditions expected to be satisfied when the process ends.

The PISA model requirements are divided into three (3) categories:

a. Process Requirements
b. Governance Requirements
c. Technological Requirements

PISA Model requirements are prioritized in terms of impact on Adequacy evaluation. With this aim, requirements are classified as high-priority or low-priority. In Appendix A an example of PISA Model requirement is provided. For more details on processes and related requirements refer to [12].

6   Adequacy Measurement System

Evaluation and rating within the PISA Model is governed by the PISA Rating System (PISA-RS). The PISA-RS works according to a bottom-up approach. The PISA Model contains the demonstration of compliance of PISA-RS with the ISO/IEC 33003 requirements [17]. Figure 2 shows the conceptual path towards the project evaluation in terms of Adequacy.

As Fig. 2. shows, the PISA-RS provides a step-wise, bottom-up mechanism to project evaluation that is based on process-specific sets of requirements belonging to three categories (process, governance, and technological).

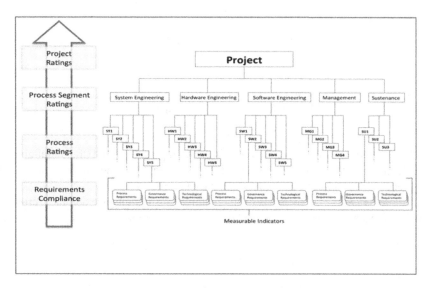

Fig. 2. PISA model adequacy measurement approach

Table 6 describes the rating scale of the Adequacy attribute and associated semantics.

Table 6.

Adequacy rating value	Meaning
Adequate - **A**	Project is run in a sound fashion and project objectives are not at risk Process improvement opportunities are limited in scope and criticality
Sufficient - **S**	Project is run satisfactorily and project objectives are largely not at risk Process improvement opportunities are present
Incomplete - **I**	Project is deployed nearly satisfactorily and project objectives are exposed to some noteworthy risk Significant Process improvement opportunities are present
Inadequate - **N**	Project objectives are at risk Process improvement opportunities are important and require immediate improvement action items

Table 7 summarizes the rating attribute related to each element under evaluation at each step of the PISA-RS.

Table 7.

PISA model rating level	Attribute
Project	Adequacy
Process segment	
Process	
Requirement	Compliance

Step 1: Compliance to process requirements. Compliance to all the requirements (Process, Governance, Technology) is verified starting from the analysis of related work products. Compliance is rated by a binary scale.

Step 2: Process rating. On the basis of the requirements compliance and their priority, the rating of each process in terms of Adequacy is determined (Table 8).

Table 8.

Process Requirements		Governance Requirements		Technological Requirements		Process Ratings
High prior.	Low prior.	High prior.	Low prior.	High prior.	Low prior.	
ALL	*	ALL	*	ALL	*	A
ALL	*	>0	*	>0	*	S
ALL	*	>0	*	>0	*	I
otherwise						N

Step 3: Segment rating. The weighted aggregation of process ratings determines the relevant process segment rating (segment rating level). It is possible that not all the processes belonging to a Process Segment are applicable (i.e. it is possible that, because the project characteristics, some activities are not executed and, consequently, some evidences are not available for rating a process). According to that, N_p represents the number of applicable processes in a Process Segment.

For System Engineering, Hardware Engineering, Software Engineering, and Management Segments if $N_p < 3$ the whole Process Segment is not applicable and, consequently, it cannot be rated. For sustenance Process Segment if $N_p < 2$ the whole Process Segment is not applicable and, consequently, it cannot be rated.

Table 9 summarizes the rating rules at for a Process Segment:

Table 9.

Number of occurrencies of process ratings				Segment Rating
A	S	I	N	
N_p	0	0	0	A
N_p - 1	1	0	0	A
*	>1	0	0	S
*	*	1	0	S
*	*	>1	0	I
*	*	0	1	I
*	*	>0	1	N
*	*	*	>1	N

Step 4: Project rating. The combination of the process segments ratings determines the project rating in terms of Adequacy attribute.

The Rating of a Project in terms Adequacy is based on the ratings of the three (3) Technical Segments (System Engineering, Hardware Engineering, Software Engineering) and on the ratings of the two (2) Coordination Segments (Management and Sustenance).

It is possible that not all the Technical Process Segments are applicable (i.e. it is possible that, because the project characteristics, some activities are not executed and, consequently, some processes are not performed).

The PISA–RS allows to evaluate a project in terms of Adequacy also in the case of one or two Technical Process Segments are not applicable.

Project rating	Ratio
A	(All Segments rated A) || (All Technical Segments A) && (Coordination Segments rated A or S)
S	(Project Not Rated A) && (No Technical Segments rated I or N) & (No Coordination Segments rated I or N)
I	(Project Not Rated S) && (No Technical Segments rated N) & (No Coordination Segments rated N)
N	Otherwise

In addition, a set of argumentations are provided in the PISA-RS on how to use the project-level Adequacy characteristic in the context of organizations benchmarking. These argumentations support the exploitation of the PISA Model to give a risk-based evaluation that is specifically referred to the involved organization (e.g. an ECU supplier). A mechanism to extend the Adequacy rating to the whole organization is provided in [12]. This mechanism can be used to qualify an organization, and consequently as a mean for benchmarking. The mechanism is based on the concept of project representativeness (that for space reasons is not described in this paper).

7 Conclusions and On-going Activities

In this paper we presented the mechanism to evaluate an automotive software-intensive development project from a process perspective. The quality characteristic under evaluation is named Adequacy. A project is said being adequate (i.e. fulfill the quality characteristic of Adequacy) when the project performance includes the deployment of a core set of technical and managerial practices and when state-of-the-art technology is used.

The Adequacy evaluation mechanism is part of the PISA Model, a novel model aimed at providing the automotive community with a quality model with innovative features that targets the specific needs of the automotive industry in the context of the development of electronic systems.

The authors, on the basis of their wide experience in automotive, recognized that the existing standards and schemes used in automotive to assess and improve the development of electronic components for automobiles present some weaknesses and their application is not always respondent to players demands. The PISA Model has been conceived with the aim of overtaking such lacks. Therefore, the PISA Model's processes are synthetically defined and embrace the whole product development life-cycle including development processes at system, hardware, software level.

Though the PISA Model has been released recently, it is going to be applied on real projects in order to get feedbacks on its suitability for the intended use.

The authors are conducting several trial PISA Model assessments with the aim of:

- Evaluating the ease of use, the completeness and the correctness of the PISA Model;
- Assessing the capability of the PISA Model to serve as a driver for improvement;
- Assuring its alignment with the State of the Art and Practice
- Spreading the knowledge of the PISA Model in the automotive community;
- Studying possible relationships and dependencies with other automotive-relevant standards.

The trial assessments with PISA Model are carried out on real projects in parallel with Automotive SPICE assessments. Data are collected during the trial PISA Model assessments and a related empirical study will be provided in a next paper. The evidences collected so far show that achieving the A rating in terms of Adequacy according to the PISA Model rating mechanism assures the achievement of the Capability Level 2 on the processes belonging to the assessment scope of the major OEMs. We are also noticing that there is an increasing interest by OEMs in the PISA Model to include it in their supplier qualification mechanisms.

Appendix A

In this Appendix an example of Process Requirement is provided in order to show the structure of PISA Model Requirements. The exemplar requirements is related to the SW2 Software Design process. Each requirement of the PISA Model independently of its category (process, governance, technological) has the same structure of the exemplar process requirement shown below.

SW2-PR1	Develop high-level software design
Clause	Software design shall be provided in order to represent the software part of the system and its interfaces.
Elaborations	A complete architecture of software shall be elaborated and documented. It shall contain the software components and the related interfaces and relationship. The software high-level design shall provide a complete representation of software units and their interfaces and interactions. Software high-level design shall address static aspects of software, as: External interfaces of the software; Interfaces between software units/software components; Resources usage constraints for software; Allocation of system requirements to the system elements SW high-level design shall address dynamic aspects of software behavior, as: Dataflow between software units/software components; Dataflow at software external interfaces; Interrupts management; SW operating modes Software design shall specify the notation to be used. Possible notations to represent software design are: natural language; semi-formal graphical notations (as UML, SysML); informal notations In the case of model-based software development the first levels of model decomposition can be equated to high-level design. In case of artificial intelligence, the definition of the structure of neural network(s) such as layers and number of nodes, learning strategy can be equated to high-level design. LINKS TO ISO 26262 Requirement(s): ISO 26262-6:2011, clause 6.4.1, 11.2; ISO 26262-6:2011, clause 9.4. LINKS TO APQP Requirement(s): Engineering Drawings
Tip(s)	A layered representation of software design is encouraged in the case of architectural high complexity of software. The use of formal notations to represent software design is not to be encouraged, because their costs in terms of tool support and people training. To address software design dynamic aspects, the use of graphical notation is profitable.
Tailoring Criteria	High-level design can be expressed as collection of separate work-product, documental and electronic.
Notes	AUTOSAR provides a set of specifications that builds a common design methodology based on standardized exchange format.

References

1. VDA QMC Working Group 13/Automotive SIG "Automotive SPICE Process Assessment/Reference Model", ver. 3.1, Verband der Automobilindustrie (2017). http://www.automotivespice.com/fileadmin/software-download/AutomotiveSPICE_PAM_31.pdf
2. Hoermann, K., Mueller, M., Dittman, L., Zimmer, J.: Automotive SPICE in Practice: Surviving Implementation and Assessment. Rocky Noor (2008). ISBN 978-1933952291
3. Fabbrini, F., Fusani, M., Lami, G., Sivera, E.: A SPICE-based supplier qualification mechanism in automotive industry. Softw. Process Improvement Practice J. **12**, 523–528 (2007)
4. ISO 26262 - Road Vehicles - Functional Safety, International Organization for Standardization (2018)
5. Niazi, M., Wilson, D., Zowghi, D.: Critical success factors for software improvement implementation: an empirical study. Softw. Process Improvement Practice **11**, 193–211 (2006)
6. Niazi, M., Ali, B.M., Verner, J.M.: Software process improvement barriers: a cross-cultural comparison. Inf. Softw. Technol. **52**(2010), 1204–1216 (2010)
7. Fabbrini, F., Fusani, M., Lami, G., Sivera, E.: Software engineering in the european automotive industry: achievements and challenges. In: COMPSAC, pp. 1039–1044. IEEE Computer Society (2008)
8. Falcini, F., Lami, G., Costanza, A.M.: Deep learning in automotive. software. IEEE Softw. **34**(3), 56–63 (2017)
9. Kreiner, C., et al.: Automotive knowledge alliance AQUA – integrating automotive SPICE, six sigma, and functional safety. In: McCaffery, F., O'Connor, Rory V., Messnarz, R. (eds.) EuroSPI 2013. CCIS, vol. 364, pp. 333–344. Springer, Heidelberg (2013). https://doi.org/10.1007/978-3-642-39179-8_30
10. Lami, G., Falcini, F.: Is ISO/IEC 15504 applicable to agile methods? In: Abrahamsson, P., Marchesi, M., Maurer, F. (eds.) XP 2009. LNBIP, vol. 31, pp. 130–135. Springer, Heidelberg (2009). https://doi.org/10.1007/978-3-642-01853-4_16
11. Johannessen, P., Halonen, Ö., Örsmark, O.: Functional safety extensions to automotive SPICE according to ISO 26262. In: O'Connor, R.V., Rout, T., McCaffery, F., Dorling, A. (eds.) SPICE 2011. CCIS, vol. 155, pp. 52–63. Springer, Heidelberg (2011). https://doi.org/10.1007/978-3-642-21233-8_5
12. Falcini, F., Lami, G.: Process Improvement Scheme for Automotive - PISA Model ver. 2.0. Rapporto Tecnico ISTI n. 390840 (2018)
13. ISO/PAS 21448 - Road Vehicles - Safety of the Intended Functionality, International Organization for Standardization (2019)
14. ISO/SAE CD 21434 - Road Vehicles - Cybersecurity engineering, International Organization for Standardization (2018)
15. IATF16949:2016 Quality management system requirements for automotive production and relevant service parts organizations, International Automotive Task Force. 1st Edition
16. ISO/IEC 33001. Information Technology – Process Assessment – Concepts and terminology. International Organization for Standardization (2015)
17. ISO/IEC 33003. Information Technology – Process Assessment – Requirements for process measurement frameworks. International Organization for Standardization (2015)
18. International Assessor Certification Scheme. www.intacs.org
19. Verband der Automobilindustrie e. V. Automotive PSICE Guidelines, 1st Ed. September 2017

Establishing a User-Centered Design Process for Human-Machine Interfaces: Threats to Success

Mario Winterer[1]([✉]) [iD], Christian Salomon[1] [iD], Georg Buchgeher[1] [iD],
Martin Zehethofer[2], and Alexandra Derntl[2]

[1] Software Competence Center Hagenberg GmbH, Hagenberg, Austria
mario.winterer@gmail.com
[2] ENGEL Austria GmbH, Schwertberg, Austria

Abstract. While user-centered design (UCD) processes have widely been established in domains like end-user electronics and business-to-consumer products, such processes still lack widespread adaptation for the development of industrial human-machine interfaces (HMIs). Over a period of more than two years, we have worked as part of a development team at a company from the manufacturing domain in a pilot project to introduce a UCD process. During this period, we have - via participant observation - collected a set of observed practices and behaviors that violate well-known UCD principles. Furthermore, we derived some root causes of these violations. Our insights are that introducing a UCD processes cannot be performed isolated for a single development team but impacts the entire organization including management and requires trust as well as changes with regard to mindset, methods, technologies, and team organization.

Keywords: User-centered design · Design process · Industry 4.0

1 Introduction

User-centered design (UCD) processes are well established in development of end-consumer electronics and web-based business-to-consumer products, as a good user experience (UX) is considered as a key success factor in these domains. However, in industrial companies, most human-machine interfaces (HMIs) are still developed traditionally in a feature-oriented manner. The design of HMIs in the mechanical engineering domain, which are used to inspect and modify process parameters or to manipulate automated processes, is typically heavily influenced by the logical structure of the control system, more precisely, the information model of the programmable logic control (PLC), without taking human factors into account.

The resulting HMIs focus on data such as functional blocks and their parameters, rather than on workflows or tasks that need to be performed by their operators. This, combined with the increasing complexity of modern industrial

© Springer Nature Switzerland AG 2019
X. Franch et al. (Eds.): PROFES 2019, LNCS 11915, pp. 89–102, 2019.
https://doi.org/10.1007/978-3-030-35333-9_6

machines, leads to cumbersome HMIs that do not match the high expectations raised by modern user interfaces of business-to-consumer products like smartphones. Today, companies see user experience as differentiating factor to get competitive advantage over competitors [23]. The need for user participation to build flexible, nevertheless understandable and fault-tolerant HMIs is also motivated by the industry 4.0 initiative [6,24].

In this case study we report on our experiences of introducing a UCD process at *ENGEL Austria GmbH*, a company from the manufacturing domain. The company is manufacturer of injection molding machines and is currently in the process of developing a new generation of its software stack. As part of this software stack a new version of a *Sequence Editor* application for the programming of robot arms is being developed. This project was selected as a pilot project for introducing UCD at *ENGEL*. As part of an industrial research cooperation, the authors of this paper have worked over two years as project members in this pilot project to supervise the introduction of the UCD process. As a result, we have obtained deep insights in the processes and social fabric of the company which is advantageous over other inquiry approaches as for this research we considered it important to be able to look behind the facade of the organization. Based on our experiences we have collected a set of practices and behaviors we encountered during the introduction of UCD, that violate the core UCD principles.

The remainder of this paper is organized as follows: In Sect. 2 we describe the industrial context of this work. Section 3 presents a brief overview of UCD including central principles. In Sect. 4 we present malpractices we have found. Section 5 discusses related work. Section 6 concludes this paper with a summary of our main findings.

2   Industrial Context

ENGEL is a large manufacturer of injection molding machines. Such machines are used across many industry domains like consumer electronics, automotive, avionics, food industry for producing different kinds of plastic parts like enclosures of cell phones and laptops, toys, car parts, bottles, tooth brushes, etc. By using different molds and adaptable machine parameters, a single machine is able to process varying types of material and hence produce many different products. Nevertheless, certain domains require very specific adaptions of machines. Providing almost any requested customization is one of the key success factors of the company.

In 2016, the company started the development of its next generation of software for injection molding machines. This project encompasses the development of a new HMI (framework and applications), and a new middleware tier based on the OPC Unified Architecture (OPC UA) specification [19] for a unified communication with PLC control systems and auxiliary devices (e.g. robot arms and conveyor belts) of different vendors. As a consequence, large parts of the software have to be re-engineered and migrated to new technologies and frameworks. This undertaking affects many different stakeholders across several organizational units in the company. The core parts of the HMI are developed by four different agile teams in a Scrum process. Once, the HMI framework is released, several customization teams, which adapt the machine to the customer's needs, will also make use of it. In addition, many other teams are working on software products that are not directly related to the HMI, but may have influence on the overall user experience (e.g. the customer portal).

One application of the HMI is a *Sequence Editor* for the programming of industrial robots and the manipulation of machine workflows. The *Sequence Editor* supports visual motion-level programming and is used by a wide range of technicians from well-trained maintenance engineers to novice factory attendants. The company selected the *Sequence Editor* as a suitable application for piloting a UCD process.

3   User-Centered Design Principles

UCD processes focus on putting users into the center of product design and development [18]. Existing approaches aim to integrate users in the development process because user involvement is a critical factor for system acceptance and success [1,3,10]. No matter which concrete methods [4] are applied by a particular approach, they all share the following common principles:

Integrated and Comprehensive Solution. In order to provide a consistent user experience, surrounding services and products must be developed together with core functions. Therefore, the development teams should cooperate closely with surrounding departments like marketing, training, and customer service [9].

Focus on Users and Tasks. For a good and minimal system design it is necessary to understand which people are using the system and what goals they are trying to achieve [8].

Active User Participation. End-users and domain experts, which in the manufacturing domain are often end-users as well, should participate through all process stages [12] beginning with early analysis. Identifying and selecting representative users is an ongoing process [13] that is crucial for project success.

Continuous Evaluation and Iteration. Development is iterative and based on prototypes even in very early states of the project. These prototypes are incrementally evaluated by either experts or (again) in collaboration with potential users [17]. Insights of these evaluations are used to build enhanced prototypes in subsequent iterations.

Interdisciplinary Teams. As a consequence of the preceding principles, a team must allocate a broad range of skills and knowledge to satisfy the UCD process needs. Usually, (software) engineers alone cannot cover this range but must be assisted sporadically by members of other departments and supported consistently by UX designers and usability engineers [5]. It is highly recommended to integrate these experts into the development teams.

One approach that transfers these principles to agile development environments is *Lean UX* as proposed by Gothelf and Seiden [7]. Lean UX focuses on vertical prototypes and minimum viable products (MVP) to gain rapid feedback and test the relevance and usability of implemented concepts (there are a lot of different definitions for MVP [16], we agreed on the definition given by Ries [21]).

4   Experiences When Introducing UCD

In this Section, we report on our experiences of introducing a UCD process for the development of the *Sequence Editor* in the UCD pilot project after about two years. For this purpose, we identified malpractices that symptomatically violate the UCD principles and methods we presented in Sect. 3. Figure 1 gives an overview of all findings. The figure lists all observed symptoms on the left side and categorize them by the principles (see Sect. 3) violated. Outgoing arrows mean that the source item is caused by the target item. So each of the symptoms can ultimately be tracked down to at least one root cause that originates in the behavior of the project team or their surrounding (processes, supervisors, etc.). As Fig. 1 shows we have identified four major root causes:

Inappropriate Development Organization, Tools, and Mindset. User interface development based on UCD requires appropriate mindsets. As industrial companies don't see themselves as software developers, they are much more traditional concerning methods, organization, tools, and mindset than modern software development organizations. These outdated attitudes may have severe impact on UCD based software product development.

UCD Intrinsic Issues. The user-centered design process is not perfect and has also some drawbacks [2]. Issues that are related to these drawbacks are summarized by this root cause.

Domain Specific Difficulties. HMI development in the industrial domain is very special due to its tight coupling to the machinery hardware and its special usage environment. Although hard- and software must work together perfectly, the software development process differs significantly from the hardware development process. Apart from that, there is the very long product life-cycle, which can last 20 years or longer. Within this time, the company must provide support and maintenance of both, software and hardware. As many machines are not connected to the internet, updating the software system requires maintenance personnel to be on-site. So for cost reasons, updates should not be done too frequently. Last, but not least, industrial companies want to keep their production knowledge secret. Due to this and because the companies are spread worldwide, it is not too easy to perform UCD related tasks like observations or interviews with end-users.

Too Less UCD Experience. 'Exercise makes perfect' is also true for introducing a new process. The team members as well as all other people concerned have to learn new ways of doing things and - even more important - accepting that things are different now. Lack of experience is especially noticeable when something goes wrong. But even when everything runs fine, people tend to revert to old habits.

The following sections (Sects. 4.1, 4.2, 4.3, 4.4 and 4.5) systematically describe all found problems and their symptoms grouped by UCD principle. Even more, where appropriate, mitigation strategies to overcome the corresponding problem are given. These strategies arise mainly from personal experiences of the authors mixed with tried and tested statements of literature. It is important to note that currently not all of these optimal situations are already established in the pilot project, hence their effectiveness is not proven yet.

4.1   Integrated and Comprehensive Solution

Feature-Driven Vs. User-Driven Development. While the pilot project follows a user-centric approach from start, all other teams continued to work feature oriented. This situation is a continuous source of conflict in a multi-team project. In a feature-driven development process, the overall model and the feature list are specified first; then the features are implemented step-wise. This is inconsistent with the user-centered design, where new features are defined and refined gradually based on user research.

Symptom: The framework team is busy implementing components like UI controls or input dialogues without any user need. Special framework features defined by the pilot project team are postponed as they do not match the predefined feature list of the framework team. As a consequence, the pilot project team must either implement the features by themselves, or wait until the framework team is able to deliver the requested feature. As the latter is irreconcilable with the UCD process (which demands early user-testing of implemented features), the pilot project team has to do much more work than planned.

Mitigation: All teams of the multi-team project follow the UCD approach. User research is done in tight cooperation. New features can be defined on demand.

Departmental Thinking. Traditionally, there is no communication channel between departments like marketing and the development teams. As a consequence, business goals do not necessarily align with product requirements nor do they drive innovation.

Symptom: There is no general design system that covers all different communication channels between company and customer: print media, the company web page, the web based customer portal, the product, and auxiliary apps. All these parts are developed independently and tell their own story to the user. As the marketing department is not interested in HMI development, and the product manager is not informed about marketing activities, the business goals of marketing and product development do not match.

Another example is the missing link between development department and customer training. While the customer training team usually has deep knowledge

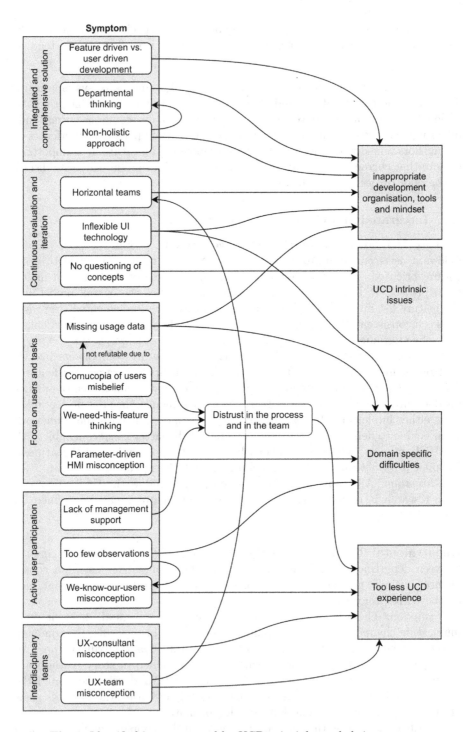

Fig. 1. Identified issues grouped by UCD principles and their causes.

about the needs and sufferings of many customers, they are not really integrated in the development process. Therefore, valuable information that is actually already within the company remains unused.

Mitigation: Development is driven by business goals. There is a clear vision for the next generation HMI which is defined interdisciplinary by UX experts, business executives, marketing experts, technicians and more. The vision is not necessarily restricted to virtual user interfaces. Every development iteration cycle generates value for the user and hence for the company.

Non-holistic Approach. Although the HMI is part of an integrated industrial environment, the HMI development is restricted to the graphical display only. This is disadvantageous in situations, where the user research findings demand a holistic approach which touches both, display and machine hardware as well. This issue is related to *Departmental thinking*, which is one of the root causes of this misconception.

Symptom: The team is presented with a *fait accompli*. Important decisions which have deep impact on user experience, are already made and cannot be (easily) changed. These may be size, orientation and position of the display panels, specification of the visualization hardware, or form and position of hardware keys. Adding additional hardware, like sensors or input devices are out of the question.

Mitigation: Due to a holistic approach, UCD means rethinking the entire machine and its environment from the point of view of user interaction. This provides an integrated solution that works best for the user.

4.2   Focus on Users and Tasks

Missing Usage Data. Due to missing usage data, the pilot project team has no idea about how the thousands of users interact with the HMI of the machines in-use. Knowledge about usage can make time-consuming observations and discussion obsolete. The reasons for the lack of data are manifold. Most industrial machines in-use are either not connected to the internet at all, or are not accessible from outside due to security reasons. So usage data has to be collected manually. Apart from that, many of the machines in-use are rather old and outdated from a technical point of view and provide too little data storage to collect user interaction data and its usage context (e.g. machine state) over time.

Symptom: Although the stakeholders pretend to know the users (see 4.3), they are not able to answer questions like 'Which UI parts are used most?', 'How many minutes/hours per day do users use the HMI?', 'Which navigation paths are used most?', 'Do the users use swipe gestures or previous/next buttons for navigating between views?', or 'What are the top ten operation errors?'. Based on such information, the development team could focus on UIs that are really relevant to the user instead of laboriously gathering such information through user research.

Mitigation: Usage data is collected automatically and periodically uploaded to a centralized cloud storage so that it can be used for detailed usage analysis. The results are an important basis for further development.

Cornucopia of Users Misbelief. The process of defining personas based on observations is regularly distrusted by stakeholders. They believe that the company has so many end-users, and all of them work differently, so it is impossible to unify their personalities in just a few personas. As a non-domain expert, these believes are hard to assess or even declare invalid, especially when there is no usage data to verify this (see *Missing usage data*).

Symptom: Experts that act as stakeholders of the project often point out the great functionality of the existing product by telling stories about a special user or use case, which, at first glance, seem to render the prospected solution impractical or incomplete.

Mitigation: Although special users and use cases are real and respected by the HMI team, they do not drive HMI development. The stakeholders have trust in the team and the process and know, that the result of a design iteration does not support all possible use cases. There are enough domain experts that defend the design iteration result against disbelievers.

We-Need-This-Feature Thinking. Stakeholders tend to use the old system as requirement reference. They demand features from this system to be transferred to the new system without taking user needs into account. As a result, they question feature-incomplete iteration results. Similar to *Cornucopia of users misbelief*, the main causes are distrust in the process and in the team, but the symptoms are different.

Symptom: Again - similar to *Cornucopia of users misbelief*, experts act as stakeholder. But instead of telling a story about individuals, they pretend a certain feature is crucial to most of the users. For non-domain experts, it is very hard or even impossible to refute this claim, hence these features are often re-implemented without any confirmation by user research or testing.

Mitigation: Stakeholders focus on the iterative progress of the team, even if they know that the current product still misses features that seem to be important at first glance. This requires a certain level of trust in the team and in the UCD process.

Parameter-Driven HMI Misconception. The PLC of *ENGEL* defines about 16.000 parameters that may be relevant to the HMI. Due to multiple product lines and individual customization, the parameters actually viewed in the HMI vary heavily. The easiest way to support this flexibility is to just visualize the logical structure of the control system, ignoring any user tasks or workflows.

Symptom: Instead of focusing on tasks, the UI focuses on parameters. Most of the views are just parameter lists without additional information. The grouping and ordering of these parameters are defined by the PLC and customer customization developers without assistance by UI/UX experts. Concepts like wizards or 'intelligent' workflow assistants are missing.

Mitigation: The HMI is two-layered. The parameter layer provides a flexible mechanism for both, the developer and the end user to define easily, which parameters should be displayed on which page and in which order. This layer is sufficient to control and operate the machine. Apart from that there is the workflow layer, that provides explicitly developed user interfaces that support important workflows and tasks. These UIs can be introduced step-by-step each improving the overall user experience.

4.3   Active User Participation

We-Know-Our-Users Misconception. As the company is unfamiliar with user-driven development, the project stakeholders are still tempted to ignore user research and demand features, they think are relevant instead. They argue this by mentioning their many years of experience. Although the company has sufficient knowledge about the customer's usage scenarios, it is almost exclusively in the minds of service technicians and customer advisers. The knowledge is not structured and therefore not directly usable.

Symptom: When presenting insights gained from user observations in the field, experienced employees, which are not part of the project team, claim that they already knew about that and this information could have easily been requested.

Mitigation: Although service technicians and customer advisers are important sources of information, the main user needs are based on user research in the fields.

Too Few User Research There are many reasons, why user research in the industrial domain is difficult. Obviously, there are safety and information security reasons. In addition, intrusive techniques like interviews keep workers away from their work, so not all companies are suitable for that. We also found that observing infrequent tasks requires good planning, so it is important to synchronize the schedule of the UX researchers with the work schedule of the participants. Hence, often the right user is not next door. Last, but not least, typical workflows often consist of many technical steps, which are less interesting to the UX expert. All in all, observing the entire workflow may take a few hours or even several days. All this causes high costs. As a result, the team tends to do less observations than necessary.

Symptom: The symptoms are obvious: for many scenarios, confirmation by observation is still pending; results from ideation workshops are not validated with end-users; colleagues are used as representative for real end-users.

Trade-off: Observations happen on a regular basis for important workflows. Missing user needs due to missing observations are mitigated by defining user need assumptions and trying to confirm or refute them early by user testing rapid prototypes. Participants are real end-users, but also service technicians, customer advisers, trainers, apprentices and other personnel of the company.

Lack of Management Support. Although the management supports the pilot project and the UCD process, it has too little knowledge about the philosophy of UCD. The consequences are lack of trust and demand for intervention.

Symptom: Time spent on user observations is criticized by supervisors (see *Too few user research*), especially if their main findings are already known by stakeholders (see *We-know-our-users misconception*).

4.4 Continuous Evaluation and Iteration

No Questioning of Concepts. Once, an early prototype has been tested and proven to work at a certain degree, it is never questioned any more. As a consequence, iterations just improve existing prototypes gradually and never raise radical changes. Although this issue is inherent to UCD methods in general, it is even worse in this industry. Due to high domain complexity, it is almost impossible to test all technical details of concepts, so there is always the risk of improving a prototype that is basically broken without knowing it. A similar issue has already been identified by [15] in 1997.

Symptom: Shortly after project start a central prototype was elaborated in detail to overcome some doubts about the user-centered approach. Even so user tests have shown that the prototype basically works for experienced users another promising concept has never been tested, because of the effort already spent.

Mitigation: Interaction concepts are tested at a very early stage. In this phase, there are often several concept proposals that can be tested against each other using A/B tests. This makes it possible to find concept errors early on and to optimally combine the best solutions. In addition, special domain expert reviews improve the prototype quality on a conceptual level.

Horizontal Teams. Currently, the multi-team project is set up with four horizontal teams. One team is responsible for the OPC UA based layer set up on top of machine and robot control, which is developed by a second team. Third, a team implements the HMI framework and the HMI base application accessing information of the OPC UA layer. Fourth, the pilot project team develops the *Sequence Editor* by means of the HMI framework and integrates it into the HMI base application. As a consequence, new interaction concepts designed by the pilot project team cannot be integrated into the system without support from the other teams. This causes latency which makes it hard to evaluate new UI concepts in time.

Symptom: A new concept that should facilitate trouble shooting in the *Sequence Editor* caused the robot control layer to provide novel data. This circumstance was not foreseen by the team implementing the *Sequence Editor* and so the group of persons participating in the technical coordination meetings on this issue has been successively increased, with a lead time of more than two Scrum sprints (3 weeks each) [22].

Mitigation: The teams are vertically organized, so they can work independently most of the time. Dependencies between teams arise only when both teams share the same user needs.

Inflexible UI Technology. Both, technology-in-use and system architecture did not support exchanging UI parts and modifying interaction concepts easily. Even more, due to the limited capabilities of the mobile touch device, interaction concepts are limited too.

Symptom: The UI framework in use does not or barely support multi-touch input. Implementing animations like fade-out of dialogs, transitions or rotations is hard and requires major code changes. Controls like text input fields, buttons or check boxes cannot be styled or skinned to be adapted to modern UI designs. Features like visualization of 3D models or embedding multimedia are missing or difficult to integrate.

Mitigation: Existing legacy components have been replaced and a more suitable UI framework has been introduced. Furthermore, a more capable mobile touch device has been prospected in favor of better user experience.

4.5 Interdisciplinary Teams

UX-Consultant Misconception. In the first months of the pilot project, the main UX work was done by external UX experts. As a result, the team had too little knowledge about UX related aspects to be able to develop the MVPs. Furthermore, external UX experts have too little domain know-how, which is necessary for a holistic understanding of scenarios.

Symptom: As the UX-consultants have only very few contact to the developer team, most of the user stories are already specified into detail when they are presented to the software developers. Although the stories might be perfect from a UX point of view, they are not technically validated, hence the developers might face several technical difficulties while implementing them. As they were not involved in the user research nor design process, they miss any reasoning and don't know if and how far they can deviate from the specification to circumvent these difficulties. Again, as the UX-consultants are separated from the development team, most of these problems are not discussed, thus the features are implemented exactly as specified - no regard to expenses. Even worse, experienced software developers often question the UX designs and concepts, which leads to disparaging opinions and disrespect toward the UX experts.

Mitigation: UX is an integrated part of the development process. The teams defines UX roles similar to the typical software development roles 'Software Architect', 'Tester' or 'DevOps Engineer'. All team members take part in UX-related tasks like user research or evaluation for the sake of knowledge transfer in both directions.

UX-Team Misconception. Separating the UX experts from the development team by building a UX team of its own was another misconception. This approach clearly conflicts with the vertical team thinking (see *Horizontal teams*). Although this keeps the UX know-how inside the company at least, it also keeps UX know-how away from the development teams.

Symptom: The symptoms are similar to *UX-consultant misconception*, although less severe, as at least there is UX know how in the company.
Mitigation: See *UX-consultant misconception*

5   Related Work

In the manufacturing industry the need for usability and user experience as explicit quality measures for user interfaces of cyber-physical systems (CPS) [24] is rather new. This need is based on changing requirements, a higher level of automation, and increasing complexity driven by the *Smart Factory* idea of the *Industry 4.0* initiative [14]. These requirements demand for appropriate and proper working UCD processes, as described by Pfeiffer et al. [20], but industry still lacks long-time experience on how to integrate these processes in their development practice.

Systematic reviews [4,11] have shown that most publications that discuss UCD processes in practice primarily discuss issues that emerge when introducing particular UCD methods (e.g. personas, user tests,...) in the context of agile processes. In [15] Lauesen investigates the introduction of UCD processes. We can confirm his findings, i.e., that early prototypes are only modified in details in later phases (see Sect. 4.4), and that there exists a friction between software developers and UX-experts (before UX-experts became part of the team). Compared to Lauesen, we have identified additional issues, which had negative impact on the project's pace.

6   Conclusion

Introducing UCD in the industrial domain represents a significant paradigm shift, since industrial HMIs are typically still developed in feature-oriented manner. UCD processes are based on a set of principles that must be followed in order to be successful. We have presented a set of issues that we have encountered when introducing UCD in a company from the manufacturing domain including symptoms and potential mitigation strategies. The root cause of most of the problems seems to be the lack of trust in the process on all organizational levels (line management, stakeholders, other teams, other departments), which itself originates from lack of knowledge about the UCD process.

Acknowledgement. The research reported in this paper has been supported by the Austrian Ministry for Transport, Innovation and Technology, the Federal Ministry for Digital and Economic Affairs, and the Province of Upper Austria in the frame of the COMET center SCCH.

References

1. Abelein, U., Sharp, H., Paech, B.: Does involving users in software development really influence system success? IEEE Softw. **30**(6), 17–23 (2013)
2. Abras, C., Maloney-Krichmar, D., Preece, J., et al.: User-centered design. In: Bainbridge, W. (ed.) Encyclopedia of Human-Computer Interaction. Sage Publications, Thousand Oaks, 37(4), 445–456 (2004)
3. Bano, M., Zowghi, D.: A systematic review on the relationship between user involvement and system success. Inf. Softw. Technol. **58**, 148–169 (2015)
4. Da Silva, T.S., Martin, A., Maurer, F., Silveira, M.: User-centered design and agile methods: a systematic review. In: 2011 AGILE conference. pp. 77–86. IEEE (2011)
5. Göransson, B., Sandbäck, T.: Usability designers improve the user-centred design process. In: Proceedings for INTERACT, vol. 99, pp. 1–4 (1999)
6. Gorecky, D., Schmitt, M., Loskyll, M., Zühlke, D.: Human-machine-interaction in the industry 4.0 era. In: 2014 12th IEEE International Conference on Industrial Informatics (INDIN), pp. 289–294. IEEE (2014)
7. Gothelf, J., Seiden, J.: Lean UX: Applying Lean Principles to Improve User Experience. O'Reilly Media, Inc., Sebastopol (2013)
8. Gould, J.D., Lewis, C.: Designing for usability: key principles and what designers think. Commun. ACM **28**(3), 300–311 (1985)
9. Gulliksen, J., Göransson, B., Boivie, I., Blomkvist, S., Persson, J., Cajander, Å.: Key principles for user-centred systems design. Behav. Inf. Technol. **22**(6), 397–409 (2003)
10. Harris, M.A., Weistroffer, H.R.: A new look at the relationship between user involvement in systems development and system success. Commun. Assoc. Inf. Syst. **24**(1), 42 (2009)
11. Jurca, G., Hellmann, T.D., Maurer, F.: Integrating agile and user-centered design: a systematic mapping and review of evaluation and validation studies of agile-ux. In: 2014 Agile Conference, pp. 24–32. IEEE (2014)
12. Kujala, S.: User involvement: a review of the benefits and challenges. Behav. Inf. Technol. **22**(1), 1–16 (2003)
13. Kujala, S., Kauppinen, M.: Identifying and selecting users for user-centered design. In: Proceedings of the Third Nordic Conference on Human-Computer Interaction, pp. 297–303. ACM (2004)
14. Lasi, H., Fettke, P., Kemper, H.G., Feld, T., Hoffmann, M.: Industry 4.0. Bus. Inf. Syst. Eng. **6**(4), 239–242 (2014)
15. Lauesen, S.: Usability engineering in industrial practice. In: Howard, S., Hammond, J., Lindgaard, G. (eds.) Human-Computer Interaction INTERACT 1997. ITIFIP, pp. 15–22. Springer, Boston, MA (1997). https://doi.org/10.1007/978-0-387-35175-9_4
16. Lenarduzzi, V., Taibi, D.: Mvp explained: a systematic mapping study on the definitions of minimal viable product. In: 2016 42th Euromicro Conference on Software Engineering and Advanced Applications (SEAA), pp. 112–119. IEEE (2016)
17. Nielsen, J.: Usability inspection methods. In: Conference Companion on Human Factors in Computing Systems, pp. 413–414. ACM (1994)
18. Norman, D.A., Draper, S.W.: User Centered System Design: New Perspectives on Human-Computer Interaction. CRC Press, Boca Raton (1986)
19. OPC Foundation: IEC 62541: OPC Unified Architecture. Standard, International Electrotechnical Commission (2015–2016)

20. Pfeiffer, T., Hellmers, J., Schön, E.M., Thomaschewski, J.: Empowering user interfaces for industrie 4.0. Proc. IEEE. **104**(5), 986–996 (2016)
21. Ries, E.: The lean startup: How today's entrepreneurs use continuous innovation to create radically successful businesses. Crown Books (2011)
22. Schwaber, K., Beedle, M.: Agile Software Development with Scrum, vol. 1. Prentice Hall, Upper Saddle River (2002)
23. Väätäjä, H., Seppänen, M., Paananen, A.: Creating value through user experience: a case study in the metals and engineering industry. Int. J. Technol. Mark. **9**(2), 163–186 (2014)
24. Wittenberg, C.: Human-CPS interaction-requirements and human-machine interaction methods for the industry 4.0. IFAC-PapersOnLine **49**(19), 420–425 (2016)

Combining GQM+Strategies and OKR - Preliminary Results from a Participative Case Study in Industry

Bianca Trinkenreich[1(✉)], Gleison Santos[1],
Monalessa Perini Barcellos[2], and Tayana Conte[3]

[1] PPGI/UNIRIO - Graduate Program in Informatics,
UNIRIO, Rio de Janeiro, Brazil
{bianca.trinkenreich, gleison.santos}@uniriotec.br
[2] NEMO Ontology and Conceptual Modeling Research Group – UFES,
Vitória, Brazil
monalessa@inf.ufes.br
[3] USES Research Group, Institute of Computing (IComp) – UFAM,
Manaus, Brazil
tayana@icomp.ufam.edu.br

Abstract. Aligning IT strategies to business goals is a top priority for CIOs. However, measuring results that IT brings to business is a challenging task. We carried out a study to help an IT director of a large mining company to define OKRs (Objective Key Results) and quantitatively monitor the achievement of goals. We performed a participative case study to define OKRs for goals and initiatives to achieve them, by using GQM+Strategies to support us in that matter. As a result, after three meetings with the IT director and IT managers, we defined OKRs for five IT goals and initiatives to achieve them. From this experience, we noticed that GQM+Strategies and OKR can be used together, working in a complimentary way: OKR gives simplicity and agility to the process, while GQM+Strategies provides useful knowledge to define OKRs and initiatives to achieve them properly.

Keywords: GQM+Strategies · Objective Key Results · OKR · Measurement

1 Introduction

Alignment between IT (Information Technology) and business goals is considered by both practitioners and researchers a management practice to enhance organizational performance. However, there is still lack of knowledge about what organizational actors really should do in practice for this alignment to happen [5]. There is a need for researchers to adapt and extend knowledge about what means IT to be aligned with business and how to measure it [6].

Measurement is a key process to support organizations in managing and improving processes, products, and services to achieve customer satisfaction [1]. Measures should be used to monitor the alignment of IT to business goals by providing useful information for decision-making [3]. However, managers face difficulties to define

© Springer Nature Switzerland AG 2019
X. Franch et al. (Eds.): PROFES 2019, LNCS 11915, pp. 103–111, 2019.
https://doi.org/10.1007/978-3-030-35333-9_7

measures, evaluate if projects are bringing expected results to business and monitor results to keep alignment between IT and business goals [3, 4].

The first author of this paper works at IT team of a large global mining company. She was asked to help the director and the five managers to define measures for goals and to review initiatives (projects and operational activities) to achieve those goals. At that point, goals were qualitative and subjective, and the director was not able to verify if the initiatives were contributing to goals achievement. We have already successfully used GQM+Strategies [2] in other areas of the organization to aid in the alignment between goals and strategies through measurement [10]. However, the IT director was running a tight schedule and needed a fast approach, which did not require training or many phases. He asked us to use OKR (Objective Key Results) [7], a method to support defining and tracking goals and their outcomes, which has been increasingly used in industry. OKR has an agile appeal, while GQM+Strategies provides detailed knowledge on how to align goals and strategies through measurement. Thus, we decided to explore the combined use of the two methods in a way that they work complementarily. As a result, after three meetings, we defined OKRs to five IT goals and initiatives to achieve them.

This paper presents the study and its main findings. It is organized as follows: Sect. 2 provides the background for the paper; Sect. 3 presents the study planning and execution; Sect. 4 addresses the process that arose from the study, Sect. 5 discusses our findings and study limitations; and Sect. 6 presents conclusions and future work.

2   Background

IT-business alignment can be considered the level of fit and integration between business, IT processes, projects, and infrastructure of an organization [13]. Aligning goals and IT projects help focus resources and projects towards value creation and requires finding the connections between them so that the links are explicit and allow for analytic reasoning about what is successful and where change is necessary [2].

The GQM+Strategies approach [2] is an extension of the Goal-Question-Metric paradigm and helps control the success or failure of strategies and goals by using a measurement system. In GQM+Strategies, strategies refer to projects, actions, or other initiatives performed to achieve goals. The GQM+Strategies model relates goals and strategies at several organizational levels. One or more strategies can accomplish the same goal. Context factors and assumptions influence goals and strategies. A GQM +Strategies element includes an organizational goal, respective strategies, context, and assumptions that influence them. GQM+Strategies elements and related models are represented in a GQM+Strategies Grid, making goals and strategies explicit, as well as measures related to them, providing a transparent correlation between goals, strategies and measurement initiatives. The GQM+Strategies process consists of an initial phase and a repeatable cycle with three stages and six phases: Develop (phases 1 and 2); Implement (phases 3 and 4) Learn (phases 5 and 6) [2].

Objective Key Results (OKR) is a collaborative goal-setting protocol to help ensure that the company is consistently focusing and prioritizing efforts on the same issues throughout the organization [8]. An OKR has two components: the Objective, qualitative and inspirational, and Key Results, quantitative and measurable. The objective should be meaningful, significant, concrete, actionable, and inspirational. Key results gauge and measure how to achieve the objective and are quantitative, usually time-bound, verifiable, and realistic. The process to define OKRs consists in setting the objectives; determining the key results for each objective, executing actions to achieve the objectives; providing regular feedbacks.

3 Study Planning and Execution

Participative case study was selected as research method as the researcher was a member of organization, she observed the particular group of organization' subjects, and was one participant in the process being observed [11]. The researcher had some control over some intervening variables and was a stakeholder in the process' outcome, as she was part of the department and would work to achieve OKRs. The participative case study report attempts to capture and communicate the biased interpretation by stakeholders of their particular environment during a particular period in time. We followed two phases Planning, for case study preparation, and Execution, for data collection.

The organization where we carried out the study is a large global mining company operating in over 30 countries, with offices, operations, exploration, and joint ventures across five continents. Information Technology (IT) department is composed of five areas: Innovation and Projects, Architecture and Technology, IT Services, Business Partners, and Strategy and Planning. At the beginning of the year, the IT director defined a set of goals, and the IT managers elicited 140 initiatives to achieve them. In April, the director realized that the goals seemed non-measurable, and he was not able to verify if initiatives elicited by IT managers were able to achieve the defined IT goals. The IT director needed a fast approach to focus efforts on the right direction and had not enough time to spend on training or following many phases of a traditional goal-setting method.

Since OKR (Objective Key Results) [8] has been increasingly used by industry to support the creation of measurable and achievable goals to foster alignment, engage the team and follow a fast cadence, the IT director showed interest in using it. The OKR literature provides knowledge (examples, good practices, tips, concepts) to build OKRs and monitor results [8]. However, there is no practical direction or procedure about how to gather contextual information and turn a qualitative objective into a measurable goal for a key result. There is also no direction about how to elicit initiatives (i.e., strategies) to achieve goals. GQM+Strategies [2] provides this kind of knowledge. We had previous experience using GQM+Strategies [2] in other departments of the company [10], and thus, we decided to combine both methods. By doing that, we expected that OKR would satisfy the need for a faster approach, while GQM+Strategies would provide complementary knowledge to perform the activities. Next, we present information about the study planning and execution.

3.1 Planning

The *goal* of the study is to analyze the combined use of OKR and GQM+Strategies to support defining measurable goals, OKRs, and initiatives for IT goals. Aligned with this goal, we defined the following *research question*: How to combine OKR and GQM+Strategies to measure qualitative goals and support their achievement? The *expected outcomes* were (i) a list of OKRs agreed by both IT director and IT managers to measure the achievement of IT goals, (ii) a process to support defining OKRs.

The technique used to collect data was document analysis and three brainstorm meetings with the IT director and IT managers. When we received the following list of five IT goals (G) defined by the IT director, it became clear for us that goals could not be easily quantified without contextual information: (G1) Become the natural provider of Operational Technology (OT) support; (G2) Continue to streamline and improve services delivery; (G3) Improve customer experience through innovation; (G4) Enable Digital Transformation journey; (G5) Be a role model for digital transformation inside IT. We also received spreadsheets containing the initiatives elicited by the IT managers and the initiative's deliverables. Meetings were scheduled to review goals in measurable terms, define OKRs, and review the initiatives.

3.2 Execution

We followed a plan of using practical work meetings, lasting between 1 and 2 h each. The IT director and the five IT managers participated in all meetings. We started by analyzing the IT goals under the perspective of OKR in order to verify if they were meaningful, significant, concrete, actionable, and inspirational. The main problem we found was that the IT goals were defined using qualitative terms (e.g., natural provider), without a rationale to explain them. This makes it difficult to measure goals achievement. We needed the information to express the goal in measurable terms. Thus, we followed practices from the Develop stage – Phase 1 of the GQM+Strategies process, which says that rationale, context factors, and assumptions characterize the environment and help define and understand goals. We asked questions to brainstorm discussion and get information to define aspects that could bring a basis to measure the achievement of qualitative objectives (e.g., aspects to explain and quantify what means to be a natural provider for the organization).

Once the aspects to be measured were identified, we used practices from the Develop stage – Phase 2 of the GQM+Strategies process to, first, define key results (KRs) and, then, elicit strategies to achieve them. To define KRs, we considered OKR guidelines (KRs should be quantitative, time-bound, verifiable, and realistic). When discussing being *verifiable*, the IT director and managers quickly defined how to collect data, as a brief measurement plan that would be further detailed. For sake of confidentiality, we used X and Y to represent current and target values, respectively, and omitted the time to achieve the result (Table 1).

Table 1. OKRs for "Become the natural provider of Operational Technology (OT) support"

Service delivery aspects to be improved	Key results
Increase availability	Reduce planned and unplanned downtime of high impact applications from X to Y
Reduce baseline costs	Reduce baseline costs from X to Y
Reduce security and operational risks	Reduce outdated components from X to Y Increase the number of components being tracked by Software Asset Manager from X to Y
Expand coverage to Location Z	Increase the maturity level of maturity model in Location Z (people, process and technologies) from X to Y

Once we had measurable goals expressed by OKRs, next step was to review elicited initiatives to verify and prioritize the ones aligned to OKRs. Due to the high number of initiatives and for the sake of confidentiality, we discuss only some of them.

First, we verified alignment between initiatives and OKRs by analyzing if the initiative deliverable could contribute to the achievement of the OKR. We also questioned the high number of initiatives (IT managers listed 140 initiatives) and their connection with the IT goals. Thus, we selected only the initiatives truly aligned with OKRs. For example, by analyzing the initiatives, it was noted that the initiative "Elaborating Software as a Services Contract Guidelines," which includes benchmarking studies, architecture guidelines and contracts review, was not aligned to any OKR, since it was not able to produce deliverables that contribute to achieving the OKRs.

We also verified the need for new initiatives. For example, there were only two initiatives related to the goal "Become the natural provider of Operational Technology (OT) support," namely: "Include scope for supporting OT users in outsourcing contract" and "Implementation of network standards to improve the security posture for OT sites." When we defined measurable goals and created OKRs, the participants realized that those initiatives were not enough, and new initiatives should be created to achieve the OKRs. The OKR goal-setting protocol does not provide any mechanism to elicit initiatives to achieve KRs. Thus, we followed an approach based on GQM +Strategies [10] to fulfill this gap. This proposal suggests that in order to elicit effective initiatives, processes related to the goals to be achieved should be analyzed. Hence, we qualitatively analyzed processes associated with each KR and investigated root-causes of problems related to these processes that impact KRs achievement. As a result, new initiatives were created to support goals achievement.

For example, we analyzed the process performed to provide the required infrastructure foundation for a new location, and we found out that the main obstacles related to the OKR "Increase the number of OT locations with foundation implemented from X to Y" are related to network and support. So, we defined two initiatives: Implement network standards and Extend the outsourcing contract to support OT users. After reviewing the initiatives to achieve each OKR, we consolidated OKRs and respective initiatives in a GQM+Strategies grid [10] to visualize results and analyze conflicts.

4   Results

The OKR provides a simple way to define and track goals and measurable results, including agile principles to help define and monitor objectives and key results, and some ideas about techniques to use during meetings to define OKRs (e.g., Design Thinking) [7]. However, it does not provide a process to guide establishing quantitative key results for qualitative objectives. Moreover, OKR does not clearly address the initiatives to be executed in order to achieve the KRs. GQM+Strategies describes a process, including a Develop stage, which can be helpful when defining quantitative KRs. Besides, GQM+Strategies gives directions on eliciting strategies to achieve goals and, once again, can be helpful to define initiatives to achieve OKRs.

OKR and GQM+Strategies have some similarities (e.g., both are concerned with defining measurable goals) and also differences (as discussed previously). In this study, we combined both practices and, together with an IT director and five IT managers, we could define OKRs and initiatives to achieve them. Figure 1 illustrates the process that arose from the study, and we briefly explain it next. Although the process is linearly presented, there can be interaction between the phases.

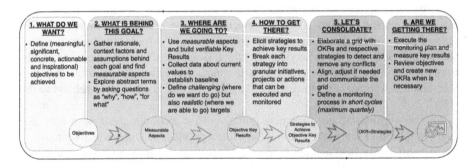

Fig. 1. Process to support defining and monitoring OKRs and strategies to achieve them.

Stage 1: What do we want? – Define objectives aligned to business (or review if they exist) being meaningful, significant, concrete, actionable, and inspirational [8].

Stage 2: What is behind this objective? – Identify measurable aspects to provide a basis to turn qualitative objectives into measurable objectives. Explore abstract terms like adjectives to understand what they mean for the organization by asking questions such as "why," "how," "for what." Gather rationale, context factors and assumptions [2] behind each goal and find measurable aspects to be measured in key results [8].

Stage 3: Where do we want to go? – Create KRs for each objective using the measurable aspects as basis. KRs should be quantitative, usually time-bound, verifiable and realistic [8]. When building KRs current values for each measurable aspect are used to establish baseline (where we are today) and challenging (where do we want to go) but also realistic (where can we go) values defined as targets [8].

Stage 4: How are we going to get there? – Elicit strategies (i.e., projects, actions or other initiatives) to achieve KRs [2]. Includes reviewing existent strategies to verify if their deliverables contribute to OKRs achievement. Process analysis, involving root-cause analysis and Pareto techniques, can be used to find obstacles to be addressed in the strategies, and that can help prioritize them [10].

Stage 5: Let's consolidate? – Elaborate a grid with OKRs and respective strategies to detect and remove any conflicts that can prevent an OKR from being achieved. Adjust the grid, if needed, and communicate to stakeholders. OKRs should be public [8] but many times, strategies may not be. Define a monitoring process instrumentation (e.g., emails, reports) and frequency in short cycles [8] to review OKRs results.

Stage 6: Are we getting there? – This stage is cyclic, as monitoring repeat following the frequency defined by organization. OKRs results, projects' deliverables, business contextual information behind goals should be regularly monitored, preferably on a short period [8]. Consolidate information, align with teams, communicate OKRs and results to all organization, review what changed and create new OKRs if needed.

5 Discussion

The results of the participative case study have initial findings to show it is possible to use GQM+Strategies and OKR together to support creating measurable goals, OKRs, and initiatives for IT goals. When asking the IT director for feedback, he said "we were stuck before your help starting with questions to demystify some terms used in goals. From there, creating measurable goals was very practical and useful to clarify meaning and make explicit how to measure it." He mentioned the approach was agile enough to provide expected results and clear enough to make the information explicit to the team.

IT goals were originally defined in a non-quantitative way, which was hard for IT managers to think about measurable attributes for them and select, from all initiatives, which ones could really deliver what was needed to achieve the goals. The culture of creating measurable goals needs to be spread through all the organization. OKRs can help with simple and actionable goals, constant monitoring, and agile changing for new OKRs when needed. By evaluating the deliverables of each initiative, we found only a few of them were truly strategic. The use of OKR and GQM+Strategies helped to make clear the alignment between initiatives and OKRs, providing a link between the actions performed by the teams and the goals the IT area wants to achieve. OKR literature suggests when OKRs are transparent, teams are senior enough to take ownership and get the work done [9]. During this study, we found a different scenario. Even for senior professionals, details about what have to be done to achieve the KRs were necessary. GQM+Strategies helped to satisfy this need. Aiming to make it easier to visualize the resulting OKRs, we built a grid. The grid was inspired by the GQM+Strategies grid proposed in [10]. Besides providing an overview of the defined OKRs and initiatives, it allows finding conflicts between them, as a monitoring and communication tool.

The process we followed to define OKRs can inspire other organizations on how measuring goals. Managers responsible for defining IT measurement processes can use information about how we defined OKRs, how we reviewed initiatives to guarantee alignment, then minimize difficulties during the definition of goals and initiatives and reduce the risk of failing in goals achievement. Furthermore, the study results can also be useful for researchers to identify practical issues to be addressed in future researches.

Regarding this study limitations, one of the biggest threats in this context is the ability to generalize from the case-specific findings to different cases [12]. Thus, the main threat to external validity in this study is about results' generalization. In case-based research, after getting results from specific case studies, generalization can be established for similar cases. Participative case study is biased [11] and subjective as its results rely on the researchers. The first author of this paper primarily conducted the study collaborating with the practitioners. She has been working at the organization for eight years. Thus, she does not provide an external view of the situation. To reduce this threat, we involved other researchers as a steering group in discussing and reflecting on the study and results. Besides, the first author had previous experience with GQM +Strategies, which may have influenced its use along with the study.

6   Conclusions and Future Work

In this paper, we reported a preliminary experience of using GQM+Strategies and OKR practices together to define measurable goals, OKRs, and initiatives for IT goals. GQM +Strategies and OKR worked in a complimentary way, where OKR provided basic concepts, simplicity, and agility to the process, while GQM+Strategies provided useful knowledge to perform activities and define initiatives. We used an informal language to avoid communication barriers between academy and industry members.

As a result of this initial study, we created a first version of a process with six stages to define OKRs and initiatives to achieve them. We used provocative questions as *What is behind this goal?* to guide a brainstorm between practitioners and help them define measurable attributes for goals; *Where do we want to go?*, to incentivize practitioners to think about targets; *How are going to get there?*, to review if existent initiatives were able to achieve key results and elicit new ones; *Let's consolidate?*, to group OKRs and initiatives; and *Are we getting there?*, to monitor results and check if goals are achieved by the elicited initiatives. This paper points out a direction for further studies to evaluate whether the proposed process could help other software organizations.

The process and knowledge provided from using OKR and GQM+Strategies practices together can be useful for practitioners to reuse or adapt the process, as well as to be inspired by our experience to define their own OKRs and initiatives. Researchers, in turn, can identify practical issues to be addressed in future research (e.g., the knowledge gaps in OKR). We did not find any work reporting the use of OKR in the IT domain combining OKR and GQM+Strategies. As future works, we intend to perform new studies applying the created process to get new data about its use and improve it.

Acknowledgment. We thank the financial support by CNPq (423149/2016-4, 311494/2017-0, 461777/2014-2, 423149/2016-4), FAPERJ (E-201.670/2017).

References

1. Forrester, E., Buteau, B., Shrum, S.: CMMI For Services, Guidelines for Superior Service. CMMI-SVC, vol. 1.3, 2nd edn. Addison-Wesley, Boston (2010). SEI
2. Basili, V., et al.: Aligning Organizations Through Measurement. TFISSSE. Springer, Cham (2014). https://doi.org/10.1007/978-3-319-05047-8
3. Jantti, M., Lepmets, M.: Proactive management of IT operations to improve IT services. J. Inf. Syst. Technol. Manag. **14**(2), 191–218 (2017). https://doi.org/10.4301/s1807-17752017000200004
4. Gacenga, F., Cater-Steel, A., Toleman, M.: An international analysis of IT service management benefits and performance measurement. J. Glob. Inf. Technol. Manag. **13**(4), 28–63 (2010)
5. Karpovsky, A., Galliers, R.D.: Aligning in practice: from current cases to a new agenda. J. Inf. Technol. **30**(2), 136–160 (2015). https://doi.org/10.1057/jit.2014.34
6. Coltman, T., Tallon, P., Sharma, R., Queiroz, M.: Strategic IT alignment: twenty-five years on. J. Inf. Technol. **30**, 91–100 (2015). https://doi.org/10.1057/jit.2014.35
7. Nivan, P.R., Lamorte, B.: Objectives and Key Results: Driving Focus, Alignment, and Engagement with OKRs, p. 224. Wiley Corporate, Hoboken (2016)
8. Doerr, J.: Measure What Matters: How Google, Bono, and the Gates Foundation Rock the World with OKRs, p. 31. Penguin Publishing Group, London (2018)
9. Wodtke, C.: Introduction to OKRs, p. 37. O'Reilly Media, Newton (2016)
10. Trinkenreich, B., Santos, G., Barcellos, M.P.: SINIS: a GQM+Strategies-based approach for identifying goals, strategies and indicators for IT services. J. Inf. Softw. Technol. **100**, 147–164 (2018)
11. Baskerville, R.L.: Distinguishing action research from participative case studies. J. Syst. Inf. Technol. **1**(1), 24–43 (1997)
12. Wieringa, R., Daneva, M.: Six strategies for generalizing software engineering theories. Sci. Comput. Program. **101**, 136–152 (2015)
13. Henderson, J.C., Venkatraman, H.: Strategic alignment: leveraging information technology for transforming organizations. IBM Syst. J. **38**(2.3), 472–484 (1999)

Software Development Practices and Frameworks Used in Spain and Costa Rica: A Survey and Comparative Analysis

Ignacio Díaz-Oreiro[1], David Chaves[1], Brenda Aymerich[1],
Julio C. Guzmán[1], Gustavo López[1(✉)], Marcela Genero[2],
and Aurora Vizcaíno[2]

[1] University of Costa Rica, San José, Costa Rica
{ignacio.diazoreiro,david.chavescampos,
brenda.aymerich,julio.guzman,
gustavo.lopez_h}@ucr.ac.cr
[2] University of Castilla-La Mancha, Ciudad Real, Spain
{marcela.genero,aurora.vizcaino}@uclm.es

Abstract. Software development has been impacted by the arrival of agile frameworks, especially in the last two decades. The HELENA Project (Hybrid dEveLopmENt Approaches in software systems development) was developed to identify the use of these frameworks in relation to more traditional ones. As part of this project, a survey was carried out in 55 countries, including Spain and Costa Rica. This paper presents the comparison of the results of these two countries, particularly in relation to two topics: the degree of agility of the activities of the software development life cycle and what are the most used methods and frameworks in each country. The results show similarities in both topics for the two countries, such as the fact that the most agile-oriented activities are Implementation/Coding and Integration/Testing, or the widespread use of agile frameworks with Scrum in the first place, followed by Iterative Development and Kanban. There are, however, some differences, such as a greater presence in Spain of scaling agile frameworks.

Keywords: Software development approach · HELENA project · Scrum · Waterfall · Agile

1 Introduction

Software development evolves continuously and in the last 25 years it has been impacted by the arrival of agile frameworks. However, despite the impact generated by agile frameworks such as Scrum, the process of converting to agile has not been unanimous through organizations in the software industry. Even within an organization it is common to find combinations of agile and traditional methods and practices, what has been called Hybrid approaches. To understand the current state of practice in the use and combination of different software development approaches, a group of researchers initiated an international research project called HELENA (Hybrid dEveLopmENt Approaches in software systems development) [1, 2]. HELENA Project

© Springer Nature Switzerland AG 2019
X. Franch et al. (Eds.): PROFES 2019, LNCS 11915, pp. 112–119, 2019.
https://doi.org/10.1007/978-3-030-35333-9_8

had a first stage in which an evaluation tool was built on the use of different practices and frameworks in software development. In a second stage, an online survey was conducted that gathered information from 55 countries and almost 1,500 products or projects.

The overall goal of this international study is to investigate the current state of practice in software and systems development. This paper presents and compares the results of two countries represented in this survey (i.e., Spain and Costa Rica).

With 505 000 Km2 and 47 million inhabitants, Spain is ten times larger and more populated than Costa Rica. Sharing cultural correspondences and having a similar number of responses, comparing the results of these two countries could provide insights into the differences between a sizeable European country and a small Latin American country.

Spain has become an important center of nearshore outsourcing for Europe due to several factors: it is part of the European Union and the Schengen Agreement, it has a significant number of IT and Telecommunications schools, the salaries are competitive compared to the rest of Europeans countries and share a good part of the working hours with these countries. On the other hand, Costa Rica has remained as an offshore and nearshore software development center for almost two decades, mainly for the US market. Subcontracting in Costa Rica is reinforced by proximity to the United States, a shared central time zone and competitive salaries compared to the United States. Many technology companies have operations in Costa Rica [3], among which are Amazon, Deloitte, IBM, Hewlett Packard Enterprise, Intel and Microsoft. In addition, around 50 companies are dedicated exclusively to software development.

This paper reports the main findings of the comparison between Spain and Costa Rica according to these key questions: (1) Which is the degree of agility in the activities of the software development lifecycle? and (2) Which frameworks and methods are used for software development?

2   Related Work

Teams of researchers have presented the results of the HELENA survey in their respective countries [4–6]. However, given the global nature of the HELENA Project, authors have also compared countries and regions. For example, Nakatumba-Nabende et al. [7] compared the results of Sweden and Uganda, showing that respondents from Uganda were mostly developers, while in Sweden, the most represented roles were architect and project/team managers. The main finding of this research is that neither country adheres to one development model but rather employ hybrid approaches. Scott et al. [8] conduct the comparison between Estonia and Sweden. Regarding development frameworks and methods, Estonian responses state a clear preference for agile frameworks, with Scrum "always used" by 58% of the respondents. In Sweden, although the use of Scrum is also frequent, only 8% indicate that it is always used, and Kanban, Iterative Development, and the Classic Waterfall Process are used as often as Scrum.

3 Results and Discussion

In both Spain and Costa Rica, the survey was conducted by academic teams of the University of Castilla La Mancha and University of Costa Rica, respectively. The online survey was forwarded to several software development companies and networks interested in agile approaches. Hereafter, the results presented are extracted from the responses 51 responses received in Costa Rica and the 50 responses obtained from Spain. The individual results of the HELENA Survey for Costa Rica are presented in [9]. Regarding the size of the companies, four categories were defined: small (fewer than 50 employees), medium (between 50 and 250), large (between 250 and 2500) and very large (more than 2500 employees). The distribution of companies in Costa Rica and Spain are similar for the small (18% and 16% respectively) and medium (28% and 25% respectively) categories. However, large and very large companies differ significantly. In Costa Rica, 39% of the companies are large while in Spain only 12% are in this category. Furthermore, 42% of Spanish companies are very large while only 20% of Costa Rican companies fall into this category.

Additionally, as for the team geographical distribution of the teams, 27% of Costa Rican companies carry out their projects in a single location, 22% distribute them within the same country, 16% within the same continent and 35% globally. On the other hand, in Spain, 24% of companies concentrate their software development in one place, 48% distribute them throughout the country, only 8% regionally and 20% globally. It is interesting to notice that Costa Rica works in a highly communicative and cooperative way with other countries to develop software products. In Spain, 72% of the projects are carried out locally, which is also conditioned by the size and population of the country, which could be since Spain would have a larger group of software builders available in the local environment.

With respect to the company business area, the answers were classified into five categories: Software Development, System Development, Consulting, Research & Development, and "Other". Table 1 shows the distribution of companies by business area and size both for Spain and Costa Rica.

In Costa Rica, large and very large companies operate mostly in Software Development and in the "Other" category, being "Other" predominantly companies that serve the financial sector. In Spain, on the other hand, the largest companies focus on Software Development and Consulting. The most representative business area in both countries is Software Development (around 40%). Consulting is another significant business area (24% for Costa Rica and 34% in Spain).

Table 1. Company business area and size for Spain and Costa Rica.

Company size	Costa Rica						Spain					
	Software Dev.	System Dev.	Consulting	R&D	Other	Total	Software Dev.	System Dev.	Consulting	R&D	Other	Total
Small	3	0	2	2	1	8	4	0	3	1	2	10
Medium	6	0	6	0	0	12	6	0	5	3	0	14
Large	8	1	2	0	9	20	3	0	2	0	1	6
Very large	2	3	2	1	3	11	9	1	7	2	1	20
Total	19	4	12	3	13	51	22	1	17	6	4	50

3.1 Which Is the Degree of Agility in the Activities of the Software Development Lifecycle?

In the following sections we will present the findings of the HELENA survey along the key questions presented above. This section focuses on the practices and frameworks used in Spain and Costa Rica to develop software. In the survey we focused on the level of agility of every stage of the software development lifecycle using SWEBOK [10] as guide. Table 2 shows the distribution of these results. Some stages such as Implementation/Coding, Integration/Testing, Change Management, and Maintenance and Evolution tend to be agile.

Configuration Management is an interesting activity since in Costa Rica most projects are conducted mainly traditional in this stage. In contrast, in Spain this stage is more balanced between traditional and agile.

In Spain, three stages tend simultaneously towards Mainly Traditional and Mainly Agile: Risk Management, Quality Management, and Transition and Operations. This shows that some projects are conducted in a traditional manner and other are agile, but with a similar weight to both sides. In Costa Rica this behavior is not observable. As it was expected, activities that are conducted mainly or Fully Agile are the same for both countries. These are: Implementation/Coding, and Integration/Testing, although Costa Rica with slightly higher numbers in these two activities.

Table 2. Degree of agility in each stage of the software development lifecycle. Each cell represents the number of companies in that category.

	Country	Fully Traditional	Mainly Traditional	Balanced	Mainly Agile	Fully Agile
Implementation /Coding	Costa Rica	1	4	4	16	9
	Spain	2	4	9	13	5
Integration and Testing	Costa Rica	1	3	8	15	7
	Spain	3	4	7	14	5
Change Management	Costa Rica	2	4	12	10	4
	Spain	2	5	9	11	5
Maintenance and Evolution	Costa Rica	1	4	9	11	4
	Spain	1	9	8	9	4
Configuration Management	Costa Rica	5	8	9	3	3
	Spain	1	12	6	8	4
Risk Management	Costa Rica	3	9	8	6	2
	Spain	3	10	4	7	4
Requirements Analysis/Engineering	Costa Rica	2	9	7	12	5
	Spain	3	9	6	11	3
Quality Management	Costa Rica	3	9	8	6	4
	Spain	3	11	3	11	3
Transition and Operation	Costa Rica	2	3	14	6	3
	Spain	2	9	4	8	3
Architecture and Design	Costa Rica	4	8	8	11	2
	Spain	4	6	8	11	3
Project Management	Costa Rica	2	4	2	11	2
	Spain	1	1	3	3	1

Regarding the profile of respondents, in Costa Rica 49% have the role of developer, while only 32% of Spanish respondents are developers. On the other hand, 30% of Spanish respondents are Project/Team managers, for only 6% of Costa Rican respondents in this category. Years of experience also show differences between both countries: 84% of Spanish respondents have 6 years or more of experience (26% between 6 and 10 years and 58% with more than 10 years), while only 53% of Costa Rican respondents have 6 years or more of experience (20% between 6 and 10 years and 33% with more than 10). The largest group of Costa Rican respondents is formed by people with between 3 and 5 years of experience (35%).

To delve in the effect of the company size on the degree of agility for different stages, we analyzed how the participants rate their way of implementing the SWEBOK stages. Figure 1 shows the result of this analysis for Costa Rica and Spain, using the averaged ratings grouped by company size.

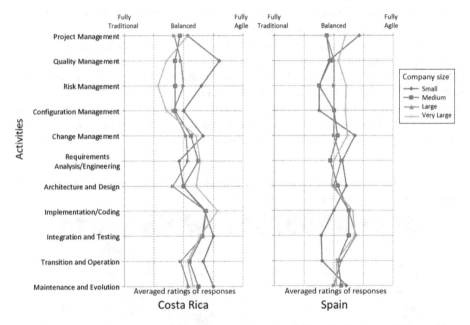

Fig. 1. Respondents rating on the implementation of activities for Spain and Costa Rica, grouped by company size.

It can be seen that there are no significant divergences for the different company sizes, with some exceptions in small companies: in Costa Rica Quality Management tends to be more agile in small companies, while in Spain, Integration/Testing tends towards "Traditional" slightly more than the rest of company sizes.

3.2   Which Frameworks and Methods Are Used for Software Development?

The use of different frameworks and methods in software development is shown in Fig. 2, which compares the results of both countries. Although the survey offered seven possible answers for this question, the chart presents only 5 of them. The remaining two (not representative) are indicated with percentages in the left side of the figure.

One of the main insights of the chart is the extended use of the agile framework Scrum in both countries. The use of Scrum in Costa Rica is, however, more widespread than in Spain, with 39% of respondents stating, "We often use it" and 41% "We Always use the framework" (compared to 22% and 26% for Spain, respectively). Another important fact is the balanced use in both countries of Iterative Development, Kanban and Test-Driven Development, which are also agile paradigms. On the contrary, in the chart we can identify frameworks or practices such as Nexus and PRINCE, which show some use in Spain and in Costa Rica are practically unknown. In the case of PRINCE, these numbers may be due to it is a project management methodology widely used in the United Kingdom, where many Spanish companies carry out software projects. On the contrary, Costa Rican companies have little participation in that market.

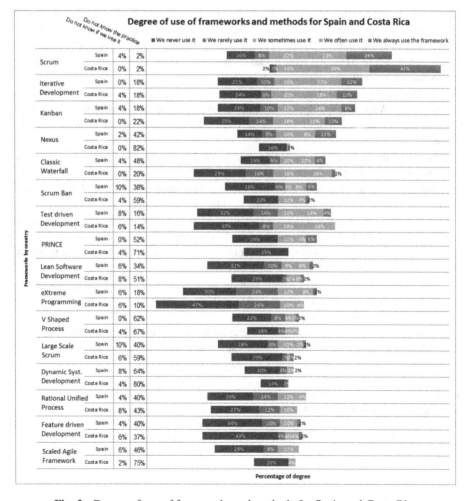

Fig. 2. Degree of use of frameworks and methods for Spain and Costa Rica

The classic waterfall process is still used in both countries, to a greater extent in Costa Rica than in Spain, despite current trends towards agile frameworks. It is important to note, however, that its use is much lower compared to software developed through agile frameworks and practices.

Regarding scaling agile frameworks, Nexus, SAFe and LeSS are better known in Spain than in Costa Rica. Accordingly, the use of these frameworks is practically non-existent in Costa Rica. In Spain, although the use is somewhat greater, only Nexus is used significantly: 8% of respondents answered "We often use it", and 12% "We always use the framework".

4   Conclusions

Results of the second stage of the HELENA Project show interesting similarities and differences between the usages of development frameworks, methods and practices when comparing responses from Spain and Costa Rica. Regarding the geographical distribution of companies, 72% of Spanish companies have their development centers within Spain, while 51% of Costa Rican respondents work in companies with offices distributed throughout the region or globally.

As for the business area, both countries are primarily involved in Software Development. Additionally, Spain dedicates a good part of its industry to Consulting, while in Costa Rica this component is surpassed by its involvement in the Financial sector.

Analyzing the size of the companies, this factor does not seem to influence the trend towards agile or traditional frameworks, both for Costa Rica and Spain. The most agile-oriented software development activities are Implementation/Coding and Integration/Testing for both countries, although with slightly higher numbers in Costa Rica.

Finally, in relation to the frameworks and practices used, it is important to mention that Scrum is the most widely used in both countries. Iterative Development and Kanban occupy the second position as most commonly used frameworks, both in Spain and Costa Rica. Classic Waterfall still has a presence, especially in Costa Rica, although in a reduced way. Regarding scaling agile frameworks, the survey identifies uses of Nexus, SAFe and LeSS frameworks, with more presence in Spain than in Costa Rica, where its use is still incipient.

As future work, we hope to broaden the analysis to include other features addressed in the survey, as well as to continue collaborating with other research teams, comparing the results of different countries that took part in the survey.

Acknowledgements. The research work presented in this paper has been developed within the following projects financed by "Ministerio de Ciencia, Innovación y Universidades, y FEDER": ECLIPSE (RTI2018-094283-B-C31) and BIZDEVOPS-GLOBAL (RTI2018-098309-B-C31). It was also partially supported by CITIC at the University of Costa Rica, Grant No. 834-B4-412.

References

1. Kuhrmann, M., Münch, J., Diebold, P., Linssen, O., Prause, C.R. On the use of hybrid development approaches in software and systems development: construction and test of the HELENA survey. In: Proceedings of the Annual Special Interest Group Meeting Projektmanagement und Vorgehensmodelle (PVM). (Lecture Notes in Informatics), vol. 263, pp. 59–68 (2015)
2. Kuhrmann, M., et al.: Hybrid software and system development in practice: waterfall, scrum, and beyond. In: Proceedings of the 2017 International Conference on Software and System Process - ICSSP 2017, pp. 30–39. ACM Press, New York (2017)
3. CAMTIC: Camara de Tecnologias de Informacion y Comunicacion. https://www.camtic.org
4. Felderer, M., Winkler, D., Biffl, S.: Hybrid software and system development in practice: initial results from Austria. In: Felderer, M., et al. (eds.) PROFES 2017. LNCS, vol. 10611, pp. 435–442. Springer, Cham (2017). https://doi.org/10.1007/978-3-319-69926-4_33
5. Paez, N., Fontdevila, D., Oliveros, A.: HELENA study: initial observations of software development practices in Argentina. In: Felderer, M., et al. (eds.) PROFES 2017. LNCS, vol. 10611, pp. 443–449. Springer, Cham (2017). https://doi.org/10.1007/978-3-319-69926-4_34
6. Tell, P., Pfeiffer, R.-H., Schultz, U.P.: HELENA stage 2—Danish overview. In: Felderer, M., Méndez Fernández, D., Turhan, B., Kalinowski, M., Sarro, F., Winkler, D. (eds.) PROFES 2017. LNCS, vol. 10611, pp. 420–427. Springer, Cham (2017). https://doi.org/10.1007/978-3-319-69926-4_31
7. Nakatumba-Nabende, J., Kanagwa, B., Hebig, R., Heldal, R., Knauss, E.: Hybrid software and systems development in practice: perspectives from Sweden and Uganda. In: Felderer, M., Méndez Fernández, D., Turhan, B., Kalinowski, M., Sarro, F., Winkler, D. (eds.) PROFES 2017. LNCS, vol. 10611, pp. 413–419. Springer, Cham (2017). https://doi.org/10.1007/978-3-319-69926-4_30
8. Scott, E., Pfahl, D., Hebig, R., Heldal, R., Knauss, E.: Initial results of the HELENA survey conducted in Estonia with comparison to results from Sweden and worldwide. In: Felderer, M., Méndez Fernández, D., Turhan, B., Kalinowski, M., Sarro, F., Winkler, D. (eds.) PROFES 2017. LNCS, vol. 10611, pp. 404–412. Springer, Cham (2017). https://doi.org/10.1007/978-3-319-69926-4_29
9. Aymerich, B., Díaz-Oreiro, I., Guzmán, Julio C., López, G., Garbanzo, D.: Software development practices in Costa Rica: a survey. In: Ahram, Tareq Z. (ed.) AHFE 2018. AISC, vol. 787, pp. 122–132. Springer, Cham (2019). https://doi.org/10.1007/978-3-319-94229-2_13
10. IEEE Computer Society: About SWEBOK. https://www.computer.org/web/swebok

Does the Migration of Cross-Platform Apps Towards the Android Platform Matter? An Approach and a User Study

Maria Caulo[1], Rita Francese[2]([✉]), Giuseppe Scanniello[1], and Antonio Spera[2]

[1] University of Basilicata, Potenza, Italy
{maria.caulo,giuseppe.scanniello}@unibas.it
[2] University of Salerno, Fisciano, SA, Italy
francese@unisa.it, a.spera18@studenti.unisa.it

Abstract. We present an approach to migrate cross-platform apps toward a native platform (i.e., Android). The approach is tailored to Ionic, i.e., an open-source framework providing a mobile UI (User Interface) toolkit for developing high-quality cross-platform apps. The validity of our approach has been validated on an open-source app developed by means of Ionic (i.e., Movies-app). In such a way, we had two versions of the same app: one developed in Ionic (the original one) and the other in Android (the migrated one). To investigate if there is a difference in the user experience when using these two versions, we conducted a user study. This user study also aimed at assessing the presence of possible differences in the affective reactions of users when using these two versions of Movies-app. The results suggest that the user experience is better when users deal with the migrated app. Similar results were achieved with respect to the affective reactions of users. We can then conclude that the migration from Ionic towards Android matters.

Keywords: Android · Cross-platform · Ionic · Migration · Sentiment analysis · User experience

1 Introduction

Migration means transferring an application to a new target environment holding the same features as the original application [5]. Migration is relevant to consolidate past knowledge and to preserve past investments [7]. In addition, the use of the migrated application should not negatively affect how the end-user perceives it as compared with its original version. Therefore, the migration is successful from the end-user perspective if she does not note any difference.

The development of apps based on cross-platform solutions (e.g., Titanium, PhoneGap, and Ionic) are free from the operating system. That is, the developer writes the code of an app once and deploys it to the different (supported) hardware/software platforms (e.g., iOS and Android). Among the cross-platform solutions, Ionic is receiving great interest because it provides tools and services

© Springer Nature Switzerland AG 2019
X. Franch et al. (Eds.): PROFES 2019, LNCS 11915, pp. 120–136, 2019.
https://doi.org/10.1007/978-3-030-35333-9_9

to easily build Mobile UIs (User Interfaces) with a native look and feel. Ionic also provides full access to native functionality of the device (behaving in this case as a hybrid platform). On the other hand, native development means developing the mobile app specifically for each hardware/software platform. For example, Android apps have to follow a Model View Controller pattern closely tied to the Android operating system architecture.

The results from an industrial survey [8] indicated that cross-platform development is largely adopted because it is less risky than the native development. Respondents in this survey also thought that a cross-platform (or hybrid) app should be preferred when no much money can be invested in the native development. The use of cross-platform frameworks is also a valuable means to the rapid prototyping of apps to be run in different hardware/software platforms. Once the value of these apps has been assessed with real users (e.g., through beta-testing), these apps could be re-implemented or migrated towards native platforms (e.g., Android or iOS). As an example, a Stack Overflow user asks some suggestions on how to substitute an Ionic app with a native Android one in the Google Play store, because he is *"planning to start a startup and currently he is not in a position to afford individual development for various platforms."*[1]

In this paper, we present an approach to migrate Apps developed with Ionic towards Android platform. To assess the validity of this approach and its underlying process, we applied both of them on a real open-source app, i.e., Movies-app.[2] Finally, to assess if the migration from Ionic to Android is valuable from the end-user perspective, we conducted a qualitative investigation with 18 users with different experience and background. The main goal of this investigation was to study affective reactions[3] and user experience[4] of the involved participants on both the versions of Movies-app. In particular, we first assessed the difference (if any) in the affective reactions of users when using Ionic and Android versions. Affective reactions were measured using a lightweight yet powerful tool, Self-Assessment Manikin (SAM) [4]. Later, we asked the participants in our study to fill a questionnaire to assess user experience [17]. The general goal of the study was to investigate whether affective reactions and user experience are affected by the used version of the app. This is to say that in case the end-user does not perceive any difference in terms of affective reactions and user experience between the original version of the app and its migrated version the migration is successful and then migration matters. It is even better if affective reactions and user experience are more positive in the case of the migrated version of the app.

---

[1] https://stackoverflow.com/questions/34986098/migrating-from-hybrid-app-to-native-app-at-later-point-of-time.

[2] https://github.com/okode/movies-app.

[3] Affect is a concept used in psychology to describe the experience of feeling or emotion.

[4] In the ISO 9241-210 [10], the user experience is defined as "a person's perceptions and responses that result from the use or anticipated use of a product, system or service."

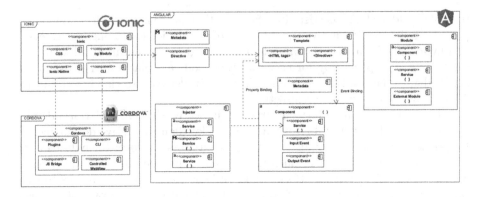

Fig. 1. Architecture of an Ionic app.

This paper provides the following main contributions:

- An approach to migrate Ionic apps towards the Android platform and its validation on open-source app developed with Ionic;
- A user study to assess if the migration from Ionic towards the Android platform matters.

In Sect. 2, we present related work and background information. We present the migration approach and the results of its application on a real case in Sect. 3. The design of the study to assess affective reactions and user experience is shown in Sect. 4. In this section, we discuss the obtained results. We conclude the paper in Sect. 5.

2   Background and Related Work

In the following of this section, we highlight some differences (at a high granularity level) between the architectures of Ionic and Android apps (depicted in Figs. 1 and 2, respectively). We conclude presenting the migration of the apps.

2.1   Ionic App Architecture

An *Ionic* app is based on web technologies, such as HTML5 and CSS, and developed on the top of Angular, a component-based platform for building mobile and desktop web applications [3]. An Ionic app is structured in pages (screens of the mobile app). Each page of the application is represented by an Angular component. The content of a component is described in an HTML file named *template*, the style in *CSS* and the behavior in *Typescript*, the development language adopted by Angular, that is derived by Javascript and enhanced with classes and a stronger type definition. The template of a component together with HTML tags contains instructions for modifying the app HTML, the app status and the DOM data, and tags related to other components or data binding.

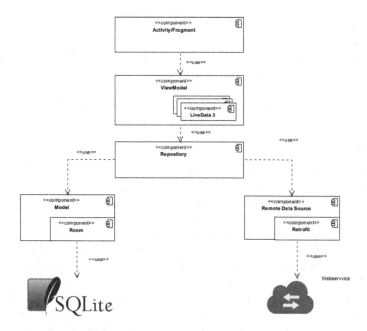

Fig. 2. Architecture of an Android app.

The modular architecture of an Angular application is based on *NgModules*: each application contains a root module called *AppModule*, and is constituted by components and service providers. It may export functionality which may be used by other *NgModules* and imports functionality offered by other *NgModules*, as shown in the right-hand part of Fig. 1. In Angular, service providers are used to share logic or data between components and for calls to server-side web services. Ionic accesses to the native device features through the Cordova plugins, written in the native language on the native platform.

2.2 Android App Architecture

Android apps architecture follows a Model-View-Controller pattern closely tied to the Android operating system architecture. It is good practice in Android app development to put in UI-based classes (Activity or Fragment) only the logic for handling the User Interface, by maintaining the separation of concerns [1]. As shown in Fig. 2, the architecture is composed of the following elements [9]:

- The *View* layer is responsible for interacting with the user and is performed by Activity and Fragment which only configure the view. It shows LiveData taken from the ViewModel.
- The *ViewModel* observes the Lifecycle state of Activities and Fragments (the view), by maintaining consistency during configuration changes and other Android life-cycle events. It gets LiveData from the Repository and makes them available to be observed by the view.

- The *Repository* is a class responsible for getting data from different sources, such as databases and web services. It handles all this data, in terms of observable LiveData, and let them be available to the ViewModel, which can monitor changes through the design pattern observer.
- *Room* is a persistence library on the top of SQLite providing more robust database access and returning queries with observable LiveData.

2.3   Migration

One of the most followed migration approaches is the one proposed by Brodie and Stonebraker, named "chicken little" [5]. It consists of an iterative migration of separable functionality. We also follow this approach, by identifying which aspects of the migration process may be automatized.

Klima and Selingerer [15] consider that many Android apps exist and that the use of cross-platform development tools is suitable for app development from scratch. To reuse existing Android apps, they propose an automated approach to convert them into Web applications by using the Google Web Toolkit (GWT), a Java to Javascript converter. For the functionality not supported by HTML5, Android wrappers are created. No evaluation is provided and only the description of the converter is discussed. Also, Stehle and Riebisch [20] approach the problem of porting a system from a single to multi-platform development platform by proposing a transformation method. Both the apps on the two different architectures evolve, by establishing traceability across the two versions. They present three case studies of porting applications with different operating systems to evaluate the extent of code conversion and structural equivalence achieved by the application. Unlike previous papers, we perform a user study aiming at evaluating the presence of possible differences in the affective reactions and user experience when using the original and the migrated app.

3   The Migration Approach

The proposed approach is conceived to migrate an app from the Ionic-Angular-Cordova to the Android native technology. The migration follows an incremental process, conducted by performing small steps, as shown in Fig. 3 by the UML activity diagram with object-flow depicting the process. To assess and describe the migration approach, we used an open-source application developed by using Ionic4-Angular-Cordova technologies. Among the ones available on GitHub we selected Movies-app, an application aiming at providing information on the most popular movies. We opted for this app because its source files were available for the download and because it is not very complex (although not obvious) and its problem domain can be considered familiar.

Some screens of Movies-app are shown in Fig. 4. The app starts from the screen in Fig. 4(a). It is possible to select three types of filters on the movies (i.e. *Populares, Top* and *Proximamente*) by tapping on the tab buttons in the lower part of the screen. Once selected a movie, it is possible to examine its detailed

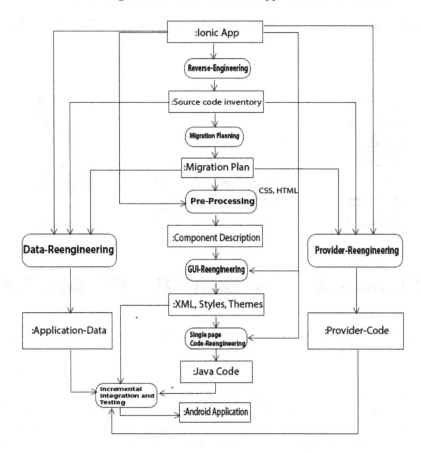

Fig. 3. The migration process.

description (Fig. 4(b)) and get details on one of its actors. In the following we examine in detail the various migration steps.

Reverse Engineering. In this phase, we analyze the functionality of the application by executing it and by examining the project structure. We identify the Ionic pages involved in the accomplishment of a given functionality and group together in modules that functionality logically related. Each Ionic page is composed of content formatting (html), style (SCSS) and behavior (TypeScript). It also imports other components, directives, and providers (or services) which are listed in the *pagName.module.ts* file available in the *pageName* folder. The output of this phase is the *Source Code Inventory* document, which lists the app modules and, for each of them, the related pages and services.

Migration Planning. Starting from the *Source Code Inventory* document, we individuate a migration order of the various functionality and services. The following three steps are performed for each page.

Fig. 4. Two screens of the Ionic application Movies-app (Fig. 4(a) and 4(b)) and a migrated interface in Android (Fig. 4(c)).

Pre-processing. This phase provides details on the types and attributes of each component included in the page. Information on the Ionic component is collected, such as tags (e. g., $ion - list$ and $ion - alert$), its position on the screen, and the number of sub-components composing it. As a result of this phase, a list of components and the related sub-components of the considered page is provided (*Component Description* in Fig. 3).

GUI-Rengineering. The Ionic page whose layout and style are described by its *.html* and *.scss* files, respectively, has to be mapped into an Android activity, whose GUI is strictly dependent on the platform. Android layout is described in XML, the style by Android styles and themes [2]. A page can be composed of Ionic predefined sub-components (e.g., a list - *ionlist* - may represent its elements by a *ioncard*), and contain information, such as $< ioncardheader >$ and $< ion-cardcontent >$. In Android, *ionlist* has to be mapped into a *RecyclerView* widget of the Activity XML file. This shows the generic element of the list by *viewholderobjects*, which are managed by an adapter that creates view holders when needed[5]. The mapping has to be performed for each Ionic GUI component. HTML and SCSS files may be automatically mapped in XML by a translator. We test the GUI appearance on various devices or on the emulator (UI testing) each time a new widget is added.

---

[5] https://developer.android.com/guide/topics/ui/layout/recyclerview.

Single page and component Code Reengineering. The application logic of an Ionic app is written in TypeScript. Many TypeScript constructs are very similar to the corresponding in Java. The main translation rules are the following [18]:

- *Variable declaration.* In TypeScript, developers only need to manage numbers, booleans, and strings. These variables have to be associated in Java to more specific types, such as double, float, char, boolean and long. Concerning arrays, their declaration in TypeScript differs from Java only in the order in which the array and its datatype have to be written.
- *Conditional Statements.* No difference.
- *Loops.* Typescript loops have the same syntax as Java ones. Except for the *let* Typescript syntax.
- *Classes.* Both Typescript and Java support classes. The syntax has some little differences.
- *Data binding.* One of the advantages of Angular is that it provides an easy way to bind data to the views. As an example, in Ionic we declare the variable *name_person* in the Typescript page and use it freely in its HTML with the following syntax: $\{\{name\_person\}\}$. This binding approach is called *interpolation* in Angular. In Android, we bind the XML view with Java using its id: $name\_person = findViewById(R.id.name\_person\_detail)$;
- *Methods/functions.* Java methods and TypeScript functions have the same meaning, but the syntax is different. As an example, in Typescrypt the word *function* should be inserted in the name of the method.
- *Ionic native plugin calls replacement by Android API.* The Android Manifest of the migrated version has to include the appropriate permissions to allow use of the native functionality. The plugin call in the TypeScript class has to be replaced by a Java call to the same code in Android.

There exist several approaches to automatically convert Java in TypeScript, but at the moment no one is available to do the vice-versa. A quick approach may consist in using a transpiler to translate TypeScript in Javascript and then transpile it to Java. The resulting code may be difficult to read. Otherwise, a code converter from TypeScript to Java has to be implemented. Since TypeScript is continuously evolving, this solution requires continuous updating of the translator. We conduct Unit testing by using JUnit for validating the behavior of each class of the app. Test cases available in Ionic may be reused as a guide.

Data-Reengineering. The Data Reengineering step is made independently from page migration. In both systems, the app may store key/value pairs in the local storage, on the device file system and SQLite is adopted as local DBMS.

Provider-Reengineering. Ionic providers (i.e., services) are mapped into Java classes in Android.

Incremental Integration and Testing. Each page is progressively integrated with the pages and providers of the same module. Test cases can be derived from the Ionic app and used to exercise the target system in order to identify eventual behavior differences. Once the Ionic application has been migrated, it has to be customized for the various type of Android devices, with different screen sizes and resolutions.

Table 1. Descriptive statistics for the Ionic Movies-app and its Android version.

Ionic		Android	
Screen Number	4	Screen Number	4
Typescript Class Number	27	Java Class Number	65
Typescript LOC	665	Java LOC	31748
SCSS file number	6	XML file number	75
SCSS LOC	611	XML LOC	7930
HTML file number	6		
HTML LOC	611		

3.1 Resulting Metrics

Some descriptive metrics on the source code of the original Ionic app and the migrated one are reported in Table 1. LOC data revealed that Ionic code is lighter than Android one, this is due to the fact that many tasks are performed by Angular libraries.

4 User Study

To conduct our user study, we followed the guideline by Wohlin et al. [24] and Juristo and Moreno [22]. We report the planning of the user study following the template suggested by Jedlitschka et al. [11].

4.1 Goals

We investigated the following main Research Question (RQ):

– *Does the migration of cross-platform Apps developed by means of Ionic towards the Android platform matter?*

   To answer this RQ, we had to compare from the end-user point of view the original version of an app (i.e., Movies-app) with that migrated to Android. To this end, we considered two main perspectives: affective reactions of users (i.e., pleasure, arousal, dominance, and liking) and user experience. In particular, we speculate that the migration from Ionic to Android matters if we observe a difference in favor of the Android version of a given app (Movies-app) with respect to the affective reactions and the user experience. Therefore, we detailed our main RQ as follows:

– *RQ1. Is there an effect (either positive or negative) on pleasure, arousal, dominance, and liking when using the (Android) migrated version of an app developed by means of Ionic?*
– *RQ2. Is there an effect (positive or negative) on the user experience when using the (Android) migrated version of an app developed by means of Ionic?*

   If the effect is positive for both the RQs, we can conclude that the migration of a cross-platform app towards Android matters.

4.2   Experimental Units

Initially, 19 people accepted to take part in the experimental study; however, 18 actually participated. The participants in the study had a different background: 12 people had a Bachelor Degree (10 in Computer Science and two in Mathematics); four people had a Master's Degree (three in Computer Engineering and one in Mathematics); one had a Ph.D. in Computer Science and one had a Scientific High School Diploma. The average age of participants is 27. Except for one of them that owned a smartphone with iOS, the others owned an Android smartphone. On average, participants install two apps a month. Most participants complain of sudden crashes and lags of apps, and irreversible blocks of the smartphone, as main annoyances during the use. This information was collected through a pre-questionnaire (i.e., a Google form) we asked the participants to fill in a few days before the actual study.

4.3   Experimental Study Material and Tasks

The experimental objects consisted of the two versions of Movies-app: the original one and the migrated one. Movies-app is a real-world App small enough to allow a good control over the participants while completing the study.

To gather affective reactions, we relied on SAM [4]. It is a questionnaire that consists of a nine-point rating scale for each of the following dimensions: pleasure, arousal, and dominance. The pleasure scale ranges from affective states associated with unhappiness/sadness to happiness/joyfulness. The arousal scale varies from calm/bored to stimulated/excited. Finally, the dominance scale ranges from submissive to dominant, i.e., from "without control" to "with control". As Koelstra et al. [16] did, we included the liking dimension on top of the SAM dimensions ones. Also, liking consists of a nine-point rating scale and varies from dislike to like.

As for user experience, we relied on the 26 statements by Laugwitz et al. [17]. These authors defined these statements to evaluate the quality of interactive products (e.g., software). Each statement is made of two adjectives that describe some opposite qualities of products. According to their objectives, these statements are grouped into the following six categories: Attractiveness, Perspicuity, Efficiency, Dependability, Stimulation, and Novelty. The scale for each adjective ranges from 1 to 7. The original set of statements from the User Experience Questionnaire[6] was in German, and then it was translated in 20 other languages, Italian included. In our experimental study, we administered the questions in the Italian version provided by the authors.

As for the experimental tasks, we asked the participants to freely use both the versions of the app according to the design described in Sect. 4.5. Right after the use of each version of the app, we asked the participants to fill in the SAM questionnaire and to respond to the 26 UEQ statements.

---

[6] https://www.ueq-online.org.

Table 2. Experiment design

Order/Group	Period	
	Period 1	Period 2
G1	Android	Ionic
G2	Ionic	Android

4.4 Hypotheses and Variables

We considered two independent variables: Technology and Order. The first indicates the technology used to implement the app. Therefore, Technology is a categorical variable with two values: Android and Ionic. The Order variable indicates the order in which a participant used the version of the app (also known as *sequence* in the literature). Similarly to Technology, Order is categorical and can assume the following two values: First and Second. For example, First indicates that the Android version has been used first and then the Ionic one. We analyzed Order to study learning effect on affective reactions and user experience.

To measure affective reactions, we used four dependent variables (one for each dimension of SAM). To measure user experience, we used six dependent variables, one for each of the six categories of UEQ (e.g., Attractiveness). To obtain a single value for each category we summed the scores of each statement in that category. For example, the Attractiveness category, which is composed of six statements, can assume values in between 6 (if all the statements are scored 1) and 42 (if all the statements are scored 7). This practice to aggregate scores from single statements is widespread (e.g., [23]). To answer the defined RQs, we formulated and tested the following parameterized null hypothesis.

- HO_X: *There is no statistically significant difference between the Android and Ionic Apps with respect to X.*

Where X is one of the considered dependent variables. Because we could not postulate an effect of Technology in a specific direction, either positive or negative, our alternative hypotheses are two-tailed.

4.5 Experimental Study Design

The design of our experimental study (see Table 2) was a *factorial crossover* [21]. In this design, the number of periods (i.e., Order) and treatments (i.e., Technology) is the same, and the treatment applies to participants once and only once [21]. The participants were divided into two groups, G_1 and G_2, both made of nine members. The assignment to the groups was randomly performed. Each participant used both the versions of the app, but participants in G_1 firstly used the Android version and then the Ionic one, while vice-versa was applied to G_2. The use of this design mitigated the effect of the app on the results.

4.6   Procedure

The study procedure included the following sequential steps.

1. We invited Ph.D. and Master's students in Computer Science and Mathematics at the University of Basilicata and students enrolled in the course of Advanced Software Engineering of the Master Degree in Computer Engineering from the same University. We also invited people working in the Software Engineering Laboratory at the University of Basilicata. They had to fill in a pre-questionnaire to gather demographic information. This design choice allowed us to have participants with heterogeneous backgrounds.
2. We randomly split the participants into two groups: G_1 and G_2.
3. The study session took place under controlled conditions in a research laboratory. We avoided interactions among participants by exploiting one-to-one sessions, namely each participant accomplished the study tasks under the supervision of one of the authors (the first one). This author did not interact with the participants to accomplish the tasks and applied the same procedure/steps for each participant.
4. Each participant performed the first task and then filled in the SAM questionnaire (first) and UEQ (later).
5. Each participant performed the second task and then filled in the SAM questionnaire (first) and UEQ (later).
6. Finally, we collected for each participant some free comments about the overall experience, through voice recordings.

All the participants used the same smartphone[7] in both the tasks. No other apps were open in the background at the beginning of each experimental session.

4.7   Analysis Procedure

To test null hypothesis, we used the ANOVA Type Statistic (ATS) [6]. It is used (e.g., in medicine) to analyze data from rating scales in factorial designs [12]. We built ATS models as: $X \sim Technology + Order + Technology : Order$. Where the dependent variable is X and Technology and Order are the manipulated ones. Technology:Order indicates the interaction between Technology and Order. This model allows determining if Technology, Order, and Technology:Order had statistically significant effects on the given dependent variable X. To verify if an effect is statistically significant, we fixed α to 0.05. That is, we admit 5% chance of a Type-I-error occurring [24]. If a p-value is less than 0.05, we deemed the effect is statistically significant.

---

[7] Umidigi A3, a Dual-Sim smartphone equipped with Android 8.1.0, 5.5" screen with 720×1440 resolution points, 3300mAh capacity battery, 2 GB RAM, 16 GB of expandable memory, MediaTek MT6739 processor.

Table 3. Summary of the results for affective reactions.

Dep. Var	Indep. Var.		
	Technology	Order	Technology:Order
Pleasure	0.3496	0.9165	**0.0140**
Arousal	0.4011	0.8178	0.1519
Dominance	0.1454	0.1454	0.7665
Liking	**0.0494**	0.6376	**0.0494**

Table 4. Summary of the results for user experience.

Dep. Var.	Indep. Var.		
	Technology	Order	Technology:Order
Attractiveness	0.0968	0.3683	0.2523
Perspicuity	0.4153	0.0851	0.8293
Efficiency	**0.0004**	0.3061	0.6581
Dependability	0.0610	0.0874	0.6849
Stimulation	0.2489	0.5606	0.1437
Novelty	0.2539	0.7532	**0.0109**

4.8   Results

RQ1. Android Vs Ionic with Respect to Affective Reactions. In Table 3, we summarize the results of the statistical inference with respect to RQ1. We can observe a statistically significant difference with respect to Liking with a *medium* effect size (0.383). We quantified effect size by means of the Cliff's delta.[8]

The median values for G_1 are 8 for Android and 7 for Ionic, while the median values for G_2 are 5 for Ionic and 6 for Android. Therefore, we can assert that the participants liked more the migrated version of Movies-app than its original version for Ionic. As for Liking, we also observed a significant interaction between the two independent variables. This interaction is significant also for Pleasure. This means that there is a combined positive effect of Technology and Order.

RQ2. Android Vs Ionic with Respect to User Experience. In Table 4, we summarize the results of the statistical inference with respect to RQ2. We can observe a statistical difference with respect to Efficiency with a *large* effect size (0.67). The median values for G_1 are 23 for Android and 17 for Ionic, while the median values for G_2 are 18 for Ionic and 23 for Android. Therefore, we can assert that the participant found the Android version of the app more efficient

---

[8] We used this kind of effect size because it is conceived to be used with ordinal variables [13]. It is: *negligible* if $|\delta| < 0.147$, *small* if $0.147 \leq |\delta| < 0.33$, *medium* if $0.33 \leq |\delta| < 0.474$, or *large* if $|\delta| \geq 0.474$ [19].

than its original version for Ionic. We also observed a significant interaction between the two independent variables for Novelty.

4.9   Further Analysis

To analyze data from the interviews, we used TAT (Thematic Analysis Template) [14]. For space constraint, we do not provide details on how we applied TAT. We report identified themes and excerpts of the interviews carried out at the end of the experimental study with the participants.

Reactivity. *The apps implemented with Android is more reactive than the other and this makes it more enjoyable.*

We can justify this pattern in the data because in Ionic the use of the browser may cause prolonged app loading and a deteriorated responsiveness and there may be performance issues when several callbacks are sent to the native code.

Fluidity. *The scroll is not fluid when sliding the results of a query. This happens for the app implemented in Ionic.*

This theme can be considered related to the previous one. The highlighted issue should depend on the resources to execute the Ionic version of the app.

User Interface, Contents, and Functionality. *The two versions of the app look quite the same, have the same functionality, and show the same contents.*

This result might be in relation to the absence of a statistically significant difference in three out of four dependent variables for affective reactions, and in five out of six dependent variables for user experience.

4.10   Discussion

On the basis of the obtained results, it seems that the main research question can be positively answered: the migration of cross-platform Apps developed by means of Ionic towards the Android platform matters. According to our study, end-users' opinions are in favor of the Android version of the app in terms of Liking and Efficiency, with respect to Technology. This is evidenced by a medium effect size for Liking and a large effect size for Efficiency. Variables related to how the two apps appear (e.g. Attractiveness includes couples of adjectives such as: Annoying/Enjoyable, Good/Bad, Unlikable/Pleasing, Unpleasant/Pleasant, Attractive/Unattractive, Friendly/Unfriendly) seem to measure no preferences for any of the versions. We conjecture that Liking might be influenced by the performance of the apps perceived by end-users (measured by Efficiency) and this is supported by free comments collected. This might also imply that the migration approach was carried out successfully, because such an approach did not negatively affect the perceived performance, indeed, the Android version has been reputed more efficient over the same experimental conditions. The Order seems not to affect the users' opinions in any of the two cases (SAM and UEQ), while Technology and Order seem to interact each other in cases of Pleasure (SAM), Liking (SAM) and Novelty (UEQ), in favor of the Android version.

4.11   Threats to Validity

We discuss the threats that could have affected the validity of the results in the user study. We ranked these threats from the most to the least sensible for the goal of our study (i.e., Internal Validity).

Internal Validity. A possible threat is voluntary participation in the study (*selection threat*). To deal with *threat of diffusion or treatments imitations*, the first author of this paper monitored participants and asked back material to prevent them from exchanging information.

Construct Validity. Each of the investigated constructs was quantified by means of one assessment at the end of the task, which can affect the results (i.e., participants tend to assess the affective state closer to when we provided them the SAM). Although the participants were not informed about our RQs, they might guess them and change their behavior accordingly (*threat of hypotheses guessing*). To mitigate *evaluation apprehension threat*, we reassured participants that their data were treated anonymously and in aggregate form. It is worth mentioning that we asked the participants to sign a consent form to use their data. We also acknowledge the presence of a *restricted generalizability across constructs*. That is while having an impact on the affective states, the approach can affect other relevant constructs which we did not observe (cognitive load).

Conclusion Validity. *Threat of random heterogeneity of participants* could be present since we involved participants with a different background. *Reliability of measures* is another threat to conclusion validity. To deal with it, we used well known and widely used measures.

External Validity. The experimental objects might affect the external validity of the results (i.e., *threat of the interaction of setting and treatment*). They could be not representative of real-world tasks. The selected mobile device on which the user study is performed was a mid-range device, because not all the real-world users own the most performing devices.

5   Conclusion and Final Remarks

We presented an approach to migrate Ionic apps towards Android. The validity of this approach has been assessed on an open-source app (i.e., Movies-app). We also studied if the application of our approach matters from the end-user perspective. To this end, we conducted an empirical investigation to study both user experience and affective reactions of possible users. The main goal was to identify differences when using both the versions of Movies-app: the Ionic and the Android ones. The results suggest that a better user experience was achieved when dealing with the Movies-app version implemented in Android. Similar results were achieved with respect to the affective reactions of users. Summarizing, it seems that the migration from Ionic towards Android matters.

References

1. Android Developers: Guide to app architecture. https://developer.android.com/jetpack/docs/guide
2. Android Styles and Themes. https://developer.android.com/guide/topics/ui/look-and-feel/themes
3. Angular. https://angular.io
4. Bradley, M.M., Lang, P.J.: Measuring emotion. The self-assessment manikin and the semantic differential. J. Behav. Ther. Exp. Psychiatry **25**(1), 49–59 (1994)
5. Brodie, M.L., Stonebraker, M.: Legacy Information Systems Migration: Gateways, Interfaces, and the Incremental Approach. Morgan Kaufmann, San Francisco (1995)
6. Brunner, E., Dette, H., Munk, A.: Box-type approximations in non parametric factorial designs. J. Am. Stat. Assoc. **92**, 1494–1502 (1997)
7. De Lucia, A., Francese, R., Scanniello, G., Tortora, G.: Developing legacy system migration methods and tools for technology transfer Software. Pract. Exp. **38**(13), 1333–1364 (2008)
8. Francese, R., Gravino, C., Risi, M., Scanniello, G., Tortora, G.: Mobile app development and management: results from a qualitative investigation. In: Proceedings of the 4th IEEE/ACM International Conference on Mobile Software Engineering and Systems, pp. 133–143. IEEE Press (2017)
9. Hossain, T.: Android Application Architecture. https://medium.com/oceanize-geeks/android-application-architecture-189b4721c7c5
10. International Organization for Standardization: Ergonomics of human system interaction - Part 210: Human-centered design for interactive systems (formerly known as 13407). ISO FDIS **9241–210** (2009)
11. Jedlitschka, A., Ciolkowski, M., Pfahl, D.: Guide to Advanced Empirical Software Engineering. Springer, London (2008). https://doi.org/10.1007/978-1-84800-044-5. Ch. Reporting Experiments in Software Engineering
12. Kaptein, M.C., Nass, C., Markopoulos, P.: Powerful and consistent analysis of likert-type rating scales. In: Proceedings of the SIGCHI Conference on Human Factors in Computing Systems, pp. 2391–2394. ACM, New York (2010)
13. Cliff, N.: Ordinal Methods for Behavioral Data Analysis. Erlbaum, New York (1996)
14. King, N.: Using templates in the thematic analysis of text. In: Cassell, C., Symon, G. (eds.) Essential Guide to Qualitative Methods in Organizational Research, pp. 256–270. Sage, Thousand Oaks (2004)
15. Klima, P., Selinger, S.: Towards platform independence of mobile applications. In: Moreno-Díaz, R., Pichler, F., Quesada-Arencibia, A. (eds.) EUROCAST 2013. LNCS, vol. 8112, pp. 442–449. Springer, Heidelberg (2013). https://doi.org/10.1007/978-3-642-53862-9_56
16. Koelstra, S., et al.: Deap: a database for emotion analysis using physiological signals. IEEE Trans. Affect. Comput. **3**(1), 18–31 (2012)
17. Laugwitz, B., Held, T., Schrepp, M.: Construction and evaluation of a user experience questionnaire. In: Holzinger, A. (ed.) USAB 2008. LNCS, vol. 5298, pp. 63–76. Springer, Heidelberg (2008). https://doi.org/10.1007/978-3-540-89350-9_6
18. McKenzie, C.: What Java developers need to know about TypeScript syntax. https://www.theserverside.com/tutorial/What-Java-developers-need-to-know-about-TypeScript-syntax

19. Romano, J., Kromrey, J., Coraggio, J., Skowronek, J.: Appropriate statistics for ordinal level data: should we really be using t-test and Cohens d for evaluating group differences on the NSSE and other surveys? In: Annual Meeting of the Florida Association of Institutional Research, pp. 1–3 (2006)
20. Stehle, T., Riebisch, M.: A porting method for coordinated multiplatform evolution. J. Softw. Evol. Process **31**(2), e2116 (2019)
21. Vegas, S., Apa, C., Juristo, N.: Crossover designs in software engineering experiments: benefits and perils. IEEE Trans. Softw. Eng. **42**(2), 120–135 (2016)
22. Juristo, N., Moreno, A.: Basics of Software Engineering Experimentation. Kluwer Academic Publishers, Dordrecht (2001)
23. Watson, D., Clark, L.A., Tellegen, A.: Development and validation of brief measures ofpositive and negative affect: the panas scales. J. Pers. Soc. Psychol. **54**(6), 1063–1070 (1988)
24. Wohlin, C., Runeson, P., Host, M., Ohlsson, M.C., Regnell, B., Wessln, A.: Experimentation in Software Engineering. Springer Publishing Company, Incorporated, Heidelberg (2012)

Software Knowledge Representation to Understand Software Systems

Victoria Torres$^{(\boxtimes)}$ (iD), Miriam Gil (iD), and Vicente Pelechano (iD)

Universitat Politècnica de València, València 46022, Spain
{vtorres,mgil,pele}@pros.upv.es

Abstract. A software development process involves numerous persons, including customers, domain experts, software engineers, managers, evaluators and certifiers. Together, they produce some software that satisfies its requirements and its quality criteria at a certain point in time. This software contains faults and flaws of different levels of severity and at different phases of its production (specification, design, etc.) so maintenance is needed in order to correct it. Perfective and adaptive maintenance is also needed to cope with changes in the environment or with new requirements, e.g. new functionalities. In this work, we introduce the Persistent Knowledge Monitor (PKM), which is being developed within the DECODER H2020 project for handling (i.e. storing, retrieving, merging and checking for consistency) all kinds of knowledge and information related to a software project. The PKM will be part of a platform capable of taking advantage of all the artefacts available in a software ecosystem, not only the source code, but also its version control system, abstract specifications, informal documents or reports, etc. for representing the software knowledge and improving the workflow of software developers.

Keywords: Persistent Knowledge Monitor · Software engineering · Traceability

1 Introduction

Software maintenance and improvement are very costly and consuming tasks especially when there is an intense use of legacy code or third-party libraries, which usually lack of documentation or when available, it is out-of-date from the current version of the associated piece of software. However, properly performing these maintenance and improvement tasks requires a deep understanding not just of the source code but also of the critical information bound to the code and the process that led to its production.

A key aspect to achieve such deep understanding is to discover knowledge by analyzing all the available artefacts of a given software project. Then, based on the

This work has been developed with the financial support of the European Union's Horizon 2020 research and innovation programme under grant agreement No. 824231 and the Spanish State Research Agency under the project TIN2017-84094-R and co-financed with ERDF.

© Springer Nature Switzerland AG 2019
X. Franch et al. (Eds.): PROFES 2019, LNCS 11915, pp. 137–144, 2019.
https://doi.org/10.1007/978-3-030-35333-9_10

obtained knowledge, stakeholders can be provided with different views of the system at different levels of abstraction that may be more appropriate to achieve the understanding of the underlying system. However, prior to the creation of such system views, knowledge has to be properly represented according to a well-defined schema or meta-model. Such meta-model must represent, in the most accurate way, all the elements that conform to a software system and all the existing relationships between them. Regarding these relationships, it is important to have a clear understanding at the most fine-grain level, where specific sections or portions of a given artefact (e.g., class x implementation in a java source file) may relate to a different one (e.g., class x definition in a uml class diagram).

In the literature we can find different meta-models targeted to represent the knowledge that can be extracted from software artefacts. These include the Knowledge Discovery Meta-model (KDM) [1] and Abstract Syntax Tree Metamodeling (ASTM) [2] (specifications developed by the OMG ADM task force [3]), FAMIX [4], the Pattern and Abstract-level Description Language (PADL) [5], or the OASIS Static Analysis Results Interchange Format (SARIF) [6]. All these meta-models put their focus on artefacts such as source code, models, and specifications to extract knowledge from the software project. However, in addition to these artefacts, there are other less formal sources that are not usually considered and that can be processed and analyzed to get some extra knowledge about the software project being maintained or improved. These include forum discussions, issue tracker items, reports, etc.

Therefore, taking as reference these meta-models, and considering these less formal sources, in this work we present an overview of the meta-model of the Persistent Knowledge Monitor (PKM), a central infrastructure to store, access, and trace all the persistent data, information and knowledge related to a given software or ecosystem. This PKM is being developed within the DECODER H2020 project[1], whose major objective is to provide powerful tools for developers to get thorough understanding of a given piece of software.

The remainder of the paper is organized as follows. Section 2 identifies the type of sources considered in DECODER to populate the PKM. Section 3 provides an overview over the existing literature found regarding meta-models representing software artefacts. Then, Sect. 4 provides an overview over the PKM meta-model, describing its main components and the relationships among them. Finally, Sect. 5 provides some conclusions and outlines future work.

2   Knowledge Sources to Populate the PKM

One of the major functionalities of the PKM is storing the knowledge generated by the DECODER toolset, toolset targeted to process/analyze the different software project artefacts. Besides this storage functionality, the PKM should also provide the capabilities to allow the DECODER toolset to query, update, and reason over the stored knowledge. Specifically, the information that will be stored in the PKM includes:

---

[1] https://www.decoder-project.eu/.

- Some form of the abstract syntax tree (and concrete trees) related to the source code and the libraries used.
- Some derived or normalized form of the code (after pre-processing, GIMPLE or Generic/Tree internal representations provided by GCC, or CIL representation for Frama-C [7]).
- Some generated or manually written annotations (e.g. in ACSL/ACSL++ for C or C++ code, in JML for Java code).
- Natural language documentation or comments, related to some particular chunk of source code or of a global nature.
- Historical information, extracted from version control systems and bugzillas.
- Information produced by static source code analysis, by optimization passes of compilers, by natural language processing and machine learning techniques.
- Any other relevant information that contributes to enrich the system representation.

Examples of processing/analyzing activities performed by the DECODER toolset are extracting features from source code, annotating code comments and issues with entities, predicates, arguments, etc. Therefore, as Fig. 1 shows, the PKM is expected to interact with several tools, some targeted to process different artefacts to generate knowledge and populate the PKM and others to consume such knowledge and assist stakeholders in their respective tasks within the process lifecycle.

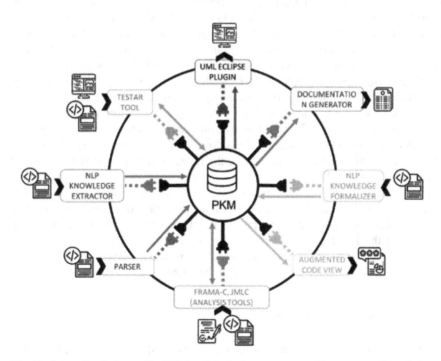

Fig. 1. Interaction between the PKM and tools that generate and/or consume knowledge

3 Meta-Models for Software Knowledge Representation

The knowledge extraction process refers to one of the major tasks of the reverse engineering, which was defined by Chikofsky and Cross II in [10] as "the process of analyzing a subject system to identify the system's components and their interrelationships and create representations of the system in another form or at a higher level of abstraction". Big efforts have been made in the area of Model-Driven software modernization where several works have been proposed in order to create a common repository structure for representing information about existing software assets. The OMG's Architecture Driven Modernization (ADM) initiative [3] defines a set of standard meta-models which represent the information normally managed in modernization tasks. Specifically, the Knowledge-Discovery Metamodel (KDM) [1] provides the ability to document existing systems, discover reusable components in existing software, support transformations to other languages and MDA, or enable other potential transformations. KDM is partitioned into several packages, each one representing different kinds of software artifacts as entities (e.g., code entities, data entities, UI entities, environment entities). An implementation of this meta-model is provided by MoDisco [11], an Eclipse-based framework that was developed to provide support to the software modernization process. In addition, to better support source code analysis activities, ADM also defined the Abstract Syntax Tree Metamodel (ASTM) metamodel [2], to represent the Abstract Syntax Tree (AST) of any programming language. This model defines a Generic ASTM (GASTM) with definitions that apply to ASTs of most programing languages, and Specialized ASTM (SASTM) with features specific to a single programming language. More recently, other meta-models have been defined to support structured metrics (SSM) [8], or software patterns (SPMS) [9]. Other meta-models focused specifically on the object-oriented languages are FAMIX [4], which also allows representing procedural languages, and the Pattern and Abstract-level Description Language (PADL) [5], which also focus on patterns, allowing the description of motifs. Mainly conceived to detect software defects and vulnerabilities, the OASIS Static Analysis Results Interchange Format (SARIF) [6] defines a standard specification to capture the range of data produced by commonly used static analysis tools.

In DECODER, for the definition of the PKM meta-model we will make use/reference all those existing meta-models when possible. For example, GASTM and FAMIX will be used to define the part of the PKM meta-model where the AST is kept. However, in the PKM we consider other less formal sources of knowledge that are poorly structured, incomplete, and sometimes incorrect. After a process of knowledge extraction, this information will be stored in the PKM.

4 The PKM Meta-Model

The PKM provides the representation of a general and specific knowledge about the artefacts of a software project. In order to manage the complexity of the PKM, it is defined by a collection of meta-models according to the categories of the artefacts and a core package that defines the general knowledge of them. The defined packages are the following (see Fig. 2):

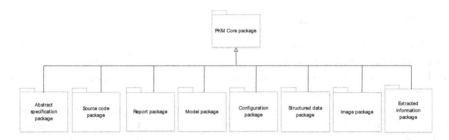

Fig. 2. Organization of the PKM Packages

- *Core package*: it defines the core part of the PKM representing the concept of artefact and its related concepts such as the project use case in which the artefact belongs to, the tools that can manage the artefacts (specification and management tools), the development phases in which artefacts are used during the development process, and the stakeholders that are involved.
- *Abstract specification package*: it defines the meta-model elements of the formal specification describing, by means of pre, post and invariants, the behavior of an associated source code. This abstract specification can be automatically generated or manually written by means of annotations (e.g., in ACSL, ACSL++, JML, etc.).
- *Source code package*: it defines the part of the meta-model that refers to the artefacts that list human-readable instructions written by a programmer with the objective of being executed in a computing device. A source code artefact belongs to one programming language, it relates to a set of referenced libraries and with history data extracted from version control systems and bugzillas.
- *Report package*: it defines the part of the meta-model that represents the artefacts containing a structured content in natural language, related to some particular chunk of source code or of a global nature.
- *Model package*: it defines the part of the meta-model that represents abstract representations of a specific aspect from a given domain (e.g., a uml class model describes the structure – concepts, properties of the concepts, relationships between concepts- of a specific domain).
- *Configuration package*: it defines the meta-model that represents artefacts describing, in plain text, the parameters that define or execute a specific software program.
- *Structured data package*: it defines the meta-model that represents artefacts that store data structures and that are usually used as interchange format.
- *Image package:* it defines the meta-model that describes binary representation of visual information such as drawings, pictures, graphs, etc.

- *Extracted information package*: it defines the meta-model that represents information produced by static source code analysis, by optimization passes of compilers, by natural language processing or by machine learning techniques.

4.1   The PKM Core Package Overview

The PKM Core package, as shown in Fig. 3, is built around the *artefact* concept, which is specialized into the different types of artefacts considered in DECODER use cases, which are *abstract specifications, source code, reports, models, configuration artefacts, structured data,* and *images*.

Artefacts are digital products or documents created during the software development process. It can be presented in different formats (plain text, key-value structures, markup documents), and levels of abstraction (high, medium, and low). Moreover, artefacts can be related to other artefacts with the same (or similar) semantic intention (e.g., a java file may be related to a uml diagram describing a class from a given domain).

An artefact belongs to a *project use case*, which defines a set of artefacts of different nature (source code, documents written in natural language, configuration files, etc.) organized (or not) according to a logical structure (e.g., directories) and provided (or not) as a compressed file. These artefacts are consumed or created during the project development and maintenance process.

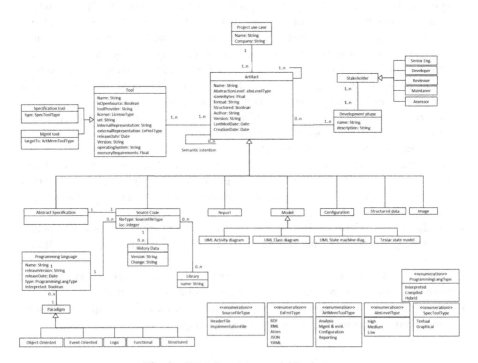

Fig. 3. PKM Core Metamodel Package

Artefacts are managed by *tools* that are used by any stakeholder to analyze, transform, refine, etc. them and produce new or modified artefacts. Tools can be categorized into *specification tools*, which are tools that allow to create, modify, and refine artefacts, and *management tools*, which are tools that assist/guide the stakeholder in the task of analyzing, managing, evolving, and configuring a specific tool as well as tools that act as back-ends to the previous tools categories to generate various kinds of reports.

Artefacts are related to *development phases* in which they are used during the development process, i.e., requirements, design, implementation, testing, deployment, maintenance. Finally, in each development phase, different *stakeholders* take part to develop a specific task within the project. These stakeholders can be senior engineers, developers, reviewers, maintainers, or assessors.

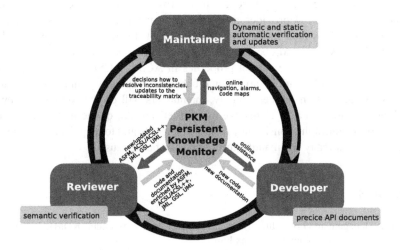

Fig. 4. An overview of the development life cycle

5   Conclusions and Future Work

As we have pointed out, the PKM has been built within the DECODER project with the goal of store, access, and trace all the persistent data, information and knowledge related to a given software project or ecosystem. This knowledge will be useful for the different actors involved during the life span of a software, especially new persons, to keep project information and knowledge in the most accessible and unambiguous way. This living repository can be queried and enriched by the actors involved in the project, in order to maintain consistency and keep the most updated and precise information about it.

This work constitutes a first step in the formalization process of the PKM meta-model, which will be in charge of gathering all the data, information and knowledge that can be extracted from a given software project. As future work such meta-model will be implemented as a database having in mind that the potential and diverse processing tools that may interact with the PKM demands for a dynamic and flexible data schema that could be modified according to the new interaction needs. Such flexibility would allow extending the schema with new types based on the processing results produced by new interacting tools. For this reason, we are planning to use JSON as the interchange mechanism between tools and the PKM. Once complete and implemented, the PKM will be validated empirically with four different use cases proposed in the DECODER H2020 project. These refer to OS drivers provided by SYSGO (https://www.sysgo.com/), the openCV library commonly used by Tree Technology (http://www.treetk.com/es/index.html) in its developments, general purpose Java code hosted in the OW2 (https://www.ow2.org) open-source software community, and My-Thai-Star showcase application, developed by CAPGEMINI (https://www.capgemini.com/es-es/service/agile-delivery-center-valencia/).

In addition, the knowledge gathered in the PKM should be also used along the different stages of the software lifecycle to improve and assist stakeholders in their respective tasks. Figure 4 provides an overview over the different roles involved in DECODER as well as their interaction with the PKM. First, developers will feed the PKM with the bulk code and documentation of the use cases where they are involved. Second, reviewers will write correct properties in ACSL, ACSL++ (the extension of ACSL for C++) or JML with invariants and behaviors implicitly connected to a model based on abstract state machines. Finally, maintainers will do the work of reviewing and taking decisions on how to resolve inconsistencies. An online traceability matrix will be used to control the consistency of these elements and to help deciding when the software becomes ready for manufacturing and for being reused.

References

1. Object Management Group, Inc.: Knowledge discovery meta- model (KDM) (2012). http://www.omg.org/technology/kdm/index.htm
2. Architecture-Driven Modernization: Abstract Syntax Tree Metamodel (ASTM), OMG document formal/2011-01-05, OMG, January 2011. http://www.omg.org/spec/ASTM
3. ADM initiative website. http://adm.omg.org. Accessed 5 July 2019
4. Tichelaar, S., Ducasse, S., Demeyer, S.: FAMIX and XMI. In: Proceedings Seventh Working Conference on Reverse Engineering, Brisbane, Queensland, Australia, pp. 296–298 (2000). https://doi.org/10.1109/wcre.2000.891485
5. Guéhéneuc, Y.G.: PTIDEJ: promoting patterns with patterns. In: 1st ECOOP Workshop on Building Systems using Patterns, pp. 1–9 (2005)
6. Static Analysis Results Interchange Format (SARIF). https://www.oasis-open.org/committees/sarif. Accessed 9 July 2019
7. Frama-C software analyzer website. https://frama-c.com/. Accessed 9 July 2019
8. Structured Metrics Meta-model (SMM): OMG document formal/2016- 04-04, OMG, April 2016. http://www.omg.org/spec/SMM/
9. Structured Patterns Metamodel Standard (SPMS): OMG document ptc/16-03-13, OMG, March 2016. http://wwwomg.org/spec/SPMS/1.1
10. Chikofsky, E.J., James, H.: Cross II: reverse engineering and design recovery: a taxonomy. IEEE Softw. **7**(1), 13–17 (1990)
11. Brunelière, H., Cabot, J., Dupé, G., Madiot, F.: MoDisco: a model driven reverse engineering framework. Inf. Softw. Technol. **56**(8), 1012–1032 (2014)

When NFR Templates Pay Back?
A Study on Evolution of Catalog
of NFR Templates

Sylwia Kopczyńska[✉], Jerzy Nawrocki, and Mirosław Ochodek

Faculty of Computing, Poznan University of Technology, Poznań, Poland
{sylwia.kopczynska,jerzy.nawrocki,miroslaw.ochodek}@cs.put.poznan.pl

Abstract. [*Context*] Failures in management of non-functional requirements (NFRs) (e.g., incomplete or ambiguous NFRs) are frequently identified as one of the root causes of software failures. Recent studies confirm
that using a catalog of NFR templates for requirements elicitation positively impacts the quality of requirements. However, practitioners are
afraid of templates as the return on investment in this technique is still
unknown.
[*Aim*] Our aim was to investigate how the usefulness of catalog of
NFR templates and its maintenance costs change over time.
[*Method*] Using 41 industrial projects with 2,231 NFRs, we simulated
10,000 different random evolutions of a catalog of NFR templates. It
allowed us to examine the distribution of catalog value, maintenance
effort, catalog utilization over a sequence of projects (a counterpart of
elapsing time).
[*Results*] From the performed analysis it follows that after considering
about 40 projects we can expect catalog value of 75% or more and maintenance effort of 10% or less. Then one could expect about 400 templates
in the catalog, but only about 10% of them would be used by a single
project (on average).
[*Conclusions*] Usefulness and maintenance costs of catalog of NFR
templates depend on the number of projects used to develop it. A catalog of high usefulness and low maintenance effort need to be developed
from about 40 projects. Since high variability of studied projects, this
number in practice might be lower. From the perspective of a large or
medium software company it seems not a big problem.

Keywords: Non-functional requirements · Templates · Catalog ·
Empirical study · Simulation

1 Introduction

Non-functional requirements (NFRs) are those that state conditions under which
the functionality of a software product is useful (e.g., they describe how fast a

This work was partially supported by the Young Staff grant 09/91/SBAD/0683.

© Springer Nature Switzerland AG 2019
X. Franch et al. (Eds.): PROFES 2019, LNCS 11915, pp. 145–160, 2019.
https://doi.org/10.1007/978-3-030-35333-9_11

system shall work, the security rules, the environments in which the system is expected to work).

NFRs are important not only in traditional approaches to manage software projects, but also in agile ones, which has been confirmed in the recent studies, e.g., by Kopczynska et al. [16] or by Alsaqaf et al. [3]. However, NFRs are often neglected, especially those that are difficult to write or ostensibly obvious. It is an important risk factor, as in many cases a project failure can be traced, amongst others, to improper management of them (see e.g., [5,6,18,20]).

Several recent studies provide evidence that using a catalog of NFR templates for requirements elicitation and specification results in requirements of higher quality (e.g., [10,14,15,27]). Moreover, many experts recommend preserving the best practices concerning requirements in the form of templates. According to their experience, using templates improves consistency and testability of requirements, reduces ambiguity [4],[19], [30], makes elicitation and specification easier [30], and saves the effort of specification [22].

Using NFR templates seems simple. They are expressed in natural language as statements with some gaps (parameters) to be filled in and optional parts to select while formulating a requirement. During NFRs specification one can select templates from a catalog and provide the values of the parameters they define, which is called template-supported elicitation.

However, there exists a problem with applying templates in software projects. We can hear the opinion of practitioners who are afraid of using templates (see e.g., the study by Palomares et al. [21]). They perceive them as a complex method and do not know what would be the return on investment. Thus, more evidence is needed about benefits, costs, and effectiveness of the investment in NFR templates.

We focused in the paper on how the characteristics of catalog change over time. Since a catalog of NFR templates evolves, i.e., it is subject to change resulting from the lessons learned from the past projects, it is practical to assume that after each project some templates that have been found missing are added, and others are modified. Dynamics of catalog characteristics is the process of change of those characteristics over time, and we are interested in the following research questions concerning the subject:

- **RQ1.** What is the dynamics of *value* of catalog of NFR templates for a project (i.e., the percentage of NFRs it can help to derive)?
  NOTE: Initially the catalog is small and will cover only a small fraction of NFRs, so its value for an analyst is low. It is interesting to know how many projects are needed to make it cover a reasonable fraction of the NFRs.
- **RQ2.** What is the dynamics of *maintenance effort* the catalog of NFR templates needs after a single project (i.e., the percentage of NFR templates that require to be added or modified to incorporate the lessons learned)?
  NOTE: The actual maintenance effort strongly depends on a person performing the task. To get free of this dependency, the maintenance effort is expressed as the percentage of templates that must be added or modified.

- **RQ3.** What is the dynamics of *utilization* of catalog of NFR templates (i.e., the percentage of NFR templates that get used in a single project to derive NFRs)?

  NOTE: The lower the utilization of the catalog the lower the speed of finding the templates one really needs.

To answer the stated research questions, we decided to conduct an empirical study. Using over 2,000 NFRs from 41 different industrial projects, we simulated 10,000 different random evolutions of a catalog of NFR templates. It allowed us to examine the distribution of catalog value, maintenance effort, catalog utilization over a sequence of projects (a counterpart of elapsing time). For the design of our study see Sect. 4, and in Sect. 3 some definitions and terminology are provided. The threats are discussed in Sect. 6, the results are reported in Sect. 5, while the findings are summarized in Sect. 7.

2   Related Work

The works on NFR templates concern:

▷ *Proposals of templates.* The idea of using templates was proposed a long time ago, e.g., in the famous book on Requirements Engineering from 1997 by Somerville and Sawyer [29]. Since then, there have been proposed several types of templates: (1) syntax templates that preserve a correct and common syntax of a statement to express a requirement, e.g., Rupp's [23], EARS [19]; (2) statement templates that preserve small statements (parts) that can be combined to build the full statement expressing a requirement, e.g., Denger et al. [8]; (3) syntax and semantic templates that preserve a correct and common syntax of a statement that can express a requirement and contain knowledge how to express specific requirements, e.g., statements/words used to correctly state the maximum system response time, e.g., Hull et al. [12], Kopczynska et al. [14], and they are also parts of the solutions proposed in the PABRE approach [26] and in the approach by Withall [30]; (4) structure templates that preserve the attributes that need to get assigned values to specify a requirement, frequently in the form of a table, e.g., Volere Snow Card [28], use case template [2], Planguage [11].

▷ *Reports on experience and research studies.* From experience of some authors we can learn that using templates improves consistency and testability of requirements, reduces ambiguity [4,19,30], makes elicitation and specification easier [29,30], and saves the effort of specification [22].

Worth attention are the empirical studies that deliver more specific observations. For example, Riaz et al. [27] conducted a series of experiments focused on security requirements templates. They showed statistically significant results regarding the increase of completeness, and better quality of NFRs elicited with the use of the template-supported approach. Kopczynska et al. [15] conducted an experiment in which they investigated templates concerning all ISO 25010 [13] characteristics. They also provided statistically significant results that using catalog of NFR templates improves quality and completeness of requirements,

but do not speed up the elicitation process. Then, Doerr et al. [9] investigated
the IESE NFR method that utilizes templates in a structured elicitation approach, which resulted in the conclusion on the improvement of completeness
of NFRs. Eckart et al. [10] showed that well-grounded templates can improve
the completeness of performance requirements meant as the completeness of all
necessary information in a single requirement.

▷ *Maintenance of catalog of NFR templates.* According to our up-to-date knowledge, there is only one study that tackled the problems concerning the maintenance of a catalog of NFR templates. Kopczynska et al. [15] carried out an early
investigation of one evolution of their catalog. Although this study provides some
idea of how characteristics of catalog of NFR templates might change over time,
the results might be biased by the order in which the projects were analyzed.
In this paper, we fill the gap by investigating how usefulness and maintenance
effort change over time in multiple different random evolutions.

3   Terminology

In this section the definitions used further on are stated. Although they were
given in the paper by Kopczynska et al [15], we provide them here so the paper
is self-contained.

We consider an **NFR template** as a regular expression over literals and
parameters that allows to *derive* a sentence which constitutes an NFR for some
software product.

The process of **direct deriviation** (deriving for short) an NFR from a template comprises the following steps: (1) Derive a sequence of literals and parameters from the regular expression, e.g., decide which literal best suits the current
context, decide on the multiplicity of a parameter, adjust sentence structure;
(2) Replace all the parameters with their actual values, e.g., provide concrete
numbers and names. Such definition of an NFR template allows the flexibility
of choosing the notation to document templates, e.g., VOLERE Snow Card [28],
QUPER's approach [25], the NoRT notation [14]. The latter, which aims at supporting the NFRs documentation in the form of natural language statements, is
used in the paper. An example of an NFR template would be:

> (Initial | After reset | All | <type >) **passwords shall be of length from** <min. num-
> ber> **to** <max. number> **characters.**

It consists of **core** which is stable during derivation (not taking into account
inflexion), parameters to be replaced with exact values (e.g., <min number>);
alternatives (options) to choose from (e.g., (Initial | After reset...).

Then, by a **catalog of NFR templates** ('catalog' for short), further denoted
as K, we understand a finite set of NFR templates. Its **size** ($|K|$) is defined as
the number of templates it contains. In the paper the considered catalogs are
organized into categories using the ISO 25010 standard [13].

While an organization executes a sequence of software development projects
P_1, P_2, ..., its catalog evolves from K_0 to K_1, K_2, ... More precisely, lessons

learned from each consecutive project P_i allow the owner to improve the templates transforming catalog from version K_{i-1} to K_i. For the sake of simplicity we assumed that each project is viewed as a finite set of its NFRs, i.e., $P_i = \{r_i^1, r_i^2, \cdots r_i^{n_i}\}$. Then, the process of considering these requirements, one by one, and modifying or adding templates to the catalog whenever necessary can be viewed as **catalog maintenance**. During the process we might meet the following situations.

- *Perfect match.* If requirement r_i^j (or its equivalent) can be directly derived from template t contained in catalog K_{i-1}, no maintenance action is required. One can say that there is a *perfect match* between requirement r_i^j and template t. Every such template will be included into new catalog K_i.
- *Template extension and indirect derivation.* It can happen that no template in old catalog K_{i-1} perfectly matches requirement r_i^j. Then template needs extension e.g., add some parameters and modify the static text or the options of template t' in such a way that there is a perfect match between r_i^j and new template t, and new template t is *backward compatible* with the old one. We say then that requirement r_i^j can be *indirectly derived* from template t.
- *Missing template.* The third situation is when requirement r_i^j (or its equivalent) cannot be directly or indirectly derived from any of the templates contained in old catalog K_{i-1}. Then, the only solution is to add new template to K_i.

To characterize the catalog maintenance, it seems useful to split the templates of new catalog K_i into the following subsets:

- *Perfect$_i$*: If template t belongs to *Perfect$_i$* then t belongs also to old catalog K_{i-1} and in P_i there is at least one requirement r_i^j such that there is perfect match between r_i^j and t. In this case the maintenance effort is negligible.
- *Modified$_i$*: Each template t of the set is an extension of a template from old catalog K_{i-1}, i.e., there is requirement r of project P_i that perfectly matches t and there is no template t' in old catalog K_{i-1} such that r perfectly matches t'.
- *Added$_i$*: If template t belongs to *Added$_i$* then there is requirement r in P_i such that r perfectly matches t and there is no template t' in old catalog K_{i-1} that r could be directly or indirectly derived from t'.
- *Sleeping$_i$*: It contains all the templates from old catalog K_{i-1} which are not used to directly or indirectly derive any requirement of project P_i. Those templates are unnecessary for the current project, but they can prove useful in the future. The maintenance effort associated with these templates is negligible.

4   Method

To answer the research questions stated in Sect. 1 concerning the dynamics of three characteristics of catalog of NFR templates, we investigated random catalog evolutions. In each evolution we simulated as the catalog is maintained based on the lessons learned from a random sequence (permutation) of the industrial projects described in Sect. 4.1. (We considered a sequence of projects as a counterpart of elapsing time.) The catalog was maintained according to the procedure presented in Sect. 4.2. In our study, we analyzed 10,000 catalog evolutions as the order of project might impact the dynamics of the characteristics of catalog of NFR templates.

4.1   Projects

We collected and analyzed NFRs from 41 sources (see Table 1 for a brief description of the projects). 40 of them were software development projects—26 of which were industry projects whose stakeholders shared the data with the authors (denoted as Ind), and 15 came from the projects shared in the Open Science teraPROMISE repository [7] (denoted as Pro). Additionally, we included one literature position claimed to be based on industry projects [28]. The majority of the projects aimed at developing web applications (Web), some of them concerned desktop applications (Desktop), and one project – an integrated information system (ZSI) with many web applications and web services. Altogether, we collected 2,231 NFRs. They concerned the development of business applications (B), i.e., software supporting some business processes in different domains.

For each project, we analyzed all the statements, but some which were not NFRs such as definitions of some terms, schedules of transitions, functional requirements, etc. (see the full list in [1]) were excluded.

4.2   Catalog Evolutions

The initial version of the catalog (K_0) was created based on the results of our previous study [14] and consisted of 83 templates. Together with the requirements, they were uploaded into a web application that allowed their analysis according to the following procedure. For each project P_i and for each requirement $r \in P_i$:

1. The contents of catalog K_{i-1} was analyzed to find template t that could be used to derive r (perfect match) and if such t was found, it was included into the next version of the catalog, K_i.
2. If such a template was not found, K_{i-1} was searched for a template t that could be modified (extended) to new version t' and t' could be used to directly derive r—then t' was included into K_i.
3. Otherwise, a new template to catalog K_i was added.

All the sleeping templates of K_{i-1} (i.e., not used, directly or indirectly, by any r from P_i) were included in K_i. This procedure was first executed manually, which we called *initial evolution* (see [15] for details). It allowed us to represent each NFR template as a set of parts (core, parameters, alternatives) and each NFR as composed of those parts. As a result, we could execute *multiple evolutions* using the software application (see [1] for details) to minimize the influence of the order of projects on the results.

Table 1. Description of the projects included in the study ("–" means that the data was not available, B – Business type of application, M – Multiple types of application).

Project	#NFRs	Source	Arch.	Application Type	Domain	Project	#NFRs	Source	Arch.	Application Type	Domain
1	76	Lit	Multiple	M	Multiple	22	139	Ind	Web	B	Banking
2	55	Ind	Web	B	Administration	23	31	Ind	Web	B	Banking
3	36	Ind	Desktop	B	Services	23	37	Ind	Web	B	Banking
4	24	Ind	Web	B	Administration	24	641	Ind	ZSI	B	Education & Financial
5	100	Ind	Web	B	Health Care	25	33	Ind	Web	B	Pharmacy
6	10	Ind	Desktop	B	Services	26	65	Ind	Web	B	Pharmacy
7	48	Ind	Desktop	B	Services	27	15	Pro	–	B	Media
8	32	Ind	Desktop	B	Services	28	24	Pro	Mobile	B	Real Estate
9	33	Ind	Web	B	Oil and Gas	29	25	Pro	Web	B	Education
10	68	Ind	Web	B	Financial	30	32	Pro	Web	B	Trade
11	32	Ind	Web	B	Banking	31	37	Pro	Web	B	Insurance
12	41	Ind	Web	B	Banking	32	47	Pro	Web	B	Services
13	11	Ind	Web	B	Education	33	11	Pro	Desktop	B	Trade
14	60	Ind	Web	B	Research	34	72	Pro	Web	B	Entertainment
15	89	Ind	Web	B	Banking	35	11	Pro	–	B	Services
16	10	Ind	Web	B	Banking	36	14	Pro	Web	B	Entertainment
17	43	Ind	Web	B	Banking	37	13	Pro	Web	B	Communication
18	20	Ind	Web	B	Banking	38	19	Pro	–	B	Software & Hardware
19	108	Ind	Web	B	Banking	39	19	Pro	Web	B	Services
20	18	Ind	Web	B	Banking	40	15	Pro	Web	B	Sport
						41	16	Pro	Web	B	Financial

To analyze the dynamics of variables in multiple catalog evolutions, we use box plots (e.g., Fig. 1). Each chart has a set of boxes each with a band inside the box which depicts the median value. The lower and upper "hinges" of the boxes correspond to the first and third quartiles, the whiskers extend from the hinge to the highest and lowest value that is within 1.5*IQR of the hinge, where IQR is the inter-quartile range (roughly speaking, the whiskers correspond to the 5th and the 95th percentiles [24]).

Moreover, to study how the diversity of projects influences the results of our analysis, we performed additional analyses. In each one, we excluded some projects which we called pseudo-outliers. *Pseudo-outliers* are those projects in the pool that use the highest number of unique (specific) NFR templates (in that sense each real outlier is also a pseudo-outlier but not vice-versa). To determine pseudo-outliers first, we ranked the projects from the most specific to the least specific by determining the number of unique NFR templates (used only by a given project).

Base on this ranking (see Table 2) we generated 5 mutations of multiple evolutions (each of size 10,000 as it was before). Each mutated multiple evolution $Evol_i$ was base on 41 projects but first i projects from the ranking were replaced by copies of randomly chosen other projects from the pool.

Table 2. The ranking used to identify pseudo-outliers.

Project	Num. of unique templates	Rank	Num. of excluded projects	Project	Num. of unique templates	Rank	Num. of excluded projects
6	40	2	3	27	2	14	–
20	19	2	3	7	1	19	–
22	17	2	3	9	1	12	–
2	15	3	5	12	1	8	–
11	15	3	5	16	1	10	–
25	13	4	7	17	1	18	–
15	11	4	7	23	1	16	–
1	10	5	9	28	1	15	–
4	10	5	9	32	1	15	–
24	8	6	11	34	1	18	–
5	7	9	11	37	1	17	–
10	6	7	–	41	1	12	–
13	4	6	–	19	0	20	–
18	4	8	–	21	0	20	–
39	4	10	–	29	0	20	–
31	3	14	–	30	0	20	–
33	3	9	–	36	1	20	–
35	3	7	–	38	0	20	–
8	2	11	–	40	0	13	–
14	2	16	–	42	0	20	–
26	2	13	–				

5 Results

5.1 Dynamics of Catalog Value

Let us define Value of catalog K_{i-1} as the percentage of NFRs of project P_i that can be directly (perfect match) or indirectly (after extension of some templates) derived from the templates of catalog K_{i-1}. Using the subsets $Perfect_i$ and

Modified$_i$ of new catalog K_i, one can define value of catalog K_{i-1} in the following way:

$$Value(i-1) = \frac{|Perfect_i \cup Modified_i|}{|P_i|} * 100\% \tag{1}$$

As mentioned earlier, project P_i is treated as a set of NFRs, thus $|P_i|$, i.e., its cardinality, denotes the number of NFRs of that project.

In practical terms, one can treat catalog value as the degree to which the catalog is useful as a prompt list for a given project.

Observation 1. *After considering about 40 projects one can expect catalog value of 75% or more.*

Justification. The distribution of catalog value for multiple evolutions is depicted in Fig. 1A as a box plot (a very brief explanation of the box plot representation of data is presented in Sect. 4.2). From the chart, it is pretty clear that for the considered set of 40 projects, independently of their order, one can expect 75% NFRs to be "covered" by templates of the catalog. Moreover, we fitted simple linear regression models for each evolution. We found significant regression equations with positive slopes—the mean value of slopes was 0.58, the median equal to 0.57, and min. and max. equal to 0.27 and 1.01, respectively (the p-value was smaller than 0.05). The intercept ranged from 60.00 to 80.00, with the mean value of 71.25 and median value of 71.27. The results indicate the increasing tendency in the data.

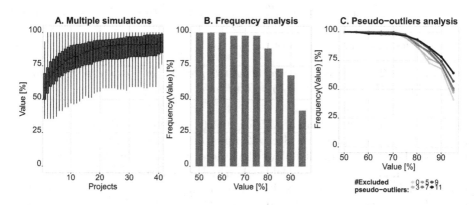

Fig. 1. (A) Distribution of catalog value, (B) Analysis of frequency after considering 40 projects for catalog value, (C) Analysis of pseudo-outliers for catalog value.

Our observation is also supported by another analysis. Let *Frequency(Value)* be a function describing the percentage of catalog evolutions for which catalog value is not less than a given *Value*. The function is depicted in Fig. 1A. From the chart presented in the figure, it follows that after considering all the 40 projects catalog value of at least 75% was achieved almost always. This chart also shows what is the chance of obtaining other catalog values, e.g., the value of 80% or more has been achieved in about 80% of cases (evolutions).

We have also examined the impact of pseudo-outliers on the catalog value, i.e., on the *Frequency* function (see Sect. 4.2 for the procedure of identifying pseudo-outliers). In Fig. 1C, there are several charts of the *Frequency* function for a given catalog value. Each of them corresponds to a different number of pseudo-outliers excluded from the original set of projects. The general conclusion is that the smaller the number of pseudo-outliers (i.e., projects that importantly differ from the rest of the portfolio of projects) the greater the chance of getting higher catalog value. What is perhaps more interesting, up to the catalog value of at least 75% the impact of pseudo-outliers is almost negligible. In other words, after considering about 40 projects the catalog value of 75% is very probable, even in the presence of pseudo-outlier projects.

5.2   Dynamics of Maintenance Effort

When considering maintenance of a catalog of NFR templates two operations seem the most important and time consuming: (1) adding new templates to the catalog and (2) modifying (extending) the existing ones. The former requires effort more or less proportional to the cardinality of the set $Added_i$ (i.e., the number of added templates), and for the latter the required effort is proportional to the cardinality of $Modified_i$ which represents the number of modified templates. Thus, one can assume the following indicator of maintenance effort $ME(i-1)$:

$$ME(i-1) = \frac{|Added_i \cup Modified_i|}{|K_i|} * 100\% \qquad (2)$$

where K_i denotes a new version of the catalog.

Observation 2. *After considering about 40 projects one can expect maintenance effort, ME, to amount up to 10% of catalog size.*

Justification. The distribution of ME for 10,000 random evolutions is presented in Fig. 2A as a box plot (see Sect. 4.2 for a description of how to read this box plot). From the figure, it follows that there is a decreasing tendency in the data. The simple regression models were fitted to confirm the observation. We found significant regression equations with the negative slopes with the mean value of -0.45, median equal to -0.44, and min. and max. equal to -0.17 and -0.69, respectively (the p-value was <0.05). The intercept ranged from 11.63 to 22.13, with the mean value of 16.95 and median value of 16.99. Moreover, from the chart in Fig. 2B, it is pretty visible that for the considered set of projects, independent of their order, one can expect that less than 10% of NFR templates require updates during maintenance process after a project.

Observation 2 is also supported by frequency analysis. Let *Frequency(ME)* be a function returning percentage of catalog evolutions for which maintenance

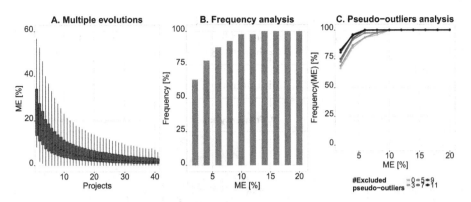

Fig. 2. (A) Distribution of maintenance effort, (B) Analysis of frequency after considering 40 projects for maintenance effort, (C) Analysis of pseudo-outliers for maintenance effort.

effort was *ME* or less. This function is depicted in Fig. 2B. From the chart, it follows that after considering all the projects, maintenance effort of 10% or less was achieved in 97.7% of evolutions. The chart also presents the frequencies for other values, e.g., one might expect that there is 78% chances that the maintenance effort would be up to 5%.

We have also examined the impact of pseudo-outliers on the value of the *Frequency* function (see Sect. 4.2 for the procedure of identifying pseudo-outliers). In Fig. 2C, there are several charts of the *Frequency* function. Each of them corresponds to a different number of pseudo-outliers excluded from the original set of projects. The general conclusion is that the impact of pseudo-outliers on maintenance effort is not very big and after considering about 40 projects the maintenance effort of 10% or less is very probable, even in the presence of pseudo-outlier projects.

5.3 Dynamics of Catalog Utilization

The simplest approach to NFRs elicitation in the presence of a catalog of NFR templates is *brute force*, i.e., going from one template to another and checking if a given template could be used to formulate an NFR for the project at hand. In this context, the following question arises: what is the percentage of considered templates that will be used to specify NFRs for a project P_i? We will refer to this percentage as *catalog utilization* and its precise definition is presented below:

$$U(i-1) = \frac{|Perfect_i \cup Modified_i|}{|K_{i-1}|} * 100\% \tag{3}$$

where K_{i-1} denotes the old (previous) version of the catalog.

Observation 3. *After considering about 40 projects one can expect catalog utilization, U, to be below 10%.*

Justification. The distribution of catalog utilization for multiple evolutions is presented in Fig. 3A as a box plot (see Sect. 4.2 for a description of how to read this box plot). From the figure, it follows that the expected value of Utilization (median value) is below 10% for the considered set of 41 projects, independent of their order (average ca. 7%, median ca. 6%, minimum ca. 1%, maximum ca. 38%).

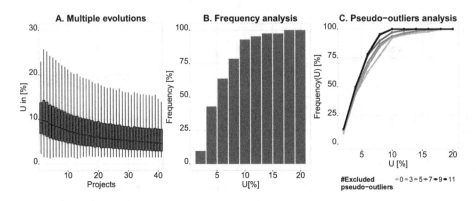

Fig. 3. (A) Distribution of utilization, (B) Analysis of frequency after considering 40 projects for utilization, (C) Analysis of pseudo-outliers for utilization.

Observation 3 is also supported by frequency analysis. Let *Frequency(U)* be a function describing percentage of the catalog evolutions for which catalog utilization was less or equal *U*. The function is depicted in (Fig. 2B). From the chart, it follows that after considering all the projects, catalog utilization of 10% or less was achieved in 93.7% of evolutions. The chart also presents the frequencies for other values, e.g., the utilization of 20% or less was practically in all the observed evolutions of the catalog.

We have also examined the impact of pseudo-outliers on the value of the *Frequency* function (see Sect. 4.2 for the procedure of identifying pseudo-outliers). In Fig. 2C, there are several charts of the *Frequency* function. Each of them corresponds to a different number of pseudo-outliers excluded from the original set of projects. The general conclusion is that the smaller the number of pseudo-outliers (i.e., the projects that differ from each other) the greater the chance of getting higher utilization.

6   Threats

In the following paragraphs, we discussed the threats to the validity of the study according to the guidelines by Wohlin et al. [31].

Conclusion validity

Reliability of Measures. To minimize the influence of inherent ambiguity of natural language that might have been introduced during the identification of the need of improvement of the catalog, the detailed procedure and definitions were created and discussed beforehand.

While conducting the initial catalog evolution as well as representing each NFR template and NFR as sets of parts (core, parameters, options) for multiple catalog evolutions we could have introduced some errors, e.g., while identifying parts of templates or identifying which part of a given template is present in a given requirement. Next, it shall be taken into account that in the multiple evolutions we used computer programs to simulate multiple maintenance processes, which might have contained some errors. To mitigate the threats concerning the multiple evolutions we also conducted simulation using the coarse-grained approach. The approach is based on the following question: *Is it true that a requirement r (from a considered project) can be derived from template t of the final version of the catalog resulting from the initial evolution?*. Thus, it is based only on the relationships between templates and requirements identified in the initial catalog simulation. In report available at website on NFR templates [1] we compared the results obtained using both the approach described in the paper and the coarse-grained approach. Based on these results, we argue, that our observations should not be visibly affected by the mentioned threats.

Fishing. To minimize the threat that the experimenters would search for a specific result when analyzing the data, the researchers did not see any information on a project, the order number of each requirement, and values of the investigated variables.

Internal Validity

Selection. The minimum requirement towards all NFRs' sets was that they contain requirements from industrial projects and most likely developing web business applications. Although we selected the source organizations by convenience, they represent a quite broad range of possible cases. Additionally, the NFRs obtained by the authors were combined with the publicly available sets [7].

Another threat relates to the homogeneity of projects (and NFRs). Since they were taken from different organizations, the abstraction levels vary, which might have boosted the size of the catalog, e.g., some people specify only that the Web Content Accessibility Guidelines (WCAG) shall be satisfied, while the others, instead, list concrete guidelines.

Construct Validity

Design Threat. The researchers did not participate in the projects for which they analyzed NFRs. Although they do have more than 5 years of experience in RE, focusing on NFRs, they might have misinterpreted some parts of requirements.

Moreover, the analyzed NFRs satisfy the definition of an NFR from [15], and we decided to use NFR templates as defined in Sect. 3. Since one might use other existing definition of an NFR, their results might vary from ours. Also using an approach that requires from an NFR to be documented with more extensive information, e.g., Gilb's Planguage [11] (it suggests that a requirement shall have a scale, measure or authority) might also drive to other results.

External validity

Interaction of Setting and Treatment. In our study, we mimicked the behavior of an organization that maintains its catalog of templates over time. The catalog maintenance procedure was aligned with the known industry practices that show the steps towards systematic requirements reuse executed in Rolls Royce [17]. Thus, we perceive the settings as realistic-enough to generalize the conclusions.

Although our goal was to provide analysis independent of the domain, type of application, we evaluated only 41 sets of requirements. Therefore, we need to accept the threat that the conclusions might be true only for the analyzed domains and types of applications.

7   Conclusions

Non-functional requirements (NFRs) are important not only when a software product is developed using traditional but also agile approaches. Since, failures in the management of NFRs, such as incomplete, ambiguous NFRs, etc., are one of the root causes of failures in transitions of software products, elicitation methods and techniques that help to overcome these issues are needed. However, first, to apply any elicitation method, knowledge of benefits and costs associated with using it must be known.

In this paper, we focused on the elicitation of NFRs using a catalog of NFR templates. We investigated the issues of usefulness and maintenance cost that are important from the perspective of the maintenance of such catalog measured with catalog value, maintenance effort, and catalog utilization by a single project. The study is based on 41 industrial projects with 2,231 NFRs (26 industry projects whose stakeholders shared the data with us and 15 projects shared in the Open Science tera-PROMISE repository [7]; Sect. 4 contains all the details). To analyze the maintenance process, i.e., how catalog of NFR templates changes using lessons learned from the previous project, we simulated 10,000 different random evolutions of a catalog of NFR templates.

Here are the observations that follow from our study:

▷ (*Observation 1.*) After considering about 40 projects one can expect catalog value of 75% or more.
▷ (*Observation 2.*) After considering about 40 projects one can expect maintenance effort (measured in number of updates) amounting up to 10% of catalog size.
▷ (*Observation 3.*) After considering about 40 projects one can expect catalog utilization to be below 10%.

The observations confirmed our initial investigation based on a single manual evolution of a catalog and improved the generalizability of study [15].

It seems reasonable to assume that a catalog of NFR templates of *catalog value* at the level of *75%* (or more) and *maintenance effort* at the level of *10%* (or less) is attractive from the point of view of practitioners. As these values were achieved in the study after about 40 projects this number of projects becomes a kind of break-even point in which the investment in catalog development highly pays back. It is worth to take into account that the projects were quite heterogeneous (e.g., they come from different organizations, describe systems from different domains). However, if an organization works on much more homogeneous projects (e.g., it implements only e-commerce systems) it would require fewer projects to achieve the benefits at the mentioned level.

From the perspective of a large software company, the requirement of conducting about 40 projects seems not a big deal; it might be even achieved within a year. For micro or small companies having such number of projects might be more difficult. Then, it might prove valuable to share a catalog of NFR templates between several companies, e.g., within a consortium or while cooperation with a research institution.

Catalog utilization below 10% seems low from the perspective of elicitors, especially in the context of catalogs containing about 400 templates. From our study it follows that after considering about 40 projects it is quite probable that the number of templates useful for a particular project will be 20 or even less. It resembles looking for a needle in a haystack. Thus, a method of searching for NFR templates faster than brute force executed manually would be valuable.

Acknowledgments. We would like to thank the companies that shared their data with us especially ATREM S.A., Consdata Sp. z o.o., Currency One S.A., IT Department of Poznan City Hall, Roche Sp. z o.o., TALEX S.A.

References

1. Website of NoRTs. http://norts.cs.put.poznan.pl
2. Adolph, S., Bramble, P., Cockburn, A., Pols, A.: Patterns for Effective Use Cases. Addison-Wesley, Boston (2002)
3. Alsaqaf, W., Daneva, M., Wieringa, R.: Quality requirements challenges in the context of large-scale distributed agile: an empirical study. Inf. Softw. Technol. **110**, 39–55 (2019)
4. Berry, D.M., Kamsties, E., Krieger, M.M.: From Contract Drafting to Software Specification: Linguistic Sources of Ambiguity. A Handbook. Ver 1.0. https://cs.uwaterloo.ca/~dberry/handbook/ambiguityHandbook.pdf. Accessed 07 Sept 2015
5. Boehm, B., In, H.: Identifying quality-requirement conflicts. IEEE Softw. **13**(2), 25–35 (1996)
6. Breitman, K.K., Leite, J.C.S., Finkelstein, A.: The world sa stage: a survey on requirements engineering using a real-life case study. J. Braz. Comput. Soc. **6**(1), 13–37 (1999)
7. Cleland-Huang, J., Mazrouee, S., Liguo, H., Port, D.: Open-Science teraPROMISE repository. http://openscience.us/repo/requirements/other-requirements/nfr. (2010). Accessed 26 June 2017
8. Denger, C., Berry, D.M., Kamsties, E.: Higher quality requirements specifications through natural language patterns. In: IEEE International Conference on Software: Science, Technology and Engineering, pp. 80–90 (2003)
9. Doerr, J., Paech, B., Koehler, M.: Requirements engineering process improvement based on an information model. In: 2004 Proceedings of 12th IEEE International Requirements Engineering Conference, pp. 70–79. IEEE (2004)
10. Eckhardt, J., Vogelsang, A., Femmer, H., Mager, P.: Challenging incompleteness of performance requirements by sentence patterns. In: International Requirements Engineering Conference (RE), pp. 46–55. IEEE (2016)

11. Gilb, T.: Competitive Engineering: A Handbook for Systems and Software Engineering Management Using Planguage. Butterworth-Heinemann, Oxford (2005)
12. Hull, E., Jackson, K., Dick, J.: Requirements Engineering (2005)
13. ISO/IEC: ISO/IEC 25010 - Systems and software engineering - Systems and software Quality Requirements and Evaluation (SQuaRE) - System and software quality models. Technical report, ISO/IEC (2010)
14. Kopczynska, S., Nawrocki, J.: Using non-functional requirements templates for elicitation: a case study. In: IEEE International Workshop Requirements Patterns (2014)
15. Kopczynska, S., Nawrocki, J., Ochodek, M.: An empirical study on catalog of non-functional requirement templates: Usefulness Maintenance Issues. Inf. Softw. Technol. **103**, 75–91 (2018)
16. Kopczyńska, S., Ochodek, M., Nawrocki, J.: On importance of non-functional requirements in agile software projects—a survey. In: Jarzabek, S., Poniszewska-Marańda, A., Madeyski, L. (eds.) Integrating Research and Practice in Software Engineering. SCI, vol. 851, pp. 145–158. Springer, Cham (2020). https://doi.org/10.1007/978-3-030-26574-8_11
17. Lam, W., McDermid, T., Vickers, A.: Ten steps towards systematic requirements reuse. In: Intenational Symposium on Requirements Engineering, pp. 6–15. IEEE (1997)
18. Lindstrom, D.R.: Five ways to destroy a development project. IEEE Softw. **10**(5), 55–58 (1993)
19. Mavin, A., Wilkinson, P.: Big Ears (The Return of "Easy Approach to Requirements Engineering"). In: Requirements Engineering Conference, pp. 277–282 (2010)
20. Nuseibeh, B.: Ariane 5: who dunnit? IEEE Softw. **14**(3), 15–16 (1997)
21. Palomares, C., Quer, C., Franch, X.: Requirements reuse and requirement patterns: a state of the practice survey. Empirical Softw. Eng. **22**, 1–44 (2015)
22. Pohl, K.: Requirements Engineering: Fundamentals, Principles, and Techniques. Springer, Heidelberg (2010)
23. Pohl, K., Rupp, C.: Requirements Engineering Fundamentals. Rocky Nook, San Rafael (2011)
24. R Documentation: Box Plots. www.rdocumentation.org/packages/graphics/versions/3.5.1/topics/boxplot. Accessed 28th Sept 2018
25. Regnell, B., Svensson, R.B., Olsson, T.: Supporting roadmapping of quality requirements. IEEE Softw. **25**(2), 42–47 (2008)
26. Renault, S., Méndez Bonilla, Ó., Franch Gutiérrez, J., Quer Bosor, M.C., et al.: A pattern-based method for building requirements documents in call-for-tender processes. IJCSA **6**(5), 175–202 (2009)
27. Riaz, M., et al.: Identifying the implied: findings from three differentiated replications on the use of security requirements templates. Empirical Softw. Eng. **22**, 2127–2178 (2016)
28. Robertson, S., Robertson, J.: Mastering the Requirements Process: Getting Requirements Right, 3rd edn. Addison-Wesley, Boston (2012)
29. Sommerville, I., Sawyer, P.: Requirements Engineering: A Good Practice Guide. Wiley, Hoboken (1997)
30. Withall, S.: Software Requirement Patterns (Developer Best Practices). Microsoft Press, Redmond (2007)
31. Wohlin, C., Runeson, P., Höst, M., Ohlsson, M.C., Regnell, B., Wesslén, A.: Experimentation in Software Engineering. Springer, Heidelberg (2012). https://doi.org/10.1007/978-3-642-29044-2

Improving Quality of Data Exchange Files. An Industrial Case Study

Günter Fleck[1], Michael Moser[2(✉)], and Josef Pichler[2]

[1] Siemens Transformers Austria, 8160 Weiz, Austria
guenter.fleck@siemens.com
[2] Software Competence Center Hagenberg, 4232 Hagenberg, Austria
{michael.moser,josef.pichler}@scch.at

Abstract. In the development of electrical machines users run a batch of command line programs by providing text-based data exchange files as input. The required structure and content of these files is often only informally documented and implicitly enforced by programs. Therefore, users are forced to execute programs without prior syntactic and semantic verification. To improve the quality of data exchange files, users need editor support that allows syntactic and semantic verification using grammar-based analyzers. In order to reduce the effort for creating grammars, we use *grammar recovery* which analyzes software artifacts and makes the retrieved knowledge visible as a language grammar. The assessment and completion of the extracted grammar requires both knowledge in software-language engineering and in the application domain. This paper examines whether the integration of grammar recovery with domain-specific languages is suitable for creating editor support for data exchange files. In particular, we are interested in whether we can recover (1) a grammar and validation rules from documentation and a corpus of example files. Furthermore, we are interested in whether (2) a domain-specific language (DSL) allows domain experts to provide missing details and evolve grammars. To answer these questions, we conducted an industrial case study on three different types of data exchange files. Results show that about 45% of the grammar rules could be recovered automatically and that the completion of the extracted grammars by end-users is a promising means to provide correct and maintainable grammars for data exchange files.

Keywords: Software evolution · Data quality · Grammar recovery · Domain-specific languages

1 Introduction

IT systems of various domains are traditionally designed following a batch architecture. Single programs in a batch fetch input data, process the provided data and produce output data processed in turn by a subsequent program. In the

© Springer Nature Switzerland AG 2019
X. Franch et al. (Eds.): PROFES 2019, LNCS 11915, pp. 161–175, 2019.
https://doi.org/10.1007/978-3-030-35333-9_12

field of engineering software, we frequently encounter human-readable, semi-structured data exchange files which are utilized as input for command-line-based engineering tools. Human-readable text files using a non-standardized, proprietary file format have been introduced to facilitate both writing and reading program input and output using common text editors and to avoid dependencies to specific data formats or tools. The flexibility with respect to editing text files goes along with the disadvantage that no validation on input files is done prior program execution and even minor lexical or syntactical errors cause the program to stop abnormally without delivering results. In the context of engineering software, this is all the more problematic as engineers have to analyze, extend, and manually forward the data output from an engineering tool as input to other command line-based engineering tools.

To tackle these problems, engineers require tool support with adequate lexical, syntactic, and semantic validation of text files for writing and reading input/output files. As required tool support must be based on formal language specifications such as context-tree grammars, one key question is how we can efficiently create context-free grammars which correctly specify the structure of existing data exchange files with respect to individual batch programs. Previous experiments [5] revealed that substantial parts of the required grammar can be automatically inferred by means of a Minimal Adequate Teacher (MAT) [2] method together with specific preprocessing. However, the inferred grammar required refactoring towards a suitable and most important maintainable basis for the desired editor support. Since this is not feasible for the targeted industrial setting, we investigate whether a combination of grammar recovery [9] and end-user driven development [8] using a domain-specific language (DSL) [13] is suitable for data exchange files. Grammar recovery addresses the problem of reconstructing a grammar by recovering language structure from existing software artefacts. It is not only successfully applied to recover grammars of legacy programming languages but as well of modern languages [10] or semi-formally specified data structures [14].

In this paper, we investigate whether a development approach can be applied that engages end-users and software developers not familiar with language engineering in the creation and maintenance of editor support for data exchange files. In particular we are interested in the following two research questions (RQs):

RQ1: Can we automatically recover grammars and semantic validation from documentation and a corpus of data exchange files?

RQ2: Can we present the extracted grammars and validation rules in a domain-specific representation so that domain experts are in the position to assess and complete grammars?

To answer these questions we conducted an industrial case study on three different sets of data exchange files at Siemens AG Austria. The remainder of this paper is organized as follows. In Sect. 2 we present the industrial context, in particular the characteristics and commonalities of data exchange files used in engineering software. Section 3 gives and overview of our approach and selectively shows recovery by example. In Sect. 4 we present the industrial case study

```
1   TEXT Input for winding calculation
2   NORM IEEE
3   ACEQ 1 80
4   BAST S 6 B 64.7 14.7
5   CLAC 15*12.0 13*3.0
6   COOL 10 3.4 12
7   BEGIN_WINDING HV
8   DISC 6*[6 A 6 B B 6]
9   DISC 6*[3 A 3 2*B B 3]
10  LOSS [12.0 15.0 15.0] [12 * 1.5]
11  TEXT ins-ax ins-rad ins(both sided)
12  WIRE A 14.5 20.65 1.1 7 6 1.6 0.01 2
13  WIRE B 16.5 17.7 1.3 7 7 1.32
14  END_WINDING
```

Listing 1.1. Example data exchange file of engineering software.

and discuss results therefrom. Section 5 lists related approaches and Sect. 6 lists threats to validity. Section 7 concludes this paper.

2   Industrial Context

Siemens AG Austria, Transformers Weiz is a manufacturer of large power transformers. To calculate the thermal, geometrical, mechanical, and electrical properties of a power transformer, 50 software programs are developed and maintained at a single subsidiary. These engineering tools are generally available as command line tools and used by the company's engineering departments around the world. In the course of software modernization efforts, Siemens AG - Austria identified data exchange between engineering software to be of high potential for improving the quality of engineering software. Engineers calculate designs of a power transformer by running a batch of engineering tools. Data output by one engineering tool is typically extended and manually forwarded as input to other engineers tools. This process is not fixed, neither in the order in which engineering tools are executed nor from which sources (e.g. other engineering tools or real measurement data) input data are obtained. Data exchange is largely based on semi-structured files using a non-standardized, proprietary file format. Engineers create and evaluate data files using text editors. Therefore, input of engineering software cannot be validated prior program execution. Consequently, even minor lexical and syntactic errors cause software programs to terminate without delivering the desired results. Moreover, error reporting is highly program-specific and tracing error messages from program output to data files is a challenge for engineers. To uplift usability of engineering software, it was decided to develop editor support with adequate lexical, syntactic and semantic validation. A basic prerequisite for the development of state-of-the editing support is the availability of language grammars, which facilitate the generation of adequate parsing infrastructure. However, as the creation, maintenance and evolution of language grammars is seen as a substantial effort, Siemens AG - Austria seeks to find ways to automate this process.

Data Exchange Files. Files for data exchange are generally referred to as KEY- WORD files. All 50 engineering tools support variants of this format. A concise definition of the format does not exist. Developers of engineering software share a common understanding of the basics of the format and adapt it to their needs. Each engineering software provides its own implementation for reading and writing KEYWORD files. Listing 1.1 shows content of a KEYWORD file. KEYWORD is a row based file format. Rows start with a keyword identifier followed by the content part of an entry. Keyword identifiers are not fixed, vary across different applications, and typically consist of 4 letters. The content part holds values of type character, string, numeric or list. Numeric values are specified as integer or real values. List of values are generally specified using square brackets ([]) as shown in lines 8 and 9. However, this is not always necessary, as the keyword CLAC in line 5 shows. Moreover, custom data encoding is used to provide input in a compact way. These encodings come in different styles and are highly pro- gram specific. An instruction which is recognized across most applications is the expansion operator (*) as used in lines 5, 8, 9, and 10. The operator expands the expression on the right side by the number on the left side. The operator can be applied to numeric values, words, or lists. Depending on the keyword the number of values per keyword is either fixed, bound by a minimum and maximum number of values, or unbound as in the case of a list of values. Key- word entries can be logically grouped within section. Section are opened with a BEGIN_<identifier> line and closed by an END_<identifier> line as shown in lines 7 and 14. The same identifiers for keywords and groups of keywords may appear in data exchange files of different engineering tools, usage however is most likely to differ.

3   Approach

Our approach to create editor support for data exchange files is based on two cornerstones. First, we automatically create parsing infrastructure from a lan- guage model recovered from existing documentation and a corpus of example files. Second, the extracted language model is assessed and completed by domain experts, i.e. developers and power users of engineering software, using a textual DSL. Figure 1 shows an overview of our approach. In short the process to create and evolve editor support can be described as follows: (1) Recovery of an initial language model from existing documentation. (2) Analysis of example input files and update of the language model. (3) Generation of a context-free attributed grammar, that is the foundation for (4) the generation of parsing infrastructure. The parsing components are automatically deployed within a generic editor for keyword files. (5) Iterative, end-user driven adaption, refinement and evolution of the extracted language model using a DSL. End-users modify the language model

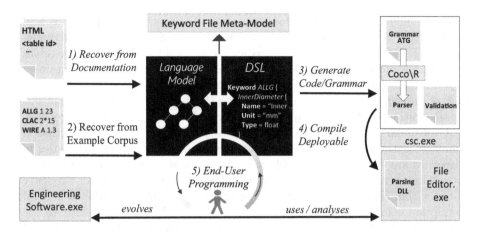

Fig. 1. Process to recover and maintain editor support

and generate updated versions of parsing components by executing step three (i.e. regenerating production rules) and four (automatic generation and deployment of parsing infrastructure) of the presented process. Subsequent sections provide details on prerequisites and technical details for our implementation.

3.1 Prerequisites and Foundations

A prerequisite to create editor support for a specific engineering software is to collect existing documentation for data exchange files and collect example files. Moreover, understanding basic concepts of the keyword file format is foundational to our approach. We use that understanding to provide a generic meta-model for capturing the essential concepts of keyword files. For the sake of brevity we omit full details, however major abstractions are a *Keyword* having a set of *Properties* reflecting the possible values of a line in a keyword file. *Properties* are described by name, data type, unit, description, and whether they are required or not. Supported data types are **string, char, integer, float,** and **list**. For list types we distinguish several sub-types reflecting element data type, e.g. string or float, and structural patterns like the usage of expansion separators as shown in Listing 1.1. Moreover, we capture the usage of keywords within named sections as a *Keyword Group*.

3.2 Recovery from Documentation

Documentation for input files is provided as a set of HTML documents and has a similar structure across different engineering software. This is for two reasons. First, department wide efforts to improve software quality led to a standardization of software documentation. Second, creation of documentation is typically done by clone-and-own of existing documentation. We exploit the structural similarity between software documentation to extract grammar and semantic validation rules from documentation. To identify descriptions of keywords within documentation the extraction mechanism searches for `table` elements in HTML sources. Simple heuristics are applied to answer whether tables contain keyword descriptions. Heuristics evaluate if (1) `id` attribute contains a known identifier (e.g. *legend*), (2) column headers contain labels such as *name*, *unit*, or *description* or synonyms thereof, or (3) table structure and content hint documentation of keywords, for example, through the usage of units or geometrical vocabulary like *diameter*, *length*, or *width*. For each keyword description found, we extract name and general description of the keyword. Properties of a keyword are extracted from table rows. For each keyword property we try to extract index, name, description and unit. These attributes are either explicitly stated within separate table columns or extracted from text within a general description column. The thereby created keyword definitions are added to the language model. Language models recovered from documentation are expected to be incomplete, out-of-date, or missing at all. Therefore subsequent analysis steps (e.g. the recovery from an example corpus) must not rely on the existence of a language model.

3.3   Recovery from Example Corpus

To parse a corpus of data exchange files we implemented a generic parsing strategy for keyword files. The strategy exploits common properties of the keyword file format. Properties common to all input files of different engineering software are, (1) line-based, (2) keyword identifier starts a line, (3) usage of `begin` and `end` identifiers to mark a group of keywords, and (4) specification of keyword properties by a space delimited list of values. Recovery from example corpus contributes the following elements to the language model: (1) keywords not contained within documentation, (2) keyword groups, (3) usage of keywords within keyword groups, and (4) data type information. During the recovery process each file in the corpus is analyzed line by line. Occurrences of keyword entries within keyword groups are collected and used to model multiplicity constraints on keywords. Moreover, for any keyword occurrence data types of keyword properties are derived and updated from the comma separated list of input values. We apply a pattern-based approach for the detection of list types. Patterns match expansion separators (i.e. *) and structural patterns within a sequence of input values. To update type information for existing keyword properties we apply a set of update rules, which direct this process. E.g. integer data types must not override a previously detected float data type, or a detected list type must override base data types. In general we rate correctness of data recovered from example files better than correctness of data recovered from documentation. Therefore, contradictory results (e.g. number of keyword parameters) are resolved in favor of the recovery from example data exchange files.

```
 1   WIREEntry<Entry entry> =    ("WIRE"
 2   CharProperty<out fcr>       (. entry.Add(fcr); .)
 3   NumeriProperty<out fdo>     (. entry.Add(fdo); .)
 4   NumberProperty<out fdo>     (. entry.Add(fdo); .)
 5   NumberProperty<out fdo>     (. entry.Add(fdo); .)
 6   NumberProperty<out fdo>     (. entry.Add(fdo); .)
 7   NumberProperty<out fdo>     (. entry.Add(fdo); .)
 8   NumberProperty<out fdo>     (. entry.Add(fdo); .)
 9   [NumberProperty<out fdo>    (. entry.Add(fdo); .)
10   [IntProperty<out fun> (. entry.Add(fun);.)]]).
```

Listing 1.2. Grammar for the keyword WIRE in Coco/R input format.

3.4   Generation of Parsing Infrastructure

The recovered language model is input for the generation process. The generation process creates production rules of a context-free grammar and code to validate semantic correctness of keyword file data. To create an executable syntax analyzer for a given language model we utilize the compiler Coco/R[1]. Hence, the grammar definition to be generated from a language model must conform to the input format of Coco/R. We use .net T4 text templates to generate the grammar definition. Templates contain a frame which already contains definitions of generic tokens and production rules. For each keyword and keyword group the generator adds new production rules. Listing 1.2 shows the production rule generated for the WIRE keyword. The token "WIRE" is expected to be followed by a character value, 6 number values (i.e. float or integer), an optional 7th number value and an optional 8th integer value. Using the generated grammar definition as input, Coco/R generates C# source code for scanner and parser components.

Next to syntax validation our approach facilitates semantic validation of keyword file data. From data constraints provided by end-users and the extracted multiplicity model we generate C# code that validates minimum and maximum occurrences of keywords within keyword groups and value ranges of numeric keyword properties. Again, we use T4 to embed validation code within a template holding the implementation frame of the validation component. As a last step, we generate a plug-in component which provides convenient access to parsing and validation facilities. All generated sources are compiled using csc.exe and packaged and deployed as DLL component.

3.5   End-User Programming of Parser Component

The generated parsing infrastructure does not always handle syntax and semantics of data exchange files correctly. This is due to missing or outdated documentation, an incomplete example corpus, and specifics in data exchange files

---
[1] http://www.ssw.uni-linz.ac.at/Coco/.

```
1   Keyword WIRE {
2       WireIdentifier {
3           Name = "Wire identifier"
4           Description = "Wire identifier (e.g. A)"
5           Type = character
6       }
7       InsulatedAxialHeight {
8           Name = "Insulated Axial Height"
9           Description = "The axial height of..."
10          Type = float
11          Unit = "mm"
12      }
13      ...
```

Listing 1.3. Definition of WIRE keyword in textual DSL

not handled by our extraction mechanism. To keep our approach as general as possible and overcome shortcomings we let developers of engineering software assess and complete the automatically recovered language model, see step 5 in Fig. 1. Developers are experts in the domain of power transformers and typically have a formal education in physics or mathematics. However, domain experts are by no means language engineers. Therefore, we present language models in a textual DSL that abstracts from language engineering specifics (e.g. creation of production rules, or building a semantic model). Listing 1.3 shows a DSL snippet of the recovered language model for the WIRE keyword. The textual DSL presents the model in a declarative style allowing engineers to modify the provided model.

To further improve usability we integrated an editor component for the presented DSL with a generic editor for keyword files. The editor displays results of syntactic and semantic validation of an keyword file. Moreover, the editor can be used to start recovery of a language model by selecting example corpus and documentation artifacts. As Fig. 2 shows, the automatically recovered language model is presented in the textual DSL and can be displayed alongside with a keyword file. By this, engineers can edit a language model using the DSL, regenerate and compile parsing infrastructure, dynamically load the generated DLL components, and explore the new behavior of the parsing component by example.

4 Evaluation

In this section we present the evaluation of our approach. To evaluate recovery of input grammars for data exchange files used in engineering software we conducted an industrial case study at Siemens AG Austria, Transformers Weiz.

Fig. 2. Editor for end-user driven language evolution

4.1 Case Study Design

The objective of this case study is to explore and analyze the application of grammar recovery to data exchange files used at Siemens AG Austria. Moreover, we want to answer if a domain-specific language is a suitable mean to correct and complement the automatically extracted grammars. This case study is driven by the following two research questions (RQs):

RQ1: Can we automatically recover language grammars from documentation and a corpus of data exchange files? Moreover, to which extend is manual rework required until a grammar suitable for building tool support exists?

RQ2: Can we present extracted grammars in a domain-specific representation so that even domain experts are in the position to assess and complete grammars without assistance from software language experts?

Units of Analysis. The units of analysis of this case study are three different sets of data exchange files for engineering software P1, P2, and P3. Selection of programs was mainly driven by a single engineering department. All engineering software are actively used and evolved for more than 10 years. For each program we collected an example corpus of data exchange files. Moreover, we collected current versions of end-user documentation for all programs.

Table 1. Example Corpus and Results for Programs *P1*, *P2*, and *P3*.

Program	P1	P2	P3
Keywords expected	39	26	10
Files in documentation	63	21	8
Files in example corpus	11	81	76
Keyword example in corpus	9562	16044	1715
Infrastructure generated	Yes	Yes	Yes
Keywords succ. recovered	46.2%	42.3%	40.0%
E1: Missing properties	28.6%	33.3%	16.7%
E2: Optional properties	23.8%	6.7%	16.7%
E3: Invalid type info	47.6%	26.7%	0.0%
E4: Missing type info	80.9%	26.7%	33.3%
Manual changes/keyword	0.82	0.69	0.2

Data Collection. To answer RQ1 we applied steps 1 to 4 of our approach as described in Sect. 3. The authors of this paper applied and evaluated recovery of language grammars and generation of parsing infrastructure. We verified the following: (1) on a coarse level we checked whether the generated parsing components could be integrated with a generic editing component. This basically verifies that the generated production rules used by a parser generator, i.e. CoCo/R, are correct and software integration is working. (2) On the level of keywords we verified correctness of the recovered grammar by instructing the generated parsing components to parse keywords found within the corpus of data exchange files. Parsing errors indicated incorrect grammar recovery. (3) To further classify errors the authors of this paper analyzed the causes of parsing errors. By this a fine grained classification of errors in grammar rules could be created. (4) Finally, to detect overly admissive grammar rules we manually analyzed and evaluated production rules together with lead developers.

To answer RQ2 the lead developer of the components was asked to complete and corrected invalid data using the declarative DSL integrated within the generic keyword file editor as described in Sect. 3. The experiment was carried out in collaboration with the authors of this paper.

4.2 Quantitative Analysis

Table 1 presents quantitative data on the three units of analysis. The number of expected keywords was collected from latest versions of engineering software and verified by lead engineers of software. Files in example corpus range from 11 to 81. Number of single keyword entries contained within all example files of a corpus range from 1715 to 16044. Moreover, Table 1 presents quantitative result for all three units. For all three programs a ready to use parsing infrastructure is generated. Between 40% to 46.2% of keywords could be correctly recovered without any manual completion and correction of grammars needed. The remaining keywords contain errors which fall into four different error categories (i.e. E1-E4). 16.7% to 28.6% of extracted keyword definitions miss specification of one or more properties. Failing to recovery optionality of properties for a keyword ranges from 6.7% to 23.8%. For P1 and P2 invalid recovery of type information was the case in 47.6% and 26.7% of incorrectly recovered keywords. For 26.7% to 80.9% of incorrectly recovered keywords, type information is missing at all. To quantify effort for completing incorrect grammar rules Table 1 lists the number of changes experts provided manually. Manual changes range from 0.2 to 0.82 per keyword. The type of change depends on the type of error, e.g. missing properties were added or invalid type information was corrected. Changes to property names, descriptions, and units were explicitly excluded from this evaluation.

4.3   Qualitative Analysis

RQ1: Can Automatic Grammar Recovery Be Applied and to Which Extend Is Manual Rework Required? In general, we state that the presented approach for grammar recovery is applicable to data exchange files. As we showed, for all three programs a ready to use parsing infrastructure is generated, providing definitions for *all* expected keywords of the analyzed systems. Roughly 40% of recovered grammar rules can be integrated with editing support as is and do not require manual completion or corrections. However, still the majority of keyword definitions could not be successfully recovered. Missing property specifications are mainly due to invalid or outdated documentation (E1). Failing to recover property specification from documentation leads to wrong assumptions during recovery from corpus data. To correctly recover optionality (E2) of properties from software artefacts, a sufficiently rich and diverse set of example data is needed. Our data sets failed to provide this diversity. A large part of errors refers to invalid (E3) or missing type information (E4). Again, missing type information can be traced back to incomplete example data. If a property is recovered from documentation, outdated or not, and example data fails to provide examples, our type inference mechanism cannot deliver results. Invalid type information is mostly due to inefficiencies and generalizations of our type inference. Especially structural patterns, e.g. line 4 in Listing 1.1, require specific information for a single keyword.

RQ2: End-User Driven Grammar Completion. For answering RQ2 we asked a lead developer to correct and complete the automatically recovered grammars. The expert iterativley updated the language grammar until the grammar could successfully parse all examples within the corpus. Completion of grammars was carried out under supervision of the authors of this paper. Effort to complete and correct generated production rules was in all three cases between 1 to 4 h.

Feedback from domain experts revealed that the declarative presentation of keyword definitions helped to read and update specifications. Moreover, domain experts noted that editing grammar definitions in a DSL alongside with a running example helped to understand concepts of the DSL. However, to further improve acceptance the concrete syntax of the DSL should be redesigned together with end-users.

In summary, we can state that semi-automatic recovery of grammar from data exchange files is feasible. Using multiple sources as input for grammar recovery, i.e. documentation and a corpus of examples files, is found beneficial for our case. In all three cases the grammar of at least 40% of keywords could be automatically recovered. Still, roughly 60% of keywords require manual adaption and correction. This seems rather low when compared to results of approaches in grammar inferences like [2]. However, approaches which fully automatically infer grammars often yield overly complex grammars with many production rules, which are therefore hard to understand and maintain [5]. In comparison, production rules generated by our approach closely match the structure of a keyword and therefore can be easily assessed and completed by domain experts.

5   Related Work

Improvement of data exchange, e.g. through standardization of exchange formats, is the goal of many industrial initiatives. Recent advances in the automation industry resulted in approaches like *AutomatationML*[2] or *OPC UA*[3]. For instance, *AutomationML* supports standardized data exchange in the engineering process of production systems [12]. Obviously, in the presented case the support of these standardized formats would require changes to engineering tools, which is not desirable. Moreover, data exchange files as used in the presented industrial context are analyzed, extended and manually forwarded by engineers as command line input of another engineering tool.

Reverse engineering structure of input formats from examples is a well studied topic in research. [1,3,6], or [11] are only some examples to that. Fisher et al. [6] for example present a system that automatically infers the structure of an ad-hoc data source. The system creates format specifications in a data description language (PADS). From PADS descriptions a compiler generates .h and .c files that together implement the data structures and operations to manipulate declared types.

A grammar recovery approach used to recover grammar specifications of online wikis is presented by [14]. Steps are reported to semi-automatically extract a grammar from a community maintained semi-formal grammar definition using different notations. Recovery of schema information from XML files is a topic which is related to our use case. However, syntactic structure is far more stable than in the presented case. [1] presents an inference approach to recreate XML-schema definitions from examples. An alternative approach to grammar creation from examples is the development of grammars by programming-by-example. In [11] an programming-by-example environment is present that supports the

---

[2] https://www.automationml.org.
[3] http://www.opcfoundation.org.

synthesis of parsers and lexers from examples. This clearly lowers the threshold to grammar development, however would still be to high for our case.

6   Threats to Validity

A threat to internal validity is the selection of software systems for which grammar of data exchange files is recovered. Selection was mainly driven by a single engineering department. Obviously, this bears the risk that structure and content of data exchange files are more similar than compared to data exchange files used in software from other engineering departments. We tried to mitigate this risk by scanning structure of data exchange files from various other software systems, however an in-depth analysis like presented in our industrial case study is missing. Moreover, manual review of production rules bears the risk of being incomplete or erroneous.

Evaluation of the presented DSL bears several risks. Studies on best practices for DSL development [4] show that usability evaluations should be executed at early design stages and involvement of end-users is recommended for the development of a DSL. Evaluation of the presented DSL by end-users was only performed during the course of this case study and no feedback has been incorporated into language design. Experts to complete grammars using the DSL comprised users which were involved during initial discussion of the approach. Therefore, biased feedback of end-users is a risk.

7   Conclusion

In this paper we present our approach to improve quality of data exchange files used in engineering software. To support the manual creation of data exchange files, high quality editor support needs to provide syntactic verification by means of language grammars. To lower effort for the creation of grammars of data exchange file formats, we propose to create parsing infrastructure by a combination of semi-automatic grammar recovery [9] and end-user driven completion of grammars.

Obviously, our approach is largely influenced by concepts and ideas of grammar recovery [9]. In the presented industrial context, grammar recovery seems promising for several reasons. First, the effort to manually create grammars would overburden affected engineering departments. Moreover, software developers responsible for targeted programs are no experts in language engineering, and therefore the threshold to build infrastructure to parse end verify data exchange files by means of context-free grammars seemed too high.

However, from previous experiments [5] we have learned that we need to include software developers in the process of grammar creation. Approaches which fully automatically infer grammars from existing software artefacts (e.g. data, source code, documentation) exist, however often yield complex grammars, which are hard to understand and maintain. In the presented industrial context this was a show stopper for these approaches. To facilitate the maintenance and evolution of grammars, we enable domain experts with no language engineering skills to actively contribute in the assessment and completion of recovered grammars by means of a DSL.

The presented approach recovers grammars and validation code from a corpus of example files and end-user documentation. Other sources information on the structure of data-exchange files were not considered. For instance, the engineering tools itself could be used as a source for grammar recovery. As shown in [7] a combination of static and dynamic analysis can be used to recover understanding of legacy source code. For the presented context this would mean to analyze *fortran* implementations of parsing components used in engineering tools.

The main reason to conduct this case study was to answer whether semi-automatic grammar recovery could substantially lower the effort for grammar creation and maintenance in the presented industrial context. Grammars extracted from documentation and example input data are sufficiently rich and correct to let domain experts assess and complete grammars. From the presented cases and feedback from stakeholders in Siemens AG Austria we conclude, that the approach is suitable to be rolled out to other engineering software. will be further improved by including static analysis of source code, e.g. to derive property types, within our automatic extraction process. Most importantly, we want to pick up feedback from end-users to redesign concrete representation of the DSL and include long-term evaluation of usage within the provided infrastructure.

Acknowledgment. The research reported in this paper has been supported by the Austrian Ministry for Transport, Innovation and Technology, the Federal Ministry for Digital and Economic Affairs, and the Province of Upper Austria in the frame of the COMET center SCCH.

References

1. Chidlovskii, B.: Schema extraction from XML data: a grammatical inference approach. In: KRDB 2001 Workshop (Knowledge Representation and Databases (2001)
2. Clark, A.: Distributional learning of some context-free languages with a minimally adequate teacher. In: Sempere, J.M., García, P. (eds.) ICGI 2010. LNCS (LNAI), vol. 6339, pp. 24–37. Springer, Heidelberg (2010). https://doi.org/10.1007/978-3-642-15488-1_4
3. Cui, W., Peinado, M., Chen, K., Wang, H.J., Irun-Briz, L.: Tupni: automatic reverse engineering of input formats. In: Proceedings of the 15th ACM Conference on Computer and Communications Security, CCS 2008, pp. 391–402. ACM, New York (2008). https://doi.org/10.1145/1455770.1455820
4. Czech, G., Moser, M., Pichler, J.: A systematic mapping study on best practices for domain-specific modeling. Softw. Qual. J. (2019). https://doi.org/10.1007/s11219-019-09466-1
5. Exler, M., Moser, M., Pichler, J., Fleck, G., Dorninger, B.: Grammatical inference from data exchange files: an experiment on engineering software. In: 2018 IEEE 25th International Conference on Software Analysis, Evolution and Reengineering (SANER), pp. 557–561, March 2018. https://doi.org/10.1109/SANER.2018.8330259

6. Fisher, K., Gruber, R.: Pads: a domain-specific language for processing ad hoc data. In: Proceedings of the 2005 ACM SIGPLAN Conference on Programming Language Design and Implementation, PLDI 2005, pp. 295–304. ACM, New York (2005). https://doi.org/10.1145/1065010.1065046
7. Kirchmayr, W., Moser, M., Nocke, L., Pichler, J., Tober, R.: Integration of static and dynamic code analysis for understanding legacy source code. In: 2016 IEEE International Conference on Software Maintenance and Evolution (ICSME), pp. 543–552, October 2016. https://doi.org/10.1109/ICSME.2016.70
8. Ko, A.J., et al.: The state of the art in end-user software engineering. ACM Comput. Surv. **43**(3), 21:1–21:44 (2011). https://doi.org/10.1145/1922649.1922658
9. Lämmel, R., Verhoef, C.: Semi-automatic grammar recovery. Softw. Pract. Exp. **31**(15), 1395–1448 (2001). https://doi.org/10.1002/spe.423
10. Lämmel, R., Zaytsev, V.: Recovering grammar relationships for the java language specification. CoRR abs/1008.4188 (2010). http://arxiv.org/abs/1008.4188
11. Leung, A., Lerner, S.: Parsimony: An IDE for example-guided synthesis of lexers and parsers. In: Proceedings of the 32nd IEEE/ACM International Conference on Automated Software Engineering, ASE 2017, pp. 815–825. IEEE Press, Piscataway (2017)
12. Lüder, A., Schmidt, N., Drath, R.: Standardized information exchange within production system engineering. In: Biffl, S., Lüder, A., Gerhard, D. (eds.) Multi-Disciplinary Engineering for Cyber-Physical Production Systems, pp. 235–257. Springer, Cham (2017). https://doi.org/10.1007/978-3-319-56345-9_10
13. Mernik, M., Heering, J., Sloane, A.M.: When and how to develop domain-specific languages. ACM Comput. Surv. **37**(4), 316–344 (2005). https://doi.org/10.1145/1118890.1118892
14. Zaytsev, V.: Mediawiki grammar recovery. CoRR abs/1107.4661 (2011). http://arxiv.org/abs/1107.4661

Containers in Software Development:
A Systematic Mapping Study

Mikael Koskinen[1]([⊠]) (iD), Tommi Mikkonen[2] (iD),
and Pekka Abrahamsson[1] (iD)

[1] Faculty of Information Technology, University of Jyväskylä,
Jyväskylä, Finland
mikael.koskinen@student.jyu.fi,
pekka.abrahamsson@jyu.fi
[2] Department of Computer Science, University of Helsinki, Helsinki, Finland
tommi.mikkonen@helsinki.fi

Abstract. Over the past decade, continuous software development has become a common place in the field of software engineering. Containers like Docker are a lightweight solution that developers can use to deploy and manage applications. Containers are used to build both component-based architectures and microservice architectures. Still, practitioners often view containers only as way to lower resource requirements compared to virtual machines. In this paper, we conducted a systematic mapping study to find information on what is known of how containers are used in software development. 56 primary studies were selected into this paper and they were categorized and mapped to identify the gaps in the current research. Based on the results containers are most often discussed in the context of cloud computing, performance and DevOps. We find that what is currently missing is more deeply focused research.

Keywords: Containers · Software engineering · Systematic mapping studies

1 Introduction

Over the past decade, continuous software development has become a common place in the field of software engineering. New toolchains have emerged to manage the complexity in continuous deployment activity. Containers are a lightweight solution that developers can use to deploy and manage applications [1]. Containers are often seen as a more light-weight alternative to Virtual Machines (VMs) [2]. Virtual Machines include the operating system where containers don't, allowing the containers to provide system resource usage advantages when compared against VMs [3].

The usefulness of containers is not limited to them being a more lightweight version of Virtual Machines. One interesting feature of the containers is that they provide portability [1] and thus modularity, making them suitable for working as software components [4] or as autonomous microservices [5]. When software systems grow, they encounter three problems:

© Springer Nature Switzerland AG 2019
X. Franch et al. (Eds.): PROFES 2019, LNCS 11915, pp. 176–191, 2019.
https://doi.org/10.1007/978-3-030-35333-9_13

1. Maintaining the software becomes harder
2. Adding new features to the system slows down
3. The resource requirements for the software grow

One option to address these problems is to make systems modular [6]. In modular systems software is split into smaller modules and the full software systems are built by combining different modules [7]. Component-based software architecture and microservice architecture allow developers to build more modular software [7, 8]. In component-based architecture systems are created by connecting different software components [9]. Components are required when the system is compiled, and they are loaded when the system starts. Because of this, component-based systems don't help with the growing resource requirements, but it makes maintaining the software easier.

Similar to components, microservices are autonomous services that together fulfill a business requirement [5]. Also, like component-based architecture, each microservice is required for the system to be fully functional. Since containers are not compiled as part of the software system, they could be used as way to build plug-in based architecture where containers-based plugins could provide new functionality into existing software and they could be added and removed runtime [10–12]. Based on our observation, containers are used to build both component-based architectures and microservice architectures [1, 5]. Still, containers are often viewed as way to lower resource requirements compared to Virtual Machines [3].

As using containers in software development is a new research area, the need for a systematic mapping study is crucial in order to summarize the progress so far and identify the gaps and requirements for future studies. In this paper we present a systematic mapping study of how containers are used in software development. In this research, we conducted a systematic mapping study to find information for the key question: What is currently known of **how containers are used in software development.** This paper is the first part of a larger study. The aim of this study is to learn if containers are used mainly as a lightweight replacement for the virtual machines or if their portability and low resource usage is used to build container-based software components. Next parts of this study will include a multi-vocal study [13] and a case-study [14].

The rest of this paper is structured as follows. Section 2 introduces the research methodology. Section 3 presents our key results. Section 4 provides discussion based on the results. Section 5 presents threats to validity of this research. Section 6 draws conclusions.

2 Research Methodology

Systematic Mapping Study (SMS) [15] is used in this paper to identify the gaps in the literature and identify where new or better primary studies are needed for using containers. This paper follows systematic mapping guidelines provided by [15–18].

The process of systematic mapping study can be split into multiple phases:

1. Defining the research questions
2. Conducting search

3. Study selection (Screening the papers)
4. Defining the classification scheme
5. Data extraction
6. Systematic mapping of the data using the classification scheme

The following Fig. 1 illustrates the process of this systematic mapping study:

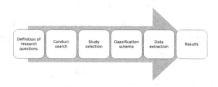

Fig. 1. Systematic mapping study process

The following sections are used to describe SMS from this study's perspective.

2.1 Definition of Research Questions

First task was the definition of research question (RQ). The research questions are listed in Table 1.

Table 1. Research questions

RQ number	Question	Motivation
RQ 1	How Containers are used in Software Development?	The question allows us to get the what is known of how containers are used in software development. What technologies are used and what software development problems are containers used to tackle
RQ 1.1	Are containers used to modularize software system, either through component-based architecture or through microservices architecture?	Based on our observation, containers could be used to architecture software systems. Still, the practitioners mostly seem to discuss containers as a technology for handling software's infrastructure
RQ 1.2	Are containers used to provide plugin-support for software systems?	Based on our observation, containers could be used to extend existing plugin-architecture based software systems

2.2 Conduct Search

After defining the research questions relevant search terms and data sources were defined.

Search Terms. Without correct search terms correct literature and research cannot be found. Table 2 lists the search terms used in this study. The following steps were used to create the search terms, as defined in [19]:

- Derive major terms from the questions by identifying the population, intervention and outcome.
- Identify alternative spellings and synonyms for major terms.
- Check the keywords in any relevant papers we already have.
- Use the Boolean OR to incorporate alternative spellings and synonyms.
- Use the Boolean AND to link the major terms from population, intervention, and outcome.

Table 2. Search terms

"container" OR "containers" OR "docker" OR "Kubernetes"
AND
"software engineering" OR "software design"

Data Sources and Search Criteria. For this research only formal data sources were considered. These included papers and journals from the four digital libraries: IEEEXplorer, ScienceDirect, SpringerLink and ACM Digital Library. The reason for selecting these sources is that they are important sources of computer science related research. Search terms were matched against title, keywords and abstract.

The search was performed between 22th of May and 5th of June in 2019. In total 3504 results were found. Results were exported into bibtex-format and loaded into reference manager (Table 3).

Table 3. Results before study selection process

Library	Results
IEEEXplorer	120
ScienceDirect	1095
SpringerLink	889
ACM Digital Library	1400

Study Selection. After finding the initial results, the next phase of the SMS was study selection. The main goal of the study selection is to find select relevant studies that properly address the research questions. As displayed in Table 4, in this study 5 inclusion criteria and 7 exclusion criteria were used.

Table 4. Study selection criteria

Inclusion criteria	Exclusion criteria
• Studies that are presented as full paper • Studies that focus on using modern containers in software development • Studies that compare containers and virtualization • Studies that are related to Docker • Studies that are related to Kubernetes	• Studies that are duplicate • Studies that are presented as short paper • Studies that do not provide abstract • Studies that are not peer-reviewed • Studies that are not written in English • Studies that are not related to the software engineering • Studies that are not related to modern Docker-style containers. For example, articles related to Java containers or Inversion of Control Containers

Of the 3504 results, 60 were removed as duplicates. Two-step selection process was used to filter out the irrelevant studies for this paper. First of each study the title was reviewed using inclusion and exclusion criteria. Each excluded study was marked as such. After this step, 3308 studies were filtered out and the second step was applied to the remaining 136 studies. In this step of each study abstract was skimmed through. In this second step, 80 studies were excluded.

In total, 56 studies [20–75] were selected as the primary studies of this paper.

Classification Schema. The selected primary studies and the research questions were used to create the classification scheme for this study. Based on a qualitative assessment, research classification approach from [76] was used to classify the papers. The classifications are listed in more detail in Table 5.

Table 5. Research type facet adapted from [76]

Research type	Description
Evaluation research	Type of paper which investigates a problem in practice
Solution proposal	A paper which presents a solution for a problem. Benefits of the solution are described
Validation research	Paper which investigates the properties of a solution that has not yet been implemented
Experience report	Paper based on work done in practice. Describes what and how something has been done personally by the author
Opinion	Paper based on the opinion of the author. Opinion articles do not rely on research methodology

Data Extraction. After using the primary studies and the research questions to create the classification schema, relevant data was extracted from the studies based on the classification schema. Title, author (first), year of publication, keywords, abstract and research type were extracted from each paper.

3   Results

In this section the results are presented found in this mapping study are presented. Of the initial amount of 3504 papers, 56 were selected as the primary papers for this study.

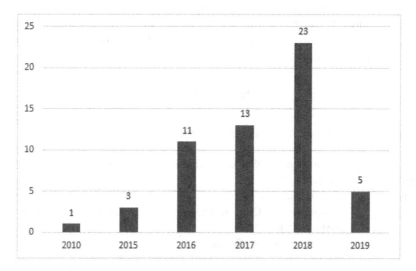

Fig. 2. Articles by year

Papers were mapped into the classification schema presented earlier in this study. The results presented in Fig. 3 of this mapping indicate that solution proposal is the most common paper when containers are discussed.

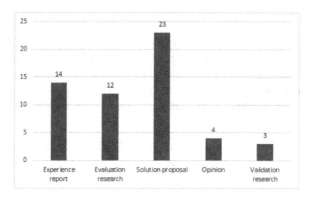

Fig. 3. Paper research types

Experience reports and evaluation research complete the top 3 of research types. Also, few validation research and opinion papers were found. Next, results are validated against the research questions.

3.1   RQ 1 How Are Containers Used in Software Development?

First research question was set to assess how containers are used in software development. The initial opinion of this study was that containers are often used as a lightweight alternative to virtual machines.

Keywords were extracted from each article's title and abstract. These keywords were then grouped together into different categories which were identified by generalizing the keywords. Table 6 presents the list of generalized categories. Each study belongs to one or more categories.

Table 6. Categories

Focus	Keywords
Software components	Modules, Packages, Artifacts, Bundle, Component
Cloud computing	Cloud, PaaS, SaaS, Cloud Infrastructure, Cloud environment, Cloud platforms
DevOps	DevOps, CI, CD
Performance	Scalability, I/O, CPU, Scaling, Replication, resources, GPU, Resource contention, performance
Security	Security, Password, Secure
Microservices	Microservice-architecture, Microservices, Micro-service
Legacy software	Modernization, Legacy
Orchestration	Orchestration, Docker Swarm, Kubernetes
Testing	Testing, Benchmark, Software Quality
IoT	IoT, Internet of Things
Plugin	Plugins, Addon, Extensions
Virtualization	Virtualization, Virtual Machine, VM

Based on the results, containers are most often discussed in relation to cloud computing, performance and devops (Fig. 4). More than 50% of the papers discussed containers in context of cloud computing. Performance related aspects and devops discussed in 45% of the papers. Most of the papers do not focus on a single category. Instead, only 13 papers belong to a single category as shown in Table 7.

Table 7. Number of categories and number of papers

# of categories	# of papers
2	14
3	14
1	13
4	8
6	4
5	3

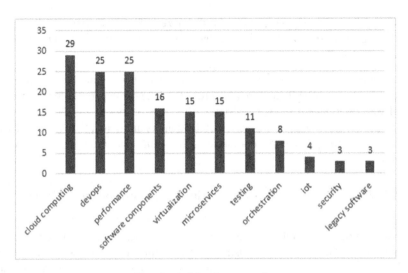

Fig. 4. Articles by categories

If we look at specific technologies (Fig. 5) and companies discussed in the papers, we can see that Docker dominates the field. More than 57% of articles mention Docker in their abstract or in their title.

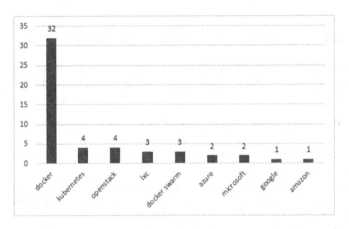

Fig. 5. Articles by container technology or organization

3.2   RQ 1.1 Are Containers Used to Modularize Software System, Either Through Component-Based Architecture or Through Microservices Architecture?

The motivation of the first sub research question was to find out if containers are discussed in relation of software architecture. 16 of the 56 papers discuss containers from software component's point of view. Also, microservices are discussed in 15 papers (Fig. 4). This clearly indicates that containers used to modularize software system, either through component-based architecture or through microservices architecture.

3.3   RQ 1.2 Are Containers Used to Provide Plugin-Support for Software Systems?

The motivation of the second sub research question was based on our observation that containers could be used to extend existing plugin-architecture based software systems. Even though 20% of the articles mentioned software components, we didn't find any indications that containers are used to create plugin-based software architecture.

4   Discussion

The implications of this systematic mapping study are described in the following sub sections.

4.1   Research in Using Containers in Software Development

Results indicate that the number of container related articles is growing (Fig. 2). 70% of the studies have been released between 2017 and 2019. There are multiple indicators that research on using containers in software development is a new research area:

1. First primary study found for this research is from 2010.
2. Number of research papers is rapidly growing.
3. Current research often covers multiple software development categories instead of focusing into a single category.
4. Research papers often start by describing what software containers are. This is an indication that the technology is seen as new by researchers and an introduction to the technology is required.
5. Most of the research focuses on a single container technology, Docker.

In summary it can be said that containers are a new research area. The amount of research has been growing steadily and there's no indication that in 2019 research related to containers is going to slow down (Fig. 6).

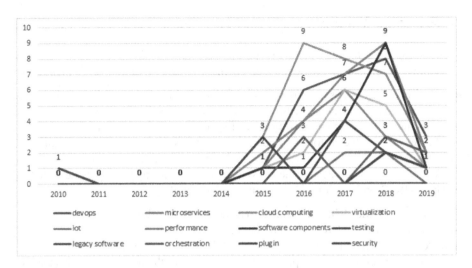

Fig. 6. Trends of using containers in software development

4.2   More Focused Research

Only 13 of the selected 56 primary studies focus their research on one category. 52% of the primary studies are related to three or more categories. It's clear that there is room for more focused research. Many of the categories are large topics and instead of research covering multiple large categories, research could focus on a single category like container security, container performance and using containers for devops.

4.3   Potential Research Avenues

As seen in Fig. 4, cloud computing, devops and performance related discussion are most common in current container research. There are multiple gaps or less-researched categories which provide potential research avenues:

- Container security
- Legacy applications and containers
- Container-based plugin technologies

Solution proposals, experience reports and evaluation research are currently the most popular research types. Together they make 88% of the primary studies selected for this research. This may indicate that containers are currently used to solve existing problems related to software development. The lack of validation research supports this as validation research could be used to test new ideas.

Figure 5 shows that Docker is the dominant technology used in research. Even though there are studies like [74] which compare Docker to other container tech-nologies, there's room for more research. Best practices-based papers are helpful for the industry: they help those organization who are already using containers and those who are just starting to use them. Only [35] provides best practices of using containers.

5 Threats to Validity

In this section the threats of validity of this research are discussed. Also selected mitigation strategies are discussed. Three potential threats of validity were identified:

Search. This study is based on the search results provided by research databases and their search engines. Because of this, the results are subject to the limitations of the search engines. We mitigated this by using four different research databases.

The keywords selected for this study are subject to search term bias. Two different container related technologies were named in the search terms and this may have affected search results, causing these two technologies to be more prevalent in the search results. Search term bias was mitigated by including generic search terms.

Identification of the Primary Studies. The selected inclusion and exclusion criteria listed in Table 4 may have affected the identification of the primary studies. For example, only papers written in English were selected. Also, not all the studies related to containers in software development are available from the used research databases. Risk of excluding primary studies was mitigated by using multiple research databases.

Data Extraction. Categories in chapter 7 were selected by the researcher after keywords were extracted. Researcher acknowledges that if there are errors in keyword extraction, this may invalidate the categorization of the keywords. To mitigate the keyword extraction and categorization, keywords were extracted multiple times and the selected categories were identified only after keyword extraction.

6 Conclusion

This paper is a part of larger study. The aim of the study is to learn if containers are used mainly as a lightweight replacement for the virtual machines or if their portability and low resource usage is used to build container-based software components. In this paper a systematic mapping was performed to examine what is known of how containers are used in software development. The next part of this research is a multi-vocal study. The research will conclude with a case study.

Four research databases were used to locate 3504 papers of which 56 were selected as the primary studies. The results indicate that cloud computing, devops and performance are the driving forces of container related discussion. Of the 56 primary studies 52% discussed cloud computing, 48% performance and 45% devops. Docker is currently the leading technology in container-based software development. 57% of the papers mentioned Docker in their title or in their abstract. Other container related technologies were mentioned at most in 7% of the papers.

As an answer to RQ 1.1, 55% of the primary studies mentioned software components or microservices. This clearly indicates that containers are used to modularize software system, either through component-based architecture or through microservices architecture. As the examination of RQ 1.2 indicated, no papers discussing the usage of containers for plugin-based architectures were found.

The findings of this paper indicate that using containers in software development is a new research area. Most of the studies don't focus on a single software development category. Instead, they often present introduction on what containers are, clearly indicating that software containers are seen as a new technology. Also, best practices-based research is not yet widely available.

References

1. Paraiso, F., Challita, S., Al-Dhuraibi, Y., et al.: Model-driven management of docker containers, pp. 718–725. IEEE (2016)
2. Dua, R., Raja, A.R., Kakadia, D.: Virtualization vs Containerization to support PaaS, pp. 610–614. IEEE Computer Society, Washington, DC (2014)
3. Hoenisch, P., Weber, I., Schulte, S., Zhu, L., Fekete, A.: Four-fold auto-scaling on a contemporary deployment platform using docker containers. In: Barros, A., Grigori, D., Narendra, N.C., Dam, H.K. (eds.) ICSOC 2015. LNCS, vol. 9435, pp. 316–323. Springer, Heidelberg (2015). https://doi.org/10.1007/978-3-662-48616-0_20
4. Lau, K.-K., Wang, Z.: Software Component Models. TSE **33**(10), 709–724 (2007). https://doi.org/10.1109/TSE.2007.70726
5. Jaramillo, D., Nguyen, D.V., Smart, R.: Leveraging microservices architecture by using Docker technology, pp. 1–5. IEEE (2016)
6. Woodfield, S.N., Dunsmore, H.E., Shen, V.Y.: The effect of modularization and comments on program comprehension, pp. 215–223. IEEE Press, Piscataway (1981)
7. Card, D.N., Page, G.T., McGarry, F.E.: Criteria for software modularization, pp. 372–377. IEEE Computer Society Press, Los Alamitos (1985)
8. Völter, M.: Pluggable component – a pattern for interactive system configuration
9. Crnkovic, I.: Component-based software engineering? New challenges in software development (2003)
10. Birsan, D.: On plug-ins and extensible architectures. Queue **3**(2), 40–46 (2005). https://doi.org/10.1145/1053331.1053345
11. Mayer, J., Melzer, I., Schweiggert, F.: Lightweight plug-in-based application development. In: Aksit, M., Mezini, M., Unland, R. (eds.) NODe 2002. LNCS, vol. 2591, pp. 87–102. Springer, Heidelberg (2003). https://doi.org/10.1007/3-540-36557-5_9
12. Marquardt, K.: Patterns for Plug-Ins. In: EuroPLoP (1999)
13. Garousi, V., Felderer, M., Mäntylä, M.V.: Guidelines for including grey literature and conducting multivocal literature reviews in software engineering. Inf. Softw. Technol. **106**, 101–121 (2019). https://doi.org/10.1016/j.infsof.2018.09.006
14. Eisenhardt, K.: Building theory from case study research. Acad. Manag. Rev. **14**, 532–550 (1989). https://doi.org/10.2307/258557
15. Petersen, K., Feldt, R., Mujtaba, S., et al.: Systematic mapping studies in software engineering, pp. 68–77. BCS Learning & Development Ltd., Swindon (2008)
16. Kitchenham, B.: Guidelines for performing systematic literature reviews in software engineering. EBSE Technical report EBSE-2007-01 (2007)
17. Kitchenham, B., Charters, S.: Systematic reviews (2009). https://www.york.ac.uk/crd/guidance/
18. Kitchenham, B., Brereton, P.: Using mapping studies in software engineering. Inf. Softw. Technol. **55**(12), 2049–2075 (2013). https://doi.org/10.1016/j.infsof.2013.07.010

19. Kitchenham, B.A., Mendes, E., Travassos, G.H.: Cross versus within-company cost estimation studies: a systematic review. TSE **33**(5), 316–329 (2007). https://doi.org/10.1109/TSE.2007.1001
20. Stillwell, M., Coutinho, J.G.F.: A DevOps approach to integration of software components in an EU research project. In: Proceedings of the 1st International Workshop on Quality-Aware DevOps, pp. 1–6. ACM, New York (2015)
21. Tuo, F., Bai, Y., Long, S., et al.: A new model of docker-based E-learning in Hadoop. In: Proceedings of the 2018 International Conference on Distance Education and Learning - ICDEL 2018, pp. 22–31. ACM Press, New York (2018)
22. Kozhirbayev, Z., Sinnott, R.O.: A performance comparison of container-based technologies for the cloud. Future Gener. Comput. Syst. **68**, 175–182 (2017). https://doi.org/10.1016/j.future.2016.08.025
23. Telschig, K., Schonberger, A., Knapp, A.: A real-time container architecture for dependable distributed embedded applications. In: 2018 IEEE 14th International Conference on Automation Science and Engineering (CASE), pp. 1367–1374. IEEE (2018)
24. Syed, M.H., Fernandez, E.B.: A reference architecture for the container ecosystem. In: Proceedings of the 13th International Conference on Availability, Reliability and Security, pp. 1–6. ACM, New York (2018)
25. Rahman, M., Chen, Z., Gao, J.: A service framework for parallel test execution on a developer's local development workstation. In: Proceedings - 9th IEEE International Symposium on Service-Oriented System Engineering, IEEE SOSE 2015, vol. 30, pp. 153–160 (2015)
26. Kratzke, N.: About the complexity to transfer cloud applications at runtime and how container platforms can contribute? In: Ferguson, D., Muñoz, V.M., Cardoso, J., Helfert, M., Pahl, C. (eds.) CLOSER 2017. CCIS, vol. 864, pp. 19–45. Springer, Cham (2018). https://doi.org/10.1007/978-3-319-94959-8_2
27. Song, M., Zhang, C., Haihong, E.: An auto scaling system for API gateway based on Kubernetes. In: 2018 IEEE 9th International Conference on Software Engineering and Service Science (ICSESS), pp. 109–112 (2018)
28. Cito, J., Schermann, G., Wittern, J.E., et al.: An empirical analysis of the docker container ecosystem on GitHub. In: IEEE International Working Conference on Mining Software Repositories, pp. 323–333. IEEE Press, Piscataway (2017)
29. Zhang, Y., Yin, G., Wang, T., et al.: An insight into the impact of dockerfile evolutionary trajectories on quality and latency. In: 2018 IEEE 42nd Annual Computer Software and Applications Conference (COMPSAC), vol. 1, pp. 138–143. IEEE (2018)
30. Naughton, T., Sorrillo, L., Simpson, A., Imam, N.: Balancing performance and portability with containers in HPC: an OpenSHMEM example. In: Gorentla Venkata, M., Imam, N., Pophale, S. (eds.) OpenSHMEM 2017. LNCS, vol. 10679, pp. 130–142. Springer, Cham (2018). https://doi.org/10.1007/978-3-319-73814-7_9
31. Naik, N.: Building a virtual system of systems using docker swarm in multiple clouds. In: ISSE 2016 - 2016 International Symposium on Systems Engineering - Proceedings Papers, pp. 1–3 (2016)
32. Shah, J., Dubaria, D.: Building modern clouds: using Docker, Kubernetes & Google cloud platform. In: 2019 IEEE 9th Annual Computing and Communication Workshop and Conference (CCWC), p. 184. IEEE (2019)
33. Klinaku, F., Frank, M., Becker, S.: CAUS: an elasticity controller for a containerized microservice. In: Companion of the 2018 ACM/SPEC International Conference on Performance Engineering, pp. 93–98. ACM, New York (2018)

34. Kehrer, S., Riebandt, F., Blochinger, W.: Container-based module isolation for cloud services. In: 2019 IEEE International Conference on Service-Oriented System Engineering (SOSE), pp. 177–186 (2019)

35. Berger, C., Nguyen, B., Benderius, O.: Containerized development and microservices for self-driving vehicles: experiences & best practices. In: Proceedings - 2017 IEEE International Conference on Software Architecture Workshops, ICSAW 2017: Side Track Proceedings, pp. 7–12 (2017)

36. Sharma, P., Chaufournier, L., Shenoy, P., et al.: Containers and virtual machines at scale: a comparative study. In: Proceedings of the 17th International Middleware Conference, pp. 1–13. ACM, New York (2016)

37. Révész, Á., Pataki, N.: Continuous A/B testing in containers. In: Proceedings of the 2019 2nd International Conference on Geoinformatics and Data Analysis - ICGDA 2019, pp. 11–14. ACM, New York (2009)

38. Barna, C., Khazaei, H., Fokaefs, M., et al.: Delivering elastic containerized cloud applications to enable DevOps. In: Proceedings of the 12th International Symposium on Software Engineering for Adaptive and Self-Managing Systems, pp. 65–75. IEEE Press, Piscataway (2017)

39. Bahadori, K., Vardanega, T.: DevOps meets dynamic orchestration. In: Bruel, J.-M., Mazzara, M., Meyer, B. (eds.) DEVOPS 2018. LNCS, vol. 11350, pp. 142–154. Springer, Cham (2019). https://doi.org/10.1007/978-3-030-06019-0_11

40. Dhakate, S., Godbole, A.: Distributed cloud monitoring using Docker as next generation container virtualization technology. In: 2015 Annual IEEE India Conference (INDICON), pp. 1–5 (2015)

41. Naik, N.: Docker container-based big data processing system in multiple clouds for everyone. In: 2017 IEEE International Symposium on Systems Engineering, ISSE 2017 - Proceedings, pp. 1–7 (2017)

42. Martin, A., Raponi, S., Combe, T., et al.: Docker ecosystem – vulnerability analysis. Comput. Commun. 122, 30–43 (2018). https://doi.org/10.1016/j.comcom.2018.03.011

43. Nardelli, M., Hochreiner, C., Schulte, S.: Elastic provisioning of virtual machines for container deployment. In: Proceedings of the 8th ACM/SPEC on International Conference on Performance Engineering Companion, pp. 5–10. ACM, New York (2017)

44. Fokaefs, M., Barna, C., Veleda, R., et al.: Enabling DevOps for containerized data-intensive applications: an exploratory study. In: Proceedings of the 26th Annual International Conference on Computer Science and Software Engineering, pp. 138–148. IBM Corp, Riverton (2016)

45. Santos, E.A., McLean, C., Solinas, C., et al.: How does docker affect energy consumption? Evaluating workloads in and out of Docker containers. J. Syst. Softw. 146, 14–25 (2018). https://doi.org/10.1016/j.jss.2018.07.077

46. Zhu, H., Bayley, I.: If Docker is the answer, what is the question?. In: 2018 IEEE Symposium on Service-Oriented System Engineering (SOSE), pp. 152–163. IEEE (2018)

47. Casalicchio, E., Perciballi, V.: Measuring Docker performance: what a mess!!!. In: Proceedings of the 8th ACM/SPEC on International Conference on Performance Engineering Companion, pp. 11–16. ACM, New York (2017)

48. Guo, D., Wang, W., Zeng, G., et al.: Microservices architecture based cloudware deployment platform for service computing. In: Proceedings - 2016 IEEE Symposium on Service-Oriented System Engineering, SOSE 2016, pp. 358–364 (2016)

49. Shadija, D., Rezai, M., Hill, R.: Microservices: granularity vs. performance. In: Companion Proceedings of the 10th International Conference on Utility and Cloud Computing, pp. 215–220. ACM, New York (2017)

50. Naik, N.: Migrating from virtualization to dockerization in the cloud: simulation and evaluation of distributed systems. In: Proceedings - 2016 IEEE 10th International Symposium on the Maintenance and Evolution of Service-Oriented and Cloud-Based Environments, MESOCA 2016, pp. 1–8 (2016)

51. Balalaie, A., Heydarnoori, A., Jamshidi, P.: Migrating to cloud-native architectures using microservices: an experience report. In: Leitner, P. (ed.) Advances in Service-Oriented and Cloud Computing. CCIS, vol. 567, pp. 201–215. Springer, Cham (2016). https://doi.org/10.1007/978-3-319-33313-7_15

52. Xu, T., Marinov, D.: Mining container image repositories for software configuration and beyond. In: Proceedings of the 40th International Conference on Software Engineering: New Ideas and Emerging Results, pp. 49–52. ACM, New York (2018)

53. Ferrer, A.J., Pérez, D.G., González, R.S.: Multi-cloud platform-as-a-service model, functionalities and approaches. Procedia Comput. Sci. **97**, 63–72 (2016)

54. Zhang, Y., Vasilescu, B., Wang, H., et al.: One size does not fit all: an empirical study of containerized continuous deployment workflows. In: Proceedings of the 2018 26th ACM Joint Meeting on European Software Engineering Conference and Symposium on the Foundations of Software Engineering, pp. 295–306. ACM, New York (2018)

55. Yarygina, T., Bagge, A.H.: Overcoming security challenges in microservice architectures. In: 2018 IEEE Symposium on Service-Oriented System Engineering (SOSE), pp. 11–20. IEEE (2018)

56. Lv, K., Zhao, Z., Rao, R., et al.: PCCTE: a portable component conformance test environment based on container cloud for avionics software development. In: 2016 International Conference on Progress in Informatics and Computing (PIC), pp. 664–668 (2016)

57. Wang, B., Song, Y., Cui, X., et al.: Performance comparison between hypervisor- and container-based virtualizations for cloud users. In: 2017 4th International Conference on Systems and Informatics (ICSAI), pp. 684–689. IEEE (2017)

58. Heinrich, R., van Hoorn, A., Knoche, H., et al.: Performance engineering for microservices: research challenges and directions. In: Proceedings of the 8th ACM/SPEC on International Conference on Performance Engineering Companion, pp. 223–226. ACM, New York (2017)

59. Jindal, A., Podolskiy, V., Gerndt, M.: Performance modeling for cloud microservice applications. In: Proceedings of the 2019 ACM/SPEC International Conference on Performance Engineering, pp. 25–32. ACM, New York (2019)

60. Siami Namin, A., Sridharan, M., Tomar, P.: Predicting multi-core performance: a case study using solaris containers. In: Proceedings of the 3rd International Workshop on Multicore Software Engineering, pp. 18–25. ACM, New York (2010)

61. Hassan, F., Rodriguez, R., Wang, X.: RUDSEA: recommending updates of dockerfiles via software environment analysis. In: Proceedings of the 33rd ACM/IEEE International Conference on Automated Software Engineering, pp. 796–801. ACM, New York (2018)

62. Gogouvitis, S.V., Mueller, H., Premnadh, S., et al.: Seamless computing in industrial systems using container orchestration. Future Gener. Comput. Syst. (2018). https://doi.org/10.1016/j.future.2018.07.033

63. Goldschmidt, T., Hauck-Stattelmann, S.: Software containers for industrial control. In: Proceedings - 42nd Euromicro Conference on Software Engineering and Advanced Applications, SEAA 2016, pp. 258–265 (2016)

64. Yin, K., Chen, W., Zhou, J., et al.: STAR: a specialized tagging approach for Docker repositories. In: 2018 25th Asia-Pacific Software Engineering Conference (APSEC), pp. 426–435. IEEE (2018)

65. Benni, B., Mosser, S., Collet, P., et al.: Supporting micro-services deployment in a safer way: a static analysis and automated rewriting approach. In: Proceedings of the 33rd Annual ACM Symposium on Applied Computing, pp. 1706–1715. ACM, New York (2018)
66. Ye, F., Jing, Z., Huang, Q., et al.: The research of a lightweight distributed crawling system. In: 2018 IEEE 16th International Conference on Software Engineering Research, Management and Applications (SERA), pp. 200–204. IEEE (2018)
67. Oh, J., Kim, S., Kim, Y.: Toward an adaptive fair GPU sharing scheme in container-based clusters. In: 2018 IEEE 3rd International Workshops on Foundations and Applications of Self* Systems (FAS*W), pp. 79–85 (2018)
68. López, M.R., Spillner, J.: Towards quantifiable boundaries for elastic horizontal scaling of microservices. In: Companion Proceedings of the 10th International Conference on Utility and Cloud Computing, pp. 35–40. ACM, New York (2017)
69. Morris, D., Voutsinas, S., Hambly, N.C., et al.: Use of Docker for deployment and testing of astronomy software. Astron. Comput. **20**, 105–119 (2017). https://doi.org/10.1016/j.ascom. 2017.07.004
70. Punjabi, R., Bajaj, R.: User stories to user reality: a DevOps approach for the cloud. In: 2016 IEEE International Conference on Recent Trends in Electronics, Information Communication Technology (RTEICT), pp. 658–662 (2016)
71. Senington, R., Pataki, B., Wang, X.V.: Using Docker for factory system software management: experience report. Procedia CIRP **72**, 659–664 (2018). https://doi.org/10.1016/j.procir.2018.03.173
72. Knoche, H., Eichelberger, H.: Using the Raspberry Pi and Docker for replicable performance experiments: experience paper. In: Proceedings of the 2018 ACM/SPEC International Conference on Performance Engineering, pp. 305–316. ACM, New York (2018)
73. Morabito, R.: Virtualization on internet of things edge devices with container technologies: a performance evaluation. IEEE Access **5**, 8835–8850 (2017). https://doi.org/10.1109/ACCESS.2017.2704444
74. Tesfatsion, S.K., Klein, C., Tordsson, J.: Virtualization techniques compared: performance, resource, and power usage overheads in clouds. In: Proceedings of the 2018 ACM/SPEC International Conference on Performance Engineering, pp. 145–156. ACM, New York (2018)
75. Ueda, T., Nakaike, T., Ohara, M.: Workload characterization for microservices. In: 2016 IEEE International Symposium on Workload Characterization (IISWC), pp. 1–10. IEEE (2016)
76. Wieringa, R., Maiden, N., Mead, N., et al.: Requirements engineering paper classification and evaluation criteria: a proposal and a discussion. Requir. Eng. **11**(1), 102–107 (2005)

Technical Debt

Empirical Analysis of Hidden Technical Debt Patterns in Machine Learning Software

Mohannad Alahdab[1,2]([✉]) and Gül Çalıklı[3]([✉])

[1] Chalmers University of Technology, Gothenburg, Sweden
mohannad@student.chalmers.se
[2] Cybercom Group, Gothenburg, Sweden
[3] Chalmers | University of Gothenburg, Gothenburg, Sweden
gul.calikli@gu.se

Abstract. [**Context/Background**] Machine Learning (ML) software has special ability for increasing technical debt due to ML-specific issues besides having all the problems of regular code. The term "Hidden Technical Debt" (HTD) was coined by Sculley et al. to address maintainability issues in ML software as an analogy to technical debt in traditional software. [**Goal**] The aim of this paper is to empirically analyse how HTD patterns emerge during the early development phase of ML software, namely the prototyping phase. [**Method**] Therefore, we conducted a case study with subject systems as ML models planned to be integrated into the software system owned by Västtrafik, the public transportation agency in the west area of Sweden. [**Results**] During our case study, we could detect HTD patterns, which have the potential to emerge in ML prototypes, except for "Legacy Features", "Correlated features", and "Plain Old Data Type Smell". [**Conclusion**] Preliminary results indicate that emergence of significant amount of HTD patterns can occur during prototyping phase. However, generalizability of our results require analyses of further ML systems from various domains.

Keywords: Machine learning · Software maintainability · Hidden Technical Debt

1 Introduction

Machine Learning (ML) applications have become integral part of software products including recommender systems (e.g., Netflix [2], LinkedIn [3]) and speech recognition systems (e.g., Apple Siri). Social media platforms such as Facebook develop ML applications for ranking posts in the news feed, speech recognition, text translation as well as real-time photo and video classification [4]. Since ML algorithms are not only being implemented in research labs, it has become obvious that it is not enough only to focus on prediction performance while developing ML software [5].

© Springer Nature Switzerland AG 2019
X. Franch et al. (Eds.): PROFES 2019, LNCS 11915, pp. 195–202, 2019.
https://doi.org/10.1007/978-3-030-35333-9_14

Since ML software also follows a lifecycle as traditional software does, the emergence of ML software, also brings maintainability challenges. Maintainability of traditional software products is still a challenge, and technical debt is an obstacle in the way of maintainability. However, existing practices, tools, and techniques to tackle technical debt are not adequate to overcome the challenges of ML software maintenance. This is due to the fact that implementation of ML algorithms is quite different compared to how traditional software is implemented. Traditional software mostly consists of a set of commands that are implemented by the developer so that the computer can follow and execute these instructions. On the other hand, ML systems learn what to do from data input to ML algorithms. ML allows the developer to work fast and the results can be delivered quickly, but in the long run, it becomes a challenge to maintain ML software. Sculley et al. [1] coined the term "Hidden Technical Debt" (HTD) to address challenges in the maintainability of ML software as an analogy to the concept of technical debt in traditional software. If those HTD patterns are detected in later stages of ML software development, it might be quite costly and infeasible to remove them in order to ensure maintainability. Therefore, early detection of HTD patterns in ML software systems is crucial.

The purpose of this paper is to empirically analyse HTD patterns during prototyping phase. Empirical analysis of HTD patterns in ML prototypes provides information to develop methods to detect and remove them. Therefore, we conducted a case study with subject systems being ML prototypes for empty parking lots prediction to be integrated into the system owned by Västtrafik. In the framework proposed by Sculley et al. [1] there are also HTD patterns that emerge in the final deployed ML system. However, in this paper, we focus on HTD patterns with the potential to emerge during prototyping phase (Throughout the paper, we call such HTD patterns "prototype-level HTD patterns). To summarize, this paper aims to answer the following research question:

RQ1: Which (prototype level) HTD patterns emerge during prototyping phase?

During the case study, we were able to detect all prototype-level HTD patterns except for "Legacy Features", "Correlated Features", and "Plain Old Data Type Smell". Our results indicate that majority of these HTD patterns can emerge even in less complex ML models that are built with small data size and number of features.

As model complexity, number of features and data size increases, emergence of these HTD prototypes become more likely, making maintainability issues in ML software products inevitable. Therefore, detection of these HTD patterns as early as possible in ML software development lifecycle (i.e., prototyping stage) is crucial. However, our case study was conducted for a specific case. Therefore, our results are preliminary and need to be supplemented by analyses of further ML systems as well as conducting workshops and interviews with practitioners.

The rest of the paper is organised as follows: Sect. 2 mentions related work. Research methodology is described in Sect. 3 and obtained results are explained in Sect. 4. Finally, Sect. 5 concludes and mentions future work.

2   Related Work

As a result of the experience gained through development and deployment of online advertising systems, D. Sculley and his colleagues at Google came up with "Hidden Technical Debt" (HTD) framework [1], to address maintainability issues of ML software. Definition of the HTD patterns that are the focus of this paper can be found in our online repository[1] and also in the original paper by Sculley et al. [1]. Referring to HTD patterns identified by Sculley et al. [1], Agarwal et al. [6] proposed a solution to reduce "direct feedback loops", which is a HTD pattern that often occurs when the deployed ML software might bias users' feedback to the software itself. This in turn, directly affects the selection of users' data for future training of that ML software [1]. The solution proposed by the authors is a complete loop for effective contextual learning consisting of the phases of deployment, exploring, logging and learning.

Breck et al. [7] indicate that testing and monitoring are crucial in order to detect and reduce HTD patterns. In order to quantify production readiness of ML systems and reduce HTD, authors present an ML Test Score rubric based on a set of actionable tests. There is also emerging research in testing Deep Learning (DL) systems reducing "prediction bias", which is a HTD pattern emerging due to behavioural changes in data. One such study is generating test cases based on a proposed a metric (i.e., Surprise Adequacy metric) that measures the distance between the behaviour of the DL model for a test input and behaviour of that model for inputs that belong to the training set [8].

3   Methodology

During the case study, we analysed prototype-level HTD patterns in ML models that were developed for Västtrafik in order to predict empty parking lots. ML models were already developed by the first author approximately two months before this research study was initiated. Moreover, while developing ML models, he did not have any knowledge about HTD patterns or how they affect ML software maintainability. The first author has 8 years of experience in software development and he is employed by Cybercom Group, an IT consultancy company. Västtrafik had outsourced the development of empty parking lot prediction prototypes to Cybercom Group. The prototypes will later be turned into production code to be deployed as integral part of Västtrafik applications.

Data analysed during this case study consists of artefacts such as ML models developed, source codes written to pre-process input data and the input data itself that is used to train and test ML models. Training/testing data contains about 6 million events that took place between years 2014–2017. Time difference between consecutive events is 15 min, and each event corresponds to a line in the dataset that is represented by a set of features values. Information about the features is given in Table 1. In order to make the features selection effective, the first author organized the features into feature sets. For instance, features

---

[1] https://github.com/gulcalikli/ProfesShortPaper.

"Weather Temperature" and "Weather Situation" both belong to set A, while features "Day after holiday" and "Day before holiday" belong to set G. Also, day and time for each event are separate features and belong to the feature set H. Each of the remaining features are assigned to a separate feature set.

Table 1. List features used in development of ML prototypes

Set	Feature name	Range	Categorical
A	Weather Temperature	[−15,30]	No
	Weather Situation	[1,30]	Yes
B	Day type	[0,1,2,3]	Yes
C	% of free spaces during previous day	[0,100]	No
D	% of free spaces during previous week	[0,100]	No
E	% of free spaces during previous 2 weeks	[0,100]	No
F	% of free spaces during the last 12 h	[0,100]	No
G	Day after holiday	[0,1]	Yes
	Day before holiday	[0,1]	Yes
H	Day name for each event	Monday..Friday]	Yes
	Time for each event	[00:00 .. 23:59]	Yes

In order to develop ML models, the first author employed boosted decision tree regression, and forest decision regression, which are among the best performing algorithms for empty parking lot prediction [9] . Sequential Forward Selection (SFS) feature selection technique was used adding one more feature set at a time, and this resulted in 16 prototypes, in total. Data corresponding to years 2014–2016 and year 2017 were used for training and testing models, respectively. Prediction performance of each prototype is shown in Table 2. In order to develop prototypes of the ML software, as ML framework, the first author used Microsoft Azure Machine Learning, which is a cloud-based service for predictive analytics. During the case study, we also used the same ML framework, in order to develop extra ML models to investigate existence of some HTD patterns. In the near future, few ML intensive systems will implement ML algorithms from scratch. Instead, for such systems training will take place in the cloud using main API and libraries. Most companies do not have enough human resources with skills required to design and implement ML algorithms. Therefore, there is a need to provide developers with APIs that allow them to embed ML functionalities into software applications. Moreover, ML systems in the cloud are cheap to operate in terms of hardware and software. Hence, using a service such as Microsoft Azure Machine Learning rather than implementing the ML algorithms from scratch is a feature in the design and implementation of this case study.

Table 2. Prediction performance results for ML models developed by employing two different regression algorithms with SFS feature selection technique (MAE: Mean Absolute Error; RMSE: Root Mean Square Error; R^2: Coefficient of Determination)

Features set	Boosted decision tree			Decision forest		
	MAE	RMSE	R^2	MAE	RMSE	R^2
A	27.80	37.60	−0.090	27.90	40.57	−0.270
A,B	25.50	35.20	0.004	26.60	38.60	−0.150
A,B,C	11.70	20.20	0.680	15.10	24.20	0.550
A,B,C,D	9.67	16.50	0.780	10.45	17.27	0.770
A,B,C,D,E	9.89	16.40	0.790	9.70	16.21	0.800
A,B,C,D,E,F	9.40	15.90	0.800	10.35	17.17	0.770
A,B,C,D,E,F,G	8.89	15.20	0.820	9.23	15.60	0.810
A,B,C,D,E,F,G,H	6.38	11.38	0.900	6.23	12.05	0.880

4   Preliminary Results

This section aims to answer RQ1 by explaining HTD patterns that are discovered in the ML models we developed, together with the data analysis techniques we employed to discover those HTD patterns. Table 2 shows prediction results for the ML models that are trained by incrementing number of features one feature set at a time according to Sequential Forward Selection (SFS) feature selection technique [10] for both boosted decision tree regression and decision forest regression algorithms.

We observed **entanglement** in the ML models we developed in the form of addition and removal of features leading to changes in models' prediction performance. As it can be seen from Table 2, adding features B, C, D and F results in a significant increase in prediction performance. Similarly, removing features A, E, G, and H also improves prediction performance. We also developed extra ML models using only features B, C, D and F resulting in a prediction performance of $RMSE = 14.4$, $R^2 = 0.84$ and $RMSE = 13.08$, $R^2 = 0.88$ for decision forest and boosted decision tree regression algortihms, respectively. Hence, using only features B, C, D and F as input features would be enough and adding the remaining features is complicating the model without any significant contribution to the prediction performance. Since the feature bundle consisting of E, G, and H had no significant effect on the accuracy performance value or the error percentages, they are **bundled features**. Moreover, feature A, and each of the features in the bundled features E, G and H are individually ϵ−**features**. We could not observe any **legacy** or **correlated features**. Figure 1 shows ML prototyping by using all features for "Boosted Decision Tree Regression" and "Decision Forest Regression" algorithms. In Fig. 1, only "Boosted Decision Tree Regression" and "Decision Forest Regression" are ML-related modules. Remaining modules, which are marked in Fig. 1, (e.g., Python script, modules to retrieve data from database and to split data into training/test sets) are all **glue code**.

Moreover, all modules make up a **pipeline jungle** (i.e., output of one module is an input to other module(s).). In Fig. 1, there are modules branching out from the module "Edit Metadata" that are marked in the figure by enclosing them with a dotted rectangular frame. This group of modules correspond to the experimentation to develop ML models with all features sets. Although not shown in Fig. 1, there were similar groups of modules branching out from the "Edit Metadata" module. Each of these groups of modules, which correspond to one of the experimentations whose result is listed in Table 2, were the **dead experimental code paths** and they were pruned from the experimentation set resulting in the pipeline jungle shown in Fig. 1.

Regarding **abstraction debt**, going through the documentations we could not come across to any design level abstraction making "feature engineering", "model definition" and "model training and evaluation" self-contained stages. On the contrary, these stages are quite coupled such that decision made in one stage affects the others. For this reason, it requires knowledge and expertise about the inner-workings of these stages. As mentioned in Sect. 3, first author had to consult an ML expert for the creation of features using domain knowledge of data and deciding on ML algorithms to be used with iterations of trial and error.

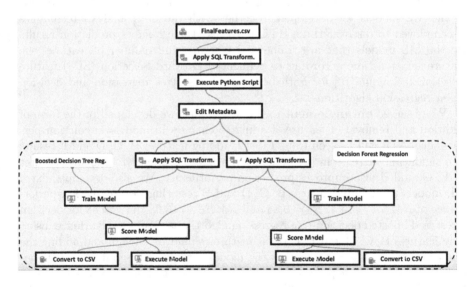

Fig. 1. ML model developed using all features resulting in pipeline jungles, and glue code in the ML model

We could not observe **plain old data type** HTD pattern, since Azure ML Studio has a drag and drop user interface and it does not allow the user to access the source code for ML algorithms. Therefore, we cannot state whether this HTD pattern exists in our prototypes or not. On the other hand, we were able to detect **multiple language smell**, since while building ML models, three programming languages were used, which are SQL, Python, and R. Multilanguage use is usually inevitable during software development. However, multilanguage use without assessment of project's language needs is not an ideal SE practice. While developing the ML prototypes analysed in the case study, first author had not made any assessment of language needs based on required functionalities taking into account the whole software system. However, Västtrafik applications are implemented in Java and JavaScript. Hence, this might lead to difficulties in the integration testing of final software system, unless this HTD pattern is reduced during production stage before deployment of ML software. During prototype development, first author tuned hyperparameters to improve prediction performance. However, this did not result in any improvement, but led to **configuration debt**.

In order to investigate emergence of **prediction bias** in subject systems of case study, we developed extra ML models in two iterations. First, we trained and tested models using datasets belonging to years 2014 and 2015, respectively. Later, models were trained and tested using datasets belonging to years 2014–2015 and 2016, respectively. We compared prediction performance of these models with the corresponding subject systems (i.e., models trained and tested with data belonging to years 2014–2016 and 2017, respectively). As training dataset size increases covering events that belong to a longer time period, Root Mean Square Error (RMSE) decreases from 12.55 to 10.48, then increases to 11.25, for the ML model developed using all features and employing boosted decision tree regression algorithm. Similarly, RMSE decreases from 13.26 to 10.95 and then increases to 12.05 when forest decision regression algorithm is employed. Increase in RMSE as training data size covers a longer time period is due to change in the data behaviour over time. **Data testing debt** was observed in the data used to train and test ML models. For instance, data contained entries with total number of empty places exceeding parking capacity. In order to detect such irregularities and remove noise from data, we converted empty parking count into percentages and set 100% as the maximum value. Also, we implemented an initial data statistics to investigate the data behaviour before starting actual data pre-processing and developing ML models. Understanding the concept of HTD, investigating patterns in ML models and realising how HTD patterns affect maintainability of resulting ML software, required time, effort and thorough discussions among authors.. It was challenging to link the effects of decisions made to develop ML algorithms on the resulting ML software that is to be deployed. Since ML models were developed by a single person, we could observe **cultural debt** up to some extent. Observation of cultural debt requires analysis of communication and interaction among members of teams consisting of ML experts, software/systems engineers working on the development of ML software.

5   Conclusions and Future Work

In order to explore the emergence of HTD patterns in ML prototypes, we conducted a case study. During our case study, we examined HTD patterns in ML models that were developed to predict empty parking lots for Västtrafik. We were able to detect all prototype-level HTD patterns except for plain old data type smell, and legacy and correlated features. Our preliminary results indicate that significant amount of HTD patterns can emerge during prototyping phase even in less complex ML models that are trained using small data size and number of features. In commercial ML applications, data size and number of features used for training purposes can get quite large, and ML algorithms employed can be quite complex (e.g., deep learning) making them more prone to emergence of HTD patterns. Therefore, removal/management of HTD patterns as early as possible in Software Development Life Cycle (SDLC) is crucial in order to improve ML software maintainability. As future work, firstly we would like to analyze additional ML software prototypes from various domains. We also would like to run workshops and interviews with practitioners to share our findings and get their feedback. In the long run, we will also conduct further case studies to investigate propagation of HTD patterns to further phases of SDLC as well as investigating their existence in deployed ML software.

References

1. Sculley, D., et al.: Hidden technical debt in machine learning systems. In: Proceedings of NIPS 2015, pp. 2503–2511. MIT Press, Montreal (2015)
2. Gomez-Uribe, C.A., Hunt, N.: The netflix recommender system: algorithms, business value, and innovation. ACM Trans. Manag. Inf. Syst. **6**(4), 13:1–13:19 (2016)
3. Kenthapadi, K., Le, B., Venkataraman, G.: Personalized job recommendation system at LinkedIn: practical challenges and lessons learned. In: Proceedings of 11th ACM Conference on Recommender Systems, Como, Italy, pp. 346–347 (2017)
4. Hazelwood, K., et al.: Applied machine learning at facebook: a datacenter infrastructure perspective. In: IEEE International Symposium on High Performance Computer Architecture Proceedings, pp. 620–629, Vienna, Austria (2018)
5. Martinez-Plumed, F., et al.: Accounting for the neglected dimensions of AI progress (2018). https://arxiv.org/abs/1806.00610
6. Agarwal, A., et al.: Making contextual decisions with low technical debt (2017). https://arxiv.org/abs/1806
7. Breck, E., Cai, S., Nielsen, E., Salib, M., Sculley, D.: The ML test score: a rubric for ML production readiness and technical debt reduction. In: BigData 2018, pp. 1123–1133. IEEE, Boston (2017)
8. Kim, J., Feldt, R., Yoo, S.: Guiding deep learning testing using surprise adequacy. In: ICSE 2019, pp. 303–314. IEEE, Montreal (2019)
9. Balzer, P.: Prediction of car park occupancy. http://mechlab-engineering.de/2015/03/vorhersage-derparkhausbelegung-mit-offenen-daten/. Accessed May 2019
10. Liu, H., Motoda, H.: Feature Selection for Knowledge Discovery and Data Mining. Springer, New York (1998). https://doi.org/10.1007/978-1-4615-5689-3

Constraining the Implementation Through Architectural Security Rules: An Expert Study

Stefanie Jasser[✉]

University of Hamburg, 22527 Hamburg, Germany
`jasser@informatik.uni-hamburg.de`

Abstract. Today, security is still considered to late in the process of software engineering. Architectural rules for security can support software architects and developers in consciously taking security into account during design and implementation phase. They allow to monitor a software system's security level. As a step towards monitoring and controlling the erosion of an architecture's security specifications we present a set of rules derived from well-known security building blocks such as patterns along with our identification process. Through these rules we aim to support architects in monitoring the implementation's conformance with security measures and, hence, in building secure software systems. The architectural security rules we identified are evaluated through expert interviews with industrial software engineers.

Keywords: Software architecture · Security by design · Secure architecture · Security constraints · Architectural constraints · Architecture erosion · Architecture violations

1 Introduction

Developing a secure software system is a very challenging task. However, software architects and developers usually are not well-educated in designing and implementing a software system with respect to security. Instead they often have only superficial knowledge about software security.

Most authors only consider two types of weaknesses in software systems:: security (design) flaws and security (implementation) bugs [1,18]. *Security design flaws* are caused on the architecture level. They often have wide impact on a system: security design flaws do not necessarily break security mechanisms but allow attackers to bypass security mechanisms. It is challenging to identify and remedy security design flaws by reason of their wide impact [29]. According to [5] avoiding security flaws significantly reduces the number and impact of successful attacks. In contrast, *security bugs* are weaknesses that are caused at the source code level. These weaknesses are easier to identify and refactor as their impact is restricted locally.

© Springer Nature Switzerland AG 2019
X. Franch et al. (Eds.): PROFES 2019, LNCS 11915, pp. 203–219, 2019.
https://doi.org/10.1007/978-3-030-35333-9_15

The authors who only consider security design flaws and security bugs assume that a secure architecture is implemented correctly, i.e. no flaw-like weaknesses but only security bugs are introduced during implementation phase. However, experience shows that the implementation usually diverges from the intended architecture. The specified architecture reflects the software architect's intention: we call it the "intended architecture" or "should-be architecture". It comprises the architect's decisions on security measures. These measures comprise rules that constrain the software system's implementation, i.e. software developers must follow them in order to avoid vulnerabilities. Hence, we consider violations of architectural security measures as a separate software weakness category. Violations may have a comparably wide impact on the system and may be identified as difficultly as security design flaws. To specify these architectural security rules explicitly would complement the architectural model.

Intended Contributions. In this paper, we give insight on architectural security measures and their impact on the implementation. The architectural security rules we found can be provided in a public catalogue. The rules contribute towards methods for security enforcement and, hence, systematic development of secure software systems.

We also enable architects to expand the rule set by adapting rules or specifying additional rules using the process we describe in Sect. 2. This process encapsulates best practices and questions that we gathered during our analysis.

Additionally, we conducted semi-structured expert interviews to assess architectural rules in general and in detail as well as the identification process we used. We further asked the participants about the idea of a public rule catalogue. Besides evaluation of our architectural security rules, the interview results we present in Sect. 4 contribute to the knowledge on the state of practice.

1.1 Background

Architectural security rules help develop secure software systems. They constrain the implementation, build security awareness and guide developers in writing secure code that actually adheres to the architecture's security measures.

Architecture-Centric Security Analysis of Software. The field of architectural security rules and security conformance checking is related to architecture-centric security analysis techniques. On the architecture level threat modelling is the most commonly used security analysis technique. The analysis is done manually mostly [32]. Besides the well-known STRIDE [17] there are others such as the approach proposed by Berger et al. [6], a tool-supported architectural risk analysis. Another well-known security modelling and analysis approach is UMLsec [20]. Despite it can be used on the architecture level, UMLsec is not explicitly designed for it. This often leads to highly complex specifications.

Security Testing. Architectural security rules are related to security testing approaches as they are a step ahead towards security conformance checking. However, architectural security rules are high-level constraints affecting the implementation. They allow for hybrid enforcement of security principles by preventive and reactive measures.

Dynamic security conformance analysis is similar to some security testing approaches. Though, in difference to testing conformance analysis is not limited to dynamic analysis and a small number of executions: Hybrid approaches allow to combine the advantages of static and dynamic analysis.

2 Identifying Common Architectural Security Rules

A software architecture defines architectural rules that constrain the software system's implementation. This definition may be implicit or explicit. Architectural rules are well known in order to improve a systems maintainability. Most of these rules are dependency rules like "*The Data Layer must not access the Application Layer.*" in a 3-Tier architecture.

A software architecture should comprise fundamental security measures such as authentication and authorization concepts which affect the whole system. These measures define architectural security rules. Architectural security rules are hardly considered in software engineering, today.

An important goal of this paper is to identify common architectural rules for security. As such common rules are hardly known today, we need to determine suitable sources of knowledge to derive such rules from. We use these sources of knowledge to identify architectural security rules, subsequently.

Database. Sources of common architectural security rules may be diverse: such rules may be derived from existing software systems, libraries, frameworks, best practices and other sources of knowledge. As architectural security rules are rarely specified today, existing software system's are inappropriate to start with. Additionally, rules derived from a limited number of existing software systems may not be valid in general but are system-specific. Unlike specific software architectures, security best practices such as architecture tactics and patterns are specified for reusability: They encapsulate security expert's knowledge and proven security solutions. We analysed architecture patterns and tactics to identify popular security rules that are valid for multiple software systems.

To complement the sources we analysed frequent security design flaws [5]. Security design flaws are fundamental security defects that have wide impact and cause weaknesses in multiple parts of a software system. We identify architectural security rules that aim to avoid the introduction of weaknesses. Prohibition rules facilitate the adherence to software security principles.

Identification Process. During our analysis we iteratively found questions that frequently helped identifying architectural security rules. We grouped these questions based on the aspects of a knowledge source they focus on[1].

---

[1] All guiding questions are available as supplementary material: https:// github.com/Granasteja/Supplementary/blob/master/PROFES-2019/2019-PROFES_Study_Supplementary_A.pdf.

Questions 1–4 are of a *general nature*. They help to identify involved architectural elements, dependencies and assumptions made by a security design pattern or flaw.

The second group of questions focus on *authentication and authorization* mechanisms. These rules are important as the identity and rights of entities form a basis for most software security functionality. Most of the analysed building blocks specify some assumptions on the authentication and authorization mechanisms they rely on: they specify at least the time when the authentication or authorization must be validated. However, some sources did not mention authentication or authorization functionality neither implicitly nor explicitly.

The questions 7–9 deal with the system's *control flow*. Control flow divergences are of particular importance as they may indicate abnormal or at least unplanned system behaviour.

The fourth group of questions examine the system's *information flow*. They investigate sensitive or untrustworthy information handled in a knowledge source. Such information could be user input, personal or mission critical such as confidential supplier contract conditions, product concepts or salary information

The guiding questions often lead to relevant architectural security rules. Hence, software architects should pay particular attention to the subjects, the rules put into focus. Architectural security rules support software engineers in developing a secure system. However, it is important to specify rules on what must not happen or exist in addition to what may or must happen or exist.

The provided questions help software architects to identify additional architectural security rules that they want to enforce, e.g. project-specific rules. Sources for project-specific architectural security rules usually are an organization's security policy, industry guidelines or requirement specification documents that deal with security requirements.

Assert Architectural Relevance. Architectural security rules ensure that the software architecture is correctly implemented. However, architects should concentrate on security rules that actually are architecturally relevant: If architecture-level security rules are mixed up with code-level security rules, the overall number of rules may overcharge software engineers. To identify architecturally relevant rules, we use the work of Eden and Kazman [9]: Eden and Kazman present two criteria to distinguish between the *architecture* and *implementation* level. The first criterion deals with a specification's *intension/extension*. According to the authors, an intensional specification has "infinitely-many possible instances". All other specifications are extensional. For instance, the rule "No SecurityLogEntry can be updated or deleted after it has-been stored" based on the sandbox design pattern is intensional. In contrast, the specification "The class MailController must not implement cryptographic algorithms itself" is extensional. The second criterion deals with a specification's *non-locality/locality*. A *non-local* specification potentially affects all or at least several parts of a system. Formally, a specification ϕ is local if the fact that ϕ is satisfied in some design model m implies that it is satisfied by every design model that subsumes m. Architecture-level specifications are both, intensional and non-local. Specifications on the implementation-level are extensional and local. Consequently, architects should apply the following two questions to all rules identified before:

– Does the rule have a local or a non-local impact?
– Does the rule have an intensional or extensional specification?

3   A Catalogue of Architectural Security Rules

Using the guiding questions we analysed security design patterns and security design flaws. Overall we derived more about 150 common architectural security rules. Table 1 presents a selected subset of these architectural security rules.

Most architectural rules used in the context of maintainability today are dependency rules. For security, we also found other rule types such as *Rule 1* which describes the expected system behaviour using temporal relations and *Rule 2* which constrains the information flow. Behavioural rules are important for security purposes as they describe how the system shall operate and react to events.

In order to provide the common architectural security rules for multiple software architects we designed a public catalogue. This catalogue supports software engineers in implementing their software system securely. It may also help to improve software engineer's awareness for software security and security measures.

In [12] the Authors present the DecisionBuddy: this tool supports software architects in making decisions during software development. We plan to extend this tool with our catalogue.

We plan to integrate both functionalities: we enable software architects to describe projects including all decisions regarding a software system. For each decision, related common architectural security rules are provided by the tool. For instance, if an architect decides to introduce a logging library the tool suggests to apply rules on secure logging behaviour to the project: for instance, log files should not include sensitive data such as implementation details. Other rules are proposed for all systems as every system should adhere to them. Many of these rules are based on security design principles or security design flaws.

Categorizing Architectural Security Rules. As a catalogue contains several solutions by nature we need to assist software architects in finding appropriate ones. Rules should be related to their sources: e.g. the rules 8 and 9 should be related to the checkpoint pattern: when an architect decides to apply this pattern to a project, he is supported with relevant architectural security rules to monitor the implementation. Ideally, the catalogue provides an API or at least a download function for the related rules.

However, we also analysed sources that are applied implicitly to a project: e.g. security design flaws such as "Authorize after you authenticate" [18]. As software systems should adhere to these common rules, too, we need additional categorization.

Table 1. Examples of common architectural security rules.

No.	Architectural security rule
1	Every exception must be sanitized before it is returned to the client
2	A sanitized Exception message must not include sensitive business information or implementation details
3	The validity of successful authentication is limited, i.e. there has to be a timeout in case the user does not actively log off
4	The user never accesses the session object
5	Every component must log all security-relevant events
6	Every security-relevant log message must be secured
7	A user can only see operations that he/she is authorized for. (limited access strategy)
8	There is at least one checkpoint initialised for both tasks: authentication and authorization
9	Every Checkpoint must provide a validation interface
10	Directly after a successful authentication, the user's authorization is validated
11	Every outbound message is sent from a central point of the system
12	Every outbound message is intercepted before it is sent
13	Messages must not be logged in debug- or info-mode in an operational environment
14	The system must not provide functionality to decrypt secured log messages
15	No common building blocks are used that have known security issues (level "critical" or "high")
16	Building blocks must not send outbound messages (e.g. to the producer)
17	Before a sensitive datum crosses a trust boundary the datums permission and the initiators rights are validated
18	All sensitive data is encrypted before storing it
19	No two instances of a microservice is deployed on the same (physical or logical) machine
20	Every validation mechanism should be based on a whitelisting approach. It may be tightened using a blacklisting approach afterwards
21	The control flow must not start within the sandbox
22	No user can have conflicting rights

During our analysis we found that architectural rules for security can be structural as well as behavioural or related to a system's data flow. These attributes build another categorization for our rules.

4   Evaluation

To evaluate our architectural security rules' relevance and usability in practice we conducted some semi-structured interviews. We further used the interviews to assess practicability of our process of finding architectural security rules.

4.1   Study Design

Participant Selection. As we aimed to receive constructive feedback only experienced software developers and software architects were interviewed. The experience in software architecture and development ranged from for 3 years up to more than 25 years. Today, all of them work in Germany, however they are multinationally software engineers with software development experience from diverse countries such as the US, Brazil, Argentina, UK, Austria. Most interviewees work in agile mode with their project teams that have 3–150 team members overall. Table 2 gives an overview of all participants.

Table 2. Interview participants and their characteristics.

#	Domain	Role(s)	Experience	Team size
A*	Enterprise	Software engineer	5–10 years	15–25
B	Logistics/enterprise	Software engineer	5–10 years	15–25
C*	Consultant/enterprise	Software architect	15–20 years	10–15
D	Banking/enterprise	Software architect	5–10 years	5–10
E	Logistics/enterprise	Software architect	5–10 years	25–50
F	Insurance/enterprise	Software engineer	<5 years	<5
G*	Enterprise	Software architect	5–10 years	10–15
H	Enterprise	Software architect	5–10 years	100–150
I	Consultant/enterprise	Software engineer	>25 years	5–10
J*	Enterprise	Software architect	10–15 years	10–15
K*	Consultant/enterprise	Software architect	>25 years	50–75
L	Consultant/enterprise	Software engineer	5–10 years	15–25

*Is a software security expert (e.g. software engineering consultant with a focus on security)

Interview Guide and Process. We used an interview guide that helped us in focussing on the relevant issues[2]. The interview guide comprised four parts: First, we investigated the participant's background and experience. We used this information to identify potential relations of answers to used technologies,

---

[2] https://github.com/Granasteja/Supplementary/blob/master/PROFES-2019/2019-PROFES_Study_Supplementary_B.pdf.

company sizes or domains. The second part deals with the examination of architectural security rules in practice as well as the assessment of the common rules we identified. The third part was about the identification process. It is asked, if it was adequate and if it may support software architects to identify project specific rules. The last part assess the idea of a public catalogue that provides architectural security rules. It mainly examines, if a catalogue would be helpful in general and what features the participants need or appreciate for such a catalogue. For this part, we use a paper prototype to get more detailed feedback. To ensure the interview guide's understandability it was tested twice.

All interviews took 1 to 2 h. The interviews were conducted either per phone, Skype or personally. We recorded them to focus on the interview.

Data Analysis. We qualitatively analysed the transcribed interviews using open coding. Such codes usually are short phrases or single words that summarize an issue in a essence-capturing way [30]. To allow reusing the codes, we generalized them after finishing the first transcript. E.g. the statements *"[architectural security] rules make it easier to implement security functionality correctly"* (Participant D) and "[architectural security rules] reduce the gap between architecture design and implementation" (Participant A) both correspond to the open code `abstraction gap`.

4.2   Study Results

Architectural Security Rules in General. We evaluated architectural security rules separately from the catalogue idea: we aimed to examine the industrial use of such rules today as well as the utility of the rules we found before. To assess the rules' utility we presented 37 architectural security rules during the interview. The rules were selected with a view to exemplify different rule types.

Nine out of twelve participants do not consider security before testing phase. Six of them report, that they *"do no security testing or analysis [of their software systems] at all"* (Participant I) except testing the authorization policy implementation. Thus, they do not consider security during software architecture design and found it *"challenging to think about security rules"* (Participant F) that could be specified for their software systems without examples. Nevertheless, all participants would appreciate an improvement of this state of industrial practice: common architectural security rules encapsulate security expert's knowledge and *"reduce the gap between architecture design and implementation."* This helps software architects and engineers in implementing a secure software system. In terms of this objective, flaw-based rules are of particular interest because they hold true for most systems (Participants A, C, D, E, G, H, K). The respondents agree with the effect of improved security awareness that is achieved by explicitly specifying architectural security rules (Participants A–K).

The participants A, D, E, G–L (9 out of 12) mentioned lack of resources to cover the high effort needed when enforce architectural security rules manually: security reviews should be conducted by software security experts for reliability reasons. However, such experts are rare and expensive today. The participants favour a tool-supported solution that indicates potential violations and, thus, narrows the manual review scope. This would further improve the effort/benefit ratio of architectural security rules: "*By identifying potential violations of architectural security rules a [conformance checking] tool can reduce the manual workload as the review may be restricted to these violations.*" (Participant G) As violations diverge from designed security measures they are potential vulnerabilities. The participants A, B, D, H, J, K consider it essential to find such violations as they "*may cause fundamental vulnerabilities*" (Participant J).

The respondents further agreed that they consider a major initial effort reasonable. However, only A, G and J indicated maximum values between 3 and 5 days for setup. However, the maintenance of the architectural security rules should be efficient (Participants B–E, I).

During the interview, the participants mentioned a number of potential impediments to the use of architectural security rules. The following list contains impediments that were stated by at least two participants:

- Intensity of labour for manual security reviews (Participant A, D, E, G–L)
- Lack of security skills may impede the identification and definition of relevant architectural security rules (Participant A, B, D, F, I)
- Insufficient security requirements specification (e.g. vague or incomplete) (Participant D, E, G, K)
- Abstract rules are hard to apply to a concrete software project (Participant C, G, J, K)

4.3   Finding Architectural Security Rules

The second issue we assessed in our interviews is the process we used to identify architectural security rules.

First, the participants were asked about the used sources of architectural security rules. The participants stated the common security building blocks, security design flaws and principles "*reasonable as there is a lack of well specified security measures in most software architectures today. [...] patterns provide good solutions for recurring security problems*" (Participant K). All participants agreed on this.

Eight out of twelve called the questions in principle "*appropriate to guide [software architects] in identifying further architectural security rules*" (Participant D, analogously participants A, B, C, F, H, I, K). This particularly holds true for inexperienced software architects as the question groups' subjects support them in focussing on frequent security issues. They consider the instruction to explicitly search for the absence of structures, data or behaviour in addition to structures, data or behaviour that must or can occur particularly helpful (Participants B, E, I). However, all participants considered project-specific architectural security rules rare: most of them expected project-specific refinement or customization more probable (e.g. defining system specifically sensitive data or trust levels) (Participants C, D, E, G, H, J, K). Besides this, they found the questions useful to extend and supplement the set of common architectural security rules we identified (e.g. by analysing additional sources of security rules).

Five participants have a lot of experience in software security from several projects (e.g. as consultants or specialists, see Table 2). Some of them suggested to add another question regarding the malicious or risky events that may occur (Participants J, K).

The Catalogue of Architectural Security Rules. We used rapid prototyping to assess the benefit of a catalogue of common architectural security rules. Ten out of twelve participants consider the catalogue helpful. Yet, they refer to the assessment of architectural rules in general (see above). The catalogue idea *"would benefit from a [conformance checking] tool"* (Participant A), that can directly access the catalogue: it could search for appropriate architectural security rules and download them from the catalogue. The rules then can be used to conduct a conformance check.

We provided some filter options based on the rules' categorization. Most participants called them supportive They were considered useful be most participants when searching for relevant architectural security rules for their projects. The participants D, I and L suggested to add additional information on the rule context (e.g. privacy, authentication and authorization etc.) or related threats (e.g. using the STRIDE categories).

5   Discussion and Future Work

5.1   Findings on Architectural Security Rules

We found many common architectural security rules that can be applied to multiple software systems. They are common as they origin from well-tried security building blocks such as security tactics and patterns and further common security knowledge sources like security design flaws. We assess the latter more important as they indicate violations of fundamental security principles. Rules derived from security design flaws affect most software systems.

We derived three types of architectural security rules: structural, behavioural and data-flow related rules. Through further analysis and the interviews we conducted we found that rules on the system's security relevant behaviour are particularly important to enforce a secure system. This is due to the vulnerability of insecure system behaviour which can be observed and exploited. In contrast, structural violations may indicate wrong system behaviour but their security impact is more ambiguous.

The interviewees verified that there is still a lack of security knowledge and awareness in industrial daily software engineering routine today. This applies in particular to architecture decisions and measures for security and their enforcement. According to the participants architectural security rules may help to close this abstraction gap: they increase the software architects' and developers' security awareness.

We presented a subset of our architectural security rules to the interviewed industrial experts. They called the rules sensible and useful for security software systems. Participants B, D, E, F, H, I, L mentioned, that the rules give them hints on security-relevant aspects on the architecture and the code level they should pay attention to: *"I did not consider log messages from the security perspective yet as they are protected through access control. However, I got some remarks from these rules which information should be secured in log messages and what can be done to do that"* (Participant B).

A catalogue supports architects in handling architectural security rules by providing search functionality to identify rules that apply for a projects current architecture (e. g. using information on architectural decisions made available from the DecisionBuddy [12]).

5.2   Towards Monitoring Architectural Security Measures

Today, the rule enforcement is done manually, i. e. by security code reviews. Due to high effort, we complement our rules with a tool-supported conformance checking approach. It supports architects in enforcing their intended security measures and provides valuable feedback to software developers in the early software development in case the approach is integrated in the daily work.

Formalizing Architectural Rules. To realize tool-support, we extended the CNL approach of Schröder et al. [33] with language support for temporal relations (extended CNL, eCNL) [19]. The CNL and, hence, the eCNL is designed for comprehensibility, expressiveness and flexibility of the architecture concept and rule specification. We use this eCNL to formally specify the architectural security rules. Temporal relations are needed to define the behavioural rules we identified above: e.g. 3 (see Table 1) could be described as: For each security session that is valid at a time t_n there will be a future state t_m $(m > n)$ in which the session will be expired. Using the eCNL this rule could be specified as follows:

> Every *SecuritySession* that (is-valid at the *Time* t_n) must be a
> *SecuritySession* that (is-invalid in the future).

As another example the following eCNL rule represents rule no. 18 formally:
> Every *SensitiveData* must be encrypted before it is stored.

Identifying Violations. We use a dynamic analysis approach to gather information on the system's actual security architecture: This approach records the system's actual security-related behaviour. A knowledge database is build from this information. Subsequently, we query this knowledge base for violations of architectural security rules. To enable such queries for rule violation, we need to map the extracted information on the actual implementation to the architectural security rule's concepts. Today, this mapping is done implicitly by the dynamic data extractor or knowledge base builder, respectively.

Currently, we refine our dynamic analysis approach by adding hybrid analysis techniques and analyzing additional source artefacts. Using hybrid analysis techniques enables a more focussed use of overhead causing dynamic analysis, e.g. by limitation to suspicious objects or system parts. Complementary static analysis further allows to identify worst case scenarios by considering all potential execution paths. In the wake of this, we aim to improve the architecture-to-code-mapping, i.e. the mapping of the intended security architecture that is represented by our rules and architecture concepts to the actual security architecture that is represented by the knowledge base.

Controlling Security Erosion. Following the well-known concept "architecture erosion" as in [16, 27] we term a system's total violations of architectural security rules "security erosion". This security erosion should not only be monitored but also controlled. Controlling security erosion comprises two general measures: first, to fix violations of the architectural security rules subsequently to an analysis regarding their actual security impact. Second, appropriate measures should be taken to avoid growing security erosion. In the future, we will intensify our work on an systematic approach for remedy vulnerabilities and improve a system's security level.

Threats to Validity. For the evaluation of qualitative research methods well-established criteria exist, e.g. dependability, transferability and confirmability [11]. There are different ways to address these criteria: confirmability may be addressed by gathering feedback on research results. We did this by discussing our architectural security rules, the identification process and the catalogue idea with industrial experts. We addressed the dependability/auditability by making our process clear. Like most qualitative studies, our evaluation has a limited sample. We argue that this is acceptable as we aimed to gather feedback from experienced software engineers. To improve transferability, we interviewed industrial experts from different domains and companies.

Yet, the interviews may have been biased by the architectural security rules that we pre-selected for evaluation. We respond to this by consciously choosing different types of architectural security rules. Furthermore, we designed the questionnaire and supplementary material with two researchers and we conducted a trial interview with another software engineer.

In case of the catalogue idea, usability issues may have prejudiced the interviewee's opinions. We addressed this by using paper prototypes: such prototypes help users to concentrate on functional aspects and overlook minor usability issues.

6   Related Work

Architectural Rules. Architectural rules are well-established in the context of software maintainability, today [1,8,10,13,37]. Mostly, they define dependencies between components that are either allowed or prohibited. Help monitoring the conformance of a system's implementation to common design principles like Modularity, Separation of Concerns and Information Hiding. However, such architectural rules do not constrain a system's behaviour, state or data flow.

In [34] the authors interviewed industrial software architects in order to identify new architectural rules that are relevant to the participants and are different to the usual dependency rules. Schröder et al. mainly asked for maintainability rules and did not find security rules.

Behavioural rules are considered rarely in existing research: Rapide [21] is an early approach that allows to constrain dependency rules considering the precise circumstances of an interaction through operational invariants. The authors defined some security related rules [22]. However, the rules are not architectural rules due to the intension and non-locality criteria. Despite most rules defined by Caracciolo are structural, he also defined some behaviour related rules [8]. Yet, the few security related rules mentioned in that work are extensional and, hence, not architectural. Abi-Antoun and Barnes specified some code-level and architecture-level rules for security in [2]. However, the authors only define structural rules based on component-connector concepts, e.g.: "KeyManager should not connect to Engine Wrapper." Few rules that are related to information flow are hard coded based on the STRIDE approach proposed in [17].

Architecture Conformance. Most conformance checking approaches are static and only consider structural dependency rules [26]. They use reflexion models [25], source code query languages (e.g. .QL [24]), structure matrices [31] and design tests [7]. Behavioural conformance checking is done rarely today.

In [1] the SECORIA approach is proposed. It allows to anticipate the structural runtime architecture through static analysis and manual code instrumentation. Conformance checks are performed on this predicted structure. The authors do not consider explicit architectural rules: Instead they compare the implementation's runtime structure to a high-level architecture diagram. In [3] the authors extend the reflexion models for tool-supported threat analysis based on the STRIDE approach. However, the threat analysis does not validate the implementation's adherence to the security measures taken in the design.

Mirakhorli et al. propose an approach to identify architecturally relevant source code using information retrieval and architectural tactics [23]. The authors use this technique to inform software engineers when they modify this code.

Sources for Architectural Security Rules. Security building blocks provide good security solutions to software engineers that are no security experts. Architecture tactics and patterns are well-known kinds of building blocks. Multiple sources for security patterns exist today, common sources are [14,15,28,35,36,38, 39]. Other papers review existing patterns, e.g. [4]. In addition to these building blocks there are other types such as reference architectures that describe security best practices, too (e.g. [22]).

However, there are further rules for architectural security rules. Examples are common security design flaws such as [5], i.e. frequently introduced weaknesses on the design level. They may be seen as building blocks in a broader sense.

7 Conclusion

We have provided common architectural security rules in this paper. Such common rules can be applied to most software systems and help to enforce security measures taken for these systems. The process we used for rule identification was iteratively improved during our work. This process is described in Sect. 2. We further proposed and evaluated the idea of a catalogue of architectural security rules to make them available to the public. Although, we already developed a first conformance checking approach, we concentrate on the use and practicability of common architecture security rules in this paper.

Through the conducted interviews we found that common architectural security rules would help architects to enforce and monitor security measures they took. Hence, they facilitate a secure software system. According to the experts, a catalogue would provide further support to the architects as many of them have only superficial knowledge on software security. Through the interviews we verified that architectural security rules may also increase software architect's and developers' awareness for security in the early phases of software development. The architectural security rules reduce the abstraction gap between the architectural level measures and their code level implementation.

In the future we will increase the benefit of architectural security rules by extending our work on security conformance checking including the extended CNL approach. We will extend it to a hybrid conformance checking to combine the advantages of static and dynamic analysis. Additionally, we work on a systematic approach to secure systems that violate security measures or principles.

References

1. Abi-Antoun, M.: Static extraction and conformance checking of the runtime architecture of object-oriented systems. In: Harris, G.E. (ed.) Companion to the 23rd ACM SIGPLAN Conference on Object-Oriented Programming Systems Languages and Applications, p. 911. ACM, New York (2008). https://doi.org/10.1145/1449814.1449904
2. Abi-Antoun, M., Barnes, J.M.: Analyzing security architectures. In: Pecheur, C., Andrews, J., Di Nitto, E. (eds.) 25th IEEE/ACM International Conference on Automated Software Engineering, pp. 3–12. ACM (2010). https://doi.org/10.1145/1858996.1859001
3. Abi-Antoun, M., Wang, D., Torr, P.: Checking threat modeling data flow diagrams for implementation conformance and security. In: Stirewalt, K., Egyed, A., Fischer, B. (eds.) Proceedings of the 22nd IEEE/ACM International Conference on Automated Software Engineering: ASE, pp. 393–396. IEEE Computer Society and ACM, New York and Los Alamitos (2007). https://doi.org/10.1145/1321631.1321692
4. Anand, P., Ryoo, J., Kazman, R.: Vulnerability-based security pattern categorization in search of missing patterns. In: 2014 Ninth International Conference on Availability, Reliability and Security, pp. 476–483. IEEE (2014). https://doi.org/10.1109/ARES.2014.71
5. Arce, I., et al.: Avoiding the top 10 software security design flaws (2014). https://www.computer.org/cms/CYBSI/docs/Top-10-Flaws.pdf
6. Berger, B.J., Sohr, K., Koschke, R.: Automatically extracting threats from extended data flow diagrams. In: Caballero, J., Bodden, E., Athanasopoulos, E. (eds.) ESSoS 2016. LNCS, vol. 9639, pp. 56–71. Springer, Cham (2016). https://doi.org/10.1007/978-3-319-30806-7_4

7. Brunet, J., Serey, D., Figueiredo, J.: Structural conformance checking with design tests: an evaluation of usability and scalability. In: 2011 27th IEEE International Conference on Software Maintenance (ICSM), pp. 143–152. IEEE, Piscataway (2011). https://doi.org/10.1109/ICSM.2011.6080781

8. Caracciolo, A.: A unified approach to architecture conformance checking. Dissertation, Universität Bern, Bern, März 2016. http://scg.unibe.ch/archive/phd/caracciolo-phd.pdf

9. Eden, A.H., Kazman, R.: Architecture, design, implementation. In: Proceedings of the 25th International Conference on Software Engineering, ICSE 2003, pp. 149–159. IEEE Computer Society, Washington, DC (2003). http://dl.acm.org/citation.cfm?id=776816.776835

10. Eichberg, M., Kloppenburg, S., Klose, K., Mezini, M.: Defining and continuous checking of structural program dependencies. In: Schäfer, W. (ed.) Companion of the 30th International Conference on Software Engineering, p. 391. ACM, New York (2008). https://doi.org/10.1145/1368088.1368142

11. Gasson, S.: Rigor in grounded theory research. In: Whitman, M., Woszczynski, A. (eds.) The Handbook of Information Systems Research, pp. 79–102. IGI Global (2004). https://doi.org/10.4018/978-1-59140-144-5.ch006

12. Gerdes, S., Soliman, M., Riebisch, M.: Decision buddy: tool support for constraint-based design decisions during system evolution. In: Proceedings of the 1st International Workshop on Future of Software Architecture Design Assistants: FoSADA, pp. 13–18. ACM Association for Computing Machinery (2015). https://doi.org/10.1145/1924421.1924451

13. Gurgel, A., et al.: Blending and reusing rules for architectural degradation prevention. In: Binder, W., Peternier, A., Ernst, E., Hirschfeld, R. (eds.) MODULARITY 2014, pp. 61–72. ACM Association for Computing Machinery, New York (2014). https://doi.org/10.1145/2577080.2577087

14. Hafiz, M.: Security pattern catalog (2016). http://www.munawarhafiz.com/securitypatterncatalog/

15. Heyman, T., Yskout, K., Scandariato, R., Joosen, W.: An analysis of the security patterns landscape. In: 2007 Third International Workshop on Software Engineering for Secure Systems, pp. 3–9. IEEE, Piscataway (2007). https://doi.org/10.1109/SESS.2007.4

16. Hochstein, L., Lindvall, M.: Combating architectural degeneration: a survey. Inf. Softw. Technol. **47**(10), 643–656 (2005). https://doi.org/10.1016/j.infsof.2004.11.005

17. Howard, M., Lipner, S.: The security development lifecycle: SDL, a process for developing demonstrably more secure software. Microsoft Secure Software Development Series, Microsoft Press, Redmond, Washington (2006). http://site.ebrary.com/lib/alltitles/docDetail.action?docID=10762138

18. Jackson Higgins, K.: 10 common software security design flaws.pdf (2014). http://www.darkreading.com/application-security/10-common-software-security-design-flaws/d/d-id/1306776

19. Jasser, S.: Security conformance checking for the detection of vulnerabilities. In: Proceedings of the 20th International Conference on Product-Focused Software Process Improvement, submitted (2019)

20. Jürjens, J.: UMLsec: extending UML for secure systems development. In: Jézéquel, J.-M., Hussmann, H., Cook, S. (eds.) UML 2002. LNCS, vol. 2460, pp. 412–425. Springer, Heidelberg (2002). https://doi.org/10.1007/3-540-45800-X_32

21. Luckham, D.C., Kenney, J.J., Augustin, L.M., Vera, J., Bryan, D., Mann, W.: Specification and analysis of system architecture using rapide. IEEE Trans. Softw. Eng. **21**(4), 336–354 (1995). https://doi.org/10.1109/32.385971
22. Meldal, S., Luckham, D.C.: Defining a security reference architecture. http://i.stanford.edu/pub/cstr/reports/csl/tr/97/728/CSL-TR-97-728.pdf
23. Mirakhorli, M., Cleland-Huang, J.: Detecting, tracing, and monitoring architectural tactics in code. IEEE Trans. Softw. Eng. **42**(3), 205–220 (2016). https://doi.org/10.1109/TSE.2015.2479217
24. Moor, O.d., Verbaere, M., Hajiyev, E., Avgustinov, P., Ekman, T., Ongkingco, N., Sereni, D., Tibble, J.: Keynote address: .QL for source code analysis. In: Korel, B. (ed.) 2007 Seventh IEEE International Working Conference on Source Code Analysis and Manipulation, pp. 3–16. IEEE Computer Society, Los Alamitos (2007). https://doi.org/10.1109/SCAM.2007.31
25. Murphy, G.C., Notkin, D., Sullivan, K.J.: Software reflexion models: bridging the gap between design and implementation. IEEE Trans. Softw. Eng. **27**(4), 364–380 (2001)
26. Passos, L., Terra, R., Valente, M.T., Diniz, R., das Chagas Mendonca, N., et al.: Static architecture-conformance checking an illustrative overview. IEEE Softw. **27**(5), 82–89 (2010)
27. Perry, D.E., Wolf, A.L.: Foundations for the study of software architecture. ACM SIGSOFT Softw. Eng, Not. **17**(4), 40–52 (1992). https://doi.org/10.1145/141874.141884
28. Rosado, D.G., Gutierrez, C., Fernandez-Medina, E., Piattini, M.: A study of security architectural patterns. In: Proceedings of the 1st International Conference on Availability, Reliability and Security: ARES, pp. 358–365. IEEE Computer Society, Los Alamitos (2006). https://doi.org/10.1109/ARES.2006.18
29. Sachitano, A., Chapman, R.O., Hamilton, J.A.: Security in software architecture: a case study. In: From the Fifth Annual IEEE SMC Information Assurance Workshop, pp. 370–376. IEEE Computer Society (2004). https://doi.org/10.1109/IAW.2004.1437841
30. Saldaña, J.: The Coding Manual for Qualitative Researchers, 2nd edn. SAGE Publications, Los Angeles (2013)
31. Sangal, N., Jordan, E., Sinha, V., Jackson, D.: Using dependency models to manage complex software architecture. In: Johnson, R. (ed.) Proceedings of the 20th Annual ACM SIGPLAN Conference on Object-Oriented Programming, Systems, Languages, and Applications, p. 167. ACM, New York (2005). https://doi.org/10.1145/1094811.1094824
32. Schaad, A., Borozdin, M.: Tam^2: automated threat analysis. In: Proceedings of the ACM Symposium on Applied Computing, SAC 2012, Riva, Trento, Italy, 26–30 March 2012, pp. 1103–1108 (2012). https://doi.org/10.1145/2245276.2231950
33. Schröder, S., Riebisch, M.: An ontology-based approach for documenting and validating architecture rules. In: Proceedings of the 12th European Conference on Software Architecture, pp. 52:1–52:7 (2018). https://doi.org/10.1145/3241403.3241457
34. Schröder, S., Riebisch, M., Soliman, M.: Architecture enforcement concerns and activities - an expert study. In: Tekinerdogan, B., Zdun, U., Babar, A. (eds.) ECSA 2016. LNCS, vol. 9839, pp. 247–262. Springer, Cham (2016). https://doi.org/10.1007/978-3-319-48992-6_19
35. Schumacher, M.: Security Patterns: Integrating Security and Systems Engineering. Wiley Series in Software Design Patterns. Wiley, Chichester, England and Hoboken (2006), http://search.ebscohost.com/login.aspx?direct=true&scope=site&db=nlebk&db=nlabk&AN=159644

36. Serrano, D., Maña, A., Sotirious, A.D.: Towards precise security patterns. In: Tjoa, A.M., Wagner, R.R. (eds.) Proceedings of the 19th International Conference on Database and Expert Systems Applications: DEXA, pp. 287–291. IEEE Computer Society, Los Alamitos (2008). https://doi.org/10.1109/DEXA.2008.36
37. de Silva, L.: Towards controlling software architecture erosion through runtime conformance monitoring. Dissertation, University of St. Andrews, St. Andrews (2014)
38. Yoder, J., Barcalow, J.: Architectural patterns for enabling application security. In: 4th Pattern Languages of Programming Conference (1997)
39. Yoshioka, N., Washizaki, H., Maruyama, K.: A survey on security patterns. Prog. Inform. **5**(5), 35–47 (2008). https://doi.org/10.2201/NiiPi.2008.5.5

Technical Debt and Waste
in Non-functional Requirements
Documentation: An Exploratory Study

Gabriela Robiolo[1]([✉]), Ezequiel Scott[2], Santiago Matalonga[3],
and Michael Felderer[4]

[1] LIDTUA (CIC), Facultad de Ingeniería, Universidad Austral,
Buenos Aires, Argentina
grobiolo@austral.edu.ar
[2] Institute of Computer Science, Tartu Unviersity, Tartu, Estonia
ezequiel.scott@ut.ee
[3] School of Computing, Engineering and Physical Sciences,
University of the West of Scotland, Paisley, UK
santiago.matalonga@uws.ac.uk
[4] Department of Computer Science, University of Innsbruck, Innsbruck, Austria
michael.felderer@uibk.ac.at

Abstract. *Background:* To adequately attend to non-functional requirements (NFRs), they must be documented; otherwise, developers would not know about their existence. However, the documentation of NFRs may be subject to Technical Debt and Waste, as any other software artefact. *Aims:* The goal is to explore indicators of potential Technical Debt and Waste in NFRs documentation. *Method:* Based on a subset of data acquired from the most recent NaPiRE (Naming the Pain in Requirements Engineering) survey, we calculate, for a standard set of NFR types, how often respondents state they document a specific type of NFR when they also state that it is important. This allows us to quantify the occurrence of potential Technical Debt and Waste. *Results:* Based on 398 survey responses, four NFR types (Maintainability, Reliability, Usability, and Performance) are labelled as important but they are not documented by more than 22% of the respondents. We interpret that these NFR types have a higher risk of Technical Debt than other NFR types. Regarding Waste, 15% of the respondents state they document NFRs related to Security and they do not consider it important. *Conclusions:* There is a clear indication that there is a risk of Technical Debt for a fixed set of NFRs since there is a lack of documentation of important NFRs. The potential risk of incurring Waste is also present but to a lesser extent.

Keywords: Non functional requirements · Technical Debt · Waste

X. Franch et al. (Eds.): PROFES 2019, LNCS 11915, pp. 220–235, 2019.
https://doi.org/10.1007/978-3-030-35333-9_16

1 Introduction

Non-functional requirements (NFRs) are of high importance for the success of a software project [8]. Nevertheless, there exists evidence that NFRs tend to come second class to functional requirements [7,8]. We see this as a pervasive problem, regardless of the methodology that the development process follows. Quality management models and standards like ISO 9001:2015 [14] and CMMI [6] require that functional and non-functional requirements are documented as way of conveying their importance. These software development models and standards take a "do as you say, say as you do" approach where documentation and upfront planning is used to mitigate the risk of not delivering the software product within the constraints of the project. In fact, the ISO/IEC/IEEE 29148:2018 standard for software and systems requirements engineering [16], prescribes that both functional and non-functional requirements have to be documented.

Agile software engineering highlights the need of "continuous attention to technical excellence" [2]. Agile software engineering methods mainly rely on immediate feedback and postulate the sufficient availability of knowledgeable software developers to mitigate potential quality risks. Unfortunately, agile values and principles often seem to be adopted naïvely [11], i.e., equating agile with avoiding documentation [25].

The starting point of the research presented in this paper is the assumption that in order to be able to adequately handle NFRs, they must be documented – otherwise developers would not know about their precise nature or even their existence. Based on a subset of data acquired from the most recent NaPiRE (**Na**ming the **P**ain in **R**equirenments **E**ngineering) survey conducted in 2018 [19], we calculate for the NFR types Compatibility, Maintainability, Performance, Portability, Reliability, Safety, Security, and Usability how often respondents state they document a specific type of NFR when they also state that this type of NFR is important. We address the following research questions:

RQ1: *Can we identify Technical Debt and Waste in requirements documentation from the responses in the NaPiRE questionnaire?* To understand the current status of Technical Debt and Waste in the context of NaPiRE, we calculate the occurrence of potential Technical Debt (i.e., NFR not documented although labeled as important) and the occurrence of potential Waste (i.e., NFR documented although labeled as not important) with regard to the different NFR types (i.e. Compatibility, Maintainability, Performance, Portability, Reliability, Safety, Security, and Usability).

RQ2: *How does the practitioners' context influence the occurrence of Technical Debt and Waste in requirements documentation?* The system type, the project size, and the type of development process are usually the first variables to be considered in exploratory studies. We explored the practitioners' responses related to these variables in order to understand how they influence the occurrence of Technical Debt and Waste in the context of NaPiRE.

Our results show a clear indication of Technical Debt in several NFRs, with Maintainability, Reliability, Usability, and Performance being the NFRs with the highest frequency of occurrence of potential Technical Debt. Furthermore, when breaking down the analysis by the type of development process, the development processes at the extremes of the spectrum (i.e., purely plan-driven or purely agile) alter the indication of the Technical Debt pattern. Furthermore, our results show that there is less risk of incurring in Waste. Less than 15% of the respondents stated that they document NFR which they do not consider important. With Security being the NFR with the highest frequency of respondents at about 15%.

2   Background

In this section, we introduce the **N**aming the **P**ain in **R**equirenments **E**ngineering (NaPiRE) initiative[1] and present an overview on research about NFRs.

2.1   The NaPiRE Project

The objective of the NaPiRE project is to establish a comprehensive theory of requirements engineering (RE) practice and to provide empirical evidence to practitioners that helps them address the challenges of requirements engineering in their projects. These objectives shall be achieved by collecting empirical data in surveys conducted world-wide and in repeating cycles. At the time of writing this paper, three rounds of the NaPiRE survey have been carried out. The first survey round was conducted in Germany and the Netherlands in 2012 [21]. The second round, conducted in the years 2014 and 2015, was extended to ten countries [20]. The third round of the survey was conducted in 2018 and collected data from 42 countries. The research presented in this paper is based on the data collected in the third round. Since the NaPiRE survey instrument has evolved since 2014/2015, a direct comparison between past analysis results and currently ongoing analyses is not always possible. This holds especially for the topic of non-functional requirements covered in this paper, which is the first one published on data from the third run.

The previous installments of the NaPiRe survey have been successful in sparking complementing research into several viewpoint of requirements engineering. For instance, to compare requirements engineering practices across geographical regions [17,22] or by development method [28,29]. We argue that, although NaPiRE data has been extensively analyzed, it has so far not been analyzed with regards to practitioners' perceptions about handling NFRs.

2.2   Published Research on Non-Functional Requirements

This section presents an overview of past directions in non-functional requirements (NFR) research with a focus on survey research in the context of software industry.

---

[1] NaPiRE web site – http://napire.org.

Borg et al. [5] presented a case study on how NFRs are dealt with in two software development organisations. The authors interviewed 14 software developers in two organisations. Their results show that, in both contexts, functional requirements take precedence over non-functional requirements.

Berntsson Svensson et al. [4] investigated the challenges for managing NFRs in embedded systems. They interviewed ten practitioners from five software companies. Their results show a widespread variation in how the respondents dealt with NFR, they also suggest a relationship between a lack of documentation of NFR and a dismissal of NFR during the project lifecycle. Behutiye et al. [3] investigated how software development teams using agile projects deal with non-functional requirements. The authors interviewed practitioners in four companies developing software with agile methodologies. Each company followed a different practices when documenting NFR (including not documenting them and relying on tacit knowledge).

Ameller et al. [1] looked at how software architects deal with non-functional requirements. Their results highlight a lack of common vocabulary among software architects to convey NFR, the two most important NFR types were performance and usability, and that NFRs are often not documented, and when documented, the documentation was usually imprecise and was rarely maintained. Also, Proot et al. [23] presented a survey about the perceived importance of non-functional requirements among software architects. Their results suggest that architects consider NFRs important to the success of their software projects.

De la Vara et al. [26] present a questionnaire-based survey capturing the more important NFRs from the point of view of practitioners. 31 practitioners from 25 organizations were selected within the industrial collaboration network of the authors. The top five NFRs identified are Usability, Maintainability, Performance, Reliability, and Flexibility. Haigh et al. [10] empirically examined the requirements for software quality held by different groups involved in the development process. She conducted a survey of more than 300 current and recently graduated students of one of the leading Executive MBA programs in the United States, asking them to rate the importance of each of 13 widely-cited attributes related to software quality. The results showed the following ranking of NFRs: Accuracy, Correctness, Robustness, Usability, Integrity, Maintainability, Interoperability, Augmentability, Efficiency, Testability, Flexibility, Portability, Reusability.

In summary, we conclude that the topic of NFRs has been extensively researched but there is few evidence of how the NFRs are documented. Furthermore, the specific relationship between importance level and degree of documentation has not yet been investigated.

3 Research Method

Before describing the research method we first present our understanding of relevant concepts and assumptions about our research. Secondly, we introduce the terminology used in this paper. Then, we present our research questions. Finally, we describe the data extraction and analysis procedure that we followed in order to answer those research questions.

3.1 Concepts and Assumptions

According to the software product quality standard ISO 25010:2011 [15], a non-functional requirement is a "requirement that specifies criteria that can be used to judge the operation of a software system" [15]. The same standard defines a model for the evaluation of quality in use and product quality of a software system. Within this quality model, the product quality attributes (also known as quality characteristics) are defined. A quality attribute is a specification of the stakeholders' needs (Functional Suitability, Performance Efficiency, Compatibility, Usability, Reliability, Security, Maintainability, Portability). We argue that both terms, NFR and product quality attribute, are related and often used interchangeably in industry, even though this is not correct according to the precise definitions of these terms. Upon careful consideration, in particular looking at how the NaPiRE survey instrument framed the questions related to NFRs, in this work we interpret NFRs to be all requirements that do not specify a functional behaviour. Furthermore, we do not differentiate between NFR and product quality attribute. We claim that (1) the NaPiRE questionnaire has not made this distinction evident, (2) most practitioners would not care for the subtleties of this differentiation, and (3) interchangeable use of terms is pervasive among practitioners and researchers [3,7,23]. In order to be consistent with the survey instrument used in the NaPiRE survey, in this paper, we use the term "quality attribute" instead of "NFR" when we present our research questions and the results of our analyses.

This research is driven by our assumption that, in agreement with [16], both functional and non-functional requirements have to be documented. In the context of software quality assurance, which is defined in ANSI/IEEE Standard 729–1983 [12], the confidence of the established technical requirements is achieved by checking the software and the documentation and verifying their consistency.

Therefore, the ideal situation is that when a quality attribute is considered as important for the development project, then it must be documented. To better convey this understanding we refer to the Technical Debt metaphor. Technical Debt, as defined by [24], is "a metaphor for immature, incomplete, or inadequate artefacts in the software development lifecycle that cause higher costs and lower quality in the long run. These artefacts remaining in a system affect subsequent development and maintenance activities, and so can be seen as a type of debt that the system developers owe the system." Also, Li et al. [18] pointed out that documentation of Technical Debt refers to insufficient, incomplete, or outdated documentation in any aspect of software development. That is, when practitioners perceive a quality attribute as important but fail to document requirements associated to the quality attribute, we will interpret this as an indication of the incurred Technical Debt. We differentiate from [9], which defines Technical Debt in requirements as the distance between the implementation and the actual state of the world.

We follow similar reasoning on the other end of the spectrum but we rely on the concept of Waste in Lean development. In Lean development, Waste is defined as anything that does not add value [13]. In the domain of software development, the types of Waste can be interpreted as: extra features, waiting, task switching, extra processes, partially done work, movement, defects, or unused employee creativity [30]. Therefore, when practitioners are investing effort in documenting requirements for artifacts (quality attributes) that they do not consider important, we are interpreting that such an effort could be better placed elsewhere in the development process, and understand it as a source of Waste.

In the most recent round of the NaPiRE survey, practitioners were asked about their perception of importance regarding a set of pre-defined quality attributes in the context of the project they were currently working on. In addition, they were asked whether they document quality attributes. The specific questions related to these aspects and their possible responses are shown in Table 1. Question Q1 asks for the level of importance of each NFR type and Q2 for its degree of documentation. Questions Q3, Q4, and Q5 request the context

Table 1. NaPiRE questionnaire items used for the analysis

ID	Questionnaire item	Possible responses	Variables
Q1	Are there quality attributes which are of particularly high importance for your development project? If yes, which one(s)?	Compatibility, Maintainability, Performance, Portability, Reliability, Safety, Security, Usability	v_6-v_13
Q2	Which classes of non-functional requirements do you explicitly consider in your requirements documentation?	Compatibility, Maintainability, Performance, Portability, Reliability, Safety, Security, Usability	v_97-v_102, v_303, v_103
Q3	How many people are involved in your project?	Free text	v_3
Q4	Please select the class of systems or services you work on in the context of your project	Software-intensive embedded systems (SIES), Business information systems (BIS), Hybrid of both software-intensive embedded systems and business information systems (HYB)	v_4
Q5	How would you personally characterize your way of working in your project?	Agile, Rather agile, Hybrid, Rather plan-driven, Plan-driven	v_24

factors project size, system type, and development process type, respectively. By combining the answers to Q1 and Q2, we can investigate if practitioners are following the requirements documentation recommendation for quality attributes in a specific context determined by Q3, Q4, and Q5.

Table 2 conveys our perception of the possible scenarios. In the ideal world, practitioners do not incur in Technical Debt (Important and Not Documented), nor do they Waste effort in documenting requirements which they do not consider important (Not Important and Not Documented (NI_ND)). However, our experience leads us to expect that, practitioners are restricted by the context of their development projects and they are bound to incur in Technical Debt and Waste. In this research, we will look for evidence of this understanding in the responses to the NaPiRE 2018 survey.

Table 2. Perception of importance and availability of documentation quadrant.

	Documentation available	
Perception of importance	Important and Documented (I_D) **Expected situation**	Important and Not Documented (I_ND) **An Indication of Technical**
	Not Important and Documented (NI_D) **An Indication of Waste**	Not Important and Not Documented (NI_ND) **Expected Situation**

3.2 Research Questions

As mentioned in Sect. 3.1, we argue that if a quality attribute is perceived important, then it should be documented. We have, therefore, divided our analysis into the following research questions:

RQ1: *Can we identify Technical Debt and Waste in requirements documentation (as interpreted in Sect. 3.1) from the responses in the NaPiRE questionnaire?* This question expresses our overarching objective of understanding the juxtaposition between the perception of the importance of a quality attribute and if it has been documented. The question is framed in the Technical Debt metaphor, as it conveys our understanding that: "If a quality attribute is considered important, then it should be documented". Any deviation in this direction should be interpreted as a project decision that, for whatever reason, lead the practitioners into not documenting a quality attribute they consider important (i.e., an expression of Technical Debt). Likewise, "if a quality attribute is not considered important, then it need not be documented". Any deviation in this direction we consider as an indication of Waste, as the effort invested in documenting the quality attribute, could have been better spent elsewhere in the development lifecycle. **RQ1** is divided into:

RQ1.1: *For which quality attributes do the practitioners' responses indicate Technical Debt?* Through this sub-question, we will explore practitioners' responses to the NaPiRE 2018 dataset an identify the quality attributes in which a deviation is present of a quality attribute is perceived important and yet, it is not documented (referred in the analysis as *I_ND*).

RQ1.2: *For which quality attributes do the practitioners' responses indicate Waste?* Through this sub-question, we will explore the practitioners' responses to the NaPiRE 2018 dataset and identify the quality attributes in which a deviation is present of a quality attribute that is not perceived as important and yet, it has been documented (referred in the analysis as *NI_D*).

RQ2: *How does the practitioners' context influence the occurrence of Technical Debt and Waste in requirements documentation?* This second research question conveys our pre-conception that practitioners fail to document some quality attributes that they consider important. **RQ2** is divided into:

RQ2.1: *How does the system type influence the occurrence of Technical Debt and Waste?* This question conveys our pre-conception that the type of system can have an influence on the perceived importance of a quality attribute, and therefore on the occurrence of Technical Debt or Waste.

RQ2.2: *How does the project size influence the occurrence of Technical Debt and Waste?* This question conveys our pre-conception that the size of the software project can have an influence on the perception of importance or the documentation needs of a quality attribute.

RQ2.3: *How does the type of development process influence the occurrence of Technical Debt and Waste?.* This question conveys our pre-conception that the development process type might have an influence on the perception of importance or the documentation needs of a quality attribute.

3.3   Data Extraction and Analysis Procedure

We base our analysis on the NaPiRE 2018 dataset and, thus, have access to the corresponding raw data as well as the pre-processed codification of the questionnaire and answers. Table 1 presents the variables included in this research.

A total of 488 responses are recorded for the NaPiRE 2018 instance of the survey. All recorded responses are complete for variables v_6 to v_13 (perceived importance of quality attributes, see Table 1) whereas only 455 responses are complete for variables v_97 to v_102, v_303, v_103 (documentation of requirements for quality attributes, see Table 1). We removed 57 responses for incompleteness in other variables of interest. Therefore, the total number of responses considered for this research is 398. Table 3 presents the distribution of responses in the aforementioned categories by the type of quality attribute.

The distribution of the contextual project information that will be analyzed for **RQ2** is shown in Table 4. It is worth mentioning that we applied a pre-processing step to variable v_3 since it represents a free-text response. We used

Table 3. Distribution of responses by quality attribute

Quality attribute	Technical Debt (I_ND)	Waste (NI_D)	I_D	NI_ND
Compatibility	70 (17.59%)	46 (11.56%)	99 (24.87%)	183 (45.98%)
Maintainability	123 (30.9%)	27 (6.78%)	105 (26.38%)	143 (35.93%)
Performance	90 (22.61%)	47 (11.81%)	143 (35.93%)	118 (29.65%)
Portability	46 (11.56%)	39 (9.8%)	31 (7.79%)	282 (70.85%)
Reliability	122 (30.65%)	31 (7.79%)	117 (29.4%)	128 (32.16%)
Safety	68 (17.09%)	31 (7.79%)	39 (9.8%)	260 (65.33%)
Security	80 (20.1%)	59 (14.82%)	125 (31.41%)	134 (33.67%)
Usability	97 (24.37%)	35 (8.79%)	158 (39.7%)	108 (27.14%)
Mean	87.0 (21.86%)	39.375 (9.89%)	102.125 (25.66%)	169.5 (42.59%)

the results from the variable coding made by the collaborators of the NaPiRE initiative during their data analysis phase. For the purpose of analysing this variable, we grouped the responses into equal-sized buckets that represent small-sized ($v\_3 < 7$), medium-sized ($7 \leq v\_3 < 15$) and large-sized projects ($v\_3 \geq 15$).

Table 4. Number of responses by variable under study. Mean and standard deviation are reported for the percentages of responses indicating Technical Debt and Waste, calculated across all the quality attributes.

Variable	Value	Responses	Technical Debt (I_ND)	Waste (NI_D)
Process type	Agile	63	26.59 ± 8.60	7.54 ± 2.91
	Hybrid	135	20.28 ± 6.07	9.81 ± 2.85
	Plan-driven	37	22.30 ± 9.88	8.78 ± 4.51
	Rather agile	95	23.16 ± 9.87	10.26 ± 4.96
	Rather plan-driven	68	18.57 ± 6.29	12.32 ± 4.30
Project size	L	123	20.93 ± 5.84	9.96 ± 3.00
	M	136	20.50 ± 6.59	11.49 ± 3.79
	S	139	24.01 ± 8.34	8.27 ± 2.49
System class	BIS	202	22.40 ± 8.87	9.65 ± 4.23
	HYB	101	23.14 ± 5.50	8.91 ± 2.80
	SIES	95	19.34 ± 5.39	11.45 ± 2.42

4   Results

This section shows the results of our analysis organized by the research questions.

RQ1: *Can we identify Technical Debt and Waste (as interpreted in Sect. 3.1) from the responses in the NaPiRE questionnaire?* To answer RQ1, we cross-reference the responses to the perceived importance of quality attributes (v_6 to v_13) with the availability of documentation (v_97 to v_102, v_303, and v_103). Important and not documented (I_ND) requirements indicate Technical Debt, whereas not important and documented (NI_D) requirements indicate Waste (see Table 2).

RQ1.1: *For which quality attributes do the practitioners' responses indicate Technical Debt?* Table 3 shows the occurrence of Technical Debt for each quality attribute. The percentage of responses showing Technical Debt (I_ND) ranges from 12% to 31%. The average percentage of responses related to Technical Debt over all quality attribute types is 22%. The quality attributes which are most likely to incur in Technical Debt are Reliability (31%), Maintainability (31%), Usability (24%), and Performance (23%).

RQ1.2: *For which quality attributes do the practitioners' responses indicate Waste?* Table 3 shows that waste also occurs in all quality attributes (albeit at a smaller response rate). The percentage of responses showing Waste (NI_D) ranges from 7% to 15%. The quality attributes which exhibit higher Waste are Security (15%), Performance (12%), and Compatibility (12%).

RQ2: *How does the practitioners context influence the occurrence of Technical Debt and Waste?* To answer RQ2, we blocked the response data by the variables type of system, project size, and development process type to investigate their influence on the occurrence of Technical Debt and Waste. Figure 1 shows the percentage of responses by quality attribute that indicate Technical Debt for each of the variables under study. Similarly, Fig. 2 shows the percentage of responses related to Waste.

RQ2.1: *How does the system type influence the occurrence of Technical Debt and Waste?* When broken down by the system type (see Fig. 1(a)) we can observe that Reliability is the most prone to Technical Debt in all types of systems. On the other end, Portability, is not prone to Technical Debt in the system types under analysis. The HYB type of system is type of system where the average percentage of responses indicating Technical Debt is the highest (23%) (see Table 4). Four quality attributes surpass the average percentage of responses for all the quality attributes (22%), namely Usability (25%), Reliability (31%), Performance (27%), and Maintainability (29%). Security (23%) can be considered a borderline case. The percentage of BIS showing Technical Debt ranges from 9% to 37% with highest values for Maintainability (37%), Reliability (32%), and Usability (26%). From Fig. 1(a) we can see that BIS systems three quality attributes surpass the average percentage of responses for all the quality attributes (22%), namely Usability (26%), Reliability (32%), and Maintainability (37%). This system type also shows the highest percentages for Maintainability (37%) and Reliability (32%). Finally, SIES systems show percentages of Technical Debt ranging from 12% to 28%, and four quality attributes surpass the average percentage of responses (19%), namely, Reliability (28%), Performance (22%), Security (21%), and Usability (21%). Maintainability (20%) can be considered as a borderline case.

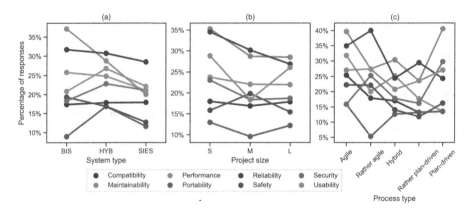

Fig. 1. Percentage of responses indicating Technical Debt by system type, project size, and process type.

Regarding Waste, the average percentage of responses for all the quality attributes is 10%, 9%, and 11% for BIS, HYB, and SIES type of systems (see Table 4). When broken down by the system type (see left-side of Fig. 2(a)), the highest percentages of responses are related to the Security of BISs (18%) and the Compatibility of SIES (16%). At the other end, the lowest percentage is related to the Maintainability of HYB systems (4%).

RQ2.2: *How does project size influence the occurrence of Technical Debt and Waste?* Figure 1(b) shows the Technical Debt for each quality attribute blocked by project size (S, M, L). Similarly, Fig. 2(b) shows the Waste. The average percentages of responses indicating Technical Debt is 24%, 20%, and 21% for projects of size S, M, and L, respectively (see Table 4).

Maintainability, and Reliability are the quality attributes which show the highest percentages of Technical Debt (regardless of project size). On the other end, Portability is the quality attribute with the lowest Technical Debt regardless of project size. Small projects incur in Technical Debt having percentages ranging from 13% to 35%. This kind of projects particularly shows high percentages related to Reliability (35%) and Maintainability (35%). As for medium-sized projects, the percentages range from 10% to 30%. In large-sized projects, the percentages of Technical Debt range from 12% to 28%.

Regarding Waste, the average percentages of responses indicating Waste is 8%, 11%, and 10% for projects of size S, M, and L, respectively (see Table 4). The percentages range from 5% to 12% for small-sized projects, from 7% to 17% for medium-sized projects, and from 7% to 16% for large-sized projects. In particular, the data points for Security and Safety seem to indicate that the number of responses showing Waste becomes larger as the project size increases.

RQ2.3: *How does type of development process influence the occurrence of Technical Debt and Waste?* Figure 1(c) shows the percentages of Technical Debt for every quality attribute organized by development process types. Similarly,

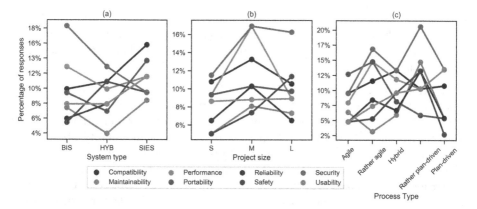

Fig. 2. Percentage of responses indicating Waste by System type, Project size, and Process type.

Fig. 2(c) shows the percentages related to Waste. Three quality attributes exhibit the highest percentages of Technical Debt regardless of the type of development process, namely Maintainability, Reliability, and Usability. On the other hand, Portability is the only quality attribute without Technical Debt for any type of development process.

Regarding Waste, the percentage responses indicating Waste related to Security is the highest. In addition, the percentage seems to increase as the projects become more plan-driven. The development process characterised as *Rather plan-driven* shows the highest overall exposure to Waste.

5 Discussion

In this section we first discuss the results achieved regarding the relation between NFRs with Technical Debt and Waste, respectively. In addition, we discuss possible threats to validity of our study.

Observations Related to NFR and Technical Debt. Our results show that the majority of the participants of the survey stated that they document NFRs when they are important and they don't document NFRs when they are not important. This is what we had hypothesized. However, we observed that there is a substantial subset of respondents who stated that they don't document (some of the) important NFRs. This is what we interpret as being at risk of Technical Debt. Certain types of NFRs were particularly prone to this phenomenon, i.e., Reliability, Maintainability, Usability, and Performance. We can only speculate what would drive practitioners into this behaviour. For example, either these NFR types are difficult to document, knowledge on how to properly document NFRs is missing, or no appropriate tool is available. Furthermore, reasons might vary by NFR type. For example with *Maintainability*, it can be argued that is left to good coding practices (i.e., avoiding code smells and focusing on refactoring). This phenomenon might also be true for other NFR types, i.e., there exist standard procedures or standard requirements that always hold and do not have to be explicitly stated in each individual project. When respondents answered the NaPiRE questionnaire, they might only have thought about project-specific documentation of NFRs.

Observations Related to NFRs and Waste. We also observed the occurrence of Waste, i.e., cases where respondents stated they document NFRs although they are not considered important. However, the observed Waste was consistently smaller than the Technical Debt (for the same quality attribute). Furthermore, when looking at the percentages observed for Waste, the proportion of Waste increases as project size increases: 5–11% for small-sized projects, 7–17% for medium-sized projects, and 7–16% for large-sized projects. This might be a signal that - consistent with common expectation - for larger projects the risk of Waste is higher than for small projects with respect to NFRs. Surprisingly, and probably against common expectation, our analyses do not give any indication that projects using rather agile or purely agile processes produce less Waste than projects using plan-driven development approaches.

Threats to Validity. We consider threats to construct, internal, external and conclusion validity according to Wohlin et al. [31] as well as measures to mitigate them.

This research is grounded on the NaPiRE 2018 survey, therefore we inherit some of the decisions taken during the development of the survey instrument. Of particular importance to the research presented in this paper is the fact that the NaPiRE 2018 survey does not differentiate between quality attribute and NFR. Both concepts are confounded in the questions on which we based our analysis. As a research team we have discussed this issue in depth and decided to accept this threat as it is in line with our shared understanding that (1) we cannot revert this decision; (2) we share the understanding that practitioners would probably not differentiate between both (and even for those who do, we can probably not guarantee a shared understanding). The latter argument is in line with the results of Eckardt et al. [8] (already mentioned in Sect. 3.1) that there is a large variety in the understanding of what is quality and what are NFRs. Continuing with inherited threats, external validity of our results highly depends on the profile of participants in the NaPiRE survey. The survey received overall 488 responses from all over the world and we have shown in a previous paper [27] that there are no significant differences in the NaPiRE data with respect to different cultural regions. Furthermore, we analyzed the data also with respect to the system type, the project size and the type of development process. We therefore think that threats to external validity are low.

An important construct validity injected by the approach described in this work relates to how the metaphor of Technical Debt and the concept of Waste were introduced into the analysis of the data set. First of all, the NaPiRE survey makes no reference to these concepts. Secondly, there is a subtle but present gap between the formulation of the questions and our interpretation. It can be argued that "which quality attribute is of particular high importance?" (as asked in the survey) is not the same as asking "List all quality attributes that are important".

Regarding internal validity, a limitation that we always have with survey research is that surveys can only reveal perceptions of the respondents that might not fully represent reality. However, the analysis stems from the well-validated NaPiRE questionnaire (see Sect. 2.1), which has continuously been improved based on piloting and the first two runs. Furthermore, we tried to be explicit in our decision about our data cleaning criteria (see Sect. 3.3) to be able to perform a thorough analysis.

6   Conclusion

This paper explored the relationship between the level of importance and the degree of documentation for the NFR types Compatibility, Maintainability, Performance, Portability, Reliability, Safety, Security, and Usability. The analysis is based on the data collected during the most recent run of the NAPiRE survey. To analyze this relationship, we refer to the Technical Debt and Waste metaphors. To the best of our knowledge, this is the first publication in which these two concepts were explored in the context of NFRs. The starting point of our analysis was the assumption that important NFRs must be documented. If a project breaks this rule, then we interpret it as a possible source of Technical Debt. Likewise, we postulated that not important NFRs should not be documented. If a project breaks this rule, then we interpret it as a possible source of Waste.

Our analyses indicate that for four types of NFR (Maintainability, Reliability, Usability, and Performance) more than 22% of the survey respondents who labelled the respective NFR type as important said that they did not document it. We interpret this as an indication that these NFR types have a higher risk of Technical Debt than other NFR types. Our analysis also indicates that the risk of Waste is less evident than the Risk of Technical Debt. Regarding Waste, NFR relating to Security exhibit the highest (about 15%) number of respondents that say that they do not consider Security important, but do document related requirements. For the remaining NFR under analysis, the respondents indicate that the problem of Waste is much less evident (when compared to Technical Debt). Additional analyses indicate that our results are not sensitive to the type of system class, the project size, or the type of development process.

Overall, we conclude that, for specific NFR types (i.e., Maintainability, Reliability, Usability, and Performance), there is a clear indication that lack of documentation of important NFRs occurs regularly, pointing to the risk of Technical Debt. Regarding Waste, with the exception of Security, we conclude that the manifestation of Waste is not as clear as the manifestation of Technical Debt. We discussed several potential reasons for the occurrence of this phenomenon. However, investigating the true causes of Technical Debt and Waste requires more empirical research, which we consider as future work.

Acknowledgments. The authors would like to thank all practitioners who took the time to respond to the NaPiRE survey as well as all colleagues involved in the NaPiRE project. The authors further acknowledge Dietmar Pfahl's contribution to research process described in this paper. Ezequiel Scott is supported by the Estonian Center of Excellence in ICT research (EXCITE), ERF project TK148 "IT Tippkeskus EXCITE". Gabriela Robiolo is supported by Universidad Austral.

References

1. Ameller, D., Ayala, C., Cabot, J., Franch, X.: How do software architects consider non-functional requirements: An exploratory study. In: 2012 Proceedings of the 20th IEEE International Requirements Engineering Conference, RE 2012, Chicago, USA (2012)
2. Beck, K., et al.: Manifesto for agile software development (2001)
3. Behutiye, W., Karhapää, P., Costal, D., Oivo, M., Franch, X.: Non-functional requirements documentation in agile software development: challenges and solution proposal. In: Felderer, M., Méndez Fernández, D., Turhan, B., Kalinowski, M., Sarro, F., Winkler, D. (eds.) PROFES 2017. LNCS, vol. 10611, pp. 515–522. Springer, Cham (2017). https://doi.org/10.1007/978-3-319-69926-4_41
4. Berntsson Svensson, R., Gorschek, T., Regnell, B.: Quality requirements in practice: an interview study in requirements engineering for embedded systems. In: Glinz, M., Heymans, P. (eds.) REFSQ 2009. LNCS, vol. 5512, pp. 218–232. Springer, Heidelberg (2009). https://doi.org/10.1007/978-3-642-02050-6_19
5. Borg, A., Yong, A., Carlshamre, P., Sandahl, K.: The bad conscience of requirements engineering: an investigation in real-world treatment of non-functional requirements. In: Third Conference on Software Engineering Research and Practice in Sweden (SERPS 2003), Lund (2003)
6. Chrissis, M.B., Konrad, M., Shrum, S.: CMMI: Guidelines for Process Integration and Product Improvement. Addison-Wesley, Upper Saddle River (2007)
7. Chung, L., do Prado Leite, J.C.S.: On non-functional requirements in software engineering. In: Borgida, A.T., Chaudhri, V.K., Giorgini, P., Yu, E.S. (eds.) Conceptual Modeling: Foundations and Applications. LNCS, vol. 5600, pp. 363–379. Springer, Heidelberg (2009). https://doi.org/10.1007/978-3-642-02463-4_19
8. Eckhardt, J., Vogelsang, A., Fernández, D.M.: Are "non-functional" requirements really non-functional? In: Proceedings of the 38th International Conference on Software Engineering - ICSE 2016, pp. 832–842. ACM Press, New York (2016)
9. Ernst, N.A.: On the role of requirements in understanding and managing technical debt. In: Proceedings of the Third International Workshop on Managing Technical Debt, Piscataway, NJ, USA, pp. 61–64 (2012)
10. Haigh, M.: Software quality, non-functional software requirements and it-business alignment. Softw. Qual. J. **18**, 361–385 (2010)
11. Hoda, R., Noble, J.: Becoming agile: a grounded theory of agile transitions in practice. In: Proceedings - 2017 IEEE/ACM 39th International Conference on Software Engineering, ICSE 2017 (2017)
12. IEEE: IEEE standard glossary of software engineering terminology. IEEE Std 610.12-1990, pp. 1–84, December 1990
13. Ikonen, M., Kettunen, P., Oza, N., Abrahamsson, P.: Exploring the sources of waste in Kanban software development projects. In: 2010 36th EUROMICRO Conference on Software Engineering and Advanced Applications, pp. 376–381 (2010)
14. ISO: ISO 9001:2015. Quality Management Systems - Requirements (2015)
15. ISO/IEC Standard: ISO/IEC 25010:2011 Systems and software engineering - systems and software Quality Requirements and Evaluation (SQuaRE) - System and software quality models (2011)

16. ISO/IEC/IEEE: ISO/IEC/IEEE 29148:2018 Systems and software engineering - life cycle processes - requirements engineering. Technical report, International Standards Organization (2018)
17. Kalinowski, M., et al.: Preventing incomplete/hidden requirements: reflections on survey data from Austria and Brazil. In: Winkler, D., Biffl, S., Bergsmann, J. (eds.) SWQD 2016. LNBIP, vol. 238, pp. 63–78. Springer, Cham (2016). https://doi.org/10.1007/978-3-319-27033-3_5
18. Li, Z., Avgeriou, P., Liang, P.: A systematic mapping study on technical debt and its management. J. Syst. Softw. **101**, 193–220 (2015)
19. Méndez Fernández, D.: Supporting requirements-engineering research that industry needs: the NaPiRE initiative. IEEE Softw. **35**(1), 112–116 (2018)
20. Fernández, D.M., et al.: Naming the pain in requirements engineering. Empir. Softw. Eng. **22**(5), 2298–2338 (2017)
21. Fernández, D.M., Wagner, S.: Naming the pain in requirements engineering: design of a global family of surveys and first results from Germany. In: EASE - 17th International Conference on Evaluation and Assessment in Software Engineering, Porto de Galinhas (2013)
22. Fernández, D.M., et al.: Naming the pain in requirements engineering: comparing practices in Brazil and Germany. IEEE Softw. **32**(5), 16–23 (2015)
23. Poort, E.R., Martens, N., van de Weerd, I., van Vliet, H.: How architects see non-functional requirements: beware of modifiability. In: Regnell, B., Damian, D. (eds.) REFSQ 2012. LNCS, vol. 7195, pp. 37–51. Springer, Heidelberg (2012). https://doi.org/10.1007/978-3-642-28714-5_4
24. Seaman, C., Guo, Y.: Chapter 2 - measuring and monitoring technical debt. Adv. Comput. **82**, 25–46 (2011)
25. Stettina, C.J., Heijstek, W.: Necessary and neglected? An empirical study of internal documentation in agile software development teams. In: Proceedings of the 29th ACM International Conference on Design of Communication (SIGDOC 2011), Pisa, Italy, 3–5 October 2011 (2011)
26. de la Vara, J.L., Wnuk, K., Berntsson Svensson, R., Sanchez, J., Regnell, B.: An empirical study on the importance of quality requirements in industry. In: Proceedings of 23rd International Conference on Software Engineering and Knowledge Engineering, New York, NY, USA, pp. 311–317 (2010)
27. Wagner, S., et al.: Status quo in requirements engineering: a theory and a global family of surveys. ACM Trans. Softw. Eng. Methodol. (TOSEM) **28**(2), 9:1–9:48 (2019)
28. Wagner, S., Méndez Fernández, D., Felderer, M., Kalinowski, M.: Requirements engineering practice and problems in agile projects; results from an international survey. In: 2017 Iberoamerican Conference on Software Engineering (CiBSE 2017) (2017)
29. Wagner, S., Méndez-Fernández, D., Kalinowski, M., Felderer, M.: Agile requirements engineering in practice: status quo and critical problems. CLEI Electron. J. **21**(1) (2018). https://doi.org/10.19153/cleiej.21.1.6
30. Wang, X., Conboy, K., Cawley, O.: "Leagile" software development: an experience report analysis of the application of lean approaches in agile software development. J. Syst. Softw. **85**, 1287–1299 (2012)
31. Wohlin, C., Runeson, P., Höst, M., Ohlsson, M.C., Regnell, B., Wesslén, A.: Experimentation in Software Engineering. Springer, Heidelberg (2012). https://doi.org/10.1007/978-3-642-29044-2

Technical Debt in Costa Rica: An InsighTD Survey Replication

Alexia Pacheco[1(✉)], Gabriela Marín-Raventós[1,2],
and Gustavo López[2]

[1] Computer Science Graduate Program (PPCI), University of Costa Rica (UCR),
San José, Costa Rica
{alexia.pacheco,gabriela.marin}@ucr.ac.cr
[2] Research Center for Communication and Information Technologies (CITIC),
University of Costa Rica (UCR), San José, Costa Rica
gustavo.lopez_h@ucr.ac.cr

Abstract. InsighTD is a globally distributed family of industrial surveys on causes and effects of Technical Debt (TD). We are currently analyzing the data gathered from the independent replication of the questionnaire in Costa Rica. In total, 156 professionals from the Costa Rican software industry answered the survey. Initial results indicate that there is a broad familiarity with the concept of TD. For the examples reported, it seems that the type of TD were product of situations that could have been prevented. TD was monitored for slightly more than half of cases, and TD was not paid in most cases. In future articles, we will report causes and the effects of TD in Costa Rica.

Keywords: Technical debt · Survey · Family of surveys

1 Introduction

Technical debt is a current and critical issue in the software development industry [1, 2]. Many studies have focused on technical debt management [3–5]. In 2016, Dagstuhl Seminar 16162 - Managing Technical Debt in Software Engineering was held, whose goal was to establish a common understanding of key concepts of technical debt. At that seminar, a definition for technical debt was proposed: "*In software-intensive systems, technical debt is a collection of design or implementation constructs that are expedient in the short term, but set up a technical context that can make future changes more costly or impossible. Technical debt presents an actual and contingent liability whose impact is limited to internal system qualities, primarily maintainability and evolvability*" [6].

This research is part of an international study to investigate the causes and implications of technical debt called InsighTD [7]. This study is a globally distributed family of industrial surveys on TD to understand TD from the practitioners' perspective. InsighTD goal is to investigate the state of practice and industry trends in the TD area including: the status quo, the causes that lead to TD occurrence, the effects of its existence, how these problems manifest themselves in the software development

© Springer Nature Switzerland AG 2019
X. Franch et al. (Eds.): PROFES 2019, LNCS 11915, pp. 236–243, 2019.
https://doi.org/10.1007/978-3-030-35333-9_17

process, and how software development teams react when they are aware of the presence of debt items in their projects. [8].

In this paper, we present the first results of InsighTD survey replication in Costa Rica. In total, 156 professionals from Costa Rican Software Industry answered the online survey. We are completing the survey analysis. Here, we describe a characterization of the professionals who answered the survey, organizations where they work, and the projects gave as an example. Furthermore, we present initial results about familiarity with TD concept and team reactions when they know that there is technical debt. Several participant roles and levels of experience are represented. Furthermore, organizations of different sizes are also represented. Also, projects of different process models, team size, age, and size are represented.

This paper is structured as follows. Section 2 discusses related work. Section 3 presents the methods for the study. Sections 4 include the results. Section 5 discusses the results. Finally, Sect. 6 presents the conclusion of the paper.

2 Related Work

The research about technical debt is broad since it is a significant concern in the software engineering industry. There are several secondary studies about technical debt. The first tertiary study on technical debt is presented by Rios et al. [1]. Authors systematically identified 13 secondary studies dated from 2012 to March 2018. Using this compilation, they developed a taxonomy of technical debt types. Also, they identified a list of situations in which debt items can be found in software projects. Furthermore, they organized a map about the state of the art of activities, strategies, and tools to support TD management.

Managing technical debt requires to recognize its leading causes because one way to reducing the problems is trying to prevent them. However, the available evidence is still limited [8]. To address the lack of empirical evidence, a group of researchers conceived InsighTD Survey – Investigating causes and implications of TD. InsighTD is a globally distributed family of industrial surveys on TD. It will provide valuable insights into the main causes and effects of TD across many countries around the world. While writing this paper, researchers from twelve countries (Brazil, Chile, Colombia, Costa Rica, Finland, India, Italy, Netherlands, Norway, Saudi Arabia, Serbia, and United States) have already joined to this project.

The first execution of InsighTD was for the Brazilian software industry. Rio, N et al. published the results of InsighTD in Brazil [8]. For this case, 107 practitioners answered the questionnaire. Authors report that there is a broad familiarity with the concept of TD in Brazil. In addition, authors indicate that deadlines, inappropriate planning, lack of knowledge, and lack of a well-defined process are among the top 10 cited and most likely causes. On the other side, authors mention low quality, delivery delay, low maintainability, rework, and financial loss are among the top 10 most commonly cited and impactful effects of TD [8].

3 Methods

The initial results of the InsighTD survey performed in Costa Rica are presented in this paper. An online survey was conducted using Google Docs. We applied non-probability sampling, specifically purposive sampling and snowball sampling. To invite the professionals involved in software development, we contacted the Computer Science and Informatics Professional Association of Costa Rica, and they sent an invitation by email to their members. Additionally, we sent an email to the personal contacts of the research group of the University of Costa Rica to invite them to take the survey and asked them to invite their partners to take the survey.

InsighTD is designed to answer the four research questions presented in Table 1 [8]. The questionnaire has 28 questions, and it is available in the instruments section of the website td-survey.com. Researchers from InsighTD Costa Rica team and InsighTD Colombia team translated to Spanish the questionnaire to apply in Costa Rica. Fully bilingual Computer Science professionals evaluated the translated instrument for readability.

Table 1. Research questions

RQ1	Are software professionals familiar with the concept of TD?
RQ2	What causes lead software development teams to incur TD?
RQ3	What effects does TD have on software projects?
RQ4	How do software development teams react when they are aware of the presence of debt items in their projects?

4 Results

This section presents the initial results of InsighTD survey in Costa Rica. First, we will describe the demographics of the participants. Later we will describe the results in Costa Rica about familiarity with TD Concept (RQ1) and the reaction of development teams when they are aware of TD (RQ4). Regarding the causes (RQ2) and effects (RQ3) of TD, we are still processing the answers to the corresponding survey questions.

4.1 Demographics

The questionnaire was online from February 26th until April 12th, 2019. One hundred fifty-six professionals from the Costa Rican software industry answered the survey. Eight participants who answered the poll were not working in Costa Rica at the time. Therefore, they were excluded from the final dataset. Hence our analysis is based on 148 answers.

Diverse types of expertise were found (Table 2). Most participants work as developers, followed by managers, testers, requirements analysts, process analysts, and software architects. In relation with the level of experience in their role, the participants indicated that they are competent (49%), followed by proficient (26%), beginners (14%), experts (8%) and novice (3%).

Table 2. Participant roles

Role	#	%
Developer	91	61%
Project Leader/Program Manager	22	15%
Tester Manager/Tester	9	6%
Requirements Analyst	7	5%
Process Analyst	6	4%
Software Architect	6	4%
DBA/Data Analysis	4	3%
Business Analyst	2	1%
Consultant	1	1%

Likewise, organizations of different sizes were represented (Fig. 1). They are distributed among small (21%), mid (47%) and large size (32%). Most of the participants (mode) work in organizations of 51–250 employees and more than 2000 employees. The median size is 251–500 employees. Consequently, participants tend to work in larger organizations; however, all company sizes are represented.

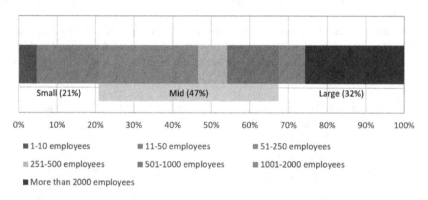

Fig. 1. Organization's size measured by number of employees

Participants were asked to choose a project and characterize it according to the development process model and team size. Most of the projects were described as agile (45%), followed by hybrid (41%), and the traditional cascade model was the least common (15%). Project teams usually consists of 5 to 9 persons (38%), followed by teams of less than five members (28%), teams of 10–20 employees (17%), teams of 21–30 employees (5%) and teams of more than 30 employees (11%). The median is teams of 5 to 9 persons. Therefore, participants tend to work in smaller teams, but all team sizes are represented.

Furthermore, participants were asked to characterize the system according to their size and age. The most common system age was 2–5 years (32%), followed by 1–2 years (21%), less one year (20%), 5–10 years (16%) and more than ten years (11%).

Finally, the system size was usually between10 K LOC and 1 million SLOC. However, there are representations of smaller (<10 KLOC – 15%) and more extensive system (>10 MLOC – 8%).

Thus, the collected data seems to be a good representation of Costa Rican software industry diversity, grasping (a) several participants' roles and levels of experience, (b) organization of different sizes, and (c) projects of different process models, team size, age, and size.

4.2   Familiarity with TD Concept

Initially, the survey asks *how familiar with the concept of TD the participant is*. Most participants (67%) are somewhat familiar with the concept (Fig. 2, left side). The third part of the participants answered that they have *never heard the term* (33%). In the questionnaire, subsequently, all participants were requested *to define TD in their words*. The idea must grasp what they understand by TD. Later, TD definition adapted from McConnell [9] was presented. Next, participants were asked about *how close the definition of technical debt they gave is to McConnell's*. Most participants (74%) answered that their definition was *very close* or *close* to McConnells' definition (Fig. 2, right side). Only a fifth of the participants (20%) indicated that they *had no prior knowledge*.

Comparing the results about *how familiar with the concept of TD the participant is* and *how close the definition of technical debt they gave is to McConnell's* (Fig. 2), participants indicated that they had never heard the term.

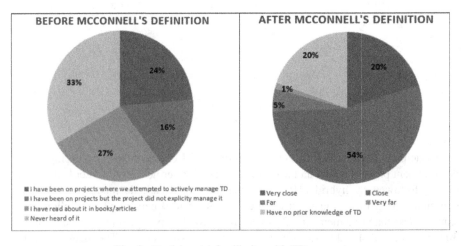

Fig. 2. Participants' familiarity with TD concept

Also, participants were asked to give an example of TD that had a significant impact on their chosen project.

Next, they were asked about *why they chose that TD example*. The four most cited reasons are *most remembered* (25%), *very common* (17%), *lot of rework* (11%) and *recent work* (10%). Later, participants were asked about *how representative their example of TD was in terms of their occurrence frequency*. Participant's answers are distributed among *happens sometimes* (49%), *often occurs* (40%), and *a unique situation* (11%).

The results suggest that the cases of technical debt grasped through the survey are real and recurring. Therefore, the results on the causes and effects of TD that we will obtain from our study, there will be built on empirical evidence that reflects real and recurring technical debt problems in software projects.

4.3   Reaction of Development Teams When They Are Aware of TD

In order to grasp the reactions of development teams when they are aware of TD, participants were asked about if it would be possible to prevent the type of debt of the event that they cited previously. Most participants (91%) answered *yes*. These results suggest that participants recalled mainly projects where TD is possible to prevent.

Next, continuing with questions about the example, they were asked *if the technical debt was monitored* and *if the technical debt was paid*. In Fig. 3, the distribution of participants answers are shown in four quadrants. Those quadrants are obtained from crossing possible answers of the following questions: *was the debt item monitored?* (x-axis), and *was the debt item paid off* (y-axis)? Most participants (36%) indicates that their technical debt item was neither monitored nor paid. Most participants (36%) indicates that their technical debt item was neither monitored nor paid. Followed by those who indicated that their technical debt item was monitored and paid (28%). Further, there are cases where although the debt was monitored, it has not been paid. Also, there are cases (10%) where the debt was not monitored, but still it was paid.

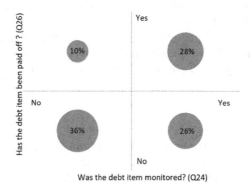

Fig. 3. Four quadrant matrix showing technical debt monitoring and payment.

When analyzing separately the answers to questions shown in Fig. 3, we found that almost half of participants (46%) indicated that technical debt was not monitored, and most participants (62%) answered that technical debt was not paid off. These results suggest that there are cases where the debt was identified, but it was not well managed.

5 Discussion

The collected data seems to be a good representation of Costa Rican software industry diversity. We found (a) several participant roles and levels of experience, (b) organization of different sizes, and (c) projects of different age and size, team size, and process models.

The main finding so far related to the question *Are software professionals familiar with the concept of TD?* is that there is a broad familiarity with TD concept. However, only a quarter of the participants involved in projects where they attempted to manage TD actively. This fact suggests the topic is recognizable in Costa Rica software industry, although, there is low adoption of technical debt management practices. Additionally, some participants recognized TD concept despite not handled the term for it. This is evidenced when we compare the results shown in Fig. 2. If we compare these findings with those reported in [8] about InsighTD Brasil, we observe that in both countries, the TD concept is known by the software industry. However, the term is not yet widely used.

Regarding the research question: *How do software development teams react when they are aware of the presence of debt items in their projects?* the types of reactions are diverse. We find the presence of the four possible combinations concerning the activity of monitoring and pay off the debt. In most cases, TD item was neither monitored nor pay off. In a little less than a third of the cases, they did monitor and pay off the TD item. Also, there are cases where TD item was either monitored or pay. These results complement the finding of the first research question, in the sense that there is still low adoption of technical debt management as work practice. For this research question, it is not possible to compare our results with the situation in Brasil. Their results about it have not been published yet.

Moreover, a vast majority of participants (90%) considered that their technical debt type could be prevented. Thus, educating professionals on technical debt management practices for contributing to TD prevention seems to make sense.

6 Conclusion

Technical debt is a real and current problem in the software industry. Understanding its causes and effects are essential to evaluate actions to prevent and manage it properly. InsighTD is a globally distributed family of industrial surveys on causes and effects of Technical Debt (TD). We applied the survey in Costa Rica and gathered 156 answers. In this paper, we presented the initial results. We focused on familiarity with TD concept and team reactions when they know that there is technical debt. However, we also present a characterization of participants, companies where they work, and their selected project for the examples.

The survey database for Costa Rica contains 148 responses and constitutes a reasonable basis for analysis because contain (a) several participants' roles and levels of experience, (b) organization of different sizes, and (c) projects of different process models, team size, age, and size.

Initial results suggest that there is a broad familiarity with the concept of TD. The types of TD of the examples reported were product of situations that could have been prevented. Furthermore, TD was monitored for slightly more than half of cases, and TD was not paid in most cases.

We will continue analyzing data to obtain the causes and effects in Costa Rica. We will share those results with Costa Rican Software Industry professionals and InsighTD project team. Also, the results from our investigation will be an input for our ongoing investigation about technical debt visualization to improve communication between stakeholders in decision making related to the software development process.

Future work includes the analysis of InsighTD results in other countries compared with Costa Rica to assess common causes and effect of TD and to identify possible specific causes and effect for Costa Rica context.

Acknowledgments. We want to thank all the participants of the survey and the researches from Costa Rica team promoting this international initiative (InsighTD).

References

1. Rios, N., de Mendonça Neto, M.G., Spínola, R.O.: A tertiary study on technical debt: types, management strategies, research trends, and base information for practitioners. Inf. Softw. Technol. **102**, 117–145 (2018)
2. Besker, T., Martini, A., Bosch, J.: Time to pay up technical debt from a software quality perspective. In: Proceedings of the 2017 20th Ibero-American Conference on Software Engineering, pp. 235–248. CibSE, Argentina (2017)
3. Li, Z., Avgeriou, P., Liang, P.: A systematic mapping study on technical debt and its management. J. Syst. Softw. **101**, 193–220 (2015)
4. Alves, N.S.R., Mendes, T.S., de Mendonça, M.G., Spínola, R.O., Shull, F., Seaman, C.: Identification and management of technical debt: a systematic mapping study. Inf. Softw. Technol. **70**, 100–121 (2016)
5. Becker, C., Betz, S., Mccord, C.: Trade-off decisions across time in technical debt management: a systematic literature review. In: Proceedings of the 2018 International Conference on Technical Debt, pp. 85–94. ACM, Gothenburg (2018)
6. Avgeriou, P., Kruchten, P., Ozkaya, I., Seaman, C.: Managing technical debt in software engineering. Dagstuhl Rep. **6**(4), 110–138 (2016)
7. InsighTD Project. http://td-survey.com/. Accessed 05 Aug 2019
8. Rios, N., Spinola, R., Mendonça, M., Seaman, C.: The most common causes and effects of technical debt: first results from a global family of industrial surveys. In: Proceedings of Empirical Software Engineering and Measurement (ESEM). ACM, Oulu (2018)
9. McConnell, S.: Managing technical debt. In: Best Practices White Papers. Construx Software, Washington, United States (2008)

Estimations

Exploring Preference of Chronological and Relevancy Filtering in Effort Estimation

Sousuke Amasaki[(✉)] [ID]

Okayama Prefectural University, 111 Kuboki, Soja, Okayama, Japan
amasaki@cse.oka-pu.ac.jp

Abstract. BACKGROUND: Effort estimation models are often built based on history data from past projects in an organization. Filtering techniques have been proposed for improving the estimation accuracy. Chronological filtering relies on the time proximity among project data and ignores much old data. Relevancy filtering utilizes the proximity of characteristics among project data and ignores dissimilar data. Their interaction is interesting because one would be able to make more accurate estimates if a positive synergistic effect exists.

AIMS: To examine whether the chronological filtering and the relevancy filtering can contribute to improving the estimation accuracy together.

METHOD: moving windows approaches as chronological filtering and a nearest neighbor approach as relevancy filtering are applied to a single-company ISBSG data.

RESULTS: we observed a negative synergistic effect. Each of the filtering approaches brought better effort estimates than using the whole history data. However, their combination may cause worse effort estimates than using the whole history data.

CONCLUSIONS: Practitioners should care about a negative synergistic effect when combining the chronological filtering and the relevancy filtering.

Keywords: Effort estimation · Moving windows · Relevancy filtering

1 Introduction

Effort estimation is still a challenging activity for software development projects. Practitioners have suffered from overruns and cancellations caused by overestimation and underestimation. As the estimation accuracy is an essential aspect of effort estimation, not a few researchers have focused on developing practices for accurate estimation. Model-based effort estimation is one of the popular topics in software effort estimation research.

Effort estimation models are often built based on history data from past projects in an organization. A reason for inaccurate estimation is the dissimilarity

© Springer Nature Switzerland AG 2019
X. Franch et al. (Eds.): PROFES 2019, LNCS 11915, pp. 247–262, 2019.
https://doi.org/10.1007/978-3-030-35333-9_18

between the history data and a target project data. One cause of the inaccuracy is that a part of the history data is too old and no longer a representative of the organization. Another cause is that a target project is of a new domain for the organization and the history data may have different characteristics.

A promising solution for the causes is filtering techniques that only keep a useful part of the history data. Chronological filtering relies on the time proximity among project data and ignores much old data. For example, Lokan and Mendes [13] proposed moving windows that filtered out old data. It does not look in any characteristics and is expected to catch changes not appeared on metrics. In contrast, relevancy filtering utilizes the proximity of characteristics among project data and ignores dissimilar data. A study [17] is an example that a k-nearest neighbor approach was used as a relevancy filtering.

As different techniques worked well for improving estimation accuracy, a question arises whether the chronological filtering and the relevancy filtering can contribute to better effort estimation together. Furthermore, if a positive synergistic effect exists beyond the mere summation of the filtering techniques, practitioners using one filter technique should adopt another one.

In this paper, we explore the effects of chronological filtering and relevancy filtering with a single-company ISBSG data, which was often used for evaluating the moving windows, for answering the following research questions:

RQ1: Does the chronological filtering improve the estimate accuracy?
RQ2: Does the relevancy filtering improve the estimate accuracy?
RQ3: Does the combination of chronological filtering and the relevancy filtering improve the estimate accuracy?

RQ1 and RQ2 were set ahead of RQ3 for the following reason though some past studies have already answered to them with the same project data. It was shown that different effort estimation techniques could cause different effects (e.g., [3,4]) when using filter approaches. The fact implies that filtering techniques do not necessarily improve estimation accuracy when one uses different effort estimation techniques. In this study, we adopted two simple effort estimation techniques, namely, average and median, to remove the effects and to focus on the effects of the filtering approaches. It may lead to a different conclusion to the past studies that used the same project data. We thus need to confirm the effects of filtering techniques again even if we used the same project data.

2   Related Work

2.1   Chronological Filtering

Although research in software effort estimation models has a long history, relatively few studies have taken into consideration the chronological order of projects. Therefore, chronological filtering has not been studied well compared with other topics in effort estimation.

To our knowledge, Kitchenham et al. [8] were first to suggest the use of chronological filtering. They built four linear regression models with four subsets, each of which comprised projects from different ranges of time duration. As the coefficients of the models were different from each other, they allowed to drop out older project data. Lokan and Mendes [13] were the first to study the effect of using moving windows in detail. They used linear regression (LR) models and a single-company dataset from the ISBSG repository. Training sets were defined to be the N most recently completed projects. They found that the use of a window could affect accuracy significantly; predictive accuracy was better with larger windows; some window sizes were particularly effective. Amasaki and Lokan also investigated the effect of using moving windows with Estimation by Analogy [1] and CART [2]. They found that moving windows could improve the estimation accuracy, but the effect was different than with LR.

Recent studies also showed the effect and its extent could be affected by windowing policies [14] and software organizations [15]. Lokan and Mendes [14] investigated the effect on accuracy when using moving windows of various ranges of time duration to form training sets on which to base effort estimates. They also showed that the use of windows based on duration could affect the accuracy of estimates, but to a lesser extent than windows based on a fixed number of projects [15].

2.2   Relevancy Filtering

Relevancy filtering is considered as a type of transfer learning approaches. While many filtering approaches have been proposed for cross-project defect prediction (e.g., [7]), a few studies on cross-company effort estimation have evaluated the effects of relevancy filtering approaches.

Turhan and Mendes [17] applied brings a so-called NN-filter [18] to cross-company effort estimation of web projects. They showed that an estimation model based on raw cross-company data was worse than that based on within-company data but was improved as comparable one by using the NN-filter. Kocaguneli et al. [9–11] also introduced a transfer learning approach called TEAK for improving cross-company effort estimation. They applied it to transfer old project to a new project and found that TEAK was effective not only for cross-company effort estimation but also for cross-time effort estimation [12].

NN-filter is based on a nearest neighbor algorithm. In that sense, a study by Amasaki and Lokan [1] can be considered as an evaluation study of the combination of the relevancy filtering and the chronological filtering. In that study, the combination worked well to improve estimation accuracy for a narrow range of window sizes. While that study used a wrapper approach for feature selection and logarithmic transformation in addition to the nearest neighbor algorithm, our study aims to explore the effects of the combination without such complicated factors. For that purpose, we adopted two simple estimation techniques that were not adopted in [1], described in the next section.

3   Methodology

3.1   Effort Estimation Techniques

Many effort estimation techniques have been proposed so far. Those often became complicated and have many parameters to be tuned for achieving higher estimation accuracy. Even a simple nearest neighbor algorithm (known as estimation by analogy in software effort estimation research) brings several options other than the number of neighbors [11].

As we aim to explore the effects of the chronological filtering and the relevancy filtering, we decided to use simple approaches, namely, a median and an average of a training set. An average uses the whole training set and is sensitive to the distribution of the training set. A median uses one effort value and is robust the change of distribution. These contrasting characteristics contributed to explore the effects of filtering approaches.

3.2   Chronological Filtering

This study adopted fixed-size moving windows [13] and fixed-duration moving windows [15]. In estimation, the latest N finished projects were selected by the fixed-size moving windows. The latest projects finished within N months were selected by the fixed-duration moving windows. As N influence on the effectiveness of moving windows, we explored various values as well as past studies.

3.3   Relevancy Filtering

This study used a nearest neighbor algorithm as a relevancy filtering approach. It is also called NN-filter [18]. NN-filter finds k nearest neighbors of a target project from history data based on unweighted Euclidean distance. Each feature of project data was normalized with min-max normalization before the distance calculation. As the synergistic effect could be observed with effective filtering, the relevancy filtering had to be configured as effective enough. If the relevancy filtering works well, increasing k would lead to worse estimation. We roughly confirmed it with $k = 3$ and $k = 1/3$ of training data and adopted $k = 3$, which is the smallest number which can make average and median estimations estimate distinct efforts. It could not be the best but was more effective enough than larger ks. Detailed analyses should be conducted in future work.

3.4   Dataset Description

This study used the single-company subset of the ISBSG dataset that was analyzed in [1,2,4,13–15]. This data set is sourced from Release 10 of the ISBSG Repository. Release 10 contains data for 4106 projects; however, not all projects provided the chronological data we needed (i.e. known duration and completion date, from which we could calculate start date), and those that did varied in data quality and definitions. To form a data set in which all projects provided the necessary data for size, effort and chronology, defined size and effort similarly, and had high quality data, we selected projects according to the following criteria:

- The projects are rated by ISBSG as having high data quality (A or B).
- Implementation date and overall project elapsed time are known.
- Size is measured in IFPUG 4.0 or later (because size measured with an older version is not directly comparable with size measured with IFPUG version 4.0 or later). We also removed projects that measured size with an unspecified version of function points, and whose completion pre-dated IFPUG version 4.0.
- The size in unadjusted function points is known.
- Development team effort (resource level 1) is known. Our analysis used only the development team's effort as well as the past studies for maximizing comparability of results.
- Normalized effort and recorded effort are equal. This should mean that the reported effort is the actual effort across the whole life cycle.
- The projects are not web projects. (This is because there is evidence that web projects are different enough in nature to other projects that they should not be analyzed together [16]; further, Function Points do not capture some features affecting the effort required for web applications [6].)

In the remaining set of 909 projects, 231 were all from the same organization and 678 were from other organizations. We only selected the 231 projects from the single organization, as we considered that the use of single-company data was more suitable to answer our research questions than using cross-company data. Preliminary analysis showed that three projects were extremely influential and invariably removed from model building, so they were removed from the set. The final set contained 228 projects.

We do not know the identity of the organization that developed these projects.

Release 10 of the ISBSG database provides data on numerous variables; however, this number was reduced to a small set that we have found in past analyses with this dataset to have an impact on effort, and which did not suffer from a large number of missing data values. The remaining variables were size (measured in unadjusted function points), effort (hours), and four categorical variables: development type (new development, re-development, enhancement), primary language type (3GL, 4GL), platform (mainframe, midrange, PC, multiplatform), and industry sector (banking, insurance, manufacturing, other).

Table 1 shows summary statistics for size (measured in unadjusted function points), effort, and project delivery rate(PDR). PDR is calculated as effort divided by size; high project delivery rates indicate low productivity. In [13], the authors examined the project delivery rate and found it changes across time. This finding supports the use of a window.

The projects were developed for a variety of industry sectors, where insurance, banking and manufacturing were the most common. Start dates range from 1994 to 2002, although only 9 started before 1998. 3GLs are used by 86%

Table 1. Summary statistics for ratio-scaled variables in data from single ISBSG organization

Variable	Min	Mean	Median	Max	StDev
Size	10	496	266	6294	699
Effort	62	4553	2408	57749	6212
PDR	0.53	16.47	8.75	387.10	31.42

of projects; mainframes account for 40%, and multi-platform for 55%; these percentages for language and platform vary little from year to year. There is a trend over time towards more enhancement projects and fewer new developments. Enhancement projects tend to be smaller than new development, so there is a corresponding trend towards lower size and effort.

3.5   Experiment Procedure

As the chronological filtering relies on the time proximity, our experiment needs to assume a situation that a development organization needs to respond to continuously coming new projects. The size of windows influences on where our experiment starts. As same as the past studies, our experiment with a specific window size was conducted as follows:

1. Sort all projects by starting date.
2. For a given window size N, find the earliest project p_0 for which at least $N+1$ projects were completed prior to the start of p_0 (projects from p_0 onwards are the ones whose training set is affected by using a window, so they form the set of evaluation projects for this window size. For example, with a window of 20 projects, at least 21 projects must have finished for the window to differ from the growing portfolio.)
3. For every project p_i in chronological sequence, starting from p_0, form estimates using moving windows and the growing portfolio (all completed projects).
   - For the growing approach (i.e., without moving windows), the training set is all projects that finished before p_i started.
   - For fixed-size moving windows, the training set is the N most recent projects that finished before p_i started. If multiple projects finished on the same date, all of them are included.
   - For fixed-duration moving windows, the training set is the most recent projects whose whole life cycle had fallen within a window of D months prior to the start of p_i.
4. Estimate an effort of a target project based on past project data.
   - For relevancy filtering, the training set is a subset selected by a nearest neighbor.
   - Without relevancy filtering, the training set is all projects from the previous step.
5. Evaluate the estimation results.

Note that the growing portfolio means using the whole history data without any filtering approaches.

We explored window sizes from 20 to 120 projects for the size-based moving windows and from 12 to 84 months for the duration-based moving windows as well as the past study [3].

3.6   Performance Measures

The accuracy statistics that we used to evaluate the effort estimation models are based on the difference between estimated effort and actual effort. We used Mean Absolute Error (MAE), which is widely used to evaluate the accuracy of effort estimation models, as it is an unbiased measure that favours neither under- nor over-estimates.

We concentrate first on the statistical significance of differences in accuracy that arise from using the filtering approaches. To test for statistically significant differences between accuracy measures, we use the two-sided Wilcoxon signed-rank test (`wilcoxon` function of the `scipy` package for Python) and set the statistical significance level at $\alpha = 0.05$. The setting of this study is a typical multiple testing, and the p-values of the tests must be controlled. Bonferroni correction is a popular method for this purpose. However, the adoption of this simple correction results in the lack of statistical power, especially for not large effects. We thus controlled the false discovery rate (FDR) of multiple testing [5] with the "`multipletests`" function of the `statsmodels` package in Python. FDR is a ratio of the number of falsely rejected null hypotheses to the number of rejected null hypotheses.

4   Results and Discussion

4.1   Effects of Chronological Filtering

Tables 2 and 3 show the effect on MAE of using moving windows, compared to always using the growing portfolio, using evaluation windows of different sizes[1]. As the past studies did not examine the effect of moving windows with simple average and median estimations, we followed the same comparison procedure based on the growing portfolio. The first column of Tables 2(a) and 3(a) and shows window sizes. The second column shows the total number of projects used as testing projects with the corresponding window size. The third and fourth columns show accuracy measures for the growing portfolio and the moving windows, for the corresponding window sizes. The number of testing projects depends on window size, and the measures resulted in different values among window sizes even for the growing portfolio. The fifth column shows the difference in percentages. The sixth column shows the p-value from statistical tests on accuracy measures between the growing portfolio and the moving windows.

---

[1] The tables only show results for every tenth window size, due to space limitations. Graphs show results for all window sizes.

The last column shows the effect size compared to using the growing portfolio. Positive values mean a preference for the growing portfolio. Tables 2(b) and 3(b) omitted the fist and the second columns as those are the same as the results with the mean estimation.

Table 2. Residuals with different fixed-size windows

(a) Average Estimation   (b) Median Estimation

Window Size	Test Prjs.	GP	MW	Diff.(%)	p-val.	Eff. Size	GP	MW	Diff.(%)	p-val.	Eff. Size
20	201	4322	4118	−4.72	0.14	−0.07	3196	3341	4.54	0.19	0.04
30	178	4105	3631	−11.57	0.00	−0.18	3033	2998	−1.16	0.47	−0.01
40	165	4125	3780	−8.34	0.00	−0.13	2948	2992	1.48	0.55	0.01
50	153	4221	3747	−11.24	0.00	−0.17	2944	2937	−0.25	0.88	−0.00
60	136	4118	3538	−14.07	0.00	−0.23	2885	2885	0.01	0.98	0.00
70	126	3946	3420	−13.31	0.00	−0.25	2617	2566	−1.92	0.38	−0.02
80	126	3946	3638	−7.79	0.00	−0.15	2617	2574	−1.65	0.23	−0.02
90	111	3975	3635	−8.57	0.00	−0.16	2616	2570	−1.77	0.45	−0.02
100	88	3789	3364	−11.21	0.00	−0.20	2599	2486	−4.33	0.01	−0.04
110	75	3593	3133	−12.80	0.00	−0.23	2236	2103	−5.93	0.00	−0.06
120	71	3520	3217	−8.63	0.00	−0.15	2242	2158	−3.73	0.00	−0.04

Figure 1 has 4 plots showing the difference in mean absolute error against window sizes. The x-axis of each figure is the size of the window, and the y-axis is the subtraction of the accuracy measure value with the growing approach from that with the moving windows at the given x-value. The moving windows is advantageous where the line is below 0. Circle points mean a statistically significant difference, with the moving windows being better than the growing portfolio. Square points mean a statistically significant difference, with the moving windows being worse than the growing portfolio. At these points, the corresponding FDR-controlled p-value is below $\alpha = 0.05$.

Regarding the fixed-size moving windows, Figs. 1(a) and (b) and Table 2 reveal the effect of using moving windows, compared to always using the growing portfolio as follows:

- With average estimation, the difference in MAE is almost always statistically significant regardless of window sizes.
- With median estimation, the line gets going down around 60 projects and implies the preference of the fixed moving windows. However, the difference is not statistically significant for all window sizes.
- The average estimation was worse in the estimation accuracy than the median estimation regardless of using fixed-size moving windows, as shown in Tables 2(a) and (b).

Table 3. Residuals with different fixed-duration windows

(a) Average Estimation   (b) Median Estimation

Window Months	Test Prjs.	GP	MW	Diff.(%)	p-val.	Eff. Size	GP	MW	Diff.(%)	p-val.	Eff. Size
12	165	4125	3368	−18.35	0.00	−0.28	2948	2808	−4.75	0.07	−0.04
18	193	4224	3766	−10.85	0.00	−0.17	3121	3081	−1.27	0.60	−0.01
24	201	4322	4116	−4.77	0.00	−0.08	3196	3116	−2.50	0.02	−0.02
30	202	4313	4252	−1.41	0.14	−0.02	3197	3183	−0.45	0.52	−0.00
36	206	4319	4284	−0.80	0.45	−0.01	3188	3160	−0.87	0.02	−0.01
42	206	4319	4387	1.59	0.39	0.03	3188	3211	0.73	0.16	0.01
48	206	4319	4409	2.09	0.05	0.03	3188	3217	0.93	0.09	0.01
54	206	4319	4444	2.91	0.00	0.05	3188	3214	0.83	0.00	0.01
60	198	4332	4438	2.45	0.00	0.04	3214	3238	0.75	0.00	0.01
66	184	4167	4234	1.61	0.00	0.03	3130	3136	0.20	0.03	0.00
72	153	4221	4274	1.25	0.00	0.02	2944	2938	−0.22	0.18	−0.00
78	126	3946	3980	0.87	0.00	0.02	2617	2603	−0.51	0.00	−0.01
84	80	3750	3769	0.50	0.00	0.01	2442	2429	−0.54	0.00	−0.01

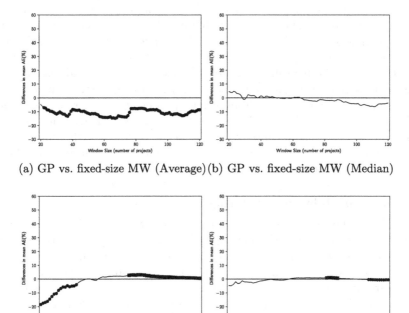

(a) GP vs. fixed-size MW (Average) (b) GP vs. fixed-size MW (Median)

(c) GP vs. fixed-duration MW (Average) (d) GP vs. fixed-duration (Median)

Fig. 1. The difference of accuracy measures between growing portfolio and moving-windows

Regarding the fixed-duration moving windows, Figs. 1(c) and (d), Table 3 reveal the effect of using moving windows, compared to always using the growing portfolio as follows:

- With average estimation, the difference in MAE is statistically significant before 30 months and implies the preference of fixed-duration moving windows. Then, the line gets going up over 0 and supports the growing portfolio. The differences are often statistically significant.
- With median estimation, the line looks similar to the one of the average estimation but modest. It gets going up and supports the growing portfolio around 60 months and then supports the fixed-duration moving windows around 80 months. The differences are statistically significant around there but the degree is trivial.
- The average estimation was worse than the median estimation regardless of using fixed-size moving windows.

From those observations, it seems that fixed-size and fixed-duration moving windows could extract a better subset for effort estimation if one uses the average estimation. In contrast, the median estimation could not gain significant benefits from the moving windows. A possible reason is that the median estimation is not sensitive to the change of training set distribution. It uses only a single project for effort estimation. The average estimation uses all training projects and is inclined to be sensitive to the change of distribution. The worse performance of the average estimation seems due to a well-known tendency that effort distribution is skewed.

In summary, a better subset can be obtained by moving windows and helps estimates by simple averaging to be more accurate. In contrast, a simple median is too robust to obtain benefits from distribution change. However, the median gave more accurate estimates. The answer to RQ1 is thus that the moving windows could improve significantly the estimation accuracy with some window sizes if one uses the average estimation. For the median estimation, the change of distribution was not sufficient.

4.2   Effects of Relevancy Filtering

Tables 4 and 5 show the effect on MAE of using the relevancy filtering approach, compared to always using the growing portfolio. For easy comparison to the previous results, the results are summarised using the same fixed-size window sizes and fixed-duration windows as well as Tables 2 and 3. The difference is in the third and fourth columns that show accuracy measures for the growing portfolio and the nearest neighbor, for the corresponding window sizes.

Figures in Fig. 2 plot the difference in mean absolute error against window sizes. The x-axis of each figure is the size of the window, and the y-axis is the subtraction of the accuracy measure value with the growing approach from that with the nearest neighbor at the given x-value.

Regarding the nearest neighbor filtering with $k = 3$ summarized with fixed-size windows, Figs. 2(a) and (b) and Table 4 reveal the effect of using relevancy filtering, compared to always using the growing portfolio as follows:

Table 4. Residuals with different k-nearest neighbor (k = 3) summarized with fixed-size windows

(a) Average Estimation

Window Size	Test Prjs.	GP	KNN	Diff.(%)	p-val.	Eff. Size
20	201	4322	3098	−28.32	0.0	−0.45
30	178	4105	2872	−30.04	0.0	−0.46
40	165	4125	2738	−33.61	0.0	−0.51
50	153	4221	2762	−34.56	0.0	−0.53
60	136	4118	2668	−35.21	0.0	−0.57
70	126	3946	2551	−35.33	0.0	−0.67
80	126	3946	2551	−35.33	0.0	−0.67
90	111	3975	2653	−33.26	0.0	−0.63
100	88	3789	2632	−30.54	0.0	−0.53
110	75	3593	2365	−34.18	0.0	−0.63
120	71	3520	2352	−33.19	0.0	−0.59

(b) Median Estimation

GP	KNN	Diff.(%)	p-val.	Eff. Size
3196	3117	−2.47	0.20	−0.02
3033	2815	−7.18	0.11	−0.06
2948	2682	−9.04	0.07	−0.08
2944	2663	−9.56	0.07	−0.08
2885	2563	−11.15	0.07	−0.10
2617	2395	−8.46	0.16	−0.09
2617	2395	−8.46	0.16	−0.09
2616	2476	−5.35	0.25	−0.05
2599	2517	−3.14	0.47	−0.03
2236	2293	2.54	0.63	0.03
2242	2322	3.59	0.74	0.04

Table 5. Residuals with different k-nearest neighbor (k = 3) summarized with fixed-duration windows

(a) Average Estimation

Window Size	Test Prjs.	GP	KNN	Diff.(%)	p-val.	Eff. Size
12	165	4125	2738	−33.61	0.0	−0.51
18	193	4224	3006	−28.84	0.0	−0.46
24	201	4322	3098	−28.32	0.0	−0.45
30	202	4313	3093	−28.28	0.0	−0.45
36	206	4319	3129	−27.54	0.0	−0.44
42	206	4319	3129	−27.54	0.0	−0.44
48	206	4319	3129	−27.54	0.0	−0.44
54	206	4319	3129	−27.54	0.0	−0.44
60	198	4332	3109	−28.23	0.0	−0.44
66	184	4167	2945	−29.33	0.0	−0.46
72	153	4221	2762	−34.56	0.0	−0.53
78	126	3946	2551	−35.33	0.0	−0.67
84	80	3750	2622	−30.08	0.0	−0.54

(b) Median Estimation

GP	KNN	Diff.(%)	p-val.	Eff. Size
2948	2682	−9.04	0.07	−0.08
3121	2991	−4.14	0.15	−0.04
3196	3117	−2.47	0.20	−0.02
3197	3114	−2.61	0.18	−0.02
3188	3132	−1.74	0.27	−0.02
3188	3132	−1.74	0.27	−0.02
3188	3132	−1.74	0.27	−0.02
3188	3132	−1.74	0.27	−0.02
3214	3133	−2.54	0.19	−0.02
3130	2910	−7.02	0.09	−0.06
2944	2663	−9.56	0.07	−0.08
2617	2395	−8.46	0.16	−0.09
2442	2522	3.29	0.69	0.03

- With average estimation, the difference in MAE is almost always statistically significant.
- With median estimation, the line almost always stays below 0 and implies the preference of the nearest neighbor filtering. However, the difference is not statistically significant for all window sizes.
- The average estimation was almost always worse than the median estimation as shown in Tables 4(a) and (b).

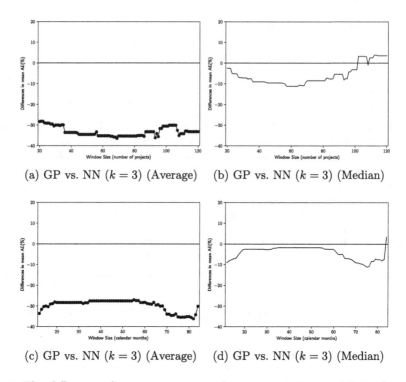

(a) GP vs. NN ($k = 3$) (Average)   (b) GP vs. NN ($k = 3$) (Median)

(c) GP vs. NN ($k = 3$) (Average)   (d) GP vs. NN ($k = 3$) (Median)

Fig. 2. The difference of accuracy measures between growing portfolio and nearest neighbor filtering

Regarding the nearest neighbor filtering with $k = 3$ summarized with fixed-duration windows, Figs. 2(c) and (d) and Table 5 reveal the effect of using relevancy filtering, compared to always using the growing portfolio as follows:

- With average estimation, the difference in MAE is almost always statistically significant and implies the preference of the nearest neighbor filtering.
- With median estimation, the line always stays below 0. There is no clear difference.
- The average estimation was worse than the median estimation.

From those observations, it seems that the nearest neighbor approach could extract a better subset for effort estimation if one uses the average estimation. Although the median estimation could gain benefits from the nearest neighbor approach, the effect was not significant. As same as the chronological filtering, a possible reason for the ineffectiveness for the median estimation is that the median estimation is not sensitive to the change of training set distribution. It is surprising that the median estimation with a small number of similar projects is not so better than that with all projects.

The answer to RQ2 is thus that the nearest neighbor algorithm could improve the estimation accuracy significantly if one uses the average estimation. The median estimation could only gain small benefits.

Table 6. Residuals with different fixed-size windows & KNN (k = 3)

(a) Average Estimation

Window Size	Test Prjs.	GP	CB	Diff. (%)	p-val.	Eff. Size
20	201	4322	3739	−13.48	0.00	−0.21
30	178	4105	3153	−23.19	0.00	−0.36
40	165	4125	3156	−23.48	0.00	−0.36
50	153	4221	3040	−27.98	0.00	−0.43
60	136	4118	2752	−33.17	0.00	−0.53
70	126	3946	2462	−37.59	0.00	−0.71
80	126	3946	2614	−33.75	0.00	−0.64
90	111	3975	2803	−29.50	0.00	−0.56
100	88	3789	2980	−21.36	0.00	−0.37
110	75	3593	2730	−24.02	0.00	−0.44
120	71	3520	2760	−21.59	0.01	−0.38

(b) Median Estimation

GP	CB	Diff.(%)	p-val.	Eff. Size
3196	3819	19.49	0.03	0.17
3033	3094	2.01	0.79	0.02
2948	3065	3.94	0.90	0.03
2944	3072	4.33	0.89	0.04
2885	2731	−5.34	0.32	−0.05
2617	2482	−5.13	0.34	−0.05
2617	2581	−1.35	0.61	−0.01
2616	2709	3.55	0.98	0.04
2599	2955	13.72	0.46	0.13
2236	2797	25.13	0.29	0.26
2242	2929	30.66	0.34	0.31

Table 7. Residuals with different fixed-duration windows & KNN (k = 3)

(a) Average Estimation

Window Months	Test Prjs.	GP	CB	Diff.(%)	p-val.	Eff. Size
12	165	4125	3200	−22.40	0.0	−0.34
18	193	4224	3166	−25.04	0.0	−0.40
24	201	4322	3074	−28.88	0.0	−0.46
30	202	4313	3153	−26.89	0.0	−0.42
36	206	4319	3231	−25.18	0.0	−0.40
42	206	4319	3124	−27.67	0.0	−0.44
48	206	4319	3144	−27.20	0.0	−0.43
54	206	4319	3150	−27.06	0.0	−0.43
60	198	4332	3117	−28.03	0.0	−0.44
66	184	4167	2924	−29.83	0.0	−0.47
72	153	4221	2737	−35.16	0.0	−0.54
78	126	3946	2517	−36.21	0.0	−0.69
84	80	3750	2622	−30.08	0.0	−0.54

(b) Median Estimation

GP	CB	Diff.(%)	p-val.	Eff. Size
2948	3127	6.06	0.80	0.05
3121	3171	1.60	0.66	0.01
3196	3140	−1.76	0.38	−0.02
3197	3219	0.67	0.40	0.01
3188	3168	−0.62	0.52	−0.01
3188	3040	−4.65	0.29	−0.04
3188	3112	−2.37	0.32	−0.02
3188	3143	−1.42	0.31	−0.01
3214	3117	−3.03	0.16	−0.03
3130	2888	−7.72	0.06	−0.07
2944	2632	−10.62	0.04	−0.09
2617	2354	−10.03	0.10	−0.10
2442	2522	3.29	0.69	0.03

4.3 Effects of Chronological and Relevancy Filtering

Tables 6 and 7 show the effect on MAE of using the chronological filtering and the relevancy filtering together, compared to always using the growing portfolio, using evaluation windows of different sizes. Figures in Fig. 3 plot the difference in mean absolute error against window sizes. Note that the combination selected $k = 3$ projects after applying the chronological filtering.

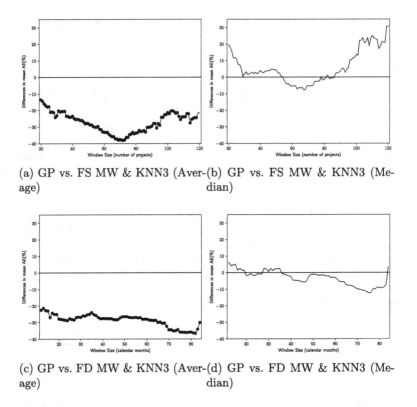

(a) GP vs. FS MW & KNN3 (Average)   (b) GP vs. FS MW & KNN3 (Median)

(c) GP vs. FD MW & KNN3 (Average)   (d) GP vs. FD MW & KNN3 (Median)

Fig. 3. The difference of accuracy measures between growing portfolio and combination of moving windows and nearest neighbor (k = 3)

Regarding the fixed-size moving windows, Figs. 3(a) and (b) and Table 6 reveal the effect of using the combination of filtering, compared to always using the growing portfolio as follows:

- With average estimation, the difference in MAE is almost always statistically significant regardless of window sizes.
- With median estimation, the line rarely gets going down below 0 and implies the preference of the growing portfolio. The difference is not statistically significant for all window sizes.
- The average estimation was competitive to the median estimation when using the combination as shown in Tables 6(a) and (b).

Regarding the fixed-duration moving windows, Figs. 3(c) and (d) and Table 7 reveal the effect of using the combination of filtering, compared to always using the growing portfolio as follows:

- With average estimation, the difference in MAE is almost always statistically significant regardless of window sizes.

- With median estimation, the line gets going down below 0 around 35 month and stays there before 80 months. The figure supports the combination around 80 months. However, the differences are not statistically significant.
- The average estimation was a bit worse than the median estimation regardless of using the combination.

From those observations, it seems that the combination could extract a better subset for effort estimation if one uses the average estimation. In contrast, the median estimation could not gain significant benefits from the combination.

From Figs. 1(d) and 2(d), we can see that the effects of fixed-duration windows and the nearest neighbor were compromised. The statistically significant window sizes in Fig. 1(d) were diminished. That is, there was no positive synergistic effect. In contrast, we can see that the growing portfolio got more advantageous in Fig. 3(b) in comparison to Figs. 1(b) and 2(b). That is, the combination caused a negative synergistic effect.

The answer to RQ3 is that the combination of chronological and relevancy filtering made the performance worse than the independent application if one uses the fixed-size windows as a chronological filtering. Even if one uses the fixed-duration windows, no positive synergistic effect occurs.

5 Conclusion

We explored the effects of chronological filtering and relevancy filtering for effort estimation. We confirmed the moving windows and the k-nearest neighbor could extract a better subset. However, only the average estimation got statistically significant benefits from the subset. Furthermore, the combination of the chronological filtering and the relevancy filtering did not cause a positive synergistic effect. Rather, the combination may cause a negative synergistic effect. We thus recommend not to combine them.

We also observed that the median estimation was better than the average estimation probably for skewed effort distribution. The observation does not necessarily imply that the filtering was insufficient because the change in distributions of feature variables was not reflected to effort estimation process by such as feature selection. Further investigation considering the change is in future work. As relevancy filtering is a type of transfer learning, it is also interesting to examine a combined effect between other transfer learning approaches and the moving windows. We could not describe why the combination technique could not work. Additional experiments with other data sets will help to reason and validate the present results.

Acknowledgment. This work was supported by JSPS KAKENHI Grant #18K11246.

References

1. Amasaki, S., Lokan, C.: The effects of moving windows to software estimation: comparative study on linear regression and estimation by analogy. In: Proceedings of IWSM-MENSURA 2012, pp. 23–32. IEEE (2012)

2. Amasaki, S., Lokan, C.: The effect of moving windows on software effort estimation: comparative study with CART. In: Proceedings of IWESEP 2014, pp. 1–6. IEEE (2014)
3. Amasaki, S., Lokan, C.: A replication of comparative study of moving windows on linear regression and estimation by analogy. In: Proceedings of PROMISE, pp. 1–10. ACM Press (2015)
4. Amasaki, S., Lokan, C.: Evaluation of moving window policies with CART. In: Proceedings of IWESEP 2016, pp. 24–29. IEEE (2016)
5. Benjamini, Y., Yekutieli, D.: The control of the false discovery rate in multiple testing under dependency. Ann. Stat. **29**(4), 1165–1188 (2001)
6. Ferrucci, F., Gravino, C., Martino, S.D.: A case study using web objects and cosmic for effort estimation of web applications. In: Proceedings of SEAA, pp. 441–448. IEEE Computer Society (2008)
7. Herbold, S.: CrossPare: a tool for benchmarking cross-project defect predictions. In: Proceedings of 30th IEEE/ACM International Conference on Automated Software Engineering Workshops (ASEW), pp. 90–95. IEEE (2016)
8. Kitchenham, B., Lawrence Pfleeger, S., McColl, B., Eagan, S.: An empirical study of maintenance and development estimation accuracy. J. Syst. Softw. **64**(1), 57–77 (2002)
9. Kocaguneli, E., Gay, G., Menzies, T., Yang, Y., Keung, J.W.: When to use data from other projects for effort estimation. In: Proceedings of ASE, pp. 321–324. ACM (2010)
10. Kocaguneli, E., Menzies, T.: How to find relevant data for effort estimation? In: Proceedings of ESEM, pp. 255–264. IEEE, September 2011
11. Kocaguneli, E., Menzies, T., Bener, A.B., Keung, J.W.: Exploiting the essential assumptions of analogy-based effort estimation. IEEE Trans. Softw. Eng. **38**(2), 425–438 (2012)
12. Kocaguneli, E., Menzies, T., Mendes, E.: Transfer learning in effort estimation. Emp. Softw. Eng. **20**(3), 813–843 (2015)
13. Lokan, C., Mendes, E.: Applying moving windows to software effort estimation. In: Proceedings of ESEM 2009, pp. 111–122 (2009)
14. Lokan, C., Mendes, E.: Investigating the use of duration-based moving windows to improve software effort prediction. In: Proceedings of APSEC 2012, pp. 818–827 (2012)
15. Lokan, C., Mendes, E.: Investigating the use of duration-based moving windows to improve software effort prediction: a replicated study. Inf. Softw. Technol. **56**(9), 1063–1075 (2014)
16. Mendes, E., Mosley, N. (eds.): Web Engineering. Springer, Heidelberg (2006). https://doi.org/10.1007/3-540-28218-1
17. Turhan, B., Mendes, E.: A comparison of cross-versus single-company effort prediction models for web projects. In: Proceedings of SEAA, pp. 285–292. IEEE (2014)
18. Turhan, B., Menzies, T., Bener, A.B., Di Stefano, J.: On the relative value of cross-company and within-company data for defect prediction. Emp. Softw. Eng. **14**(5), 540–578 (2009)

Automated Functional Size Measurement: A Multiple Case Study in the Industry

Christian Quesada-López[1]([⊠]), Alexandra Martínez[1], Marcelo Jenkins[1],
Luis Carlos Salas[1,2], and Juan Carlos Gómez[2]

[1] Universidad de Costa Rica, San José, Costa Rica
{cristian.quesadalopez,alexandra.martinez,marcelo.jenkins}@ucr.ac.cr
[2] Grupo Asesor en Informática, San José, Costa Rica
{lsalas,jgomez}@grupoasesor.net

Abstract. Automating functional size measurement (FSM) for software applications that use specific development frameworks is a challenge for the industry. Although FSM automation brings benefits such as savings in time and costs, and better measure reliability, it is difficult to implement. In this paper, we present a multi-case study that evaluates the accuracy of an automated procedure for software size estimation in the context of a software development company. This procedure is implemented by a tool called FastWorks FPA, which obtains the IFPUG FPA function point estimation of software applications modeled in the company's FastWorks framework. We describe the measurement process used by the tool, and discuss the results of the case studies. The accuracy (magnitude of relative error) of the measurements computed by the tool ranged between 3.9% and 12.9%, based on the total unadjusted function points. These results provide evidence for the feasibility of automating the counting process, as the tool's estimated functional size reasonably approximates the result of specialists' manual counting.

Keywords: Functional size measurement · Functional size estimation · IFPUG FPA · Empirical study

1 Introduction

Functional size measurement (FSM) has demonstrated its usefulness in different software development phases [26]. The accuracy of FSM is critical in software project management, being one of the key inputs for effort and cost estimation models [13]. However, FSM highly depends on the knowledge of the measurer, thus requiring a significant level of expertise. A widely used FSM method is IFPUG FPA [18]. This method considers product functionality from the user's perspective, and it is independent from the technology used to implement it.

Having accurate software size estimation for its applications is a challenging task for any software organization [10]. Differences in measuring may occur because FSM inherently entails subjectivity in the application of some method

© Springer Nature Switzerland AG 2019
X. Franch et al. (Eds.): PROFES 2019, LNCS 11915, pp. 263–279, 2019.
https://doi.org/10.1007/978-3-030-35333-9_19

rules [10], and some decisions are left to the measurers. This might result in variations of size estimates by different counters on the same application [35]. Moreover, FSM methods are still considered time consuming and expensive [21].

To take advantage of the benefits of FSM, it is necessary to provide solutions that generate measurements faster, with less human subjectivity [15,28], and with an acceptable degree of variation in accuracy [15,34]. To address these issues, a number of studies on FSM automation have been conducted in recent years [28,35], yielding benefits such as savings in time and costs, and better reliability and repeatability of measures [15]. To ensure the consistency and repeatability, the FSM automation must be performed from the consistent interpretation of measurement rules [25]. Automating functional size measurement for software applications that use specific development frameworks is a challenge for industry [10]. Any organizations that wants to introduce function points (FP) for estimating size and determine development effort, must collect a data baseline to allow for benchmarking, and the construction of effort estimation models based on historical data [10].

We have investigated automatic estimation of IFPUG FPA functional size for software models expressed in the FastWorks (FW) framework in collaboration with University of Costa Rica and *Grupo Asesor IT Services Group* [29,30]. FW is a development framework that has been developed and maintained internally by this software organization. We presented the FSM procedure and its automation with the measurement prototype tool [29], and empirically validated the functional size estimation results through a case of study in industry [30].

In this paper, we examine the automated function point estimation procedure implemented in FastWorks (FW) by sizing the models of six software applications independently developed by a software architect of the organization. We conducted a multi-case study to evaluate the accuracy of the measurements obtained by the prototype tool. The process of measurement is described, and the differences between the unadjusted function points (UFP) obtained by the tool and those obtained by a specialist are examined. This includes an analysis of the differences in identification and sizing basic functional components (BFC) used in the IFPUG method.

The remainder of the paper is organized as follows. Section 2 presents an overview of FSM. Section 3 presents the related work. Section 4 briefly describes the measurement tool. Section 5 presents the case studies and the results. Finally, Sect. 6 outlines the conclusions.

2   Background

Albrecht presented the first Functional Size Measurement (FSM) method to size software from the user point of view, quantifying the functional requirements [5]. FSM is the process of measuring functional size, its concepts and principles for application are defined in the ISO/IEC 14143-1 standard [17]. There are five standardized methods for FSM based on functional user requirements: COSMIC-FFP (ISO/IEC 19761), IFPUG FPA (ISO/IEC 20926), MkII (ISO/IEC 20968),

NESMA (ISO/ IEC 24570) y FiSMA (ISO/IEC 29881). FSM enables a software project to be measured at the early phases, based on the requirements and facilitates the benchmarking of different projects [13].

The International Function Point Users Group (IFPUG) refined Albrecht's proposal and presented the FPA counting practice manual. IFPUG FPA measurement method classifies user requirements using a set of basic functional components (BFC) called transactional (TF) and data functions (DF). Data functions (DF) are classified into internal logic files (ILF) and external interface files (EIF). Transactional functions (TF) are classified into external inputs (EI), external outputs (EO), and external inquires (EQ). Functions are then counted according to a defined complexity criteria based on the data element types (DET), the file types referenced by a transaction (FTR), and the record element types (RET) within a data group. The measurement process in FPA involves the identification and count of these BFC types: EI, EO, EQ, ILF, and EIF, in order to obtain the unadjusted function points (UFP). Historically, IFPUG FPA has been the most popular FSM method [12].

A functional size measurement (FSM) method is a logical sequence of operations that are described generally [1,3]. A FSM procedure on the other hand, provides a set of operations, described specifically, to obtain a measurement according to one or more measuring principles and to a given FSM method. A FSM procedure requires the identification of a number of elements and the correct application of several rules to ensure that the measurement results meet the quality criteria [1,3].

A FSM procedure follow the steps of the process model for FSM methods proposed by Abran [3]. This process model is divided in three stages: (1) the design of the measurement procedure, (2) the application of the procedure, and (3) the exploitation of the results. In the first step, the concept to be measured, the FSM method and the procedure rules are defined. This includes the definition of the objectives, the characterization of the concept, the selection of the metamodel and the definition of the mapping and counting rules. In the second step, the FSM procedure is applied to the software artifacts. This includes the artifacts gathering, the construction of the functional model and the application of the rules. In the third step, the measurement results are presented and used, for example, in estimation models. The verification activities are carried out for each of the 3 stages to ensure a sufficient degree of reliability of the procedure.

The measurement procedure conducted and evaluated in this study was implemented following these stages of the process model for FSM methods [3].

3   Related Work

Research on automation of FSM has increased in recent years [28]. Several studies have analyzed different aspects of the automation of FSM [25,28]. These studies aim to automate the counting of the functional size from different software artifacts such as the requirements specification, the design models, the source code, or the test cases, among others [25,28]. To systematically obtain the functional size, these works defined mapping rules between the concepts that describe the artifacts and the components of the selected FSM method [33].

Uemura et al. [36] proposed a FPA measurement rules for design specifications based on UML. They developed a function point measurement tool to count design models on Rational Rose and evaluated its applicability. Kusumoto et al. [19] examined the possibility of measuring FP from source code automatically for object-oriented programs written in Java. The function point measurement tool was applied to practical Java programs and the difference between the FP values obtained by the tool and those of an FP measurement specialist were compared. Edagawa et al. [10] proposed a procedure to automatically measure the functional size based on IFPUG FPA. This approach count the data and transactional functions from the screen transitions and database accesses of web applications.

Lamma et al. [20] presented a tool for measuring IFPUG FPA from entity relationship and data flow diagrams. The FP counting rules were translated into systematic rules expressing the properties of the ER–DFD and the results were evaluated. Abrahao and Pastor [1] proposed a FSM procedure and tool to calculate the IFPUG FPA size from object oriented models based on IFPUG FPA and the Object-Oriented Hypermedia method (OO-H). Abrahão et al. [2] defined a measurement procedure for the OO-H Web applications based on COSMIC FFP. They presented the mapping and measurement rules to automatically derive functional size. Živkovič et al. [38] automated the software size estimation based on function points using UML models. The mapping rules was formally described to enable the automation. Besides, they defined a formal representation of functional size measurement methods [16]. Lavazza et al. [22] proposed a technique for building FPA-oriented UML models to measure function points. The technique was validated in a controlled experiment and a set of pilot applications.

Marín et al. [23] analyzed FSM proposals and tools to provide a guide for practitioners and researchers. They detailed procedures based on COSMIC FFP using conceptual models as input artifacts. They concluded that the formalization of the models are essential. Mapping rules between the COSMIC concepts and model concepts should be clearly defined and accuracy verification should be conducted. Barkallah et al. [6] propose a framework on how to apply COSMIC FFP using UML models.

Akca and Tarhan [4] proposed a measurement library to measure COSMIC FFP in Java business applications at runtime. In [14], Tarhan presented a FSM prototype tool using java source on runtime and functional execution traces. Finally, They proposed a set of requirements that need to be considered for FSM automation tools [35].

In 2014, the Object Management Group [15] proposed the Automated Function Points specification to count function points based on IFPUG FPA. The specification is used to measure transaction oriented applications with persistent data. The approach differs from IFPUG FPA when subjective judgments have to be replaced by the rules needed for automation.

Özkan [24] proposed a FSM approach for three tier object architecture and a measurement prototype tool based on COSMIC. Ungan et al. [37] presented a COSMIC functional measurement automation tool ScopeMaster. The tool automatically generates a size estimation from textual requirements and provides detailed reports on measurement details. De Vito et al. [9] designed and automated the COSMIC measurement based on UML models. To assess the measurement procedure they carried out two case studies and compared the results provided by the tool with the ones obtained by experts applying the COSMIC method.

In this study, we evaluated a FP size measurement tool for the FastWorks framework [29,30]. The FSM procedure and prototype tool were implemented mostly based on [10,15,16,20,35]. Our measurement tool attempts to measure the UFP from the FastWorks model based on the IFPUG FPA method.

4   Measurement Prototype Tool

In this section, we overview the measurement process and prototype tool that were described in detail in our previous work [29,30].

FastWorks (FW) is the development framework of the organization in which this study was conducted. This organization own framework has been used to develop Microsoft.NET information systems for the governmental sector for 15 years. FW allows the automatic generation of software from the model of the application. It provides a graphical environment that supports the modeling of transactional systems, generating a standardized architecture for the different modules and their functionalities, and thus increasing the productivity of the development process.

Figure 1 shows the FW "Model Specifier" component and the "Generator" component. The modeling process is performed in the "Model Specifier". This component provides a set of work spaces to perform the model specification based on the user functional requirements. The "Generator" component is used to produce the source code based on the model.

In the "Model Specifier" the following elements and their relationships are modeled to represent a software application: (1) *Module:* represents the application. It has one or more windows and a main window is defined for each module. (2) *Window:* is a screen in the module that contains one or more frames with interaction between them. (3) *Frame:* has one or more sentences that manage the data and one or more controls, actions and events. It is classified as a list that only contains a table control or as a form that contains multiple controls. (4) *Database:* describes the persistent entities of the application. (5) *Statement:* is a programming statement for data management (i.e. SQL statements). A statement could be linked to a frame or an action and resolve calls to CRUDL operations, stored procedures, functions and views based on and linked to the database. (6) *Control:* allows the input or output of data in a frame. A control may contain other controls and may have one or more related events associated. (7) *Action:* allows to perform the execution of transactions in a frame using one

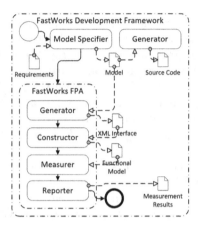

Fig. 1. Measurement prototype tool [29,30].

or more statements and also could perform operations with other controls. (8) *Event:* allows to perform the execution of transactions in response to the user events and also could perform operations with other controls. (9) *Hierarchy:* allows the organization of parent windows. Finally, (10) *Context:* represents the global information of the application environment. For example, a parent window could write a set of values and child windows could read these values.

The framework model comprises all the software application end-user functionalities. From the model, the application is automatically generated. In our case, the model is used not only to generate the source code, but also to produce the information for the construction of the functional model used as input in the FSM procedure. The functional model in FastWorks contains all the information required to estimate the functional size of the final application.

"FastWorks FPA" (FW-FPA) automatically estimates the IFPUG FPA size from the model of the target application. FW-FPA was implemented as part of the framework using the .Net platform and the MS ScriptDom assemblies to parse the transactions. The Neo4j API was used to manage the graph representation and to calculate the functional size. Figure 2 depicts the FW-FPA prototype tool components and the measurement process. The prototype tool includes the following components [29,30]:

Generator: this component generates an XML interface file from the FW model that details all required information for the construction of the functional model. The interface file is generated from the instantiated objects of the application and implements a set of features for the automation of the identification of trigger events handling, functional processes, persistent data, and type of access from functional processes to persistent data. The instrumentation libraries allow the user events tracking and the database analysis.

Constructor: this component constructs the functional model (event, data and transactional model) based on the information provided for the interface file.

It simulates the execution of transactions and generates the graph that represents the functional model of the application. While the execution of transactions is simulated, the traces are processed and the meta-model components are mapped between the FW components and the measurement procedure components.

Measurer: this component (a) enables the mapping between the IFPUG FPA and the concepts of the functional model of the measurement procedure, (b) identifies unique, cohesive and independently functions and data groups, and (c) calculates the functional size according to the mapping and counting rules for each functional process. It enables viewing and editing the FSM mapping and recalculating the results.

Reporter: this component shows the details of the FSM results. It details all the stages of the process and the breakdown of the measurements keeping traceability with the application model and presents a visualization of the functional model. The results provided by this component allows to apply the accuracy verification protocol.

Our measurement procedure define the functional meta-model required and the rules to map this model with the IFPUG FPA meta-model [29,30]. The functional meta-model used in the procedure is instantiated based on the identification of the set of elements from the application modeled in FW. The elements of the meta-model needed to be identified are the following: (1) *Application:* represents the target application to measure that could have one or more controls. (2) *Control:* is a user interface component such as: screens, buttons, edit text, data grids, containers and others. The user executes functionality with events associated to the controls. (3) *Event:* allows the execution of end user functionality. It could be classified as a navigation or as a function. (4) *Function:* represents a functional process and could be classified as transaction or data entity. (5) *Transaction:* represent a unique, cohesive and independently function based on database operations. It access data entities and could be classified as read or write. (6) *Data entity:* represents a table or a group of tables in the database representing a logical group. (7) *Data element:* represents a data attribute or database column. It could be classified as a data or as a calculated. (8) *Database:* represent any database or persistent data used by the application (internal or external).

The FSM procedure was implemented following the process model for FSM methods proposed in [3]. To measure a software application, the following four steps are conducted:

(S1) Generating the functional model elements: Based on the application modeled in the framework, the information for the construction of the functional model is extracted. This process extract and convert the required elements of the application model in the elements of the functional meta-model.

(S2) Constructing the functional model: Based on the extracted elements in S1, the functional model is automatically generated. The construction of the functional model is made simulating the execution of the end-user functionality.

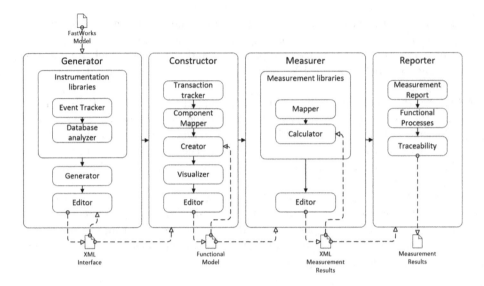

Fig. 2. The measurement process.

First, an event model is constructed based on the application, control, event and function elements. After that, a data model is constructed based on the database, data entity and data element elements and finally, with the execution of functional transactions between the event and data model, the transactional model is constructed adding the transaction elements where access to persistent data exists. The event, data and transactional models conforms the functional model. This functional model is represented as a graph (directed, labeled and weighted) that denotes the functionality of the application. The functional graph is composed of eight types of nodes, one for each meta-model element. The edges represent the relationship between each node showing the functional processes.

(S3) The mapping phase: Based on the functional model, each element is mapped to the IFPUG FPA meta-model. First, the data function (DF) candidates are identified and classified. This includes the identification of the logical groups based on the relationships between the data entities and how the transactions access these data entities. In addition, the classification of each data entity as an internal logic file (ILF) or an external interface file (EIF) is performed based on the type of access in the transactions (read/write). Finally, the identification of technical entities is completed checking if the data entity and its data elements are not reached by the user interface. Second, the transactional function (TF) candidates are identified and classified. Each TF is extracted from the function nodes. A function could be composed by a set of transactions that are executed simultaneously. The classification of each function as an external input (EI), external output (EO) or external inquiry (EQ) is performed based on the type of access of the functions (read/write) based on

the transactions. This includes the identification of calculated data elements to distinguish be-tween EO and EQ functions. Finally, based on the classification of the DF and TF, data element types (DET), record element types (RET) and file types referenced (FTR) are identified. Due space limitations the specific mapping rules are not detailed.

(S4) The measurement phase: Based on the classification of IFPUG FPA elements, the complexity of each TF and DF is determined and each function is weighted. Finally, the counting of the unadjusted function points (UFP) is calculated. This step is based on the counting rules specified in the IFPUG FPA counting practice manual. Adjusted function points are not considered.

The accuracy verification protocol [27] was used to calibrate the measurement procedures and the automated measurement tool. After that, the protocol allowed the validation of the measurement results. The verification process was conducted in three main phases: *(P1) Overall FP comparison:* the overall measurement results for the counting process are compared against the "true value". *(P2) Accuracy detailed comparison:* the measurement results for each step in the process is checked and the BFC are compared against the "true value". This phase identify the place where a difference in the counting process is presented. Each step in this phase represents a deep analysis of the measurement process. At the end of this phase, any assignable cause responsible for an error is isolated, linked, and reported based on the P3. *(P3) Error identification and recovery:* the reason for a difference is identified. An inspection on the quality of requirements, input artifacts, and process is conducted to identify where the error comes from and the differences are recorded and reported.

5   Case Studies

To assess the FastWorks FPA tool, a multi-case study was conducted to evaluate the accuracy of an automated software size measurement procedure. The structure of the report follows the guidelines for empirical studies proposed in [32].

5.1   Planning

We used the FastWorks FPA tool to automatically estimate the size of six software applications modeled in FW. We then compared those estimations against those obtained by a specialist using the requirement specification documents. Our objective was to evaluate the accuracy of an automated measurement procedure that uses the FastWorks FPA tool. The case studies were performed to answer the following research questions:

RQ1. Are the overall results measured by the tool similar to the ones measured by the specialist using the requirements specifications?

RQ2. Are the basic functional (BFC) results measured by the tool similar to the ones measured using the requirements specifications?

Systems Under Measurement. The target applications were independently modeled in FastWorks by a software architect of the organization. The first target application is the Contoso University System (CoU, 164 UFP) [29,30]. The second application is the Project Management System (PMS, 152 UFP) [1]. The third application is the Point of Sale Software (PoS, 35 UFP). The fourth application is the Registration System (REG, 146 UFP) [7,8]. The fifth application is the Warehouse Management System (WMS, 118 UFP) [11]. Finally, the sixth application is the Employee Management System (EMS, 95 UFP) [13]. The applications were modeled based on the requirements specification document written using the IEEE Recommended Practice for Software Requirements Specifications standard. The requirements were described in terms of functionality. All applications are transactional systems that mostly performs create, read, update, delete, and list (CRUDL), and assignment, search and filter operations. Additionally, these applications implement more complex functionalities that involves reports and business processes associated with each problem domain. All applications could be coded in ASP.NET C# code and use relational databases. The measurements of the target applications have been reported in previous measurement studies.

Instrumentation. The experimental instruments were prepared in advance and the whole experimental package was based on the used in previous studies [27,29–31]. For each application, a software requirement specification was prepared and validated, and the functional size was manually validated by two specialists based on previous counts [1,7,8,11,13,29,30]. The applications were modeled in FW and then their functional size was estimated by the FastWorks FPA tool. The results were processed and compared in a standardized results sheet against the "true value". Verification of the measurement accuracy was done in different phases applying the verification protocol [27].

Threats to Validity. The six software applications are small but their requirement specifications are regular examples of current practices used in industry. The effect of the artifacts can influence the study outcomes. Since we applied the tool to only six applications, the accuracy might depend on the characteristics of these applications. The applications were selected by convenience and were not a random selection. The size of the applications ranged from 35 to 164 UFPs and results could not be generalized to other domains or larger applications. Two researchers collected and validated the IFPUG FPA functional sizes used as a "true values", but they are not certified as function point specialists. However, they have more than 10 years of experience in measurement, and the applications had been previously measured and reported in similar studies. The results can only be generalized to the development framework used in this software organization and the functional models described in this study. The FSM procedure was calibrated according to the modeling standards of the organization, the development framework, and its unique characteristics. The scope of the count is limited to the functional model generated for the system modeled

Table 1. Results of functional size measurement.

Proj	App	Count	UFP(Qty)	DF			TF			
				ILF	EIF	Total	EI	EO	EQ	Total
P1	CoU	Manual	164 (37)	35 (5)	0 (0)	35 (5)	58 (15)	21 (4)	50 (13)	129 (32)
		Tool	155 (35)	35 (5)	0 (0)	35 (5)	61 (15)	9 (2)	50 (13)	120 (30)
P2	PMS	Manual	152 (40)	28 (4)	0 (0)	28 (4)	90 (27)	10 (2)	24 (7)	124 (36)
		Tool	146 (38)	28 (4)	0 (0)	28 (4)	86 (26)	10 (2)	22 (6)	118 (34)
P3	PoS	Manual	35 (9)	7 (1)	5 (1)	12 (2)	4 (1)	0 (0)	19 (6)	23 (7)
		Tool	31 (7)	7 (1)	5 (1)	12 (2)	6 (1)	7 (2)	6 (2)	19 (5)
P4	REG	Manual	146 (35)	28 (4)	20 (4)	48 (8)	60 (14)	12 (6)	26 (7)	98 (27)
		Tool	135 (27)	28 (4)	10 (2)	38 (6)	64 (14)	10 (2)	23 (5)	97 (21)
P5	WMS	Manual	118 (27)	21 (3)	20 (4)	41 (7)	34 (9)	14 (3)	29 (8)	77 (20)
		Tool	113 (27)	21 (3)	20 (4)	41 (7)	31 (9)	0 (0)	41 (11)	72 (20)
P6	EMS	Manual	95 (22)	21 (3)	5 (1)	26 (4)	38 (10)	19 (4)	12 (4)	69 (18)
		Tool	100 (22)	21 (3)	5 (1)	26 (4)	41 (10)	19 (4)	14 (4)	74 (18)

in this specific framework, that is a non-public framework. The way a system is modeled in the framework could impact the measurement outcome. Although the development teams obeyed their standards for modelling, the several decisions on the implementation of the database model can influence the identification of some logical groups, this affecting the final count.

5.2 Analysis of Results

Results of size measurement for each application are shown in Table 1. This table contains the project (Proj), the application (App), the type of count (manual or automated by the tool), the measurement results in unadjusted function points (UFP) together with the quantity of functions (Qty), as well as the functional size and functions from each basic functional component (BFC): data (DF) and transactional (TF) functions, internal logic files (ILF), external interface files (EIF), external inputs (EI), external outputs (EO), and external inquires (EQ).

Table 2 shows the accuracy results per application. For each project (Proj) and its associated application (App), we show four metrics: the magnitude of relative error (MRE), the magnitude of error relative (MER), the balanced relative error (BRE), and the differences in results (Diff). These results are given for total UFP and for each basic functional component.

Measurements estimated by the tool yielded an accuracy (in terms of MRE) between 3.9% and 12.9%, based on the total UFP. For Contoso University System (CoU, 164 UFP), the accuracy (MRE) was 5.5%, for Project Management System (PMS, 152 UFP), the accuracy was 3.9%, for Point of Sale Software (PoS, 35 UFP), it was 11.4%, for Registration System (REG, 146 UFP), an accuracy of 7.5% was attained, for Warehouse Management System (WMS, 118 UFP), the accuracy was 4.2%, and finally, for the Employee Management System (EMS, 95 UFP), it was 5.3%. These results indicate that, in the context of FastWorks,

Table 2. Results of accuracy.

Proj	App	Metric	UFP	DF			TF			
				ILF	EIF	Total	EI	EO	EQ	Total
P1	CoU	MRE	5.5%	0.0%	–	0.0%	5.2%	57.1%	0.0%	7.0%
		MER	5.8%	0.0%	–	0.0%	4.9%	133.3%	0.0%	7.5%
		BRE	5.8%	0.0%	–	0.0%	5.2%	133.3%	0.0%	7.5%
		Diff	−9	0	0	0	3	−12	0	−9
P2	PMS	MRE	3.9%	0.0%	–	0.0%	4.4%	0.0%	8.3%	4.8%
		MER	4.1%	0.0%	–	0.0%	4.7%	0.0%	9.1%	5.1%
		BRE	4.1%	0.0%	–	0.0%	4.7%	0.0%	9.1%	5.1%
		Diff	−6	0	0	0	−4	0	−2	−6
P3	PoS	MRE	11.4%	0.0%	0.0%	0.0%	50.0%	–	68.4%	17.4%
		MER	12.9%	0.0%	0.0%	0.0%	33.3%	100.0%	216.7%	21.1%
		BRE	12.9%	0.0%	0.0%	0.0%	50.0%	–	216.7%	21.1%
		Diff	−4	0	0	0	2	7	−13	−4
P4	REG	MRE	7.5%	0.0%	50.0%	20.8%	6.7%	16.7%	11.5%	1.0%
		MER	8.1%	0.0%	100.0%	26.3%	6.3%	20.0%	13.0%	1.0%
		BRE	8.1%	0.0%	100.0%	26.3%	6.7%	20.0%	13.0%	1.0%
		Diff	−11	0	−10	−10	4	−2	−3	−1
P5	WMS	MRE	4.2%	0.0%	0.0%	0.0%	8.8%	100.0%	41.4%	6.5%
		MER	4.4%	0.0%	0.0%	0.0%	9.7%	–	29.3%	6.9%
		BRE	4.4%	0.0%	0.0%	0.0%	9.7%	–	41.4%	6.9%
		Diff	−5	0	0	0	−3	−14	12	−5
P6	EMS	MRE	5.3%	0.0%	0.0%	0.0%	7.9%	0.0%	16.7%	7.2%
		MER	5.0%	0.0%	0.0%	0.0%	7.3%	0.0%	14.3%	6.8%
		BRE	5.3%	0.0%	0.0%	0.0%	7.9%	0.0%	16.7%	7.2%
		Diff	5	0	0	0	3	0	2	5

the functional size estimated by the tool could reasonably approximate manual counting performed by specialists.

The accuracy of the total function points count for IFPUG FPA could be considered acceptable in industry (±10%). However, given a ±30% variance, the accuracy of some BFCs (EIF, EO, EQ) was not sufficiently low in some applications. As reported in previous studies [10,30], the total function point count could be relatively accurate, although some classifications of BFCs failed. For this reason, both the total FP count and the BFC count should be tested and analyzed. In our case, it is necessary to calibrate the EO and EQ component mapping rules to ensure accuracy of measurement results.

Table 3 shows the aggregated accuracy results across all six applications. We present the mean, median, min and max of the magnitude of the relative

Table 3. Summary of aggregated accuracy results.

Metric		UFP	DF			TF			
			ILF	EIF	Total	EI	EO	EQ	Total
MRE	Mean	6.3%	0.0%	12.5%	3.5%	13.8%	34.8%	24.4%	7.3%
	Median	5.4%	0.0%	0.0%	0.0%	7.3%	16.7%	14.1%	6.7%
	Min	3.9%	0.0%	0.0%	0.0%	4.4%	0.0%	0.0%	1.0%
	Max	11.4%	0.0%	50.0%	20.8%	50.0%	100.0%	68.4%	17.4%
MER	Mean	6.7%	0.0%	25.0%	4.4%	11.0%	50.7%	47.1%	8.1%
	Median	5.4%	0.0%	0.0%	0.0%	6.8%	20.0%	13.7%	6.9%
	Min	4.1%	0.0%	0.0%	0.0%	4.7%	0.0%	9.1%	1.0%
	Max	12.9%	0.0%	100.0%	26.3%	33.3%	133.3%	216.7%	21.1%
BRE	Mean	6.8%	0.0%	25.0%	4.4%	14.0%	38.3%	49.5%	8.1%
	Median	5.5%	0.0%	0.0%	0.0%	7.3%	10.0%	14.9%	7.1%
	Min	4.1%	0.0%	0.0%	0.0%	4.7%	0.0%	0.0%	1.0%
	Max	12.9%	0.0%	100.0%	26.3%	50.0%	133.3%	216.7%	21.1%
Diff	Mean	−5	0	−2	−2	1	−4	−1	−3
	Median	−6	0	0	0	3	−1	−1	−5
	Min	−11	0	−10	−10	−4	−14	−13	−9
	Max	5	0	0	0	4	7	12	5

error (MRE), the magnitude of error relative (MER), the balanced relative error (BRE), and the absolute difference (Diff). The variation is presented for the total function points count (UFP), and each basic functional component (BFC).

The results show an accuracy (mean of MRE) of 6.3% based on the total UFP. This is an acceptable variation in industry. In total, the accuracy (mean of MRE) for transactional functions (TF) was 7.3%, data functions (DF) was 3.5%, internal logic files (ILF) was 0.0%, external interface files (EIF) was 12.5%, external inputs (EI) was 13.8%, and external outputs (EO) and external inquires (EQ) 34.8% and 24.4%. The EO and EQ balanced each other and the accuracy for TF was 7.3%. Considering a ±30% variance, the accuracy of the BFCs are promising for the organization. However, the accuracy at the BFC level must be improved in order to achieve strength results.

In summary, the measurement results obtained by the tool present some deviations from the ones calculated manually. Although the total number of UFPs (RQ1) can be measured with an acceptable level of accuracy, this is not possible for the UFP counts for all the BFCs (RQ2). Hence, the classification and counting of each BFC should be improved.

5.3 Discussion

Hereinafter, we discuss the reasons for deviations in measurement results, identifying and analyzing the main causes (factors of influence) of such deviations. The case studies confirmed our previous results and added new findings as well.

The FastWorks FPA tool extracted most of the transactional functions, although some function classifications were confounded between EOs and EQs. The difference was presented by the mapping rules that identify EO elements when it finds calculated fields implemented in the data accesses of the transactions. The requirements identified as EQ corresponded to reports that the development framework (FW) implemented without the need to add calculated fields.

Differences identified in some requirements were caused by the identification of extra DET, RET and FTR elements. This differences were caused by technical implementations in the FW that add attributes to the database entities for integrity control. In the calibration process, some data tables and technical columns were identified that are not part of the user's requirements. In some cases, functionality was duplicated from other requirements. The analysis of the functional model allows the identification of these elements to calibrate the results. We considered these cases as duplicated functionality, but also reported them to the professional for consideration during the decision making processes.

Finally, FW implements some default functionality to the final user and this should be taken into account. Moreover, some functions classified as EQ were not identified because the default implementation of the FW coupled some requirements and provided, for example, filter options without access to the data functions.

6 Conclusion

In this paper, we evaluated the automated function point estimation tool Fast-Works FPA. Six software applications were automatically counted by this tool. Such applications were independently modeled by a software architect from the organization.

The results show that the values of the automatic and manual measurement were convergent. The accuracy (mean of MRE) was 6.3% based on the total unadjusted function points (UFP). Functional size measurements were obtained with an acceptable level of accuracy that might allow the organization to implement a metrics program based on the functional size.

In the near future, we plan to conduct more experimentation with software applications of higher complexity, to aggregate evidence on the tool's performance. To that aim, we would like to use the tool with the organizational portfolio of applications and validate the measurement results. Also, we would like to analyze in detail the classification of functions, since eliminating some of those will greatly enhance the counting results. In addition, we will carry out studies to analyze the possibility of obtaining IFPUG FPA and COSMIC FFP countings from early models using the framework.

Acknowledgments. This work was partially supported by the University of Costa Rica No. 834-B8-A27. We thank the Empirical Software Engineering Group at UCR.

References

1. Abrahao, S.: On the functional size measurement of object-oriented conceptual schemas: design and evaluation issues. Universidad Politecnica de Valencia (2004)
2. Abrahão, S., DeMarco, L., Ferrucci, F., Gomez, J., Gravino, C., Sarro, F.: Definition and evaluation of a cosmic measurement procedure for sizing web applications in a model-driven development environment. Inf. Softw. Technol. **104**, 144–161 (2018)
3. Abran, A.: Software Metrics and Software Metrology. Wiley, Hoboken (2010)
4. Akca, A., Tarhan, A.: Run-time measurement of cosmic functional size for java business applications: is it worth the cost? In: IWSM-MENSURA, pp. 54–59. IEEE (2013)
5. Albrecht, A.: Measuring application development productivity. In: Joint Share, Guide, and IBM Application Development Symposium (1979)
6. Barkallah, S., Gherbi, A., Abran, A.: COSMIC functional size measurement using UML models. In: Kim, T., et al. (eds.) ASEA 2011. CCIS, vol. 257, pp. 137–146. Springer, Heidelberg (2011). https://doi.org/10.1007/978-3-642-27207-3_14
7. Bundschuh, M., Dekkers, C.: The IT Measurement Compendium: Estimating and Benchmarking Success with Functional Size Measurement. Springer, Heidelberg (2008). https://doi.org/10.1007/978-3-540-68188-5
8. COSMIC: The COSMIC Functional Size Measurement Method Versión 4.0.1 Course Registration (C-REG) System Case Study. Version 2.0. COSMIC (2015)
9. De Vito, G., Ferrucci, F., Gravino, C.: Design and automation of a COSMIC measurement procedure based on UML models. Softw. Syst. Model. (2019). https://doi.org/10.1007/s10270-019-00731-2
10. Edagawa, T., Akaike, T., Higo, Y., Kusumoto, S., Hanabusa, S., Shibamoto, T.: Function point measurement from web application source code based on screen transitions and database accesses. J. Syst. Softw. **84**(6), 976–984 (2011). https://doi.org/10.1016/j.jss.2011.01.029
11. Fetcke, T.: The warehouse software portfolio: a case study in functional size measurement. Citeseer (1999)
12. Fingerman, S.: Practical software project estimation; a toolkit for estimating software development effort & duration. Sci-Tech News **65**(1), 28 (2011)
13. Garmus, D., Herron, D.: Function Point Analysis: Measurement Practices for Successful Software Projects. Addison-Wesley Publishing Inc., Boston (2001)
14. Gonultas, R., Tarhan, A.: Run-time calculation of COSMIC functional size via automatic installment of measurement code into Java business applications. In: 2015 41st Euromicro Conference on Software Engineering and Advanced Applications, pp. 112–118. IEEE (2015). https://doi.org/10.1109/SEAA.2015.30
15. Group, O.M.: Automated Function Points (AFP) Version 1.0, OMG Document Number: formal/2014-01-03. OMG (2014). http://www.omg.org/spec/AFP
16. Heričko, M., Rozman, I., Živkovič, A.: A formal representation of functional size measurement methods. J. Syst. Softw. **79**(9), 1341–1358 (2006)
17. ISO: Information Technology, Software Measurement, Functional Size Measurement: Definition of Concepts. ISO/IEC (2007)
18. ISO: ISO/IEC 20926:2009 Software and systems engineering - Software measurement - IFPUG functional size measurement methods. ISO/IEC (2009)

19. Kusumoto, S., Imagawa, M., Inoue, K., Morimoto, S., Matsusita, K., Tsuda, M.: Function point measurement from java programs. In: Proceedings of the 24th International Conference on Software Engineering, ICSE 2002, Orlando, Florida, pp. 576–582. ACM, New York (2002). https://doi.org/10.1145/581339.581412

20. Lamma, E., Mello, P., Riguzzi, F.: A system for measuring function points from an ER-DFD specification. Comput. J. **47**(3), 358–372 (2004)

21. Lavazza, L.: Automated function points: critical evaluation and discussion. In: 2015 IEEE/ACM 6th International Workshop on Emerging Trends in Software Metrics, pp. 35–43. IEEE (2015). https://doi.org/10.1109/WETSoM.2015.13

22. Lavazza, L.A., del Bianco, V., Garavaglia, C.: Model-based functional size measurement. In: Proceedings of the Second ACM-IEEE International Symposium on Empirical Software Engineering and Measurement, ESEM 2008, Kaiserslautern, Germany, pp. 100–109. ACM, New York (2008). https://doi.org/10.1145/1414004.1414021

23. Marín, B., Giachetti, G., Pastor, O.: Measurement of functional size in conceptual models: a survey of measurement procedures based on COSMIC. In: Dumke, R.R., Braungarten, R., Büren, G., Abran, A., Cuadrado-Gallego, J.J. (eds.) IWSM/Mensura/MetriKon -2008. LNCS, vol. 5338, pp. 170–183. Springer, Heidelberg (2008). https://doi.org/10.1007/978-3-540-89403-2_15

24. Özkan, B.: Automated functional size measurement for three-tier object relational mapping architectures. Coll. Econ. Anal. Ann. (43), 51–68 (2017). https://ideas.repec.org/a/sgh/annals/i43y2017p51-68.html

25. Özkan, B., Demirörs, O.: Formalization studies in functional size measurement. In: Modern Software Engineering Concepts and Practices: Advanced Approaches, pp. 242–262. IGI Global (2011)

26. Özkan, B., Demirors, O.: On the seven misconceptions about functional size measurement. In: IWSM-MENSURA, pp. 45–52. IEEE (2016)

27. Quesada-López, C., Jenkins, M.: Applying a verification protocol to evaluate the accuracy of functional size measurement procedures: an empirical approach. In: Abrahamsson, P., Corral, L., Oivo, M., Russo, B. (eds.) PROFES 2015. LNCS, vol. 9459, pp. 243–250. Springer, Cham (2015). https://doi.org/10.1007/978-3-319-26844-6_18

28. Quesada-López, C., Jenkins, M.: Procedimientos de medición del tamaño funcional: un mapeo sistemático de literatura. In: Ibero-American Conference on Software Engineering, pp. 141–154 (2017)

29. Quesada-López, C., Jenkins, M., Salas, L.C., Gómez, J.C.: Fastworks FPA: Una herramienta para automatizar la medición del tamaño funcional. In: Simposio Argentino de Ingeniería de Software, pp. 48–57. Sociedad de Informática (2017)

30. Quesada-López, C., Jenkins, M., Salas, L.C., Gómez, J.C.: Towards an automated functional size measurement procedure: an industrial case study. In: IWSM-MENSURA, pp. 138–144. ACM (2017)

31. Quesada-López, C., Madrigal-Sánchez, D., Jenkins, M.: An empirical evaluation of automated function points. In: Ibero-American Conference on Software Engineering, pp. 151–165 (2016)

32. Runeson, P., Höst, M., Rainer, A., Regnell, B.: Case study research in software engineering. In: Guidelines and Examples. Wiley Online Library (2012)

33. Sag, M., Tarhan, A.: Measuring cosmic software size from functional execution traces of Java business applications. In: IWSM-MENSURA, pp. 272–281. IEEE (2014)

34. Soubra, H., Abran, A., Ramdane-Cherif, A.: Verifying the accuracy of automation tools for the measurement of software with COSMIC-ISO 19761 including an AUTOSAR-based example and a case study. In: IWSM-MENSURA, pp. 23–31. IEEE (2014)
35. Tarhan, A., Özkan, B., İçöz, G.: A proposal on requirements for cosmic FSM automation from source code. In: IWSM-MENSURA, pp. 195–200. IEEE (2016)
36. Uemura, T., Kusumoto, S., Inoue, K.: Function point measurement tool for UML design specification. In: International Software Metrics Symposium, pp. 62–69. IEEE (1999)
37. Ungan, E., Hammond, C., Abran, A.: Automated cosmic measurement and requirement quality improvement through scopemaster® tool. In: IWSM-MENSURA (2018)
38. Živkovič, A., Rozman, I., Heričko, M.: Automated software size estimation based on function points using uml models. Inf. Softw. Technol. **47**(13), 881–890 (2005)

Can Expert Opinion Improve Effort Predictions When Exploiting Cross-Company Datasets? - A Case Study in a Small/Medium Company

Filomena Ferrucci and Carmine Gravino[✉]

University of Salerno, Fisciano, Italy
{fferrucci,gravino}@unisa.it

Abstract. Many studies have shown that the accuracy of the predictions obtained by estimation models built considering data collected by other companies (cross-company models) can be significantly worse than those of estimation models built employing a dataset collected by the single company (within-company models). This is due to the different characteristics among cross-company and within-company datasets. In this paper, we propose an approach based on the opinion of the experts that could help in the context of small/medium company that do not have data available from past developed projects. In particular, experts are in charge of selecting data from public cross-company datasets looking at the information about employed software development process and software technologies. The proposed strategy is based on the use of a Delphi approach to reach consensus among experts. To assess the strategy, we performed an empirical study considering a dataset from the PROMISE repository that includes information on the functional size expressed in terms of COSMIC for building the cross-company estimation model. We selected this dataset since COSMIC is the method used to size the applications by the company that provided the within-company dataset employed as test set to assess the accuracy of the built cross-company model. We compared the accuracy of the obtained predictions with those of the cross-company model built without selecting the observations. The results are promising since the effort predictions obtained with the proposed strategy are significantly better than those obtained with the model built on the whole cross-company dataset.

Keywords: Effort estimation · Cross-company estimation models · Expert opinion · Delphi approach

1 Introduction

Effort estimation is a key management activity which goes on throughout a software project being fundamental for accurate project (re)planning and for allocating resources adequately [6,46]. Thus, the competitiveness of a software

© Springer Nature Switzerland AG 2019
X. Franch et al. (Eds.): PROFES 2019, LNCS 11915, pp. 280–295, 2019.
https://doi.org/10.1007/978-3-030-35333-9_20

company heavily depends on the ability of its project managers to accurately predict in advance the effort required to develop software system. Several techniques, which rely on a more formal approach, have been proposed to support project managers in estimating software development effort. These include the application of some algorithms to a number of factors that influence the development cost, such as the size, to produce an estimate or a prediction model providing the estimation in an objective way.

The paper focuses on the problem of having an effort prediction model in the context of small/medium software companies that do not have data to build their own models [39]. In this scenario companies can approach the problem by employing estimation models obtained by considering data collected by other companies (cross-company models) and obtained from publicly available dataset (e.g., PROMISE [1]). However, many studies have shown that the accuracy of the obtained predictions can be significantly worse than those of estimation models built employing datasets collected by the company from past projects (within-company models) [10,16,22,26,27,32,33]. This is due to the different characteristics of the software developed by the single company or due to specific development context. Some approaches have suggested to prune data from publicly available datasets, however, they require datasets with many observations and the availability of some data of the single company as well as sophisticated learning strategies [37,38].

In this paper, we propose an approach based on the opinion of the experts that could help in the context of small/medium company that do not have data available from past developed projects. In particular, company experts are in charge of selecting data looking at the information available in the public dataset about employed software development process and software technologies (e.g., programming languages). The proposed strategy is based on the use of a Delphi approach to reach consensus among experts involved in the selection and the use of an estimation technique to build the estimation model using the selected data.

To assess the strategy, we performed an empirical study considering a dataset from the PROMISE repository that includes information on the functional size expressed in terms of COSMIC and other information on the development process to be exploited for building the cross-company estimation model. This dataset was obtained by extracting information from ISBSG repository [2]. We selected this dataset since COSMIC is the method used to size the applications by the company that provided us the test set we used to assess the accuracy of the built cross-company estimation models. As for the estimation technique we used simple linear regression since the company involved in our study was interested in estimating the effort by exploiting only the functional size information as independent variable. Furthermore, simple linear regression can be considered one of the most widely used estimation technique in studies similar to ours [18].

In the following we name the strategy based on expert opinion used to select data as CCexpert, while the approach based on the use of the information contained in a publicly available dataset is named CCoriginal. To assess the accuracy of CCexpert, we compared the effort predictions obtained using it with those achieved exploiting the cross-company model built without selecting the observations.

To this aim, we defined the following research questions:

RQ: Are the effort predictions obtained with CCexpert better than those achieved with CCoriginal?

Structure of the Paper. Background on the use of cross-company effort estimation models is presented in Sect. 2. In Sect. 3 we provide a description of the design of the performed study, while the results are presented and discussed in Sect. 4. Section 5 concludes the paper with final remarks.

2   Background and Related Work

In the last 20 years several studies have been performed to assess the usefulness of cross-company effort estimation models [5,12,13,21,43], many of them in the context of Web effort estimation which are discussed in [8,37]. Furthermore, some literature reviews have also highlighted main results of those studies and discussed differences, e.g., [16,18,31]. Many of the studies found that cross-company estimation models provided results significantly worse than those of within-company estimation models [10,16,22,26,27,32,33]. The reasons highlighted by the performed studies are mainly related to the differences between the data in the cross-company dataset and the data in the within-company dataset. Indeed, software project data of a company can differ significantly from data of different companies, due to differences in the adopted processes and practices [26,27]. Thus, researchers highlighted that cross-company datasets should be analyzed and partitioned in order to select the observations that could match within-company development practices and ensure a random sample representative of a well-defined population [33].

To addresses the above issues some recent studies proposed strategies to select the cross-company dataset more similar to the within-company dataset. Some of these proposals exploited widely used machine learning approaches, such as analogy-based technique [19] and Nearest cc filtering (NN-filtering) with stepwise regression [10,47] to select observations to be used for the cross-company effort estimation models. The results of the performed studies revealed that for the majority of the cross-company models built predictions achieved were comparable with those obtained with within-company models. However, in some cases predictions worse than those achieved with the simple baseline based on the median of previous project efforts were obtained.

Other two studies [38] and [37] analyzed the use of a framework to build cross-company models to be exploited by a single company. The framework is based on a learning task that aims to highlight relationship between the single company and the companies whose data forms the cross-company dataset. In particular, the selection of the cross-company models is done by exploiting a limited number of within-company training examples. The first study validated the proposed framework exploiting data from traditional software projects [38], while the second study investigated the framework using data from Web software projects [37].

Differently, in this paper, we propose an approach based on the opinion of the experts that could help in the context of small/medium company that do not have data available from past developed projects. In particular, company experts are in charge of selecting data looking at the information available in the public datasets about employed software development process and software technologies (e.g., programming languages).

In the literature several studies have shown that effort predictions based only on the opinion of experts usually fail (see e.g., the review reported in [14]). However, there are some studies that have proposed to exploit opinions of experts in combination with model-based effort prediction strategies to improve. In particular, Mendes *et al.* proposed the use of Bayesian Networks to construct an expert-based Web effort model [35]. The performed study showed that the involved Web Company can benefit since the built model allowing the representation of uncertainty (which is inherent in effort estimation) outperformed expert-based estimates. Furthermore, other previous studies investigated Web effort estimation models that explicitly consider uncertainty, which is inherent to effort estimation, applying Bayesian Networks [24,28,29]. The analyses were based on data about 150 projects from the Tukutuku dataset to built Hybrid Bayesian Network models (structure expert-driven and probabilities data driven) [35]. The results were encouraging since the Hybrid Bayesian Network models provided results better than baselines, such as mean- and median-based effort, and widely used estimation techniques, such as multivariate regression, classification and regression trees. These analyses were successively extended by considering further data from the Tukutuku dataset and both Hybrid and data-driven different Bayesian Network models [30,34].

In our approach we involved experts in the selection of the data, about employed software development process and software technologies (e.g., programming languages), to be included in the cross-company dataset and not in the selection of the effort estimation techniques/models.

3   Study Design

The *goal* of this study is to investigate whether the use of expert opinions for selecting data from a cross-company dataset to be employed for building cross-company estimation models can improve the accuracy of the obtained predictions.

In the following we describe the employed datasets, data selection strategy, estimation technique, validation method, and evaluation criteria and discuss threats to validity of the study.

3.1   Datasets

In this section we first describe the dataset from PROMISE repository used to build the cross-company effort estimation models (i.e., the training set). Then, we present the within-company dataset used to validate the obtained cross-company models (i.e., the test set).

Training Set. The dataset employed to build the cross-company models was selected from the PROMISE repository. For each observation it includes information on the functional size expressed in terms of COSMIC and other information on the development process that are exploited for building the cross-company estimation model. It was obtained by extracting information from ISBSG repository [2]. We selected this dataset since COSMIC is the method used to size the applications by the company that provided us the test set we used to assess the accuracy of the built cross company models.

Table 1 shows some summary statistics related to the applications included in the cross-company dataset. The variables are EFF, i.e., the actual effort expressed in terms of person-hours, and CFP, expressed in terms of number of COSMIC Function Points. Obs indicates the number of observations in the dataset, while Min, Max, Mean, Median, and Std. Dev. denote the minimum, maximum, mean, median, and standard deviation of the considered variables (i.e., Var). Other information about this dataset are provided in Sect. 3.2 where we describe the selection of the cross-company dataset.

Test Set. Data to validate the built cross-company models was provided by an Italian small/medium-sized software company, whose core business is the development of enterprise information systems, mainly for local and central government. Among its clients, there are health organizations, research centers, industries, and other public institutions. The company is specialized in the design, development, and management of solutions for Web portals, enterprise intranet/extranet applications (such as Content Management Systems, e-commerce, work-flow managers, etc.), and Geographical Information Systems. It is certified ISO 9001:2000, and it is also a certified partner of Microsoft, Oracle, and ESRI.

The dataset includes information on 25 applications, such as e-government, e-banking, Web portals, and Intranet applications. All the projects were developed with SUN J2EE or Microsoft .NET technologies. Oracle has been the most commonly adopted DBMS, but also SQL Server, and MySQL were employed in some of these projects. As for the collection of the information, the software company used timesheets to keep track of the development effort. In particular, each team member annotated the information about his/her development effort on each project every day, and weekly each project manager stored the sum of the efforts for the team. To collect all the significant information to calculate the values of the size measure in terms of COSMIC, a template is filled in by the project managers and the functional size is determined by the company measurers.

The summary statistics related to the 25 applications employed in our study[1] are shown in Table 2.

Table 1. Descriptive statistics of training set

Var	Obs	Min	Max	Mean	Median	Std. Dev.
EFF	42	40	47493	5671.6	2937	9552.55
CFP	42	2	2003	340.05	104.5	508.23

Table 2. Descriptive statistics of test set

Var	Obs	Min	Max	Mean	Median	Std. Dev.
EFF	25	782	4537	2577	2686	988.14
CFP	25	163	1090	602.04	611	268.47

3.2 Data Selection Strategy

To select observations, i.e., projects, from the cross-company dataset that have characteristics more close to the ones developed by the single company involved in our study, we exploited the Delphi method, which allowed us to bring together the opinions of the company experts. The Delphi method is a structured communication technique, originally developed as a systematic, interactive forecasting method which relies on a panel of experts. The experts answer questions in two or more rounds. After each round, an anonymous summary of all judgments is provided by a facilitator. Then, experts are encouraged to revise their previous answers taking into account the opinions of the other participants involved. The process can be stopped according to a predefined stop criterion (e.g., achievement of consensus, stability of results). Delphi is based on the principle that forecasts (or decisions) from a structured group of individuals are more accurate than those from unstructured groups [41].

3.3 Estimation Technique

To build the cross-company prediction models we have employed as an estimation technique the simple linear regression, which is a model-based approach widely and successfully employed in the industrial context and in several researches to estimate development effort (see e.g., [3, 9, 16, 23, 25, 36]).

---

[1] Raw data cannot be revealed because of a Non Disclosure Agreement with the software company.

Simple linear regression allows us to build estimation models to explain the relationship between the independent variable, denoting the employed size measure (i.e., CFP), and the dependent variable, representing the development effort (EFF). Thus, simple linear regression allows us to obtain models of this type:

$$EFF = a + b \times CFP \tag{1}$$

where b is the coefficient that represents the amount the variable EFF changes when the variable CFP changes 1 unit, and a is the intercept. Once such a model is obtained, given a new software project for which an effort estimation is required, the project manager has to size it using the same unit of measure of the model, and to use this value in the regression equation to get the effort prediction.

3.4   Validation Method

To validate the obtained cross-company effort estimation models we have exploited two different datasets. The estimation models have been built by exploiting a first dataset (from PROMISE repository) that contains information from projects developed by different software companies in the past. A second dataset that contains information from software projects developed by a company in our research network has been used to validate the built estimation models.

3.5   Evaluation Criteria

We decided to employ Mean of the absolute residuals (MAR) obtained for the 25 observations in the test set as evaluation criteria [46]. Furthermore, to answer our research question we applied the Wilcoxon test [7] on the distribution of the 25 absolute residuals obtained with CCexpert and the distributions of the 25 absolute residuals achieved with CCoriginal. For all the statistical tests performed in our analysis, we decided to accept a probability of 5% of committing a Type-I-Error, as is customary in Software Engineering empirical studies [49].

To have also an indication of the practical/managerial significance of the results, we verified the effect size. Effect size is a simple way of quantifying the standardized difference between two groups [15]. In particular, we employed the Vargha and Delaney's A12 statistics as non-parametric effect size measure [48]. According to Vargha and Delaney, a difference between two populations can be classified in small, medium, and large as in Table 3. An effect size less than or equals to 0.56 can be considered negligible.

3.6   Threats to Validity

The results of our empirical study could be affected by some threats, that should be taken into account in future investigations [17,50].

Table 3. Effect size classification

Effect size	A12 statistics
Negligible	Less than or equals to 0.56
Small	Greater than 0.56
Medium	Greater than 0.64
Large	Greater than 0.71

The measurement and the collection of the information included in our datasets could affect the construct validity. As reported above, we employed a publicly available dataset included in the PROMISE repository [1]. It has been extracted from ISBSG repository, thus it respects all the criteria established by the ISBSG proponents. As an example, the selected observations are all scored as A and B regarding the data quality variable [2]. As for the dataset used as test set, it was obtained from small/medium software company in our network. The collection of the effort is done using timesheets: each team member annotated the information about his/her development effort on each project every day, and weekly each project manager stored the sum of the efforts for the team. The significant information to calculate the value of the size measure in terms of COSMIC is obtained from questionnaire filled-in by the project managers. The company measurers determine the functional size of the projects on the base of the information collected. One of the authors analyzed the filled templates and the analysis and design documents, in order to cross-check the provided information. The same author calculated the values of the size measure to cross-check the work done by the company measurers.

As for the employed within-company dataset, we are aware that we considered one dataset to test the approach and more tests should be exploited to generalize the results.

Concerning the conclusion validity, we carefully applied the statistical tests performed by verifying all the required assumptions.

A evaluation criteria we decided to use a single measure, widely used in studies similar to ours (e.g., [20,45,46]), i.e., Mean of the absolute residuals. Of course we are aware that other measures could be used (e.g., Median of absolute residuals). We did not use summary measures like MMRE and Pred(25), since their use has been strongly discouraged in recent simulation studies, showing that MMRE wrongly prefers a model that consistently underestimates [40].

As for the threats regarding reliability validity, all the information exploited in our study to select the observations in the training set (used to build the effort estimation model) are available on the web, i.e., PROMISE repository.

4   Results and Discussion

We first present the results about the data selection strategy introduced in Sect. 3.2, then we describe the construction of the cross-company effort prediction models and discuss the accuracy of the obtained predictions.

4.1   Cross-Company Dataset Selection

As for the selection of the cross-company dataset, three managers of the selected company were involved int the application of the Delphi method described in Sect. 3.2. They were selected by the company taking into account their experience in managing software development process and their knowledge about software measures/metrics to summarize software process/products.

We applied the Delphi method two times. The first time we asked experts to decide what variables of the selected PROMISE dataset should be considered to select observations for the construction of the cross-company estimation model. As suggested by the method, we applied two rounds. In the first round they were asked to select which variables among those specified in the cross-company dataset have to be considered for the selection of the observations. Then, in the second round one of the authors acted as facilitator and summarized the selected variables and asked again to experts to express their opinions. Table 4 shows the variables selected by the experts after the first round among those available in the cross-company dataset[2]. At the end of the second round they decided to consider four variables: (1) Primary Programming Language (PPL); (2) Language1; (3) DBS1; OS1; (4) Architecture; and (5) OS1.

The second time, using the same procedure of two rounds they selected the observations shown in Table 5 looking at the variables selected above[3]. These observations were selected since the values of the selected variables are close to the ones that characterize the projects that usually the company develop. Indeed, the company employs SUN J2EE or Microsoft .NET technologies for the software development. Furthermore, Oracle has been the most commonly adopted DBMS. However, also SQL Server and MySQL are employed.

From the summary of the facilitator, we can observe that many observations were not considered since they do not included information about Architecture and DBS1 (e.g., such as observations: 3199, 27927, 27913, 3133, 24302, 27917, 31448, 31240, 31451, 30879, 30719, 27547, 27537, 29893, 31512, 28129, 30611). Similarly, observations not specifying the value for Language1 were not considered. Even if observation 28020 was characterized by Java as PPL, Client server as Architecture, and Oracle as DBS1 it was not included due to the value of Language1. Observation 29834 was not selected since the values of PPL and Language1 are COBOL and Owner script, respectively. Similarly for observations 30333 and 32064 since the values for those variables are COBOL and

---

[2] See the PROMISE repository web site for the description of all the variables: https://terapromise.csc.ncsu.edu/repo/effort/isbsg/isbsg10/isbsg-attribute-info.txt.

[3] See the PROMISE repository web site to see the remaining observations: http://openscience.us/repo/effort/isbsg/cosmic.html.

Table 4. First application of the Delphi method: variables selected by experts after the first round

Var	Description
IS	A derived field which attempts to summarize Organization Type of the project
PPL	The primary language used for the development: JAVA, C++, PL/1, Cobol etc.
Language1	The primary technology programming language used to build or enhance (the software, i.e., that used for most of the build effort)
OS1	The primary technology operating system used to build or enhance the software (i.e., that used for most of the build effort)
Architecture	A derived attribute for the project to indicate if the application is: Stand alone, Multi-tier, Client server, Multi-tier with web public interface
DBS1	The primary technology database used to build or enhance the software (i.e. that used for most of the build effort), otherwise (if known) it is whether the project used a DBMS

VB.NET and COBOL and ASP.NET C#, respectively. Observation 27934 has no value for DBS1, while Language1 is equal to RPG3. So, it was not considered. Other observations were not selected due to the value of Architecture (e.g., 25271), Language1 and DBS1 (e.g., 27553), or they miss the value of DBS1 (e.g., 28884).

It is important to mention that this second application of Delphi method to select the observations could be automated in the future, for example exploiting similarity measures and machine learning approaches. This could help to reduce the effort of the experts involved in the process and to avoid having strong dependency on expert intuition.

4.2 Model Construction and Validation

To build the cross-company effort prediction model using the data presented in Table 1 we first verified the linear regression assumptions, i.e., the existence of a linear relationship between the independent variable and the dependent variable (linearity), the constant variance of the error terms for all the values of the independent variable (homoscedasticity), the normal distribution of the error terms (normality), and the statistical independence of the errors, in particular, no correlation between consecutive errors (independence). To this aim, we performed statistical analyses, of course considering 95% confidence level. Both Pearson's correlation test (statistic = 0.182 with p-value > 0.05) [11] and the Spearman' rho test (statistic = 0.234 with p-value > 0.05) [7] revealed that the EFF (i.e., dependent variable) and CFP (i.e., independent variable) are not correlated since the statistics is not close to 1 or (−1). The homoscedasticity assumption was verified by performing the Breush-Pagan Test [4]. The Shapiro test [42] revealed

Table 5. Second application of the Delphi method: observations selected by experts

obs	CFP	EFF	PPL	Language1	OS1	Architecture	DBS1
29331	210	204	Java	C++ Java	UNIX Windows NT	Multi-tier	Oracle
25081	237	600	C++	Java	Windows	Multi-tier with web public interface	MySQL
29471	61	669	Java	Java	Linux	Multi-tier with web public interface	MySQL
30658	5	784	ABAP	Java	Windows	Multi-tier with web public interface	MySQL
31895	82	903	C#	Java	Windows XP	Client server	SQL Server
27505	118	1488	Script Language	Java	Linux	Multi-tier with web public interface	MySQL
29311	643	4224	Java	Java	Windows 2000	Client server	Oracle
29310	441	47493	ASP.Net	Java 2EE	Windows XP	Client server	Oracle

that the two distributions of EFF and CFP as well as the distribution of residuals (i.e., error terms) are not normal since a p-value less than 0.05 was obtained (i.e., the normality of the distribution was the null hypothesis). The Durbin-Watson test revealed that the residuals for consecutive errors are not so uncorrelated since the obtained statistic was less than 2. Taking into account the results of the performed analysis to verify linear regression assumptions, we decided to apply a log transformation to the variables [27].

The equation of the regression model obtained considering Log(CFP) as independent variable and Log(EFF) as dependent variable is (named CCoriginal):

$$Log(EFF) = 6.604 + 0.228 * Log(CFP) \tag{2}$$

and when it is transformed back to the original raw data scale we obtain:

$$EFF = 738 * CFP^{0.228} \tag{3}$$

Similarly, we obtained the regression model for the cross-company dataset resulted from the data selection strategy described in Sect. 3.2 (named CCexpert):

$$EFF = 161 * CFP^{0.456} \tag{4}$$

To evaluate the prediction accuracy of CCoriginal and CCexpert and answer to research questions RQ, we performed the validation as described in Sect. 3.4 employing the single-company dataset summarized in Table 2. The results of the validation in terms of MAR values are reported in Table 6, while Fig. 1 shows the boxplots of absolute residuals achieved with the two effort prediction models.

From Table 6 we can observe that the MAR value achieved with CCexpert is more than 1.5 times lower than the one obtained with CCoriginal, thus highlighting much better results for CCexpert. Furthermore, the result of the performed

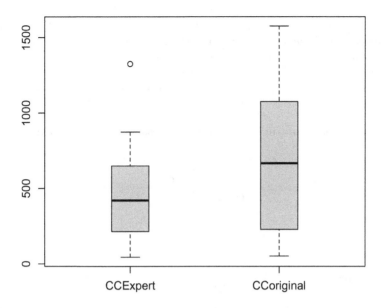

Fig. 1. Absolute residuals

Wilcoxon test revealed that the estimations obtained with CCexpert are significantly better than those obtained with CCoriginal (p-value < 0.001) with a small effect size (0.64).

Thus, we can positively answer our research question:

> The effort predictions obtained with CCexpert are better than those achieved with CCoriginal

4.3   Main Findings

From the results presented above we can conclude that the proposed strategy based on the opinion of experts for selecting cross-company dataset has provided interesting results for the software company involved in our study.

The main take away for researchers is that the identification of a strategy to select from publicly available data the information useful to build good effort estimation models can be crucial. Of course, the proposed strategy can be improved by automating the selection of variables. This could be a direction for the future work.

As for the point of view of practitioners, our study has shown that by employing a widely recognized approach (i.e., Delphi) can allow to improve significantly the effort predictions, with a minimal effort, in a context of small/medium company which does not have data available from past developed projects. To consolidate the contribution highlighted for practitioners, we think some aspects require further investigation. Indeed, from the decision taken by the experts in the selection of independent variables (i.e., predictors) we noted that factors such as the application area of the projects, the size of the available development group, or performance and security requirements were not considered. Thus, it could be interesting verify these decisions in other (similar) contexts.

Table 6. Results in terms of Mean of Absolute Residuals (MAR)

Model	MAR
CCoriginal	701
CCexpert	467

5   Conclusion

We have proposed an approach based on the opinion of the experts (provided through the Delphi method) to build cross-company effort prediction models. In particular, experts are in charge of selecting data from public cross-company datasets looking at the information about employed software development process and software technologies, before to apply an estimation technique to build the prediction models. This strategy could help in the context of small/medium company which does not have data available from past developed projects. The performed empirical study, involving a software company that exploits COS-MIC as functional size measurement method, has provided encouraging results. Indeed, the effort predictions obtained with the proposed strategy are significantly better than those obtained with the model built on the whole cross-company dataset.

As future work, we have planned to replicate this study with other publicly datasets and with other companies of our research network, with the aim of consolidate and improve the findings of the present study. We also intend to further assess the proposed strategy considering different estimation techniques, e.g., when software companies are interested to build prediction models based on several independent variables. Indeed, in the presented study we employed only a functional size measure, i.e., COSMIC, since the company measured the projects made available for the study with this measure. Also, sensitivity analysis could be used to test for the effect of including or excluding observations/values. Moreover, as mentioned above, we could automate the selection of the observations to be included in the cross-company dataset for the construction of the estimation model, after the selection of the variables through the Delphi approach. To this aim, similarity measures and machine learning approaches could be exploited. The application of search-based strategy could also be considered [44]. Finally, it could be interesting to verify the managers' opinions of the cost-benefit of the approach, by performing a qualitative research study.

References

1. The promise repository of empirical software engineering data (2015)
2. ISBSG: www.isbsg.org (2017)
3. Abualkishik, A.Z., et al.: A study on the statistical convertibility of IFPUG function point, COSMIC function point and simple function point. Inf. Softw. Technol. **86**, 1–19 (2017)
4. Breush, T., Pagan, A.: A simple test for heteroscedasticity and random coefficient variation. Econometrica **47**, 1287–1294 (1992)
5. Briand, L., El Emam, K., Surmann, D., Wiekzorek, I., Maxwell, K.: An assessment and comparison of common software cost estimation modeling techniques. In: Proceedings of International Conference on Software Engineering, pp. 313–322. IEEE Press (1999)
6. Briand, L.C., Wieczorek, I.: Software resource estimation. In: Encyclopedia of Software Engineering, pp. 1160–1196 (2002)
7. Conover, W.J.: Practical Nonparametric Statistics, 3rd edn. Wiley, Hoboken (1998)
8. Corazza, A., Martino, S.D., Ferrucci, F., Gravino, C., Mendes, E.: Investigating the use of support vector regression for web effort estimation. Empirical Softw. Eng. **16**(2), 211–243 (2011)
9. Di Martino, S., Ferrucci, F., Gravino, C., Mendes, E.: Comparing size measures for predicting web application development effort: a case study. In: Proceedings of Empirical Software Engineering and Measurement, pp. 324–333. IEEE Press (2007)
10. Ferrucci, F., Mendes, E., Sarro, F.: Web effort estimation: the value of cross-company data set compared to single-company data set. In: Proceedings of the 8th International Conference on Predictive Models in Software Engineering, pp. 29–38 (2012)
11. Freund, J.: Mathematical Statistics. Prentice-Hall, Upper Saddle River (1992)
12. Jeffery, R., Ruhe, M., Wieczorek, I.: A comparative study of two software development cost modeling techniques using multi-organizational and company-specific data. Inf. Softw. Technol. **42**, 1009–1016 (2000)
13. Jeffery, R., Ruhe, M., Wieczorek, I.: Using public domain metrics to estimate software development effort. In: Proceedings of International Software Metrics Symposium, pp. 16–27. IEEE Press (2001)
14. JøRgensen, M.: A review of studies on expert estimation of software development effort. J. Syst. Softw. **70**(1–2), 37–60 (2004)
15. Kampenes, V., Dyba, T., Hannay, J., Sjoberg, I.: A systematic review of effect size in software engineering experiments. Inf. Softw. Technol. **4**(11–12), 1073–1086 (2007)
16. Kitchenham, B., Mendes, E., Travassos, G.: Cross versus within-company cost estimation studies: a systematic review. IEEE Trans. Softw. Eng. **33**(5), 316–329 (2007)
17. Kitchenham, B., Pickard, L., Pfleeger, S.: Case studies for method and tool evaluation. IEEE Softw. **12**(4), 52–62 (1995)
18. Kitchenham, B., Mendes, E., Travassos, G.H.: A systematic review of cross- vs. within- company cost estimation studies. In: Proceedings of the 10th International Conference on Evaluation and Assessment in Software Engineering, EASE 2006, pp. 81–90. BCS Learning & Development Ltd., Swindon (2006)
19. Kocaguneli, E., Menzies, T., Mendes, E.: Transfer learning in effort estimation. Empirical Softw. Eng. **20**(3), 813–843 (2015)

20. Langdon, W.B., Dolado, J., Sarro, F., Harman, M.: Exact mean absolute error of baseline predictor, MARP0. Inf. Softw. Technol. **73**, 16–18 (2016)
21. Lefley, M., Shepperd, M.J.: Using genetic programming to improve software effort estimation based on general data sets. In: Cantú-Paz, E., et al. (eds.) GECCO 2003. LNCS, vol. 2724, pp. 2477–2487. Springer, Heidelberg (2003). https://doi.org/10.1007/3-540-45110-2_151
22. Lokan, C., Mendes, E.: Cross-company and single-company effort models using the ISBSG database: a further replicated study. In: Proceedings of International Symposium on Empirical Software Engineering, pp. 75–84. IEEE Press (2006)
23. Martino, S.D., Ferrucci, F., Gravino, C., Sarro, F.: Web effort estimation: function point analysis vs. COSMIC. Inf. Softw. Technol. **72**, 90–109 (2016)
24. Mendes, E.: Predicting web development effort using a Bayesian network. In: Proceedings of Evaluation and Assessment in Software Engineering, pp. 83–93. IEEE Press (2007)
25. Mendes, E., Counsell, S., Mosley, N.: Comparison of Web size measures for predicting Web design and authoring effort. IEE Proc.-Softw. **149**(3), 86–92 (2002)
26. Mendes, E., Di Martino, S., Ferrucci, F., Gravino, C.: Effort estimation: how valuable is it for a Web company to use a cross-company data set, compared to using its own single-company data Set? In: Proceedings of the 6th International World Wide Web Conference, pp. 83–93. ACM Press (2007)
27. Mendes, E., Kitchenham, B.: Further comparison of cross-company and within-company effort estimation models for web applications. In: Proceedings of International Software Metrics Symposium, pp. 348–357. IEEE Press (2004)
28. Mendes, E.: A comparison of techniques for web effort estimation. In: Proceedings of the First International Symposium on Empirical Software Engineering and Measurement, ESEM 2007, Madrid, Spain, 20–21 September 2007, pp. 334–343 (2007)
29. Mendes, E.: The use of a bayesian network for web effort estimation. In: Baresi, L., Fraternali, P., Houben, G.-J. (eds.) ICWE 2007. LNCS, vol. 4607, pp. 90–104. Springer, Heidelberg (2007). https://doi.org/10.1007/978-3-540-73597-7_8
30. Mendes, E.: The use of Bayesian networks for web effort estimation: further investigation. In: Proceedings of International Conference on Web Engineering, pp. 203–216 (2008)
31. Mendes, E., Kalinowski, M., Martins, D., Ferrucci, F., Sarro, F.: Cross- vs. within-company cost estimation studies revisited: an extended systematic review. In: Proceedings of the 18th International Conference on Evaluation and Assessment in Software Engineering, EASE 2014, pp. 12:1–12:10. ACM, New York (2014)
32. Mendes, E., Lokan, C.: Investigating the use of chronological splitting to compare software cross-company and single-company effort predictions: a replicated study. In: Proceedings of the 13th International Conference on Evaluation and Assessment in Software Engineering, EASE 2009 (2009)
33. Mendes, E., Martino, S.D., Ferrucci, F., Gravino, C.: Cross-company vs. single-company web effort models using the Tukutuku database: an extended study. J. Syst. Softw. **81**(5), 673–690 (2008)
34. Mendes, E., Mosley, N.: Bayesian network models for web effort prediction: a comparative study. IEEE Trans. Softw. Eng. **34**(6), 723–737 (2008)
35. Mendes, E., Pollino, C.A., Mosley, N.: Building an expert-based web effort estimation model using Bayesian networks. In: 13th International Conference on Evaluation and Assessment in Software Engineering, EASE 2009, 20–21 April 2009. Durham University, UK (2009)

36. Menzies, T., Chen, Z., Hihn, J., Lum, K.: Selecting best practices for effort estimation. IEEE Trans. Softw. Eng. **32**(11), 883–895 (2006)
37. Minku, L., Sarro, F., Mendes, E., Ferrucci, F.: How to make best use of cross-company data for web effort estimation? In: 2015 ACM/IEEE International Symposium on Empirical Software Engineering and Measurement (ESEM), pp. 1–10 (2015)
38. Minku, L.L., Yao, X.: How to make best use of cross-company data in software effort estimation? In: Proceedings of the 36th International Conference on Software Engineering, ICSE 2014, pp. 446–456. ACM (2014)
39. Minku, L.L., Yao, X.: Which models of the past are relevant to the present? A software effort estimation approach to exploiting useful past models. Autom. Softw. Eng. **24**(3), 499–542 (2017)
40. Myrtveit, I., Stensrud, E.: Validity and reliability of evaluation procedures in comparative studies of effort prediction models. Empirical Softw. Eng. **17**(1–2), 23–33 (2012)
41. Rowe, G., Wright, G.: Expert opinions in forecasting: the role of the Delphi technique. In: Armstrong, J.S. (ed.) Principles of Forecasting. ISOR, vol. 30, pp. 125–144. Springer, Boston (2001). https://doi.org/10.1007/978-0-306-47630-3_7
42. Royston, P.: An extension of Shapiro and Wilk's W test for normality to large samples. Appl. Stat. **31**(2), 115–124 (1982)
43. Ruhe, M., Wieczorek, I.: How valuable is company-specific data compared to multi-company data for software cost estimation? In: Proceedings of the International Software Metrics Symposium, pp. 237–246. IEEE Press (2002)
44. Sarro, F., Ferrucci, F., Gravino, C.: Single and multi objective genetic programming for software development effort estimation. In: Proceedings of the ACM Symposium on Applied Computing, SAC 2012, Riva, Trento, Italy, 26–30 March 2012, pp. 1221–1226 (2012)
45. Sarro, F., Petrozziello, A.: Linear programming as a baseline for software effort estimation. ACM Trans. Softw. Eng. Methodol. **27**(3), 12:1–12:28 (2018)
46. Shepperd, M.J., MacDonell, S.G.: Evaluating prediction systems in software project estimation. Inf. Softw. Technol. **54**(8), 820–827 (2012)
47. Turhan, B., Mendes, E.: A comparison of cross-versus single-company effort prediction models for web projects. In: 40th EUROMICRO Conference on Software Engineering and Advanced Applications, EUROMICRO-SEAA 2014, Verona, Italy, 27–29 August 2014, pp. 285–292 (2014)
48. Vargha, A., Delaney, H.D.: A critique and improvement of the CL common language effect size statistics of McGraw and Wong. J. Educ. Behav. Stat. **25**(2), 101–132 (2000)
49. Wohlin, C., Runeson, P., Host, M., Ohlsson, M., Regnell, B., Wesslen, A.: Experimentation in Software Engineering - An Introduction. Kluwer, Dordrecht (2000)
50. Yin, R.K.: Case Study Research: Design and Methods. Sage Publications, Thousand Oaks (1984)

Continuous Delivery

Excellence in Exploratory Testing: Success Factors in Large-Scale Industry Projects

Torvald Mårtensson[1]([⊠]) [iD], Antonio Martini[2] [iD], Daniel Ståhl[3] [iD],
and Jan Bosch[4] [iD]

[1] Saab AB, Linköping, Sweden
torvald.martensson@saabgroup.com
[2] University of Oslo, Oslo, Norway
antonima@ifi.uio.no
[3] Ericsson AB, Linköping, Sweden
daniel.stahl@ericsson.com
[4] Chalmers University of Technology, Gothenburg, Sweden
jan@janbosch.com

Abstract. Based on interviews with 20 interviewees from four case study companies, this paper presents a list of key factors that enable efficient and effective exploratory testing of large-scale software systems. The nine factors are grouped into four themes: "The testers' knowledge, experience and personality", "Purpose and scope", "Ways of working" and "Recording and reporting". According to the interviewees, exploratory testing is a more creative way to work for the testers, and was therefore considered to make better use of the testers. Exploratory testing was also described as a good way to test system-wide and to test large-scale systems, especially exploratory testing with an end-user perspective. The identified key factors were confirmed by a series of follow-up interviews with the 20 interviewees and a cross-company workshop with 14 participants. This strengthens the generalizability of the findings, supporting that the list of key factors can be applied to projects in a large segment of the software industry. This paper also presents the results from a systematic literature review including 129 publications related to exploratory testing. No publication were found that summarizes the key factors that enable efficient and effective exploratory testing, which supports the novelty of the findings.

Keywords: Continuous delivery · Continuous integration · Exploratory testing · Large-scale systems · Software testing

1 Introduction

Exploratory testing is described in different ways in published books and research papers. Gregory and Crispin [1] describe the test technique with the following words: "Exploratory testers do not enter into a test session with predefined, expected results. Instead, they compare the behavior of the system against what they might expect, based on experience, heuristics, and perhaps oracles. The difference is subtle, but meaningful." The test technique is focused on learning, shown in for example Hendrickson's [2] definition of exploratory testing: "Simultaneously designing and executing tests to

X. Franch et al. (Eds.): PROFES 2019, LNCS 11915, pp. 299–314, 2019.
https://doi.org/10.1007/978-3-030-35333-9_21

learn about the system, using your insights from the last experiment to inform the next."

Hendrickson [2] splits the domain of testing into two complementing test forms: exploring and checking. In a similar way, Gregory and Crispin [1] describe how exploratory testing and automated testing complement each other: "Exploratory testing and automation aren't mutually exclusive but rather work in conjunction. Automation handles the day-to-day repetitive regression testing (checking), which enables the exploratory testers to test all the things the team didn't think about before coding."

In our previous work [3] we have developed a test method for exploratory testing of large-scale systems. From a study based on both quantities and qualitative data, we showed that exploratory testing plays a role in the continuous integration and delivery pipeline for a large-scale software system (with automated testing and exploratory testing complementing one another). Quantitative data collected in the study showed that the exploratory test teams in the case study produced more problem reports than other test teams, proving exploratory testing as being an efficient test technique.

Since our previous study on exploratory testing [3], we have identified a growing interest in exploratory testing from several of the companies we as researchers work with, and an interest to improve how the test technique is used in the companies. Based on this, the topic of this research paper is to answer the following research question: *What are the key factors that enable efficient and effective exploratory testing of large-scale software systems?*

The contribution of this paper is three-fold: First, it presents an extensive literature review, which summarizes published work related to exploratory testing. Second, the paper provides interview results from four case study companies, showing how exploratory testing is used in large-scale industry projects. Third, it presents a list of key factors that can enable efficient and effective exploratory testing of large-scale software systems.

The remainder of this paper is organized as follows: In the next section, we present the research method. This is followed in Sect. 3 by a study of related literature. In Sect. 4 we present the analysis of the interview results (the list of key factors), followed by a summary of the follow-up interviews and the cross-company workshop in Sect. 5. Threats to validity are discussed in Sect. 6. The paper is then concluded in Sect. 7.

2   Research Method

An overview of the research method is presented in Fig. 1. The study started with a systematic literature review, in order to look for answers to the research question (presented in Sect. 1) in published literature. A review protocol was created, containing the question driving the review, and the inclusion and exclusion criteria (presented in Sect. 3.1). The review was conducted according to the stages for a systematic literature review as presented by Kitchenham [4].

In parallel, a series of interviews were conducted with 20 interviewees from four case study companies (which we will refer to as Company A, Company B, Company C and Company D). The interviews were conducted as semi-structured interviews, using an interview guide with pre-defined specific questions. The purpose of the first series of

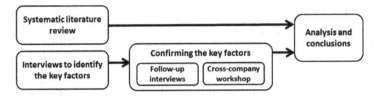

Fig. 1. An overview of the research method.

interviews was to *identify the key factors* that enable efficient and effective exploratory testing of large-scale software systems. The interview results were analyzed based on thematic coding analysis as described by Robson and McCartan [5]. The interview responses were coded and collated into themes, resulting in a thematic map with four main themes that in turn consist of several sub-themes: a list of key factors which can enable efficient and effective exploratory testing.

This was followed by *follow-up interviews* with the same 20 individuals as the first series of interviews (to collect feedback in order to strengthen the validity of the identified key factors in all four case study companies). In order to achieve method and data triangulation [6], the follow-up interviews was complemented with a *cross-company workshop* with 14 participants representing all four case study companies (discussing the results from the two series of interviews). The purpose of the follow-up interviews and the cross-company workshop was to confirm that the interpretation of the first series of interviews was correct, as well as looking for negative cases. The final step of the study consisted of *analysis and conclusions*, including a summary of threats to validity.

The case study companies involved in the study (Company A, Company B, Company C and Company D) are all multi-national organizations with more than 2,000 employees. All companies develop large-scale and complex software systems for products which also include a significant amount of mechanical and electronic systems. The case study companies operate in the following industry segments:

- Company A: Aeronautical systems
- Company B: Cars and services for cars
- Company C: Transport solutions for commercial use
- Company D: Video surveillance cameras and systems.

3   Reviewing Literature

3.1   Criteria for the Systematic Literature Review

In order to look for solutions related to the research question (as described in Sect. 1) in related work, a systematic literature review [4] was conducted. The question driving the review was "How are key factors that enable efficient and effective exploratory testing of large-scale software systems described in literature?" The inclusion criterion and the exclusion criterion for the review are shown in Table 1.

Table 1. Inclusion and exclusion criteria for the literature review.

Inclusion criterion	Yield
Publications matching the Scopus search string `TITLE-ABS-KEY` (`"exploratory testing"`) on October 27, 2018	129
Exclusion criterion	**Remaining**
Excluding duplicates and conference proceedings summaries	122
Excluding publications not related to development of software systems	71
Excluding publications with no available full-text	65

Our previous work [3] includes a similar systematic literature review, covering 52 publications. For the literature review in this study we expanded the search scope, which yielded 129 publications. After removing duplicates and conference proceedings summaries, the abstract of the remaining 122 publications were reviewed manually. Publications not related to development of software systems were excluded, i.e. removing publications related to archeology, chemistry et cetera. As a final stage, publications for which we could not find any available full-text were excluded from the literature review.

Characteristics and content of the remaining 65 research papers were then documented in a consistent manner in a data extraction protocol: for each paper a summary of how the paper was related to the research question, and representative keywords and quotes (sorted into categories which emerged during the process). The process was conducted iteratively to increase the quality of the analysis. Finally, the results from the review were collated and summarized.

3.2   Results from the Literature Review

An overview of the publications found in the systematic literature review is presented in Table 2. The review of the 65 publications retrieved from the search revealed that nine of the publications were not directly related to exploratory testing (only mentioning exploratory testing in passing while discussing other test techniques).

Ten of the publications are comparing exploratory testing and other test techniques, typically comparing exploratory testing and scripted testing (also referred to as test case based testing, specification based testing or confirmatory testing). The comparisons were based on literature reviews, true experiments, and case studies from industry projects. The papers describe or touch upon the strengths and weaknesses of exploratory testing (e.g. Shah et al. [7]), but do generally not define key factors for efficient or effective exploratory testing. One paper touch upon the subject: Thangiah and Basri [8] state that "exploratory testing is a testing approach that allows you to apply your ability and skill as a tester in a powerful way".

Twenty publications propose new methods that in different ways involve or include a reference to exploratory testing. Eleven of those publications present new methods or approaches, which combine exploratory testing and another test technique [9–19].

Table 2. An overview of the publications found in the systematic literature review.

Topic of the publications	Number of papers
Not relevant	9
Comparing exploratory testing and other test techniques	10
Methods	20
Tools	7
How exploratory testing is used	9
Reporting experiences	10
Summary	**65**

These methods try to combine the flexibility of exploratory testing with the structure provided by scripted test cases. As one example, Frajtak et al. [11] describe that the testers can use "their skills and intuition to explore the system", but "it is hard to measure the effectiveness of the [exploratory] testing". As a solution, Frajtak et al. proposing a technique where recording of the (exploratory) testers actions are used to create test case scenarios. Ghazi et al. [20] provide a different kind of structure, aiming to support practitioners in the design of test charters through checklists. Sviridova et al. [21] discuss effectiveness of exploratory testing and propose to use scenarios. The level of freedom in exploratory testing is discussed by Ghazi et al. [22], presenting a scale for the degree of exploration and defining five levels. Raappana et al. [23] report the effectiveness of a test method called "team exploratory testing", which is defined as a way to perform session-based exploratory testing in teams. One of the papers is our previous work [3], presenting a test method for exploratory testing of large-scale systems (as described in Sect. 1). Finally, Shah et al. [24] take a somewhat different approach, describing exploratory testing as a source of technical debt, and propose (as a solution to this problem) that exploratory testing should be combined with other testing approaches.

Seven of the publications present different types of tools, developed to increase the efficiency in exploratory testing. However, three of the papers does not include any validation of the presented tool. The remaining four papers describe tools developed to visualize how the executed testing covers the system under test [25, 26], visualize code changes in the system under test [27], and refine system models based on recorded testing activities [28].

Nine publications describe in different ways how exploratory testing is used by the testers. Four of those publications [29–32] focus on the tester's knowledge and experience: Itkonen et al. [31] discuss how testers recognize failures based on their personal knowledge without detailed test case descriptions ("domain knowledge, system knowledge, and general software engineering knowledge"). Gebizli and Sozer [29] present results from a study showing that both educational background and experience level has "significant impact" on the efficiency and effectiveness of exploratory testing. In contrast to that, two papers [33, 34] focus on the tester's personality: Shoaib et al. [34] simply conclude that "people having extrovert personality types are good exploratory testers". Pfahl et al. [33] analyzes the results from an online survey, and finds that exploratory testing "is as an approach that supports creativity during testing and that is effective and efficient". Tuomikoski and Tervonen [35] embrace both approaches, stating that "the effectiveness of exploratory testing is strongly based on individual test engineer's skills and ability to analyze system and its behavior" but also that "exploratory testing doesn't fit for everyone, and really requires experienced test engineers".

Finally, ten papers report experiences from exploratory testing in industry, but without presenting any documented quantitative or qualitative data. Pichler and Ramler [36] present experiences from development of mobile devices, and find that "tool support enhances the capability of human testers". Kumar and Wallace [37] describe that for the exploratory tester, it is "easy to get lost in a thicket of well-intentioned heuristics", and proposes the use of "problem frames" as a solution for this problem.

In summary, we found no publication with a complete summary of key factors that enable efficient and effective exploratory testing. Instead, published work tend to focus on one aspect, leaving out areas that other authors consider to be the core issues.

4   Identifying the Key Factors

4.1   Background Information

Twenty individuals participated in the interviews, with an average of 13 years of experience of industry software development (spanning from 4 to 46 years). All interviewees had experiences from exploratory testing as testers, and in some cases also as test leaders. Some of the interviewees were working in development teams, which incrementally developed new functions or systems (working only part-time as testers). Some of the interviewees had dedicated roles as testers in independent test teams (continuously testing the software updates coming from the development teams).

Interviewees from all four case study companies described that exploratory testing was used for two purposes in their organization: to find bugs during development of new functions and systems, and for testing of the complete system. The interviewees described that exploratory testing was used primarily for new functions, whereas automated testing and manual scripted testing was used primarily for regression tests.

The interviewees had a very positive attitude towards exploratory testing, responding 4 or 5 (on a Likert scale from 1 to 5) when they were asked to rate the value of exploratory testing as a test technique for large-scale software systems. The interviewees were then asked to describe strengths and weaknesses with exploratory testing. Generally, the interviewees described that exploratory testing is a good way to find problems fast and efficient. Exploratory testing is also a more creative way to work for the testers, and was therefore considered to make better use of the testers. Exploratory testing was also described as a good way to test system-wide and to test large-scale systems, especially exploratory testing with an end-user perspective. The interviewees also described a few weaknesses with exploratory testing: Some interviewees described that they believed that exploratory testing was more difficult for new testers. Another viewpoint was that it could be more difficult to describe what you have tested, compared to if you follow a scripted test case.

4.2   Key Factors for Efficient and Effective Exploratory Testing

The main question of the first series of interviews was: "What are the key factors that you think enable efficient and effective exploratory testing of large-scale software systems?" The responses for this question included a large amount of statements and comments. Extracts from the interview responses were coded and collated into themes. A thematic network were constructed [5], resulting in a thematic map with four main themes, which in turn consist of several sub-themes: a list of key factors which can enable efficient and effective exploratory testing.

The four main themes and their sub-themes are shown in Table 3, together with information about how many interviewees provided statements that supported each theme and sub-theme.

Table 3. Key factors which can enable efficient and effective exploratory testing, and the number of interviewees providing statements that supported each theme and sub-theme.

	Interviewees
The testers' knowledge, experience and personality	**20**
- The testers know how the system is built, and the correct behavior of the system	14
- The testers know how the product is used by the end-user (or the end user is represented in the test team)	12
- The testers are curious and want to learn about the system	16
Purpose and scope	**18**
- A well-defined purpose and scope for the tests (system functions ready to be tested) which the testers can transform into e.g. scenarios or focus areas	10
- Regression testing secure basic stability and integrity in the system (before exploratory testing)	11
Ways of working	**14**
- An established way of working, including e.g. planning meetings, preparations, test strategies and heuristics (a balance between structure and freedom)	10
- Testers with different experiences and competences work together as a team, helping each other with new ideas and knowledge about different parts of the system	12
Recording and reporting	**17**
- Test environments that support debugging and recording	10
- A well-defined way to report the test results, including a description of areas covered by the tests and a list of identified problems	12

All 20 interviewees talked about the importance of *the testers' knowledge, experience and personality*. In order to test the system, the testers must *know how the system is built, and the correct behavior of the system*. One interviewee asked for "testers with different types of experiences". Another voice asked for "good system knowledge". One interviewee described that the tester must have "test confidence", meaning that as a tester you should "trust your instinct that this is wrong". The testers must also *know how the product is used by the end-user* (or the end user should be represented in the test team). To quote one of the interviewees: "If you have the end-user perspective, then you know if a problem is a problem". One interviewee even stated that "you should always have the end-user perspective". The testers must also *be curious and want to learn about the system*. This means that even if the tester has good system knowledge, he/she still wants to learn more. The interviewees described that this calls for certain types of personalities, e.g. "the right personality, to be interested in new perspectives, curiosity, imagination". Some of the interviewees also described this as an interest in tracking down the problems in the system, e.g. "someone who want to find the bugs – curious and creative people".

As many as 18 interviewees did in different ways talk about the *purpose and scope* of the tests. This includes a *well-defined purpose and scope for the tests (system functions ready to be tested)* which the testers can transform into e.g. scenarios or focus areas. One interviewee described that "you should have a list of functions that should be tested". Several interviewees clarified that this should not be interpreted as that exploratory testing only could be used at a final stage of a project, and that this also affect development planning: "Test when the function is ready, and not too early. You must build the function in steps so it can be tested." Another interviewee had a similar comment: "Do exploratory testing early, but test complete functions". A related area is *regression testing to secure basic stability and integrity in the system* (before exploratory testing). Efficient regression testing finds problems in legacy functions (introduced due to dependencies between functions or systems). If this works well, skilled exploratory testers will not waste their time investigating and reporting problems with legacy functions, but can instead focus on testing the new functions. As one of interviewees put it: "Simple problems should be identified and corrected from automated testing". In the same way, the testers' time is not wasted at trouble-shooting problems that has already been analyzed. To quote one of the interviewees: "what is the status of the product, what are the known errors or problems").

Ways of working were discussed by 14 of the 20 interviewees. The interviewees requested *an established way of working*, including planning meetings, preparations, test strategies and heuristics (a balance between structure and freedom). The statements from the interviewees were quite general, e.g. "some kind of structure for the testing". However, the interviewees also emphasized that this structure should never be at the same detailed level as manual test-case-based testing, described e.g. by one of the interviewees as to "find the balance between freedom and traceability". One interviewee stated that "You must have fun – play around with things". The interviewees particularly emphasized advantages from that *testers with different experiences and competences work together as a team*, helping each other with new ideas and knowledge about different parts of the system. Some interviewees asked for that the testers should do the testing together ("test together with colleagues"). Others focused on that testers should help each other with new ideas, preparations et cetera ("a structure for how testers should support each other"). Generally, the interviewees asked for individuals with different knowledge and experience ("a team with a mix of individuals").

Seventeen of the 20 interviewees talked about *recording and reporting*. The interviewees *described test environments that support debugging and recording* as a prerequisite for efficient testing, in order to provide detailed data about the identified problems. The interviewees also asked for recording in order to document the testing. Quoting one of the interviewees: "An efficient way of documenting what you do". The interviewees also asked for *a well-defined way to report the test results*, including a description of areas covered by the tests and a list of identified problems. Reporting should not be limited to only problem reports, as it is also important to describe which areas of the product that has been tested. This is important in order to avoid that testers (or test teams) spend time testing the same things, and to secure that the purpose and scope of the testing is fully covered. As one of the interviewees phrased it: "You must document in a good way what you have done, otherwise you might miss important areas". There were different opinions about how the results from the testing should be reported. One interviewee explained that test results should be visualized, i.e. not only described in text. Another interviewee argued that the best way is to "involve the people interested in the test in the test".

In summary, we find that the thematic coding analysis of the interview results resulted in nine factors, all supported by statements or comments from at least ten of the interviewees. The nine factors were arranged in four groups, each group supported by between fourteen and twenty interviewees.

5   Confirming the Key Factors

5.1   Follow-up Interviews

In order to strengthen the validity of the findings from the first series of interviews, a second series of interviews was conducted. The list of key factors (presented in Table 3) were presented to the interviewees. The interviewees were then asked to rate the importance of each factor on a Likert scale from 1 ("not important") to 5 ("very important"). This means that the interviewees did not only provide feedback on the interpretation of their own responses, but were also providing feedback on the input from 19 other interviewees from four companies.

The interviewees generally confirmed the list of factors, rating the importance of each factor as 4 or 5. The interviewees often added comments like "All factors seem to be very important" or "All factor are relevant and good – they describe prerequisites for good testing". The interviewees were also asked to explain if they had not for example talked about e.g. test environments in the first interview, but now rated this factor as very important. Generally, the interviewees explained this with e.g. "the things I did not talk about [at the first interview] was what I took for granted" or similar comments. Four interviewees commented on the factor "established way of working", and the importance of balance between structure and freedom, e.g. "How much planning is this? It must be some, but not too much. I rate this as 2 on a scale from 1 to 5 if it means too much planning."

Three interviewees commented on that the factors seem to be correlated, e.g. to work together as a team is less important if every single tester covers all types experiences and competences. One interviewee rated five of the factors as 2 or 3, and suggested changes such as "I want to include the term domain knowledge in this factor". However, the same interviewee concluded with "the list is great, but it can be better".

We find that the second series of interviews confirm the results from the first series of interviews, showing that the key factors presented in Table 3 in a good way reflect the interviewees' positions and viewpoints.

5.2 Cross-Company Workshop

To complement the second series of interviews, a cross-company workshop was organized with participants from all four case study companies. Fourteen individuals participated in the workshop, five of them with roles as manager, test leader or test specialist. Four of the participants at the workshop had also been participating as interviewees in the two series of interviews. At the workshop, two of the researchers presented the results from the literature review and the two series of interviews. The workshop participants discussed the presented key factors (from Table 3) but had only minor comments regarding the factors (e.g. "to talk to the developers is probably better than just to write a problem report").

The researchers also presented a summary of differences between the case study companies: All factors were supported by comments or statements from interviewees from all case study companies, except for the factor "A well-defined purpose and scope for the tests" (coming from three of the four companies). However, workshop participants from the fourth company commented that "We work with purpose and scope. This is important." Another difference between the companies identified in the first series of interviews was that "Work together as a team" was implemented differently in the case study companies: In two of the companies the testers worked together in the test facilities. In the other two companies the testers tested separately, but worked together and supported each other as a team in other ways.

The workshop participants were asked to rate their current situation with regards to each factor. This revealed differences between the companies, and encouraged discussions related to some of the factors, e.g.:

- Should the exploratory test teams cover all types of end-users (such as e.g. a service technician), or focus only on the primary user (e.g. the driver of the car)?
- How are stability and integrity best maintained in the system – with e.g. 100% code coverage on component level, or a mix of component tests and system tests?
- What does reporting actually mean – does it include to follow up that the information has actually been received by the R&D department?

Participants representing all four case study companies showed interest in a continued study, with the purpose to construct a method or a model based on the identified nine key factors. The method/model could then be used to evaluate the current situation in an organization, and provide input to improvement initiatives related to exploratory testing. The workshop participants discussed if such a model could include the stakeholders who can enable solutions for the different key factors. It then became evident that the workshop participants had quite different opinions, also among participants from the same company. As it seems, it is difficult to identify one single role who can enable a factor. Instead, many roles are involved, or it could be difficult to identify any relevant role or part of the organization.

The workshop participants also discussed how the key factors are correlated, e.g. if the testers have the right knowledge, experience and personality (the first three factors), they probably need less support from an established way of working (the sixth factor). Generally, almost all of the identified connections pointed towards the first two key factors (related to the testers' knowledge and experience). We interpret this as that factors related to "the right people" should be considered to be more important than factors related to "the right structure".

Finally, the workshop participants discussed how exploratory testing is related to Agile methodologies. The individuals participating at the workshop expressed very different opinions. One voice had the opinion that exploratory testing harmonize well with Agile development ("exploratory testing is enabling Agile"). Another individual had a somewhat opposite opinion ("Agile is killing exploratory testing") based on that Agile methodologies often tend to focus on automated testing.

We find that the cross-company workshop confirmed the findings from the two series of interviews, and that the identified key factors are valid for all four case study companies. The interest from the workshop participants in the construction of an actionable method or model based on the nine key factors shows that the results from the study are considered to be useful in practice. One workshop participant concluded the workshop with the words "It was a good thing to see the nine factors, and to see that also other companies find these things to be important. This makes it easier for us to change things back home".

6   Threats to Validity

6.1   Threats to Construct Validity

One must always consider that a different set of questions and a different context for the interviews can lead to a different focus in the interviewees' responses. In order to handle threats against construct validity, the interview guide was designed with open-ended questions. In this paper, we also present background material for both the interviewees and the case study companies in order to provide as much information as possible about the context and enable reproducibility of the study.

It is conceivable that the interviewees' perception of the key factors for effective and efficient exploratory testing is affected by the current situation in the case study companies (e.g. which type of questions or topics that are currently in focus in each company). Therefore, it is plausible that the exact description of the key factors should have been different if the study had included other case study companies. However, all factors are based on comments and statements from at least 10 of the 20 interviewees, and are considered to be valid for all four case study companies (based on the follow-up interviews and the cross-company workshop). Due to this, we argue that this threat to construct validity should be seen as acceptable.

Another threat to construct validity is researcher bias during the interpretation of the interview results. This threat was mitigated with member checking (the follow-up interviews) and a focus group (the cross-company workshop), following the guidelines from Robson and McCartan [5] who consider this to be "a very valuable means of guarding against researcher bias" and a good way to "amplify and understand the findings".

6.2   Threats to Internal Validity

Of the 12 threats to internal validity listed by Cook, Campbell and Day [38], we consider Selection, Ambiguity about causal direction and Compensatory rivalry relevant to this work:

- *Selection*: All interviewees and workshop participants were purposively sampled (selected as good informants with appropriate roles in the companies) in line with the guidelines for qualitative data appropriateness given by Robson and McCartan [5]. Based on the rationale of these samplings and supported by Robson and McCartan who consider this type of sampling superior for this type of study in order to secure appropriateness, we consider this threat to be mitigated.
- *Ambiguity about causal direction*: While we in this study in some cases discuss relationships, we are very careful about making statements regarding causation. Statements that include cause and effect are collected from the interview results, and not introduced in the interpretation of the data.
- *Compensatory rivalry*: When performing interviews and comparing scores or performance, the threat of compensatory rivalry must always be considered. The questions in our interviews were deliberately designed to be value neutral for the participants, and not judging performance or skills of the interviewee or the interviewee's organization. Generally, the questions were also designed to be opened-ended to avoid any type of bias and ensure answers that were open and accurate. However, our experiences from previous work is that we found the interviewees more prone to self-criticism than to self-praise.

6.3   Threats to External Validity

The list of key factors was confirmed by series of follow-up interviews and a cross-company workshop with participants from the same case study companies as the first series of interviews. Due to this, it is conceivable that the findings from this study are only valid for these companies, or for companies that operate in the same industry segments (presented in Sect. 2).

The follow-up interviews and the workshop showed that the list of key factors is valid for all four case study companies. Because of the diverse nature of these four companies, the case study companies represent a good cross-section of the industry (as described in Sect. 2). Based on this, it is reasonable to expect that the identified key factors that can enable efficient and effective exploratory testing are also relevant to a large segment of the software industry at large (analytic generalization). However, we consider external validation in other case study companies (preferably in different industry segments) to be a natural suggestion for further work.

7   Conclusion

In this paper, we have presented interview results from 20 interviewees with an experience of 4–46 years (on average more than 13 years). The interviewees come from four case study companies, all developing large-scale software systems. The interviewees described that exploratory testing was used for two purposes in their organization: to find bugs during development of new functions and systems, and for testing of the complete system. Exploratory testing was used primarily for new functions, whereas automated testing and manual scripted testing was used primarily for regression tests.

The interviewees had generally good experiences from using exploratory testing. According to the interviewees, exploratory testing is a more creative way to work for the testers, and was therefore considered to make better use of the testers. Exploratory testing was also described as a good way to test system-wide and to test large-scale systems, especially exploratory testing with an end-user perspective.

Based on the analysis of the interview results (presented in Sect. 4) we identified nine key factors, grouped in four themes, which can enable efficient and effective exploratory testing of large-scale software systems:

- *The testers' knowledge, experience and personality*:
  - The testers know how the system is built, and the correct behavior of the system
  - The testers know how the product is used by the end-user (or the end user is represented in the test team)
  - The testers are curious and want to learn about the system
- *Purpose and scope:*
  - A well-defined purpose and scope for the tests (system functions ready to be tested) which the testers can transform into e.g. scenarios or focus areas
  - Regression testing secure basic stability and integrity in the system (before exploratory testing)
- *Ways of working:*
  - An established way of working, including e.g. planning meetings, preparations, test strategies and heuristics (a balance between structure and freedom)
  - Testers with different experiences and competences work together as a team, helping each other with new ideas and knowledge about different parts of the system
- *Recording and reporting:*
  - Test environments that support debugging and recording
  - A well-defined way to report the test results, including a description of areas covered by the tests and a list of identified problems.

The list of key factors was confirmed by a series of follow-up interviews with the 20 interviewees (presented in Sect. 5.1) and a cross-company workshop with 14 participants (presented in Sect. 5.2). The follow-up interviews and the workshop also showed that the list of key factors is valid for all four case study companies. As the four case study companies operate in different industry segments, it is reasonable to expect that the identified *key factors that enable efficient and effective exploratory testing* can be applied to projects in a large segment of the software industry.

The systematic literature review (presented in Sect. 3) identified 129 publications related to exploratory testing, with 65 publications related to exploratory testing of software systems. No publication were found that summarizes key factors that enable efficient and effective exploratory testing, which supports the novelty of the findings presented in this paper.

7.1 Further Work

As the study reported in this paper does not include any external validation, this comes as a natural suggestion for further work (as described in Sect. 6.3). The external validation is preferably conducted in case study companies that operate in other industry segments than the companies in the primary study.

Further work could also include construction of a method or a model, which can help companies to improve how exploratory testing is used in the companies (as suggested in Sect. 5.2).

Another topic for further work is to analyze the relation (described in Sect. 5.2) between exploratory testing and Agile methodologies: is it so that "exploratory testing is enabling Agile" or is it "Agile is killing exploratory testing"?

References

1. Gregory, J., Crispin, L.: More agile Testing. Addison Wesley, Boston (2015)
2. Hendrickson, E.: Explore It!, The Pragmatic Bookshelf (2013)
3. Mårtensson, T., Ståhl, D., Bosch, J.: Exploratory testing of large-scale systems – testing in the continuous integration and delivery pipeline. In: Felderer, M., Méndez Fernández, D., Turhan, B., Kalinowski, M., Sarro, F., Winkler, D. (eds.) PROFES 2017. LNCS, vol. 10611, pp. 368–384. Springer, Cham (2017). https://doi.org/10.1007/978-3-319-69926-4_26
4. Kitchenham, B.: Procedures for performing systematic reviews. Keele UK Keele Univ. **33** (2004), 1–26 (2004)
5. Robson, C., McCartan, K.: Real World Research, 4th edn. Wiley, Hoboken (2016)
6. Runeson, P., Höst, M.: Guidelines for conducting and reporting case study research in software engineering. Empirical Softw. Eng. **14**(2), 131–164 (2009)
7. Shah, S.M.A., Gencel, C., Alvi, U.S., Petersen, K.: Towards a hybrid testing process unifying exploratory testing and scripted testing. J. Softw. Evol. Process **26**(2), 220–250 (2014)
8. Thangiah, M., Basri, S.: A preliminary analysis of various testing techniques in Agile development - a systematic literature review. In: 3rd International Conference on Computer and Information Sciences, ICCOINS 2016, pp. 600–605 (2016)
9. Basri, S., Dominic, D.D., Murugan, T., Almomani, M.A.: A proposed framework using exploratory testing to improve software quality in SME's. Advances in Intell. Syst. Comput. **843**, 1113–1122 (2019)
10. Calpur, M.C., Arca, S., Calpur, T.C., Yilmaz, C.: Model dressing for automated exploratory testing. In: IEEE International Conference on Software Quality, Reliability and Security Companion, QRS-C 2017, pp. 577–578 (2017)

11. Frajtak, K., Bures, M., Jelinek, I.: Model-based testing and exploratory testing: is synergy possible? In: 6th International Conference on IT Convergence and Security, ICITCS 2016 (2016)

12. Gebizli, C.S., Sozer, H.: Improving models for model-based testing based on exploratory testing. In: 38th Annual International Computers, Software and Applications Conference Workshops, COMPSACW 2014, pp. 656–661 (2014)

13. Hellmann, T.D., Maurer, F.: Rule-based exploratory testing of graphical user interfaces. In: 2011 Agile Conference, Agile 2011, pp. 107–116 (2011)

14. Hudson, J., Denzinger, J.: Risk management for self-adapting self-organizing emergent multi-agent systems performing dynamic task fulfillment. Auton. Agents Multi-Agent Syst. **29**(5), 973–1022 (2015)

15. Kim, D.-K., Lee, L.-S.: Reverse engineering from exploratory testing to specification-based testing. Int. J. Softw. Eng. Appl. **8**(11), 197–208 (2014)

16. Kuhn, A.: On extracting unit tests from interactive live programming sessions. In: International Conference on Software Engineering, pp. 1241–1244 (2013)

17. Mihindukulasooriya, N., Rizzo, G., Troncy, R., Corcho, O., García-Castro, R.: A two-fold quality assurance approach for dynamic knowledge bases: the 3cixty use case. In: CEUR Workshop Proceedings (2016)

18. Rashmi, N., Suma, V.: Defect detection efficiency of the combined approach. In: Satapathy, S., Avadhani, P., Udgata, S., Lakshminarayana, S. (eds.) ICT and Critical Infrastructure: Proceedings of the 48th Annual Convention of Computer Society of India - Volume II. AISC, vol. 249, pp. 485–490. Springer, Cham (2014). https://doi.org/10.1007/978-3-319-03095-1_51

19. Schaefer, C.J., Do, H.: Model-based exploratory testing: a controlled experiment. In: 7th International Conference on Software Testing, Verification and Validation Workshops, ICSTW 2014, pp. 284–293 (2014)

20. Ghazi, A.N., Garigapati, R.P., Petersen, K.: Checklists to support test charter design in exploratory testing. In: Baumeister, H., Lichter, H., Riebisch, M. (eds.) XP 2017. LNBIP, vol. 283, pp. 251–258. Springer, Cham (2017). https://doi.org/10.1007/978-3-319-57633-6_17

21. Sviridova, T., Stakhova, D., Marikutsa, U.: Exploratory testing: management solution. In: 12th International Conference: The Experience of Designing and Application of CAD Systems in Microelectronics, CADSM 2013, p. 361 (2013)

22. Ghazi, A.N., Petersen, K., Bjarnason, E., Runeson, P.: Levels of exploration in exploratory testing: from freestyle to fully scripted. IEEE Access **6**, 26416–26423 (2018)

23. Raappana, P., Saukkoriipi, S., Tervonen, I., Mäntylä, M.V.: The effect of team exploratory testing - experience report from F-Secure. In: International Conference on Software Testing, Verification and Validation Workshops, ICSTW 2016, pp. 295–304 (2016)

24. Shah, S.M.A., Torchiano, M., Vetrò, A., Morisio, M.: Exploratory testing as a source of technical debt. IT Prof. **16**(3), 44–51 (2014)

25. Bures, M., Frajtak, K., Ahmed, B.S.: Tapir: automation support of exploratory testing using model reconstruction of the system under test. IEEE Trans. Reliab. **67**(2), 557–580 (2018)

26. Frajtak, K., Bures, M., Jelinek, I.: Exploratory testing supported by automated reengineering of model of the system under test. Cluster Comput. **20**(1), 855–865 (2017)

27. Reis, J., Mota, A.: Aiding exploratory testing with pruned GUI models. Inf. Process. Lett. **133**, 49–55 (2018)

28. Gebizli, C.Ş., Sözer, H.: Automated refinement of models for model-based testing using exploratory testing. Softw. Qual. J. **25**(3), 979–1005 (2017)

29. Gebizli, C.S., Sözer, H.: Impact of education and experience level on the effectiveness of exploratory testing: an industrial case study. In: 10th IEEE International Conference on Software Testing, Verification and Validation Workshops, ICSTW 2017, pp. 23–28 (2017)
30. Itkonen, J., Mäntylä, M.V., Lassenius, C.: How do testers do it? An exploratory study on manual testing practices. In: 3rd International Symposium on Empirical Software Engineering and Measurement, ESEM 2009, pp. 494–497 (2009)
31. Itkonen, J., Mäntylä, M.V., Lassenius, C.: The role of the tester's knowledge in exploratory software testing. IEEE Trans. Softw. Eng. **39**(5), 707–724 (2013)
32. Micallef, M., Porter, C., Borg, A.: Do exploratory testers need formal training? An investigation using HCI techniques. In: International Conference on Software Testing, Verification and Validation Workshops, ICSTW 2016, pp. 305–314 (2016)
33. Pfahl, D., Yin, H., Mäntylä, M.V., Münch, J.: How is exploratory testing used? A state-of-the-practice survey. In: International Symposium on Empirical Software Engineering and Measurement (2014)
34. Shoaib, L., Nadeem, A., Akbar, A.: An empirical evaluation of the influence of human personality on exploratory software testing. In: 13th International Multitopic Conference, INMIC 2009 (2009)
35. Tuomikoski, J., Tervonen, I.: Absorbing software testing into the scrum method. In: Bomarius, F., Oivo, M., Jaring, P., Abrahamsson, P. (eds.) PROFES 2009. LNBIP, vol. 32, pp. 199–215. Springer, Heidelberg (2009). https://doi.org/10.1007/978-3-642-02152-7_16
36. Pichler, J., Ramler, R.: How to test the intangible properties of graphical user interfaces? In: 1st International Conference on Software Testing, Verification and Validation, ICST 2008, pp. 494–497 (2008)
37. Kumar, S., Wallace, C.: Guidance for exploratory testing through problem frames. In: Software Engineering Education Conference, pp. 284–288 (2013)
38. Cook, T.D., Campbell, D.T., Day, A.: Quasi-Experimentation: Design & Analysis Issues for Field Settings, vol. 351. Houghton Mifflin, Boston (1979)

Comparison Framework for Team-Based Communication Channels

Camila Costa Silva⬤, Fabian Gilson(✉)⬤, and Matthias Galster⬤

University of Canterbury, Christchurch, New Zealand
camila.costasilva@pg.canterbury.ac.nz,
{fabian.gilson,matthias.galster}@canterbury.ac.nz

Abstract. Communication via instant messaging (*e.g.*, Slack) supports collaboration between software developers. It enables discussions and knowledge sharing within small groups, companies and physically distributed teams. In this paper, we introduce a comparison framework aiming at the evaluation of team-based communication channels for (a) practitioners interested in using or improving communication channels as part of their project and team communication, and (b) researchers interested in utilising team communication channels to answer research questions (*e.g.*, to analyse developer communication in mining studies). The framework includes criteria derived from other empirical works on developer communication and experience reports related to development tools. We illustrate the framework by analysing four communication tools (Microsoft Teams, Slack, Gitter, Spectrum).

Keywords: Collaborative software development · Developer communication · Instant messaging · Social media

1 Introduction

Social media support software development [13]. For example, distributed teams or individual developers can share knowledge and discuss design decisions in online developer communities (*e.g.*, Stack Overflow). In particular, instant messaging (IM) using tools such as Slack improves team communication [17]. For example, Zahedi *et al.* found that IM-based communication support formal planning (with chat history stored for latter reference) [16]. Also, IM-based communication is more suitable for ad-hoc and urgent communication in teams than emails [16] and help clarify misunderstandings and collaboratively solve problems [3]. Finally, IM communication helps team members collectively store and retrieve knowledge [4], for example, about technical details of a product under development [2]. IM communication can be project-specific (*e.g.*, developers who communicate in a private Slack channel) or topic-specific and relevant to a broader audience (*e.g.*, a public Gitter group discussing Python problems).

Previous research has explored the use of social media like Stack Overflow to share and discuss problems and solutions [11], and Slack for discussions in

ⓒ Springer Nature Switzerland AG 2019
X. Franch et al. (Eds.): PROFES 2019, LNCS 11915, pp. 315–322, 2019.
https://doi.org/10.1007/978-3-030-35333-9_22

communities of practice [6]. In this paper, we present a comparison framework for IM-based communication channels. The framework supports (1) practitioners who may want to identify the most suitable tool for their own purpose (*e.g.*, to use in their project or team), and (2) researchers studying developer communication interested in comparing tools to find the one most suitable for their research (*e.g.*, for mining studies). Practitioners and researchers may also want to understand differences between tools and extend or develop new tools.

2 Framework

The framework (see Table 1) needs to be general enough to characterise a wide range of communication channels, but including too many criteria would limit its usefulness. Therefore, criteria are based on needs and challenges described in the literature [12], needs expressed by practitioners [3,11], issues identified in empirical studies [4,14,16] as well as their relevance for the practical use of a communication channel (*e.g.*, pricing, access to conversation data). Additionally, we draw upon comparison frameworks proposed in other domains (such as product line engineering [8,9]) and integrate criteria from previously published evaluation frameworks [1].

Table 1. Comparison framework

Type	Criteria	Description
Popularity	Year of release # of users # of public groups	Describe how known and widely used tools and their groups are.
Openness	Service plans Group types Group visibility	Ability to access tools through different service plans; group types can be topic-specific or project-specific; visibility can be private or public.
Administration	User profile Permission type	Functions and resources to manage users, their profiles and access rights.
Interaction features	Interaction group/space Interaction format Message format Conversation Notifications/mentions Search capability	Spaces for interactions (public/private) and their format (*e.g.*, rich text, file sharing, videoconferencing); mechanisms for direct interactions and notifications between users; search capabilities (*e.g.*, history and file search).
Interoperability	External apps Client platforms	How tools interact with external resources and how tools can be accessed (*e.g.*, via the web, mobile and desktop apps).
API	APIs documentation	Description of APIs to extract data from groups, chat rooms and messages and/or build analysis tools or extensions.

The framework is rather qualitative and "descriptive" in nature and does not include numerical evaluation criteria. While a quantitative evaluation would allow visual representations, assigning numerical values to criteria such as popularity seems rather arbitrary and subjective, and would provide only limited insights (*e.g.,* number of users might be misleading as a sole measure for popularity if many users are inactive).

3   Case Study

We used the proposed framework in a case study [10] to compare four team communication tools. As **cases**, we selected Microsoft Teams (MS-Teams)[1] and Slack[2] because (at the time of writing this paper) they are the most popular tools for team communication [5,7]. We included Gitter[3] since it is frequently used by software developers [13]. We selected Spectrum[4] as alternative to Slack suggested in a Slack discussion. To **collect data**, the authors reviewed documentation of the tools available online and tested their features following the framework.

Popularity. In Table 2 we compare tools based on popularity.

Table 2. Popularity

Criteria	MS-Teams	Slack	Gitter	Spectrum
Year of release	2017	2013	2014	2017
# of users	≈13,000,000	≈10,000,000	≈800,000	Unknown
# of public groups	Unknown	≈2,000	≈90,000	≈5,000

MS-Teams is the latest of the four tools. It has gradually been replacing *"Office365 classrooms"* and *"Skype for Business"* and is used by more than 500,000 organisations [15]. Slack is the oldest tool and currently used by 85,000 organisations [7]. Slack has no public groups (see below), but users can request access to groups they want to join[5]. Gitter was released to assist GitHub users and was acquired by Gitlab in 2017 but kept its GitHub integration. Spectrum's number of users is unknown.

Openness. In Table 3 we compare tools based on openness. MS-Teams offers different **service plans**, *i.e.* attached to their Office365 ecosystem on top of a free plan. Slack has three plans for teams (free, standard and plus) and an enterprise grid (*i.e.* a local instance with enhanced privacy and security). Spectrum used to be a paid service, but became free when joining GitHub. Regarding **group types** and **group visibility**, groups in MS-Teams are organisation-wide and invitation-only. As MS-Teams, Slack distinguishes organisation-wide and

---

[1] https://products.office.com/en-us/microsoft-teams.

[2] https://slack.com/.

[3] https://gitter.im/.

[4] https://spectrum.chat/.

[5] See *e.g.*, https://slofile.com/ and https://standuply.com/.

Table 3. Openness

Criteria	MS-Teams	Slack	Gitter	Spectrum
Service plans	Free + 4 paid	Free + 3 paid	Free	Free
Group types	Project	Project/topic	Project/topic	Project/topic
Group visibility	Orga./Private	Orga./Private	Public/Private	Public/Private

invitation-only groups, but links to topic-related groups can be found on blogs or open sources repositories making groups on Slack both project and topic-specific. Gitter offers public or private groups that may be linked to private GitHub repositories and therefore offers project- and topic-specific groups. An open group may be restrained to GitHub users only. Spectrum offers both open and private as well as project- and topic-specific groups.

Administration. Registered users can customise their **profile** in all tools except Gitter by adding a picture (one per group in Slack) and a bio or status message. Spectrum and Gitter are tightly connected to Github accounts, MS-Teams requires a Microsoft account and Slack an email address only. All tools offer basic administrative features at least to create, delete, invite members to and ban members from groups. Slack and MS-Teams provide more advanced features with the ability to give (partial) admin **permissions** to members, *e.g.,* to add/ban users, create/delete chat rooms or connect third party components.

Interaction Features. In Table 4 we compare interaction features of tools.

Table 4. Interaction features

Criteria	MS-Teams	Slack	Gitter	Spectrum
Interact. group	Team	Workspace	Community	Community
Interact. space	Channel	Channel	Room	Channel
Private space	Yes	Yes	Yes	Yes
Interact. format	Text,audio,video	Text,audio,video	Text	Text
Message format	Rich text	Markdown	Markdown	Markdown
File posting	All types	All types	All types	Images
Conversation	Threaded	Threaded	Unthreaded	Threaded
Notif./mentions	Yes	Yes	Yes	Yes
Search capability	Content + files	Content + files	Content + users	Content

In MS-Teams, **interaction groups** are organised as *"teams"*, in Slack as *"workspaces"*, and as *"communities"* in Gitter and Spectrum. In MS-Teams, Slack and Spectrum, **interaction spaces** are called *"channels"*, while in Gitter they are called *"rooms"*.

In MS-Teams, Slack and Spectrum, public chat rooms are accessible to all users inside a group, but users can create **private interaction spaces** (private chat rooms and direct messages). In Gitter, users can join each room of a community independently. Both MS-Teams and Slack offer the possibility to invite guests into rooms. In Slack, a room can be shared with another Slack group to create a communication *bridge* between two organisations (paid plan).

Tools offer various **interaction formats** and **message formats**. MS-Teams offers a rich text editor with an optional subject and compulsory content. Messages may be formatted as *"announcements"* with dedicated icons and formatting options. In Spectrum, conversations always contain a subject and an optional content whereas in Slack and Gitter messages are simple text notes with no title. Slack, Gitter and Spectrum use a *Markdown* syntax to format messages. MS-Teams is the only tool that supports (video) calls in its free plan, while Slack requires a paid plan. Additionally, regarding **file posting**, any kind of files are supported in MS-Teams, Slack and Gitter but only images in Spectrum.

All tools but Gitter use *"threaded"* **conversations**, *i.e.* each message can have multiple replies that are indented under their parent message. However, replies cannot have their own replies, limiting the indentation to one single level. At the opposite, Gitter conversations are linear.

All tools support **notifications** and **mentions** to let other members know about: (a) answers to a conversation they were part of or (b) when referrals are made (*e.g.*, a user A calls out user B).

All four tools offer a keyword-based **search capability** to retrieve messages, files (MS-Teams and Slack) or other users (all but Spectrum). MS-Teams and Slack allow to search through mentions. Slack has the most powerful search allowing structured queries (*e.g.*, based on dates).

Interoperability. In Table 5 we compare interoperability features of tools.

Table 5. Interoperability

Criteria	MS-Teams	Slack	Gitter	Spectrum
External apps	Yes-unlimited	Yes-limited	Yes	No
Client platforms	Win/Mac Android/iOS	Win/Mac/Linux Android/iOS	Win/Mac/Linux Android/iOS	Mac

Regarding **external apps**, MS-Teams has been designed to be part of the Office365 ecosystem and may interface with Office tools (paid plan). As Slack, it offers connectors to many software development tools such as Trello, Bitbucket or GitHub, but unlike Slack, all of these connectors are free without any limitations. Gitter is highly coupled to GitLab and offers connectors to Trello, Bitbucket and GitHub, but supports fewer connectors than Slack and MS-Teams. Spectrum can connect to an existing Slack group and import its members and chat rooms, but has no connectors to any additional third-party applications. In addition to web-based user interfaces offered by all tools, **supported platforms** of clients for Slack and Gitter include Windows, Mac and Linux as well as Android and iOS mobile apps. MS-Teams offers clients for all aforementioned platforms except Linux. Spectrum only offers a client for Mac.

API. Apart from Spectrum, all tools offer APIs to retrieve messages or activity-related data from existing rooms through a REST API. They also offer more powerful hooks to integrate custom apps into groups or chat rooms (such as bots). MS-teams and Slack offer software development kits for Javascript/nodejs and C#/.NET (Microsoft only). However, Slack restricts more advanced monitoring and analysis API endpoints to their paid plans. No tool provides "out-of-the-box" statistics or analyses of messages in depth, for example, to summarise main findings about a project (*e.g.,* to "brief" users who join a channel).

4   Discussion

Summary of Findings. Following our comparison framework, MS-Teams appears to be the most complete and flexible tool even with its free plan. Slack closely follows MS-Teams, but requires a paid plan for audio/video features and limits the number of third-party plugins. Gitter specifically focuses on the software development community and integrating development tools, whereas the ecosystems of Slack and MS-Teams are more diverse. Another notable distinction is that Gitter is the only tool that still uses linear rather than threaded discussions in individual chat rooms. To that regard, MS-Teams and Slack are the most powerful tools since they support rich text formatting and any file types in messages. Lastly, all tools but Spectrum offer built-in connectors to additional apps (*e.g.,* agile software development tools or source code repositories), the ability to programmatically interact with chat rooms, to create custom apps and offer client software for a wide range of operating systems.

Applicability of Framework. Regarding the developed framework, we believe all criteria are potentially useful for both researchers studying developer communities and practitioners. This framework provides a foundation for a systematic comparison of team communication channels and helps understand the differences between those channels. The following criteria may be of particular interest to **researchers** who study developer communication:

- **Popularity:** This criterion offers a big picture of the impact of a team communication channel within a community and gives credibility to data gathered from that channel. It also helps understand how a communication tool evolves over time and how functionality impacts the number of users.
- **Interaction features:** Message threads and user mentions inside a group may give insights about the team dynamics in that group, *e.g.,* how often direct call-outs are made amongst members, the nature of these mentions or if there are any blaming issues in a particular group.
- **API:** Since researchers are often interested in mining data in an automated way, knowing about resources of a team communication tool API will help them understand how feasible it is to collect data from a channel.

For **practitioners**, the potentially most helpful criteria are:

- **Openness:** Practitioners care about the cost when choosing a team-based communication tool and how organisation members can easily be added.
- **Administration and interaction features:** It is important to manage the resources of a communication tool, understand what type of content can be shared and how such content can be retrieved. For instance, depending on the complexity of a project, practitioners will need features to ban or apply restrictions to users' access or define shared spaces between projects.
- **Interoperability:** It may be critical to integrate a team-based communication channel with other existing tools to keep a centralised source of knowledge inside an organisation or project (*e.g.*, interfaces to project management software or collaborative document repositories).
- **API:** Like researchers, practitioners would need a communication tool that offers the ability to plug in custom data mining or monitoring features from external resources (*e.g.*, to add a chat bot to trigger a software development pipeline or record tasks into a project board).

Threats to Validity. Our work is subject to various validity threats:

- **Construct validity:** When selecting the tools under review, we applied a series of selection criteria that may have influenced to what extent our framework fits the needs for such a comparison. However we do not claim that our framework includes an exhaustive list of criteria. Rather, we expect it to be modified and extended in the future.
- **Internal validity:** The influence of our personal experiences with IM-based tools may have played a role in defining the comparison criteria. However, we carefully analysed (meta) empirical studies and experience reports in order to consolidate previously identified principles into the proposed framework.
- **External validity:** The case study is limited to four team-based communication channels and the extent to which those tools are representative is unknown. However, according to latest available statistics, at least MS-Teams and Slack are widely used in the software development community.

5   Conclusions

We introduced a comparison framework for team-based communication channels that we applied in a case study involving four instant messaging tools. We identified a series of evaluation criteria from the literature covering aspects like the popularity of the tool, its features, the types of interactions and its interoperability. We do not claim that this framework is exhaustive but believe it offers a structured evaluation scheme for researchers and practitioners to assess the suitability of a particular messaging tool or identify missing features.

To expand the framework and to identify additional criteria, we could follow a design science approach to integrate practical problems relevant to developers and knowledge questions investigated by researchers to support developers.

References

1. Albrecht, C.C.: A comparison of distributed groupware implementation environments. In: Hawaii International Conference on System Sciences (HICSS), pp. 1–9. IEEE (2003)
2. Alkadhi, R., Laţa, T., Guzman, E., Bruegge, B.: Rationale in development chat messages: an exploratory study. In: International Conference on Mining Software Repositories (MSR), pp. 436–446. IEEE (2017)
3. Forsgren, E., Byström, K.: Multiple social media in the workplace: contradictions and congruencies. Inf. Syst. J. **28**(3), 442–464 (2018)
4. Kotlarsky, J., van Fenema, P.C., Willcocks, L.P.: Developing a knowledge-based perspective on coordination: the case of global software projects. Inf. Manag. **45**(2), 96–108 (2008)
5. Lardinois, F.: Microsoft says teams now has 13M daily active users. https://techcrunch.com/2019/07/11/microsoft-says-its-slack-competitor-teams-now-has-13-million-daily-active-users/. Accessed 23 July 2019
6. Lin, B., Zagalsky, A., Storey, M., Serebrenik, A.: Why developers are slacking off: understanding how software teams use slack. In: Conference on Computer Supported Cooperative Work and Social Computing (CSCW), pp. 333–336. ACM (2016)
7. Matney, L.: Slack now has more than 10 million daily active users. https://techcrunch.com/2019/01/29/slack-now-has-more-than-10-million-daily-active-users/. Accessed 23 July 2019
8. Rabiser, R., Guinea, S., Vierhauser, M., Baresi, L., Grünbacher, P.: A comparison framework for runtime monitoring approaches. J. Syst. Softw. **125**, 309–321 (2017)
9. Rieger, C., Majchrzak, T.A.: Towards the definitive evaluation framework for cross-platform app development approaches. J. Syst. Softw. **153**, 175–199 (2019)
10. Runeson, P., Host, M., Rainer, A., Regnell, B.: Case Study Research in Software Engineering: Guidelines and Examples. Wiley, Hoboken (2012)
11. Squire, M.: Should we move to stack overflow? Measuring the utility of social media for developer support. In: International Conference on Software Engineering (ICSE), pp. 219–228. IEEE (2015)
12. Storey, M., Zagalsky, A., Filho, F.F., Singer, L., German, D.M.: How social and communication channels shape and challenge a participatory culture in software development. IEEE Trans. Softw. Eng. **43**(2), 185–204 (2017)
13. Storey, M.A., Singer, L., Cleary, B., Figueira Filho, F., Zagalsky, A.: The (R)evolution of social media in software engineering. In: Future of Software Engineering at ICSE (FOSE), pp. 100–116. ACM (2014)
14. Storey, M.A., Treude, C., van Deursen, A., Cheng, L.T.: The impact of social media on software engineering practices and tools. In: Workshop on Future of Software Engineering Research (FoSER), pp. 359–364. ACM (2010)
15. Wright, L.: Microsoft teams wins enterprise connect best in show award and delivers new experiences for the intelligent workplace, March 2019. https://www.microsoft.com/en-us/microsoft-365/blog/2019/03/19/microsoft-teams-experiences-intelligent-workplace/. Accessed 29 July 2019
16. Zahedi, M., Shahin, M., Babar, M.A.: A systematic review of knowledge sharing challenges and practices in global software development. Int. J. Inf. Manag. **36**(6), 995–1019 (2016)
17. Zhang, S., Köbler, F., Tremaine, M., Milewski, A.: Instant messaging in global software teams. Int. J. e-Collab. **6**(3), 43–63 (2010)

DevOps in Practice – A Preliminary Analysis of Two Multinational Companies

Jessica Díaz[1]([⊠]) [ID], Jorge E. Perez[1] [ID], Agustín Yague[1] [ID],
Andrea Villegas[1,2], and Antonio de Antona[3]

[1] Universidad Politécnica de Madrid, 28031 Madrid, Spain
{yesica.diaz,jorgeenrique.perez,
agustin.yague}@upm.es, a.villegas@alumnos.upm.es
[2] Sistemas Avanzados de Tecnología, S. A. (SATEC), 28023 Madrid, Spain
[3] Everis Spain S.L., Madrid, Spain

Abstract. DevOps is a cultural movement that aims the collaboration of all the stakeholders involved in the development, deployment and operation of software to deliver a quality product or service in the shortest possible time. DevOps is relatively recent, and companies have developed their DevOps practices largely from scratch. Our research aims to conduct an analysis on practicing DevOps in +20 software-intensive companies to provide patterns of DevOps practices and identify their benefits and barriers. This paper presents the preliminary analysis of an exploratory case study based on the interviews to relevant stakeholders of two (multinational) companies. The results show the benefits (software delivery performance) and barriers that these companies are dealing with, as well as DevOps team topology they approached during their DevOps transformation. This study aims to help practitioners and researchers to better understand DevOps transformations and the contexts where the practices worked. This, hopefully, will contribute to strengthening the evidence regarding DevOps and supporting practitioners in making better informed decisions about the return of investment when adopting DevOps.

Keywords: DevOps · Empirical software engineering · Exploratory case study

1 Introduction

In the recent digital history, it is possible to verify that success is not always achieved by the product that is better built, more usable, or of better quality, but by the one that appears first and meets a certain need. This is why the software industry tries to be more agile, more tolerant to change, more adaptable to new needs, and above all, tries to shorten development time from request to implementation. Companies that can release software early and frequently have a higher capability to innovate and compete in the market. Innovative companies, such as Google, Amazon, Netflix, LinkedIn, Facebook, and Spotify, initiated an organizational transformation that aimed fast speed in releases and quick response time to customer demands. DevOps is an organizational transformation that had its origin at the 2008 Agile conference in Toronto, where Debois highlighted the need of resolving the conflict between developer teams and

© Springer Nature Switzerland AG 2019
X. Franch et al. (Eds.): PROFES 2019, LNCS 11915, pp. 323–330, 2019.
https://doi.org/10.1007/978-3-030-35333-9_23

operation teams when they have to collaborate to provide this quick response time to customer demands [1]. Later, at the O'Reilly Velocity Conference, two Flickr employees delivered a seminal talk known as "*10+ Deploys per Day: Dev and Ops Cooperation at Flickr*" which can be considered the starting point to extend agile beyond development [2]. Today an entire industry has been created around DevOps tools whose objective is to automate best practices, such as continuous delivery and continuous deployment, that promote fast and frequent delivery of new and changing features while ensuring quality and non-disruption of the production environment and customers [3].

But beyond all that, DevOps is a cultural movement that aims the collaboration among all the stakeholders involved in the development, deployment and operation of software to deliver a high-quality product or service in the shortest possible time. DevOps breaks down organizational silos and "*stresses empathy and cross-functional collaboration within and between teams—especially development and IT operations— in order to operate resilient systems and accelerate delivery of changes*" [4]. It is a simple concept, but its adoption by organizations is enormously complicated because of great differences in the way in which DevOps promotes to work and the traditional way in which most software companies have been working for decades. DevOps is founded on the Lean principles and shares its values, such as process optimization, search for continuous improvement, and the enhancement of customer satisfaction.

However, DevOps is relatively recent, and little is known about best practices and the real value and barriers associated with DevOps in industry. Companies have developed their DevOps practices largely from scratch—by training employees on the fly. Google, Amazon, Netflix, LinkedIn, Facebook, and Spotify are some examples of successful companies whose DevOps practices have been reported and disclosed in IT books, blogs and events. These provide a valuable information for companies, however, for most of them, it is quite difficult to match these leader companies and adopt the practices they disclose. In addition, failures are not described. Some annually reports about the state of DevOps, such as the report made by DORA (DevOps Research & Assessment association) [5] and the report made by Puppet and Splunk [6], analyze data of survey questionnaires over 30,000 technical professional worldwide, respectively. The first one identifies a set of *software delivery performance profiles* (elite, high, medium and low performance) and relates DevOps practices with these profiles. The second one identifies 5 stages of DevOps evolution (aka. the *DevOps evolutionary model*) and establishes the practices that define and/or contribute to success in that stage. These reports also provide a valuable information for companies as they provide a global picture; however, the wide range of participant companies and the great variability among participants make difficult, for a company, to find the right way for a DevOps transformation based on similarities (e.g. IT department size, business, scope, DevOps Teams size, DevOps strategy, etc.) with other companies. Erich et al. [7] and Lwakatare et al. [8] also performed exploratory studies on six companies and one company, respectively, providing a key baseline for future studies with a broader scope until achieving the saturation for qualitative studies.

Our research aims to conduct an analysis on practicing DevOps in +20 software-intensive companies to provide patterns of DevOps practices and identify their benefits and barriers. This paper presents the preliminary analysis of an exploratory case study based on the interviews to relevant stakeholders of two (multinational) companies. DevOps embodies a vast and diverse set of practices, from which some patterns can be generalized under certain conditions, depending on the environment [9]. The analysis of these two case studies may help researchers and professionals to understand the barriers and benefits (specifically, delivery software performance) when two companies of the software industry made a DevOps transformation, how these companies dealt with the transformation (specifically, DevOps team topology), and finally, it may help others to make better informed decisions based on this know-how. There are some decisions that can lead to the failure of an organization, and many others to success, so that the only way to be sure of being on the right way is to follow one that has been successfully proven on numerous occasions.

2 Exploratory Case Study

The research methodology has been previously described, discussed, and improved at the *Fostering More Industry-Academic Research in XP* (FIAREX) workshop, part of XP 2018 conference [10]. We have followed the guidelines for conducting case study research in software engineering proposed by Runeson and Höst [11]. We have established a chain of evidence by following a strict process that consists of the preparation of a questionnaire and interviews, performance and recording, transcription, coding, and analysis. To qualitatively analyze the data, we have used the thematic analysis approach [12, 13], which is one of the most used synthesis methods that consists of coding, grouping, interconnecting and obtaining patterns. The last two activities were also supported using the clustering technique, which divides samples in groups called clusters based on their similarity. The visualization of these clusters helped us to better interpret and relate the qualitative data.

2.1 Data Collection and Instruments

The interviews were conducted face-to-face by two researchers. The interview consists of 100 questions and takes about 2.5 h. The questions were collected from the existing literature conducting survey studies on DevOps state [5, 6, 14], exploratory studies [7, 8], as well as from meetings with experts in some international and national workshops (e.g. at the FIAREX workshop part of the XP conference [10] and a local industrial workshop organized by the authors[1]) and national events (e.g. DevOps Spain[2] and itSMF events[3]). The interview is structured to collect professional information from interviewees, organizations, DevOps adoption processes, DevOps teams' topology, culture related practices, team related practices, collaboration related practices, sharing related practices, automation related practices, measurement and monitoring related

---

[1] (Spanish) Workshop on DevOps located at Universidad Politécnica de Madrid, Spain, https://www.youtube.com/watch?time_continue=6&v=rDHv3dK_Am8, last accessed 2019/08/01.

[2] https://www.devops-spain.com/, last accessed 2019/08/01.

[3] https://www.itsmf.es/index.php?option=com_content&view=article&id=3133:2018-10-11-00-30-06&catid=79:noticias&Itemid=401, last accessed 2019/08/01.

practices, barriers, and results. This questionnaire includes a set of short, open, and semi-open questions in which the interviewee can choose one or more options, explain their selections, or add a new answer. Both options and questions have been refined as we gained more knowledge during the interviews, the workshops and the events. An example is question 17 about the DevOps teams' topology and its scope within the IT department. It was initially an open question, but after 4–5 interviews we realized that answers were too long and not clarified the topology, so we added some options based on the *DevOps Topologies collection of patterns* by Skelton and Pai [15] and the *organizational structures used in DevOps journey* by the State of DevOps Report [6]. After analyzing more interviews, we defined our own DevOps Teams patterns (see Sect. 2.2).

The interview also asks for the *deployment frequency*, i.e., the number of deploys to production of an application per unit of time; the *lead time for changes*, i.e., the time from a change in the code to code is successfully running in production; and the *time to recovery*, i.e., elapsed time to restore a service when an incident causes its unavailability. These metrics were defined by DORA as indicators for defining a set of *software delivery performance profiles* (elite, high, medium and low performance) [5]. We have adapted the scale that is used for these indicators to classify companies according to the profiles by DORA for the scale that is shown is Table 1. This work is required because, as mentioned before, this kind of reports analyzes massive data, and the variability of these data is huge (e.g. the lead time goes from less than one hour to six months, and the data we have managed for lead time none exceed one day). Additionally, we limited the lead time for changes affecting to one line of code as we think that asking for the lead time of a change in the code is ambiguous.

Table 1. Software delivery performance indicators.

Software delivery performance indicators	Elite	High	Medium	Low
Deployment frequency	On demand, multiple deploys per day	One deploy per day	One deploy per week	Between once per week and one per month
Lead time for changes	Less than one hour	Less than one hour	Between one hour and one day	Between one hour and one day
Mean Time to Recovery	Less than one hour	Less than one hour	Between one hour and one day	Between one day and one week

2.2   Subjects

This paper focuses on two companies (ID17 and ID18). In these interviews three people were interviewed: a consultant from Everis with +6 years of experience and +4 years in DevOps that worked for ID17 and ID18, the director of the DevOps department from organization ID17 with +12 years of experience and +6 years in DevOps, and a Scrum master from organization ID18 with +15 years of experience and +2 years in DevOps. Table 2 shows the description of these organizations. ID17 is a large company whose structure is very departmental: DevOps department (22 people), operation & cloud systems (12), operation and on-premise systems (15–20), security

(12), architecture (20), quality assurance (10), service/help desk (22), a number of development departments (4–50 people) composed by *squads* (4–9 people). Squads are similar to Scrum teams, i.e. are the basic unit of development at Spotify, who coined this concept[4]. It is necessary to highlight that these teams have also the appropriate skills to release to production. This company also adopted the concept of *chapter* to designate people having similar skills and working within the same general competency area in different squads. This company has a DevOps chapter, and Architecture chapter, and QA chapter. ID 18, despite its small size, also has departmental structure, with different departments for development, DevOps & Cloud, QA, and security.

Table 2. Organizations' subject description.

ID	Scope	Organization size	Business	Creation year	IT department size	DevOps team num & size
17	International	Large[a]	Telecommunications	Between 2000 and 2010	500	1 Team (22 members)
18	International	Large	Real state	Before 2000	30	1 Team (5 members)

[a]Spanish law 5/2015, on the promotion of business financing, states that a small company has a maximum of 49 workers and a turnover or total asset value of less than ten million euros; and medium-sized companies are those with less than 250 workers and a turnover of less than fifty million euros or an asset of less than 43 million euros. Meanwhile, large companies are those that exceed these parameters.

3 Key Findings

RQ1. *What problems do companies try to solve and what results try to achieve by implementing DevOps?* ID 17 disclosed that the organization size, the diversity of its departments (development, operations, security, service, QA, architecture, etc.) as well as the interaction between them, and the complexity of its processes, hampered reducing time to market, and made this company less competitive. ID18 disclosed that the organization devoted most of the time to maintaining legacy applications and when this organization decided substitute the core legacy application with a new one, the CEO decided to make a significant change in the methodology, interaction between teams and the delivery and releasing processes to reduce time to market.

RQ2. *What are the DevOps practices according to software practitioners?* This paper focuses on team related practices. Based on data collected from this study (+20 organizations), we have defined four patterns that describe the topology of DevOps teams and their scope within the IT department (see Fig. 1):

(1) *Interdepartmental DevOps teams' pattern* represents a close collaboration between Dev teams and Ops teams although these teams belong to different departments with different managers. Other authors called this pattern as *Dev and Ops Collaboration* [15] although we have identified two modalities: a

---

[4] https://blog.crisp.se/wp-content/uploads/2012/11/SpotifyScaling.pdf, last accessed 2019/08/01.

combination of DevOps and traditional teams/approaches (a bimodal approach for different product/services) and only DevOps teams but maintaining the departmental structure.

(2) *Native DevOps teams pattern* represents a close and efficient collaboration between Dev teams and Ops teams (also QA, security, etc.). It is an approach mainly adopted by start-up companies in which there is not separated roles for dev and ops. Other authors called this pattern as *Fully Shared Ops Responsibilities* [15].

(3) *DevOps as a Service* is typical for companies without enough staff or experience, or very departmental and large companies, which cannot initially afford a complete DevOps transformation. This pattern provides an especial DevOps chapter that facilitates and helps to spread awareness of DevOps practices. According to other topologies this pattern is considered an antipattern *DevOps Team Silo* that only has sense when the team is not permanent, lasting less than (say) 12 or 18 months [15]. If silos are broken, this pattern could be considered as *DevOps Advocacy Team* [15]. According to our study, the DevOps service team usually becomes a department with its own manager, however we did not observe the creation of a new silo. Additionally, in our study no organization outsourced this service (*DevOps as an External Service*).

(4) *Ops as a Service* represents those situations in which the traditional IT Operations department assumes the DevOps competences mainly by automating infrastructure provision (and possibly other more processes) on which applications are deployed and run. According to other topologies, this pattern could be *Ops as Infrastructure-as-a-Service (Platform)* [15].

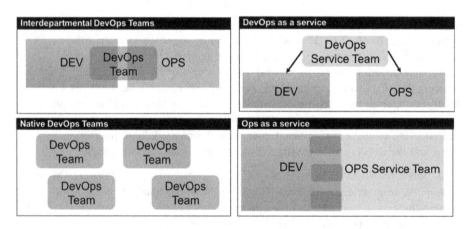

Fig. 1. DevOps team topology.

According to this classification, the organizations ID17 and ID18 implemented *DevOps as a Service* and *Ops as a service,* respectively. In the organization ID 17, the DevOps Service Team is a department composed by two squads. One of them automates processes and develops a DevOps platform for internal use, and the other one acts as a chapter so that, its members work closely with the development departments, evangelizing both DevOps practices and the use of its internal platform. In the organization ID 18, the traditional Ops (renamed as DevOps and Cloud department) provides services to other development departments. In this organization two models coexist: DevOps principles and practices for new developments and traditional approaches for core and legacy applications (bimodal approach).

RQ3. *What were the achieved results of implementing DevOps?* Table 3 shows the data for the software delivery performance. According to these data and the benchmark of Table 1, we can say that organization ID17 has achieved a medium performance (medium deployment frequency, medium lead time, and low mean time to recovery) and ID18 also achieved a medium performance (low deployment frequency, medium lead time, and medium mean time to recovery).

Table 3. Results of software delivery performance indicators.

ID	Deployment frequency	Lead time for changes	Mean time to recovery
17	One deploy per week	Between one hour and one day	Between one day and one week
18	One deploy per sprint (3 weeks)	Between one hour and one day	Between one hour and one day

RQ4. *What barriers are encountered when implementing DevOps?* ID17 disclosed about the misalignment among departments and the inflexibility of communication processes, whereas ID18 disclosed the complexity of standardizing and automating processes.

4 Conclusions and Threats to Validity

This paper presented the preliminary results of analyzing two organizations through an exploratory case study. The organizations were interviewed through a specific questionnaire to assess the state of DevOps. The data were systematically analyzed, and metrics were customized to have a better profiling of companies. The results mainly focused on analyzing the DevOps team topologies and the benefits when adopting DevOps in terms of software delivery performance. The defined questionnaire for interviews and the process defined to analyze these interviews provides a powerful tool to get results about the DevOps topics under research. The complete case study aims to tackle a significant number of software-intensive companies (+20) to give a detailed analysis of problems, barriers, benefits and practices patterns when organizations start a DevOps transformation, as well as of the relation between concepts (e.g. some practices and their resulting benefits). These patterns could provide a set of good practices when organizations decide to start DevOps transformation.

The main threat to validity is regarding with construct validity. Specifically, we used the *convenience sampling strategy*, which is a non-probability/non-random sampling technique used to create sample as per ease of access to organizations and the relevant stakeholders to the study. This could lead to organizations not fully reflecting the target audience.

Acknowledgment. This work is supported by the project CROWDSAVING (TIN2016-79726-C2-1-R).

References

1. Debois, P.: Agile infrastructure and operations: how infra-gile are you? In: Agile Conference in Toronto (2008). http://www.jedi.be/presentations/IEEE-Agile-Infrastructure.pdf. Accessed 01 Mar 2018
2. Allspaw, J., Hammond, P.: 10+ deploys per day: dev and ops cooperation at Flickr. In: O'Reilly Velocity Conference (2009)
3. Lwakatare, L.E., Kuvaja, P., Oivo, M.: Relationship of DevOps to agile, lean and continuous deployment. In: Abrahamsson, P., Jedlitschka, A., Nguyen Duc, A., Felderer, M., Amasaki, S., Mikkonen, T. (eds.) PROFES 2016. LNCS, vol. 10027, pp. 399–415. Springer, Cham (2016). https://doi.org/10.1007/978-3-319-49094-6_27
4. Dyck, A., Penners, R., Lichter, H.: Towards definitions for release engineering and DevOps. In Proceedings of the IEEE/ACM 3rd International Workshop on Release Engineering (2015)
5. DevOps Research and Assessment: Accelerate: State of DevOps 2018: Strategies for a New Economy. https://devops-research.com. Accessed 01 Aug 2019
6. State of DevOps Report 2018. https://puppet.com/resources/whitepaper/state-of-devops-report. Accessed 01 Aug 2019
7. Erich, F., Amrit, C., Daneva, M.: A qualitative study of DevOps usage in practice. J. Softw. Evol. Process **29**, e1885 (2017)
8. Lwakatare, L.E., Kuvaja, P., Oivo, M.: An exploratory study of DevOps - extending the dimensions of DevOps with practices. In: Proceedings of the Eleventh International Conference on Software Engineering Advances, pp. 91–99 (2016)
9. Ebert, C., Gallardo, G., Hernantes, J., Serrano, N.: DevOps. IEEE Softw. **33**(3), 94–100 (2016)
10. Díaz, J., Almaraz, R., Pérez, J., Garbajosa, J.: DevOps in practice: an exploratory case study. In: Proceedings of the 19th International Conference on Agile Software Development: Companion (XP 2018), p. 3, Article no. 1. ACM, New York (2018). https://doi.org/10.1145/3234152.3234199
11. Runeson, P., Höst, M.: Guidelines for conducting and reporting case study research in software engineering. Emp. Softw. Eng. **14**, 131–164 (2009)
12. Thomas, J., Harden, A.: Methods for the thematic synthesis of qualitative research in systematic reviews. BMC Med. Res. Methodol. **8**, 45 (2008)
13. Cruzes, D.S., Dyba, T.: Recommended steps for thematic synthesis in software engineering. In: 2011 International Symposium on Empirical Software Engineering and Measurement, Banff, AB, pp. 275–284 (2011). https://doi.org/10.1109/esem.2011.36
14. Kim, G., Willis, J., Debois, P., Humble, J.: The DevOPS Handbook: How to Create World-Class Agility, Reliability, and Security in Technology Organizations. It Revolution Press, Portland (2016)
15. Skelton, M., Pai, M.: DevOps Topologies collection of patterns. https://web.devopstopologies.com/. Accessed 01 Aug 2019

Implementing Ethics in AI: Initial Results of an Industrial Multiple Case Study

Ville Vakkuri$^{(\boxtimes)}$ ⓘ, Kai-Kristian Kemell ⓘ,
and Pekka Abrahamsson ⓘ

University of Jyväskylä, PO Box 35, FI-40014 Jyväskylä, Finland
{ville.vakkuri, kai-kristian.o.kemell,
pekka.abrahamsson}@jyu.fi

Abstract. Artificial intelligence (AI) is becoming increasingly widespread in system development endeavors. As AI systems affect various stakeholders due to their unique nature, the growing influence of these systems calls for ethical considerations. Academic discussion and practical examples of autonomous system failures have highlighted the need for implementing ethics in software development. However, research on methods and tools for implementing ethics into AI system design and development in practice is still lacking. This paper begins to address this focal problem by providing elements needed for producing a baseline for ethics in AI based software development. We do so by means of an industrial multiple case study on AI systems development in the healthcare sector. Using a research model based on extant, conceptual AI ethics literature, we explore the current state of practice out on the field in the absence of formal methods and tools for ethically aligned design.

Keywords: Artificial intelligence · AI ethics · AI development · Responsibility · Accountability · Transparency · Behavioral software engineering

1 Introduction

The role of ethics in software systems development has dramatically changed following the increasing influence of Autonomous Systems (AS) and Artificial Intelligence (AI) systems. AI/AS systems necessitate ethical consideration due to their unique nature. Whereas one can opt out of using conventional software systems, the very idea of being an active user in the context of AI systems is blurred.

The harm potential of these systems, as well as actual real-life incidents of AI system failures and misuse, have resulted in a growing demand for AI ethics as a part of software engineering (SE) endeavors. AI ethics studies have argued that AI/AS engineering should not be simply a technological or an engineering endeavor [1]. Specifically, it is argued that developers should be aware of ethics in this context due to their key role in the creation of the systems. Aside from discussion among the academia, public voices have also expressed concern towards unethical AI systems following various real-life incidents (e.g. unfair systems [2]).

© Springer Nature Switzerland AG 2019
X. Franch et al. (Eds.): PROFES 2019, LNCS 11915, pp. 331–338, 2019.
https://doi.org/10.1007/978-3-030-35333-9_24

Despite the increasing activity on various fronts in relation to AI ethics, a notable gap between the concerns voiced over AI ethics and SE practice in AI remains. It is known that developers are not well-informed on ethics [3]. New ethical methods and practices that take into account the behavioral and social aspects of SE are needed. Thus, AI Ethics also needs to be approached from the field of behavioral software engineering (e.g. [4]). Developers are known to prefer simple and practical methods, if they utilize any at all [5], which makes the lack of methods in AI ethics an issue. Without methods, it can be difficult for organizations to detect ethical issues during design and development, which can become costly later on.

Extant studies on AI Ethics have largely been theoretical. To provide empirical data into this on-going discussion on AI ethics, we have conducted a multiple case study on AI system development in the healthcare sector in order to further our understanding on the current state of practice. The exact research question tackled here is:

RQ: How are AI ethics taken into consideration in software engineering projects when they are not formally considered?

2   Related Work

Much of the research on AI ethics has been conceptual and theoretical in nature. These studies have e.g. focused on defining AI ethics in a practical manner through various constructs in the form of values. For the time being, this discussion on defining AI ethics has come to center around four values: transparency [6–8], accountability [6, 8], responsibility [6, 8], and fairness (e.g. [2]), as we discuss in the next section.

Following various real-life incidents out on the field, AI ethics has also begun to incite public discussion. This has caused various government, public, and private organizations to react, primarily by producing their own demands and guidelines for involving ethics into AI development. Countries such as Germany [9] have emphasized the role of ethics in AI/AS, and the EU drafted its own AI ethics guidelines [10]. Industry organizations such as Google and IBM[1] have also devised their own guidelines.

Thus far, various attempts to bring this on-going academic discussion out on the field have been primarily made in the form of guidelines and principles, with the most notable ones being the IEEE guidelines for Ethically Aligned Design (EAD) [8]. However, past experiences have shown us that guidelines and principles in the field of ICT ethics do not seem to be effective. For example, McNarama [3] argued based on empirical data that the ACM ethical guidelines had ultimately had very little impact on developers, who had not changed their ways of working at all. A recent version of the EAD guidelines acknowledged that this is likely to also be the case in AI ethics.

---

[1] Google: AI Principles: https://www.blog.google/technology/ai/ai-principles/. IBM: Everyday ethics for AI: https://www.ibm.com/watson/assets/duo/pdf/everydayethics.pdf.

3   Research Model

The field of AI ethics can be divided into three categories: (1) Ethics by Design (integration of ethical reasoning capabilities as a part of system behavior e.g. ethical robots); (2) Ethics in Design (the regulatory and engineering methods); and (3) Ethics for Design: (codes of conduct, standards etc.) [11]. In this paper, we focus on the ethically aligned development process (Fig. 1).

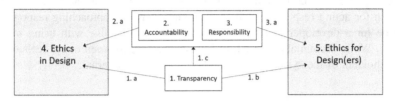

Fig. 1. Research framework

In addressing ethics as a part of the development of AI and AI-based systems, various principles have been discussed in academic literature. For the time being, the discussion has centered on four constructs: Transparency [6–8], Accountability [6, 8], Responsibility [6], and Fairness (e.g. [2]). A recent EU report [10] also discussed Trustworthiness as a value all systems should aim for, according to its authors. Out of these four main principles, we consider accountability, responsibility, and transparency (ART principles), as formulated by Dignum [6], a starting point for understanding the involvement of ethics in ICT projects.

Transparency is defined in the ART principles of Dignum [6] as transparency of the AI systems, algorithms and data used, their provenance and their dynamics. I.e. the transparency refers to understanding how AI systems work by being able to inspect them. Transparency can be argued currently to be the most important of these principles or values in AI ethics. Turilli and Floridi [7] argue that transparency is the key pro-ethical circumstance that makes it possible to implement AI ethics at all. It has also been included into the EAD guidelines as one of the key ethical principles [8].

In the research framework of this study, transparency is considered on two levels: (a) transparency of data and algorithms (line 1.a), as well as, (b) systems development (line 1.b). The former refers to understanding the inner workings of the system in a given situation, while the latter refers to understanding what decisions were made by whom during development. As a pro-ethical circumstance, transparency makes it possible to assess accountability and responsibility (line 1.c).

Accountability refers to determining who is accountable or liable for the decisions made by the AI. Dignum [6] in their recent works defines accountability to be the explanation and justification of one's decisions and actions to the relevant stakeholders. In the context of this research framework, accountability is used not only in the context of systems, but also in a more general sense.

Transparency is required for accountability (line 1.c), as we must understand why the system acts in a certain fashion, as well as who made what decisions during development in order to establish accountability. Whereas accountability can be considered to be externally motivated, closely related but separate construct responsibility is internally motivated. The concept of accountability holds a key role in aiming to prevent misuse of AI and in supporting wellbeing through AI [8].

Dignum [6] defines responsibility in their ART principles as a chain of responsibility that links the actions of the systems to all the decisions made by the stakeholders. We consider it to be the least accurately defined part of the ART model, and thus have taken a more comprehensive approach to it in our research framework. According to the EAD guidelines, responsibility can be considered to be an attitude or a moral obligation for acting responsibly [8]. A simplified way of approaching responsibility would be for a developer to ask oneself e.g. "would I be fine with using my own system?". While accountability relates to the connection between one's decisions and the stakeholders of the system, responsibility is primarily internal.

4   Study Design

This study was carried out as a multiple case study featuring three different cases where AI systems were developed for the needs of the healthcare sector. Each case was a specific AI project in a case company. All three projects were development projects focused on creating a prototype of an AI-based healthcare software solution. The combination of AI solutions used were different in each case. NLP (natural language processing) technologies played major role in cases B and C.

Table 1. Case information

Case	Case description	Respondents [Reference]
A	Statistical tool for detecting social marginalization	Data Analyst [R1], Consultant [R2], Project Coordinator [R3]
B	Speech recognition and NLP based tool for diagnostics	Developer [R4], Developer [R5], Project Manager [R6]
C	NLP based tool for indoor navigation	Developer [R7], Developer [R8]

The interviews were conducted as semi-structured, qualitative interviews, using a strategy prepared according to the guidelines of Galletta [12]. The interviews were conducted face-to-face and the audio was recorded. The records were then transcribed for the purpose of data analysis. In the transcripts, the cases and respondents were given individual references shown in Table 1. The interviews were conducted in Finland, using the Finnish language. The interview questions in their entirety can be found in an external resource[2]. We focused on the developer and project point of view by primarily interviewing developers and project managers.

---

[2] http://users.jyu.fi/~vimavakk/AIDevQuestionnaire.

The data from the transcripts were analyzed in two phases. First, we followed a grounded theory (Strauss and Corbin [13] and later Heath [14]) inspired approach. In this phase, the transcripts were coded quote by quote and each quote was given a code describing its contents. The same process was repeated for all eight interviews. In the second phase, we utilized the commitment net model of Abrahamsson [15], as analysis tool to further analyze and categorize the coded quotes from the first phase.

In using the commitment net model, we followed a similar method as in Vakkuri et al. [16] and focused on the concerns and actions of the developers in relation to software development. Each concern and any actions related to it were listed for each respondent and compared across respondents and cases.

These findings were then compared to the constructs in our research framework in order to evaluate what aspects of AI ethics were being implemented in the project. In this evaluation, actions were emphasized due to the research question of this study. I.e. we wanted to understand how they had implemented ethics in practice. In presenting our results, we present our key findings as primary empirical conclusions, PECs.

5   Empirical Results

As the interviews progressed, the developers expressed some concerns towards various ethical issues. However, these concerns were detached from their current work. Furthermore, it was evident that in none of the cases had the hypothetical effects of the system on the stakeholders been discussed. To give a practical example, a system potentially affecting memory illness diagnoses (Case B) clearly has various effects on its potential users when the test can be taken without supervision. Yet, the developers of this system felt that their users would not be curious about the workings of the system. They considered it sufficient if the responsibility was outsourced to the user and it was underlined that the system does not make the formal diagnosis.

The developers also exhibited a narrow view of responsibility in relation to harm potential. Only physical harm potential was considered relevant, and the developers felt that none of their systems had such potential.

"Nobody wants to listen to ethics-related technical stuff. [...] It's not relevant to the users" (R5)

"What could it affect... the distribution of funds in a region, or it could result in a school taking useless action... it does have its own risks, but no one is going to die because of it" (R1)

PEC1. Responsibility of developers and development is under-discussed.

In terms of transparency of algorithms and data, case A stood out with the team's mathematical knowledge. They utilized algorithms they were familiar with and which they understood on an in-depth level. In cases B and C, the companies utilized third-party components largely as black boxes. They did, however, have an in-depth understanding of any components created by the team. Even though transparency of algorithms and data was not present, case B developers acknowledged its potential importance. However, it was not pursued in projects B and C due to not being a formal requirement, as opposed to A where it was pursued due to being one.

"We have talked about the risks of decision-making support systems, but it doesn't really affect what we do" (R5)

PEC2. Developers recognize transparency as a goal, but it is not formally pursued.

Accountability was actively considered in relation to cybersecurity and data management, as well as error handling related to program code. The developers were aware that they were in possession of sensitive data, and that they were accountable for taking measures to keep it secure, as well as to abide to laws related to personal data handling. To this end, cybersecurity was considered as a part of standard company protocol, following established company practices.

"It's really important how you handle any kind of data… that you preserve it correctly, among researchers, and don't hand it out to any government actors. […] I personally can't see any way to harm anyone with the data we have though." (R2)

Developers' concerns on error handling, underlined by one of the respondents directly remarking "I aim to make error free software" (R1), also stood out. The developers were concerned about engineering quality software in terms of it being error free and considered it their professional responsibility to do so. The respondents could discuss various practices they utilized to handle and prevent errors in the project.

PEC3. Developers feel accountable for error handling on programming level and have the means to deal with it.

Through ethics were not taken into consideration on a project level, the individual developers exhibited some concern towards socioethical issues arising from their systems. While they were able to think of ways their system could negatively affect its users or other stakeholders in its current state, they lacked ways to address these concerns, as well as ways to conduct ethical analysis. Some extant SE practices such as documentation and audits were discussed as ways to produce transparency, but ultimately they offered little help in systematically implementing ethics.

PEC4. While the developers speculate potential socioethical impacts of the resulting system, they do not have means to address them.

6   Discussion

On a general level, our findings further underline a gap between research and practice in the area. Whereas research on AI ethics alongside various guidelines devised by researchers and practitioners alike has discussed various ethical goals for AI systems, these goals have not been widely adopted out on the field.

Extant literature has highlighted the importance of transparency of algorithms and data [6, 8]. Without understanding how the system works, it is e.g. impossible to establish why it malfunctioned in a certain situation in order to understand the causes of an accident that resulted in material damages. Our findings point towards transparency being largely ignored as a goal. Third-party components are utilized as black boxes, and developers do not see this as a notable problem. In this sense, we consider PEC2 to contradict existing literature. The lack of emphasis placed on transparency is interesting from the point of view of feature traceability as well. For decades, understanding the inner workings of a system was considered important in any SE endeavor [17]. In AI SE, this long-standing goal of feature traceability seems to be waning.

The situation is similar for tackling potential misuse of the systems, error handling during system operations, and handling unexpected system behavior. These goals are included into the IEEE EAD guidelines [8]. Yet, none of the case companies took any measures to address these potential issues. Error handling was simply considered on the level of program code. To this end, though we discovered various examples of ethics not being implemented, we also discovered that some existing and established SE practices can be used to support the implementation of AI ethics. Documentation, version control, and project management practices such as meeting transcripts produce transparency of systems development by tracking actions and decision-making. Similarly, software quality practices help in error handling in the context of AI ethics (PEC3), although only on the level of program code.

The developers exhibited some ethical concerns towards the systems they were developing (e.g. PEC2). Little is currently known about the state of practice out on the field, although a recent version of the EAD guidelines speculated about a gap in the area, which our findings support in relation to most aspects of AI ethics. Despite AI ethics largely not being implemented, our findings point towards it partially being a result of a lack of formal methods and tools to implement it (PEC4).

Thus, following this study, as well as a past case study [16], we suggest that future research seek to tackle the lack of methods and tooling in the area. Though developers may be concerned about ethical issues, they lack the means to address these concerns. Methods can also raise awareness of ethics, motivating new concerns.

As for the limitations of the study, the outlined research model is heavily based on ART principles of Dignum [6] and IEEE's EAD [8]. This may exclude some parts of the current AI ethics discussion (e.g. Fairness). However, the EAD can be seen as a distilled version of the ongoing AI ethics discussion that includes the most important parts of it. Finally, the sample size is quite small for making far reaching conclusions but provides much needed empirical data on a very current topic.

7 Conclusions and Future Work

In this paper, we have sought to better understand the current state of practice in AI ethics. Specifically, we studied the way AI ethics are implemented, if at all, when they are not formally considered in a software engineering project. To this end, we conducted a multiple case study featuring three case companies developing AI solutions for the healthcare sector.

We discovered that some existing good practices exist for some aspects of AI ethics. For example, current practices out on the field are already capable of producing transparency of systems development. Moreover, the developers are aware of the potential importance of ethics and exhibit some concerns towards ethical issues. Yet, they lack the tools to address these concerns. As tackling ethics is not a formal requirement in AI projects, these concerns go unaddressed for business reasons. In this light, we consider the creation of methods and tools for implementing AI ethics important. These will both help developers to implement AI ethics in practice as well as raise their awareness of ethical issues by e.g. helping them understand harm potential of AI systems.

References

1. Charisi, V., et al.: Towards moral autonomous systems. arXiv preprint arXiv:1703.04741 (2017)
2. Flores, A.W., Bechtel, K., Lowenkamp, C.T.: False positives, false negatives, and false analyses: a rejoinder to "machine bias: there's software used across the country to predict future criminals, and it's biased against blacks". Fed. Probation **80**(2), 38 (2016)
3. McNamara, A., Smith, J., Murphy-Hill, E.: Does ACM'S code of ethics change ethical decision making in software development? In: Proceedings of the 2018 26th ACM ESEC/FSE, ESEC/FSE 2018, pp. 729–733. ACM, New York (2018). https://doi.org/10.1145/3236024.3264833
4. Lenberg, P., Feldt, R., Wallgren, L.G.: Behavioral software engineering: a definition and systematic literature review. J. Syst. Softw. **107**, 15–37 (2015). https://doi.org/10.1016/j.jss.2015.04.084
5. Fitzgerald, B., Hartnett, G., Conboy, K.: Customising agile methods to software practices at Intel Shannon. EJIS **15**(2), 200–213 (2006). https://doi.org/10.1057/palgrave.ejis.3000605
6. Dignum, V.: Responsible autonomy. arXiv preprint arXiv:1706.02513 (2017)
7. Turilli, M., Floridi, L.: The ethics of information transparency. Ethics Inf. Tecnol. **11**(2), 105–112 (2009). https://doi.org/10.1007/s10676-009-9187-9
8. Ethically aligned design: a vision for prioritizing human wellbeing with autonomous and intelligent systems, first edition (2019). https://standards.ieee.org/content/ieee-standards/en/industryconnections/ec/autonomous-systems.html
9. Ethics Commission's complete report on automated and connected driving (2017). https://www.bmvi.de/SharedDocs/EN/publications/report-ethics-commission.html
10. Ethics Guidelines for Trustworthy AI (2019). https://ec.europa.eu/digital-singlemaket/en/news/ethics-guidelines-trustworthy-ai
11. Dignum, V.: Ethics in artificial intelligence: introduction to the special issue. Ethics Inf. Technol. **20**(1), 1–3 (2018). https://doi.org/10.1007/s10676-018-9450-z
12. Galletta, A.: Mastering the Semi-Structured Interview and Beyond: From Research Design to Analysis and Publication, vol. 18. NYU Press, New York (2013)
13. Strauss, A., Corbin, J.: Basics of Qualitative Research: Techniques and Procedures for Developing Grounded Theory, 2nd edn. Sage Publications Inc., Thousand Oaks (1998)
14. Heath, H., Cowley, S.: Developing a grounded theory approach: a comparison of Glaser and Strauss. Int. J. Nurs. Stud. **41**(2), 141–150 (2004)
15. Abrahamsson, P.: Commitment nets in software process improvement. Ann. Softw. Eng. **14**(1), 407–438 (2002). https://doi.org/10.1023/A:1020526329708
16. Vakkuri, V., Kemell, K., Kultanen, J., Siponen, M.T., Abrahamsson, P.: Ethically Aligned Design of Autonomous Systems: industry viewpoint and an empirical study. arXiv preprint arXiv:1906.07946 (2019)
17. Gotel, O., et al.: Traceability fundamentals. In: Cleland-Huang, J., Gotel, O., Zisman, A. (eds.) Software and Systems Traceability, pp. 3–22. Springer, London (2012). https://doi.org/10.1007/978-1-4471-2239-5_1

Agile

How Agile Is Hybrid Agile? An Analysis of the HELENA Data

John Noll[1](✉) and Sarah Beecham[2]

[1] University of Hertfordshire, Hatfield, England
j.noll@herts.ac.uk
[2] Lero, the Irish Software Research Centre, University of Limerick, Limerick, Ireland
sarah.beecham@lero.ie

Abstract. Context: Many researchers advocate "tailoring" agile methods to suit a project's or company's specific environment and needs. This includes combining agile methods with more traditional "plan driven" practices.

Objective: This study aims to assess to what extent projects actually combine agile and traditional practices.

Method: Data from the HELENA survey of nearly 700 projects were examined to assess how many projects combine agile methods and traditional *methods*, and also to what extent they used different software development *practices*.

Results: The data show that, overall, two-thirds of the projects in the survey combine agile and traditional methods to some extent. However, projects that combine agile and traditional *methods* are significantly less likely to use agile *practices* than projects that solely use agile methods.

Conclusions: We hypothesize that the mindset of an organization, rather than technical necessity, determines whether a project will adopt a hybrid vs. purely agile approach.

Keywords: Agile development methods · Empirical Software engineering · Hybrid agile development

1 Introduction

Proponents of agile software development methods assert that to be "agile" a project must follow the methodology. For example, Kent Beck claimed that, for Extreme Programming to work, a project must adopt all twelve XP practices, because they support and rely on each other [3].

But researchers and practitioners advocate tailoring agile methods to suit a project's or company's specific environment and needs [4], and empirical evidence has confirmed that projects do tailor methods in practice [7,11,12,16,20,22]. This may include combining agile methods with more traditional "plan driven" approaches, as well as combining different agile methods.

But how frequently are agile and traditional methods combined into so-called "hybrid" approaches? And, given that agile methods employ known, proven practices, but in an "agile" way [3,6,15], is there any difference in practice adoption

© Springer Nature Switzerland AG 2019
X. Franch et al. (Eds.): PROFES 2019, LNCS 11915, pp. 341–349, 2019.
https://doi.org/10.1007/978-3-030-35333-9_25

between hybrid approaches and purely agile projects? This study aims to assess to what extent projects actually combine agile and traditional methods and practices.

To find out, we analyzed data from the HELENA survey [14] of nearly 700 projects, to assess how many projects using agile methods also used traditional methods, and also to what extent projects that might be classified as "purely agile[1]" or "hybrid" use different software development practices.

The analysis shows that nearly two-thirds of projects reported in the survey combine agile and traditional methods to some degree, but 30% of projects *never* use traditional methods (Table 1, column 1). Further, projects that often use agile methods, but never use traditional methods, are significantly more likely to use agile software development *practices* than projects that combine agile and traditional methods. This suggests that hybrid projects *replace* agile practices with traditional practices, rather than *augment* agile methods with traditional practices. We hypothesize that this difference is due as much to an organization's "mindset" as to technical requirements.

The remainder of this paper is organized as follows: in Sect. 2 we introduce the background to the problem, and define our research questions. Section 3 describes the method used. In Sect. 4 we present the results; Sect. 5 discusses their implications and presents our conclusions.

2 Background

2.1 Agile and Traditional Development Approaches

Agile adoption in industry is growing year by year. According to the State of Agile Report published in December 2018 [23], the top reasons for this are to accelerate software delivery, enhance ability to manage changing priorities, increase productivity, improve business/IT alignment, enhance software quality and enhance delivery predictability. The agile philosophy, as described in the Agile Manifesto, centers around *a set of iterative and incremental software engineering practices* [10]. However, the actual practices contained within this *set* have evolved over time, and vary from project to project. They are even said to be revolutionary [7]. In a recent survey, researchers identified 36 such agile practices [14]. As coined by Bertrand Meyer [18], "every project I've seen embraces a subset of the chosen method's ideas, rejecting those that don't fit its culture or needs ...". Also, according to Meyer [18], agile methods are not a negation of what came before, and can be considered as another brick in the software development wall. Conboy concurs [6], stating that although agile methods are not entirely new or that different to development methods used before, the movement can be branded as an alternative to traditional development methods [6].

---

[1] "Purely agile" means a project often or always uses at least one agile method, but never uses any traditional methods; see Sect. 4 for details.

Kuhrmann et al. [12] argue that "hybrid approaches emerge naturally because of the challenges accompanying a migration to agile," suggesting that hybrid approaches are driven by need rather than mindset. Marinho et al. [17] also suggest that global development projects use a combination of agile and traditional methods because of the need to maintain a level of forward planning and structure while benefitting from a flexible and collaborative approach offered by agile practices. These views support Tell and colleagues' recommendation that research should focus on the practices used, rather than debate about what is the 'right' method [22].

There are hints in the empirical research to suggest that this reliance on traditional methods might be due to project size since large projects may require more coordination and heavier methodologies than offered by agile methods [1,9]. Or possibly there is a perceived need for upfront precise and comprehensive planning, and defining the architecture prior to testing and implementation, that push project managers to hold onto traditional plan driven methods [19]. It appears that in practice, adapting the development approach to the context demands a balance of methods and practices [2,4,24].

2.2 Research Questions

In light of these arguments, we seek to answer the following two research questions:

1. To what extent is a hybrid approach combining agile and traditional *methods* used in practice? In this context, we define a *method* as an approach to managing a software project that uses a set of software development *practices* in a certain way; examples of methods are Scrum, Waterfall, and Feature Driven Development (see Sect. 3 for a complete list of methods considered).
2. What *practices* are used by projects that employ such a hybrid approach? A *practice* is a particular technique for developing software, such as pair programming or model-driven development, that may be part of many different methods (see Sect. 4 for the list of practices considered).

3   Method

In attempt to answer our research questions, we used the HELENA ('Hybrid dEveLopmENt Approaches in software systems development) data set that is the result of a multi-year effort to investigate how real software projects combine agile and traditional software development methods [14]. More details can be found on the official website[2].

---

[2] HELENA Survey: https://helenastudy.wordpress.com/.

HELENA used an online survey [5, 21] to collect data from practitioners about the development methods they use in their projects, and what practices they use [13].

The survey comprises 38 questions divided into five parts: demographics (10 questions), process use (13 questions), process use and standards (5 questions), experiences (2 questions) and closing (8 questions) [14]. The survey was distributed to personal contacts of the participating researchers, through posters at conferences, and to mailing lists and social media; in total, the survey yielded 1,467 responses, of which 690 were complete [14]; the results presented in this paper are based on the 690 complete responses.

3.1   Data Analysis

The analysis in this paper focuses on two aspects of the survey: what *methods* are used by projects, and what *practices* are used. Following Kuhrmann and colleagues [13], methods were categorized as *traditional*, *agile*, or *generic*. Scrum, Safe, Lean, LESS, Nexus, XP, Kanban, DevOps, ScrumBan, Crystal, DSDM and Feature-driven development (FDD) were categorized as agile, while Waterfall, Spiral Model, V-Model, RUP, PRINCE2 and SSADM were categorized as traditional. Iterative development[3], Domain-Drive Design (DDD), Model Driven Architecture (MDA), Team Software Process (TSP), and Personal Software Process (PSP), were classified as generic, since the approach does not fit into either the agile or traditional category. Respondents were asked to rate the frequency with their project applied each of these methods on a five point scale ranging from *never* to *rarely, sometimes, often,* and *always* used. The HELENA survey also asked respondents to rate the frequency with which a project uses 36 development practices, on the same five point scale. When analyzing practice use, we followed Tell and colleagues [22] approach and classified a practice as "used" when respondents stated their projects used the practice *rarely, sometimes, often,* or *always.*

4   Results

Table 1 shows the frequency that projects use and combine agile and traditional methods. The majority (458 of 690, or 66%) of projects combine agile and traditional development methods; these are shown in **boldface** in Table 1. Conversely, 171 projects (25%) *often* or *always* use at least one agile method, but *never* use any traditional methods; these are shown in *italics* in Table 1. Finally, only 43 projects (6%) *never* use agile methods.

---

[3] While Iterative development is a key feature of agile methods some traditional approaches (RUP and the Spiral Model, for example) also incorporate iterations [15]; consequently, we followed Kuhrmann et al. [13] and classified iterative development in the generic category.

Table 1. Frequency of traditional and agile method combination.

Agile	Traditional					TOTAL
	Never	Rarely	Sometimes	Often	Always	
Never	(21) 3%	(1) 0%	(3) 0%	(10) 1%	(8) 1%	(43) 6%
Rarely	(2) 0%	**(1) 0%**	**(3) 0%**	**(13) 2%**	**(5) 1%**	(24) 3%
Sometimes	(16) 2%	**(9) 1%**	**(24) 3%**	**(24) 3%**	**(17) 2%**	(90) 13%
Often	*(55) 8%* †	**(53) 8%**	**(56) 8%**	**(82) 12%**	**(20) 3%**	(266) 39%
Always	*(116) 17%* †	**(44) 6%**	**(42) 6%**	**(33) 5%**	**(32) 5%**	(267) 39%
TOTAL	(210) 30%	(108) 16%	(128) 19%	(162) 23%	(82) 12%	(690) 100%

The TOTAL *column* indicates the total frequency with which projects perform agile methods at the level shown; the TOTAL *row* indicates the total frequency with which projects perform traditional methods at the level shown.

Entries in **bold** are classified "hybrid" while entries marked with a † are classified "pure agile."

We compared the frequency that purely agile projects use certain practices, to hybrid projects that combine agile and traditional methods. We define a *purely agile* project as one that respondents stated *often* or *always* uses at least one agile method, but *never* uses any traditional method. We define a *hybrid* project as one that respondents stated uses at least one agile method, and also uses at least one traditional method, where "uses" means at least *rarely*. In Table 1, purely agile projects are marked with a †, and hybrid projects are shown in **boldface** type.

Comparing purely agile projects to hybrid projects, Table 2 shows the difference in the fraction (as %) of projects in each category that use a given practice, and whether that difference (*diff* column) is significant according to the Chi-square comparison of proportions. A practice was considered to be "used" if respondents reported it was used more often than *never* (in other words, at least *rarely*).

This table shows that there are several practices associated with agile methods [12] – refactoring, continuous integration, continuous deployment, collective code ownership, definition of done and daily standups – that are performed by a majority of Agile projects, but significantly fewer Hybrid projects. Also, pair programming and test driven development (TDD) are performed significantly more often by purely agile projects, although not by a majority.

Conversely, formal estimates and formal specification – that are classified as traditional practices [12] – are performed by a minority of Hybrid projects, but significantly less by Agile projects.

Only four practices – release planning, iteration planning, coding standards, and end-to-end testing – are performed by a majority of projects at the same frequency whether purely agile or hybrid.

Table 2. Comparison of practices use by 171 Agile and 458 Hybrid projects.

practice (n = 36)	Agile (n = 171)	Hybrid (n = 458)	diff	p value	practice (n = 36)	Agile (n = 171)	Hybrid (n = 458)	diff	p value
Retrospectives*	68%	48%	20	***	Onsite customer*	20%	19%	1	0.8
Refactoring*	63%	43%	20	***	Iteration planning*	58%	57%	1	0.8
Cont integration*	75%	56%	19	***	Scrum-of-scrums	19%	19%	0	1
Cont deployment*	56%	38%	18	***	Coding stds	70%	71%	−1	0.9
Auto unit test	67%	50%	17	***	Auto theorem prv	2%	4%	−2	0.3
Pair programming*	30%	15%	15	***	Security testing	25%	29%	−4	0.4
Expert/team estimates	56%	41%	15	***	Burn down charts	37%	41%	−4	0.5
Backlog mgt	75%	60%	15	***	End-to-end testing	50%	55%	−5	0.3
Limit WIP	44%	30%	14	**	Auto code gen	16%	21%	−5	0.3
Collective code own*	51%	37%	14	**	Model checking	4%	10%	−6	*
Code review	73%	59%	14	**	Destructive test	6%	12%	−6	*
Velocity-based plan	36%	23%	13	**	Design reviews	36%	43%	−7	0.1
TDD*	33%	20%	13	***	Prototyping	33%	41%	−8	0.1
Def of done*	62%	49%	13	**	Formal estimates+	2%	13%	−11	***
Daily standup*	69%	56%	13	**	Use case modeling	14%	30%	−16	***
Iter/sprint reviews	69%	58%	11	*	Arch spec	32%	49%	−17	***
User stories	63%	53%	10	*	Formal spec+	6%	24%	−18	***
Release planning	69%	65%	4	0.4	Detail design/spec	16%	34%	−18	***

Values marked '%' the fraction of projects in the column that use the practice *rarely, sometimes, often,* or *always*. The practices are sorted by the difference in fractions, where $diff = Agile\% - Hybrid\%$. The statistical significance of the difference is indicated in the p value column, where '*' is p value $\leq$.05, '**' is p value $\leq$.01, and '***' is p value $\leq$.001; p values $>$.05 are shown as their actual values.

Practices marked with '*' in column 1 are classified as "agile"; marked with '+' are classified as traditional [12].

5   Discussion and Conclusions

Our results show that a majority of projects in the HELENA survey combine agile and traditional methods. This is consistent with other findings that show companies tailor methods to suit their context [7,11,12,16,20,22].

However, our results also show that a substantial number of projects are able to use only agile methods, without employing any traditional methods; this is consistent with the views of agile method advocates such as Kent Beck [3].

Further, Table 2 shows that purely agile projects – those that use agile methods often or always, but *never* use traditional methods – use agile *practices* significantly more often than hybrid projects. In addition, purely agile projects use traditional practices significantly less often than hybrid projects. This suggests that hybrid projects *replace* agile practices with traditional practices, rather than *augment* agile methods with traditional practices.

Tell and colleagues argue that agile methods have changed the mindset, but not the practices, that projects adopt, stating that their results "reveal a small core of practices used by practitioners regardless of the (hybrid) development method selected [22]." While our analysis also shows there is a set of practices – release planning, iteration planning, coding standards, and end-to-end testing – that are likely to be used by a majority of projects in both categories, our analysis also suggests that being "agile" is more than just adopting an agile mindset and method; rather, those projects that state that they solely use agile *methods* also report that they actually use agile *practices* as well.

Returning to our research questions:

RQ1: To what extent is a hybrid approach combining agile and traditional methods *used in practice?* The answer to this question is, the majority (66%) of projects in the HELENA survey combine agile and traditional methods (see Sect. 4).

RQ2: What practices *are used by projects that employ such a hybrid approach?* The answer to this question is somewhat more nuanced. All practices queried in the HELENA survey are used by at least some hybrid projects; however, some practices are used more often than others. As shown in Table 2, agile practices are used significantly less often by hybrid projects than by purely agile projects, and certain traditional practices are used significantly more often by hybrid projects than agile projects.

The HELENA survey did not provide extensive opportunities for respondents to explain why they adopt methods and practices, so we cannot say definitively why the adoption of practices is different between hybrid and purely agile projects. However, Michal Doleżel suggested a possible reason, which he called "institutional logic" [8]: organizations with an agile "logic" will view agile methods, and practices, more favorably than organizations with a traditional "logic." As such, we propose the following hypotheses based on this notion:

H1: Organizations with an agile mindset are more likely to be purely agile, and therefore adopt agile practices, regardless of technical drivers.

H2: Organizations with a traditional software development mindset are more likely to adopt a hybrid approach, and therefore adopt traditional practices, regardless of technical drivers.

Acknowledgments. This work was supported, in part, by Science Foundation Ireland grants 10/CE/I1855 and 13/RC/2094 to Lero - the Irish Software Research Centre (www.lero.ie).

References

1. Aitken, A., Ilango, V.: A comparative analysis of traditional software engineering and agile software development. In: 2013 46th Hawaii International Conference on System Sciences, pp. 4751–4760, January 2013

2. Akbar, R., Safdar, S.: A short review of global software development (gsd) and latest software development trends. In: 2015 International Conference on Computer, Communications, and Control Technology (I4CT), pp. 314–317. IEEE (2015)
3. Beck, K., Gamma, E.: Extreme Programming Explained: Embrace Change. Addison Wesley, Boston (2000)
4. Boehm, B., Turner, R.: Using risk to balance agile and plan-driven methods. Computer **36**(6), 57–66 (2003)
5. Ciolkowski, M., Laitenberger, O., Vegas, S., Biffl, S.: Practical experiences in the design and conduct of surveys in empirical software engineering. In: Conradi, R., Wang, A.I. (eds.) Empirical Methods and Studies in Software Engineering. LNCS, vol. 2765, pp. 104–128. Springer, Heidelberg (2003). https://doi.org/10.1007/978-3-540-45143-3_7
6. Conboy, K.: Agility from first principles: reconstructing the concept of agility in information systems development. Inf. Syst. Res. **20**(3), 329–354 (2009)
7. Diebold, P., Zehler, T.: The right degree of agility in rich processes. Managing Software Process Evolution, pp. 15–37. Springer, Cham (2016). https://doi.org/10.1007/978-3-319-31545-4_2
8. Doležel, M.: Possibilities of applying institutional theory in the study of hybrid software development concepts and practices. In: Kuhrmann, M., et al. (eds.) PROFES 2018. LNCS, vol. 11271, pp. 441–448. Springer, Cham (2018). https://doi.org/10.1007/978-3-030-03673-7_35
9. Dyba, T., Dingsoyr, T.: What do we know about agile software development? IEEE Softw. **26**(5), 6–9 (2009)
10. Fowler, M., Highsmith, J.: The agile manifesto. Softw. Dev. **9**(8), 28–35 (2001)
11. Klünder, J., et al.: HELENA Study: reasons for combining agile and traditional software development approaches in German companies. In: Felderer, M., Méndez Fernández, D., Turhan, B., Kalinowski, M., Sarro, F., Winkler, D. (eds.) PROFES 2017. LNCS, vol. 10611, pp. 428–434. Springer, Cham (2017). https://doi.org/10.1007/978-3-319-69926-4_32
12. Kuhrmann, M., et al.: Hybrid software development approaches in practice: a European perspective. IEEE Softw. **36**(4), 20–31 (2019)
13. Kuhrmann, M., et al.: Hybrid software and system development in practice: waterfall, scrum, and beyond. In: Proceedings of the 2017 International Conference on Software and System Process, pp. 30–39. ACM (2017)
14. Kuhrmann, M., Tell, P., Klünder, J., Hebig, R., Licorish, S., MacDonell, S.: Helena stage 2 results. Technical report, HELENA consortium (11 2018)
15. Larman, C., Basili, V.R.: Iterative and incremental development: a brief history. Computer **36**(6), 47–56 (2003)
16. Marinho, M., Luna, A., Beecham, S.: Global Software development: practices for cultural differences. In: Kuhrmann, M., et al. (eds.) PROFES 2018. LNCS, vol. 11271, pp. 299–317. Springer, Cham (2018). https://doi.org/10.1007/978-3-030-03673-7_22
17. Marinho, M., Noll, J., Richardson, I., Beecham, S.: Plan-driven approaches are alive and kicking in agile global software development. In: International Symposium on Empirical Software Engineering and Measurement (ESEM). ACM/IEEE (2019)
18. Meyer, B.: Making sense of agile methods. IEEE Softw. **35**(2), 91–94 (2018)
19. Nerur, S., Mahapatra, R., Mangalaraj, G.: Challenges of migrating to agile methodologies. Commun. ACM **48**(5), 72–78 (2005)

20. Paez, N., Fontdevila, D., Oliveros, A.: HELENA study: initial observations of software development practices in Argentina. In: Felderer, M., et al. (eds.) PROFES 2017. LNCS, vol. 10611, pp. 443–449. Springer, Cham (2017). https://doi.org/10.1007/978-3-319-69926-4_34

21. Shull, F., Singer, J., Sjøberg, D.I.: Guide to Advanced Empirical Software Engineering. Springer, Heidelberg (2007). https://doi.org/10.1007/978-1-84800-044-5

22. Tell, P., et al.: What are hybrid development methods made of?: an evidence-based characterization. In: Proceedings of the International Conference on Software and System Processes, pp. 105–114. IEEE Press (2019)

23. VersionOne Inc: 13th Annual State of Agile Development Survey (2018). https://www.stateofagile.com/#ufh-i-521251909-13th-annual-state-of-agile-report/473508. Accessed 5 August 2019. web page

24. Vinekar, V., Slinkman, C.W., Nerur, S.: Can agile and traditional systems development approaches coexist? an ambidextrous view. Inf. Syst. Manag. **23**(3), 31–42 (2006)

Challenges of Scaled Agile
for Safety-Critical Systems

Jan-Philipp Steghöfer$^{(\boxtimes)}$ (ID), Eric Knauss (ID), Jennifer Horkoff (ID),
and Rebekka Wohlrab (ID)

Software Engineering Division,
Department of Computer Science and Engineering,
Chalmers | University of Gothenburg, Gothenburg, Sweden
{jan-philipp.steghofer,eric.knauss}@gu.se, {jenho,wohlrab}@chalmers.se

Abstract. Automotive companies increasingly adopt scaled agile methods to allow them to deal with their organisational and product complexity. Suitable methods are needed to ensure safety when developing automotive systems. On a small scale, R-Scrum and SafeScrum® are two concrete suggestions for how to develop safety-critical systems using agile methods. However, for large-scale environments, existing frameworks like SAFe or LeSS do not support the development of safety-critical systems out of the box. We, therefore, aim to understand which challenges exist when developing safety-critical systems within large-scale agile industrial settings, in particular in the automotive domain. Based on an analysis of R-Scrum and SafeScrum®, we conducted a focus group with three experts from industry to collect challenges in their daily work. We found challenges in the areas of living traceability, continuous compliance, and organisational flexibility. Among others, organisations struggle with defining a suitable traceability strategy, performing incremental safety analysis, and with integrating safety practices into their scaled way of working. Our results indicate a need to provide practical approaches to integrate safety work into large-scale agile development and point towards possible solutions, e.g., modular safety cases.

Keywords: Scaled agile · Safety-critical systems · Software processes · R-Scrum · SafeScrum

1 Introduction

In the automotive domain, several dozen development teams work together in a highly coordinated fashion towards the delivery of a product. Systems and software engineering need to be combined in these cases to deliver a final product and the chosen process needs to scale across a large number of teams and different engineering disciplines. To manage this complexity, many companies have started adopting solutions such as the Scaled Agile Framework (SAFe)[1] or Large-Scale Scrum (LeSS)[2]. These agile frameworks also aim at reducing the time-to-market

---

[1] https://www.scaledagileframework.com/.
[2] https://less.works/less/framework/index.html.

© Springer Nature Switzerland AG 2019
X. Franch et al. (Eds.): PROFES 2019, LNCS 11915, pp. 350–366, 2019.
https://doi.org/10.1007/978-3-030-35333-9_26

and propose solutions for the coordination between teams, exchange of artefacts, and the prioritisation of work within an organisation.

However, these frameworks do not provide explicit support for the creation of safety-critical systems and the risk management, safety analysis, and certification activities associated with ensuring safety. On a small scale, R-Scrum [11] and SafeScrum® [13] help organisations to combine the documentation needs and the rigour required for safety-critical systems with agile development. However, the existing approaches do not describe how to scale them beyond individual teams. It is also not obvious how to tack on such activities, in particular since safety is a cross-cutting concern which needs to be addressed on all levels of the system. Preparing a release for certification in a big-bang approach, i.e., after development has mostly finished, has also proven to be infeasible. Therefore, safety should be considered continuously and integrated in the everyday work of the engineers to produce all necessary artefacts and the required audit trail in an ongoing fashion. Understanding how to do this in a practical setting is an important first step towards extending agile frameworks like SAFe and LeSS.

In parallel with the advent of methods to scale agile, variations of agile approaches that address safety-critical systems have been developed. Two well-cited examples are R-Scrum [11] and SafeScrum® [13], but other, less comprehensive approaches exist. Kasauli et al. [15] provide an overview of the literature in this area and identify a number of solution approaches to combine agile practices, mostly from Scrum and XP, with activities necessary for safety-critical systems such as risk management and hazard analysis. Other authors are addressing specific domains (e.g., medical devices [23]) to provide experiences from practice.

However, a number of challenges remain in adapting the processes of large organisations producing safety-critical systems to fulfil both the need for agility and the required rigour for certification. This is a particular problem in the automotive domain since the organisations involved in producing vehicles are very large, distributed over many disciplines and physical locations, and have established practices and tool-chains that are difficult to change [3, 7]. This leads us to the following research questions:

RQ1: Which common principles and practices can be derived from existing approaches for agile development of safety-critical systems?

RQ2: Which practical challenges exist when applying these principles and practices in a large-scale industrial setting?

To answer RQ1, we analysed existing literature with a focus on R-Scrum and SafeScrum®, as well as the overview presented in Kasauli et al. [15]. We derived the common principles *focus on traceability, safety as an ongoing set of activities, shared responsibility of the team*, as well as *involvement of assessors or auditors in ongoing development* (see Sect. 3). We also identified that existing approaches *do not address scaling beyond a single team, have no provisions for systems with mixed criticality*, and *lack concrete approaches for automation*.

Based on these findings, we conducted a focus group to answer RQ2. We presented the common principles to practitioners in the domain and elicited a number of challenges that occur in the automotive industry in practice when agile methods are used to create safety-critical systems. These challenges can be mapped to the areas of *living traceability*, *continuous compliance*, and *organisational flexibility* (see Sect. 4). There, we also compare the challenges to what is known from the literature.

Thus, the main contribution of this paper is an overview of the unsolved, practical challenges in combining agile methods with safety-critical systems with a particular focus on large-scale development efforts in the automotive domain. This will create the foundation for future work in which specific solution approaches to these challenges will be developed and evaluated.

2   Methodology

We base our findings in this paper on a focus group in which we discussed R-Scrum and SafeScrum® with practitioners. To prepare this focus group, one of the researchers extracted a list of commonalities and differences from the published accounts of R-Scrum and SafeScrum® (e.g., [11,13]). This list was discussed and refined with the other co-authors and contrasted with the findings of Kasauli et al. [15]. It was decided to focus on the commonalities of the approaches since they show the common underpinnings of how agile approaches can be applied to safety-critical products. These results provide the answer to **RQ1** and are presented in Sect. 3.

The focus group included three industrial experts, all with several years of experience in developing safety-critical systems in agile settings. These experts are leaders in the field and are all involved in strategic projects transforming their respective international organizations towards agile development. Two of the practitioners are experts on process, methods, and tools from two different automotive OEMs. One of them has a background in safety assurance and the other in scaled agile and AUTOSAR-compliant tool chains. The third practitioner is a senior software engineer in a medical device company with a background in agile in industrial, regulated environments. Although from a different domain, this expert participated in the workshop due to their experience and strong interest in scaled safety-critical agile methods. Including an expert from another domain also allowed pinpointing which challenges are specific to automotive.

As part of the focus group, we presented R-Scrum, SafeScrum®, and the findings from [15] to the practitioners and gauged their reaction to them. Based on this presentation, we invited the practitioners to share the challenges they see with applying agile methods to safety-critical systems within the large-scale development efforts in their organisations. The practitioners then brainstormed and described their own experience and the challenges they encounter. The researchers took extensive notes and collected the remarks on post-it notes. When saturation was achieved, these post-it notes were roughly sorted into topical areas by one of the researchers. These areas were then discussed in the group and topics were moved between topical areas when necessary to jointly create a clustering, thereby excluding or merging topics that were closely related.

After the conclusion of the focus group, the researchers ensured that agreement was reached on all topics when they reconstructed the discussion and recorded the findings based on their notes as well as the final clustering. They are presented in Sect. 4. These results provide the answer to **RQ2** and are presented in Sect. 4. All results were member checked with the participants of the original workshop, who corrected some details but confirmed the overall findings.

3 Existing Agile Approaches for Safety-Critical Systems

There are two agile approaches that cover the entire development lifecycle for safety-critical systems in the literature: *R-Scrum* [11] and *SafeScrum®* [13].

R-Scrum is described by Brian Fitzgerald and colleagues from their observations at the company QUMAS which builds "compliance management solutions". The paper thus does not describe a method that has been designed by researchers and evaluated in a company, but is rather a collection of the best practices at QUMAS that have proven worthwhile over the years. There are no studies to validate the usefulness of R-Scrum outside of QUMAS.

SafeScrum® in turn is a more designed process in which researchers and practitioners created a version of Scrum to fit the needs of safety-critical projects with a focus on IEC 61508:2010. The process (or rather "method framework" as the authors call it) has been used in a number of case studies. It is well-documented in a book [13] and a number of case studies (e.g., [20,25]) that demonstrate its application and efficacy.

In addition to this, Kasauli et al. [15] describe the results of a systematic mapping study and present an exhaustive list of relevant research about applying agile methods to safety-critical systems. The authors also provide challenges and solution candidates that have been reported in the literature which have been validated in a workshop with industrial practitioners. These solution candidates are, however, not embedded in a process or method framework.

A comparison of these sources shows that the proposed solutions for using agile methods to develop safety-critical systems share a number of commonalities:

Focus on traceability: Traceability is regarded as a foundation for the ability to certify software. R-Scrum makes *living traceability* a cornerstone of the method to provide "complete transparency into the development process at any point in time" [11]. SafeScrum® also emphasises traceability, in particular to fulfil the requirements of the IEC 61508:2010 standard, but also to enable change impact analysis and to perform safety testing [13]. Kasauli et al. [15] also report on two sources explicitly stating the need for traceability to ensure requirements are met and to determine which tests need to be run.

Safety as an ongoing set of activities: In order to ensure that safety is taken into consideration in all design decisions and in the daily programming and validation work, it is integrated into the process tightly and activities involving safety are performed continuously rather than at discrete points in time (e.g., immediately before a release). R-Scrum aims to achieve *continuous compliance* by including risk analysis in user story prioritisation and including a quality control board that is involved in continuously checking the developed code as well as accompanying documentation and design documents. In addition, quality assurance audits are included in each sprint and additional "hardening sprints" can be scheduled before releases. SafeScrum® likewise introduces safety into the sprint planning and the sprints themselves. An "alongside engineering team" is responsible for these activities that include updating the hazard log and safety cases, performing risk analysis and safety validation, and ensuring that safety requirements are captured. Kasauli et al. also mention suggestions from the literature to include safety considerations in Scrum ceremonies such as daily stand-up meetings, setting up a continuous integration tool-chain that includes safety builds, including relevant documents such as hazard logs in code reviews, and perform continuous risk management.

Shared responsibility of the team: Notably, all three sources suggest that the development team itself is involved in the activities to ensure safety, not a separate group of people. Even the "alongside engineering team" from SafeScrum® should not be seen as a team separate from the developers, but rather defines roles that can be fulfilled by the developers themselves. The book states, however, that this "may involve others external to the SafeScrum®team". In any case, developers are never absolved from taking responsibility for safety in the ongoing safety activities. They need to be able to work with the risk analysis, update hazard logs and other artefacts, and ensure in their design decisions that safety considerations are upheld. They are also responsible for writing appropriate test cases for safety validation. Kasauli et al. explicitly list literature that mentions collective code ownership, experts in the team, and the necessity that team members are familiar with safety standards in addition to the joint activities mentioned above.

Involvement of assessors or auditors in ongoing development: While not taken up by Kasauli et al., both R-Scrum and SafeScrum® suggest to include assessors or auditors for the final product in the development process. In the case of R-Scrum at QUMAS, these audits are performed by the customers and include the development process itself. This means that the organisation ensures that their process adheres to the standards set by the customers which usually follow the established safety standards in turn. In SafeScrum®, repeated safety audits are called for to ensure independent validation of the created product and process. In case of both methods, an established, traceable audit trail facilitates these occasions greatly.

However, there is *no notion of scaling beyond a single team*. Neither R-Scrum nor SafeScrum® provide guidance how work on safety should be divided between collaborating teams or between a product and team level. They locate the responsibility for safety of the product with the single development team (and the auxiliary "alongside engineering team"), but also assume that this team can control the entire development lifecycle of the product. This is insufficient in situations in which a complex organisational structure is used in which safety has to be ensured across large number of teams working on the same product. While a diagram describing the activities of the alongside engineering team in SafeScrum® does contain the item "subcontractor" management, this issue is not taken up in the rest of the book [13]. Likewise R-Scrum and the descriptions by Kasauli et al. lack details of how to involve suppliers apart from including external actors in planning and review meetings.

Furthermore, there is *no notion of mixed criticality*. Both R-Scrum and SafeScrum® assume that the product in its entirety is safety-critical and that all parts of the product thus need to be treated as safety-critical. In reality, however, products often consist of particular, safety-critical parts that are combined with other, non-critical components. Applying the same process to both kinds of assets can result in additional cost since the overhead necessary to ensure that the safety-critical parts can be certified is unnecessary for the non-safety-critical ones.

Finally, there are *no guidelines on the automation of safety certification*. In practical settings, tool support is required to ensure that activities concerned with safety can be embedded in the development process. This is particularly true for complex software product lines, e.g., in the automotive industry: all variants of a highly variable product need to be safe. Thus, safety cases need to be applicable to all variants and can become shared assets or even contain variability information themselves. Such scenarios require tool support and automation.

In summary, we extracted the following remaining issues that need to be addressed in mature domains such as automotive from our analysis of R-Scrum and SafeScrum® as well as the partial solutions reported by Kasauli et al.:

Scaling safe Scrum: combining the scalability of SAFe or LeSS with the safety features of R-Scrum or SafeScrum® for multi-team projects;

Mixed criticality: safety-critical parts of products need to be developed with more ceremony than parts that are not safety-critical;

Automation: automate generation of "proof of compliance" documentation within complex Continuous Integration/Deployment (CI/CD) tool-chains.

4   Open Challenges According to Industry

Upon presenting and discussing the principles and practices of currently safety-focused agile methods in our focus group, the focus group members brainstormed the challenges they encounter in their organisations. We categorised these challenges into three different areas that need to be addressed for scaled agile for safety-critical systems to become a reality in industry. The first two of these areas overlap with the solution areas of current frameworks listed in Sect. 3. However, we describe specific and detailed challenges for those and take an additional step by introducing challenges on the organisational level.

The foundation: living traceability. As recognised in both R-Scrum and SafeScrum®, traceability—and, in particular, the "living" version of it—is the foundation for an agile way of working with safety. The ability to connect the individual artefacts in the development process to each other enables the generation of the reports required by safety standards and facilitates the construction of safety cases. This goes beyond the traceability between requirements and test cases prescribed by safety standards, though: living traceability means that developers actively and continuously create, maintain, and delete trace links while they go about their development work. The resulting network of trace links not only supports safety, it also helps the developers with change impact analysis, program comprehension, and identifying technical debt.

The goal: continuous compliance. The goal for all organisations that have been a part of this study as well as for those R-Scrum and SafeScrum® have been applied to is to continuously produce the necessary safety arguments to ensure that compliance can be proven at any point in the development process. This is in contrast to the established way of working where the safety arguments are produced in a big bang approach towards the end of the development cycle or even immediately before an audit or certification. Continuous compliance enables an organisation to show at any point in time that their system complies to all necessary standards and has been developed following a process able to produce a safe system.

The next step: organisational flexibility. Once continuous compliance is achieved, the final stepping stone is to achieve flexibility in the organisation to work within a safety-critical domain in a truly agile way. This flexibility has to be achieved in three different areas: the *ecosystems* of components that are being used and exchanged with suppliers, *change management* within the organisation, and the *way of working* with critical artefacts.

4.1 Living Traceability

Continuously maintained traceability provides the foundation for scaled agile for safety-critical systems. As one of the workshop participants put it: "There are many motivators for traceability, but safety captures all of our needs", meaning that all needs for traceability from other areas of development are also present when discussing the needs for traceability to ensure safety. Our participants identified the following challenges in this area:

"Select the Right Direction for Traceability." Establishing a traceability information model (TIM) that supports safety analysis is a challenge. More fine-grained artefacts (lower-level artefacts) should contain links that link to more abstract artefacts (higher-level artefacts). One reason for this is variability: an abstract, high-level artefact can be refined into several variants on the lower level. Trace links from the high-level artefact to all variants are impractical, so instead, each variant should link to the higher-level artefact. That makes tool-support to collect the links crucial and needs to be captured in the TIM which defines the structure and semantics of the trace links. A common misunderstanding of bidirectional traceability is that trace links must exist in both

directions—instead, tools must exist that can reconstruct one direction from the other if necessary.

"Provide a Meaningful TIM for Safety-Critical Systems." Defining a traceability information model that supports the required semantics for safety-critical systems can pose a problem (see also next item). A suitable TIM needs to connect all safety-related artefacts, such as requirements, safety cases, and tests, in order to detect inconsistencies between them, to allow tracking their evolution, and to show that all safety concerns have been addressed in the design, the architecture, code, tests, and documentation. While the literature describes TIMs (e.g., Safe-TIM [21]), it is unclear how they can be adapted to an organisation and if they fit other needs for traceability (such as change impact analysis). In addition, the evolution of artefacts needs to be sufficiently captured in the information in order to track changes in both artefacts and the links and ensure consistency.

"What are Critical Decisions When Defining a TIM?" The chosen TIM (e.g., SafeTIM) has a huge impact on how the links can be used later on in the project. At this point, there is no method for how to define a TIM to address the traceability needs of an organisation. Traceability needs include the purpose of establishing trace links (e.g., for change impact analysis or for program comprehension), the process steps in which trace links should be established, maintained, and used, and an alignment with the overall process goals. Since such a method is missing, there is no clear understanding for which decisions are critical when defining a TIM and which impact these decisions will have. This makes it difficult to foresee how well a TIM will be able to support the organisation in the future. Taken together with the high cost and effort of evolving the TIM, this makes organisations reluctant to commit to a specific TIM.

"Trace Between Safety Analysis Artefacts on the Same Level of Abstraction." The item definition according to ISO 26262 [14], the standard for functional safety in the automotive domain, focuses on single vehicle functions with selected use cases and functional requirements. The hazard analysis, i.e., the activity in which the top-level safety requirements are defined, is based on this functional description. However, the high-level functional requirements and their related high-level safety requirements are defined as siblings in a hierarchy of requirements, without explicit trace links between them. In practice, however, safety-oriented concerns of different functions are related to each other and safety goals and requirements can impact the development of multiple functions. The lack of traceability makes it difficult to evolve these aspects together. In order to more easily create and maintain trace links between safety-related information, the functional description should ideally be expressed in a formalised way and tooling and concepts should allow relating cross-cutting aspects at any time during the process.

"Trace to Review Status, Changes, and Decisions." It is important to know whether reviews have been passed to understand the current state of the system.

Similar to tracing to test results, this enables engineers to see which aspects of the overall safety argument for the system are covered and what is left to do. Relevant changes that have an impact on these reviews and their status must also be traced in order to understand when a review needs to be repeated. At the same time, important decisions that impact safety need to be traceable, e.g., as design rationales, to help engineers understand why the arguments were constructed the way they are and how the underlying architecture impacts this argument.

"Creating, Storing, and Accessing Baselines." A baseline is a snapshot of all artefacts relevant at a specific point in time in the development process. Having many different, interrelated artefacts with different lifecycles, worked on by different teams at different locations, and stored in different systems [16] makes it difficult to define and store a consistent snapshot and make it available, e.g., to auditors.

4.2   Continuous Compliance

Keeping safety-related artefacts up-to-date in a scaled agile setting requires incremental safety analysis that spans all required product variants. There is also a push towards certifying the manufacturer instead of the product itself. The focus group revealed the following challenges:

"Support Delta Analysis." Changes in the system should not necessitate a complete reconstruction of the safety case. Instead, only the relevant parts should be reassessed and the current safety case should only be updated to the extent necessary. Consistent traceability is one cornerstone to solve this issue since it allows to include safety cases in change impact analysis. On the other hand, techniques used in safety analysis, such as formal hazard analysis techniques, should to be able to handle incremental changes.

"Update Safety Case on Demand." As stated above, the goal is to produce safety arguments about deltas and thus only focus on changes and their impacts. This would mean that safety analysis is near-continuous, triggered predominantly by changes. However, even if the technical challenges of delta-analysis are solved, it is currently unclear how often to create a new safety argument. Does the creation of a new or updated safety case depend on the "size" of the delta? What is the right balance between a desire for continual safety and the resources needed to produce frequent safety arguments? How often is often enough?

"Safety Case Must Cover Variants." Since automotive companies usually work with software product lines, a safety case must cover all relevant variants of a system. That means that regardless how the final system is assembled from different re-usable assets, the safety case must hold. In practice, however, many feature combinations are not relevant. Developers are not always aware of which combinations are relevant, though, and sampling strategies are often unsystematic [19]. For continuous compliance, safety cases must at least cover those variants that

are used in production and must show systematically that these variants are safe.

"Facilitate Pre-certification." In the medical device domain, where standard bodies govern and enforce the use of safety standards, such bodies have begun to allow *pre-certification*, i.e., a certification of the organisation and their development and quality assurance practices rather than the individual software in an attempt to reduce the time to market.[3] Such approaches help to avoid the "big bang", all-at-once certification process before releasing products, moving certification steps earlier in the development lifecycle. They also make it easier to push updates to existing software to the customer continuously.

4.3   (Organisational) Flexibility – Safe Ecosystem

One part of organisational flexibility for automotive OEMs is the ability to use components from suppliers with as little effort as possible in a safe ecosystem. Our participants identified the following challenges:

"Passing Safety Requirements to Suppliers." The communication between an OEM and a supplier about requirements for components at the moment is based on the exchange of documents that contain both functional and safety requirements. The supplier transfers these requirements into a requirements management tool and starts using them in the development and the construction of the safety case. However, it is not uncommon that the OEM changes functional and safety requirements. In that case, the supplier receives a new document and has to manually update the requirements database, update the trace links, and understand the impact on the current design [18]. Clearly defined software interfaces for the exchange of requirements would improve such updates. A common exchange standard, e.g., similar to the ReqIF format [8], could be a first step. A system that also supports versioning and diffing of such requirements would further reduce the effort required for suppliers.

"Treat Components as Safety Blackboxes." At the moment, safety-critical components that an OEM buys from a supplier need to be fully transparent in terms of design, safety requirements, and safety cases in order to be integrated into the safety argument for the overall system. Such components can thus not be treated as black boxes and the OEM has to invest considerable effort to integrate the relevant artefacts. In the future, it is desirable that individual components have a clearly defined *safety contract* [12], e.g., based on assumptions and guarantees, that can be used to seamlessly integrate a component into the safety argument of the overall system. While previous work on this topic exists, a standard for the exchange, verification, and use of such contracts has yet to emerge.

---

[3] See, e.g., https://www.fda.gov/MedicalDevices/DigitalHealth/DigitalHealthPreCert Program/ucm584020.htm.

4.4   (Organisational) Flexibility – Change Management

Part of an agile way of working is the ability to react to changes quickly and to adapt what is being built within a short period of time. This requires the ability to also adapt the safety case as needed. The focus group mentioned two challenges in this area:

"Support Local Decisions and Changes." Since safety is an overarching concern, decisions about safety and the construction of the safety case are often centralised, e.g., in an architecture runway team. This limits the flexibility of the individual teams to make decisions about implementation details and creates bottle necks in the certification process. Instead, local design decisions and changes should be supported when making the safety case, e.g., by modularising it and giving the individual teams the opportunity to update the safety case locally while maintaining global consistency.

"How to Decide Which Changes Need a Change Request?" A change request is a formal way to control the change process for product changes that have an impact on other development teams, downstream artefacts and, in particular, the safety case. Since change requests require certain steps to be completed and a high level of rigour to be applied, they are costly and should only be used if necessary. However, this is difficult to determine for any given product change. Organisations therefore err on the side of caution, producing more change requests than necessary. If living traceability is established, however, it should be possible for tools to provide decision support to semi-automatically identify the impact of a change on other teams and the safety case and thus reduce the number of change requests and, consequently, development cost and time.

4.5   (Organisational) Flexibility – Way of Working

As a final building block towards flexibility, the way of working needs to address a number of aspects on a fundamental level. Our participants identified the following challenges in this area:

"Mixing Safety-Critical Components and Requirements with Less or Non-Safety Critical Requirements." It is common in the automotive domain that components provide safety-critical functionality as well as functionality that is not safety-critical. At the moment, these functionalities are treated differently based on their Automotive Safety Integrity Level (ASIL) as defined in ISO 26262. Functionality assigned "QM" is not safety-critical, ASIL A or B is safety-critical and required some validation while ASIL C or D are highly safety-critical and require rigorous validation. Ideally components with different ASIL should be isolated via the architecture, but this can not always be guaranteed. Requirements management tools and practices currently do not allow a fine-grained assignment of ASIL to components, e.g., on the level of features or even code

blocks. This in turn means that all functionality of a component is treated with the same rigour, potentially using resources that could be applied elsewhere. As mentioned in Sect. 3, mixed criticality is not directly supported by R-Scrum or SafeScrum®.

"Reuse of Safety Requirements and Arguments." In many cases, safety requirements can be reused across components and functionality. Since safety requirements are often linked to functional requirements, a reuse of the functional requirement can lead to a reuse of the safety requirement. Ideally, parts of the safety argument and the information used to construct them should also be reused. This is particularly true for different variants of a system in a software product line that have slight differences in functionality but are structurally and behaviourally similar. However, an understanding of the changes needed to reuse a safety argument in different circumstances as well as tool support to detect inconsistencies in reused safety requirements and safety arguments is required.

"Coordination and Modularization." Development processes in which several hundred developers across different departments and potentially even organisations are involved require a high degree of coordination and modularisation. Since safety is a cross-cutting concern, achieving safety in a complex system composed of several subsystems is challenging. The modularisation and architectural isolation of functionality mentioned above is a first step, but distributing the work required to construct the safety argument is also necessary. A possible solution is a modularized safety argument. That means that a compositional form of discovering and including safety requirements [5] as well as constructing the safety argument [24] is required as well as automated ways of checking the argument for consistency (such as extensions of [2]). Such a modular approach will allow different teams to work on isolated parts of the safety argument and compose the individual parts into one encompassing subsystems and finally the entire system. Such an approach resembles the idea of "safety blackboxes" (cf. Sect. 4.3) and would also support the reuse of safety requirements and arguments.

5 Discussion

In this work, we have extracted common principles, practices and limitations from the literature on safety-critical agile methods and compared this to the experiences of three senior experts from industry, two of whom work in the automotive domain. What we find is an extended and refined list of principles and challenges as well as a number of solution candidates.

5.1 Challenges

In answering RQ1, we find that the literature emphasizes traceability, continuous safety, shared responsibility, and ongoing auditor involvement. Our findings echo the literature emphasis on traceability, but add specific details and challenges with implementing traceability in large-scale safety-focused agile (RQ2).

The idea of "living traceability" as an ongoing set of activities that are part of the daily work of the developers bears a strong resemblance to *ubiquitous traceability* [4], an idea championed in the traceability literature. While challenges to traceability in the automotive domain have been described elsewhere (see, e.g., [18]), this study adds additional challenges on a more technical level, e.g., about creating baselines. These challenges are nonetheless important, since their solution will decide about wide-spread adoption of traceability practices in industry.

The focus on scaling is missing in the literature on agile processes for safety-critical systems and current approaches that take scaling into account do not cater to the needs of safety-critical systems [22]. To address safety in an agile way of working, it should be possible to view traceability in both a bottom-up and top-down way, TIMs should be specific for safety concepts and should come with guidance for design, safety-related traceability should extend horizontally across requirements, should include review statuses, and should account for baselines.

Our findings also confirm and expand on the area of continuous safety. On this topic, we can also add specific technical challenges (RQ2). In particular, safety should be analyzed on the delta of small changes with guidance provided on the size of such deltas, safety cases should account for software variants, and the possibility of pre-certification should be considered. This last point bears similarity to the ongoing auditor involvement practice extracted from the literature. However, in general, the involvement of auditors was not emphasized, as this practice is less relevant in the automotive domain. Our participant from the medical device industry emphasised this aspect, however, as pre-certification and the ongoing involvement of auditors in the development process can be a key contributor to reduce the time to market in this domain.

While the literature emphasized shared safety responsibility, our workshop findings placed more emphasis on organizational flexibility, including ecosystems, change management, and ways of working. This is a direct result of the more complex organisational structure present in the scaled agile environments our practitioners work in. Again, these findings were broken down into more specific challenges (RQ2). In the area of ecosystems, identified challenges centred on passing safety information to suppliers, and receiving safety information from components in a clear and easily understandable format.

From the change management perspective, decision making should be local when possible, and decision making concerning invoking change requests should be better supported. The former point most closely echoes the shared responsibility emphasis from the literature, but puts it into the context of a hierarchical organisation in which responsibilities need to be distributed to development teams and some decisions, e.g., about architecture, are made on a product-level [9].

Practical challenges related to ways of working include dealing with a mix of safety- and non-safety-critical components, reuse of safety requirements and arguments, how to the level of abstraction of safety arguments, and how to manage coordination and modularization. These challenges are at a level of specificity not found in the current literature.

5.2 Possible Solutions

Before consulting with our industrial partners, we noted that the literature on safety-focused agile does not consider scale, mixed criticality, or automation. Our industrial challenges confirmed the first two observations. Although many of our identified challenges can lead to automation or benefit from it, this was not identified as a direct challenge in practice. This might be due to the fact that an *increased degree of automation* might be seen as one of the solutions for these challenges. A tool-chain that supports living traceability, helps identify if a safety case needs to be changed, and integrates variants into the handling of safety arguments would be highly beneficial.

Another possible solution, in particular to the challenges associated with continuous compliance, are techniques that allow the *incremental update of the safety case*. Industry needs the ability to update small parts of the safety case based on individual change requests to reduce the cost and time required for changes and to allow integrating components from suppliers into the system The need for such techniques has also been acknowledged in the defense industry "as a means of reducing the impact and hence cost of re-certification of changes to systems" [10]. While some work on incremental safety assessment exists, it is either focused on describing formal refinement relations [17] or make an argument for first modularising the safety case [26] before taking further steps in this direction. The variability inherent to complex product lines, e.g., in the automotive industry also needs to be taken into account.

The *modularisation of the safety case* also came up as a crucial building block to address the challenges in our data. While a number of solutions have been proposed for modular safety cases (see, e.g., [1,6,27]), they are not used in practice by our participants, presumably since they are tightly coupled to an underlying architecture [1] or prescribe a specific notation and toolset [6,27]. None of the approaches addresses the needs of a complex product line. Our industrial partners require more generic guidelines that they can adapt to their existing processes, architecture, and tool-chain instead.

6   Conclusion

In this paper, we summarise our findings of challenges of applying agile methods to the development of safety-critical systems in large-scale industrial settings. Based on a focus group, we identify a number of challenges in three areas and compare them with what is known from the literature, in particular to R-Scrum and SafeScrum®.

We have noted the lack of work combining large-scale agile practices with safety-critical agile practices, even though such a combination is currently required in many automotive organizations. Overall, our findings summarize the limitations with current safe agile practices, and list practical, grounded challenges of using such methods in a large-scale context, with a focus on the automotive domain. These challenges can be a foundation for future work and for combining the rigorous approach to safety analysis and verification of R-Scrum and SafeScrum® with the scaled agile practices of SAFe and LeSS. In particular, a better understanding of establishing traceability throughout the development lifecycle is needed. In addition, the ability to proof continuous compliance based on updates of safety cases is a necessity. Finally, safe ecosystems, an integrated change management approach, and a way of working based on reuse, coordination, and modularisation will ensure organisational flexibility.

We also identify candidates for solution approaches and point out related work in the area. The exploration of traceability information models for safety-critical applications is one such starting point, but currently suffers from limited guidance on how to apply this in a practical setting. The ability to incrementally update the safety cases based on small changes and the incorporation of variability in the safety analysis are further pre-requisites to achieve organisational flexibility. Furthermore, a modularisation of the safety case would help organisations in including externally sourced components and build incremental safety arguments based on small change requests.

We hope that our findings spur future work in expanding and refining agile methods: to support developing safety critical products at scale, and to consider further challenges as reported by our industrial partners.

Acknowledgement. We thank all participants in our focus group for their insights and their engagement. This work was supported by Software Center (www.software-center.se).

References

1. Althammer, E., Schoitsch, E., Sonneck, G., Eriksson, H., Vinter, J.: Modular certification support – the DECOS concept of generic safety cases. In: 6th IEEE International Conference on Industrial Informatics, pp. 258–263, July 2008. https://doi.org/10.1109/INDIN.2008.4618105
2. Antonino, P.O., Trapp, M.: Improving consistency checks between safety concepts and view based architecture design. In: PSAM12, Honolulu, Hawaii, USA 282 (2014)
3. Broy, M., Krüger, I.H., Pretschner, A., Salzmann, C.: Engineering automotive software. Proc. IEEE **95**(2), 356–373 (2007)
4. Cleland-Huang, J., Gotel, O.C., Huffman Hayes, J., Mäder, P., Zisman, A.: Software traceability: trends and future directions. In: Proceedings of the on Future of Software Engineering, pp. 55–69. ACM (2014)
5. Cleland-Huang, J., Vierhauser, M.: Discovering, analyzing, and managing safety stories in agile projects. In: IEEE 26th International Requirements Engineering Conference (RE), pp. 262–273, August 2018. https://doi.org/10.1109/RE.2018.00034
6. Denney, E., Pai, G.: Towards a formal basis for modular safety cases. In: Koornneef, F., van Gulijk, C. (eds.) SAFECOMP 2015. LNCS, vol. 9337, pp. 328–343. Springer, Cham (2015). https://doi.org/10.1007/978-3-319-24255-2_24

7. Ebert, C., Favaro, J.: Automotive software. IEEE Softw. **34**(3), 33–39 (2017). https://doi.org/10.1109/MS.2017.82
8. Ebert, C., Jastram, M.: ReqIF: seamless requirements interchange format between business partners. IEEE Softw. **29**(5), 82–87 (2012)
9. Eckstein, J.: Architecture in large scale agile development. In: Dingsøyr, T., Moe, N.B., Tonelli, R., Counsell, S., Gencel, C., Petersen, K. (eds.) XP 2014. LNBIP, vol. 199, pp. 21–29. Springer, Cham (2014). https://doi.org/10.1007/978-3-319-14358-3_3
10. Fenn, J.L., Hawkins, R., Williams, P., Kelly, T., Banner, M., Oakshott, Y.: The who, where, how, why and when of modular and incremental certification. In: IET Conference Proceedings, pp. 135–140(5), January 2007
11. Fitzgerald, B., Stol, K.J., O'Sullivan, R., O'Brien, D.: Scaling agile methods to regulated environments: an industry case study. In: International Conference on Software Engineering, ICSE 2013, pp. 863–872. IEEE Press, Piscataway (2013)
12. Gallina, B., Carlson, J., Hansson, H., et al.: Using safety contracts to guide the integration of reusable safety elements within ISO 26262. In: 21st Pacific Rim International Symposium on Dependable Computing (PRDC), pp. 129–138. IEEE (2015)
13. Hanssen, G.K., Stålhane, T., Myklebust, T.: SafeScrum®-Agile Development of Safety-Critical Software. Springer, Cham (2018). https://doi.org/10.1007/978-3-319-99334-8
14. International Organization for Standardization: Road vehicles - functional safety. ISO 26262:2011, November 2011
15. Kasauli, R., Knauss, E., Kanagwa, B., Nilsson, A., Calikli, G.: Safety-critical systems and agile development: a mapping study. In: 2018 44th Euromicro Conference on Software Engineering and Advanced Applications (SEAA), pp. 470–477, August 2018
16. Knauss, E., Pelliccione, P., Heldal, R., Ågren, M., Hellman, S., Maniette, D.: Continuous integration beyond the team: a tooling perspective on challenges in the automotive industry. In: 10th ACM/IEEE International Symposium on Empirical Software Engineering and Measurement, p. 43. ACM (2016)
17. Lisagor, O., Bozzano, M., Bretschneider, M., Kelly, T.: Incremental safety assessment: enabling the comparison of safety analysis results. In: 28th International System Safety Conference (ISSC) (2010)
18. Maro, S., Steghöfer, J.P., Staron, M.: Software traceability in the automotive domain: challenges and solutions. JSS **141**, 85–110 (2018)
19. Mukelabai, M., Nešic, D., Maro, S., Berger, T., Steghöfer, J.P.: Tackling combinatorial explosion: a study of industrial needs and practices for analyzing highly configurable systems. In: 33rd IEEE/ACM International Conference on Automated Software Engineering (ASE) (2018)
20. Myklebust, T., Stålhane, T., Lyngby, N.: An agile development process for petrochemical safety conformant software. In: 2016 Annual Reliability and Maintainability Symposium (RAMS), pp. 1–6. IEEE (2016)
21. Nair, S., de la Vara, J.L., Melzi, A., Tagliaferri, G., de-la-Beaujardiere, L., Belmonte, F.: Safety evidence traceability: problem analysis and model. In: Salinesi, C., van de Weerd, I. (eds.) REFSQ 2014. LNCS, vol. 8396, pp. 309–324. Springer, Cham (2014). https://doi.org/10.1007/978-3-319-05843-6_23
22. Putta, A., Paasivaara, M., Lassenius, C.: Benefits and challenges of adopting the scaled agile framework (SAFe): preliminary results from a multivocal literature review. In: Kuhrmann, M., et al. (eds.) PROFES 2018. LNCS, vol. 11271, pp. 334–351. Springer, Cham (2018). https://doi.org/10.1007/978-3-030-03673-7_24

23. Schooenderwoert, N.V., Shoemaker, B.: Agile Methods for Safety-Critical Systems: A Primer Using Medical Device Examples. CreateSpace Independent Publishing Platform, Scotts Valley (2018)
24. Sharvia, S., Papadopoulos, Y.: Integrated application of compositional and behavioural safety analysis. In: Zamojski, W., Kacprzyk, J., Mazurkiewicz, J., Sugier, J., Walkowiak, T. (eds.) Dependable Computer Systems. AINSC, vol. 97, pp. 179–192. Springer, Heidelberg (2011). https://doi.org/10.1007/978-3-642-21393-9_14
25. Stålhane, T., Myklebust, T., Hanssen, G.: The application of safe scrum to IEC 61508 certifiable software. In: 11th International Probabilistic Safety Assessment and Management Conference and the Annual European Safety and Reliability Conference, pp. 6052–6061 (2012)
26. Wilson, A., Preyssler, T.: Incremental certification and integrated modular avionics. IEEE Aerosp. Electron. Syst. Mag. **24**(11), 10–15 (2009)
27. Zimmer, B., Bürklen, S., Knoop, M., Höfflinger, J., Trapp, M.: Vertical safety interfaces – improving the efficiency of modular certification. In: Flammini, F., Bologna, S., Vittorini, V. (eds.) SAFECOMP 2011. LNCS, vol. 6894, pp. 29–42. Springer, Heidelberg (2011). https://doi.org/10.1007/978-3-642-24270-0_3

On the Benefits of Corporate Hackathons for Software Ecosystems – A Systematic Mapping Study

George Valença[1]([⊠]), Nycolas Lacerda[1], Maria Eduarda Rebelo[1],
Carina Alves[2], and Cleidson R. B. de Souza[3]

[1] Departamento de Computação, Universidade Federal Rural de Pernambuco,
Recife, Pernambuco, Brazil
{george.valenca, eduarda.rebelo}@ufrpe.br,
nycolas.lacerda@ufrpe.com
[2] Centro de Informática, Universidade Federal de Pernambuco, Recife,
Pernambuco, Brazil
cfa@cin.ufpe.br
[3] Faculdade de Computação, Universidade Federal do Pará, Belém, Pará, Brazil
cleidson.desouza@acm.org

Abstract. Software companies have increasingly organised hackathons since the early 2010s. These time-bounded, intensive, collaborative and solution-oriented events enable companies to generate several ideas, some of which can be used to evolve their products and services. Hackathons are means to gather feedback from outside to innovate. Companies also follow such open innovation trend by raising software ecosystems via a platformisation process. They create platforms so that third parties can develop new software solutions and in doing so extend the current product portfolio. In this scenario, a hackathon can be seen as a strategy to support ecosystem evolution. Therefore, we decided to conduct a systematic mapping study to investigate the benefits that hackathons can provide to software ecosystems. This paper presents our analysis of twenty-seven papers on corporate hackathons in the software industry. As main findings, we (i) describe a set of fourteen social, technical and business benefits; as well as (ii) discuss how companies can leverage ecosystem health by conducting hackathons. We address the scarcity of research around the outcomes of corporate hackathons. Besides, we conclude that hackathons are alternative modes of production and innovation, which can catalyse a software ecosystem.

Keywords: Corporate hackathons · Open innovation · Software ecosystems · Systematic mapping study

1 Introduction

The phenomenon of platformisation has altered the dynamics of the IT industry in the last decade. The software ecosystem paradigm created a new business environment in which third parties can develop their products or services by relying on a platform [19]. The ecosystem company, who also owns the platform, leverages these products or

© Springer Nature Switzerland AG 2019
X. Franch et al. (Eds.): PROFES 2019, LNCS 11915, pp. 367–382, 2019.
https://doi.org/10.1007/978-3-030-35333-9_27

services to increase its revenues. Hence, companies span traditional boundaries via a fertile open innovation approach that creates a shift towards a distributed process of product innovation and development [10]. Such value co-creation initiative is based on knowledge and resources from outside the company, the third parties. One way to attract such parties is through hackathons [7]. A hackathon is a time-bounded event in which people come together to collaboratively build, and potentially launch, a new solution to solve a particular problem built on top of new or existing technology [16].

Corporate or industrial hackathons have become widespread due to their potential to foster innovation by disseminating new technologies and fostering collaboration. Large companies such as Facebook and Google, as well as small ones, run multiple smaller internal and external hackathons yearly [12]. Internal hackathons promote creative thinking of employees, who are stimulated to think of new projects, reflect on the challenges faced by the company and present new ideas. In external hackathons (i.e. opened to participants that are not formally or directly related to the company), the focus of the company is to obtain novel ideas from people that are not acquainted with the context and routine of the business. Hence, the company gains new insights on how to solve problems, expand its product line, and gather new developers to work on its ecosystem.

The increasing interest of companies to conduct hackathons reveals that such events hold great chances to generate commercial advantage, enabling an ecosystem to evolve [12]. However, reports about the benefits of hackathons are still scarce and spread in different venues [4]. Moreover, the literature largely focuses on civic and educational hackathons, causing the need for studies addressing corporate hackathons [1, 14, 17]. This scenario motivated us to conduct a systematic mapping study on the benefits of corporate hackathons for software ecosystems. This method offers a coarse-grained view of the type of reports and results that have been published in a given research field by categorising and often representing them as a visual map [13]. As main findings, we describe 14 social, technical and business benefits, which emerged from the analysis of 27 primary studies. We also discuss these benefits from the perspective of ecosystem health [8] to denote their contribution to productivity, robustness and niche creation. Hence, we lay the foundations for a systematic understanding of corporate hackathons.

The rest of this paper is structured as follows. Section 2 describes relevant concepts on software ecosystems and hackathons. In Sect. 3, we describe the protocol of the systematic mapping study. Section 4 details our results in a general manner, with demographic data, and more specifically by answering our research question. Finally, we discuss our findings in Sect. 5 and present final considerations in Sect. 6.

2   Theoretical Background

2.1   Software Ecosystems

Software companies have increasingly appreciated the movement from single to multiple-products in a platform approach [10]. In a platform business model, companies open their platforms for third parties/potential partners to integrate their specific solutions and/or develop new ones [2]. We can understand a **software ecosystem** as a set of businesses functioning as a unit and interacting with a shared market for software and services, together with the relationships among them [6]. In this setting, companies invest in innovative business models to co-create value for the ecosystem and promote knowledge sharing among the community of participants. Well-known examples of ecosystems are Google's Android, Microsoft's Dynamics CRM, and Apple's iOS.

Software ecosystems can be understood over three **dimensions** [18]. The *social dimension* encompasses the actors participating in the ecosystem with their respective roles, relationships, skills, motivations, among other factors that regulate the interactions within the network. The *technical dimension* is mainly concerned with the software platform, which is a software-based system that provides core features shared by a portfolio of products or services that interoperate with each other. These solutions can be extended via boundary resources, such as application programming interfaces (APIs) and software development toolkits (SDKs) [10]. This dimension also comprises product management and development processes that discipline how solutions are collaboratively planned, evolved and released to customers. Finally, the *business dimension* deals with the strategies to capture value and generate revenue for ecosystem participants. It involves the platform business model, with definitions about entry barriers, intellectual property rights; in addition to innovation directions.

Broadly speaking, we can divide the ecosystem in two main groups of **actors**. Those in charge of controlling and those subsumed to the current rules. A company called *keystone* [9] governs the evolution of the ecosystem by defining rules of access to the platform and orchestrating the creation of new solutions (e.g. apps). In parallel, a group of *complementors* can co-create value on top of such platform by combining their solutions to address market needs for additional features or services.

The overall **health** of a software ecosystem depends on the actions and decisions taken by each participant. We can assess it via three key measures [5]. *Productivity* is the ability of the ecosystem to transform inputs into products and services, which may happen by increasing the number of applications in an app store. *Robustness* means the capacity of the ecosystem to deal with interferences and pressure from competitors. It comprises the number of participants in the ecosystem, as well as their active contribution and survival rate. Finally, *niche creation* involves the business opportunities that the ecosystem can provide to its participants. It lies on increasing the number of players that use the platform, producing valuable resources and creating new market niches. Thereby, by assessing these aspects, we can establish strategies that will enable all ecosystem participants to co-evolve, i.e. a win-win approach [8].

2.2 Corporate Hackathons

The notion of hackathon appeared in the 2000s as a collaborative software method that relies on the crowd to solve problems [12]. It is commonly seen in teaching (*educational hackathon*) and government (*civic hackathons*) initiatives. In the first case, IT courses introduce hackathons as a contest for graduating students to solve real-life issues in a challenging and fun scenario. They must intensively collaborate with each other, think of innovative solutions and develop specific skills [14]. In the second case, public organisations promote such competitions to create value from open data [17].

In their turn, *corporate hackathons* are industry-oriented events, focused on business activities. Tech companies from all sizes have increasingly integrated hackathons into their software development work to support product test and evolution. The collaborative practices of hackathons generate new ideas, early prototypes, and even business plan development, thereby promoting innovation [12]. Such hackathons can be broadly divided in two subtypes: *internal* and *external*.

Internal hackathons promote creative thinking of employees who are stimulated to think of new projects, reflect on the challenges faced by the company, and present new ideas. Nolte et al. [11] present an example of an internal industrial hackathon at Microsoft and discusses what happened to some projects after the event took place. Meanwhile, *external* hackathons are open to participants that are not formally or directly related to the company. In this case, the focus of the company is to gather novel ideas from outsiders, who can provide insights on how to solve the company's problems and/or expand its product line. Furthermore, an external hackathon is an opportunity for a company to present its products to developers, who can extend its products using the company's APIs. In short, hackathons also allow a company to gather new developers for its ecosystem. Raatikainen [15] present an example of an external hackathon from F-Secure, a company who developed a cloud-based ecosystem. Big players such as Facebook and Google run multiple internal and external hackathons each year [12].

3   Research Method

3.1   Research Question

Our interest on the interplay of hackathons and software ecosystems resulted from our observation that IT companies were increasingly investing in these time-bounded events. Although hackathons can be employed as recruitment events to promote specific technologies, we speculated that companies might also be employing them to foster innovation and evolve their product portfolios. Based on such assumption, we decided to perform a mapping study on corporate hackathons.

Our study aimed at answering the following **research question** (RQ): *what benefits hackathons can provide to software ecosystems?* Through this RQ, we could examine the perceived benefits of a hackathon for a software ecosystem, considering the perspective of keystones (i.e. those responsible for ecosystem coordination) and complementors (i.e. players who create extensions and new solutions in the ecosystem).

3.2   Data Collection

We started the **search process** by analysing seminal papers on hackathons to get a better understanding of the main concepts encompassed by this topic. The relevance of this step lies in the lack of agreement among researchers regarding terms and notions to adopt while addressing this phenomenon [7]. To start the automatic search process, we created an initial search string and performed trial searches on databases such as Google Scholar and IEEEXplore. This string involved the term 'ecosystem', which restricted our results, given that many authors discuss the idea of hackathons within ecosystems but not necessarily combine these terms. Hence, we adopted the following expression with a more open structure that could provide us with a wider and richer set of results: *(hackathon OR hackfest OR code camp OR hack day OR codefest)*.

We performed the automatic searches between 08/03/19 and 17/03/2019. This procedure involved four digital libraries: ACM Digital Library (DL), IEEEXplore, Science Direct, and Wiley Interscience. These are specific and complementary engines, which index multiple events and journals. Hence, they enabled a broad search coverage. The search procedure explored three fields of the papers (title, abstract and keywords) and considered a timeframe of 20 years. The reasoning for such period of time lies in the origin of the term 'hackathon', which appeared in 1999 at an event held in California, which gathered developers to work on legal issues related to software [12].

The automatic search procedure provided us with 2769 papers. We remark that 75% of the papers (2084) stemmed from ACM DL. Such high number of results is caused by two main reasons: (i) this engine has computer programming as a pillar, causing the term 'code' to gain multiple hits, and (ii) it creates variations for each term (e.g. 'code' also became 'coding'). Both facts introduced multiple out-of-scope papers. Then, we performed an initial filter via the following inclusion (ICi) and exclusion criteria (ECi):

- IC_1: papers describing industrial or corporate IT hackathons (internal or external).
- EC_1: papers discussing other forms of hackathons (e.g. civic, educational or conference hackathons) or corporate hackathons outside IT/software development field.
- EC_2: papers not written in English.
- EC_3: grey literature (including theses and books) and papers available as posters.

To apply the former criteria, we read the title and abstract of the papers. As a result, we maintained a subset of 27 papers. We also considered this list to conduct a manual snowballing search. We started this step with a backwards search, analysing the list of references of the each paper. Then, a forward search focused on verifying the papers that cite each item of our list. The resultant list of the snowballing search encompassed 22 papers. By combining these two lists, we generated a set of 49 papers.

3.3   Data Analysis

After aggregating the list of 49 papers, we started the **extraction process** by creating a spreadsheet with general demographic information about the papers (first set) in addition to specific information related to the research questions (second set). The first set involved papers' *ID, title, author(s), year, publication* (i.e. event or journal name) *name* and *type*, and *paper type*. The last information item involved the six main types of study proposed by Wieringa et al. [20]: evaluation research, proposal of solution, validation research, philosophical paper, opinion paper, and personal experience paper.

The extraction process involved a full reading of the papers, generating a deeper understanding of their content. Three researchers conducted this process and excluded additional 22 papers in light of our criteria, resulting in a final list of 27 primary studies (cf. Appendix). We represent the complete process in Fig. 1 as follows.

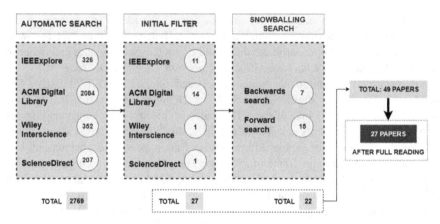

Fig. 1. Search process results.

The final phase of our mapping study consisted of an **analysis process**. We gathered all information regarding each extraction item in a separate file to create specific syntheses by using thematic analysis guidelines. This method aims at analysing and classifying data, which is categorised in derived themes [3]. It enabled us to identify the 14 different benefits of hackathons and to further combine them in three different categories. Such conceptual grouping also supported simple counts, from the distribution of papers per year to the number of evidence/papers that cite a given benefit. Hence, it helped us to organise the dataset in rich detail, preparing it for our interpretation.

4   Results

4.1   Overview of Existing Research on Corporate Hackathons

The distribution of the primary studies per **year** is presented in Fig. 2. The set of 27 papers range from 2007 to 2019. It is noteworthy that there seems to be a growing interest in investigating corporate hackathons: 37% (10) of the papers were published between 2018 and 2019. In particular, our results could reveal even more the current focus on corporate hackathons if our search had covered the whole year of 2019. Most of these papers (17; 63%) were presented in events (e.g. conferences, workshops). In addition, the set of journals papers (10; 37%) within our list were published between 2015 and 2019, which enables us to speculate that research on this topic is getting more attention from researchers.

Regarding the **type of papers**, almost all primary studies (25; 93%) were evaluation papers. These papers described one or more hackathons investigated in practice (either as their focus or briefly in the text). The other two primary studies consisted of a philosophical paper (S5) and a validation paper (S25). This result denotes the current focus of researchers to describe the hackathon phenomenon, which may anticipate new proposals of solutions or philosophical discussions.

Finally, we could observe that a relevant part of the **authors** (39; 43%) belong to industry. They work on software companies such as IBM (S12), Microsoft (S1, S13) and F-Secure (S9), which reveals the important role that hackathons current play in industry setting. From the perspective of academia, James D. Herbsleb, Marko Komssi and Mikko Raatikainen are frequent authors, with three papers each.

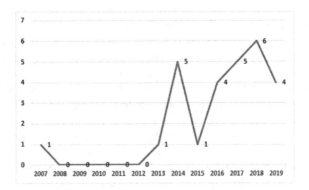

Fig. 2. Distribution of primary studies per year, from 2007 to 2019.

4.2   Research Question Analysis

Our thematic analysis of the 27 primary studies provided a rich set of benefits of hackathons for software ecosystems. Only two papers did not present inputs to answer the RQ (S6, S27). We classified the 14 resultant elements (Fig. 3) as social (SB_X), technical (TB_X) and business (BB_X) benefits, representing the dimensions of an ecosystem [8].

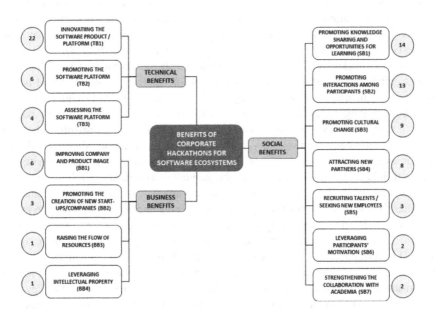

Fig. 3. Technical, business and social benefits of corporate hackathons for software ecosystems.

Social Benefits. The social dimension of an ecosystem involves the collaboration within the different actors of an ecosystem.

Promoting knowledge sharing and opportunities for learning (SB₁) is the most frequent reported social benefit (14 papers; 52%). Corporate hackathons provide participants with a low-risk environment in which they can (i) learn or try something new, as well as (ii) teach what they do and how they do it (S9, S11, S13). Therefore, hackathons foster shared learning in two manners (S8, S16). First, through their dynamics, which involves face-to-face discussions and overall interactions (S4), ground-breaking technology and challenges to be solved and participants that often come excited to learn something new and useful (S10). Second, through a common initial phase in which participants receive technical training or independently explore (e.g. by reading tutorials or asking mentors) software tools, APIs, programming languages, techniques and artefacts to adopt in their projects (S3, S7, S9). Participants also earn or exercise soft skills, such as team collaboration, leadership and presentation abilities (S1, S12, S13).

In internal hackathons, employees can develop a shared understanding via information exchange among different team members (S16). In their turn, external hackathons enable companies to communicate and obtain ideas and experiences from people with different backgrounds. From an ecosystem view, hackathons create a knowledge flow in a privileged and structured way between third parties and a keystone (S22, S23). Therefore, these events establish a process of knowledge transfer (S16, S17) and recognition, since participants also prove their skills (S8).

Another relevant social benefit is *promoting interactions among participants* (SB₂), which we observed in 13 papers (48%). Once companies organise a hackathon, they bring people together and provide opportunities for network expansion (S1, S24). Participants get the opportunity to interact in a different context and establish new and deeper relationships (S16). The dynamics of hackathons also favours informal conversations among attendees, and sustains cooperation even after the event (S3). Participants recognise the advantage of interacting with diverse people that may hold varying types of knowledge from different fields of expertise (S10, S18).

In internal hackathons, the intensive work during the event is a seed for more efficient collaboration and stronger team bond in future projects (S9). External hackathons generate an additional benefit. They enable co-creation of novel solutions and new connections among companies involved, i.e. those organising, supporting or participating (e.g. start-ups, SMEs, external developers adopting or experimenting the API) (S13, S20). Participants gain visibility and meet new partners and suppliers through their common interests (S23). For instance, S11 cited a company that plans to invite tech partners to join its hackathon. We detail this context of community evolution in SB₄.

In general, in the context of ecosystems, hackathons can foster longer collaborations after the event (S13). Smaller companies perceive hackathons as a chance to join an ecosystem by interacting with bigger players – who can shop for ready-made solutions from start-up firms, for instance (S8). They may also partner with similar firms: S11 reported on the continued collaboration between two companies to further develop the hackathon idea, while S12 analysed the emergence of ecosystems formed by start-ups (S12). For the ecosystem to flourish, it is paramount that the keystone understands the hackathon as a strategy to share a larger portion of conception and development (S23).

The primary studies also reinforced that hackathons are means of ***promoting cultural change*** (**SB₃**) (9 papers, 33%). They are eye-opening events (S23) that foster innovative thinking (S5) and entrepreneurial spirit towards new business opportunities (S10, S11). Participants not only gain new skills, but also start to embrace a solution-oriented and self-directed mind-set (S11). In light of that, a growing number of businesses are adopting hackathons as innovation contests that can introduce a result-driven innovation culture (S2, S17). Internally, hackathons can transform corporate culture (S20) by introducing (i) an agile and flexible way of working (S4), (ii) freedom to create new solutions based on participants own ideas (S10) and (iii) a more open culture that allows everyone to see opportunities outside their current positions, even in other areas (S23).

Hackathon also lead software development towards agile and integrated processes. For instance, in internal hackathons, teams from different areas work together for a common goal (S23). Moreover, hackathons promote continuous development and integration for solutions to be created in a short timeframe (S2). Such principles are a path to turn passive users into active participants in a software ecosystem (S21).

Another frequent social benefit of hackathons mentioned in the studied papers is ***attracting new partners*** (**SB₄**) (8 papers, 30%). Most students in a corporate hackathon are getting their first contact with the IT industry. The positive and motivating environment of the event may turn them into new hackathon mentors, or active contributors and users of the platform (S3, S12). For instance, S18 reported on hackathon teams that expressed their interest to continue working on their projects until completion. They intended to add further refinements and features to the platform, which was the centre of the hackathon (S4). In particular, participants may act as evangelists once they seek visibility for their projects or for the ecosystem itself (S17). In a hackathon reported by S3, students created blogs to promote their projects and posted links to their source-code in mailing lists. Therefore, hackathons entail ecosystem growth by building a (i) community of users and experts, as well as (ii) strategic business-to-business networks (S8, S11, S24). The event can shape or define the ecosystem by evolving its community with new complementors, partners and suppliers (S23). These actors will contribute for product development and improvement via open innovation and co-creation (S4).

An additional benefit of a corporate hackathon is the possibility of ***recruiting talents/seeking new employees*** (**SB₅**) (3 papers, 11%). The literature revealed that recruitment is not usual in hackathons. However, players organising the event may perceive it as a good opportunity to attract skilled workers (S8, S24). S23 reported on a company that used the hackathon to recruit developers for their subsidiary. Hackathons usually bring IT passionate and skilled people closer to companies (S24). Participants may look for (new) positions in the companies involved in the event or within their ecosystems (e.g. to nurture the network with new solutions by acting as complementors).

Final benefits from a social perspective involve ***leveraging participants' motivation*** (**SB₆**) (2 papers, 7%) and ***strengthening the collaboration with academia*** (**SB₇**) (2 papers, 7%). The first one reveals that hackathons reinforce a positive and motivating work environment (S1) with challenges that foster a "sense of achievement" (S24). The second one denotes that universities may not simply act as co-organisers or places to locate the event (S8). For instance, in S11, a company organised a hackathon to collaborate with students of business, well-being, and game development, i.e., the company collaborated with a university of applied science.

Technical Benefits. In the technical dimension of an ecosystem, we explore the solutions provided by participants, generally built and integrated via a common platform.

Most of the primary studies denote that hackathons are initiatives for *innovating the software product/platform* (**TB₁**) (22 papers, 81%). The premise of a corporate (external) hackathon is to enhance software development by using the point of view of external professionals (S23). Hence, companies can identify new business opportunities due to new product or service ideas raised by such outside world (S17). Hackathons favour innovation by acting as time-based contests that accelerate development, using agile software practices, new ways of collaborating, in addition to multiple social and technological resources (S21). They gather people from diverse backgrounds, who hold a "can-do" and "hands-on" mind-set to solve focused challenges (S2, S4, S18). With varied and interdisciplinary stakeholders in the same location, hackathons enable some sort of requirements elicitation, discussion and refinement (S8, S16). The creative, real-world grounding, and semi-structured process of a hackathon fosters self-disruption by helping participants to "think outside the box" (S7, S16, S24).

Hackathons frontload and speed up the innovation process, comprising their whole flow, from identifying and assessing relevant problems to unexpected solutions and their (often partial) implementation (S4, S5, S11, S20, S23, S24). This process can be based on a platform or product, with organisers supplying participants with a public database or SDK, for instance. As an example, S25 analysed a hackathon around an ecosystem, in which Microsoft and Samsung provided tools and SDKs for augmented reality and Internet-of-Things for attendees to combine them with a media API.

Hackathon participants deliver different forms of innovation to improve a company's platform or portfolio. Outcomes range from fresh ideas to proofs-of-concept and (early) prototypes (to be integrated into existing products) or even Minimum Viable Products (MVPs) (S3, S12, S13). Companies may also collect suggestions for new business models or feedback on current ideas and/or products (S4, S10, S19, S23, S24).

S17 argues the organising company can also see hackathon participants as customers, understanding how and why they use its products or services (S17). S1 and S11 reported on promising ideas that can receive funding for further development in the form of projects and even become future products. In S9, attendees reported several issues and improvement requirements for a 3rd party API. They also used the API to develop working prototypes. S4 and S12 described hackathons in which the winning team was supposed to refine and finish the application after the event, in order to make it available in an "app store". In S23, the hackathon organiser archived ideas and concepts that were not be implemented during the event to explore them based on markets and available resources. In S26, the hackathon enabled participants to watch, via social media, as their ideas speed from mind to market.

An additional result of hackathons is product documentation. Organising companies can benefit from synopses for the resulting solutions, as well as descriptions in terms of how to use these solutions (S3, S18). For instance, S3 reported on a hackathon in which participants created extensive documentation (including use cases) of the tools in use and for those developed during the event.

Hackathons are also means of ***promoting the software platform*** (**TB$_2$**) (5 papers; 19%). Platform owners can expose an API as the underlying technology upon which new solutions will be created. In particular, partner companies supporting the event gain the same advantage. Both keystone and its partners often prepare the participants by explaining their platforms in detail. Since most participants of hackathons are professional users of SDKs and APIs, companies may perceive them as a valuable group of influencers (S25). It means hackathons are useful to reach out to talented third-party developers and market the platforms, which can then be adopted as a basis for future development, therefore evolving the ecosystem (S11). In S10, organisers described a SDK, focused on the APIs, which participants were required to use at the hackathon. In a similar fashion, in the case presented by S12, students had basic training on Bluemix, the cloud platform as a service from IBM. In another hackathon at IBM, globally distributed researchers and engineers interacted with the "API ecosystem" (S15). Finally, in S25, we identified a case in which a VR start-up sent an enthusiastic representative to the hackathon to demonstrate their platform in a short breakout session.

The innovating ideas and preliminary applications developed by the teams during the event prove to be a catalyst in ***assessing the software platform*** (**TB$_3$**) (4 papers; 15%) by providing feedback about the platform's technical details (e.g. bottlenecks, bugs) and/or design (S9, S10). In S9, the key contributions concerned higher-level design decisions and understanding of the developers' experience. A similar result was reported by S22, which described that enablers and obstacles to third-party development were perceived during a hackathon: a security feature proved to be challenging to use, which caused developers to adopt workarounds and change their initial idea (S22). In S14, a keystone analysed the acceptance of a new platform feature, which proved to be popular during the event: all teams used it for app development.

Business Benefits. The business dimension of ecosystems involves the strategies (e.g. business and revenue model), vision and customer base, among other elements.

From a business perspective, the most relevant benefit is ***improving company and product image*** (**BB$_1$**) (6 papers; 22%). Promoting hackathons will position the organisers (the company itself, its partners, the university hosting the event, etc.) in the trending scope (S12). This suggests these parties are enablers of innovation (S4), maintaining *"their cool profile"*, stated S25. Corporate and product brand promotion steams from good publicity in local media, for instance (S8, S11, S20). Another important and natural marketing channel lies in participants, who can raise the visibility of the platform owner by telling about their experience to their peers (S25).

We also observed corporate hackathons as initiatives of ***promoting the creation of new start-ups/companies*** (**BB$_2$**) (3 papers; 11%). This means hackathons can act as an incubation of start-ups (S21, S25). Although participants focus on problem solving and product development, the instruments (e.g. agile practices, list of challenges, etc.) and conditions (e.g. creative thinking, performance under pressure, etc.) experienced in a hackathon naturally shape a start-up or intra/entrepreneurial spirit (S11).

Finally, hackathons are forms of ***raising the flow of resources*** (**BB$_3$**) (1 paper; 4%) within the ecosystem. According to S4, in these events, it is possible to find new investors for the company, product or platform (S4). Moreover, the several solutions developed during a hackathon are also ***leveraging intellectual property*** (**BB$_4$**) (1 paper;

4%). Participants and the companies themselves can benefit from IP development (S20), depending on hackathon terms (e.g. joint ownership, assignment agreement, etc.).

We can conclude that, from a *technical* perspective, hackathons can accelerate the early phases of the development of new creative solutions, ultimately contributing to the creation a new codebase (S3, S4, S5, S7). In a *social* perspective, hackathons are means to change companies' culture toward a more rapid, responsive, and innovative direction (S11). Finally, from a *business* perspective, keystones can bring direct value to ecosystems by leveraging hackathons to advance their technologies (S9, S10).

5 Discussion

Our analysis revealed that social aspects prevail among the reported benefits that companies may gain by conducting a hackathon. The **social benefits** was the greater (7 benefits; 50% of the total) and the most frequent (51 text excerpts/citations) set among the primary studies. A corporate hackathon enables participants (either employees or outsiders) to learn or expand their technical expertise (SB_1), which is particularly important for a software ecosystem. This is necessary for a software developer to become fluent in the technical requirements necessary to create third party solutions in the ecosystem. Hackathons also bring new knowledge inside the company. The stimulating and highly participative environment of corporate hackathons stimulates the creation of new ideas and the analysis of the problem from different viewpoints. Hence, hackathons support innovative efforts. They are fruitful scenarios to raise ecosystem *productivity*, as the company can transform its current technology (accompanied by "materials of innovation" such as an API) into new solutions (e.g. new third-party apps, services), at lower costs and in a faster pace [5].

Companies must also observe hackathons as means to gradually rely on a wide network of partners and individuals. The event demands participants to interact during solution development, which may also occur in breakout sessions and other moments for networking (SB_2). The company should structure the event to guarantee such collaboration among participants, who may become part of the ecosystem (SB_4). Therefore, it is possible to argue that hackathons contribute to the *robustness* of the existing ecosystem by extending its "social ecosystem" and promoting its connectedness [9, 18].

From the perspective of **technical benefits**, hackathons pave the way for companies to promote their platforms, showing they can be used to solve varied issues (TB_2). By using such platforms, hackathon teams may lead to important innovations for the ecosystem. We observed that these teams could post their solutions in the app store once they had a MVP (TB_1). Participants then generate an increase in ecosystem *productivity*. Besides, once perceiving the usefulness of the technology made available in the software platform, hackathon teams can act as evangelists and attract new players to the software ecosystem. In short, hackathons support ecosystem *robustness*.

Hackathons also establish an efficient and effective way of holistically testing the ecosystem (TB_3). In other words, hackathon participants can assess the software platform by identifying bugs and providing feedback on the ease of third-party application development. In this way, they provide future directions for the development of the software platform, and consequently of the ecosystem, from the perspective of complementors. For instance, they allow platform owners to verify to what extent the requirements for applications are fulfilled. In doing so, participants contribute to ecosystem *productivity*, as a result from overall improvements in the shared platform.

Finally, among **business benefits**, we noticed that hackathons can be an effective publicity campaign. They help positioning the product or company brand (BB_1), which can expand to a larger public. Thereby, it will also support an increase in the community of users and complementors of the software ecosystem, raising its *robustness*. Furthermore, corporate hackathons promote the emergence of new start-ups/companies (BB_2), thereby, allowing *niche creation* in software ecosystems.

As mentioned in Sect. 2.1, it is important to understand and monitor the health of a software ecosystem. According to our literature review, hackathons provide benefits that allow the three health measures (i.e. productivity, robustness and niche creation) to increase. However, ecosystem health is influenced by other factors, such as consistent and lasting partnerships, platform security, product quality and customer care [17]. Therefore, hackathons alone are not enough to guarantee the sustainability of a software ecosystem. This raises an interesting research question for future work about the extent to which hackathons contribute to software ecosystem health.

6 Conclusion

Our systematic mapping study suggested that hackathons majorly bring social benefits for an ecosystem by promoting knowledge sharing and learning opportunities, enhancing collaboration among ecosystem participants and growing the community. We drew on ecosystem health elements to discuss what software companies can gain while promoting these events. We revealed the extent to which hackathons can act as a method to leverage a software ecosystem. Therefore, we help practitioners to better understand the context of hackathons and gain insights on how to adopt them as a collaborative and exploratory method for innovation.

In addition, we contribute to the literature on open innovation by shedding light on factors not previously described by authors. Related literature on hackathons have mostly focused on events leaded by government organisations. The recent systematic reviews conducted by Attard et al. [1] and Safarov et al. [17] analysed hackathons on open government data. These journal papers focus on civic hackathons, which reinforces the relevance of a mapping study that addresses a complementary view on the topic. Our findings improve the theoretical conversation about corporate hackathons and provide relevant inputs to approach the topic in future studies.

As a possible construct validity of our method, we acknowledge the risk of having neglected some search terms that could have led us to new results. To address this issue, we calibrated the search string by including terms identified in well-recognised literature (i.e. relevant papers on hackathons from well-known/renowned events or journals). We also tried to encompass specific or commercial terms coined by hackathons promoted by big companies. Besides, we guaranteed that two researchers performed each phase of the search process. Thereby, we established a continuous validation strategy, which involved discussions between the researchers. To cope with conclusion validity, we carefully organised the extraction files, creating different versions of our analysis to enable an audit trial by checking how we generated a given finding.

We found a large emphasis on descriptive studies about corporate hackathons. Hence, we see a current need for future research specifically in two areas:

- **Techniques or methods to support corporate hackathons**. To contribute towards this research avenue, we aim to conduct ethnographic studies of hackathons in IT industry to derive (i) facilitators/enablers and barriers/challenges and (ii) lessons learned. Our goal is to elaborate a set of recommendations for organising hackathons, highlighting their interrelation with the software engineering process. For instance, exploring how these events enable an initial requirements phase, as we reported while discussing the technical benefits of hackathons.
- **Theories and conceptual models on corporate hackathons.** We seek to address this need by deepening our analysis of the benefits to interrelate them. For instance, *can a social benefit (e.g. attracting new partners [SB₄]) promote a given technical benefit (e.g. raising the flow of resources [BB₃])?* Then, we will continue examining the primary papers to map and combine additional aspects of hackathons, such as place of occurrence, main goals and steps. This will enable us to identify possible patterns, e.g. *a corporate hackathon performed at a university tends to focus on brand positioning and enables an effective recruitment process*. To discuss these findings, we shall perform an expert review with organisers of hackathons.

Acknowledgements. This project was financially supported by the Brazilian National Research Council (CNPq), processes [430905/2018-1], [420801/2016-2] and [311256/2018-0].

Appendix

ID	Paper information
S1	Nolte, A., et al. You Hacked and Now What? Exploring Outcomes of a Corporate Hackathon. ACM on Human-Computer Interaction. 2018
S2	Alkema, P. J., et al. Agile and hackathons: a case study of emergent practices at the FNB codefest. South African Institute of Computer Scientists and Information Technologists. ACM, 2017
S3	Trainer, E. H., et al. Community code engagements: summer of code & hackathons for community building in scientific software. Int'l Conf. on Sup. Group Work. 2014
S4	Frey, F. J. and Luks, M. The innovation-driven hackathon: one means for accelerating innovation. European Conf. on Pattern Languages of Programs. 2016
S5	Grace, L. Deciphering Hackathons and Game Jams through Play. Int'l Conf. on Game Jams, Hackathons, and Game Creation Events. 2016
S6	Izvalov, A., et al. Comparison of game creation and engineering hackathons on the global and local levels. Int'l Conf. on Game Jams, Hackathons, and Game Creation Events. 2017
S7	Thomer, A. K., et al. Co-designing scientific software: Hackathons for participatory interface design. CHI Conf. Extended Abstracts on Human Factors in Computing Systems. 2016

(continued)

(continued)

ID	Paper information
S8	Porras, J., et al. Hackathons in software engineering education: lessons learned from a decade of events. I'l Workshop on Software Eng. Education for Millennials. 2018
S9	Raatikainen, M., et al. Industrial experiences of organizing a hackathon to assess a device-centric cloud ecosystem. Annual Computer Soft. and Applications Conf. 2013
S10	Rosell, B., et al. Unleashing innovation through internal hackathons. Innovations in Technology Conference. 2014
S11	Komssi, M., et al. What are hackathons for? IEEE Software 32 (5). 2015
S12	Avalos, M., et al. Hackathons, semesterathons, and summerathons as vehicles to develop smart city local talent that via their innovations promote synergy between industry, academia, government and citizens. Int'l Smart Cities Conf. 2017
S13	Pe-Than, E., et al. Designing Corporate Hackathons With a Purpose: The Future of Software Development. IEEE Software 36 (1). 2019
S14	Tsukada, M., et al. Software defined media: Virtualization of audio-visual services. Int'l Conf. on Communications. 2017
S15	Wittern, E., et al. A graph-based data model for API ecosystem insights. Int'l Conf. on Web Services. 2014
S16	Saravi, S., et al. A Systems Engineering Hackathon – A Methodology Involving Multiple Stakeholders to Progress Conceptual Design of a Complex Engineered Product. IEEE Access 6. 2018
S17	Kan, S., et al. Customer Experience Transformation in the Aviation Industry: Business Strategy Realization through Design Thinking, Innovation Management, and HPT. Performance Improvement 58 (1). 2019
S18	Busby, B. and Lesko, A. M. Closing gaps between open software and public data in a hackathon setting: user-centered software prototyping. F1000Research 5. 2016
S19	Helander, M., et al. Looking for great ideas: Analyzing the innovation jam. Workshop on Web Mining and Social Network Analysis. 2007
S20	Flores, M., et al. How can hackathons accelerate corporate innovation?. Int'l Conf. on Advances in Production Management Systems. 2018
S21	Lindtner, S., et al. Emerging sites of HCI innovation: hackerspaces, hardware startups & incubators. Conf. on Human Factors in Computing Systems. 2014
S22	Dal Bianco, V., et al. The role of platform boundary resources in software ecosystems: A case study. Conf. on Software Architecture. 2014
S23	Herala, Antti, et al. Strategy for Data: Open it or Hack it?. Journal of Theoretical and Applied Electronic Commerce Research 14 (2). 2019
S24	Granados, C. and Pareja-Eastaway, M. How do collaborative practices contribute to innovation in large organisations? The case of hackathons. Innovation. 2019
S25	Zukin, S. and Papadantonakis, M. Hackathons as Co-optation ritual: Socializing workers and institutionalizing innovation in the "new" economy. Precarious work. 2017
S26	Alänge, S. and Steiber, A. Three operational models for ambidexterity in large corporations. Triple Helix 5 (1). 2018
S27	Menon, K., et al. Industrial internet platforms: A conceptual evaluation from a product lifecycle management perspective. Journal of Eng. Manufacture 233 (5). 2018

References

1. Attard, J.: A systematic review of open government data initiatives. Gov. Inf. Q. **32**(4), 399–418 (2015)
2. Che, M., Perry, D.E.: Architectural design decisions in open software development: a transition to software ecosystems. In: Australian Software Engineering Conference, pp. 58–61 (2014)
3. Cruzes, D.S., Dyba, T.: Recommended steps for thematic synthesis in software engineering. In: IEEE International Symposium on Empirical Software Engineering and Measurement, pp. 275–284 (2011)
4. Herala, A.: Strategy for data: open it or hack it? J. Theor. Appl. Electron. Commer. Res. **14**(2), 33–46 (2019)
5. Iansiti, M., Levien, R.: Strategy as ecology. Harvard Bus. Rev. **82**(3), 68–81 (2004)
6. Jansen, S., Finkelstein, A., Brinkkemper, S.: A sense of community: a research agenda for software ecosystems. In: 31st International Conference on Software Engineering, pp. 187–190 (2009)
7. Komssi, M., et al.: What are hackathons for? IEEE Softw. **32**(5), 60–67 (2015)
8. Manikas, K., Hansen, K.M.: Reviewing the health of software ecosystems – a conceptual framework proposal. In: International Workshop on Software Ecosystems, pp. 33–44 (2013)
9. Manikas, K., Hansen, K.M.: Software ecosystems – a systematic literature review. J. Syst. Softw. **86**(5), 1294–1306 (2013)
10. Nambisan, S., Siegel, D., Kenney, M.: On open innovation, platforms, and entrepreneurship. Strateg. Entrep. J. **12**(3), 354–368 (2018)
11. Nolte, A., et al.: You hacked and now what? - Exploring outcomes of a corporate Hackathon. In: PACMHCI 2(CSCW), pp. 1–23 (2018)
12. Pe-Than, E., et al.: Designing corporate Hackathons with a purpose: the future of software development. IEEE Softw. **36**(1), 15–22 (2019)
13. Petersen, K., et al.: Systematic mapping studies in software engineering. In: International Conference on Evaluation and Assessment in Software Engineering, pp. 68–77 (2008)
14. Porras, J., et al.: Hackathons in software engineering education: lessons learned from a decade of events. In: 2nd International Workshop on Software Engineering Education for Millennials, pp. 40–47 (2018)
15. Raatikainen, M. et al.: Industrial experiences of organizing a hackathon to assess a device-centric cloud ecosystem. In: IEEE Annual Computer Software and Applications Conference, pp. 790–799 (2013)
16. Rosell, B., Kumar, S., Shepherd, J.: Unleashing innovation through internal Hackathons. In: IEEE Innovations in Technology Conference, pp. 1–8 (2014)
17. Safarov, I.: Utilization of open government data: a systematic literature review of types, conditions, effects and users. Inf. Polity **22**(1), 1–24 (2017)
18. Soussi, L.: Health vulnerabilities in software ecosystems: five cases of dying platforms. MS thesis. Utrech University (2018)
19. Valença, G., Alves, C.: A theory of power in emerging software ecosystems formed by small-to-medium enterprises. J. Syst. Softw. **13**, 76–104 (2017)
20. Wieringa, R.: Requirements engineering paper classification and evaluation criteria: a proposal and a discussion. Requir. Eng. **11**(1), 102–107 (2006)

Agile in the Era of Digitalization: A Finnish Survey Study

Petri Kettunen[1]([⊠]) [iD], Maarit Laanti[2], Fabian Fagerholm[1,3] [iD],
and Tommi Mikkonen[1] [iD]

[1] Department of Computer Science, University of Helsinki, Helsinki, Finland
{petri.kettunen, fabian.fagerholm,
tommi.mikkonen}@helsinki.fi
[2] Nitor Delta, Helsinki, Finland
maarit.laanti@nitor.com
[3] Blekinge University of Technology, Karlskrona, Sweden
fabian.fagerholm@bth.se

Abstract. Agile software development has been applied since the early 2000s. It is now mainstream industrial practice in information and communication technology (ICT) companies and IT organizations. However, recently increasing and even disruptive digitalization has brought new drivers and needs for agility both in software organizations as well as in traditional companies, which are becoming more and more software-intensive. Following that line of developments, based on our recent survey conducted in Finland in 2018, in this paper we explore the current state of the affairs with respect to how different organizations currently address agility and agile development in both IT and non-software industrial sectors. The results show that operative goals (productivity, quality) are considered the most important ones to achieve by agile means. Scrum, Kanban and DevOps are the most frequently reported methods, and SAFe is the dominant scaling model. Lead time metrics are the most typically followed measurements. The operative goals as well as responsiveness are also the most highly ranked future aims. The impacts of digitalization are considered substantial but agile developments are seen to address them well. As a conclusion of this survey study, there is no "one agile way" for all. Different organizations seem to emphasize multiple aspects of agility when they develop, adapt and even transform themselves. Yet, also many commonalities were indicated.

Keywords: Agile software development · Enterprise agility · Transformation · Digitalization · Survey

1 Introduction

Agile methods and practices are nowadays mainstream in software development organizations. Agile practices and ways of working are also increasingly applied in other functional areas and operations of large companies in different industry sectors. Moreover, modern software-intensive companies facing digitalization are transforming to become agile enterprises with business agility [1].

© Springer Nature Switzerland AG 2019
X. Franch et al. (Eds.): PROFES 2019, LNCS 11915, pp. 383–398, 2019.
https://doi.org/10.1007/978-3-030-35333-9_28

When agile software development methods and practices are extended and scaled up to enterprise levels, new competences and organizational capabilities beyond software engineering are required. It is thus important for each particular organization be able to understand their specific needs and agile means in order to achieve the goals of agility in their cases [2, 3].

There is a need for more empirical research to understand the current state of the agile practice in order to advance relevant software engineering research [4]. In this paper, we present current results about agility in mostly large organizations based on our recent survey study done in Finland. Various agile surveys have been conducted earlier, but current factors like disruptive digitalization may bring agile software development and business agility more topical for different organizations [5–7]. Compared to previous studies, we are interested not only in measuring how widely agile methods are currently applied in industrial practice but we want also to understand why and how different companies want to be(come) agile and how agility will possibly be evolving in the future in different software-intensive industries.

Previously, we have published selected results of the survey focusing on questions about Scaled Agile Framework (SAFe) adoption and agile transformation [8, 9]. This continuation paper examines primarily different questions of the survey data.

The rest of this paper is organized as follows. Section 2 charters the research background and Sect. 3 describes the survey design. In Sect. 4 designated results of the survey data are presented followed by comparative discussion in Sect. 5. In Sect. 6 we conclude with pointers to planned further work.

2   Background

2.1   Current State of Practice and Trends

Agile software development (ASD) has been practiced in industry – also in Finland – for two decades now since the publication of the Agile Manifesto in the early 2000s. Since then agile development has evolved considerably [10].

One of the main development trends since the early days is that ASD has expanded from small colocated team setups to large-scale and distributed settings. Scaling frameworks – particularly Scaled Agile Framework (SAFe) – have been developed to assist in large-scale agile. However, many challenges are still faced [11–13].

Furthermore, agile has been expanded beyond software development to other business processes and organizational functions. Such agile transformations in organizations are conducted to achieve enterprise-level agility particularly in large, established companies [5, 6]. Notably, agile adoptions are not just something that took place in the early era of ASD (2001–2010) but they are also currently ongoing in many organizations [14].

ASD methods and practices are nowadays applied also in hardware and systems engineering functions in product development organizations. That requires adapting the lightweight agile ways of working with the inherent constraints and requirements of complex systems development in the specific domains (e.g., automotive) [15, 16].

In all, since the early days 2000s both the technical and the business environments of software organizations and companies in different industry sectors and domains have changed considerably – sometimes even radically. Digitalization is nowadays a potential impact factor in many industry sectors, not limiting to the ICT sector alone.

Those are the underlying motivations for our empirical research. What agile software development has previously been may not reflect fully the actual state today and trends in the foreseeable future [4, 10].

2.2 Research Streams

In addition to the progressed state of the practice (Sect. 2.1), agile software development related research has advanced in many avenues both conceptually and empirically although it may have been lagging behind practice [4]. In general, agility is not specific to software development, and agile enterprises have been considered much before the Agile Manifesto in 2001 – particularly in manufacturing industries [17]. Some seminal works to ground and define information systems development (ISD) agility conceptually have been published [18]. Harmonized and consistent understanding of what constitutes agility in software systems development would make it possible to define comparable measures for rigorous empirical agile research [19, 20]. However, even the agile terminology is still not fully settled and different terms are sometimes used interchangeably for the same concepts in research literature [13].

Current popular agile research themes include large-scale agile software development and organizational transformations for enterprise agile [4, 13, 21]. DevOps is one of the recent topics.

At the enterprise level recent research is advancing towards strategic agility and, ultimately, to agile software enterprises [7]. Like agile practice, agile research is gradually expanding beyond software to address strategic enterprise agility in software organizations and software-intensive companies. That research stream is our overarching and guiding motivation with the intention to contribute empirical evidence with this survey study. In essence, we are continuing here our agile research work started in early 2000s [2, 22].

Overall, we do recognize that our research themes are broad and partially multidisciplinary. In particular, there are additional foundational reference areas such as management and organization sciences addressing organizational transformations and digitalization in industries. It is not possible to cover such broad topics in here, but we consider them important for framing and comprehending agile development and agility in software-intensive company contexts with various contingencies [1].

2.3 Prior and Related Studies

Considering prior and related survey works, probably one of the most internationally known ones is the annual State of Agile survey by VersionOne Inc. [14]. It covers agile adoption, benefits of adopting agile, agile methods and practices used, success metrics of agile initiatives/agile transformations and agile projects, and scaling agile.

The European HELENA study initiated in 2016 has surveyed software systems development organizations for their agile development methods and practices with respect to their different combinations (hybrid approaches) in different industry domains [23]. It also explores the reasons for implementing hybrid development approaches and the ways they are formed in practice.

In Finland, a particular scientific survey study was done in 2012 [24]. It explored the usage of agile and lean methods, practices and principles, the goals for agile and lean adoptions, their challenges and limiting factors, and the perceived improvement effects of adoptions. Also the future plans were enquired. Furthermore, the Finnish Software Industry Survey examined agility in 2014 [25]. The results indicated differences in agility (e.g., flexibility) in different types and sizes of software organizations.

We have been experiencing industrial agile practice and changes in Finland during the period 2012–2018 (i.e., since the study in [24] and our survey). However, we are not aware of comparable longitudinal research about agile evolution in Finland.

3 Research Design

On the whole, the purpose of our survey research was to examine the current state of agile development and enterprise agility in Finland. We are interested in measuring how widely agile methods and practices are currently applied in industrial practice and how that is evolving. Moreover, we want to understand why different companies want to change – even transform – with agile means and how beneficial and successful their particular changes have been. Digitalization is one of our intriguing context factors. The target population was intentionally not limited to software companies since we were also interested in non-software companies (i.e., companies in other industries than IT) currently facing digitalization and becoming more software-intensive as "software houses". We aimed to investigate not only the current whereabouts but also the future intentions of the companies.

The survey questionnaire was composed by starting from our selected main research themes of interests. The questionnaire structure comprised the following primary sections: Company's state of agile, Agile company transformation, Agile future of the company.

The specific questions were compiled on the one hand by referring to prior surveys for comparison purposes (e.g., [24, 26]) and by deriving from our industrial experiences and our prior works (e.g., [2, 22]) on the other hand. The draft questionnaire was first piloted both in our industrial and academic organizations. The final version consisted of total of 50 questions (including background information items). Certain questions were only applicable depending on their preceding selector questions (e.g., whether SAFe is in use or not). The questions were stated both in Finnish and in English. Table 1 presents the question items selected for analysis in this paper.

For data collection, the survey was implemented as a web-based online questionnaire with the Finnish/English language choice. We considered several potential distribution channels in order to reach a wide, representative sample population. However, due to pragmatic constraints we decided to use convenience sampling. The questionnaire was distributed with one Finnish consulting company mailing list mass postings to over 600 people collected from people interested in the company's offering of software consultancy and agile transformation services, and with social media. It was open for responding for 4 weeks in Nov–Dec 2018. We received 118 finished responses.

4 Results

Due to the space constraints, we cannot cover all the questions of our survey in here. In order to investigate the research themes of agility and agile development changes, in this paper we focus on the question items shown in Table 1.

Table 1. Questionnaire main sections and selected question items

Company's state of agile
– What agile methods and models are there in use in Your company?
– What particular (agile) measurements does the company follow up?
Agile company transformation
– Why does Your company want to become more agile?
– Where is the current overall focus of agility in Your company?
Agile future of the company
– What goals does the company attempt to achieve by agile means?
– How much does digitalization impact the agile development of Your company?
Background information (organization and respondent)
– What is the primary sector (line of business) of Your company?
– What is your primary role in Your organization?

4.1 Background Information

The majority (75%) of our respondents in this sample were in large organizations: 44 reported that their organization is very large (more than 5000 persons) and also 44 large (more than 250 persons; In Finland companies with < 250 employees are SMEs).

The respondents were also asked to designate the industry/business sector of their companies. The survey question listed 23 answering choices (denoted here as C1–C23) and an open choice field. Our respondents represented more than 15 different domains with ICT sector being the most frequent one as shown in Table 2. However, notably, taking together the majority of the respondents reported their companies to be in other sectors than the ICT.

Table 2. What is the primary sector (line of business) of Your company?

(top 5) (multi choice not allowed)	n (N = 115, 'No answer' choice N/A = 0)	% (out of N)
C1 ICT sector (including consulting), information technology	38	33
C2 Financial sector (banking, insurance)	27	23
C4 Telecom services	13	11
C17 Traffic, logistics	8	7
C3 Retail sector	4	3

The questionnaire included also a few question items concerning the respondent's whereabouts and viewpoints of the company. Because our overall aim is to understand agility in software development organizations and companies as a whole, it is illuminating to have such contextual background information for analysis. Table 3 shows that our sample includes respondents with diverse roles. However, most of the respondents are directly involved with software development.

Table 3. What is your primary role in Your organization?

(top 10) (multi choice not allowed)	n (N = 117, N/A = 2)	% (out of N)
Software development or supporting it (including project management)	38	32
Software process development, organizational development (coach)	20	17
Architecture and technology development	11	9
Software development management (R&D)	10	9
Product management	8	7
Business management	6	5
Business process development	4	3
Sales, marketing, customer relationships or equal	4	3
Information/Knowledge management	3	3
Personnel management (HR and supervising excluding top management)	2	2

4.2   Company's State of Agile

To begin with, one of the first questions of the questionnaire was about the agile methods and models usage in companies. The question presented 13 choices and an open field as shown in Table 4. Notably the choices included typical software methods (e.g., Scrum, XP) but also more organizational ones including scaling agile.

The majority of the respondents reported that Scrum, Kanban and DevOps are widely used. Also Lean methods appeared to be commonplace. Considering the agile scaling methods, Scaled Agile Framework (SAFe) was reported by more than half of our respondents while Large Scale Scrum (LeSS) and Disciplined Agile Delivery (DAD) are clearly less frequently used. In-house scaled agile models are not extremely unusual. We have earlier published more detailed results of the SAFe adoption elsewhere [9].

Table 4. What agile methods and models are there in use in Your company (multi choice)? (All methods and models which Your company uses in software development at least partially)

Choice	n (N = 116, N/A = 3)	% (out of N)
Scrum	101	89
Kanban	97	86
DevOps	73	65
Scaled Agile Framework (SAFe)	71	63
Lean methods	66	58
Agile portfolio management	20	18
In-house scaled agile development model (what kind)	16	14
Agile rolling budgeting (or no budgeting at all)	14	12
Extreme Programming (XP)	13	12
Spotify model	11	10
Large Scale Scrum (LeSS)	7	6
Agile Modelling	7	6
Disciplined Agile Delivery (DAD)	1	1
Other	1	1

In addition to the agile method and model usage, we enquired also what particular measurements and metrics the companies use. The question was fully open with no prescribed choices given except 'No metrics'. Table 5 presents the different measurements that the respondents indicated. Note that some respondents reported many. Because of the open answering form, the responses (some of them were in Finnish) are here coded and grouped as qualitative data.

Development process operational measurements (lead time, cycle time; outcomes) appear to be the most typically followed internal attributes. However, also some external customer-related measurements (value, NPS) seem to be in place.

Table 5. What particular (agile) measurements does the company follow up?

(open choice)	n (N = 114, N/A = 22)	% (out of N)
Key measurements (what):	46	40
– Lead time (features, epics, issues), cycle time, release cycle	29	
– Value	9	
– Defects	6	
– Outcomes, releases, deployments	4	
– Velocity	4	
– Automation (test, release)	4	
– Employee experience, "happy-or-not"	4	
– Predictability	3	
– NPS, customer experience	3	
– MISC. (several nominations, other than the ones above)	<3	
No metrics	47	41

4.3   Agile Company Transformation

In this survey, we were especially interested in discovering how extensively companies have performed agile adoptions and even company-wide agile transformations. The questionnaire included one specific question about when there has been executed or planned agile transformation in the company most recently and another question of how the company is/has been executing agile transformation. We have presented those results earlier elsewhere [8].

In this paper, we address the fundamental question for what reasons and purposes companies need and want to be or become more agile. Table 6 shows the responses for that question. There were 15 choices listed and an open choice field. Operative productivity and quality were reported most often, but overall there was a lot of variance in the reasons for agile adoption. That is, companies have many reasons for being or becoming (more) agile. We return to this in Sect. 4.4 (Table 10).

Table 6. Why does Your company want to become more agile (multi choice)?

Choice	n (N = 86, N/A = 2)	% (out of N)
(4) Productivity and quality (operative)	62	72
(3) Responsiveness to customer/market changes (new features)	56	65
(8) Job satisfaction	46	53
(12) Fast/continuous organizational learning in rapidly changing operating environments	44	51
(2) Competitive and desirable products (new product development)	41	48
(9) Project manageability	41	48
(6) Customer experience	38	44
(11) Strategic and organizational flexibility	38	44
(5) Customer satisfaction	37	43
(1) New business (product and service innovation)	28	33
(7) User experience (UX)	27	31
(15) Employer brand	25	29
(10) Continuous budgeting, resourcing	18	21
(14) Company image	18	21
(13) Customers require/wish (agile development)	13	15
(16) Other	3	3

Table 7. Why does Your company want to become more agile (multi choice)? – BY INDUSTRY SECTOR (see Tables 2 and 6 for the choices)

Industry sector	Rank				
	#1	#2	#3	#4	#5
C1 ICT sector (including consulting), information technology	(4)	(3)	(8)	(2)	(9), (12)
C2 Financial sector (banking, insurance)	(3), (4), (8)			(6)	(5)
C4 Telecom services	(4)	(3)	(9)	(1), (2), (5), (12)	

Table 7 brings a comparative view of the relative importance of different reasons in different industry sectors (top 3, c.f., Table 2). The productivity and quality (choice 4) is ranked high in all the ICT (C1), financial (C2) and telecom service (C4) sectors, followed by responsiveness (choice 3). There appears to be some emphasis on also customer-related reasons (choices 5, 6) and employees (choice 8). Competitive and desirable products are also important reasons (choice 2). However, no statistical significance in those industry sectors can be conjectured here.

In addition to asking for the specific reasons for being or becoming agile, we inquired also more broadly, where the companies put currently weight on their agility in general. The question item listed 7 choices including 'No particular focusing' and an open choice field. Note that we did not give any prescribed definition of 'agility'. Table 8 shows that the respondents indicated operative goals most frequently. Both organizational and technological means are utilized.

Table 9 gives an industry-specific (top 3, c.f., Table 2) view of the agility emphasis. The ICT sector (C1) appears to put noticeable weight also on strategic goals while in the financial sector companies (C2) the overall agility of the company seems to be important. Again, no statistical significance in those sectors can be conjectured here.

Table 8. Where is the current overall focus of agility in Your company (multi choice)? (Evaluate the goals and means of the company from your point of view in your opinion)

Choice	n (N = 86, N/A = 2)	% (out of N)
(2) Operative goals (e.g., internal efficiency)	44	51
(4) Organizational means (e.g., self-organizing teams)	41	48
(5) Scaling agile development	35	41
(3) Technological means (e.g., improved work methods)	34	40
(6) Overall agility of the company	27	31
(1) Strategic goals (e.g., speed advantage in the business sector)	20	23
(8) No particular focusing	4	5
(7) Other	2	2

Table 9. Where is the current overall focus of agility in Your company (multi choice)? – BY INDUSTRY SECTOR (see Tables 2 and 8 for the choices)

Industry sector	Rank				
	#1	#2	#3	#4	#5
C1 ICT sector (including consulting), information technology	(2)	(3), (4)		(1)	(5)
C2 Financial sector (banking, insurance)	(6)	(2), (4)		(3), (5)	
C4 Telecom services	(5)	(2)	(3)	(1)	(6)

4.4   Agile Future of the Company

In addition to probing the current state of agile and agility in companies, we are also interested in understanding their pictures of futures and the developmental scenario paths. For that, we asked the respondents to portray the time period 2018–2020 from their company's point of view.

Table 10 presents the responses of what the respondents see important that their companies attempt to achieve by agile means. The question item listed 13 different choices and an open choice. The basic agile goals of productivity, quality and responsiveness are the most indicated ones. However, there appear to be a wide range of other aims to attain covering both external customer-facing items (e.g., customer experience) and internal organizational ones (e.g., job satisfaction).

Table 10. What goals does the company attempt to achieve by agile means (multi choice)? (Appraise the 3 most important ones (weight, urgency))

Choice	n (N = 111, N/A = 4)	% (out of N)
Responsiveness to customer/market changes (new features)	55	50
Productivity and quality (operative)	55	50
Competitive and desirable products (new product development)	28	25
Customer experience	27	24
Job satisfaction	27	24
Project manageability	26	23
Fast/continuous organizational learning in rapidly changing operating environments	23	21
Customer satisfaction	21	19
Strategic and organizational flexibility	18	16
New business (product and service innovation)	12	11
User experience (UX)	11	10
Continuous budgeting, resourcing	3	3
Company image	3	3
Other	0	0

Finally, addressing directly the factor of digitalization, we asked the respondents to evaluate the impacts of digitalization and how effectively their agile development fit with them. The answering form was a 2-dimensional grid like depicted in Fig. 1. In addition, there was an open field for specifying particular factors of digitalization. Note that we did not give any prescribed definition of 'digitalization'.

The distribution in Fig. 1 shows that, overall, the respondents consider both the impacts of digitalization and the matching of agile developments in their companies substantial. For the particular digitalization impact factors AI, robotics (automation) and IoT were identified most frequently as presented in Table 11. Because of the open answering form, the responses (some of them were in Finnish) are here coded and grouped as qualitative data.

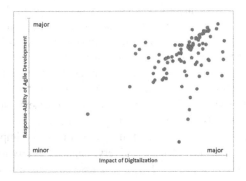

Fig. 1. How much does digitalization impact the agile development of Your company? (Net impact of the different factors and the corresponding usefulness of agile development) – (N = 111, N/A = 20)

Table 11. What factors of digitalization (e.g., artificial intelligence, IoT) affect in particular? – (N = 58)

(open comment)	n	% (out of N)
AI	25	44
Automation, robotics, RPA	20	34
IoT, IIoT	18	32
Data	10	18
VR, AR, XR	5	9
Analytics	4	7
ML	4	7
5G	4	7
Blockchain	4	7
MISC. (several nominations, other than the ones above)	<4	

5 Discussion

5.1 Comparative Analysis

Goals. Overall, the respondents indicated a wide range of targets for their companies to pursuit by becoming more agile (see Table 6). Not surprisingly, operative goals (productivity, quality) were the most often reported ones but also customer-facing goals (responsiveness to customer/market changes and competitive, desirable products) were ranked high which aligns with the agile value of satisfying customers. Those ones are also emphasized as the future targets (Table 10). Notably also internal goals of job satisfaction and organizational learning were reported to be important ones (Table 6). However, overall there appear to be no profound differences in Tables 6 and 10. This could be investigated further in different industry sectors (e.g., the choice Customer experience). One explanatory factor may also be how different respondents have interpreted the terms "more agile" and "agile means" and perceived the timeframe ("become", "future of the company") in these questions.

Comparing and contrasting with related prior research, Rodríguez et al. reported that the most important goals in agile and lean adoption are to increase productivity, improve product and service quality and to reduce development cycle times and time-to-market [24]. Those results are similar to our ones, operative productivity and quality being the top in Table 6. VersionOne found that the most important reasons for adopting agile are to accelerate software delivery, enhance ability to manage changing priorities and to increase productivity [14, 26]. Those ones are also close to our results in Table 6.

Measurements and Metrics. Interestingly enough, a substantial share (41%) of our respondents indicated that the company follows up no particular metrics (see Table 5). It could be due to the particular phases of the agile transformations in the companies with no specific metrics selected yet. It could possibly also depend on the formulation of the question – agile measurements and metrics could mean different things in different roles (Table 3) and company contexts. This is an area of a further study.

Comparing the current focus of agility in companies and the key metrics, there appear to be an alignment with operative goals being the main focus area (Table 8) and lead time metrics being the most frequently used measurements (Table 5). Furthermore, operative productivity and responsiveness were reported most often as the company agile targets (Table 6) which also aligns with the lead time and outcome metrics being the key ones in Table 5.

In the prior related research, Rodríguez et al. does not cover any particular metrics [24]. However, their results include the perceived effects of adoption of agile and lean including for instance accelerated time-to-market/cycle time. We could expect those organizations to somehow measure that. In our results (Table 5) lead time, cycle time and velocity are related metrics.

VersionOne reports how success is measured with agile initiatives and with agile projects [26]. For the latter, customer/user satisfaction is indicated most. In our results, NPS and customer experience had only few occurrences.

Velocity and Effort estimates were found to be the most highly influential metrics reported in industrial agile studies included in one systematic literature review (SLR) [27]. In our results, velocity was not ranked high and effort estimates did not appear. The potential reason could be that these are rather team level metrics, and agile development has evolved to be a subject for the whole company. Lead time was the most often cited metric in our study while in contrast it was not ranked especially high in the abovementioned SLR.

Innovation. Facilitating innovation is one of the principal underlying goals of agile development methods, and empirical research evidence has been called for [19]. In our survey, the following question item choices address innovation in particular (see Tables 1, 6, 7 and 10):

– Why does Your company want to become more agile?
– What goals does the company attempt to achieve by agile means?

• New business (product and service innovation)
• Competitive and desirable products (new product development)

Interestingly, the goal 'Competitive and desirable products (new product development)' is ranked relatively high while the higher-level goal 'New business (product and service innovation)' appears to be less important (see Tables 6 and 10).

Future of Agile. Agile software development has been practiced for the past two decades. During that time, there have been considerable evolution and expansion from small colocated teams to large-scale agile and agile enterprise transformations. Some of the most current and future trends foreseen are to join agile software development with new emerging technologies including AI, IoT, Big data and AR/VR [10]. Table 11 in our results indicate similar factors.

5.2 Implications

Managerial Implications. Following our findings and the analysis in Sect. 5.1, we suggest the following recommendations for practitioners of agile software production and for organizational agility development:

• Goals and means: Each organization should consider both the ends (agility) and the means (agile development) strategically and systemically in their specific business context. Each company should know why and how to change (Table 7).
• Measurements and metrics: The key measurements (Table 5) to follow should match with the agile goals to be attained (Table 10). The metrics should be defined unambiguously across the organization (e.g., "value" [28]).
• Innovation: Is there an overemphasis of (short-term) operative goals? Could fast/ continuous organizational learning be leveraged more for competitive and desirable products (new product development) and new business (product and service innovation) – c.f., Table 10? Each company should realize not only operative agility but also enterprise (business) agility strategically and manage accordingly [1].

- Future of agile: Each company should continuously realize possible impacts of digitalization – which may be even disruptive – in its business domain(s) and industry sector (Table 11). The selected agile means should be fitting (Fig. 1).

Theoretical Implications. Our survey instrument can be elaborated with theoretical viewpoints of agility:

- Certain different questions (currently 50 items in the questionnaire) could be analyzed in combinations in order to form higher-level understanding of their potential relationships in different organizations. For instance, the goals (Tables 6 and 10) and measurements (Table 5) could conceptually be linked together. We had such an initial conceptual research model underlying the current questionnaire design.
- Considering the focus areas of agility (Table 8), the results could be viewed from different perspectives such project/process perspective vs. product perspective vs. organizational perspective. That could be used to profile agility in different organizations. We have earlier designed a provisional agility profiler instrument and now this survey questionnaire could possibly be coupled with that [2]. In addition, we have earlier proposed an agile transformation model, which could also be joined [3].
- In general, digitalization may bring both internal (e.g., automation) and external (e.g., user experience) impacts to different software-intensive organizations in different industry sectors. Understanding the whole in different companies needs holistic frames and models in order to be able to align the strategic ends and to assess how the selected agile means contribute in the specific contexts (c.f., Table 11).

5.3   Threats to Validity and Limitations

Considering the comparability and generalization, we acknowledge that a construct validity concern in our questionnaire is whether all the respondents have interpreted and conceived all the terms in the survey questionnaire in the same way (e.g., 'agile transformation'). However, also for instance Rodríguez et al. did not limit the usage of agile with specific definitions [24]. A similar exploratory strategy by not giving preset terminology definitions has been used also for instance in the HELENA survey [23]. We do not consider internal validity to be a significant concern since the purpose of the survey is primarily exploratory rather than explanatory. We have thus been cautious not draw decisive conclusions in this study. External validity is limited by the background information collected (see Sect. 4.1). Research comparisons with industrial surveys (e.g., VersionOne [14]) should take possible biases into account.

The design of our web-tool based questionnaire was such that the respondents could skip questions. This produced a considerable amount of partially filled responses – not every respondent replied to all questions. In this paper, our inclusion criteria has been to take into account only finished respondents.

Due to the company-specific call-out (Sect. 3), sampling bias is a threat. With the social media distribution, the response rate is unspecified. A general limitation is that we did not ask the respondents to identify their organizations. Consequently, we cannot tell the number of different responding companies. Rodríguez et al. acknowledged the same constraint [24]. Due to those restrictions we refrain from evaluating how representative our respondent sample is with respect to all Finnish industries and companies. However, the respondents represented several domains (see Table 2).

6 Conclusions

In this paper we have presented and analyzed selected results of the survey study, that we have recently (2018) conducted in Finland. We examined how different software organizations currently perform agile software development, how they consider organizational agility and how they change. Digitalization in different industry sectors was one of our interest factors. The research results indicate that usual operative goals (productivity, quality) and responsiveness are the most important targets to attain by agile means. However, companies pay attention also to higher-level organizational goals and transformational aims for their agility.

Our current survey data opens up room for further research. There are several questions (50 altogether in the questionnaire) which were not covered in this paper. They deserve further analysis. One potential approach could be to use the industry sector (Table 2) and company size as the context variables, and to calculate possible correlations. In addition, more cross-tabulations could be done (c.f., Tables 7 and 9). One of our research hypotheses is that when the company management is committed and actively participating, the enterprise-level agile transformation becomes strategic and leads to determined, measured and sustainable effects (c.f., Table 8).

Furthermore, our future work plans include replicating the survey in other Nordic countries and annually in Finland. That would make it possible to conduct further comparative analysis and ascertain longer-term trends and evolutions – considering especially such factors as digital transformations in different industrial domains.

References

1. Kettunen, P., Laanti, M.: Future software organizations – agile goals and roles. Eur. J. Futures Res. **5**, 16 (2017)
2. Kettunen, P.: Systematizing software-development agility: toward an enterprise capability improvement framework. J. Enterp. Transform. **2**(2), 81–104 (2012)
3. Laanti, M.: Agile transformation model for large software development organizations. In: Tonelli, R., (ed.) Proceedings of the XP2017 Scientific Workshops, Article No. 19. ACM, New York (2017)
4. Mishra, A., Garbajosa, J., Wang, X., Bosch, J., Abrahamsson, P.: Future directions in Agile research: alignment and divergence between research and practice. J. Softw. Evol. Proc. **29**, e1884 (2017)
5. Ronzon, T., Buck, J., Eckstein, J.: Making companies nimble – from software agility to business agility. IEEE Softw. **36**(1), 79–85 (2019)
6. Prikladnicki, R., Lassenius, C., Carver, J.C.: Trends in agile: perspectives from the practitioners. IEEE Softw. **33**(6), 20–22 (2016)
7. Prikladnicki, R., Lassenius, C., Carver, J.C.: Trends in agile: from operational to strategic agility. IEEE Softw. **36**(1), 95–97 (2019)

8. Kettunen, P., Laanti, M., Fagerholm, F., Mikkonen, T., Männistö, T.: Finnish enterprise agile transformations: a survey study. In: Hoda, R. (ed.) XP 2019. LNBIP, vol. 364, pp. 97–104. Springer, Cham (2019). https://doi.org/10.1007/978-3-030-30126-2_12

9. Laanti, M., Kettunen, P.: SAFe adoptions in Finland: a survey research. In: Hoda, R. (ed.) XP 2019. LNBIP, vol. 364, pp. 81–87. Springer, Cham (2019). https://doi.org/10.1007/978-3-030-30126-2_10

10. Hoda, R., Salleh, N., Grundy, J.: The rise and evolution of agile software development. IEEE Softw. 35(5), 58–63 (2018)

11. Ebert, C., Paasivaara, M.: Scaling agile. IEEE Softw. 34(6), 98–103 (2017)

12. Kalenda, M., Hyna, P., Rossi, B.: Scaling agile in large organizations: practices, challenges, and success factors. J. Softw. Evol. Proc. 30, e1954 (2018)

13. Dikert, K., Paasivaara, M., Lassenius, C.: Challenges and success factors for large-scale agile transformations: a systematic literature review. J. Syst. Softw. 119, 87–108 (2016)

14. Version One 13th Annual State of Agile Report. https://stateofagile.versionone.com. Accessed 21 May 2019

15. Knauss, E.: The missing requirements perspective in large-scale agile system development. IEEE Softw. 36(3), 9–13 (2019)

16. Prikladnicki, R., Lassenius, C., Carver, J.C.: Trends in agile updated: perspectives from the practitioners. IEEE Softw. 35(1), 109–111 (2018)

17. Goldman, S.L., Nagel, R.N., Preiss, K.: Agile Competitors and Virtual Organizations: Strategies for Enriching the Customer. Van Nostrand Reinhold, New York (1995)

18. Conboy, K.: Agility from first principles: reconstructing the concept of agility in information systems development. Inf. Syst. Res. 20(3), 329–354 (2009)

19. Abrahamsson, P., Conboy, K., Wang, X.: 'Lots done, more to do': the current state of agile systems development research. Eur. J. Inf. Syst. 18, 281–284 (2009)

20. Dingsøyr, T., Dybå, T., Abrahamsson, P.: A preliminary roadmap for empirical research on agile software development. In: Melnik, G., Kruchten, P., Poppendieck, M. (eds.) Proceedings of the Agile 2008 Conference, pp. 83–94. IEEE, Los Alamistos (2008)

21. Moe, N.B., Dingsøyr, T.: Emerging research themes and updated research agenda for large-scale agile development: a summary of the 5th international workshop at XP2017. In: Tonelli, R., (ed.) Proceedings of the XP2017 Scientific Workshops, Article No. 14. ACM, New York (2017)

22. Laanti, M., Salo, O., Abrahamsson, P.: Agile methods rapidly replacing traditional methods at Nokia: a survey of opinions on agile transformation. Inf. Softw. Technol. 53(3), 276–290 (2011)

23. Kuhrmann, M., et al.: Hybrid software development approaches in practice: a European perspective. IEEE Softw. 36(4), 20–31 (2019)

24. Rodríguez, P., Markkula, J., Oivo, M., Turula, K.: Survey on agile and lean usage in finnish software industry. In: Runeson, P., Höst, M., Mendes, E., Andrews, A., Harrison, R. (eds.) ESEM 2012 ACM-IEEE International Symposium on Empirical Software Engineering and Measurement, pp. 139–148. ACM, New York (2012)

25. Finnish Software Industry Survey. http://www.softwareindustrysurvey.fi/focus-on-flexibility-agility-in-software-development/. Accessed 10 Mar 2019

26. Version One 12th Annual State of Agile Report. https://stateofagile.versionone.com. Accessed 10 Mar 2019

27. Kupiainen, E., Mäntylä, M.V., Itkonen, J.: Using metrics in agile and lean software development – a systematic literature review of industrial studies. Inf. Softw. Technol. 62, 143–163 (2015)

28. Alahyari, H., Berntsson Svensson, R., Gorschek, T.: A study of value in agile software development organizations. J. Syst. Softw. 125, 271–288 (2017)

Project Management

What's Hot in Product Roadmapping?
Key Practices and Success Factors

Jürgen Münch[1]([⊠]), Stefan Trieflinger[1]([⊠]), and Dominic Lang[2]([⊠])

[1] Reutlingen University, Alteburgstraße 150, 72768 Reutlingen, Germany
{juergen.muench,
stefan.trieflinger}@reutlingen-university.de
[2] Department of IT Coordination, Robert Bosch GmbH,
71636 Ludwigsburg, Germany
dominic.lang2@bosch.com

Abstract. Context: Organizations are increasingly challenged by dynamic and technical market environments. Traditional product roadmapping practices such as detailed and fixed long-term planning typically fail in such environments. Therefore, companies are actively seeking ways to improve their product roadmapping approach. **Goal:** This paper aims at identifying problems and challenges with respect to product roadmapping. In addition, it aims at understanding how companies succeed in improving their roadmapping practices in their respective company contexts. The study focuses on mid-sized and large companies developing software-intensive products in dynamic and technical market environments. **Method:** We conducted semi-structured expert interviews with 15 experts from 13 German companies and conducted a thematic data analysis. **Results:** The analysis showed that a significant number of companies is still struggling with traditional feature-based product-roadmapping and opinion-based prioritization of features. The most promising areas for improvement are stating the outcomes a company is trying to achieve and making them part of the roadmap, sharing or co-developing the roadmap with stakeholders, and the establishing discovery activities.

Keywords: Product management · Product strategy · Product roadmap · Roadmapping · Product discovery · Agile transformation · Product design · Innovation

1 Introduction

For each company it is essential to provide a strategic direction, in which the product offering will be developed over time in order to achieve the corporate vision. In general, the purpose of a roadmap is to provide essential understanding, proximity, direction and some degree of certainty regarding the planning of a journey [1]. In companies, roadmaps are strategic tools, which can take various forms such as product roadmaps, technology roadmaps, industry roadmaps or science roadmaps [2]. From the point of view of product management, a product roadmap describes how an organization intends to achieve a product vision. It should focus on the value it aims to deliver to its customers and the organization itself in order to rally support and coordinate

© Springer Nature Switzerland AG 2019
X. Franch et al. (Eds.): PROFES 2019, LNCS 11915, pp. 401–416, 2019.
https://doi.org/10.1007/978-3-030-35333-9_29

effort among stakeholders [3]. Currently, the product roadmaps of many organizations cover long time horizons and concrete products, features or services together with precise release dates [4]. These so-called feature-based roadmaps are created to inform stakeholders or customers about the point in time a product, feature or service is expected for market launch [5]. This approach worked well in market environments that are predicable, stable and reliable. However, through increasing market dynamics, rapidly evolving technologies and shifting user expectations, coupled with the adoption of lean and agile practices it becomes almost impossible to predict which product, feature or services will satisfy the need of the customer and the organization. Thus, companies are increasingly struggling with their ability to plan their product portfolio and it seems that the traditional process of product roadmap creation does not fulfill its purpose anymore [3, 5].

This article aims at identifying the state-of-the-practice of mid-sized and large German companies with respect to current product roadmapping practices. This includes challenges and success factors regarding the product roadmapping process. The outline of the paper is as follows: Sect. 2 sketches related work. Section 3 presents the study approach including the research questions, the applied research method, the execution of the study as well as the discussion of validity. The results of the study are discussed in Sect. 4. Finally, the main findings are summarized, and further research is outlined.

2   Related Work

Roadmapping is known as a flexible technique for exploring and communicating the dynamic linkage between markets, products and technologies over time [6, 7]. Groenveld defines roadmapping as a process that contributes to the integration of business and technology by displaying the interaction between products and technologies over time and taking into consideration short- and long-term product and technology aspects [8]. The practice of roadmapping typically involves social mechanisms as this process connects people of different functions and allows them to share different information and perspectives [1, 9]. According to Groenveld roadmapping must be seen as an ongoing process and differs from one company to another [8]. Several studies exist that focus on analyzing challenges with respect to roadmapping. Example studies are:

DeGregorio interviewed 500 companies in order to identify the key problems regarding product roadmapping. The author pointed out that the information and the knowledge in order to create the roadmap is often missing or incorrect. Typical examples are, that the information is nonexistent, hidden in documents or that roadmap elements are not tied to actual product plans and product requirements. Furthermore, the author mentioned that more problems exist, and the findings are just the tip of the iceberg [10].

Komssi et al. conducted an action research study and identified the following problems with respect to roadmapping [11]: (1) trouble with linking business strategy to solution planning; (2) a feature-driven mindset, i.e., the discussion about long-term planning focuses too much on low-level components; (3) the difficulty to understand the customer needs in order to develop services. Overall the author recommends that companies have to link their strategy and release planning and improve their roadmapping practice.

Pora et al. identified challenges and categorized them into the three categories "people", "process", and "data" [12]. The challenges in the category "people" are the commitment of the management and the selection of the right key players in order to create a roadmap. The category "process" consists of the six challenges: (1) initialization of the roadmapping process; (2) choosing and customizing the appropriate roadmapping approach; (3) facilitation of workshops to generate and share the knowledge required for the roadmapping process; (4) alignment of organizational KPIs with roadmapping; (5) current rules and work procedures in an organisation do not support a rapidly changing business environment; (6) the prediction of future events based on limited availability of data. Challenges in the category "data" consist of (1) prediction of future events due to limited availability of data on new and emerging technologies or market forces; (2) frequent updates to reflect changes; (3) disruptive changes are irrelevant for ongoing roadmaps.

Most of the existing studies are not focussing on companies developing software-intensive products in dynamic technical and market environments. This is the focus of the study presented in this article. An exception is the study by Pora et al. [12]. Pora et al. conducted a case study in a similar context. However, only four companies were investigated in this study and thus further research is necessary. Moreover, the study presented in this article focuses on German companies.

3 Study Approach

Based on the study goals, the following research questions were defined:

RQ1: What approaches, procedures and methods for creating and updating a product roadmap are currently applied at companies developing software-intensive pro ducts in dynamic and technical market environments?
RQ2: What challenges are associated with product roadmapping?
RQ3: What are the success factors of product roadmapping?

It should be mentioned that RQ1 is intentionally defined for a broader scope than the one covered in this study in order to consider also future research. The precise version of RQ1 that is addressed in this article is: "what approaches, procedures and methods for creating and updating a product roadmap are currently applied at the 13 case companies?".

In order to achieve our objective a qualitative study design was chosen as the study aims at identifying new insights. Therefore, the experience, opinions and views of experts needed to be obtained. The qualitative interview study was preferred over a quantitative method. Fink identifies several opportunities, in which a qualitative method is appropriate. The following four aspects are relevant regarding this study: (1) the study is focused on investigating the knowledge and opinions of experts in a particular field; (2) the study intends to collect information through interviews with own words rather than with using predefined choices; (3) there is not enough prior information of the study subject to enable either the use of standardized measures of the construction or a formal questionnaire; (4) the sample size is limited due to access or resource constraints [13]. Semi-structured individual expert interviews with industry practitioners were used to collect data since it provides a mixture of open-ended and specific questions and is flexible enough to allow unforeseen types of information [14]. Moreover, semi-structured expert interviews allow interviewees to share their own opinion by using free speech, but at the same time provide a similar structure for all interviews, which makes results comparable and patterns visible [15]. In order to focus and structure the interviews and to ensure thematic comparability, an interview guide was developed (the complete interview guide is available on Figshare [16]). The interview guide aims at assuring that important aspects are not ignored. For preparation purposes the interview guide was sent to the interviewees in advance. An evaluation of the interview guide was conducted with four experts with different roles at the Robert Bosch Smart Home GmbH in the context of a pilot study [5].

Study Execution

We recruited 15 experts from 13 companies, which operate in a dynamic and uncertain market environment. We selected the interviews based on their experience regarding product roadmapping. The search for suitable participants and the subsequent establishment of contact was conducted via a social business platform in order to find appropriate business contacts. We conducted preliminary discussions with each potential participant to ensure that the selected interviewees are suitable for our research. Table 1 gives an overview of the participants who voluntarily participated in this study. The column "Experience" refers to the amount of years in which the person was involved in roadmapping activities. The range spanning of experience was between 2 and 17 years with an average of 7 years.

The interviews took place from February to April 2019. Two interviews were conducted face-to-face in the office of the case company, while 13 interviews were conducted via phone. All interviews were led by the same researcher. The average length of the interviews was 38 min, with the range spanning between 32 and 57 min. All interviews were conducted in German language. The audio was recorded for accurate data analysis. We analyzed the data by creating transcriptions word by word, highlighting main responses and interpreting and extracting keywords and key quotes.

Table 1. Participants of the expert interviews

Interviewee	Position	Experience	Company size by no. of employees
Interviewee 1	Product manager	4 years	Small
Interviewee 2	Product manger	9 years	Medium
Interviewee 3	Innovation manager	3 years	Large
Interviewee 4	Product manager	10 years	Large
Interviewee 5	Product manager	2 years	Medium
Interviewee 6	Product manager	7.5 years	Medium
Interviewee 7	Product manager	7 years	Medium
Interviewee 8	Head of product management	6 years	Large
Interviewee 9	Head of product management	8 years	Medium
Interviewee 10	Head of product management	17 years	Medium
Interviewee 11	Head of product management	7 years	Medium
Interviewee 12	Head of product management	5 years	Small
Interviewee 13	Head of product management	11 years	Medium
Interviewee 14	Head of product management	6 years	Medium
Interviewee 15	Head of product management	8 years	Medium

Validity

Different frameworks exist for assessing the validity and trustworthiness of qualitative studies. We use the framework proposed by Yin [17] as the basis for the discussion of the validity of our study. Internal validity is not discussed since causal relationships were not examined in the present study. **Construct validity:** As a means for establishing construct validity the goal and the purpose of the interviews were explained to the interviewees before the interviews. In addition, the way of data collection through semi-structured interviews allowed for asking clarifying questions and avoiding misunderstandings. **External validity:** The external validity is restricted due to the limited number of participants and because the results are derived from German companies that operate in an uncertain and dynamic market environment (e.g., smart home). Thus, the results are not directly transferable to other industry sectors. **Reliability:** The reliability was supported by providing an interview guide that is publicly available. The analysis has been conducted in a systematic and repeatable way. Therefore, a replication of the study and a reduction of researcher bias is supported.

4 Results

4.1 Product Roadmapping Practices

In order to answer RQ1 we analyzed the information from interviews and figured out that despite there are a lot of common practices, the companies have a quite individual approach to roadmapping. In order to compare the different practices, we used an existing schema for describing the nine main dimensions of product roadmapping approaches [18]. In the following, the results are described along these dimensions:

Roadmap Items: First of all, we analyze which items (i.e., which kind of information artifacts) have been found in the roadmaps. Typical examples for roadmap items are outputs (i.e., products, features, deliverables), goals/outcomes, topics (i.e., generic subject), or themes (i.e., high-level user need, or system need). The study shows that seven out of 13 companies are using products or features without goals. The roadmap of two companies includes goals such as "increase the number of payed users of our digital service" or "Increase the value of in-app purchases by 15%." The roadmap of two companies contains topics such as "development of a solution in the area of smart home". Two companies are using themes such as "feeling safe at home" or "check your home, wherever you are" as roadmap items. Only few companies actively use goals or outcomes in the roadmap. For instance, one head of product stated that their *"roadmap includes goals because the management or the customer considers a feature as a commitment. However, the roadmap is a living document that can frequently change at any time"* (head of product management). Another product manager mentioned that outcomes are more suitable as a basis to create product roadmaps: *"When we talk about goals or visions, we don't want to mix them up with solutions. That means that we [...] aim at delivering value for the business and for the customers. Therefore, we emphasize outcomes over outputs on our roadmap."* (product manager).

Adequacy of Item Detailing Based on the Timeline: The adequacy of the item detailing answers the question how detailed the items are planned with respect to short-, mid-, and long-term timeframes. This dimension is important because in dynamic environments with high uncertainty it often does not make sense to have a fine-grained planning of all the details in the long-term timeframe. The analysis of the interviews shows that companies whose roadmap contains only features or products without goals or outcomes typically use a detailed planning over a long-time horizon. This means that all features and all respective tasks for developing those features are planned and worked out in detail for short-, mid-, and long-term. Companies that are using goals as part of their roadmap have different levels of planning detail for different timeframes. This means, that the planning of items is more detailed the closer they are in time. One participant said: *"I would never plan the roadmap in detail for one year. In this case, the high level of market dynamic would lead to a lot of effort in order to adjust the roadmap. My planning is only for short-term items in detail, the mid- and long-term consists only of topics or ideas. In general, only as detailed as necessary."* (head of product management). This indicates that roadmaps are likely to fail when their level of detailing is not adequate. Another participant mentioned that *"due to the dynamic and uncertain market environment, detailed planned roadmaps over a long time-horizon* *make no sense as the predicted planning will not be achieved. Therefore, our roadmap contains a detailed planning for the short-term, the mid-term includes so-called candidate features, which are under evaluation and the long-term roadmap involves only ideas or high-level topics." (product manager).*

Reliability: The reliability can be seen as the trustworthiness of a roadmap and its ability to provide direction for an organization and its teams. This very much depends on the amount and frequency of changes and the way how changes are done. Five companies reported that their roadmaps are subject to frequent ad hoc adjustments. Within two companies the adjustments of the product roadmap are done in regular review cycles: *"The roadmap is usually changed after our quarterly planning meetings, in which we analyze the current market situation." (product manager)* Six companies change their roadmap through a systematic change management and adjustments are done reactively: *"A typical situation for an adjustment is that we must react to a market launch of an innovative product of a competitor. In such a case the product owner proposes how the change should be conducted and coordinates this change with the management." (product manager).* The analysis shows that frequent ad hoc changes of the roadmap occur in such companies where products are planned in detail over a long-time horizon. These problems decrease the acceptance of a roadmap and it is likely that *"each product owner has, in addition to the official roadmap, a separate backlog. This is sorted by priority, relevance, return on invest, outcome and so on." (product manager).* The analysis shows that roadmaps containing goals, topics or outcomes are more likely to be subject to systematic adjustments and less subject to ad hoc changes. These systematic adjustments increase the reliability of roadmaps, which can be seen as a prerequisite for their successful usage.

Confidence: The confidence describes the ability of a feature in the roadmap with regards to the fulfillment of the expected goals/outcomes at acceptable cost. In consequence, the confidence should significantly affect the probability that a feature is decided to be implemented. One participant mentioned that *"the product management has the task to ensure that every product contributes to our goals and vision." (product manager).* Another participant said: *"Before we include a product in the roadmap, we have a strategic meeting which includes the validation of the contribution a product delivers in order to achieve our goals." (product manager).* 12 out of 13 companies consider the impacts of roadmap items on goals. This is done mainly based on assumptions and estimates and rarely on empirical facts. One participant mentioned that they try to evaluate the cost and impact of features through expert interviews. He mentioned that *"regarding features where [they] are not sure about the costs and value creation for customers, [they] conduct interviews with experts." (product manager).* One company is using advanced product discovery methods in order to validate the impacts of products or features upfront. Thereby it increases the confidence that the product or feature will have the expected effect after implementation and delivery.

Discovery: The dimension discovery describes the ability of a company to identify and validate items on the roadmap before implementation. In six companies no product discovery is conducted at all. Four companies assess features based on expert knowledge without further validation. A participant said: *"I think product discovery is not relevant for a service platform. In our processes the product manager determines which product will be put onto the roadmap"* (head of product management) Another interviewee mentioned: *"We don't talk with the customer, but the product managers estimate whether the product will be successful in the market. Very often I hear: 'The product is innovative; I think the customer will buy it.'"* (head of product management). Two companies decide about product roadmap items based on customer requests. One interviewee explained: *"We have the service or sales team, which the customers can contact in the case of questions, problems and wishes. I interview these people in regular time intervals in order to identify the wishes of our customers."* (head of product management). Seven companies are conducting some kind of discovery activities by involving the customer more actively. One participant, for instance, mentioned: *"We organize workshops in which we invite a selection of users to participate. The purpose of such workshops is identifying what pain points the customers have, how the customers are solving their problems today and what kind of solution we must provide, that leads to a change of customer behavior."* (head of product management) Another participant explained: *"We invite potential customers to visit us and test our prototypes for new product ideas. While testing we observe the customers and conduct an interview with each person after the observation. The result of the observation and the feedback is used in order to improve our prototypes."* (product manager).

Prioritization: This dimension addresses how roadmap items are prioritized and which factors are taken into consideration. Nine companies prioritize the roadmap items mainly based on expert opinions. One company conducts the prioritization of the roadmap items based on the capability to deliver: *"I prioritize the features mainly according to "quick wins", as they can be quickly implemented and deliver quickly a value to our business. Furthermore, I discuss the prioritization with the engineering and adjust it if necessary."* (head of product management) Three companies conduct the prioritization based on a process with the focus on delivering value to customer and the business. One approach is *"[...] to answer the question: Which items deliver the most value to the company? Therefore, a team consisting of me, the product manager, the product owner and the head of engineering conducts the evaluation process. We choose these different participants as they consider the items from different views. In more detail, the product manager is responsible for all products and evaluates that all products contribute to achieve our goals, the product owner manages the requirements to build each product and the head of engineering is responsible for the technical implementation of the products. Within the evaluation we score each item with points from one to four according to the following criteria: 'development effort', 'costs', 'value for the customer', 'feasibility', 'market relevance' and 'strategic alignment'. After the evaluation, the total score of each item is calculated and compared with the other items. The higher the total number of points, the higher is the value of the item in the context of the company's vision and thus also the prioritization within the roadmap."* (product manager). Another participant reported about their approach: *"We developed a metric using the following criteria: customer and market value and positioning in relation to our competition and profitability. On the basis of these* *criteria we calculate the value of each item and this determines the prioritization."* *(product manager).* Estimation procedures are often applied. In the words of one participant: *"In order to conduct the prioritization we estimate the following criteria: What is the business value of the outcome? How high is the effort and which uncertainty factors are existing? We put these three criteria into relation and prioritize the items accordingly." (head of product management).* The analysis of the interviews showed that prioritization procedures foster the creation of customer value and an optimized resource allocation. However, the prioritization is usually based on subjective estimations or expert opinions and not on empirical facts.

Extent of Alignment: This dimension specifies the width and depth of alignment of the roadmap, i.e., how good the stakeholder coverage is and how deep they are involved and how well they understand their respective roles. When talking about alignment, most of the analysed companies understand the benefits of stakeholder alignment and referred to the number of roadmaps that they are using. Nine companies are using several roadmaps that cover different views, e.g., the engineering or the sales view. One participant reported: *"Each department that delivers services to the customer has its own product roadmap and there is another roadmap for the management that contains all products." (product manager).* Four companies are using only one roadmap that is used as orientation for all departments and teams and one of them is having *"a central roadmap that everybody knows. Based on this roadmap, every department is aligning its tasks and measures." (head of product management).*

Ownership and Responsibility: Ownership refers to the question "Who owns the roadmap and is accountable, i.e., signs off and approves the roadmap?" Responsibility refers to the question "Who is responsible for the definition of the roadmap and the conduction of the product roadmapping process?" This dimension can influence the success of the whole roadmapping process. One interviewee mentioned: *"After the development of the roadmap [...] usually the head of product management presents the roadmap to the management and based on the opinion of the management adjustments take place. After the management has approved the roadmap it will be communicated across the company as well as to customers or stakeholders." (product manager).* Overall, the approach that the management approves the roadmap and releases budget for further activities regarding the roadmap items is applied by each company participating in the study. In each company, product management creates, maintains, and manages the product roadmap.

4.2 Challenges

The uncertain and dynamic market environment poses different challenges: *"Currently we have to deal with many uncertainties and permanent changes of requirements." (product manager).* Furthermore, there are internal processes and stakeholders that lead to unforeseen changes of the roadmap: *"Due to the rapid changes of the market it happens that a department has the feeling that it is no longer valuable for the company. Therefore, it wants to show, that it is still important. And suddenly, a new product pops up with the demand to introduce it into the market. Usually this leads to a shifting of capacity and leads to the circumstances that other planned and approved products are not delivered on time." (head of product management).* Rapid market changes require the ability to face and manage uncertainties. However, many companies lack a process that is able to cope with uncertainty: *"Our current process is designed for the entry and change of requirements once or twice a year, and this is not often enough." (product manager).*

The roadmap of seven companies covers a long time-horizon. Thus *"[..] one challenge is to provide a reliable roadmap over a long time period [although] there are a lot of uncertain variables [...]. As result we have to frequently update our roadmap." (product manager).* This decreases the reliability of the roadmap and employees consider the roadmap not as a trusted planning tool. Moreover, replanning consumes a lot of capacity of the participating employees which could be used more efficiently. In a nutshell: *"As soon as a roadmap is planned in detail and in long-term, it becomes difficult. For example, during development you learn a lot about the customer and their needs. This means a shifting of the requirements and deadlines, which leads to a constant adjustment of the roadmap." (product manager).*

The behaviors of the management, marketing, and sales also provide several challenges. *"One challenge are the members of the management of the various business areas who know exactly which feature the customer needs." (head of product management).* Typically, the management defines concrete features based on its own opinion without validation. Moreover, management is often only willing to provide budget for products and features it proposed itself. This often leads to the development of product and features that are not or rarely used. In addition, management and sales often see the roadmap as an obligation that all products or features are available at the specified release dates, e.g., for a market launch. *"The management or the sales department think that the data in the roadmap is always correct and never changing. However, the roadmap is a living document that frequently changes during a month. The problem is if they communicate specific dates to the customer. This leads to long discussions and disappointments [...]." (head of product management).* Moreover, the prediction of the expected market launches of a product is also considered as a challenge. *"The management or the stakeholders expect an exact information to which point in time a product is ready to market launch. However, predictions over a long time period are very difficult to make and in the most cases this information is wrong [...].".* This leads to circumstances where the roadmap contains incorrect but binding information. Typical consequences are missing deadlines, budget overruns, poor quality or decreasing team motivation which in turn lead to disappointed customers and stakeholders. The pressure to still fulfil the roadmap promises keeps the team from doing the right things. Adding to that, another interviewee mentioned: *"Often management has a precise idea how a roadmap must look like. I have observed that product managers know that the current product roadmapping process doesn't work, but they are afraid to try out new methods." (product manager).* This triggers frustration and leads to a culture in which the employees are trying to avoid mistakes.

However, the interviews have shown that this case also occurs vice versa. *"Our culture is very experimental, and we always try to introduce new methods. This is often difficult for [employees]. Because they are habitual to use a standard procedure."* (product manager).

The interviews also revealed conflicts between the business and the engineering. One participant mentioned, for instance, that *"the engineering has no understanding for the achievement of short-term business goals such as a quick and small product launch in order to enter quickly into a market. The reason is that they would like to deliver a complete functional product. On the other hand, the sales department has no understanding for technological limitations. They have their requirements and expect that the engineering department integrates these requirements without any delay. This leads again and again to conflicts."* (head of product management). However, for sales and marketing the reliability of the roadmap is an important topic in order to plan activities such as campaigns. *"If sales or marketing people look into the roadmap, the data it contains has to be reliable, especially the information to which point in time a product, feature or service will be available."* (product manager).

Another challenge is to identify and apply a method for prioritizing the items in the roadmap. *"We have developed a metric with different factors in order to determine the prioritization for each product. Sometimes I get results and think: That can't be correct. In my opinion the other product is more important in order to reach our goals. Thus, the use of mathematical methods with respect to roadmapping is very limited."* (head of product management). Besides that, there are also challenges to obtain the information for the prioritization process. *"In order to prioritize the requirements, I am missing important information such as: By how much would the product increase our margin? – or – which time is estimated to finish the product development? Such input is often missing, and this makes it very difficult to prioritize all the requirements."* (product manager).

Several challenges occur in the case of systems (such as an IoT system consisting of several hardware components, sensors and an app). *"A challenge is to identify the dependencies of the products (which components are required at which point of time) in an early phase and to document them in the roadmap. Furthermore, the different components are delivered by different teams. For this reason, it is difficult to obtain the current state of the implementation from each team in order to react to delays in an early stage."* (product manager). This might, for instance, increase the risk of a delayed market launch. A related challenge is to align the development of different products that belong together: *"Our organization is focused on the development of individual products, not systems. This means, each department has its own roadmap. In order to deliver all required products at the same time the challenge is to merge the different information in one central roadmap."* (product manager).

Another challenge is to motivate all relevant stakeholders to be an active part of the development of the product roadmap. It is difficult to integrate the relevant stakeholder and employees in a way that they are aligned to the roadmap and collaborate. Table 2 gives an overview of the main challenges that were mentioned in these interviews.

Table 2. Challenges of product roadmapping

Product roadmapping – current challenges
Technologies and markets change rapidly
Feature-based-roadmaps need to be changed frequently
Frequent changes consume a lot of capacity and employees lose trust in the roadmap
The internal processes are not suitable to handle frequent changes of the roadmap
Need for differentiation with respect to short-, mid- and long-term timeframe is made
Roadmap contains unrealistic and incorrect information
Marketing and sales ask for accurate long-term predictions for release dates in order to plan their activities (such as campaigns, industry events)
The roadmap owner prescribes roadmap features and overrules product management.
Relevant information for prioritizing the roadmap is missing
The management of dependencies is difficult
It is difficult to motivate stakeholders to actively participate in the roadmapping process
Management assesses its employees by how well they implement a feature-based roadmap regarding time and scope
The employees do not trust in the roadmap, i.e., the roadmap is not reliable

4.3   Success Factors

Several participants mentioned that it is important to customize new roadmapping practices to their specific context (including higher-level processes, development environment, organizational structures, roles). The usage of off-the-shelf approaches without tailoring them to the company context is not seen as an appropriate way in order to establish roadmapping practices successfully. One participant mentioned that *"[...] there is no standard process for roadmapping. It is important to test, evaluate and adapt the product roadmapping process [..]."* (head of product management). Several participants also highlighted that the process of adapting a new roadmapping approach is an incremental process that might take a longer time period and cannot be done at one go.

Another important success factor that was mentioned by several participants is that a roadmap should look differently for different timeframes. Different timeframes in the roadmap should have different planning levels (e.g., more detailed planning for the short term) and different types of items (e.g., planning of themes instead of features for the long term). A participant said that *"in a dynamic and uncertain market environment it makes no sense to create a detailed roadmap for one year. In my opinion the suitable period of time for a roadmap depends on the market in which a company operates. Very important is the quality of the information provided in order to determine the different roadmap items."* (product manager). These aspects significantly affect the necessity for frequent changes of the roadmap and thereby influence the reliability of the roadmap. Only if the time horizon, the level of detail, and the item type are adequate to the timeframe, the need of changes is low, and they can be managed systematically. This allows managers and employees to feel comfortable working with the roadmap and they can rely on it as an instrument which is providing orientation and guidance.

Another major success factor that was mentioned is that clear strategic objectives should be specified and communicated. A participant mentioned that *"each product to be developed should contribute to achieve our goals and vision. If this is not the case, there are always ambiguities and misunderstandings that lead to frequent adjustments of the roadmap." (product manager).* In this context it is essential to define a clear and understandable vision and communicate it across the company. Furthermore, the business and customer objectives should be derived from this vision. The contribution of roadmap items to these objectives should be clearly expressed and evaluated. It should be clear which value each feature on the roadmap delivers in order to contribute to achieve the company's goals. A clear vision and goals that contribute to that vision also help to prioritize items on the roadmap.

Several participants mentioned that it is important for the success of a roadmap that roadmap items are validated with respect to their underlying assumptions (such as "Is there a customer need for that feature?", "Is the problem to be solved important?", "Are there enough customers that have this problem?", "Is it feasible to implement the feature?", "Does the feature have the expected outcome?") before implementation. This should be done on a continuous basis. A participant mentioned the following: *"In the past we saw again and again that we developed a product which had little demand from the market. Therefore, we need a process that identifies the problems and needs of the customer. It is not enough to talk with the key account manager about customers. Moreover, periodical checks regarding the roadmap should be conducted in order to review that the roadmap still correspond to current market conditions." (head of product management).* A thorough validation of roadmap items before implementation requires the integration of discovery activities in the product development process.

Involving all relevant stakeholders was also considered as a key success factor for the roadmapping process. One interviewee mentioned that *"[...] a clear process to determine the items for the roadmap is necessary. This means a cross-functional collaboration of the different stakeholders and departments (e.g., management and discovery). It does not make sense that one person is responsible to fill the roadmap based on his opinion. Moreover, meetings are also not suitable to talk about the topic 'product roadmap', because usually the time is too short. Rather the roadmap should be discussed in the context of two or three full-day sessions." (product manager).* A participant mentioned that you can see the success of alignment if *"a stakeholder looks at the roadmap and [] understands it immediately." (product manager)*

Different representations of the roadmap are an important factor for meeting the requirements of the various stakeholder and for keeping the roadmap understandable. A participant mentioned: *"The management does not have the time to read all the detailed information that is important for product management. For this reason, we create a management summary in which only the most important information is included." (head of product management).* Also, several interviewees mentioned the quality of the communication and alignment as success factor: *"In order for the roadmapping process to work, it is essential that there is good communication among all stakeholders. For example, in order to manage the product roadmap a product manager requires all information and must know all dependencies of the products."* *(product manager).*

The right mindset of the organization is another key factor for success. A participant mentioned that *"freedom and responsibility are very important for roadmapping and product development processes. This means that employees should not be put under pressure but receive the freedom to unfold."* *(product manager).* Top-level management should be involved early in the product roadmapping process and should give product management the necessary freedom to create and manage the product roadmap. Furthermore, the decisions regarding the roadmap (e.g., prioritization of a new item) should not be taken emotionally. One participant said: *"Usually the idea finder is very enthusiastic about the implementation of his idea. However, it might be that the management or other colleagues have the opinion that the proposed product does not fit into the overall strategic direction. This leads to many discussions on an emotional level."* *(product manager).*

Last but not least, several interviewees mentioned the culture and values lived in a company as success factors. Important for the success of a roadmap is a *"management that doesn't expect a one-year roadmap and then measures the employees how well this roadmap has been executed by the initial plan, but a management that has understood that there is a dynamic and uncertain market, in which long-term planning is almost impossible. Moreover, values such as openness, respect or honesty are important for the roadmapping process, which leads to a good working atmosphere and to more collaboration among different stakeholders."* *(product manager).* Table 3 gives an overview of the identified success factors.

Table 3. Success factors for product roadmapping

Product roadmapping – success factors
Management does not expect a detailed planned roadmap over a long time-horizon
The level of planning detail and the item types in the roadmap vary with different timeframes
Changes to the roadmap are clearly justified
The roadmap is aligned with the company vision and the product vision
The product vision and strategic objectives are clearly stated and communicated
The contribution of roadmap items to higher-level goals (up to the vision) is determined
The contribution of roadmap features with respect to their outcomes is validated before implementation (especially for the short-term timeframe)
Product discovery methods are integrated into the roadmapping process
A clear process for prioritization and decision making is established based on high quality information input
All relevant stakeholders are involved in the creation and evolution of the roadmap
Different consistent representations of the roadmap for different stakeholders exist
The organizational culture values openness, respect, and honesty

5 Conclusion

The results of the study show that those companies that have already implemented fairly mature product roadmapping practices are especially strong with respect to the dimensions "roadmap items", "adequacy of item detailing based on the timeline" and roadmap "reliability". This means, that they treat different timeframes differently with respect to the detailing level and the type of items in the roadmap. Companies that show a high level of product roadmapping maturity change or update their roadmaps in a way that stakeholders trust these changes and can reliably use the roadmap for their tasks. The study revealed that frequent ad hoc adjustments usually occur in organizations where products or features are planned in detail over a long-time horizon. These frequent adjustments of the roadmaps typically lead to a decrease in reliability and trustworthiness of the product roadmap. Reliability and trust can be seen as indispensable for the acceptance and successful usage of a roadmap. The study shows that many of the participating companies see product discovery activities as a necessity to identify and validate features. However, many of the companies participating in the study currently have not yet integrated product discovery activities systematically in their roadmapping process. The study also shows that the right prioritization fosters the creation of customer value and an optimized resource allocation. The most promising areas for improvement are stating outcomes a company is trying to achieve and making them part of the roadmap, sharing or co-developing the roadmap with stakeholders, and establishing discovery activities. Overall, many companies have already a good understanding of success factors for roadmapping processes in dynamic environments. However, they are currently struggling with overcoming key challenges. Further research is planned to increase the external validity of the findings and to explore possible ways to improve product roadmapping practices in different organizational contexts. In detail the authors use the findings of this study to develop a maturity model with which practitioners can assess their current product roadmapping practices. This maturity model also aims at identifying potentials for a sustainable improvement of their product roadmapping process.

Acknowledgements. We wish to thank the participants in the study for their time and contributions.

References

1. Kostoff, R.N., Schaller, R.: Science and technology roadmaps. IEEE Trans. Eng. Manag. **48**(2), 132–143 (2001)
2. Kameoka, A., Kuwahara, T., Li, M.: Integrated strategy development: an integrated roadmapping approach. In: PICMET 2003: Portland International Conference on Management of Engineering and Technology Management for Reshaping the World, Portland, OR, USA, pp. 370–379 (2003)
3. Lombardo, C.T., McCarthy, B., Ryan, E., Conners, M.: Product Roadmaps Relaunched - How to Set Direction While Embracing Uncertainty. O'Reilly Media Inc., Gravenstein Highway North, Sebastopol (2017)

4. Münch J., Trieflinger S., Lang, D.: Product roadmap – from vision to reality: a systematic literature review. In: ICE/IEEE ITMC: International Conference on Engineering, Technology and Innovation, Valbonne, France (2019)
5. Münch J., Trieflinger S., Lang, D.: Why feature based roadmaps fail in rapidly changing markets: a qualitative survey. In: International workshop on Software-Intensive Business: Start-Ups, Ecosystems and Platforms, Espoo, Finland, pp. 202–218 (2018)
6. Euiyoung, K., Beckman, S.L., Agogino, A.: Design roadmapping in an uncertain world: implementing a customer-experience-focused strategy. Calif. Manag. Rev. **61**(1), 43–70 (2018)
7. Phaal, R., Farrukh, C.J.P., David, R.: Technology roadmapping—A planning framework for evolution and revolution. Technol. Forecast. Soc. Change **71**(1–2), 5–26 (2004)
8. Groenveld, P.: Roadmapping integrates business and technology. Res.-Technol. Manag. **40**(5), 48–55 (1997)
9. Lehtola, L., Kauppinen, M., Kujala, S.: Linking the business view to requirements engineering: long-term product planning by roadmapping. In: 13th IEEE International Conference on Requirements Engineering, RE 2005, Paris, France, pp. 439–443 (2005)
10. DeGregorio, G.: Technology management via a set of dynamically linked roadmaps. In: Proceedings of the 2000 IEEE Engineering Management Society, Albuquerque, NM, USA, pp. 184–190 (2000)
11. Komssi, M., Kauppinen M., Töhönen H., Lehtola L., Davis, A.M.: Integrating analysis of customers processes into roadmapping: the value-creation perspective. In: 2011 IEEE 19th International Requirements Engineering Conference, Trento, Italy, pp. 57–66 (2011)
12. Pora, U., Thawesaengskulthai, N.: Data-driven roadmapping turning challenges into opportunities. In: 2018 Portland International Conference on Management of Engineering and Technology (PICMET), Honolulu, HI, USA, pp. 1–11 (2018)
13. Fink, A.: Analysis on Qualitative Surveys. In: Fink, A. (ed.) The Survey Handbook, pp. 61–78. SAGE Publications, Thousand Oaks (2003)
14. Edwards, R., Holland, J.: What is Qualitative Interviewing?. Bloomsbury, London, New York (2013)
15. Bryman, A., Bell, E.: Business Research Methods, 4th edn. Oxford University Press, New York (2015)
16. Published on Figshare. https://figshare.com/s/2f872ac9997d6860640c. Accessed 14 June 2019
17. Yin, R.K.: Case Study Research: Design and Methods, 5th edn. SAGE Publications Inc., London (2014)
18. Münch, J., Trieflinger, S., Lang D.: DEEP: the product roadmap maturity model. In: Submitted to: International Workshop on Software-Intensive Business: Start-Ups, Ecosystems and Platforms, Tallinn, Estonia (2019)

Integrating Data Protection into the Software Life Cycle

Ralf Kneuper$^{(\boxtimes)}$ ID

IUBH University of Applied Sciences—Distance Learning,
Kaiserplatz 1, 83435 Bad Reichenhall, Germany
r.kneuper@iubh-fernstudium.de

Abstract. Data protection has become increasingly important in recent years, partly due to the EU General Data Protection Regulation (GDPR) and similar legislations in other countries, but also because of various privacy scandals which led to bad press for the affected companies. Since most of the processing of the relevant personal data is performed by software, data protection needs to be addressed in the development of software. This paper therefore investigates how to incorporate data protection in the software life cycle. Based on a simple default life cycle model, the main questions to ask and issues to address in the various phases are summarized. These questions and issues are independent of the exact life cycle model used, whether plan-driven, agile or some hybrid, and can therefore easily be mapped to some other model. Not surprisingly, data protection mainly affects the analysis and design of software systems ("privacy by design") when the data to be processed and stored as well as the form of processing and the protection mechanisms to be used are defined. Nevertheless, to some extent the entire life cycle down to withdrawal is affected.

Keywords: Data protection · Software life cycle · Data protection by design · Privacy

1 Introduction

With the increasing amount of (personal) data collected and processed over the last decades, rules limiting the collection and processing of personal data and ensuring fair use have become increasingly important. This is reflected by the fact that most countries today have some form of data protection legislation defining what is considered adequate and fair, based on similar but not identical concepts across the different countries.

One of the most widely known and arguably most important such data protection legislation is the *General Data Protection Regulation (GDPR)*, which came into effect in the European Union in May 2018. Although most of its requirements are not really new, the GDPR has made it far more visible that data protection needs to be taken into account when processing (personal) data,

© Springer Nature Switzerland AG 2019
X. Franch et al. (Eds.): PROFES 2019, LNCS 11915, pp. 417–432, 2019.
https://doi.org/10.1007/978-3-030-35333-9_30

to some extent by defining serious penalties for infringements. However, it is important to not only look at how to satisfy legal requirements but also keep in mind that—apart from the legal consequences—a data protection scandal in a company may lose the trust of their customers, which eventually may hurt even more.

To ensure that data protection is not just an after-thought but considered from the start, the concept of *Privacy by Design* was developed by Cavoukian when she was Information and Privacy Commissioner of Ontario [1,2]. Under the name *Data Protection by Design*, this expectation of addressing data protection from the start of creating a system is also included in the GDPR. Since most of the relevant processing is performed by software, this is particularly relevant in the development of software, and needs to be taken into account both in the definition of software requirements and of the software processes used.

The current paper addresses the second of these aspects and analyses how to integrate data protection by design and the resulting requirements into the software processes and the software life cycle used. (A second paper discussing the software requirements resulting from data protection is under preparation by the author.)

Method Used. To identify the software process steps needed to incorporate data protection by design, the following approach was used. First, a systematic analysis of GDPR identified the relevant requirements, starting from the summary of the relevant parts of GDPR described below in Sect. 2. These requirements were translated into steps or questions to be answered in the software process, which in turn were then assigned to the appropriate life cycle stage, see Sect. 3.

Next, these results were validated by comparing them against relevant literature to check that all relevant requirements stated there are indeed included in the appropriate life cycle stage, as described in Sect. 4. With few exceptions, the literature on data protection only talks about the software processes and life cycle on a very high level, if at all, and one of the goals of this paper is to bring these documents together and provide more detail.

2   Data Protection and the General Data Protection Regulation

To get started, the main concepts of data protection and of GDPR are introduced. Note that the GDPR is used as an example data protection legislation here, but other data protection legislations will lead to similar results.[1]

---

[1] In some countries, such as the USA, the relevant legislation does not go under the name of data protection but under the name of *privacy*, a very similar concept.

2.1   Basic Concepts of Data Protection

In spite of its name, data protection is not concerned with the protection of (confidential or sensitive) *data* as such, but with the protection of *individuals* against misuse or unfair use of their personal data. While for example the design of a new product may be considered highly confidential, this is not covered by data protection which only refers to personal data.[2]

According to GDPR, Art. 4(1), personal data are defined as "any information relating to an identified or identifiable natural person". (In other contexts, for example ISO/IEC 29100:2011[3], the name "personally identifying information" PII is used to describe the same concept.) Examples of such personal data range from very simple data such as "person X has the email address Y", via "the user with IP address X has visited the website Y at time T", or "the smartphone of user X was at position P at time T", to rather critical and confidential data such as health data, for example "person X visited a hospital at time T and was diagnosed to suffer from disease Y". As can be seen, the level of protection needed may vary considerably. Data protection in general starts from the premiss that it should be up to the person concerned to decide whether and how such information may be used, and not to the entity that happens to have this information available for whatever reason.

The term "identifiable" leaves a lot of room for interpretation, and some legislations other than the GDPR will for example not count an IP address as personal data. Below, this will be reflected by the need to identify the personal data processed in a certain context as part of analysis, where the result will not only depend on the data themselves but also on the relevant legislation.

In addition to the personal data as defined in the previous paragraph, the GDPR also introduces "special categories of personal data" which require a higher level of protection and are defined as "personal data revealing racial or ethnic origin, political opinions, religious or philosophical beliefs, or trade union membership, and the processing of genetic data, biometric data for the purpose of uniquely identifying a natural person, data concerning health or data concerning a natural person's sex life or sexual orientation" (Art. 9(1) GDPR).

There is an important difference between data protection and IT security: IT security considers how to protect the organisation's own data and other IT assets. In data protection, the organisation needs to consider how to protect information about other people, often outside the organisation, against threats which may come from the organisation itself. This is the main reason why data protection is required by law and not left to the organisations involved. Data protection and IT security are both concerned with protecting information, but against different types of threats, and IT security is an important tool necessary (but not sufficient) for implementing data protection.

---

[2] Since data protection is only concerned with personal data, when we talk about "data" in the remainder of this paper this will always refer to personal data.

[3] ISO/IEC 29100:2011 *Information technology—Security techniques—Privacy framework*.

2.2   The General Data Protection Regulation (GDPR)

In May 2018, after a two-year transition period, the GDPR came into effect in the European Union (EU), defining requirements on how to handle personal data of EU citizens. This section will give a short summary of the GDPR as needed to understand its implications on software processes.

The GDPR Roles. The GDPR defines three main roles involved in the processing of personal data:

– The *data subject* (in ISO/IEC 29100:2011 called the "PII principal") is the (natural) person whose data are processed and who needs protection. Typical examples include customers, employees, and visitors to a company website.
– The *controller* is the entity that decides on how data are processed within an organisation, and therefore is responsible for this processing.
– The *processor*, finally, is the entity that performs the actual processing of data, following the rules set by the controller.

The processor and controller may be the same entity, in which case GDPR just talks about the controller, or they may be different entities, in which case a contract between the two is required to ensure that the controller does actually control the processing, and the processor processes the data as defined by the controller.

Based on these roles, GDPR defines a number of requirements to be addressed in any processing of personal data and therefore by any software that performs such processing. In the following, these will be grouped as follows: first of all, the GDPR defines general principles that need to be satisfied. Based on these principles, the rights of the data subjects are specified. Additionally, there are some further requirements which belong to neither of these groups.

The GDPR Principles. The following principles are defined by Art. 5 of GDPR:

– *Lawfulness, fairness and transparency*: in particular, these principles state that the processing of personal data is forbidden unless one of six lawfulness conditions defined in Art. 6 GDPR is satisfied, such as consent by the data subject or "processing is necessary for the purposes of the legitimate interests pursued by the controller".
– *Purpose limitation* requires that in general, personal data may only be used for the purpose for which they were originally (and lawfully) collected.
– *Data minimisation*: the use of personal data is to be reduced to the minimal extent necessary for its purpose. Storing personal data "just in case ..." is forbidden, which can become a major challenge in the context of big data.
– *Accuracy*, i.e. the controller and/or processor need to ensure that the personal data are accurate.
– *Storage limitation* is closely related to data minimisation and requires that personal data are stored no longer than necessary.

- *Integrity and confidentiality* require that personal data are protected adequately to ensure that only people that are entitled to do so can read or write these data.
- *Accountability*, finally, requires that the controller does not just comply to the above principles but is able to demonstrate this compliance.

The Rights of the Data Subject. In addition to the principles described above, the GDPR defines a number of rights of the data subject. The main important ones are:

- Right of *transparent information* (Art. 12 GDPR): data subjects are entitled to information about the handling of personal data in a transparent and easy-to-understand way.
- Right of *information* (Art. 13, 14 GDPR): data subjects have the right to be informed about the processing of their personal data.
- Right of *access* (Art. 15 GDPR): data subjects have the right to ask for the personal data stored about them, and the processing performed on these data.
- Right to *rectification* (Art. 16 GDPR): data subjects have the right to request the correction of incorrect data stored about them.
- Right to *erasure* (also called the "right to be forgotten"; Art. 17 GDPR) and right to restriction of processing (Art. 18 GDPR): data subjects have, under certain conditions, the right to request that personal data about them is deleted or—if for some reason this is not possible, for example because the data need to be stored for legal reasons—that processing of these data is restricted.
- Right to *data portability* (Art. 20 GDPR): data subjects have the right to transfer data provided by them to a different processor, e.g. if they want to move to a different provider for a certain service.
- Right to *object* (Art. 21 GDPR): data subjects have, under certain conditions, the right to object to the processing of personal data about them. This is for example relevant if they have given their consent to such processing earlier, and now want to withdraw that consent.

These rights can be translated more or less directly into functional requirements on the software system to be developed.

Other GDPR Requirements. The most important requirement asks for data protection by design (Art. 25(1) GDPR), which does not state any explicit requirements on the resulting product but points to the need to address the principles and rights described above from the start of designing a process and the software to support it. In spite of its name, data protection by design does not only apply to the design phase of software development but to all phases across the software life cycle, though with a focus on analysis and design.

Closely related is data protection by default (Art. 25(2) GDPR), stating that systems must be configured such that privacy is the default and the user may change these settings to explicitly allow less privacy, rather than vice versa.

The rules on automated decision-making and profiling set a limit to the usage of software systems (Art. 22 GDPR). Although decision-making solely based on automated processing is allowed, the individuals affected are entitled to obtain human intervention in such decisions, for example decisions about whether or not they are considered credit-worthy.

To help ensure the transparency of the data processing performed, "records of processing activities" need to be kept, documenting the processing performed, the data processed, the steps taken to protect these data etc. (Art. 30 GDPR).

If there is expected to be a high risk to the data subjects from a new technology or system, a data protection impact assessment (DPIA) needs to be performed to assess the impact of this new technology or system and identify measures to reduce this risk to an acceptable level. Performing the DPIA is the responsibility of the controller, but the controller will often need help from software development for this task.

3   Data Protection in the Software Life Cycle

In order to assign the different data protection tasks to the software life cycle, the simple life cycle model shown in Fig. 1 is used as a starting point. This life cycle model is not taken from any standard publication but a summary of the phases that are commonly used in any such model. As a result, this is just one of many possible such models, see [10] for a thorough discussion of software life cycle models. However, the tasks described below are largely independent of the life cycle model used, and could therefore aligned to different models without problems, including iterative-incremental or agile approaches as described in Sect. 3.9.

Fig. 1. A sample software life cycle

The life cycle used by the Norwegian data protection office *Datatilsynet* in [4] uses very similar phases (though somewhat different names), but starts with a phase "Training" that covers training of employees on the relevant regulatory and mandatory requirements, the development methodology and the life cycle and tools used for IT security. Since this training will usually be performed on an organisational level, largely independent of any specific software project, and therefore is not included here.

Even though IT security forms an important foundation for data protection, the implications of IT security on the software processes are outside the scope of this paper and therefore will not be covered here. (See [10, Sect. 3.11] for more detail about this topic.)

3.1   Analysis (Requirements)

As is to be expected, the main task of analysis regarding data protection is to clarify the general set-up, answering in particular the following questions:

1. Which data protection roles are involved in the processing? Who is the controller, and are there any separate processors? Is there a single controller or joint controllership, that is multiple controllers who are jointly responsible?
2. Who are the data subjects?
3. Which data protection legislation is applicable? If processing is to be performed within the EU, this will be the GDPR, but there is likely to be additional legislation such as a national data protection act, and/or some industry-specific legislation. If data are to be processed or moved outside the EU, other or additional national legislation will apply.
4. Which personal data are needed (not just considered useful) for the intended functionality? Remember that the answer to this question not only depends on the data needed but also on the relevant legislation and its interpretation of the term "personal data".
   (a) Do the personal data processed include any special categories of personal data (Art. 9 GDPR), or data of children (Art. 8 (2) GDPR)?
   (b) Would it be possible to do without these data, at least some of them?
   (c) If not, would it be possible to turn them into anonymous or at least pseudonymous data?
   (d) Are there any relevant meta-data to be processed, i.e. data about data? E.g. even though the contents of a certain message may not be known, date and time of the message or the identity of its sender and receiver still describe personal data.
5. Which lawfulness condition according to Art. 6(1) GDPR is going to form the legal basis for processing the personal data? What implications does this lead to—which steps are allowed, required or forbidden?
   (a) If consent is to be used as the legal basis: what is going to be covered by this consent? What happens if a user does not give his consent, or only partial consent, or withdraws it at a later stage? Consent is only considered as a legal basis for data processing if it is genuinely voluntary, implying that one also has to deal with the case that it is not given.
   (b) If the legitimate interests are to be used as the legal basis: which interests of the data subjects are relevant and need to be considered? What does that imply for the design and implementation of the system? Where are the limits of those legitimate interests?
   (c) If relevant, the legal basis must also cover the special categories of personal data and the personal data of children.
6. What need for protection and what risks result from the answers to the previous questions? What data protection damage could be caused by the software system to be developed? The answer to these questions should take into account both the usage as intended, and any possible misuse, for example by an attacker who steals the data. Who can access the data—legitimately or

illegitimately? This could include own employees, external suppliers (processors), external attackers, and other third parties who happen to run across the data by accident.

7. Which (functional or non-functional) software requirements resulting from data protection are relevant and need to be considered? This includes functions such as gathering, managing and applying consent by the data subject where adequate, or the deletion of personal data once they are no longer needed. In particular, the rights if the data subjects lead to many such software requirements. An analysis of these is planned to be published in a separate paper by the author.

8. Based on the data protection roles identified in question 1, to what extent are data going to be exchanged with third parties, for example by using cloud or other third-party services?

9. Is the system under development expected to lead to a high risk for the data subjects, which would imply that a DPIA needs to be performed?

The answers to these questions should be discussed with a data protection specialist, for example the Data Protection Officer of the controller organisation, in order to ensure correct interpretation of the data protection concepts and completeness of the data protection requirements.

3.2   Design (Architecture)

The main task in design regarding data protection is to define suitable technical and organisational measures (commonly known as TOMs) to adequately implement the requirements identified in analysis. In particular, the following questions need to be addressed:

1. What role do the data protection or GDPR principles play in the system under development, and how can these principles be implemented? To achieve this so-called *Privacy-Enhancing Techniques* (PETs) are usually used, such as access restrictions, encryption and anonymisation [3]. Some of the most important PETs will be discussed below.
   Similarly, *privacy (design) patterns* can be used to design implementations of these principles, see e.g. [5].

2. An aspect that is easily overlooked: what personal data are transferred to third parties by the libraries, SDKs and other tools or services planned to be used. This is closely related to question 8 in analysis, but while in analysis the focus was on deliberate sharing of data with third parties, design also has to identify the data sharing that is not needed to provide the intended functionality but introduced by the tools used. See below for more detail.

3. Are there any existing frameworks or other information that should be taken into account? In the case of web tracking, this includes for example the do-not-track flag and the *IAB GDPR Transparency & Consent Framework* [8].

4. Finally, it should be checked whether the results of analysis regarding data protection are still up-to-date, complete, and fully addressed by design.

Similar to the analysis phase, the results of the design phase should be discussed and validated with the Data Protection Officer to ensure that the relevant data protection requirements are interpreted correctly.

Managing and Complying to User Consent. An important type of legal basis for processing personal data is consent by the user, i.e. by the data subject concerned. Since this user consent must be genuinely voluntary, some users may give it, some may only consent to certain types of processing, and some may not consent at all. Software design therefore must be able to handle these different cases, keeping track of consent given or refused, and comply to this consent by only processing data if consent has been given (or processing is performed on a different legal basis and the user has not objected to it).

Identification, Authentication and Authorization. Performing identification (who is the user?), authentication (is he really the user he claims to be?) and authorization (what rights does the user have?) is a standard task of IT security which needs to be integrated into the design of almost any system, and forms one basis for data protection. Data protection puts additional restrictions on the authorization step, requiring restrictive handling of authorizations for the processing of personal data.

Using Libraries, SDKs and Web Services. A major challenge may be the selection of libraries, SDKs etc., in the following just summarised as "libraries". This mainly applies to the development of mobile apps and of services and plug-ins for web applications, where it is quite common to use external libraries which sometimes share data with their provider and other third parties, often without the developer knowing about them [7,11].

Even if the library does not include any explicit functionality to share personal data, just calling it at run-time will, if no explicit steps are taken to prevent this, usually pass at least the IP address of the user to the provider of the library.

To address these issues, the following steps are needed when using any third-party libraries (or SDKs or other run-time services):

- Find out about any personal data passed on by the library to any third parties.
- Check whether the library can be configured such as to prevent or at least reduce this passing-on of data. Often, the libraries support suitable parameters, even though these may be well-hidden. According to the data protection principle "data protection by default", the default library configuration should be such that a high level of data protection is ensured, but in practice this often is not the case, in particular when the library was developed outside the EU.
- When a library is called at run-time, it may be possible to deploy this library on one's own server rather than call it from somewhere else.

- Analyse and decide whether the remaining passing-on of personal data is acceptable and covered by the legal basis used for the processing. A new analysis of the legal basis used may be needed, in particular if the "legitimate interest" is used which requires a weighing of interests. In some cases, this will lead to the decision that the legal basis is no longer adequate and the functionality planned must be based on a different library, or reduced or even withdrawn altogether.
- Document this decision incl. the reasoning used. Ensure that the users (data subjects) are informed about any data still passed on.

The same is true when embedding information from other web sites such as videos, fonts, or social media buttons. If no suitable steps are taken to prevent this, at least the IP address of the user will be transferred to the provider, often more.

So far, this discussion assumed that the developers under consideration *use* the libraries. Of course, someone has to develop these libraries in the first place. Developers creating libraries, SDKs etc. to be used by someone else also need to address data protection and make life easy for their colleagues using their libraries, e.g. by allowing a data protection-friendly configuration and making this the default.

Encryption of Data. GDPR mentions encryption multiple times as a tool to be used to protect data and ensure security (e.g. Art. 6(4)e, Art. 32(1)a), but without any detailed statements about when and how to use it. In this context it is important to remember that encrypted personal data are still personal data that are subject to data protection, and encryption is just one step to protect these data.

Encryption is a complex topic with many unexpected traps, and one should not try to define one's own encryption algorithm, actually not even implement an existing algorithm oneself, but rather use standard libraries provided by specialist cryptographers.

An important question to consider in this context is how long the encrypted data need to be kept confidential, since this affects the configuration of the crypto-algorithms, in particular key lengths, and to some extent even the selection of the algorithms themselves.

Anonymity and Pseudonymity. A useful approach to protect personal data is to anonymize them, or at least to work with pseudonyms, and both approaches are therefore mentioned repeatedly in the GDPR as tools to protect data.

Legally speaking, there is a fundamental difference between anonymous and pseudonymous data. With *anonymous data*, it is not possible to identify the individuals concerned. Therefore, anonymous data do not count as personal data, and data protection requirements do not apply. With pseudonymous data, identification is still possible but requires additional information such as a mapping table. This additional information must be stored separately and well-protected.

Pseudonymous data therefore still count as personal data which are subject to data protection, but working with pseudonyms is a method to protect data which may help to satisfy the data protection requirements.

In practice, it is often difficult to distinguish between anonymous and pseudonymous data since, given enough additional information, it is always possible to identify the individuals concerned. Also, there are different opinions about what counts as "identification" in this context. For example, in Europe permanent cookies are usually considered as identifiers since they allow to identify repeated visits of the same individual, while in the USA these are usually considered as anonymous data since in general it is not possible to identify the individual's name etc.

Apart from these legal aspects, ensuring that data are genuinely anonymous is a complex technical task, and there are a number of well-known examples where it turned out that "anonymous" data could in fact be de-anonymised. For example, just knowing the ZIP or post code plus the birth date of a person may seem anonymous but is, in many cases, sufficient to reduce the candidate individuals to a very small group of people, possibly just one. A common approach to apply this knowledge is to join the "anonymous" data set, possibly containing sensitive personal data, with a second data set which is publicly available but in itself does not contain any sensitive data. The join can then be done via a joint key, such as ZIP code plus birth date [16].

This and many other examples show that anonymisation of data is a difficult task which requires much more than just leaving out the name of the person involved. There is a number of approaches to systematically anonymise data, such as k-anonymity [16] and differential privacy [6], which are however fairly difficult to apply, at least for non-specialists. A less systematic approach, which is in turn far easier to apply, is described in [12] in the context of health data. Whenever data are to be anonymised, it is important to use such a thorough approach and thus ensure that the results are indeed anonymous.

3.3   Implementation

The main task regarding data protection in the implementation phase is to ensure that the analysis and design results are correctly incorporated into development. Any revisions and extensions of the results of analysis and design need to take into account the data protection issues discussed above, such as the decision to use a certain SDK or embed any third-party services.

3.4   Test and Acceptance

The main data protection tasks in test and acceptance are to verify that the requirements identified in analysis and design are indeed implemented in the resulting system. Remember that this does not imply the use of a sequential process model. Test and acceptance may also be performed iteratively, for example as part of checking the "definition of done" after implementing individual user stories, and/or as part of sprint reviews.

Using Production Data for Testing. Sometimes, organisations want to use production data for test and acceptance, which provides particular challenges regarding data protection and may only be performed under certain restrictive conditions. As the name implies, production data are provided for some production purpose, and usually not for testing. Using these data for testing therefore implies a change of purpose, bringing up the principle of purpose limitation. Since the new purpose still supports the original purpose, this in general is a minor change and may still be legal, assuming the following conditions are satisfied.

First of all, any processing of personal data requires a lawfulness condition according to Art. 6 GDPR to be satisfied. In the case of test acceptance, this is usually the "legitimate interest" of the controller. In addition to the legitimate interest itself, this lawfulness condition requires that the processing is *necessary* rather than just useful for the purpose, in this case testing, and the interest of the processor must be *balanced* against the interests of the data subjects:

- Necessity: as one typical example, using production data for testing may be necessary in the case of testing complex data migration procedures, in particular in a regulated environment where the organisation has to prove that data migration is performed properly. Another example is the test whether the software system can handle complex, possibly inconsistent, input data such as contained in the production data. Of course, before any such tests based on production data are performed the "normal" functional tests based on artificial test data must have been completed successfully.

  For functional testing, the use of production data in general is neither legal nor useful, since for proper functional testing, one needs to know the expected results for comparison with the actual results. In case of production data, these will however not be available.

  Even when the use of production data for testing is considered necessary, it is important to limit the impact on the data subjects. This involves applying adequate IT security measures, in particular internally limiting access to these test data, and protecting the data against outside attacks. As far as reasonably possible without impacting the goals of the test, the data should be anonymised or at least pseudonymised before using them for testing.
- Balance: in most cases, the data subjects will themselves have an interest that the software used for processing their data is tested thoroughly, and it remains to analyse the risks involved. Based on the IT security measures taken, the risks involved for the data subjects must be considered to below.

The main alternative is consent by the data subject, which is more difficult to handle, but needs to be acquired if the conditions for legitimate interest are not fully satisfied. In particular, this applies to the processing of special categories of personal data, such as health data, where the legitimate interest is not defined as a lawfulness condition.

3.5 Transition

The transition from development to operations has to ensure that the data protection measures set up earlier are indeed implemented in operations, and relevant documentation is set up. This involves in particular:

1. Train the users regarding the data protection functionality
2. Ensure that the processing is made transparent for the data subjects, for example by documenting it in the relevant data protection declaration
3. Ensure that the processing is incorporated into the "records of processing activities"
4. Ensure that data protection contracts are agreed with external suppliers (processors)
5. Set up processes for incident response and handling of personal data breaches.

3.6 Operations

Ensure Data Security. The main data protection task to perform during operations is to ensure adequate security of data, based on the concepts and methods defined during the earlier phases of the software life cycle. To a large extent, this security will address the entire IT infrastructure and not be limited to the specific system under consideration.

Handle Personal Data Breaches. Even when all data protection measures have been implemented correctly, problems may occur where individuals and their data are not protected as expected, called a "personal data breach" in GDPR. In this case, notification to the relevant supervisory authority may be required within a narrow time frame of 72 h (Art. 33 GDPR), as well as information of the data subjects affected (Art. 34 GDPR). Not a legal requirement but possibly at least as important is the adequate handling of questions from the press and the general public in case a breach has become public. It is therefore important to set up a process beforehand so that data breaches can be handled properly under pressure. At least all employees should know whom to inform immediately should they encounter a personal data breach.

Data Collected in Operations. To some extent, operations itself collects and processes personal data, mainly in various log files which, apart from many other data, often also contain personal data. This may lead to a conflict of interests, when from the IT security point of view, extensive logging of user activities is expected, while at the same time data protection asks to keep logging to a minimum. In this case, logging needs to be kept to the minimum required for the purpose, and an analysis of the legitimate interests performed, similar to the analysis described for testing with production data.

3.7   Change Control

Change control[4] describes the systematic handling of changes and change requests when the software under consideration is in productive use. Regarding data protection, the relevant tasks to be performed are largely independent of whether a certain change is performed during initial development or later, when the system is already in operation. This leads to the following question for any change performed:

- Does the change have any impact on the processing of personal data? This may be a change of functionality, or a technical impact, for example using a different SDK.
  - If the change does have any such impact, this should be analysed in more detail, based on the questions listed above for analysis and design.

3.8   Withdrawal

At the end of the software life cycle, software is withdrawn once it is no longer needed. This phase requires less work regarding data protection than most of the previous phases, but still a few questions need to be addressed:

1. Will the system's personal data still be needed? Should they be migrated to another system or deleted?
2. If the personal data are to be migrated, how are they protected on their way to as well as within the new system?
3. In either case, how can the personal data be deleted securely in the old system, including backup versions?

3.9   Agile Development

Independent of the life cycle model used, the questions above need to be answered in any software development effort. An important challenge in agile development is that many data protection requirements are non-functional requirements or constraints, and therefore difficult to describe using standard agile methods such as user stories. Techniques to resolve this challenge and adequately incorporate data protection in agile development include:

1. As far as functional requirements are concerned, these should be described in the standard format agreed, such as user stories.
2. Non-functional requirements and constraints need to be communicated clearly within the team, and integrated into the quality assurance measures used, such as the *definition of ready* (DoR) and the *definition of done* (DoD). Furthermore, the DoR should include check items derived from the questions and issues listed above for the early development phases, and be checked whenever a functionality is transferred to the sprint backlog, including for example

---

[4] The term "change control" is used here, following the recent ITIL v4. Alternatively, this process is often known under the name "change management".

(a) Have the relevant roles (data subject, controller, processor) been identified?

(b) Have the personal data been identified which are to be processed?

(c) Are only those personal processed that are genuinely needed for the functionality to be developed?

(d) Has the legal basis for processing been identified? What exactly is
included, what is not?

(e) ...

Similarly, the DoD and/or the sprint review should include check items such
as

(a) Have the personal data been identified and documented which are to be
exchanged with other systems?

(b) Has the processing of personal data been documented, including the purpose? Is that consistent with the identified legal basis?

4   Validation of Results

Since the GDPR requirements are expressed in a very different way compared to
software and software process requirements, there is no formal way to validate
the results in this paper. To ensure the correctness of the results, they are checked
against the text of the GDPR itself, supported by some legal commentaries such
as [9].

More difficult is the completeness of the results. To validate the completeness,
the results were compared against different publications that address the effects
of data protection and GDPR requirements on software development, in particular [3,4,13–15]. The results of these comparisons were directly integrated into
the results described above, so that the version reported here already includes
all requirements that had been identified as missing.

5   Conclusion

Data protection has become increasingly important in today's economy, both
due to a number of data scandals that led to a loss of trust in the affected
companies, and, partly triggered by such scandals, due to data protection and
privacy legislation such as the GDPR. As indicated by the concept of "data
protection by design", implementing data protection requires that this topic is
addressed from the start, including the development of any software used for the
processing of personal data. Different activities are needed at different times in
the software life cycle, mainly in the early development phases but—though to
a lesser extent—also in the later phases down to operations and eventually the
withdrawal of the software. It is therefore important to have a good understanding of these necessary activities in order to incorporate them into the relevant
project plans, product backlogs or software process models as appropriate.

References

1. Cavoukian, A.: Privacy by design. The 7 foundational principles. Technical report, Information and Privacy Commissioner of Ontario (2011). https://www.ipc.on.ca/wp-content/uploads/Resources/7foundationalprinciples.pdf
2. Cavoukian, A., Taylor, S., Abrams, M.E.: Privacy by design: essential for organizational accountability and strong business practices. Ident. Inf. Soc. **3**(2), 405–413 (2010). https://doi.org/10.1007/s12394-010-0053-z
3. Danezis, G., et al.: Privacy and data protection by design–from policy to engineering. Technical report, ENISA, December 2014. https://doi.org/10.2824/38623
4. Datatilsynet: Software development with data protection by design and by default (2017). https://www.datatilsynet.no/en/about-privacy/virksomhetenesplikter/innebygd-personvern/data-protection-by-design-and-by-default/
5. Drozd, O.: Privacy pattern catalogue: a tool for integrating privacy principles of ISO/IEC 29100 into the software development process. In: Aspinall, D., Camenisch, J., Hansen, M., Fischer-Hübner, S., Raab, C. (eds.) Privacy and Identity 2015. IAICT, vol. 476, pp. 129–140. Springer, Cham (2016). https://doi.org/10.1007/978-3-319-41763-9_9
6. Dwork, C.: Differential privacy: a survey of results. In: Agrawal, M., Du, D., Duan, Z., Li, A. (eds.) TAMC 2008. LNCS, vol. 4978, pp. 1–19. Springer, Heidelberg (2008). https://doi.org/10.1007/978-3-540-79228-4_1
7. Englehardt, S., Acar, G., Narayanan, A.: Website operators are in the dark about privacy violations by third-party scripts, January 2018. https://freedom-to-tinker.com/2018/01/12/website-operators-are-in-the-dark-about-privacy-violations-by-third-party-scripts/
8. Interactive Advertising Bureau (IAB Europe): IAB Europe and IAB Tech Lab release cross-industry Transparency & Consent Framework for adoption, April 2018. https://www.iabeurope.eu/all-news/press-releases/iab-europe-and-iab-tech-lab-release-cross-industry-transparency-consent-framework-for-adoption/
9. Kühlung, J., Buchner, B. (eds.): Datenschutz-Grundverordnung/BDSG. Kommentar. C.H. Beck, 2. edn. (2018)
10. Kneuper, R.: Software Processes and Life Cycle Models. An Introduction to Modelling, Using and Managing Agile, Plan-Driven and Hybrid Processes. Springer, Cham (2018). https://doi.org/10.1007/978-3-319-98845-0_3
11. Lindsey, N.: Popular Android apps are sharing personal data with Facebook without user consent, January 2019. https://www.cpomagazine.com/data-privacy/popular-android-apps-are-sharing-personal-data-with-facebook-without-user-consent/
12. Office for Civil Rights (OCR): Guidance Regarding Methods for De-Identification of Protected Health Information in Accordance with the Health Insurance Portability and Accountability Act (HIPAA) Privacy Rule (2012). https://www.hhs.gov/hipaa/for-professionals/privacy/special-topics/de-identification/index.html
13. Reid, G.: How to navigate the software development life cycle under the GDPR (2017). https://iapp.org/news/a/how-to-navigate-the-software-development-life-cycle-under-the-gdpr/. International Association of Privacy Professionals (IAPP)
14. Santala, A.: What should software engineers know about GDPR? (2017). https://www.infoq.com/articles/gdpr-for-software-devs/
15. Simon, K., Moucha, C.: Sicherheit und Datenschutz im Lebenszyklus von Informationssystemen. DuD Datenschutz und Datensicherheit **43**(2), 97–101 (2019)
16. Sweeney, L.: k-Anonymity: a model for protecting privacy. Int. J. Uncertain. Fuzziness Knowl.-Based Syst. **10**(5), 557–570 (2002)

Revisiting the Product Configuration Systems Development Procedure for Scrum Compliance: An i* Driven Process Fragment

Yves Wautelet[1]([⊠]) [iD], Sara Shafiee[2] [iD], and Samedi Heng[3] [iD]

[1] KU Leuven, Leuven, Belgium
yves.wautelet@kuleuven.be
[2] Danmarks Tekniske Universitet, Kongens Lyngby, Danmark
sashaf@dtu.dk
[3] Université de Liège, Liège, Belgium
samedi.heng@uliege.be

Abstract. Product Configuration Systems (PCS) are software applications supporting the design of products tailored to the individual desiderata of customers. PCS development does not follow the same procedure as traditional software: indeed, due to its nature, specific knowledge needs to be collected, a set of custom engineering stages have thus been built-up. Within these stages, special requirements representation and design artifacts are used notably to deal with features interdependencies. More specifically, the Product Variant Master (PVM) has been specifically created for PCS knowledge representation while Class-Responsibility-Collaboration (CRC) cards and a UML Class Diagram are often indispensable for PCS object-oriented design. PCS development projects have gradually started to use agile methods like the Scrum. This paper presents a process fragment for conducting PCS development projects with Scrum; it overviews how the development team of a specific organization adapted the agile process to the PCS context. This process fragment has indeed been built on the basis of practitioners knowledge collected through 5 qualitative interviews (inductive approach) and exhaustively depict the activities performed by the team on PCS development projects of various size and context. Because of the possibility to represent social (role) dependencies, the fragment is visually represented using an i* Strategic Rationale Diagram. The main contribution of the paper is the fragment itself, it is intended to be dynamically used as an initial guidance for PCS development teams willing to conduct projects using Scrum; it can be tailored to any project/sprint and enriched at will.

Keywords: Product Configuration Systems · Agile development · Scrum · DevOps · i-star · Feature dependencies

© Springer Nature Switzerland AG 2019
X. Franch et al. (Eds.): PROFES 2019, LNCS 11915, pp. 433–451, 2019.
https://doi.org/10.1007/978-3-030-35333-9_31

1   Introduction

A Product Configuration Systems (PCS) is a software-based system to support configuring a product at will (automatically or on the basis of user input) to match the customers' needs while satisfying technical constraints. Often the amount of possible configurations is huge because it increases exponentially with the number of configurable parameters. Also, constraints are often numerous and complex to express requiring specific modeling artifacts. PCS enable companies to propose alternatives to facilitate their sales and production processes by integrating information about the product's features, structures, constraints, costs and prices. Using the PCS, the client can build the exact product he wishes and by the same time make the first step in its production process. Widely used in various industries, PCS can bring substantial benefits [12,13,26] such as shorter lead times for generating quotations, fewer errors, increased ability to meet customers' requirements regarding product functionality, the use of fewer resources, optimized product designs, less routine work and improved on-time delivery. A PCS can for example be developed for configuring a car; the customer buying a new car is then capable of selecting the type of body, the color, the type of engine, etc. (Fig. 1).

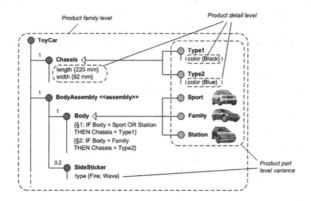

Fig. 1. Car Product Configuration System (from [25]).

PCS being first and foremost software systems, their development have followed the evolution in software development life cycles. At first they were developed using a (sequential) seven steps procedure (see [14]) executed in a waterfall fashion. Later on, the procedure has been integrated in the Rational Unified Process (RUP) [15] life cycle for iterative development. With the growing popularity of Scrum, the question of using agile development within PCS development has been raised. Several internal characteristics of PCS nevertheless induce that the adoption of Scrum in such developments need to be handled with care. Scrum essentially prioritizes sprints on the basis of the business value induced by the development of user stories [31]. The latter are filling the so-called Product Backlog. Because of the high amount of dependencies among the configurable features in the product supported by the PCS, sprints cannot be managed on the basis of user stories exclusively. Indeed, more knowledge is required in order to ensure that constraints are handled adequately; this has an impact on the prioritization of developments. In other words, the constraints from the features' dependencies induce that the sprints' content cannot be driven by value only. Also, because of the complexity in the production process resulting from virtually infinite product configuration choices, domain experts (among which production engineers) constantly need to be consulted in the building and the validation of the PCS. Also, documentation on the state of the PCS needs to be produced and kept up-to-date to ensure all of the possible configurations are supported and non-supported configurations are prescribed. Finally, short time release integration deliver significant added value, especially when new configurations of the product are made possible/available or existing configurations should be updated. Also, when new configurations need to be tested on small customers groups, immediate (even if they are partial) deployments have proven to be of value (because they allow to immediately attract customers and constitute life-sized evaluation environment). For these reasons and because they often need to be integrated in a broader software ecosystem, members of the operation team are involved in the execution of each sprint. This is in line with the DevOps [2] approach.

The aim of the research is to depict how the Scrum process has been adopted in a large organization specialized in the such developments. Due to the proven benefits in general software development, the adoption of Scrum has been, into the case organization, pushed by the top-management more than 3 years ago. Through a set of interviews, we aimed to understand what are the current activities and practices performed into a PCS development project conducted with Scrum. More specifically, we are interested in how the organization manages the elements identified in the previous section. On the basis of the data collected through interviews, we have built a process fragment. The latter is, with respect to the case organization, exhaustive (it depicts all of the activities) but not exclusive (not all of these activities are necessarily performed in each project and other activities can be added if found relevant). The process fragment is expressed with i* (i-star) [32] in order to highlight the social dependencies between the involved roles. The process fragment itself constitutes main contribution of the paper and can be used as a reference for PCS development professionals willing to conduct projects using Scrum. We nevertheless do not consider it as a fixed scientific truth but rather as a first reference that can be further used, tailored and validated by other PCS development teams and/or cases.

2   Theoretical Background

2.1   PCS Projects Specifics

There are enough differences between general software development projects and PCS ones for studying the impact of agile adoption in this specific field.

First of all, knowledge complexity and the possible extensions of PCS make the project scoping determinant [24]. This is done by identifying the requirements, evaluating the time and budget, and prioritizing the different products and functions. In PCS projects, goals and stakeholders' requirements are mostly determined in the first steps because of the complexity and dependencies found in the product's features, the range of involved stakeholders (from end-users desiderata to production specialists determining the possible combinations), and other functional and non-functional requirements.

Secondly, because of the differences in the nature of the knowledge to be represented, PCS are formalized, combined, modeled and communicated differently than in general software development projects. The knowledge modeled in PCS is indeed extensive and has to be continually validated by domain experts and production specialists [25]. Strong communication between the PCS development team and these experts is thus vital. Without proper validation, very minor misunderstandings could lead to significant errors in the calculations and outputs.

Thirdly, clear and comprehensive documentation of the developed PCS has to be produced and needs to be understandable by all stakeholders in a non-technical language [11]. Also, PCS often need to be integrated in a complex software ecosystem; this requires propagation of related knowledge. In addition, frequent changes/updates in the supported product(s) requires continuous updates and maintenance [6].

Because of the aforementioned elements, PCS require the development of specific artifacts (see Sect. 2.2) furnishing the data/information required by the PCS development team to perform its activities properly. The smooth integration of these artifacts into a Scrum-based project is addressed by the process fragment.

2.2 Product Configuration Systems, the Traditional Center Product Modeling Procedure

Hvam et al. [14] propose the *Center Product Modeling (CPM)* procedure for PCS development; the latter consists of seven stages called phases in the initial version to be executed in a waterfall fashion. These phases are to be mapped into disciplines following the terminology of the RUP when integrated in the latter life cycle[1]. Several extensions of CPM have been proposed (2001) (2003) (2006) (2008) over the years. The different stages of the CPM framework include (1) *development of the specification processes*, (2) *analysis of the product range*, (3) *object-oriented modeling*, (4) *object-oriented design*, (5) *programming of the PCS*, (6) *plan for implementation, and finally* (7) *plan for maintenance and further development*. For each of the stages artifacts are defined in order to represent/document relevant knowledge to fulfill the stage. Among those, we

---

[1] The phases in RUP are indeed groups of iterations which are opposed to the stages of [14] that constitute waterfall steps for the development (deployment and maintenance of a PCS).

are particularly interested in the *Product Variant Master* (*PVM*) and *Class-Responsibility-Collaboration* (*CRC*) cards because these allow to represent constraints and dependencies in PCS knowledge representation.

The terminology used into the CPM framework is not entirely aligned with the terminology commonly used in Software Engineering (SE). Indeed, what is refereed to as *Programming* in [14] is what SE generally refers to as *Implementation* (i.e., the physical coding of the product using a programming language). Similarly, what is refereed to as *Implementation* in [14] is known as *Deployment* in SE. In the rest of this paper we adopt the terminology of general SE so that we use *Implementation* for the coding of the solution; the *Deployment* stage is outside the scope of the process fragment that we introduce in this paper so we do not refer to it later on.

2.3 Artifacts Traditionally Required in Product Configuration Systems Development Projects

The Product Variant Master. To obtain an overall view of the products in the CPM framework, the product range is drawn up in a PVM to represent the *phenomenon model* [14]. The PVM consists of two structures, which are the *part-of* structure and the *kind-of* structure. The *part-of* structure represents the parts that appear in the entire product family. The classes are defined as object classes which include the *name of the class*, *description*, *attributes* and *constraints*. The *kind-of* structure describes the different variants the individual parts can have. Furthermore, the PVM contains a description of the most important connections between parts, i.e., the rules for how parts are permitted to be combined. To preserve the overview of the PVM, CRC cards are associated with the PVM to describe the individual parts in more detail (see hereunder). The PVM represents knowledge from different domains, which include customers, engineering and part/production view [10]. The causal connection can then be drawn between the views to identify complexity and non-value adding variety in the product range. The PVM is very important for scoping the project. It indeed determines what components are part of the PCS and what are not, the level of granularity and the modularization. All of the theoretical possibilities of product customization are not necessarily included due to complexity and economic reasons. Figure 2 shows an illustrative example of the PVM.

The Class Diagram. In the CPM framework, the UML class diagram [20] is used to represent the *information model*. Its individual classes are defined from the PVM using transformation rules. Aggregation and association structures are used for relationships between objects. The aggregation structure corresponds to the *part-of* structure in the PVM. The association structure is used if objects are associated with each other. Multiplicities can be used with the aggregation and association structures to represent the number of sub-parts needed to make a super-part [14]. Generalization and package structures describe relationships

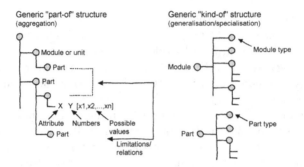

Fig. 2. Structure of the PVM regarding part-of and kind-of structure (adjusted from [10]).

between classes. The generalization structure corresponds to the *kind-of* structure in the PVM. Forward engineering rules allow to generate a class diagram directly from the PVM structure (see [14]).

Class-Responsibility-Collaboration Cards. The CRC cards, which are associated with both the PVM and the class diagram, describe the classes in more detail. The CRC card was first proposed as a way to teach object-oriented thinking. Later, they were developed for use in PCS projects, where they describe the individual object classes of the PVM and the class diagram in more details [14]. In other words, the CRC card defines the class, including the class name and its possible place in the hierarchy, together with a date and the name of the person responsible for the class. Also, the class task (responsibility), the class attributes and methods, and with which classes it collaborates (collaboration) is given. Furthermore, a sketch of the product part represented by the class is included. The purpose of the CRC cards is to document detailed knowledge about the attributes and methods for the individual object classes and to describe the classes' mutual relationships. The CRC cards serve as documentation for both domain experts and system developers.

3   Research Method and Process Fragment Validation

In order to gather specific knowledge on how PCS teams apply Scrum in practice and build a process fragment, we proceeded through different stages.

First, the research team – composed of two specialists of the Scrum process into general software development projects and one specialist into Scrum and PCS development – made a preliminary brainstorming session to identify what elements are typically needed in PCS development and potentially poorly supported by Scrum. A general presentation of Scrum was made, for each point, the adequacy for PCS developments was discussed. This allowed to build-up a series of questions. The first one asks for a very general description of all of the activities, the next ones result from the specifics discussed by the research team. This leads to the following list of questions:

- *Describe all the activities that you are doing during a typical sprint;*
- *How do you gather domain knowledge? After initial start is it frequent to ask for clarifications? Who is the interface to obtain these then?*
- *Do you systematically need an evaluation of the AS-IS situation? What is the trigger to start with the modeling of the TO-BE situation?*
- *What are the models, tools to represent the (software/PCS) problem and solution?*
- *Do systematically need the PVM and CRC cards in addition to User Stories to depict the structure and functions of the PCS? Could User Stories be sufficient? Could you avoid using User Stories in a Scrum project?*
- *Do you use a class diagram to model the (PCS) Object Oriented application? What are your preferred sources of documentation (e.g., interviews, technical documents, workflows, etc.) to build it?*
- *How do you proceed with the testing of the output in a sprint? How do you select the end-users to be part of tests?*
- *How do you cascade/incorporate the feedback of users in the deliverable of the next sprints?*
- *How do you prioritize the developments for the next sprint? How do you manage the product's features dependencies? Who sets the priorities and on what basis?*
- *How do you manage the deployment of the PCS release? Is the release put in production at the end of each sprint or is it included into a production backlog?*

Second, five qualitative interviews of members of a PCS development team (working within a single organization) have been conducted. The interview process involved people that have been playing all of the different roles of a Scrum team in the studied organization. The latter team has more than ten years of experience in PCS development with both the RUP and Scrum. In that company, since the 3 last years, RUP has nevertheless been totally abandoned to exclusively focus on Scrum. The interviews consisted in the open set of questions that has been depicted above.

Third, the qualitative data collected during the interviews was analyzed using concept-driven coding [7] leading to build a first version of the process fragment. It required crossing all the information (and more specifically the project management and engineering related concepts) retrieved from the interviews. When there were ambiguities, they were discussed with a member of the research team that has been Scrum master in PCS projects for more than 6 years. The Scrum-based PCS development approach has been formalized using the process fragment concepts of [23] and graphically represented in i* in the same fashion as in [30]. The choice of i* has been made because it highlights the social dependencies between the actors/roles but is not sequential. We indeed did not want to document a sequence of activities in the process fragment because we observed that there is a high variability in their sequence and/or parallelism from project to project. This implicitly also shows the flexibility in the adoption of the process fragment by a new development team. Multiple activities can indeed be performed at the same time, some activities can be omitted, some others added and the sequence can be chosen in function of the field requirements/constraints. Workflow-based notations that are more directive in terms of sequence, do not highlight social dependencies and are less tailorable/customizable and thus less relevant; the i* notation better allows to deal with the variability in the activities' execution and selection.

Fourth, the "candidate" version of the process fragment built in the former stage has been presented to the practitioners involved in the interview stage (acting as a focus group) within the context of a workshop. The latter was meant to serve as an evaluation/validation for the "candidate" process fragment. Concretely the process fragment and its notation were presented and explained followed by a group discussion on the accuracy, correctness and completeness. Their feedback/comments/ideas have been collected and the final version of the process fragment has been built; this version is the one presented in this paper (see Sect. 4). The activities included in the process fragment vary from project to project and more specifically from sprint to sprint essentially in function of the PCS's complexity, size and the desiderata of the development team. This final version is exhaustive meaning that it includes all of the possible activities reported by the development team. It is meant to be tailored to each project sprint. Activities can be selected dynamically in function of the scope and needs; new activities can also be added if required/found relevant by the adopting team. The process fragment is thus not prescriptive but rather customizable in function of the sprint's context.

4   The Software Process Fragment

Table 1 documents all of the process fragment elements defined in Seidita et al. [23] that are instantiated onto our contribution.

To graphically represent the process fragment's elements, we use an i* Strategic Rationale (SR) diagram of Fig. 3. For clarity, we insist that, in a same project, each of the **Roles** can be played by several individuals and a same individual can also play different **Roles**. Moreover, the *Scrum Master* role is not part of the process fragment because its responsibilities and activities are generic in Scrum; we here focus on the aspects that are (PCS-)project related in the studied organization.

Specifically, because of the arrows present in the i* representation, the process fragment may seem to be directed, sequential and highly structured. The arrows nevertheless only represent dependencies between the involved roles and do not prescribe the sequence of execution of activities. Similarly, it presents all of the activities that have been reported as useful in the development of a PCS using Scrum but not all of them necessarily need to be performed in a specific sprint nor Scrum project. If used as a reference, the process fragment can be tailored at will to each specific sprint into a project. We distinguish several types of stakeholders having various goals and expectations, i.e.:

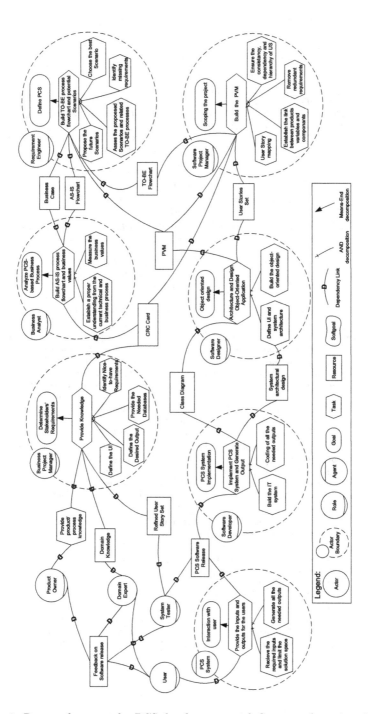

Fig. 3. Process fragment for PCS development with Scrum: exhaustive view.

Table 1. Instantiation of our Process Fragment.

Element	Definition (from [23])	Instantiation to our process fragment	i* Representation
Design Process	*Design process from which the fragment has been extracted*	*The Scrum Agile Method*	N/A
Phase	*A specification of the fragment position in the design workflow. Usually referring to a taxonomy*	*Determine Stakeholders' Requirements, Process Analysis, Product Analysis, Manage Product Backlog, Object oriented Analysis and Design, PCS System Implementation, PCS System Release Deployment, Test*	Goal
Goal	*The process-oriented objective of the fragment*	*The integration of PCS development in Scrum*	N/A
Activity	*A portion of work assignable to a performer (role)*	*Gather Knowledge, Build AS-IS process flowchart and business values, Define PCS, Plan Release, Architecture and Design Object-Oriented Application, Implement PCS System and Generate Output, Test Integration of Release, Test Release*	Task
Work Product	*The resulting product of the work done in the fragment; it can be realized in different ways also depending on the specific adopted notation*	*Business Case, AS-IS Flowcharts, TO-BE Flowcharts, User Stories Set, Class-Responsibility-Collaboration Cards, Product Variant Master, User Stories for Sprint, Class Diagram, System architectural design, PCS Software Executable Release, Refined User Story Set*	Resource
Role	*The stakeholder performing the work in the process and responsible of producing a work product (or part of it)*	*Domain Expert, Product Owner, Business Analyst, Requirements Engineer, Software Designer, Software Developer, Infrastructure Engineer, System Tester, User*	Role
Description	*It is the textual and pictorial description of the fragment; it provides a bird-eye on the whole process the fragments come from and the fragment overview in terms of tasks to be performed, roles and work product kind to be delivered*	The i* Process Model of Fig. 3	A Strategic Rationale Diagram
Composition Guideline	*A set of guidelines for assembling/composing the fragments with others*	The transformation of the PVM to a class diagram as presented in [14]. The transformation rules from a PVM to a User Story Set	N/A

- The *Product Owner (PO)* **Role** is a senior manager that is mainly in charge of developing a vision of the PCS that needs to be built and propagate that vision over the development team; it is a key stakeholder of the project. He does not provide a detailed specification of the PCS but rather a coarse-grained vision of how the PCS will be developed and integrated in the software ecosystem. The first process fragment **Activities** are performed by this role. These are performed in the context of the *Determine Stakeholders' Requirements* **Phase** which is represented as an i* Goal in Fig. 3. A means-end decomposition then allows to refine the i* Goal representing the **Phase**. Indeed, to fulfill this i* Goal, the *PO* **Role** performs the **Activity** *Gather Knowledge*. In itself, the latter **Activity** requires a set of other **Activities** to be achieved (as shown through the decompositions in Fig. 3). These are *Define the Desired Output, Provide the Needed Databases* and *Identify Nice to-have Requirements*; the output of these **Activities** is compiled into the *Business Case* **Work Product**). In addition, the *PO* **Role** also performs activities in the context of the *Manage Product Backlog* **Phase** which is represented as an i* Goal. A means-end decomposition then allows to refine the i* Goal representing the **Phase**. Indeed, to fulfill this i* Goal, the *PO* **Role** performs the **Activity** *Plan Release* [21]. The latter **Activity** allows to select a specific sub-set of User Stories (from the entire set of User Stories) to be developed/prototyped within the next Sprint. This allows to build the *User Stories for Sprint* **Work Product** used by the *Software Designer* **Role** to fulfill the *Architecture and Design Object-Oriented Application* **Activity**;
- The *Domain Expert* **Role** is played by all of the experts of the organizations' business processes and/or product and is thus in charge of participating to the *Provide Domain Knowledge* **Activity** fulfillment;
- The *Business Analyst* **Role** performs is activities in the context of the *Process Analysis* **Phase** which is represented as an i* Goal in Fig. 3. A means-end decomposition then allows to refine the i* Goal representing the **Phase**. Indeed, to fulfill this i* Goal, the *Business Analyst* **Role** performs the **Activity** *Build AS-IS process flowchart and business values*. In itself, the latter **Activity** requires a set of other **Activities** to be achieved (as shown through the decompositions in Fig. 3). These are *Establish a proper understanding from the current technical and business process*, and *Measure the business values*; the output of these **Activities** is compiled into the *AS-IS Flowcharts* **Work Product**). In the particular domain of PCS, we indeed proceed through an evaluation of the AS-IS business processes before defining the PCS. This practice is adopted by agile teams as well;
- The *Requirements Engineer* **Role** performs activities in the context of the *Product Analysis* **Phase** which is represented as an i* Goal in Fig. 3. A means-end decomposition then allows to refine the i* Goal representing the **Phase**. Indeed, to fulfill this i* Goal, the *Requirements Engineer* **Role** performs the **Activity** *Define PCS*. In itself, the latter **Activity** requires two **Activities** to be achieved. These are *Build TO-BE process flowchart and potential Scenarios* and *Build the Product Variant Master and CRC Cards*.

Both **Activities** requires a set of other **Activities** to be achieved (as shown through the decompositions in Fig. 3). More specifically:

- To achieve the *Build TO-BE process flowchart and potential Scenarios* **Activity**, one need to perform the **Activities** *Propose the future Scenarios, Asses the proposed Scenarios and related TO-BE processes, Identify missing requirements* and *Choose the best Scenario*. This allows to build the *TO-BE Flowcharts* **Work Product** later used by the *Software Designer* **Role** to fulfill the *Architecture and Design Object-Oriented Application* **Activity**;

- To achieve the *Build the Product Variant Master and CRC Cards* **Activity**, one need to perform the **Activities** *Establish the link between products variables and components, Remove redundant requirements* and *Ensure the consistency, dependency and hierarchy of User Stories*. This allows to build the *CRC Cards* as well as the *PVM* **Work Products** used by the *Software Designer* **Role** to fulfill the *Architecture and Design Object-Oriented Application* **Activity**.

Also the output of these **Activities** allow to build the *User Story Set* **Work Product** later used by the *PO* **Role** to fulfill the *User Story mapping* **Activity**.

- The *Software Designer* **Role** is in charge of transforming the specifications into a software architecture and design. He performs his activities in the context of the *Object-Oriented Analysis and Design* **Phase** which is represented as an i* Goal in Fig. 3. A means-end decomposition then allows to refine the i* Goal representing the **Phase**. Indeed, to fulfill this i* Goal, the *Software Designer* **Role** performs the **Activity** *Architecture and Design Object-Oriented Application*. The latter **Activity** allows to design the application. In itself, the latter **Activity** requires a set of other **Activities** to be achieved (as shown through the decompositions in Fig. 3). These are *Define User Interface, Build system architecture* and *Build the object-oriented design*. This allows to build the *Class Diagram* and the *System architectural design* **Work Products** used by the *Software Developer* **Role** to fulfill the *Implement PCS System and Generate Output* **Activity**;

- The *Software Developer* **Role** is in charge of transforming the software architecture and design into an executable PCS. He performs his activities in the context of the *PCS System Release Implementation* **Phase** which is represented as an i* Goal in Fig. 3. A means-end decomposition then allows to refine the i* Goal representing the **Phase**. Indeed, to fulfill this i* Goal, the *Software Developer* **Role** performs the **Activity** *Implement PCS System and Generate Output*. The latter **Activity** allows to build an executable release ready to be tested. In itself, the latter **Activity** requires a set of other **Activities** to be achieved (as shown through the decompositions in Fig. 3). These are *Build the IT system* and *Coding of all the needed outputs*. This allows to build the *PCS Software Executable Release* **Work Product** used by the *System Tester* **Role** to fulfill the *Test Release* **Activity**;

- The *Infrastructure Engineer* **Role** is in charge of ensuring that the release of the PCS built during the Sprint can be put in production through a smooth integration in the software infrastructure. He performs his activities in the context of the *PCS System Release Deployment **Phase*** which is represented as an i* Goal in Fig. 3. A means-end decomposition then allows to refine the i* Goal representing the ***Phase***. Indeed, to fulfill this i* Goal, the *Infrastructure Engineer **Role*** performs the ***Activity** Test Integration of Release*. In itself, the latter ***Activity*** requires a set of other ***Activities*** to be achieved (as shown through the decompositions in Fig. 3). These are *Perform Infrastructure Compatibility Testing for New Release* and *Perform Load Testing for New Release*. This allows to build the *PCS Software Executable Release **Work Product*** used by the *System Tester **Role*** to fulfill the *Test Release **Activity*** and the *Refined User Story Set **Work Product*** used by the *Requirements Engineer **Role*** to fulfill the *Build TO-BE process flowchart and potential Scenarios **Activity***;

- The *System Tester **Role*** is in charge of testing the developed PCS release. He performs his activities in the context of the *Testing **Phase*** which is represented as an i* Goal in Fig. 3. A means-end decomposition then allows to refine the i* Goal representing the ***Phase***. Indeed, to fulfill this i* Goal, the *System Tester **Role*** performs the ***Activity** Test Release*. The latter ***Activity*** allows to evaluate the output of the Sprint; for this the *System Tester **Role*** depends on the (end) *User **Role*** for fulfilling the *Provide Feedback on Software Release **Activity***. This allows to build the *Refined User Story Set **Work Product*** used by the *Requirements Engineer **Role*** to fulfill the *Define PCS **Activity***. We here refer to refining the business processes and the PCS analysis for the next Sprint;

- The (end) *User **Role*** uses the PCS and is thus in charge of participating to the *Feedback on the Software Release **Activity*** fulfillment.

5   Discussion: Requirements Representation and Backlog Management Within Scrum

Scrum traditionally manages its backlog on the basis of user stories. User stories written for the development of a PCS nevertheless requires to be accompanied with product structural details. To be able to create the configuration solution space for a specific product, one needs to be aware of the whole product architecture, the sequence (and importance) of the selection (which feature impacts others and should be chosen first), the constraints on product components (e.g., if the customer can order a car with 6 doors the whole product should be adjustable), etc. Consequently, the user stories are most often completed with a series of constraints. For example, the user story *As an online customer, I want to be able to choose the size of engine so that I can choose my preferred car capacity*, are accompanied with the scenario(s) *Given motor size is valid, When it is chosen from "2, 2.3, 2.5 liter". Then the: (i) Selection 2 is not valid is car has 4 doors; (ii) Selection 2.5 is not valid if car is 2 doors*. Since these constraints are difficult to express fully and efficiently in (structured) natural language, the PVM (with CRC cards) are used as a complementary documentation for the development team. Systematically these need to be built for any complex PCS development project and are consulted when filling the sprint backlog to ensure the constraints and dependencies are respected. There is redundancy between the constraints found with the user stories and the PVM; user stories serve for quick reference and the PVM is used for formal support.

In practice, in a PCS development project, the user stories drive the sprint backlog on the basis of their value but the the precedence constraints and dependencies lead to form groups of US that need to be implemented in the same release/sprint. In PCS, the prioritization of the user stories indeed depends on the structure of the product itself as well as the technical constraints. The product components which are the major variables controlling the solution space need to be developed and positioned at the beginning of PCS project. Moreover, from the technical perspective, the main attributes cannot be positioned after the minor ones as they should be located in a higher level of abstraction to be able to control the minor attributes range. For example, if we want to write the user stories to develop a PCS for a car, first of all, we should know about the product and which components have a higher priority; e.g., we cannot go to the details of the leather in the interior design before determining the main elements of the car. This has a significant impact on the management of the software process; these precedence constraints are the main driver of the release delivery in every Scrum-based PCS project.

Setting-up precedence/dependency constraints and ensuring they are respected is currently done manually in the studied organization. Also, no tool support is ensuring traceability between the user stories and the PVM requiring substantial domain knowledge to consistently fill the product/sprint backlogs. A Computer Aided Software Engineering (CASE) tool for backlog management is under development; it ensures traceability and consistency between the so-called *user story view* and *PVM view*. Based on the formal linkage between user stories and PVM parts, the tool automatically validates that all the constraints are respected when a sprint backlog is filled.

6   Towards a Revised Process Pattern for Product Configuration Systems Development and Threats to Validity

As shown process in the fragment, PCS development practices with Scrum subsequently evolved from the classical CPM procedure of [14]. Analysis practices remain rather aligned with that framework; indeed, in our process fragment we start with the *Process Analysis* including the evaluation of the situation AS-IS and the *Product Analysis* that includes the evaluation of the TO-BE processes and a first specification of the PCS. This remains aligned with the first and second stages of the traditional PCS development framework. At design stage we nevertheless have a significant difference with the latter framework. Our process fragment indeed considers *Object Oriented Analysis and Design* in one stage. The main reason that can be evoked here is that agile practices focus on fast development and do not advice to spend a lot of time on software architecture and design but rather prescribes to re-factor the architecture later on in the development if required. The *Implementation* stage of our process fragment corresponds to the *Programming* stage of the classical PCS development framework. Also, no explicit project management is evoked in the framework from [14]; in the proposed process fragment, the content of the Sprints are defined by the *PO* in the *Manage Product Backlog* stage. Finally, for an optimal integration of the PCS into the software ecosystem, practitioners include operators at the implementation stage. This allows to include the deployment constraints into the release development to ensure the PCS a smooth integration; this is a genuine practice not present in the CPM procedure.

Even if we do not strictly speaking conduct an experiment nor ask specific research questions so we do not draw formal conclusions (statistical or otherwise), we include some threats to validity related to the data collection that might lead to errors and hazards into the process fragment that we have presented.

With respect to the **construct validity**, the main threat is that interview questions are not interpreted by interviewees the way intended by the interviewers. To manage this, we conducted several interviews with people playing or having played each role. This allowed to collect multiple opinions on the same question/aspect so that the reliability on what we have inferred increases. Similarly, the process fragment has been validated with the interviewees in order to reduce the impact of this particular treat.

As far as the **internal validity** is concerned, the major threat is that answers from interviewees reflected their personal opinion(s) on how the organization should behave rather than how it empirically behaves. Also, the interviewees' roles have an influence on the knowledge he/she has on the asked questions. To deal with this we also asked the same set of questions each relating to different area of knowledge to each of the interviewees. This allowed to have the answer of the specialists (the roles involved in specific activities we ask a question on) as well as the ones of people that are not performing the activities but interact with the people performing them. Consequently, we have a more credible global picture of the organizational behavior.

The treat to **external validity** is that the results may not be generalizable to other organizations than the one studied. This threat to validity should be taken very seriously. We have presented the whole contribution as the results of the modeling of a single organization having experience on multiple projects. The process fragment has been made exhaustive meaning that it documents a set of practices that can or cannot be adopted in a single project/sprint. It should of course be further extended/validated on the basis of interviews in other organizations but we aimed to have a first study here showing how a complex PCS development is managed with Scrum into a mature organization.

7 Related Work

To the best of our knowledge, no scientific study reported on the use of Scrum or any agile method in the context of PCS. Other studies have nevertheless been made where other artifacts were used for software analysis in combination with user stories because of domain specifics (e.g., [27,29]). PCS and Software Product Line Engineering (SPLE) nevertheless do share common characteristics [17]. While PCS mainly support traditional engineering products (e.g., mechanical, electronic, etc.), software product families and SPLE are used in the engineering of software variants. These approaches all target to design new variants for a product family to meet customer requirements. To represent product knowledge, SPLE mostly uses feature models [16], a tree-like graphical model comparable to the PVM since it represents elements and their dependencies. Because of this similarity and the impact of this similarity on the management of the software development, we overview work relating SPLE and Agile Development (AD).

By definition, SPLE and AD can be seen as water and oil; as opposed to AD, SPLE focuses on upfront design [4]. Several works have nevertheless been conducted to combine SPLE and AD (e.g., [5,8,9,18,19]). In SPLE, two engineering phases are existing, Domain Engineering (DE) relating the domain knowledge and Application Engineering (AE) relating the customer needs; AD could be applied in these two phases of SPLE. However, the adoption of AD in DE requires more effort than in AE [4] because of the features dependencies (represented in the features model and requiring upfront design). This issue can immediately be related to the one of building the PVM in PCS.

O'Leary et al. (2012) [19] developed an *Agile Process model for Product Derivation* (*A-Pro-PD*). The latter aims at minimizing upfront investments. It combines the core assets of SPLE such as feature models, architecture models, code artifacts with AD. PuLSE-I [3] proposes to adopt agile practices such as planning games and incremental design into Product Derivation. Diaz et al. (2014) [5] customize the Scrum process for SPLE. User stories are used for describing software product-line features; they are prioritized on the basis of business value and assigned to sprints. The research in [22] aims at aligning SPLE artifacts from Kunbang [1] with AD artifacts from Agilefant [28]. More specifically, they relate leaf features (not composed of other features) to a feature backlog itself composed of the product backlog. The feature backlog is thus composed through elements on the lowest granularity level and recomposed into the product backlog for iteration (sprint) management.

8   Conclusion

The specifics of PCS make them an interesting but complicated application domain for a software development based on agile methods. PCS constitute the primary interface with the customer so that they are user-centered systems requiring feedback and validation to be aligned at best with their expectations. In such a context, proceeding through sprints would turn out to be very beneficial. PCS are nevertheless narrowly tight with the constraints inherent to the product they allow to customize so that there is less latitude in their development than in general software systems. Short releases immediately deployed allow testing the impact of new configurations on some particular customer sets to collect relevant sales data and efficiently support the production process.

This paper's main contribution is a process fragment for PCS development using Scrum. The latter has been built on the basis of data gathered from a PCS development team having substantial experience in such developments; it has been made exhaustive to include all of the reported activities of the case organization and aligned with the knowledge, syntax and semantics of SE concepts found in literature. This allowed to build a first reference of a process fragment tailorable to any PCS development project and more particularly its sprints. As such, it does not constitute a unique truth/pathway to be adopted/used faithfully but rather a guidance to be dynamically tailored for each project/sprint in function of their specifics and the desiderata of the development team. It nevertheless constitutes a consistent whole that can be used as a starting point for PCS development teams willing to adopt Scrum, agile and some DevOps practices in their projects. Finally, the process fragment has to evolve by (i) the study of more settings where the application of an agile method has to deal with software with much dependencies and technical constraints and (ii) by its active application on case studies. More roles, activities, tasks and artifacts can of course be added but the process fragment needs to remain easy to use in order not to hamper the agility of the project. We point to the development of a CASE tool to support activity selection to dynamically tailor it to a specific project/sprint. This way variability in the roles, activities and work products when adopting the fragment can be actively supported.

References

1. Asikainen, T., Männistö, T., Soininen, T.: Kumbang: a domain ontology for modelling variability in software product families. Adv. Eng. Inform. **21**(1), 23–40 (2007)
2. Bass, L., Weber, I., Zhu, L.: DevOps: A Software Architect's Perspective. Addison-Wesley Professional, Boston (2015)
3. Carbon, R., Lindvall, M., Muthig, D., Costa, P.: Integrating product line engineering and agile methods: flexible design up-front vs. incremental design. In: 1st International Workshop on Agile Product Line Engineering (APLE 2006), Maryland, USA (2006)
4. Díaz, J., Pérez, J., Alarcón, P.P., Garbajosa, J.: Agile product line engineering - a systematic literature review. Softw. Pract. Exp. **41**(8), 921–941 (2011)
5. Díaz, J., Pérez, J., Garbajosa, J.: Agile product-line architecting in practice: a case study in smart grids. Inf. Softw. Technol. **56**(7), 727–748 (2014)
6. Friedrich, G., Jannach, D., Stumptner, M., Zanker, M.: Knowledge Engineering for Configuration Systems. Elsevier, Amsterdam (2014)
7. Gibbs, G.R.: Thematic coding and categorizing. Anal. Qual. Data **703**, 38–56 (2007)
8. Haidar, H., Kolp, M., Wautelet, Y.: An integrated requirements engineering framework for agile software product lines. In: 13th International Conference on Software Technologies, ICSOFT 2018, Porto, Portugal, 26–28 July 2018, pp. 124–149 (2018). Revised Selected Papers
9. Hanssen, G.K., Fægri, T.E.: Process fusion: an industrial case study on agile software product line engineering. J. Syst. Softw. **81**(6), 843–854 (2008)

10. Harlou, U.: Developing product families based on architectures. Department of Mechanical Engineering, Technical University of Denmark (2006)
11. Haug, A., Hvam, L.: The modelling techniques of a documentation system that supports the development and maintenance of product configuration systems. Int. J. Mass Cust. **2**(1–2), 1–18 (2007)
12. Haug, A., Hvam, L., Mortensen, N.H.: The impact of product configurators on lead times in engineering-oriented companies. AI EDAM **25**(2), 197–206 (2011)
13. Hvam, L., Haug, A., Mortensen, N.H., Thuesen, C.: Observed benefits from product configuration systems. Int. J. Ind. Eng. Theory Appl. Pract. **20**(5–6), 1–6 (2013)
14. Hvam, L., Mortensen, N.H., Riis, J.: Product Customization. Springer, Heidelberg (2008). https://doi.org/10.1007/978-3-540-71449-1
15. IBM: The Rational Unified Process, Version 7.0.1 (2007)
16. Kang, K.C., Cohen, S.G., Hess, J.A., Novak, W.E., Peterson, A.S.: Feature-oriented domain analysis (foda) feasibility study. Technical report, Carnegie-Mellon University, Pittsburgh, PA, Software Engineering Institute (1990)
17. Männistö, T., Soininen, T., Sulonen, R.: Product configuration view to software product families. In: 10th International Workshop on Software Configuration Management (SCM-10), Toronto, Canada, pp. 14–15 (2001)
18. Noor, M.A., Rabiser, R., Grünbacher, P.: Agile product line planning: a collaborative approach and a case study. J. Syst. Softw. **81**(6), 868–882 (2008)
19. O'Leary, P., McCaffery, F., Thiel, S., Richardson, I.: An agile process model for product derivation in software product line engineering. J. Softw. Evol. Process **24**(5), 561–571 (2012)
20. OMG: Omg unified modeling language (omg uml). version 2.5. Technical report (2015)
21. Patton, J., Economy, P.: User Story Mapping: Discover the Whole Story, Build the Right Product. O'Reilly Media Inc, Newton (2014)
22. Raatikainen, M., Rautiainen, K., Myllärniemi, V., Männistö, T.: Integrating product family modeling with development management in agile methods. In: Proceedings of the 1st International Workshop on Software Development Governance, pp. 17–20. ACM (2008)
23. Seidita, V., Cossentino, M., Chella, A.: A proposal of process fragment definition and documentation. In: Cossentino, M., Kaisers, M., Tuyls, K., Weiss, G. (eds.) EUMAS 2011. LNCS (LNAI), vol. 7541, pp. 221–237. Springer, Heidelberg (2012). https://doi.org/10.1007/978-3-642-34799-3_15
24. Shafiee, S., Hvam, L., Bonev, M.: Scoping a product configuration project for engineer-to-order companies. Int. J. Ind. Eng. Manag. **5**(4), 207–220 (2014)
25. Shafiee, S., Hvam, L., Haug, A., Dam, M., Kristjánsdóttir, K.: The documentation of product configuration systems: a framework and an IT solution. Adv. Eng. Inform. **32**, 163–175 (2017). https://doi.org/10.1016/j.aei.2017.02.004
26. Trentin, A., Perin, E., Forza, C.: Product configurator impact on product quality. Int. J. Prod. Econ. **135**(2), 850–859 (2012)
27. Trkman, M., Mendling, J., Trkman, P., Krisper, M.: Impact of the conceptual model's representation format on identifying and understanding user stories. Inf. Softw. Technol. **116**, 106169 (2019)
28. Vähäniitty, J.: Do small software companies need portfolio management, too. In: 2006 Proceedings of the 13th International Product Development Management Conference, Milan, Italy, pp. 1471–1486, EIASM. Citeseer (2006)
29. Wautelet, Y., Heng, S., Hintea, D., Kolp, M., Poelmans, S.: Bridging user story sets with the use case model. In: Link, S., Trujillo, J.C. (eds.) ER 2016. LNCS,

vol. 9975, pp. 127–138. Springer, Cham (2016). https://doi.org/10.1007/978-3-319-47717-6_11

30. Wautelet, Y., Heng, S., Kiv, S., Kolp, M.: User-story driven development of multi-agent systems: a process fragment for agile methods. Comput. Lang. Syst. Struct. **50**, 159–176 (2017)

31. Wautelet, Y., Heng, S., Kolp, M., Mirbel, I.: Unifying and extending user story models. In: Jarke, M., et al. (eds.) CAiSE 2014. LNCS, vol. 8484, pp. 211–225. Springer, Cham (2014). https://doi.org/10.1007/978-3-319-07881-6_15

32. Yu, E., Giorgini, P., Maiden, N., Mylopoulos, J.: Social Modeling for Requirements Engineering. MIT Press, Cambridge (2011)

Microservices

Kuksa: A Cloud-Native Architecture for Enabling Continuous Delivery in the Automotive Domain

Ahmad Banijamali[1]([✉])[iD], Pooyan Jamshidi[2][iD], Pasi Kuvaja[1][iD], and Markku Oivo[1][iD]

[1] M3S Research Unit, ITEE Faculty, University of Oulu, Oulu, Finland
{ahmad.banijamali,pasi.kuvaja,markku.oivo}@oulu.fi
[2] Computer Science and Engineering Department,
University of South Carolina, Columbia, USA
pjamshid@cse.sc.edu

Abstract. Connecting vehicles to cloud platforms has enabled innovative business scenarios while raising new quality concerns, such as reliability and scalability, which must be addressed by research. Cloud-native architectures based on microservices are a recent approach to enable continuous delivery and to improve service reliability and scalability. We propose an approach for restructuring cloud platform architectures in the automotive domain into a microservices architecture. To this end, we adopted and implemented microservices patterns from literature to design the cloud-native automotive architecture and conducted a laboratory experiment to evaluate the reliability and scalability of microservices in the context of a real-world project in the automotive domain called Eclipse Kuksa. Findings indicated that the proposed architecture could handle the continuous software delivery over-the-air by sending automatic control messages to a vehicular setting. Different patterns enabled us to make changes or interrupt services without extending the impact to others. The results of this study provide evidences that microservices are a potential design solution when dealing with service failures and high payload on cloud-based services in the automotive domain.

Keywords: Microservices · Cloud-native architecture · Cloud computing · Automotive

1 Introduction

In recent years, there has been an increased focus from industry and academia to investigate cloud platform architectures that enable continuous software delivery (CD) in vehicles [10]. Many industries have started to look for CD solutions as they need to release quality software more frequently, better respond to automotive market changes, avoid vehicle recalls, improve productivity, and increase customer satisfaction [28]. For this purpose, vehicular software and information resources are being virtualised and designed as services in the cloud [17]. Cloud

© Springer Nature Switzerland AG 2019
X. Franch et al. (Eds.): PROFES 2019, LNCS 11915, pp. 455–472, 2019.
https://doi.org/10.1007/978-3-030-35333-9_32

platforms in the automotive domain (ACPs) provide the possibilities to exchange data beyond vehicles [19], connect vehicles to other objects in the environment, update automotive software using wireless communications systems (over-the-air) [33], and enable many more business services in the cloud (Fig. 1).

Fig. 1. Cloud platforms in the automotive domain

Nevertheless, the migration of software delivery to ACPs has raised new research challenges. For example, vehicle-to-cloud (V2C) data transmission requires low latency and high reliability to satisfy the requirements of real-time systems [21]. Scalability is another challenge that demands the decomposition of functionalities and efficient data management [15]. Furthermore, the resiliency configuration explains runtime behaviour and faulty components [15], and security is a major requirement for protecting vehicles from malicious attacks [34].

In addition, as for the migration process towards distributed systems, such as cloud-native architectures, many architecture designs fail as long as their goal is to only replace the existing legacy architecture with a virtualised environment in the cloud [3]. The reasons may include but are not limited to a lack of solid business cases for cloud migration, neglecting adequate support teams, migrating at once to the cloud, and not considering applications' architecture refactoring [4,5]. Consequently, the benefits from migration to the cloud platforms could be trivial, as the failure can happen anytime [3].

Despite the importance of CD and the mentioned quality challenges in ACPs, there has been insufficient focus from research that provides practical insights into designing software architectures that address those quality concerns [6]. Due to the impact of microservices on cloud-native architectures with respect to quality requirements, such as reliability, scalability, availability, and fault-tolerance [4,5], microservices can be a potential solution for the existing challenges in ACPs. In relation to this, the ultimate objective of our paper is to investigate whether microservices *can enable over-the-air (OTA) continuous delivery in ACPs while improving reliability and scalability in this domain*. We have proposed a microservices architecture based on a real-world project in the automotive domain called Eclipse Kuksa and conducted a laboratory experiment to evaluate the architecture with respect to the mentioned quality attributes.

The results of this study can benefit industrial practitioners and academic researchers in the domains of automotive software engineering and cloud platform design. The study is aimed at researchers who would like to gain insight into the application of microservices in the domain of ACPs. From the practitioners' perspective, the findings provide experimental results for the reliability and scalability of microservices in a real-world industrial case in the automotive domain. The key contributions of the study are: (1) assessing the relative extent to which cloud-native architecture can enable continuous delivery in the automotive domain and (2) evaluating the role of microservices patterns in improving the reliability and scalability of services in this context.

2   Background

2.1   Microservices

Monolithic architectures are usually successful when the whole system is small and the number of functions is low [9]. Increasingly, the number of end users requires more deployment in the cloud [9], as every time that we apply a change to a small part of an application, we need to build and deploy the whole monolithic system again [3]. Furthermore, scalability means scaling the whole application rather than a part of the components that requires more resources [13]. As a consequence, many companies, such as Netflix, Amazon, and Atlassian, have migrated to more scalable and reliable architectures like microservices.

As for distributed systems, microservices are used to design fine-grained, modular services that have different life cycles but work together [23]. Each service deploys independently [2] using a potentially different deployment framework typically in the cloud [25], scales independently [31], is tested individually, and accomplishes responsibilities independently [31] while communicating through lightweight mechanisms, such as RESTful APIs [13]. The relevant architecture breaks down a system into services, each as a business capability [13].

Microservices promote a DevOps philosophy about separated small teams working together to meet the objectives of a large mission-critical system [5]. On the other hand, DevOps provides the framework for developing, deploying, and managing the microservices container ecosystem [11]. In this architecture, a microservice is developed and maintained by one small team while coordination among the teams is minimised [35]. It is noted that the largest size of the teams usually follows Amazon's notion of the "Two Pizza Team", meaning not a large group of people [13].

Despite all the advantages that microservices bring to the architecture designs, they have several challenges that should carefully be addressed. For example, replacing a monolithic architecture with a large number of interconnected microservices can increase latency and other performance issues [5]. Having a system that is currently being used in production, it is necessary to make the migration incrementally [35] without data loss and interruption [5], during which we need adequate frameworks and experience in how to proceed

[35]. Eventually, inconsistencies among microservices is another relevant challenge [13].

2.2 Software Architectures of Automotive Cloud Platforms

Convergence of the internet of things and cloud computing has enabled innovative business use cases, ecosystems, and players in the automotive domain [17]. ACPs' application includes but is not limited to advanced vehicle connectivity, infotainment applications, voice and video data streaming, fleet management services, remote diagnostics and maintenance, and telematics services [14,18].

Due to the increasing number of connected vehicles, the security, reliability, availability, robustness, and scalability of services are becoming new quality requirements in ACPs [16]. The extent of architectures in ACPs ranges from multi-layered architectures [7] to service-oriented architectures (SOA) [22,32]. Datta et al. [8] designed a framework for connected vehicles to offer consumer-centric services and a uniform mechanism for describing and collecting vehicular sensors' data. The designed architecture applies technologies such as road side units (RSUs) and machine-to-machine (M2M) gateways, including the fog computing platform [8]. The authors argued that using fog computing technologies can improve the fault tolerance, reliability, and scalability of the system [8]. Scalability and interoperability have been addressed in another study [26] in a modular architecture built upon DevOps practices to enable vehicle-to-everything (V2X) applications. The authors divided real-time applications for managing traffic into small modules to validate the functionality of the architecture [26].

A scalable and fault-tolerant data-processing design for real-time traffic-based routing was proposed by another study [27]. It argued that the designed architecture can serve a wide range of workloads and use cases with low-latency requirements [27]. Real-world scenarios of intelligent traffic system applications demonstrated the need for scalable big data analysis, service encapsulation, dynamic configuration, and optimisation strategies in this context [12]. Due to the technological variety in ACPs, architecture designs must assure stakeholders [5] that provisional services will meet the quality requirements at a specific level of cost and risk that is enforced by service level agreements (SLAs) [24].

3 Research Questions and Method

This section describes the study's objective, research questions, and research method.

3.1 Objective and Research Questions

The main objective of our study was to evaluate whether microservices can address CD in the context of ACPs and whether they can improve the reliability and scalability of services in this context. The research questions (RQs) for this study were as follows:

- RQ1: Can the microservices architecture design enable over-the-air continuous delivery from cloud platforms in the automotive domain?
- RQ2: How can the microservices architecture design improve the reliability and scalability of services in cloud platforms in the automotive domain?

3.2   Research Method

To design the target microservices architecture, we adopted a software architecture from a real-world project in the context of ACPs called Eclipse Kuksa (see Sect. 4). It was important to initiate the migration process based on an existing project to review how the new architecture design could improve reliability and scalability in this domain. For the migration and refactoring process of the current architecture of Eclipse Kuksa, we applied microservices patterns from literature (e.g., [4]). Each refactoring represented a small and controlled change, so it was possible to identify how the quality attributes changed. The codes are available on GitHub[1].

Recent research [29] has explained that although it is critical to evaluate the requirements of a new software system to ensure system acceptance by users, real context evaluations are often complex. Before operating newly designed systems in real dynamic and complex environments, it is reasonable to assess them in laboratory setting experiments [29]. Thus, to evaluate the designed microservices architecture, we used laboratory experiments as the research method to answer the RQs of this study.

To date, there are several domain-specific services designed in Eclipse Kuksa. Among them, this study selected a service that is used for the purpose of motion control. Previous studies [4,5,20,23,30] have proposed frameworks and parameters in which architecture designers select microservices for migration, for example, according to their value to end users (e.g., improved user experience regarding the availability of services) or the project organisation (i.e., information exchange scalability and resiliency support) [5]. We selected the *motion control service* because of its value to end users and applicability in different scenarios. Furthermore, it demonstrates how end users can send control commands to vehicles from the cloud platform in Eclipse Kuksa using different user interfaces. It is a general service that can be part of many scenarios in this domain. The primary business driver for this service is to demonstrate OTA updates and messaging from the cloud to vehicles. This creates suitable grounds for future studies, e.g., on driver behaviour optimisation, natural language processing in vehicles, or OTA driver authentication.

Section 5 provides more details of our evaluation setting and the technology stacks used in our experiment.

---

[1] https://github.com/ahmadbanijamali/Rover-Control-Experiment.git.

4   Eclipse Kuksa

The Eclipse Kuksa[2] utilises open, vehicle-independent protocols, ensuring life-time value for vehicles through upgradable applications. It addresses application systems, software solutions, and services for the mass differentiation of vehicles. The ecosystem of Eclipse Kuksa is comprised of three main platforms, including the (1) in-vehicle platform, (2) cloud platform, and (3) an app IDE. The Eclipse Kuksa is supported by a wide range of integrated open source software technologies and development environments, such as automotive grade Linux (AGL) and Eclipse Paho for the in-vehicle platform and Eclipse-Hono, Eclipse Hawkbit, Eclipse MosQuitto, Keycloak, and InfluxDB in the cloud back-end.

4.1   The Existing Architecture of Eclipse Kuksa

Figure 2 shows the components and services in the Eclipse Kuksa architecture. The architecture only provides information about the necessary components and services that we needed in our experiment in the scope of this paper. It neglects other parts of Eclipse Kuksa ecosystem, such as device management and representation, authentication and authorisation, and the app store.

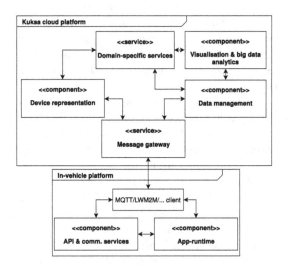

Fig. 2. Software architecture of Eclipse Kuksa

Message Gateway. The Eclipse Kuksa cloud platform (EKCP) sends and receives different types of messages from and to various sources, such as vehicles, devices, and third-party services. In general, messages include "telemetry messages" that depict data stemming from vehicles, devices, and sensors and "commands and

---

[2] https://projects.eclipse.org/projects/iot.kuksa.

controls messages" that are dedicated to the vehicles and device management components. The message gateway provides remote service interfaces for connecting vehicles and devices to the cloud back-end.

Data Storage and Management. An important part of the realisation of the EKCP is the storage and management of vehicles' and IoT devices' data in the appropriate database management system (DBMS). Although data management is a central aspect of every cloud platform architecture, due to the wide range of vehicles and devices connected to ACPs, it is necessary to establish a well-defined data management system that can handle complexities related to big data, consistency, performance, scalability, and security.

Visualisation and Big Data Analytics. The advances in the digitisation of the automotive domain have created a large amount of heterogeneous data coming from various sources. This has also yielded new requirements in terms of volume, variety, and velocity that are commonly called big data. The EKCP includes components and services to visualise and manage the big data in this domain.

Device Representation. To realise the distinct functionality of domain-specific services, a digital representation is important. Digital twin offers the possibility to access and alter the state of a vehicle's functionality in a controlled manner.

Domain-Specific Services. The domain-specific services are developed according to different use cases and business scenarios on top of the in-vehicle platform. They can handle different functions and tasks in vehicles and beyond them.

In-Vehicle Platform. The communication protocols such as MQTT and LWM2M have enabled sending different messages from vehicles to the cloud and vice versa. The in-vehicle platform in Eclipse Kuksa includes an app runtime environment that is connected to an in-vehicle gateway, enabling software delivery and deployment in vehicles.

4.2 The Proposed Microservices Architecture for the Eclipse Kuksa Cloud Platform

Connected vehicles have high demands on the exchange of data between vehicles and a variety of services in the cloud. Due to the importance of the domain-specific services in ACPs, we selected a sample telemetry service that communicates with vehicles through sending command and control messages to vehicles (see Sect. 3.2). Figure 3 shows our proposal for the refactored architecture of EKCP that is described in greater detail in this section.

The migration to a microservices architecture in EKCP is a step-by-step process including new components and modules and modifying the existing components (Fig. 4). We started the process by creating a better understanding of the existing architecture (Sect. 4.1) and introducing the CD pipeline.

Configuration Server. According to previous research [4], we required two individual and separate repositories as source code storage and software configurations storage. The configuration server is a central place to support the externalised configuration and changes without rebuilding or restarting the services.

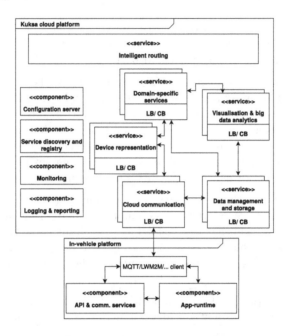

Fig. 3. The microservices architecture in Eclipse Kuksa

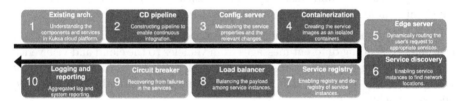

Fig. 4. The migration process to a microservices architecture

The Spring cloud configuration server is a potential technology that stores each microservice property based on the service-ID. The properties can be stored in the cloud or in other repositories, such as in GitHub.

Containerisation. The next step before establishing an intelligent routing (edge server) component was the containerisation of each service. This step is a part of the CD pipeline for building the container image for each service. The Docker and Docker Hub are the technology stacks used for this purpose.

Intelligent Routing (Edge Server). This is the layer right after the user interface (UI). Edge server dynamically routes requests to the appropriate microservices. Thus, it is possible here to monitor the service usage, as all requests pass this layer. As an instance of the technology stack, Netflix provides Zuul as the front door for all requests from devices and web sites to the back-end.

Service Discovery. Service instances dynamically find network locations of a service provider, which is critical for the service's auto-scaling and failures.

Service Registry. In addition to service discovery, service registry registers and de-registers service instances. It stores addresses of each service as the service initiates and removes the addresses once it does not receive the heartbeat or the service is terminated. Spring Eureka provides the technology stack for service discovery and registry.

Load Balancer. A purpose for migrating to a microservices architecture is to improve the scalability of each service based on the payload [5]. We used load balancers to distribute the payload among multiple instances of our services. Netflix Ribbon and Apache Zookeeper are examples of relevant technology stack.

Circuit Breaker. Once the number of consecutive failures in services crosses a specific threshold (open state), we call the circuit breaker to either invoke a response code or return the latest cached data from the service provider. Once the timeout expires, the circuit breaker allows a limited number of test requests to service providers, and, if they pass, it changes to a closed state. Hystrix and NGINX are relevant technology stacks here.

Logging and Reporting. To control what is happening in microservices, accessing the consolidated logs [5], implementing infrastructure-level metrics, and creating a holistic view of the system, we need to establish an efficient logging and reporting functionality. The system is used for a variety of purposes, such as monitoring the traffic and service usages, identifying the cause of errors, and finding performance bottlenecks. Due to the wide scope, different technologies (i.e., Hystrix, Grafana, Kibana, and fluentd) are used for specific purposes.

Continuous Delivery Pipeline. To establish a CD pipeline, we required continuous integration using following components. Jenkins was the solution used as the continuous integration server to build and deploy the applications. Docker was the tool that we used for the containerisation of applications and to isolate them from each other. The Docker Hub, as the repository of Docker container images, pulls images from Docker's public registry instance. Figure 5 shows the CD pipeline in EKCP.

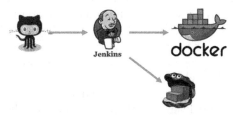

Fig. 5. The continuous delivery pipeline

5 Evaluation

5.1 Experimental Setting

To evaluate CD in the proposed architecture, we considered that our service sent automatically-generated updates as specific calls to forty vehicles in a specific region of the city. The calls were similar as they were demonstrating one released update. The software delivery cycle that the calls sent to the vehicles was one minute. In each call, we changed "next move direction" in the rover and the designed architecture should continue the message delivery without interruption. We ran the experiment for a duration of one hour to record how different microservices patterns behave in a CD environment in ACPs. We reviewed what percentages of calls is sent successfully to the rover and provide a statistics of successful and failed calls to show the CD performance in our design.

To review the scalability and reliability of the services in our designed architecture, we deployed three different scenarios. We aimed to measure metrics such as service downtime, recovery time, and load sharing behaviours. We registered four instances of Backserver service and one Client service (see Sect. 5) on a Spring Eureka server. The experimental scenarios were as follows.

1. During the first 10 min, all services were up and running. Half of the Backserver instances (two instances) shutdown automatically at 00:10 and restarted simultaneously at 00:15.
2. All service instances from the Backserver shut down automatically at 00:20 and started gradually (one by one) every five minutes until they all came up at 00:40.
3. All service instances from the Backserver went off at 00:45 and re-started simultaneously at 00:50.

Figure 6 presents the experimental setting in this study, including the different services, components, and technology stacks.

The Cloud Back-End. We developed the Backserver and Client services using Spring Boot. All microservices were running on a computer with an Intel Core i7-6600U CPU @2.6 GHz and 20 GB installed RAM. Eclipse Hono version 7.0 was used as the message broker to connect the Backserver to the in-vehicle platform via MQTT using a 4G connection. The Hono instance was placed on an Azure Kubernetes service (AKS) cluster.

The Client service automatically triggered the delivery to the Backserver instances. Each message delivered to the rover contained the "rover id", "speed control", and "next move direction". The Backserver was responsible for sending the messages to the Hono instance and from there to the rover. The microservice patterns and technologies used are shown in Table 1.

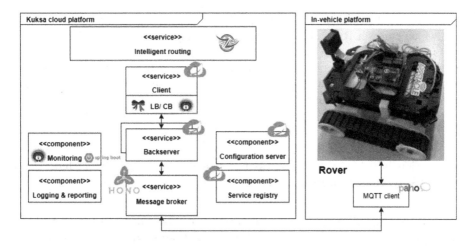

Fig. 6. The experimental setting

Table 1. Microservice patterns and technologies used in this experiment

Pattern	Technology	Customised configuration
Intelligent routing	Netflix Zuul	serviceId: backserver, serviceId: Client
Load Balancing	Netflix Ribbon	Server list refresh interval: 2s
Circuit breaker	Hystrix	Sleep window: 5s, Request volume threshold: 20, Error threshold: 50%
Configuration server	Eureka	–
Service registry	Eureka	eureka.client.register-with-eureka=false eureka.client.fetch-registry=false
Monitoring	Hystrix dashboard	–

The In-Vehicle Platform. To demonstrate the outcomes of the experiment, we used a rover, which is an open source mobile robot. The rover includes a Raspberry Pi 3 Model B (RPi3), a motor driver layer (Arduino), and a Rover-Sense layer designed for in-vehicle communication demonstrations. A customised software (called roverapp[3]) was designed that runs on a Linux-based embedded single board computer (i.e., RPi3). The roverapp includes an API to handle various functions in the rover, such as motion control.

In addition to the commands sent to the rover, the RoverSense layer sends telemetry data from different sensors, such as infrared proximity sensors, ultrasonic sensors, temperature and humidity sensors, and an accelerometer to the cloud. The roverapp creates the possibility of real-time video streaming to the cloud platforms, such as Azure or AWS. It also allows the marker detection used in platooning or autonomous driving scenarios.

---

[3] https://app4mc-rover.github.io/rover-app/.

The rover's features' applications and tooling use AGL as the operating system, which runs on RPi3. The in-vehicle Kuksa layers, including a middleware layer (containing Kuksa APIs and Eclipse Paho) and an application layer (containing a runtime and sandbox environment), run on top of AGL. These two layers enable functions such as communication to the cloud via MQTT and third party applications' implementation.

5.2   Results

This section is structured to address the research questions and includes the aggregated results of our experiment.

RQ1. Can the Microservices Architecture Design Enable over-the-air Continuous Delivery from Cloud Platforms in the Automotive Domain? CD helps teams to produce applications in short cycles and ensures that the software can be reliably released at any time. Figure 7 shows the service registry dashboard in a Spring Eureka server. It shows that four instances of the Backserver and one Client service were up and running at the time of the experiment.

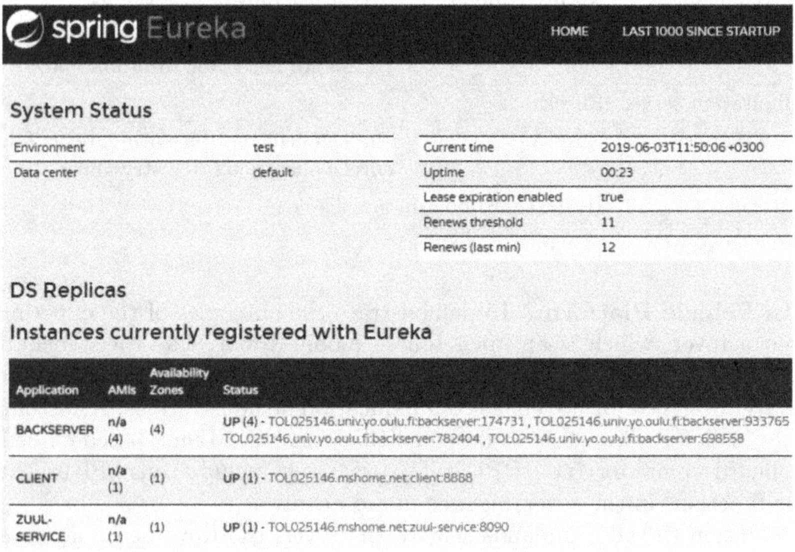

Fig. 7. Registered services for the designed architecture

Table 2 shows the aggregated results of the duration that each service instance of the Backserver was up during our designed scenarios. In addition, it shows statistical information on the service resiliency in our setting.

Table 2. Experiment results using the designed microservices architecture

		No. of running instances in three scenarios	Time
Total duration of experiment	60 min	zero (shutdown all instances)	10 min
		one	5 min
Cycle time	1 min	two	10 min
		three	5 min
		four	30 min
Circuit breaker status	No.	Circuit breaker status	No.
Success (execution completed with no errors)	22	Failure (execution threw an Exception)	24
Timeout (execution started, but did not complete in the allowed time)	4	Short-Circuited	0
Quickest time to call Backserver when came up		1 min	

During our experiment, we could make changes (shutdown, re-start, and update the code) in a service without affecting other services. According to our experimental scenarios, Backserver instances set up and down multiple times, even though it did not impact other available services. It was easy to make changes on a service, e.g., updating the listening port or rover direction, without interruption to other services.

Our findings indicated that although we had a number of failed calls and timeout errors due to the following reason, the circuit breaker could prevent cascading failures to other services. The Client service talked with the service registry to receive the IP addresses of available Backserver instances and used its load balancer to choose one of them. The Client service could not know directly that a Backserver instance was no longer available. This is the job of the service registry to continuously discover which Backserver instances are dead or alive via heartbeat mechanisms. During our experiment, the Backserver instances shutdown several times while the Client service could not get the list of the remaining instances from the service registry in real-time. In this approach, the service discovery logic tightly coupled with clients, in which it could improve through other approaches, such as server-side service discovery.

Summary. The designed architecture preserved continuous software delivery by automatic registering and de-registering service instances and continuing OTA software delivery after each change.

RQ2. How Can the Microservices Architecture Design Improve the Reliability and Scalability of Services in Cloud Platforms in the Automotive Domain? Table 3 shows a summary of the results of the total calls on each Backserver instance. The Client service sent more calls on the Backserver instances that were up for a longer time in our scenarios. In total, we had 990 successful calls distributed among four Backserver instances to control the rover speed and movement direction.

Table 3. The number of calls on the Backserver instances

		Service #1	455
Total calls sent to rover	990	Service #2	276
		Service #3	153
		Service #4	106

Figure 8 presents how the load balancing mechanism distributed the load among the different instances. In addition, it shows the circuit breaker behaviour regarding different errors to improve the reliability of the system.

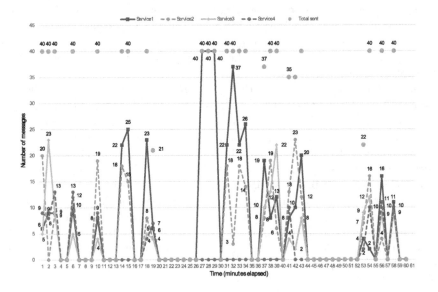

Fig. 8. The number of calls on each service in three scenarios

The client-side strategy load balancing automatically distributed concurrent calls to the available Backserver instances. The Netflix Ribbon load balancer continuously rotated a list of Backserver instances that were attached to it (the

Round Robin method). In addition, to manage failures that happened in a service (e.g., timeout), Hystrix prevented cascading failures to other services, which improved the fault tolerance of our system. Broken service instances automatically recovered and registered themselves into the Eureka service registry, which made the designed microservices recoverable.

Summary. Although failures often happen in services, load balancing mechanisms were able to skip unhealthy instances.

6   Discussions

The objective of this research was to review whether the recent architectural design styles, such as microservices, could address CD and DevOps in the automotive domain. In an experimental setting, we evaluated how quality attributes such as the scalability and reliability of services could be improved by microservices patterns.

RQ1. Can the Microservices Architecture Design Enable Over-the-air Continuous Delivery from Cloud Platforms in the Automotive Domain? A previous study [6] noted that to maintain continuous software delivery, it is necessary to address architectural challenges, such as the deployability and modifiability. Our findings showed that the proposed architecture could improve the deployability of the system as there was no need to resolve the conflicts between changes afterwards. Furthermore, we could deploy changes in different services independently and quickly without any interruption in other services.

We noticed that microservices created the possibility to make the changes localised to one service while other services were not affected. We had lightweight services that made any update in the codes easier. In safety-critical systems, such as ACPs, it is vital that changes in a service or technology do not interrupt other running services. Our findings showed that microservices could improve the modifiability of the architecture. Although the designed architecture could enable the CD in this domain by sending OTA messgaes to the rover, there were several failed and timeout calls that should be optimised with respect to different service level agreements.

RQ2. How Can the Microservices Architecture Design Improve the Reliability and Scalability of Services in Cloud Platforms in the Automotive Domain? Scalability is the property of a system that handles a growing amount of requests by adding resources to the system. The Backserver instances allowed us to support a good number of concurrent calls coming from the Client to the rover. The Backserver was also stateless, which did not retain consumer states. It enabled us to have autoscaling of the services when the load required.

The load balancing mechanism in our system could also distribute the load automatically among available service instances.

Our findings in this study showed how the fault-tolerant mechanisms, such as the circuit breaker, could handle the resiliency and reliability in our proposed architecture. We defined different thresholds such as the error threshold percentage and request volume threshold to force the circuit breaker to open and prevent slow or failed calls from interrupting other services in our architecture, which improved reliability of the architecture.

6.1   Threats to Validity

Construct validity, in our research, is concerned with using the right measures in our experiment. To assess the reliability and scalability, we used the common metrics that are widely applied in the literature (see [5,23]). Internal validity concerns the relationship between the constructs and the proposed explanation. Our implementation was run in three scenarios in a laboratory experimental setting with specific and defined objectives. Although we established a controlled environment, aspects related to the performance of Azure cloud platform or 4G network connection could not be customised or controlled. In addition, the implementation and results were discussed and reviewed among the authors of this study. In our experiment, we selected the technology stacks that are commonly used by companies and the performance analysis of those technologies are out of scope of this research.

External validity is related to the generalisability of the study. A previous study [1] noted that it is not essential to satisfy all requirements by a given benchmark candidate to be considered useful for empirical research. We applied microservices patterns from scientific literature, established a controlled experiment with three defined scenarios, and used a real-world project to evaluate the behaviour of one single microservice in the designed architecture. Future studies can replicate the experiment with multiple services in real continuous software delivery environments in the automotive domain to evaluate generalisability of the results. Reliability concerns the repeatability of the research procedure and conclusions. We explained in detail the experimental setting and all publicly available materials, which can be applied by future studies.

7   Conclusion

Automotive cloud platforms have received increasing attention from research and industrial communities. To increase the reliability and scalability in ACPs and enable continuous software delivery in the automotive domain, we proposed a microservices architecture for a real-world project called Eclipse Kuksa and ran an experiment to evaluate the designed architecture.

Our findings showed that the proposed architecture could handle CD through improving the deployability, modifiability, and availability of the architecture.

Our designed architecture could address quality issues, such as payload distribution among different instances and the resiliency of services. The research findings showed that microservices are an interesting design alternative to address quality concerns of future cloud platforms in the automotive domain.

References

1. Aderaldo, C.M., Mendonça, N.C., Pahl, C., Jamshidi, P.: Benchmark requirements for microservices architecture research. In: 1st International Workshop on Establishing the Community-Wide Infrastructure for Architecture-Based Software Engineering, pp. 8–13. IEEE (2017)
2. Balalaie, A., Heydarnoori, A., Jamshidi, P.: Microservices architecture enables devops: migration to a cloud-native architecture. IEEE Softw. **33**, 42–52 (2016)
3. Balalaie, A., Heydarnoori, A., Jamshidi, P.: Migrating to cloud-native architectures using microservices: an experience report. In: Celesti, A., Leitner, P. (eds.) ESOCC Workshops 2015. CCIS, vol. 567, pp. 201–215. Springer, Cham (2016). https://doi.org/10.1007/978-3-319-33313-7_15
4. Balalaie, A., Heydarnoori, A., Jamshidi, P., Tamburri, D.A., Lynn, T.: Microservices migration patterns. J. Softw.: Pract. Exp. **48**, 2019–2042 (2018)
5. Bass, L., Weber, I., Zhu, L.: DevOps: A Software Architect's Perspective. Addison-Wesley Professional, Boston (2015)
6. Chen, L.: Microservices: architecting for continuous delivery and DevOps. In: IEEE International Conference on Software Architecture (ICSA), pp. 39–397. IEEE (2018)
7. Contreras-Castillo, J., Zeadally, S., Guerrero-Ibanez, J.A.: Internet of vehicles: architecture, protocols, and security. Internet Things J. **5**, 3701–3709 (2018)
8. Datta, S.K., Gyrard, A., Bonnet, C., Boudaoud, K.: oneM2M architecture based user centric IoT application development. In: 3rd International Conference on Future Internet of Things and Cloud, pp. 100–107. IEEE (2015)
9. Dragoni, N., Dustdar, S., Larsen, S.T., Mazzara, M.: Microservices: migration of a mission critical system. arXiv preprint arXiv:1704.04173 (2017)
10. Ebert, C., Favaro, J.: Automotive software. IEEE Softw. **34**, 33–39 (2017)
11. Ebert, C., Gallardo, G., Hernantes, J., Serrano, N.: Devops. IEEE Softw. **33**, 94–100 (2016)
12. Fiosina, J., Fiosins, M., Müller, J.P.: Big data processing and mining for next generation intelligent transportation systems. J. Teknologi **63**, 21–38 (2013)
13. Fowler, M., Lewis, J.: Microservices. https://martinfowler.com/articles/microservices.html
14. Google Cloud: Designing a Connected Vehicle Platform on Cloud IoT Core 2019-05-07. https://cloud.google.com/solutions/designing-connected-vehicle-platform
15. Häberle, T., Charissis, L., Fehling, C., Nahm, J., Leymann, F.: The connected car in the cloud: a platform for prototyping telematics services. IEEE Softw. **32**, 11–17 (2015)
16. Haghighatkhah, A., Banijamali, A., Pakanen, O., Oivo, M., Kuvaja, P.: Automotive software engineering: a systematic mapping study. J. Syst. Soft. **128**, 25–55 (2017)
17. He, W., Yan, G., Da, X.L.: Developing vehicular data cloud services in the IoT environment. IEEE Trans. Ind. Inf. **10**, 1587–1595 (2014)
18. Jain, P.: Automotive Cloud Technology to Drive Industry's New Business Models - 2019-05-07. http://shiftmobility.com/2017/06/automotive-cloud-technology-drive-automotive-industrys-new-business-models

19. Armbrust, M., et al.: A view of cloud computing. Commun. ACM **53**, 50–59 (2010)
20. Levcovitz, A., Terra, R., Valente, M.T.: Towards a technique for extracting microservices from monolithic enterprise systems. arXiv:1605.03175 (2016)
21. Lu, N., Cheng, N., Zhang, N., Shen, X., Mark, J.W.: Connected vehicles: solutions and challenges. Internet Things J. **1**, 289–299 (2014)
22. Mietzner, R., Leymann, F., Unger, T.: Horizontal and vertical combination of multi-tenancy patterns in service-oriented applications. Enterp. Inf. Syst. **5**, 59–77 (2011)
23. Newman, S.: Building Microservices: Designing Fine-Grained Systems. O'Reilly Media Inc., Newton (2015)
24. O'Brien, L., Merson, P., Bass, L.: Quality attributes for service-oriented architectures. In: Proceedings of the International Workshop on Systems Development in SOA Environments, p. 3 (2007)
25. Pahl, C., Jamshidi, P.: Microservices: a systematic mapping study. In: Proceedings of the 6th International Conference on Cloud Computing and Services Science, pp. 137–146 (2016)
26. Rufino, J., Alam, M., Ferreira, J.: Monitoring V2X applications using DevOps and docker. In: International Smart Cities Conference, pp. 1–5 (2017)
27. Serrano, D., Baldassarre, T., Stroulia, E.: Real-time traffic-based routing, based on open data and open-source software. In: 3rd World Forum on Internet of Things, pp. 661–665 (2016)
28. Shavit, M., Gryc, A., Miucic, R.: Firmware update over the air (FOTA) for automotive industry. SAE Technical (2007)
29. Stol, K., Fitzgerald, B.: The ABC of software engineering research. ACM Trans. Softw. Eng. Methodol. **27**, 11 (2018)
30. Taibi, D., Lenarduzzi, V., Pahl, C.: Architectural patterns for microservices: a systematic mapping study. In: Proceedings of the 8th International Conference on Cloud Computing and Services Science, pp. 221–232 (2018)
31. Thönes, J.: Microservices. IEEE Softw. **32**, 116–116 (2015)
32. Yang, M., Mahmood, M., Zhou, X., Shafaq, S., Zahid, L.: Design and implementation of cloud platform for intelligent logistics in the trend of intellectualization. China Commun. **14**, 180–191 (2017)
33. Zeller, M., Prehofer, C., Krefft, D., Weiss, G.: Towards runtime adaptation in AUTOSAR. In: 5th Workshop on Adaptive and Reconfigurable Embedded Systems, vol. 10, pp. 17–20 (2013)
34. Zhang, T., Antunes, H., Aggarwal, S.: Defending connected vehicles against malware: challenges and a solution framework. Internet Things J. **1**, 10–21 (2014)
35. Zhu, L., Bass, L., Champlin-Scharff, G.: DevOps and its practices. IEEE Softw. **33**, 32–34 (2016)

Inputs from a Model-Based Approach Towards the Specification of Microservices Logical Architectures: An Experience Report

Nuno Santos[1,2(✉)] , Helena Rodrigues[1,2] , Nuno Ferreira[2,3] ,
and Ricardo J. Machado[1,2]

[1] CCG/ZGDV Institute, Guimarães, Portugal
nuno.santos@ccg.pt
[2] ALGORITMI Center, School of Engineering,
Minho University, Guimarães, Portugal
[3] i2S Insurance Knowledge S.A., Porto, Portugal

Abstract. Adopting microservices architectures (MSA) in software projects include specific concerns on design, development and deployment. Projects often struggle for taking decisions for properly bound the microservices, partition databases, address communication and messaging, among others. Proposing a model-driven approach allows abstracting microservices behavior from the business domain. However, there is still lack of modeling methods supporting architecture design alignment with business requirements that cover microservices principles. In this paper, microservices logical architectures are derived from functional requirements, which are modeled in SoaML diagrams. This paper discusses design, data management, inter-service communication and automatization based on the derived architecture diagram.

Keywords: Microservices · Modeling · Design · Data management · Inter-service communication · Automatization · UML · SoaML

1 Introduction

Microservices architectures [1] (MSA) are an architectural style oriented towards modularization, where the idea is to split the application into smaller, interconnected services, running as a separate process that can be independently deployed, scaled and tested [2]. The development of MSAs follow the following principles [1]: (i) "Model around business concepts"; (ii) "Adopt a culture of automation"; (iii) "Hide internal implementation details"; (iv) "Decentralize all the things"; (v) "Make services independently deployable"; (vi) "Isolate failure"; and (vii) "Highly observable".

Designing MSAs for a given business capability or domain, typically uses patterns such as Domain-driven Design (DDD), single responsibility principle (SRP) or Conway's Law. However, MSA design often faces challenges related to database partition,

This work was supported by FCT – Fundação para a Ciência e Tecnologia within the Project Scope: UID/CEC/00319/2019.

the proper size of the microservice, communication and messaging, which are not addressed systematically by those patterns. By applying a modeling method in the process of designing a MSA, one may model the solution foresee issues on bounded contexts for microservices, namely intra-service behavior, interfaces and data models separation, and inter-service communication and messaging requirements [1].

Accordingly, this paper proposes an approach for designing a microservices-oriented logical architecture (MSLA), *i.e.*, a logical view [3] on the behavior of microservices and relationships between microservices. This approach uses UML use cases diagrams for domain modeling, which are further used as an input for designing a MSLA in an automated way, by using an adaptation of the *Four Step Rule Set* (4SRS) method [4]. Each of these functionally decomposed UML use cases give origin to one or more components, which will then compose the microservices. The 4SRS method assures the alignment of the designed architecture with the elicited user requirements.

It is the purpose of this paper to present an adaptation of this method in order to support a proper architecture design compliant with the microservices architecture main principles, the 4SRS–MSLA. Issues such as data consistency, security, communication, deployment, and other patterns [5–8] have also been addressed and are presented in this paper, although extensive discussion on such patterns here is out of scope. For representation purposes, this approach adopts the service-oriented architecture modeling language (SoaML). Additionally, based on the premise that a proper specification of requirements benefits from multi-perspectives, the adapted method includes outputs for different SoaML diagrams, like Service Participants, Capabilities, Service Architectures, and Service Interfaces. Although there is not a common standard on modeling MSAs [9], there seems to be a tendency to use languages oriented to describe service-based architectures [10] (SoaML, SOMA, SOADL), but also UML for modeling services and operations [11–13], or both [14].

This research bases itself in an industrial running example, the *Unified Hub for Smart Plants* (UH4SP) [15], designed in the context of a funded project, where a UML use cases model regarding the requirements are the input for deriving the project's MSLA, by using the 4SRS-MSLA method.

This paper is structured as follows: Sect. 2 presents related work; Sect. 3 introduces the running example of the UH4SP project; Sect. 4 describes an approach for modeling microservices in SoaML; Sect. 5 discusses design, development and deployment issues from the modeled artifact; Sect. 6 describes the lessons learned from the experience report; and Sect. 7 describes the conclusions and future work.

2 Related Work

Although a somewhat recent trend, microservice architectures adoption has arisen the identification of patterns, from migration [16] to development and deployment of such architectures [5–8], ranging from service design, orchestration/coordination, deployment, data distribution, among others. The 'Decomposition' pattern [5] is often used as a starting point for designing microservices architectures, as it intends to assure that the given service refers to a small scope of the system. A microservice scope may relate to organization's business capabilities, or to a business domain by applying the domain-driven design (DDD) [17] approach. Our approach also uses the DDD rationale to structure boundaries within the requirements modeling, later considered as an input for the microservices design.

Also, architecture design presents many challenges in what regards microservices adoption [9]. Typically, implementation of these architectures starts by developing services for a given business process [18], making use of simplified microservices patterns [8]. In terms of microservices modeling and their granularity, DDD's bounded contexts, within requirements modeled using use cases, allow defining steps to derive a domain model for a microservice [13]. Use cases are also considered as an input to properly define microservice granularity in [7], namely based on their functional decomposition [19]. Moreover, granularity is managed using models in [20]. Other works focus in design patterns from databases [21, 22] or deployment-related [23].

Overall, designing MSAs continuously implies an iterative addition, modification and elimination of services even after the implementation has ended. For that reason, the architect must have a supportive approach for tracking changes in business needs to the MSLA. The referred approaches allow specifying and modeling an MSA but do not support alignment and traceability as the 4SRS-MSLA does. In this paper, the 4SRS-MSLA contributes to architecting microservices and their granularity, and contributes in defining associated data models and communications.

3 Running Example: The Unified Hub for Smart Plants (UH4SP)

The UH4SP project aims developing a platform or integrating data from distributed industrial unit plants, with focus in the cement domain, allowing the use of the data acquired from IoT systems for enterprise-level production management and collaborative processes between plants, suppliers, forwarders and clients. The project aimed at developing new solutions regarding the control of trucks arrival/exit as well as the load/unload activities, and for communicating with the plant's ERP and the industrial hardware. These solutions were validated within a proof of concept performed in an ecosystem of industrial unit plants using production management systems developed by *Cachapuz Bilanciai Group*, located in Braga, Portugal, as they were the leading entity of the UH4SP project consortium.

The UH4SP project arose with the need of overcoming Cachapuz solution's limitations in adopting IIoT/I4.0 paradigm. Firstly, the current solution is deployed on-premises. It has a considerable scaling and complexity, which made it not adequate and flexible to enable the development and deployment of cloud services based on modules and external access. The on-premises deployment is a difficulty for promoting a corporate-level management, since in order to the industrial group manager to have an integrated analysis of the group's plants, he was only able to access the individual plant's ERP one at a time using a remote virtualized environment. The remote business analysis was also impossible to perform in some contexts, namely within plant's located in poor Internet connectivity spaces. The current solution did not enable the incorporation of remote technical interventions. Finally, the current solution was not able to respond to a previous need of enabling third–party access (*e.g.*, forwarders, customers, suppliers) to the inclusion of collaborative tools in process execution and analysis.

In short, the UH4SP project aimed developing:

- new functionalities for providing management of corporate-level production;
- tools for supporting new collaborative processes within the supply chain;
- a microservices architecture;
- production management services, that rely on previous synchronization of Cachapuz's systems (at the industrial unit level).

4   From Business Needs to Microservices

Using a model-based approach for designing a service-oriented architecture allows identifying some microservices elements, nevertheless much information is lost as UML Use Cases relate to user requirements and these are far from the desired architecture elements. Thus, by using a software engineering method as the 4SRS method, the derived information will now relate to the system requirements. Specification refinement through model transformations [24] is an approach that promotes an overview of the overall system for afterwards having a context to elicit the technical requirements.

This section describes a model-based approach for microservices architecture design, using requirements engineering approaches to design service-oriented architectures that respond to elicited requirements. This approach firstly uses typical gathered user requirements, namely functionally decomposed UML Use Cases, which are input for the 4SRS method that allows modeling a logical architecture diagram (using UML Component notation). Afterwards, by identifying the domains present in the architecture (DDD) we propose to refine sub-systems (regarding each domain) of the architecture iteratively, in order to identify, model and specify a set of software services in SoaML diagrams, such as Service Participants, Service Interface, Capabilities, Service Data, Service Architecture, Service Contracts, among others, until all logical architectural elements are supported by software services.

The 4SRS method takes as input a set of UML Use Cases describing the user requirements and derives a software logical architecture using UML Components. The logical architecture is then refined trough successive 4SRS iterations (by recurring to tabular transformations), producing progressively more detailed requirements and design specifications. An overview of the approach is depicted in Fig. 1.

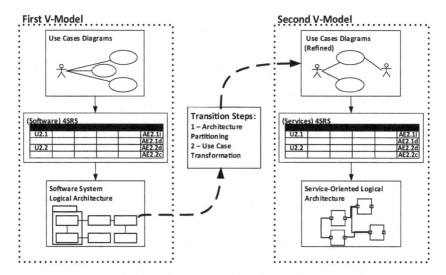

Fig. 1. Recursive architectural model transformations for service design

4.1   Setting Boundaries of Domains

The requirements engineering process followed an agile modeling process, "Agile Modeling Process for Logical Architectures" (AMPLA) [25] that, based on successive model derivation, namely referring to sequence, use case and components diagrams, method allows to derivate just enough requirements/use cases into a candidate logical architecture. In AMPLA, the requirements will be later refined and will emerge, in a continuous architecting (CA) way, as the 4SRS method is regularly revisited alongside the development Sprints. The use of 4SRS throughout the AMPLA process, first in the scope of the candidate architecture, and afterwards in the scope of each refinement, provides the traceability between components and the functional requirements, allowing an agile response to changing requirements.

The project's objectives are used as input for the high-level use case modeling were: (1) to define an approach for a unified view at the corporate (group of units) level; (2) to develop tools for third-party entities; (3) in-plant optimization; and (4) system reliability. The requirements elicitation started by listing a set of stakeholder expectations towards the product roadmap, encompassing the entire product but only MVP features were detailed. The expectations list of the project included 25 expectations, categorized by environment, architecture, functional and integration issues. They relate to business needs that afterwards allowed depicting functional requirements, modeled in use cases (Fig. 2).

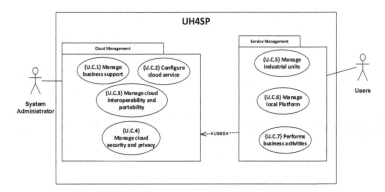

Fig. 2. UH4SP first-level Use Cases

The Use Case model was globally composed by 37 use cases after the decomposition. Use case *{UC.1} Manage business support* was decomposed in five use cases, use case *{UC.2} Configure cloud service* was decomposed in eight use cases, use case *{UC.3} Manage cloud interoperability and portability* was decomposed in five use cases, use case *{UC.4} Manage cloud security and privacy* was decomposed in three use cases, use case *{UC.5} Manage industrial units* was decomposed in two use cases, use case *{UC.6} Manage local Platform* was decomposed in five use cases, and use case *{UC.7} Performs business activities* was decomposed in ten use cases. Almost the entire model was detailed in one lower-level (*e.g.*, {UC5.1}, {UC5.2}, etc.). Only the cases of *{UC.1} Manage business support*, *{UC.2} Configure cloud service* and *{UC.7} Performs business activities* included an additional decomposition, composed with three use cases each, and are examples of bigger sized features of the MVP (based on the quantity of low–level use cases). Use cases *{UC.3} Manage cloud interoperability and portability* and *{UC.4} Manage cloud security and privacy* relate to features not addressed in the MVP, hence were not object of further decomposition. The total of 37 use cases perceive the low effort in decomposing at this phase, taking into account the large-scale nature of the project, namely the number of expectations (25) and that it is to be implemented by five separate teams.

The UH4SP logical architecture had as input 37 use cases and, after executing 4SRS method, was derived with 77 architectural components that compose it. The architecture is composed by five major packages, namely: *{P1} Configurations* – related with system configurations; *{P2} Monitoring* – related with system monitoring and services utilization measuring; *{P3} Business management* – related with logistic operations and information consults; *{P4} UH4SP integration* – related with system integration between IoT systems and the fog; *{P5} UH4SP fog data* – related with temporarily stored data in fog databases, storing all industrial local data, which are then synchronized to the cloud and available to authorized stakeholders.

This architecture was afterwards divided in a set of modules to be assigned to each of the project's teams (Fig. 3). The modularization exercise followed the DDD rationale, where the domains basically referred to main contributions that each team brings to the consortium, namely IoT, cloud infrastructure, cloud applications and sensors.

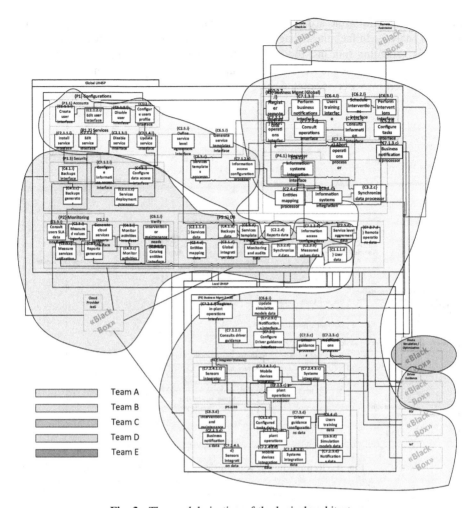

Fig. 3. The modularization of the logical architecture

The modularization depicted in Fig. 3 originated 5 modules/subsystems, each assigned for 'Team A', 'Team B', 'Team C', 'Team D' and 'Team E'. Each modularization may be refined. These techniques redefine the system boundaries, which now regards only the given module as a subsystem for design. This new subsystem now originates a new Use Case model, which now includes more detail information about a domain [26]. This Use Case model is afterwards used within a 4SRS–MSLA execution, as described in next section.

Each module could have sub-domains, which was responsibility of the assigned team to identify them. At this point, it was also important to identify dependencies and flows between domains for performing aimed business processes. The modeling support for this exercise can be, e.g., sequence diagrams as in Fig. 4, where two microservices regarding the sub-system - «Authentication» and « Authorization » -

were identified within the scope of a given business process – in this case, a remote business analysis. In fact, these diagrams are powerful tools for bordering the modules, as well as validating (not just the modules but as well the whole) architecture. Additionally, defining the sequence flows also supported eliciting communication specification between microservices (cf. Sect. 5.3).

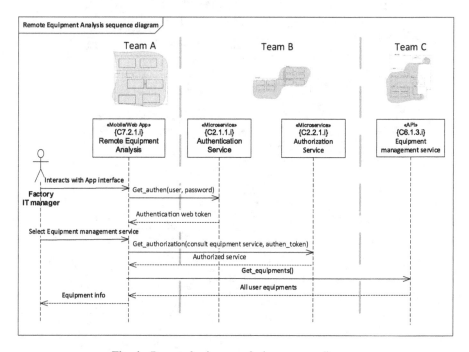

Fig. 4. Remote business analysis sequence diagram

4.2   Transforming Use Cases in Services

Resulting from the modularization, now each sub-system is refined independently. For that purpose, new UML Use Cases are identified, regarding only the sub-system, in order to refine the existing information. This section describes the steps that comprise the 4SRS-MSLA method (Fig. 5), from where each UML component is initially specified. Next, these components are identified and their behavior derived in microservices (SoaML's Service Participants), as also the channels and contracts between them. The aim for using the 4SRS-MSLA is to have a logical view of the microservices' internal behavior and communications, so that all the elicited functional requirements are met in the derived solution. The four steps of the 4SRS-MSLA are the following:

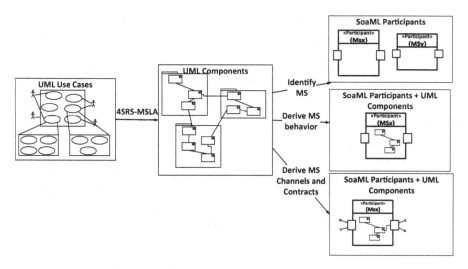

Fig. 5. Specifying microservices using 4SRS-MSLA

Step 1. Components Creation
The first step regards the creation of three components, where the 4SRS-MSLA method associates, for each use case, a component for interface with users or systems (*i-type*), a component for the data model (*d-type*), and a component for logic/control of the microservice domain (*c-type*).

Step 2. Components Elimination
In the second step, components are submitted to elimination tasks. In previous versions of the method, the redundancy identification often includes components that are functionally similar but with different usage, which result in eliminating redundant components but defining a wider representation for the retained component. This often occurs within *c*- or *i-types* components. Nevertheless, the microservices principles suggest that the microservice has only one specific purpose, hence one may suggest that a component should be eliminated only if its purpose is exactly the same as of the another one, and thus not eliminating any of them if their purpose is just similar.

Step 3. Component Packaging/Microservice Identification
The third step consists in grouping a set of components in packages, which further compose higher-level microservices. In 4SRS-MSLA, packaging is based on the use cases model obtained in the first-level refinement. Components, regardless of their category (i-, d-, or c-type), are assigned to one package (higher-level microservice) based on the process they relate to, or based on the non-leaf use case (that includes the leaf) originally derived from. Such packaging assures that the DDD pattern is followed.

Step 4. Microservices Associations
The associations between components are then generalized in order to depict the associations between microservices. In a microservices context, these associations relate to service channels that exist in order to allow communication between microservices to support a given business process or information flow. This view is

intended for identifying the need for such channels, regardless of the communication Pattern adopted, i.e., messaging between services or use of middleware such as API Gateways or lightweight message bus. Identifying such associations is based on descriptions from use cases (dependencies between functionalities at user requirements level), as well as from the components themselves, during the execution of step 2.

4.3   Service Modeling in SoaML

In this section, the inputs from the derived UML models by performing AMPLA and the 4SRS-MSLA are used to model the SoaML diagrams and their components. The modeling so far allows deriving the microservices' internal behavior, their data models, and the existing communications. These different concerns are included in different SoaML diagrams, in form of transition rules. These rules are grouped in 'Boundary', 'Data' and 'Communication', as depicted in Table 1.

Table 1. Transition from UML (within AMPLA) to SoaML

Rule	Input from UML	Output in SoaML
1. Boundary	UML Packages	Service Participants
2. Boundary	UML Packages	Service Architecture diagram
3. Boundary	UML Components (within Packages)	Service Capabilities (methods)
4. Boundary	i-types	Separate web apps from Service Participants
1. Data	d-types	Service Capabilities
1. Communication	4SRS (associations)	Service Participants (Requests/Services and Ports)
		Service Interfaces
2. Communication	UML Sequences	Service Interfaces

5   Microservices Design

5.1   Microservice Design

Each microservice identified within the 4SRS-MSLA method execution is represented as a Service Participant. Thus, the set of Service Participants compose the microservices architecture. The required invocations for the Participant (Fig. 6) were identified based on the use case description, where the interactions with other use cases were previously described. Additionally, the same interactions allowed identifying the need for methods that call those services and the properties (data) within the Capabilities.

It is during Step 2 of the 4SRS-MSLA that it is defined the expected behavior of the microservice. In order to align with typical composing layers of a microservice (UI, API, Logic and database), this approach proposes maintaining a general purpose description, but also the inclusion of HTTP verbs under which that component is called (used for defining «request» ports), the invocation of HTTP verbs required to consume services that are necessary in order to fulfill its purpose (used for defining «service» ports), and the properties that compose the dedicated database of the microservice (input for Service Data, but not discussed in this paper).

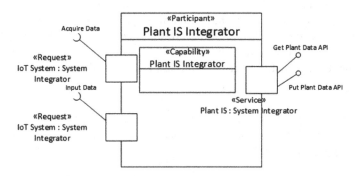

Fig. 6. Participant with ports, interfaces and capabilities (methods/properties)

In Step 3 of the 4SRS-MSLA, it is common that *i-type* components that relate to user interface (UI) actions are grouped together into one or more *i–type* components. This occurs because these components are typically part of a web application rather than a given consumed service.

5.2   Data Management

In Step 3 of the 4SRS-MSLA, *D–types* may also be grouped if the goal is to centralize the data, as in the "shared database" pattern. Alternatively, they may be included in the package from the higher-level microservice they relate to. This decision results in including within the microservice *d–type* components that are responsible for the related data access, which reflects an application of a "database per service".

If the solution uses the shared database pattern, the MSLA is likely to have a dedicated package for *d-type* components, which must be assured when performing Step 3 of 4SRS, i.e., assigning a package to *d-type* components. This package is not transformed into a microservice, but rather remains as a dedicated package (just like the UI package for web apps). If the solution uses the database per service pattern, *d–types* are assigned in Step 3 to a given service, i.e., any package except for the UI. Additional patterns are then followed, like API Composition, Command Query Responsibility Segregation (CQRS) – cf. Sect. 5.3 - and Saga. These patterns are out of the scope of this paper, but will be discussed in future research.

5.3   Inter-service Communication

Defining inter-service communication is very complex during specifications, as some informations about communication needs (parameters, formats, protocols, etc.) are not always clear during specification tasks. This section proposes defining such communication needs, by using inputs that may come from the 4SRS-MSLA method execution as from the sequence diagrams exercise (cf. Sect. 4.1). In terms of modeling,

SoaML diagrams able to be used are the ones such as Service Architecture, Service Interface and Service Channels.

From the 4SRS-MSLA, in Step 4 defining microservices associations should follow some constraints in order to prevent ineffective communication. Figure 7 represents the associations and rules that this step has to follow for proper component association. On the left side, are represented direct associations between components within the same sub-domain (*i.e.*, *i-*, *c-* and *d-type* components derived from the same use case), and, on the right side, the associations derived from use case dependencies.

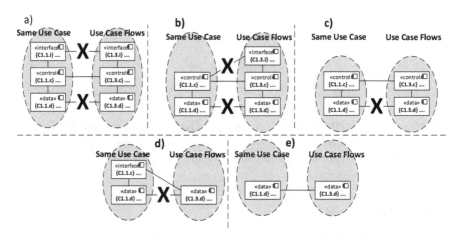

Fig. 7. Defining associations between components

In terms of the required association rules: **Scenario (a):** On the left side, if the three components are maintained, *i-type* should associate with *c–type*, and *c-type* associate with *d-type(s)*, assuring a proper intra-service flow. **Scenarios (a), (b) and (c):** Associations with the ones exemplified on the right side, referring to inter-service communications, should be always assigned between *c-types*. **Scenario (d):** No *c-types* were maintained, so use case flow-related associations are between *i-* or *d-types*. **Scenario (e):** only *d-types* were maintained, thus, in spite of being unusual scenario, the association is defined. In this case, an analysis by the architect is required, since *d-types* usually respond (in CRUD actions towards data) to another component's call.

In order to implement API Composition, modeling refers to the microservice's response to a given process, which is derived from the associations from Step 4 and depicted in Service Participant's service ports. Additionally, identifying needs for implementing CQRS refers to the dependencies between microservices, using the Service Architecture (Fig. 8). It should be referred that both patterns are typically used only in "database per service" settings.

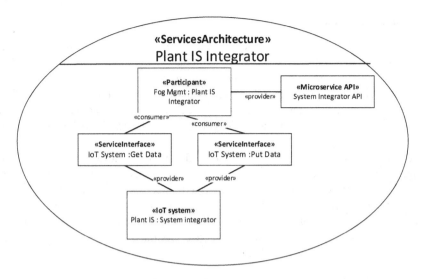

Fig. 8. Service Architecture

The approach for a given communication pattern (API gateways, remote procedure invocation, messaging or a domain-specific protocol, etc.) is not yet defined in MSLA, rather it only defines the necessity of existence of a flow between microservices. However, any design decisions on adopting a given pattern may be directly included in the components specification, the ServiceChannels, or in Service Interface diagram (Fig. 9).

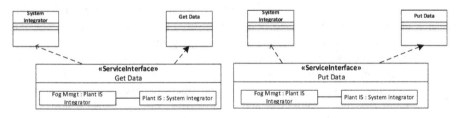

Fig. 9. Service Interface

For these interfaces, besides defining the parameters of the exchanged data, the design decisions rely in whether the communication is synchronous or asynchronous. This decision will then support the protocol for brokerage to be used (e.g., REST and gRPC for synchronous, or MQTT, AMQP, OPC-UA or Kafka for asynchronous).

5.4   Automatization

The agility provided by a microservices architecture mainly provides from having an infrastructure that supports a proper continuous integration/deployment (CI/CD) pipeline of the microservices to a production environement.

For this particular goal, obstacles refer to maximizing as possible CI/CD of the microservices, namely by performing a set of tests to the microservice. For this purpose, modeling may only provide some guidance on the expected behavior of the microservice.

Components and associations are the required input for performing several types of testing, from unit to acceptance testing. Additionally, component testing is enabled by validating the microservice behavior as described its composing components. Service integration contract testing is enabled by validating the scenarios where services invoke other services. These invokes are represented as ServiceChannels by the associations described in Step 4. Diagrams such as Service Contracts or even UML Sequence diagrams enable the contract validation.

6   Lessons Learned

It is difficult to directly jump to service specification. In the UH4SP project, requirements were typically elicited by stakeholders regarding front-end functionalities, since they are more aware of the business and not so much of the technology. Hence, starting in modeling a logical architecture based on business requirements allowed using stakeholder inputs for an initial stage and afterwards refine the information necessary to specify the MSLA.

The UH4SP was composed by 5 teams, where each one was assigned to a module from the architecture. Since a module could have one or more microservices, this research allowed to validate loosed development from different teams. Sequence diagrams were also useful for discussing and developing microservice communications that were developed by different teams.

As a disadvantage, the diagrams were only the starting point for developing and deploying the microservices. In terms of data management, inter-service communication, messaging/brokers, deployment and infrastructure, the diagrams do not provide still the necessary detail for implementing application, infrastructure application and infrastructure patterns [5].

7   Conclusions and Future Work

Microservices architectures are seen with great advantages in software development, and especially for cloud applications. Although its advantages, teams struggle with properly designing, developing, and deploying this technology. Performing traditional techniques in software engineering, in terms of requirements modeling, is still far from providing a proper level of detail for developing microservices. However, there is room for specifying services based on the elicited requirements.

This paper proposed defining a method for deriving a microservices logical architecture from functional requirements. The method has as input an UML logical components diagram, where domains (DDD) were identified within the architecture. That information was used for iterative refinement of the architecture, enabling deriving microservices specifications, afterwards modeled in SoaML diagrams. Additionally, these diagrams were basis for discussing microservices principles.

The discussion from this paper is an initial effort in designing the microservices architecture. It allowed defining the bounded contexts, separation of data models, needs for API calls. However, many issues around these concerns need to be addressed in microservices development but will be focused in future research, like data consistency, security (tokens) needs, or messaging, brokerage or API management.

References

1. Newman, S.: Building Microservices - Designing Fine-Grained Systems. O'Reilly Media Inc., Newton (2015)
2. Thönes, J.: Microservices. IEEE Softw. **32**, 116 (2015)
3. Kruchten, P.: The 4+1 view model of architecture. IEEE Softw. **12**, 42–50 (1995). https://doi.org/10.1109/52.469759
4. Machado, R.J., Fernandes, J.M., Monteiro, P., Rodrigues, H.: Transformation of UML models for service-oriented software architectures. In: Proceedings of 12th IEEE International Conference Workshops on Engineering of Computer Systems, pp. 173–182 (2005)
5. Richardson, C.: Microservice Patterns, 1st edn. Manning, Shelter Island (2018)
6. Krause, L.: Microservices: Patterns and Applications - Designing Fine-grained Services by Applying Patterns (2014). Lucas Krause
7. Namiot, D., Sneps-Sneppe, M.: On micro-services architecture. Int. J. Open Inf. Technol. **2**, 24–27 (2014)
8. Taibi, D., Lenarduzzi, V., Pahl, C.: Architectural patterns for microservices: a systematic mapping study. In: International Conference on Cloud Computing and Services Science, CLOSER. INSTICC (2018)
9. Di Francesco, P., Malavolta, I., Lago, P.: Research on architecting microservices: trends, focus, and potential for industrial adoption. In: IEEE International Conference on Software Architecture (ICSA), pp. 21–30. IEEE (2017)
10. Di Francesco, P.: Architecting microservices. In: IEEE International Conference on Software Architecture Workshops, ICSAW 2017: Side Track Proceedings (2017)
11. Rademacher, F., Sachweh, S., Zündorf, A.: Analysis of service-oriented modeling approaches for viewpoint-specific model-driven development of microservice architecture. arXiv Preprint arXiv:180409946 (2018)
12. Alshuqayran, N., Ali, N., Evans, R.: A systematic mapping study in microservice architecture. In: Service Computing (2016)
13. Kharbuja, R.: Designing a Business Platform using Microservices. Technische Universität München (2016)
14. Rademacher, F., Sorgalla, J., Sachweh, S.: Challenges of domain-driven microservice design: a model-driven perspective. IEEE Softw. **35**, 36–43 (2018). https://doi.org/10.1109/MS.2018.2141028

15. Santos, N., Rodrigues, H., Pereira, J., et al.: UH4SP: a software platform for integrated management of connected smart plants. In: 9th IEEE International Conference on Intelligent Systems (IS). IEEE, Funchal (2018)

16. Balalaie, A., Heydarnoori, A., Jamshidi, P.: Migrating to cloud-native architectures using microservices: an experience report. In: Celesti, A., Leitner, P. (eds.) ESOCC Workshops 2015. CCIS, vol. 567, pp. 201–215. Springer, Cham (2016). https://doi.org/10.1007/978-3-319-33313-7_15

17. Evans, E.: Domain-Driven Design: Tackling Complexity in the Heart of Software. Addison-Wesley, Boston (2004)

18. Lenarduzzi, V., Taibi, D.: Microservices, continuous architecture, and technical debt interest: an empirical study. In: 44th Euromicro Conference on Software Engineering and Advanced Applications (SEAA). IEEE, Prague (2018)

19. Tyszberowicz, S., Heinrich, R., Liu, B., Liu, Z.: Identifying microservices using functional decomposition. In: Feng, X., Müller-Olm, M., Yang, Z. (eds.) SETTA 2018. LNCS, vol. 10998, pp. 50–65. Springer, Cham (2018). https://doi.org/10.1007/978-3-319-99933-3_4

20. Hassan, S., Ali, N., Bahsoon, R.: Microservice ambients: an architectural meta-modelling approach for microservice granularity. In: IEEE International Conference on Software Architecture (ICSA), pp. 1–10. IEEE (2017)

21. Furda, A., Fidge, C., Zimmermann, O., et al.: Migrating enterprise legacy source code to microservices: on multitenancy, statefulness, and data consistency. IEEE Softw. **35**, 63–72 (2018). https://doi.org/10.1109/MS.2017.440134612

22. Messina, A., Rizzo, R., Storniolo, P., Tripiciano, M., Urso, A.: The database-is-the-service pattern for microservice architectures. In: Renda, M., Bursa, M., Holzinger, A., Khuri, S. (eds.) ITBAM 2016. LNCS, vol. 9832, pp. 223–233. Springer, Cham (2016). https://doi.org/10.1007/978-3-319-43949-5_18

23. Chen, L.: Microservices: architecting for continuous delivery and DevOps. In: IEEE International Conference on Software Architecture (ICSA). IEEE, Seattle (2018)

24. Santos, N., Ferreira, N., Machado, R.J.: Transition from information systems to service-oriented logical architectures: formalizing steps and rules with QVT. In: Ramachandran, M., Mahmood, Z. (eds.) Requirements Engineering for Service and Cloud Computing, pp. 247–270. Springer, Cham (2017). https://doi.org/10.1007/978-3-319-51310-2_11

25. Santos, N., Pereira, J., Morais, F., Barros, J., Ferreira, N., Machado, R.J.: An agile modeling oriented process for logical architecture design. In: Gulden, J., Reinhartz-Berger, I., Schmidt, R., Guerreiro, S., Guédria, W., Bera, P. (eds.) BPMDS/EMMSAD - 2018. LNBIP, vol. 318, pp. 260–275. Springer, Cham (2018). https://doi.org/10.1007/978-3-319-91704-7_17

26. Santos, N., et al.: Specifying software services for fog computing architectures using recursive model transformations. In: Mahmood, Z. (ed.) Fog Computing, pp. 153–181. Springer, Cham (2018). https://doi.org/10.1007/978-3-319-94890-4_8

A Modular Approach to Calculate Service-Based Maintainability Metrics from Runtime Data of Microservices

Justus Bogner[1,2]([⊠]) [iD], Steffen Schlinger[2], Stefan Wagner[2] [iD],
and Alfred Zimmermann[1]

[1] University of Applied Sciences Reutlingen, Reutlingen, Germany
{justus.bogner,alfred.zimmermann}@reutlingen-university.de
[2] University of Stuttgart, Stuttgart, Germany
{justus.bogner,stefan.wagner}@iste.uni-stuttgart.de,
mail@steffen-schlinger.de

Abstract. While several service-based maintainability metrics have been proposed in the scientific literature, reliable approaches to automatically collect these metrics are lacking. Since static analysis is complicated for decentralized and technologically diverse microservice-based systems, we propose a dynamic approach to calculate such metrics from runtime data via distributed tracing. The approach focuses on simplicity, extensibility, and broad applicability. As a first prototype, we implemented a Java application with a Zipkin integrator, 23 different metrics, and five export formats. We demonstrated the feasibility of the approach by analyzing the runtime data of an example microservice-based system. During an exploratory study with six participants, 14 of the 18 services were invoked via the system's web interface. For these services, all metrics were calculated correctly from the generated traces.

Keywords: Maintainability metrics · Dynamic analysis · Microservices

1 Introduction

Service-oriented computing [12] introduced maintainability-related benefits like increased reusability or loose coupling into the development of distributed enterprise applications. More recently, microservices [11] promise even greater advantages with respect to flexibility and sustainable evolution. However, their decentralized nature and their high degree of technological heterogeneity may pose difficulties for metric-based quality assurance, e.g. with static source code analysis. Moreover, the most critical quality aspects of microservices are concerned with architecture (e.g. coupling and cohesion) and not so much with source code [2]. While a number of service-based maintainability metrics have been proposed to address this [3], approaches to automatically collect these metrics are lacking. Because meaningful static code analysis is very complex for service-based systems, most suggestions so far have focused on programming language

X. Franch et al. (Eds.): PROFES 2019, LNCS 11915, pp. 489–496, 2019.
https://doi.org/10.1007/978-3-030-35333-9_34

independent workarounds, e.g. using SoaML [6] and service interface definitions like WSDL [1] or OpenAPI [9].

A promising alternative to gather such metrics seems to be *dynamic analysis* [14], i.e. to observe and document the system's behavior at runtime. Dynamic metrics already have a long history and a large number of them have been proposed [13]. Analyzing the system execution may also produce additional maintainability-related insights that static analysis cannot, especially in the area of dynamic coupling [7]. Furthermore, microservice-based systems highly value observability to operate the complex net of distributed services. This means that microservices usually rely on monitoring or even distributed tracing[1]. Such produced runtime data could be reused for maintainability evaluations. In this paper, we therefore propose an extensible approach to calculate service-based maintainability metrics from the runtime data of microservice-based systems.

2   Research Design

The development of our approach took place in several stages. First, we analyzed existing service-based metrics (mostly based on [3]) to understand what data attributes were necessary to calculate a broad set of maintainability metrics. We also collected and evaluated existing approaches (see Sect. 5) as well as general tools for distributed tracing in service-based environments. Based on this initial analysis, we decided that our own approach should focus on the following three principles:

- **Simplicity**: has a simple and clean data model and architecture
- **Extensibility**: can be extended with additional data sources or metrics
- **Broad applicability**: can be used with diverse service-based systems

In the second step, we then designed a modular architecture (see Sect. 3.1) and an internal data model (see Sect. 3.2). Afterwards, we decided which data sources and which metrics we would implement for the first iteration and developed the prototype of the tool (see Sect. 3.3). Lastly, we demonstrated the effectiveness of the tool-supported approach in an exploratory study with an example system that was used by six people (see Sect. 4).

3   Calculating Service-Based Metrics from Runtime Data

In this section, we describe the abstract details of our general approach as well as the concrete implementation of the first prototype. For source code and more extensive documentation, please refer to our GitHub repository[2].

---

[1] https://opentracing.io.

[2] https://github.com/xJREB/microservices-runtime-analysis.

3.1   Architecture

The analysis tool was designed as a simple command line interface (CLI) application and loosely follows a *Pipes and Filters* architecture. It consists of several
types of modules which sequentially process data (see Fig. 1). For data collection, different types of `Integrator` modules can be used. An `Integrator` queries
an external data source with runtime data (e.g. an OpenTracing server) and
produces the internal canonical data model from it. In one execution, several
different `Integrators` can be used to construct a more complete view of the
system. This model is then used as the foundation for metric calculation: each
implemented `Metric` module uses the data model to derive its metric results.
Lastly, this list of metric results is then processed by each specified `Exporter`
module. An `Exporter` transforms and forwards the results to the final location,
e.g. it may create an XML file. Likewise, several `Exporters` can be used in a
single execution. For the sake of simplicity and to ease integration into a CI/CD
pipeline, the analysis tool has no internal persistence. Upon execution, it collects
data, calculates the metrics, and finally outputs the results.

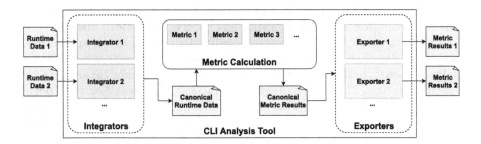

Fig. 1. General architecture of the approach (arrows indicate data flow)

3.2   Data Model

Every `Integrator` needs to produce our internal canonical representation of the
microservice-based system under analysis. This data model (see Fig. 2) includes
the services of the system, but also runtime information like the number of times
an operation was called during the analysis timeframe. In principle, it represents
a directed graph where the nodes are `Services` and the edges are `Dependencies`,
e.g. a `Dependency` could be an outgoing edge from node `Service` S_1 to node
`Service` S_2. Each `Service` in turn has a list of its offered `Operations`. They
consist of a list of input `parameters`, a list of how often other services called
this operation (`calls`), and a list of other `Operations` that were subsequently
invoked as a response to this operation (`responsesForOperation`). This simplis-
tic model enables the calculation of a large number of maintainability metrics
for e.g. coupling, cohesion, size, and complexity via efficient graph operations,
on system- as well as on service-level. It could also be easily extended with
additional attributes to facilitate the calculation of new metrics.

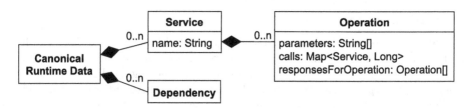

Fig. 2. Canonical data model for runtime data

3.3   Implementation

The first prototypical implementation of the approach is a Java CLI application (see Fig. 3). Apache Maven is used to manage dependencies and to create an executable JAR file that can be called with various input parameters such as the endpoints of runtime data sources. We rely on the JGraphT library[3] to create the internal model of the system as a directed graph. The plugin mechanism to dynamically include newly developed modules is realized with Java interfaces and the Java Reflection API. In the first iteration, we implemented one `Integrator`, 23 `Metrics`, and five `Exporters` (XML, JSON, CSV, Markdown, plain text).

Concerning runtime data sources, we analyzed a wide variety of approaches, among them distributed tracing frameworks like Jaeger and monitoring solutions like Prometheus[4]. In the end, we decided to implement a Zipkin `Integrator` for the first prototype. Zipkin[5] is a distributed tracing system based on the Google Dapper architecture. It implements the OpenTracing standard and is one of the most popular open source tracing implementations (over 11k stars on GitHub at the time of writing). Zipkin requires the inclusion of a small piece of application code, a `Tracer`, into each service that should be instrumented. These `Tracers` record application activity and then asynchronously send tracing information to a central Zipkin server. As opposed to non-invasive techniques like e.g. `tcpdump`, Zipkin is therefore able to gather very rich runtime data. Our implemented Zipkin `Integrator` queries the RESTful API of a Zipkin server and retrieves the list of services with their respective traces within a certain timeframe. These information are then converted to our canonical data model.

With respect to `Metrics`, we collected a set of 58 service-based maintainability metrics proposed in the scientific literature. The majority of them have been summarized in [3]. These metrics were then analyzed for their relevance and applicability to our approach. In the end, we selected 16 of these metrics for the first prototype. Since several aspects of service-based maintainability (especially dynamic coupling) were not covered, we designed and adapted seven additional

---

[3] https://jgrapht.org.

[4] For more details on tool analysis and selection, please refer to https://github.com/xJREB/microservices-runtime-analysis/tree/master/docs/tools.

[5] https://zipkin.io.

metrics. These 23 metrics were then implemented[6], among them 13 coupling, five complexity, three cohesion, and two size metrics. Eight of them are system level metrics, 14 relate to the service level, and one is collected per operation.

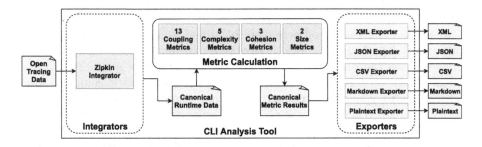

Fig. 3. Implemented architecture of the first prototype (arrows indicate data flow)

Architecture, data model, and implementation fulfill all three principles postulated for the approach (see Sect. 2). The approach is *simple* in the sense that it avoids the complexity of e.g. model-driven engineering and relies only on very few data model concepts and module types, i.e. the bare minimum of what is needed. It is *extensible* in the sense that the plugin architecture makes it very easy to develop additional `Integrators`, `Metrics`, or `Exporters`, which follows the *open/closed principle* ("open for extension, closed for modification"). Lastly, it is *broadly applicable* in the sense that it is not tied to specific service technologies or implementation frameworks. In principle, any data source with sufficient information to construct the internal data model can be integrated without having to touch any of the downstream implementation units.

4   Demonstration and Discussion

To illustrate the feasibility and effectiveness of our approach, we conducted an exploratory study with an open source example system. The goals of this demonstration were to explore if metrics are calculated correctly and to get an estimation if runtime data produced during normal usage of a system is sufficient for accurate results. We chose the Twitter-like microblogging system *ramanujan*[7], since it is of decent size (18 services) while still being simple enough for a small study and has a web frontend for convenient end-user access. Furthermore, each service already implements a Zipkin tracer so that no modifications were required. We hosted this system together with a Zipkin server in a closed environment and then instructed six test participants (master students) to use it. We divided our testers into two groups with three participants each (G_1 and

---

[6] For more details on metric analysis and selection, please refer to https://github.com/xJREB/microservices-runtime-analysis/tree/master/docs/metrics.

[7] https://github.com/senecajs/ramanujan.

G_2). The groups used the system separately and had to work on two tasks (T_1 and T_2). For T_1, they had five minutes to find and use the complete functionality offered via the web interface. For T_2, they should use the system's messaging for an additional five minutes to discuss a topic of their choosing. Afterwards, our tool calculated the metrics from the produced Zipkin data and we analyzed the results and differences per groups and tasks[8].

In total, 14 of the 18 services were identified from the combined data of both groups. The remaining four services provided functionality that could not be invoked via the web interface, e.g. the manual import of messages into the system. Based on these 14 services, all metric values for static coupling, size, and cohesion were calculated correctly (dynamic coupling metrics do not have a "correct" value). When looking at G_1 and G_2 separately, the results are the same per group. However, an analysis of the individual tasks of G_2 revealed that not all service dependencies were identified in T_1 as well as T_2, because a clustered service relied on load balancing to two instances based on chosen usernames. This led to minor inaccuracies for the static coupling metrics. Since the testers of G_2 chose different usernames per task, the combined data sets of T_1 and T_2 therefore yielded accurate results. All in all, this small case study was successful in demonstrating our approach with just six participants that used the system for a combined duration of 20 min.

However, the demonstration also highlighted weaknesses of dynamic analysis: evaluation quality depends on the richness and completeness of runtime data. Services or operations that are not used during the recording are not registered and therefore the resulting metrics may be inaccurate. This may be especially relevant for very large systems with diverse services and functionality. Similarly, a less invasive `Integrator` that does not require service modification would most likely result in even larger inaccuracies or even no values for certain metrics. In addition to the invasiveness vs. data quality trade-off, we must also consider potential performance impacts. Our small demonstration was no suitable evaluation for this. Even though modern distributed tracing like Zipkin is specifically designed for minimal performance overhead, there is still additional load in the system. Therefore, the usage of such an approach with a critical production system needs to be carefully evaluated.

5   Related Work

Several approaches have been proposed in the area of architecture reconstruction for microservice-based systems. Granchelli et al. [8] designed an approach called MicroART that combines static information from a source code repository with dynamic runtime data collected via `tcpdump`. The approach is based on model-driven engineering and requires the usage of Docker containers as well as some manual effort in the refinement phase. Similarly, Mayer and Weinreich [10] present a mixed recovery approach based on OpenAPI descriptions and runtime

---

[8] We also published the results in our repository: https://github.com/xJREB/microservices-runtime-analysis/tree/master/docs/demonstration-results.

information from HTTP calls intercepted via a custom data collection library. Their approach is limited to RESTful services using the Spring framework.

Some publications also propose quality evaluation approaches for microservices based on dynamic analysis. Engel et al. [5] created a framework (MAAT) that utilizes the OpenTracing API to create a model and visualization of the system's architecture. Afterwards, six metrics are calculated to evaluate the system's conformance to principles derived from popular microservice characteristics. While the approach promises to be very interoperable w.r.t. data sources, metric extensibility does not seem to be a high priority. The source code of MAAT is also not shared publicly. Lastly, Cardarelli et al. [4] built on the existing MicroART framework to use its output for a new customizable quality evaluation framework called MicroQuality. The complex approach employs model-driven engineering techniques as well as the object constraint language (OCL) for specifying quality attributes. The authors envision an ecosystem where such quality definitions are shared across systems and organizations.

6 Conclusion

We designed a simple, extensible, and broadly applicable approach to calculate service-based maintainability metrics from runtime data and implemented a Java prototype with a Zipkin integrator, 23 maintainability metrics, as well as export to XML, JSON, CSV, Markdown, and plain text. We demonstrated the feasibility of our approach via a small exploratory study with an example microblogging system: metrics for all used services were calculated correctly based on the produced runtime data. Future work could expand the prototypical implementation with additional `Integrators` or `Metrics`. Furthermore, an industrial evaluation with a larger system would yield important insights into metric accuracy as well as performance impact at such scale. Lastly, the dynamic approach could also be combined with static information like machine-readable system descriptions to mitigate some of its shortcomings.

Acknowledgments. This research was partially funded by the Ministry of Science of Baden-Württemberg, Germany, for the doctoral program *Services Computing* (https://www.services-computing.de/?lang=en).

References

1. Basci, D., Misra, S.: Data complexity metrics for XML web services. Adv. Electr. Comput. Eng. **9**(2), 9–15 (2009). https://doi.org/10.4316/aece.2009.02002
2. Bogner, J., Fritzsch, J., Wagner, S., Zimmermann, A.: Assuring the evolvability of microservices: insights into industry practices and challenges. In: 2019 IEEE International Conference on Software Maintenance and Evolution (ICSME). IEEE, Cleveland (2019)
3. Bogner, J., Wagner, S., Zimmermann, A.: Automatically measuring the maintainability of service- and microservice-based systems. In: Proceedings of the 27th

International Workshop on Software Measurement and 12th International Conference on Software Process and Product Measurement on - IWSM Mensura 2017, pp. 107–115. ACM Press, New York (2017). https://doi.org/10.1145/3143434.3143443

4. Cardarelli, M., Iovino, L., Di Francesco, P., Di Salle, A., Malavolta, I., Lago, P.: An extensible data-driven approach for evaluating the quality of microservice architectures. In: Proceedings of the 34th ACM/SIGAPP Symposium on Applied Computing - SAC 2019, pp. 1225–1234. ACM Press, New York (2019). https://doi.org/10.1145/3297280.3297400

5. Engel, T., Langermeier, M., Bauer, B., Hofmann, A.: Evaluation of microservice architectures: a metric and tool-based approach. In: Mendling, J., Mouratidis, H. (eds.) CAiSE 2018. LNBIP, vol. 317, pp. 74–89. Springer, Cham (2018). https://doi.org/10.1007/978-3-319-92901-9_8

6. Gebhart, M., Abeck, S.: Metrics for evaluating service designs based on SoaML. Int. J. Adv. Softw. **4**(1), 61–75 (2011)

7. Geetika, R., Singh, P.: Dynamic coupling metrics for object oriented software systems. ACM SIGSOFT Softw. Eng. Notes **39**(2), 1–8 (2014). https://doi.org/10.1145/2579281.2579296

8. Granchelli, G., Cardarelli, M., Francesco, P.D., Malavolta, I., Iovino, L., Salle, A.D.: Towards recovering the software architecture of microservice-based systems. In: 2017 IEEE International Conference on Software Architecture Workshops (ICSAW), pp. 46–53. IEEE (2017). https://doi.org/10.1109/ICSAW.2017.48

9. Haupt, F., Leymann, F., Scherer, A., Vukojevic-Haupt, K.: A framework for the structural analysis of REST APIs. In: 2017 IEEE International Conference on Software Architecture (ICSA), pp. 55–58. IEEE (2017). https://doi.org/10.1109/ICSA.2017.40

10. Mayer, B., Weinreich, R.: An approach to extract the architecture of microservice-based software systems. In: 2018 IEEE Symposium on Service-Oriented System Engineering (SOSE), pp. 21–30. IEEE (2018). https://doi.org/10.1109/SOSE.2018.00012

11. Newman, S.: Building Microservices: Designing Fine-Grained Systems, 1st edn. O'Reilly Media, Sebastopol (2015)

12. Papazoglou, M.P.: Service-oriented computing: concepts, characteristics and directions. In: Proceedings of the 7th International Conference on Properties and Applications of Dielectric Materials (Cat. No. 03CH37417), pp. 3–12. IEEE Computer Society (2003). https://doi.org/10.1109/WISE.2003.1254461

13. Tahir, A., MacDonell, S.G.: A systematic mapping study on dynamic metrics and software quality. In: 2012 28th IEEE International Conference on Software Maintenance (ICSM), pp. 326–335. IEEE (2012). https://doi.org/10.1109/ICSM.2012.6405289

14. Tosi, D., Lavazza, L., Morasca, S., Taibi, D.: On the definition of dynamic software measures. In: Proceedings of the ACM-IEEE International Symposium on Empirical Software Engineering and Measurement - ESEM 2012, p. 39. ACM Press, New York (2012). https://doi.org/10.1145/2372251.2372259

Consumer-Driven Contract Tests for Microservices: A Case Study

Jyri Lehvä[(✉)], Niko Mäkitalo, and Tommi Mikkonen

Department of Computer Science, University of Helsinki, Helsinki, Finland
{jyri.lehva,niko.makitalo,tommi.mikkonen}@helsinki.fi

Abstract. Design by contract is a paradigm that aims at capturing the interactions of different software components, and formalizing them so that they can be relied upon in other phases of the design. Such a characteristic is especially helpful in the context of microservice architecture, where each service is an independent entity that can be individually (re)deployed. With contracts, testing of microservice based systems can be improved so that also the integration of different microservices can be tested in isolation by the developers working on the system. In this paper, we study how systems based on microservice architecture and their integrations can be tested more effectively by extending the testing approach with consumer-driven contract tests. Furthermore, we study how the responsibilities and purposes of each testing method are affected when introducing the consumer-driven contract tests to the system.

Keywords: Consumer-driven contract testing · Design by contract · Microservices · Test planning · Integration testing · Test coverage

1 Introduction

Consumer-Driven Contract testing [9] is a way to test integrations between services and ensure that all the integrations are still working after new changes have been introduced to the system. The main idea is that when an application or a service (consumer) consumes an API provided by another service (provider), a contract is formed between them. The contract contains information about how the consumer calls the provider and what is being used from the responses.

As long as both of the parties obey the contract, they can both use it as a basis to verify their sides of the integration. The consumer can use it to mock the provider in its tests. The provider, on the other hand, can use it to replay the consumer requests against its API. This way the provider can verify that the generated responses match the expectations set by the consumer. With consumer-driven contracts, the provider is always aware of all of its consumers. This comes as a side product when all the consumers deliver their contracts to the provider instead of consumers accepting the contracts offered by the provider.

In this paper our objective is to study how systems based on the microservice architecture [1,12] and their integrations [8] can be tested more effectively by

© Springer Nature Switzerland AG 2019
X. Franch et al. (Eds.): PROFES 2019, LNCS 11915, pp. 497–512, 2019.
https://doi.org/10.1007/978-3-030-35333-9_35

extending the testing approach with consumer-driven contract tests. In particular, we are interested in how the responsibilities and purposes of each testing method are affected when introducing the consumer-driven contract tests to the system.

The rest of this paper is structured as follows. Section 2 provides the background for the paper, and Sect. 3 introduces the case study. Section 4 presents the results of the case study. Section 5 provides an extended discussion regarding our observations. Finally, Sect. 6 draws some final conclusions.

2   Background

Microservice architecture is a relatively new approach to architecting systems that are updated continuously [5]. The fundamental goal of microservices is to make each service self-contained, even if this means implementing similar (or even the same) functions in numerous services [6]. In other words, the goal is to minimize dependencies between the services, so that they can be designed and deployed independently of the other parts of the system [7]. Furthermore, different tools and techniques can be used when implementing microservices because they only need to interact with each other using well-defined APIs [11]. Therefore, designers can apply various techniques in testing individual services. However, when orchestration of numerous microservices is required, a common testing approach is needed to test their interaction. This is often visualized with testing pyramid (Fig. 1).

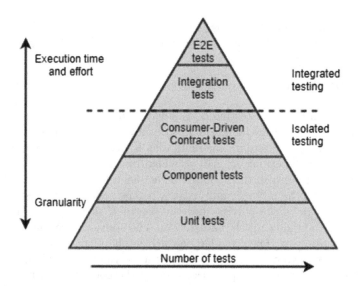

Fig. 1. Test pyramid with consumer-driven contract tests. Adapted from [3].

Since microservices are typically deployed directly to a live environment, traditional end-to-end and integration tests can be challenging to organize. Instead, a testing approach is needed where microservices can be tested in isolation from the live system, and preferably so that the developers can easily run the tests on their machines.

Consumer-driven contract testing is an approach that allows testing both sides of an integration separately and isolated from each other. It relies on consumer-driven contracts [9] between a consumer and a provider, following the design-by-contract paradigm [4]. They are created by the consumer and then shared to the provider for verification so that each contract describes a set of interactions between the consumer and the provider. A single interaction is a pair of request and response describing how the services communicate with each other. From the consumers perspective, the interaction describes the outgoing request and the response for it from the provider. From the providers perspective, the interaction defines what kind of incoming request it receives from the consumer and what kind of response the consumer expects to be generated for it.

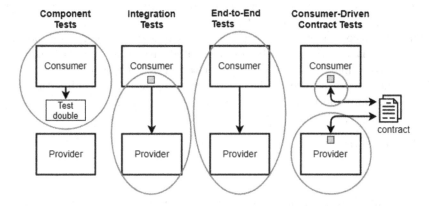

Fig. 2. Scopes of different testing methods.

From the surface, consumer-driven contract testing resembles integration testing – both involve a service provider and a service consumer, and their interaction is being tested. However, in consumer-driven contract tests, they are isolated from each other by an explicit contract instead of being directly connected, whereas in integration testing, more liberal interactions are typically allowed. The catch is that instead of forming a connection between the services, the test is divided into two independent and isolated stages (Fig. 2). *In the first stage*, the consumer creates a contract containing the details of each interaction it requires from the provider. The contract is then shared with the provider. *In the second stage*, the provider uses the contract to test its API. After the provider has successfully verified the contract with the tests, the consumer and the provider know they are compatible with each other.

The verified consumer-driven contract describes a specific state of the integration between the consumer and the provider. If that state changes from either side, there is a high chance of introducing defects to the integration. As explained earlier, the consumer and the provider can both be tested based on the contract.

The consumer testing can be achieved by comparing the newly implemented changes to the past state of the consumer. That can be done by using a mock that is based on the previous version of the contract. If the mock fails when the consumer sends the request to the provider, it means the implementation has changed, and the consumer no longer obeys the contract. If the consumer changed it on purpose, it is considered as a proposal for a new version of the contract. After that, the mock should be updated to match the changes, and the contract must be verified again by the provider to make sure it is compatible with those changes.

The provider side verification of the contract is done by playing the consumers requests from the contract against the provider and comparing the provider responses to the expected responses from the contract. If they match, the contract is satisfied, and both the consumer and the provider are compatible with each other. Sometimes the provider needs to make breaking changes. In such situations, the changes should be communicated with the consumers. After that, the consumers can create new versions of the contracts that take the breaking changes into account and enables the provider to evolve as planned.

Obviously, consumer-driven contract tests aim at a very specific point in development. Hence, they must be complemented with other types of testing that have been traditionally executed. To understand the exact benefits of consumer-driven contract testing, we conducted a case study in cooperation with a commercial company and its production system.

3   Case Study

3.1   Overview

Our case study is based on a system built on microservice architecture, consisting of eight services and four databases. The purpose of the system is to enable admin users to create custom product configurations to be sold in web stores to customers. Those web stores are consuming the APIs of the system. The system keeps track of stock levels for the products in different warehouses and provides tools for warehouse workers to fulfill orders placed by the customers.

An overview of the microservice system is shown in Fig. 3. The development team owns the microservices inside the black box. Other teams own the rest of the microservices. The arrows between the services are pointing from consumer to provider direction or in other words, from downstream to upstream. Two external calls from the Shop are highlighted with green color. Those are calling the endpoints that are in the focus of this case study. Integrations from web apps, external APIs, and the rest of the shops that act as consumers of the system have been abstracted away to reduce the noise from the two endpoints.

All databases of the system are MySQL[1] databases and the APIs are Express[2] applications written in JavaScript. The API endpoints mostly consist of CRUD

---

[1] https://www.mysql.com/.

[2] https://expressjs.com/.

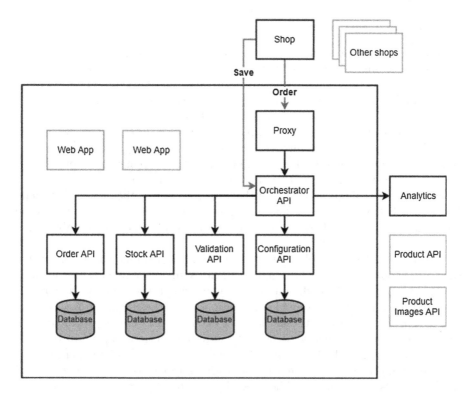

Fig. 3. High level architecture and integrations. (Color figure online)

operations, the Orchestrator API being an exception. Orchestrator API does not have direct access to the databases, and its purpose is to orchestrate the actions needed to complete the save and the order operations. Those actions consist of validation and calling the other APIs to complete the request.

The system was built to replace an old monolithic system. The transition happened gradually, one endpoint and one functionality at a time. The Proxy was implemented to help in the transition period. It used to contain logic to decide whether to forward the incoming calls to the old or the new system depending on the state of the transition. Currently, the Proxy is only used to keep the old deprecated API endpoints supported until all the consumers have been updated to use the new endpoints. Order requests from the Shop are still going through the Proxy meaning that those have not yet been integrated to use the new endpoints provided by the Orchestrator API.

The scope of the case study consists of the two endpoints: Save and Order. Both are highlighted in Fig. 3 with green color. These endpoints were chosen for the case study because they involve multiple microservices to fulfill the incoming requests. That makes them an exciting target for a spike from the integrations point of view.

3.2   Baseline Test Setup

The system of the case study has been tested with unit-, component- and end-to-end tests. The unit tests are used to test single functions within the microservices. Most commonly, they have been written to help the developers to implement more complex logic to verify that the small piece of code works as intended. They do lift off some burden from the other testing methods, but they do not test any parts of the code that is directly involved in integrations. Because of that, they are not discussed further in the scope of this case study, and the focus will be in the component- and end-to-end tests. The component tests present the majority of the tests in the system. They have been implemented for every single endpoint in every single service, and they extensively test the behavior of them. The tested behavior includes different happy case scenarios, request validation errors, and situations where the services in the upstream or the databases are not functioning correctly.

The team ended up implementing a vast number of component tests because these were comfortable and fast to implement. A single component test involves sending a request to the endpoint and then checking if the endpoint returns the expected response. All the outside integrations are always replaced with mocks. The mocks help to verify if the service calls external services correctly, and helps to emulate different scenarios where the external services behave in different ways. Most importantly, they make the tests isolated and easy to operate.

The team was quite confident in the testing strategy with just the unit- and component tests for quite a while. Together the tests were very throughout at making sure the isolated services worked as expected. The team also had a tactic to avoid making changes to the endpoints that could potentially break integrations. That meant only adding new features instead of changing or removing the existing ones. The confidence slowly faded away when the number of services, endpoints, and integrations kept growing when new features were implemented. As a result of that, the team decided to implement end-to-end tests to cover the most critical functionalities of the system.

The experience from the end-to-end tests was entirely different compared to the component tests. They required much additional effort because the tests were not isolated anymore, and they involved multiple different services and databases. To implement the tests, the developers needed to start all the associated services and databases on their machines. In addition, the end-to-end tests required planning. The whole system had to be in a specific state to make the tests pass. That meant inserting a correct set of data to all the databases – the setting and resetting of the data needed to happen before the tests were run. The team ended up implementing a couple of additional endpoints to the services which were only used by the tests. They also created a couple of seed SQL files that could be used to insert data to the databases manually.

The end-to-end tests needed to be run in the Continuous Integration (CI) system as well. The team already had an existing development environment that was used by the CI. The development environment had all the services deployed and available for testing purposes. The same errors which happened

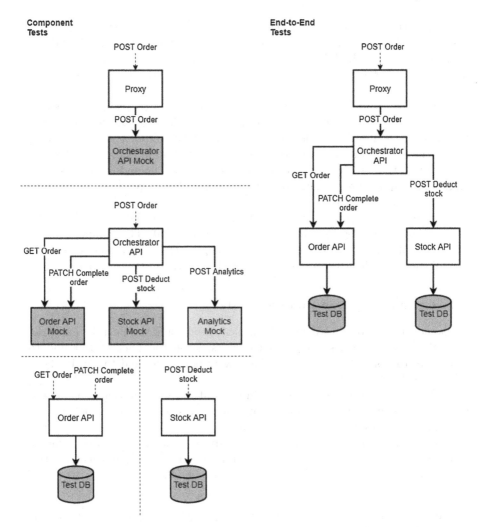

Fig. 4. Test boundaries of the order endpoint.

during developing on local machines often followed to the tests run by the CI in the development environment. Those were mainly caused by other development activities and other tests modifying the data. Often the fix required manual work to rerun the seed SQL files when something in the system had changed. The debugging of the errors became more challenging as the system grew, and the errors had to be traced from logs collected from multiple services.

The general feeling of the end-to-end tests was that they were slow, prone to errors, hard to debug, and non-deterministic in general. Sometimes it even felt like the team avoided running them because of the high effort. It was not uncommon that they failed to data errors, and no one wanted to spend time debugging them. In some cases, the errors in tests were left completely ignored if it was evident that there were no new changes to the system that could have broken the feature. It did not feel rewarding to debug and fix errors that were only related to the testing environment and not to the actual features of the system.

The above experiences and feelings guided the team to avoid implementing the end-to-end tests for every feature. It felt like the growing number of end-to-end tests would shift time and focus from other important things to just debugging false-negative errors. Because of that, they were implemented for just a handful of the most critical features of the system. The end-to-end tests only tested one happy case scenario per feature and did not even try to test all the different error scenarios.

Figure 4 introduces the testing boundaries for Order endpoint. The feature involves four microservices and two databases in total. The component tests isolate the microservices from each other using mocks and the end-to-end test tests if the Order feature works when all of the services are connected.

3.3   Consumer-Driven Contract Tests

Consumer-driven contract tests were implemented using the Pact JS[3], and they used Pact Broker[4] for sharing the contracts. Both the Pact Broker and the tests were run on a local machine. They were not attempted to run in the CI environment.

Calling the Save and Order endpoints initiates a set of interactions between the services. Following the naming convention of consumer-driven contract testing, each interaction happens between a consumer and a provider. Sometimes service can have both of the roles if it needs to consume other services to be able to respond to its consumer. The different roles for the services in this case study are broken down for both endpoints in Tables 1 and 2.

Table 1. Save endpoint roles. C and P refer to Consumer and Producer, respectively.

Service	C	P
Orchestrator API	x	
Configuration API		x
Validation API		x
Stock API		x
Order API		x

Table 2. Order endpoint roles in integrations. C and P refer to Consumer and Producer, respectively.

Service	C	P
Proxy	x	
Orchestrator API	x	x
Stock API		x
Order API		x

---

[3] https://github.com/pact-foundation/pact-js.

[4] https://github.com/pact-foundation/pact_broker.

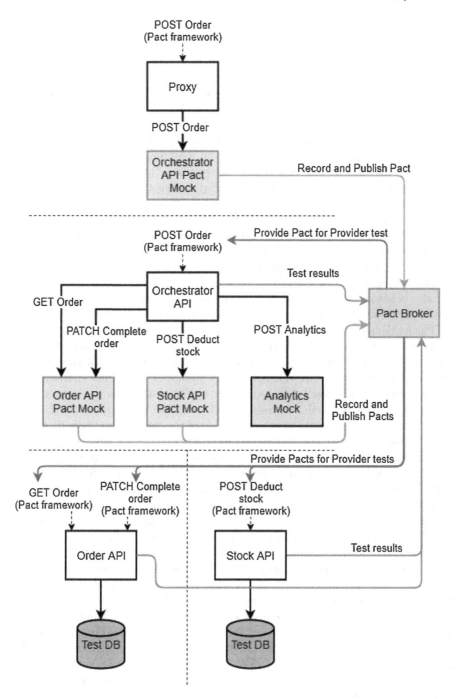

Fig. 5. Consumer-driven contract tests of the Order endpoint.

Consumer-driven contract tests break the testing boundaries between the services when compared to the component tests. This means that the services are no longer fully isolated from each other. The services are not directly connected either, like happened with end-to-end tests or would happen with integration tests. Instead, they are indirectly connected, and they communicate with each other using the contracts as a tool.

Such setting lets the consumer and the provider sides to be tested separately. There is no requirement for them both to be available and connected during the test execution. That still does not lift off the requirement of having to run the tests on both sides to fully verify the integration. Figure 5 illustrates this for Order endpoint. When it is compared to Fig. 4 with the component- and end-to-end tests, it is quick to notice that a few differences are standing out between the approaches.

The consumer tests use the mocks to achieve isolation in the same manner as component tests, but in addition to that, the Pact Broker is being utilized to share the contracts to the provider tests to fully verify both sides of the integrations. Unlike component tests, the consumer-driven contract tests do not test the behavior of the consumers. They directly trigger the parts of the code that initiate the external calls to the provider to focus solely on the integrations.

The implementation of the consumer and the provider tests with Pact differed from each other quite a lot. On the consumer side, the tests were all about implementing the Pact mocks. That meant writing a mock with the expected request and response for it. When the tests were executed, Pact compared the actual requests generated by the consumer application to the ones specified in the mock. If they matched, the tests passed, and Pact generated a contract out of the mock and considered the consumer side of the integration verified. At that point, the new contract was automatically uploaded to Pact Broker.

The provider side of tests required much less work compared to the consumer side. They ended up requiring only tens of lines of code. The implementation of the tests consisted of making sure the provider is available, and there is a correct set of data in its database. The provider tests automatically fetched all the contracts from Pact Broker. Then Pact dynamically generated tests out of the contracts and ran them against the provider. If the provider responded with the same responses the consumer specified to the contract, the tests passed. The test results were automatically reported to the Pact Broker after each test run.

Each tested integration between the services of both the Save and the Order endpoints consisted of 2–3 interactions. In total, there were 23 different interactions, and they all had a meaning to the consumers. Every single integration between the services contained the 200 OK happy case interaction. The second most common interaction was the 400 Error, which was a result of a failed request validation on the provider side. All of those interactions were important for the consumers because they had implemented behavior based on them. If the format changes, the consumers fail to handle those scenarios properly.

4   Results

4.1   Comparison of Testing Methods

The comparison of the testing methods was made by seeding defects to the integrations and studying how the tests caught them. The defects were implemented by going through all the interactions one at a time and by separately implementing them to both, to the consumer and to the provider, sides. The goal was to find out how the testing methods can catch those defects that break the integrations.

The seeded defects were violations against the contracts that were already verified on both sides. On the consumer side that meant changing the request that is sent to the provider. A few concrete examples of that would be renaming of query parameters, changing the format of request body or modifying the request headers. On the provider side the violations were changes to the API and its responses.

The comparison of the testing methods revealed that the consumer-driven contract tests were able to catch every single defect from the 23 different interactions. That was not the case with the component tests; they allowed the defects to slip through. The end-to-end tests were able to catch the defects from interactions that were part of a single happy case scenario, but the rest of the defects were left uncaught.

The comparison of the testing methods highlighted that the initial testing strategy was lacking when it came down to testing integrations. It also showed that consumer-driven contract tests were able to fill that hole from the testing strategy. The component tests from the initial testing strategy were very brittle in revealing errors in integrations. They did manage to reveal if something had changed during implementation time, but they did very little to tell if the change was an actual breaking change to a specific integration or just a change to the behavior of the service. Because of that, there is a chance to accidentally or unconsciously change the component tests to match the new functionality without realizing the implications on the other side of the integration. That leaves the integration broken while the component tests are still passing.

The end-to-end tests, on the other hand, proved to catch the breaking changes in the happy case of the Order endpoint. That is great, but there were still many different interactions that were left entirely untested. One good example is the Order endpoint, which had just one test for the happy case scenario and the different error case interactions were untested.

In conclusion, the introduction of the consumer-driven contract tests brought confidence to the testing strategy. The consumer-driven contract tests turned out to be very throughout at testing the integrations between the services. Compared to the component tests, it was not possible to make the tests pass without fixing the broken integrations first. They also caught all the different error cases which were not covered by the end-to-end tests. They were also easy and fast to run as they are always run in isolation from the other services. They did not cause any false negative errors, which proved they were very deterministic, making them convenient to use.

Integrations between the shop, the case study system, and analytics were not testable with the consumer-driven contract tests. They could and most likely should be tested that way, but they were scoped out from the case study to keep the scope more tightly on the testing method itself. Because of that, there were no attempts to contact the other teams to implement the consumer or the provider tests and to share the contracts. Therefore, the integrations with them were left tested with component tests and mocks that are not being verified in any way. That did not change the initial situation any better or worse as that was the case even before the implementation of consumer-driven contract tests.

4.2   Experiences with Consumer-Driven Contract Testing

The literature suggested that consumer-driven contract testing is a viable option to test integrations. There was just one requirement that could be hard to fulfill in some situations. The requirement was that the consumer and the provider must be able to communicate the process with each other.

The experiences from the case study supported the findings from the literature. The consumer-driven contract tests were very throughout on finding defects from integrations between services. The defects got reliably caught from both of sides of the integrations.

In addition to being a viable option for testing integrations, the literature listed further benefits for the consumer-driven contract testing, including (i) decoupling consumer from the provider and enables testing of both sides in isolation; (ii) fast, stable, and deterministic execution; (iii) ensuring that the provider knows who are consuming its API and how; enabling the provider to evolve based on real business needs from its consumers; (iv) enforcing that the provider tests always catch sudden breaking changes to the API; and (v) using contracts as a tool to improve communication between teams.

With the case study, we were able to confirm most of the listed benefits. The consumer-driven contract tests were run in isolation, which resulted in them being fast and stable. Due to that, they were also relatively easy to operate compared to the end-to-end tests even though they required the extra step to share the contracts. The sharing was made simple with Pact and the Pact Broker, which both proved out to be prominent tools in the field of implementing consumer-driven contract tests.

Especially the tooling made it possible to visualize who are the consumers for the providers and how they are consuming the APIs. In the case study, the consumer-driven contract tests were implemented after the actual services had already been implemented. That did not let the case study to examine how the provider could have been created and evolved from a scratch based on the needs of the consumers. Still, the case study was able to prove that it is possible to evolve the provider when the requirements from the consumers are visible in the contracts. In the future, consumers can use the contracts to communicate or suggest new changes to the provider.

The approach in the case study was to implement the consumer-driven contract tests in a spike by experimenting and implementing the tests for only a selected few features of the system. That was successful, and it proved that the spikes are an excellent way to experiment with the consumer-driven contract testing for already existing systems. That is an essential feature as it enables teams to experiment with the tests with a smaller scope and see if it fits their purposes. Majority of the time was spent at the beginning on learning the new way of testing and finding out proper tools for the job. After those were sorted out, the implementation of new tests became straightforward.

The spike method had another significant benefit when figuring out if the consumer-driven contract testing should be used. It can work as an excellent way to learn if there are any pain points in the communication inside the organization or between the different teams before fully committing to it. The effect of communication is a good thing to keep in mind when thinking about using the testing method. The system in the case study was initially implemented by one team so the communication would not have been a problem. It could have been challenging to extend the method to the outside consumers (the Shops) who were consuming the system or to the other APIs (the Analytics) that were consumed by the system.

The expansion of the testing coverage outside of the system developed by the team in the case study would have required communication with other teams. The first step would have been to introduce the testing method to them and then convince them that consumer-driven contract testing is something that is needed. That can be hard for many reasons. The other team can, for instance, be busy doing something else, with its own prioritized backlog. Moreover, even if the new testing method would end up to the backlog, it could take a while to get it prioritized high enough for actual implementation. Still, contracts are a great tool to communicate and share the details if all of the parties finally agree to proceed with the implementation. In another scenario, the teams could break the silos between them and cooperate so that the outside team does the initial implementation of the tests to help the other team to get started.

5   Discussion

In this paper, we have used five different testing methods split into two categories: isolated and integrated testing. Ideally, the highest number of tests should be written to the isolated category as they are easier to implement, more stable, and faster to execute, resembling a pyramid in shape (Fig. 1 given in Sect. 2). Every testing method in the pyramid has a different purpose and should focus solely on it to get the best results out of the combination of them all. Together they were said to be an ideal testing strategy for microservices [2].

It was shown that the initial testing strategy in the case study was lacking. It only included end-to-end, component, and unit tests. Compared to the testing pyramid, it was completely missing the consumer-driven contract- and integration test layers. Because of that, the errors in integrations were not caught adequately by the tests.

The component tests did give a clue if something possibly had changed in the integrations during the development time, but they did not directly reveal if the changes were breaking changes to the integrations. The change could also be related to some simple behavior such as validation rule that does not break the integration but makes the tests fail. When a new breaking change was implemented, the component tests initially failed. After that, the test could be changed without a notice that the other side of the integration is no longer compatible with the new change.

Unlike the component tests, the end-to-end tests did reveal broken integrations and prevented them from being deployed. The problem with end-to-end tests was a massive effort required to implement and operate them. These need much planning to implement, and these were prone to errors related to the testing environment, network, and test data. Debugging the reason for the test failures was troublesome and time-consuming because multiple services were involved in the process. Due to that, they had been implemented just for a couple of happy case interactions, and they lacked the coverage for different error case interactions. It would have been next to impossible to cover all the different interactions with the end-to-end tests, as there are so many different corner cases and branches to consider.

The integration tests would test the integrations using real running instances of the components in a production-like environment. These would be slower and harder to implement and execute compared to the consumer-driven contract tests. The added value would be mostly related to testing if the network and other infrastructure are working as expected. In the end, this would be testing a production-like environment but not the actual production environment. That would not guarantee that the production environment works the same way as the test environment. However, the experiences gained from the case study showed that the consumer-driven contract tests could replace the integration tests.

An open question related to integration tests is if these could help with testing the integrations with the systems that were developed by the other teams (Other shops and Analytics in Fig. 3). That is an interesting issue, as consumer-driven contract tests would have required the parties to communicate with each other to make the tests happen. In both cases, we considered the other side of the integration unreachable to reason about the impact on the testing method.

Integration tests addressing the integration with the shops would require the shops to implement the integration tests as these are the consumer. The shops were considered unreachable, so that is out of the question. Even if the shops implemented the integration tests, the testing would remain challenging. Each shop should run the tests every time there are changes to the provider. Ideally, the developer would be able to run the tests while developing the changes on a local machine. That would require having the codebase for all the shops and be able to run their tests, which further does not sound ideal and would require much unnecessary effort.

The integration with analytics was a case where the provider was considered unreachable. From the perspective of integration tests, this does not matter as long as the provider stays available for the tests to call it. Still, the integration tests would be far from ideal in this case as well. The integration tests would only be able to prove that the integration worked when the tests were run. They would not prevent the provider from changing the interface unless the provider is able to run the integration tests of the consumer. This means that the breaking change could happen in any given time, and if it happens, it could take a while until the consumer integration tests are rerun to catch the errors. With just integration tests, there is no way for the consumer to prevent the unreachable provider from publishing the breaking changes. The integration test would merely work as a tool to find out if the integration is already broken and requires fixing. That could and should be done more efficiently with a proper setup of logging, monitoring, and alerts.

To summarize, an ideal testing strategy for microservices based on the lessons learned from the case study as well as literature contains unit, component, consumer-driven contract, and end-to-end tests. The integration tests can be left out, and their responsibility should be given to consumer-driven contract tests. This leaves only end-to-end testing in the integrated testing category, while the rest of the testing methods are in the isolated testing category. An additional benefit that was gained and considered significant is reduced flakiness as a result of replacing the non-deterministic tests with deterministic tests. This enables more enhanced automation when considering debugging of the system. Finally, the ideal testing strategy is highly dependant on cooperation and communication between the teams. Therefore, good communication across the teams is something that should always be a top priority. It cannot be emphasized enough that communication is the foundation that enables the teams to build great things together.

Threats to Validity. The validity of as study is basically about the knowledge claims that can be made based on the results [10]. As our intent was to gain experiences on the usage of a particular testing methodology, one particular issue in terms of validity is that of the role of the testing methodology itself in the results achieved. The separation of the methodology used from the experience of the designers in the actions taken is fundamentally hard. This is something one may need to take into account if aiming to apply (generalise) the results in other cases. In addition, the characteristics of the system used in the case study may have an effect on the results. However, as these characteristics are somewhat typical in microservice based systems, this is not considered an overly restricting issue.

6   Conclusions

In this paper, we have studied consumer-driven contract testing in the light of a case study based on an industrial system. Our experiences gained from the case study confirmed the benefits commonly associated with such tests: (i) integrations are tested in isolation by decoupling the consumer and the provider using a contract, contributing to fast and stable tests; (ii) the provider knows who are consuming its API and how; (iii) the provider can evolve based on real business needs from its consumers; (iv) the consumer can feel safe as the provider tests always catch breaking changes to the API; and (v) contracts can work as a tool to improve communication between different development teams.

Furthermore, our experiences suggest that the consumer-driven contract tests can replace integration tests as they caught all the defects from the integrations that were implemented in the case study. In that light, it can be safely said that consumer-driven contract testing is a viable addition to testing strategies used to test integration-heavy systems, especially those based on microservices.

Acknowledgments. The work of N. Mäkitalo was supported by the Academy of Finland (project 313973).

References

1. Cerny, T., Donahoo, M.J., Trnka, M.: Contextual understanding of microservice architecture: current and future directions. ACM SIGAPP Appl. Comput. Rev. **17**(4), 29–45 (2018)
2. Clemson, T.: Testing strategies in a microservice architecture (2014). https://martinfowler.com/articles/microservice-testing. Accessed 8 Feb 2019
3. Cohn, M.: Succeeding with Agile: Software Development Using Scrum, 1st edn. Addison-Wesley Professional, Boston (2009)
4. Meyer, B.: Applying 'design by contract'. Computer **25**(10), 40–51 (1992)
5. Namiot, D., Sneps-Sneppe, M.: On micro-services architecture. Int. J. Open Inf. Technol. **2**(9), 24–27 (2014)
6. Newman, S.: Building Microservices: Designing Fine-Grained Systems. O'Reilly Media Inc., Sebastopol (2015)
7. Pautasso, C., Zimmermann, O., Amundsen, M., Lewis, J., Josuttis, N.: Microservices in practice, part 1: reality check and service design. IEEE Softw. **34**(1), 91–98 (2017)
8. Pautasso, C., Zimmermann, O., Amundsen, M., Lewis, J., Josuttis, N.: Microservices in practice, part 2: service integration and sustainability. IEEE Softw. **2**, 97–104 (2017)
9. Robinson, I.: Consumer-driven contracts: a service evolution pattern (2018). https://martinfowler.com/articles/consumerDrivenContracts.html. Accessed 21 Oct 2018
10. Shadish, W.R., Thomas, C.D., Thomas, C.D.: Experimental and Quasi-experimental Designs for Generalized Causal Inference. Houghton Mifflin Company, Boston (2002)
11. Sill, A.: The design and architecture of microservices. IEEE Cloud Comput. **3**(5), 76–80 (2016)
12. Wolff, E.: Microservices: Flexible Software Architecture. Addison-Wesley Professional, Boston (2016)

Continuous Experimentation

Data Driven Development: Challenges in Online, Embedded and On-Premise Software

Helena Holmström Olsson[1(✉)] and Jan Bosch[2]

[1] Department of Computer Science and Media Technology, Malmö University,
Malmö, Sweden
`helena.holmstrom.olsson@mau.se`
[2] Department of Computer Science and Engineering,
Chalmers University of Technology, Gothenburg, Sweden
`jan.bosch@chalmers.se`

Abstract. For more than a decade, data driven development has attracted attention as one of the most powerful means to improve effectiveness and ensure value delivery to customers. In online companies, controlled experimentation is the primary technique to measure how customers respond to variants of deployed software. In B2B companies, an interest for data driven development is rapidly emerging and experiments are run on selected instances of the system or as comparisons of previously computed data to ensure quality, improve configurations and explore new value propositions. Although the adoption of data driven development is challenging in general, it is especially so for embedded systems companies and for companies developing on-premise software solutions. Due to complex systems with hardware dependencies, safety-critical functionality and strict regulations, these companies have longer development cycles, less frequent deployments and limited access to data. In this paper, and based on multi-case study research, we explore the specific challenges that embedded systems companies and companies developing on-premise solutions experience when adopting data driven development practices. The contribution of the paper is two-fold. First, we provide empirical evidence in which we identify the key challenges that embedded systems and on-premise software solutions companies experience as they evolve through the process of adopting data driven development practices. Second, we define the key focus areas that these companies need to address for evolving their data driven development adoption process.

Keywords: Data driven development · Online software · Embedded systems · On-premise solutions · Adoption process · Challenges

1 Introduction

Over the past years, software-intensive companies in a variety of domains, with online companies leading the way, have started adopting data driven development practices to continuously assess customer value and monitor feature usage [1–3]. Using the

© Springer Nature Switzerland AG 2019
X. Franch et al. (Eds.): PROFES 2019, LNCS 11915, pp. 515–527, 2019.
https://doi.org/10.1007/978-3-030-35333-9_36

definition provided by [4], data driven development is the *ability of a company to acquire, process, and leverage data in order to create efficiencies, iterate and develop new products, and navigate the competitive landscape.* In recent studies, data driven development practices are proven useful for improving product performance, for optimizing system parameters and for evaluating new product concepts [5–8]. As a result, companies that are adept at acquiring, processing and leveraging customer and product data become more profitable as continuous assessment of customer value can have a profound impact on annual revenue [8]. As an additional benefit, data can help question, challenge, complement and confirm existing assumptions in the organization. In this way, collection and use of data is becoming an effective mechanism for replacing opinions-based decision-making with data-driven decision-making about customer value, system performance and overall product quality [2]. While the opportunities provided by data are already well-established in online companies, they are becoming increasingly recognized also in companies developing on-premise solutions and embedded systems. With products such as cars, trucks, phones, cameras, household appliances etc. being increasingly software-intensive and connected to the Internet, these companies are starting to explore the opportunities that online companies have benefitted from for more than a decade [9]. However, although there are examples of data driven development practices being used in embedded systems and on-premise companies, the adoption process of these practices is challenging. Typically, and due to complex systems with hardware dependencies, safety-critical functionality and strict regulations, these companies have longer development cycles, less frequent deployments and limited access to customer and product data.

In this paper, and based on multi-case study research, we explore the specific challenges that embedded systems companies and companies developing on-premise solutions experience when adopting data driven development practices. To achieve this, we first review contemporary literature on data driven development in online companies where these practices are fully adopted and successfully used, and we identify the typical stages these companies evolve through when adopting these practices. Second, and with the adoption stages from the online companies as a basis, we study a total of nine companies in the embedded systems and in the on-premise software domain with the intention to understand the specific challenges these companies experience when adopting the similar practices as the online companies.

The contribution of the paper is two-fold. First, we provide empirical evidence in which we identify the key challenges that embedded systems and on-premise software solutions companies experience as they evolve through the process of adopting data driven development practices. Second, we define the key focus areas that these companies need to address for further evolve their data driven development practices.

The remainder of the paper is organized as follows. In Sect. 2, we review contemporary literature on data driven development in online companies and we identify the typical stages that online companies evolve through when adopting data driven development. In Sect. 3, we describe the research method and the case companies. In Sect. 4, we present our empirical findings. In Sect. 5, we identify the key challenges that embedded systems and on-premise solutions companies experience when adopting data driven development and we define the key focus areas that these companies need to address to further evolve these practices. In Sect. 6, we conclude the paper.

2   Background

In this section, we review contemporary literature on the adoption of data driven development in online companies. We define online companies as companies providing web services and that use controlled experiments to determine which variant of a product, design or interface that performs the best. In recent studies, companies such as e.g. Facebook, Google, Booking, Amazon, LinkedIn and Skyscanner are often referred to in relation to successful use of controlled experimentation [6, 10].

2.1   Data-Driven Development

For decades, one of the primary challenges in software development has been how to shorten feedback cycles to customers [11, 12]. As outlined in previous research [13], the first step towards shorter feedback cycles is the adoption of agile development. These methods emphasize short iterations of increments rather than the long cycles as known from traditional development. More recently, technologies such as continuous integration [14] and continuous deployment [15] have enabled companies to further shorten feedback cycles. These technologies allow for frequent test and deployment of software and in combination with connectivity that enables diagnostic, performance and operations data to be collected, companies can significantly shorten the time it takes to learn from and respond to customers.

In online companies, data driven development is a well-established approach to software development [3, 8, 11, 16]. In these companies, data is the foundation for any decision regarding redesign or improvement of a feature, for prioritization of features from the backlog and for optimization of certain metrics. With techniques such as A/B testing and automated practices for data collection and analysis, customers are continuously part of experiments to help optimize the system and queries are processed frequently to provide software developers and managers with rapid feedback [5]. As recognized in our previous research [17], companies that adopt data driven development typically do this by starting to identify what key factors to optimize for. This is achieved by modeling the expected value of a feature in order to get a few metrics in place to then collect data that will help improve these. In online companies, common metrics are e.g. *'number of users'*, *'frequency of use'*, *'response time'*, *'number of successful upsells'*. In addition to identifying metrics, teams also need to identify the relative priority of these factors. This is important as some factors may improve while others decline when running an experiment. Data driven development reflects a shift from traditional development where requirements inform development [18], towards a situation in which continuous collection of data inform development throughout the lifecycle of the system [2, 5, 19]. Moreover, and as experienced in online companies, data-driven development constitutes an effective means to challenge existing assumptions held by people in the organization. Often, inaccurate assumptions result in poor decision-making, an inaccurate understanding of customer value and slow feedback cycles. As a consequence, companies end up investing development efforts in features that are not used by customers and optimizing for metrics that are no longer representative for what generates business value.

2.2 Experimentation Practices

As a critical technique in data driven development, online controlled experimentation, also known as A/B testing, allows continuous validation of value with customers [16]. Online controlled experiments constitute a practice of comparing two versions of functionality to determine which one performs better in relation to predefined criteria such as e.g. conversion rate, click rate or time to perform a certain task. In online companies, controlled experiments are the norm with companies such as e.g. Amazon, eBay, Facebook, Google and Microsoft running hundreds and even thousands of parallel experiments to evaluate and improve their services at any point in time. To achieve this, companies need an infrastructure to collect and store data from deployed products and that makes data available for analysis. There are numerous experimentation tools and platforms available on the market [6, 20]. However, the challenges of building the data infrastructure are typically not concerned with the basic technologies but rather with aspects related to customer relations, legal constraints, cost of data collection and storage. It should be noted that experimentation involves many different techniques. For example, experimentation could refer to iterations with prototypes in the startup domain, canary flying of software features, gradual rollout and dark launches [11]. With frequent experimentation, teams can adopt an increasingly iterative development approach in which features are sliced into smaller parts that can be developed in less than a sprint and for which the team collects data to guide the next steps of development. As recognized in [2], this allows teams to rapidly determine whether a feature adds value or not. In our previous research, and based on studying a large number of online experiments at Microsoft, we introduced the Experiment Lifecycle in which we outline the three main stages of every Online Controlled Experiment [11].

During recent years, online controlled experimentation has received increasing interest and there exist a number of studies describing the many benefits with this practice [8, 11, 16, 20, 21]. These studies outline the roles involved (e.g. data analysts, data scientists, product managers, software developers etc.), the task at hand (e.g. development of roadmaps, design and analysis of experiments, development of products, deployment of products etc.) and the technical infrastructure that is the platform for the experiments (e.g. the application programming interfaces, experiment databases, analytic tools, instrumentation, integration and deployment systems etc.). In particular, challenges in relation to the definition of an 'Overall Evaluation Criterion' have been carefully explored [16] as well as models that describe the experiment lifecycle in online companies [2, 8], the data collection techniques that are used [22], and the infrastructure that is required for running a successful online controlled experiment [16, 23].

2.3 Team – System – Business Metrics

As a prerequisite for an experiment, teams need to define an 'Overall Evaluation Criterion' (OEC) [11, 16]. The OEC is a structured set of metrics consisting of success, guardrail and data quality metrics that are used to define performance goals and desired outcomes of an experiment. For teams, an OEC can consist of improving conversion rate on a website, increase throughput or improve a specific feature. At a system or product level, the OECs cover system and product performance and metrics are used to track the overall product portfolio. At the highest level, business metrics are defined to track overall business goals. While metrics at the team level are leading indicators that teams can influence on a daily basis, business metrics are lagging indicators that are hard to influence in the short term but instead metrics that change over a longer period of time. In previous research [11], and based on our insights from working with four companies in the online domain, we introduced a framework for how to scale experimentation and in which the definition of OECs at the team, at the system and at the business level are critical elements. The goal is to have efforts at the team level positively influence business metrics [17]. If so, companies can effectively scale experimentation, advance their data driven development practices and successfully use data as the basis for decision-making throughout the organization.

2.4 Data Driven Development Adoption Process

Based on the learnings from our literature review, as well as from on our own experiences when studying companies in the online domain, we have identified five stages that we see online companies evolve through when adopting data driven development (Fig. 1).

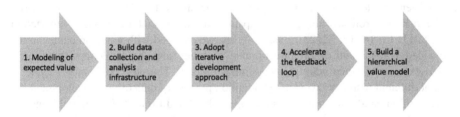

Fig. 1. Data driven development adoption process: the five stages we see online companies evolve through when adopting data driven development. The model is derived from previous literature as well as from our own experiences when studying online companies.

The first stage online companies enter when adopting data driven development is to have development teams identify what factors to optimize for. This is achieved by *modeling the expected value* of a new or existing feature and works as the basic stage in order to get a few metrics in place to then collect data to help improve these. These factors are used to guide experimentation and to track the performance of subsequent releases of the feature. In the second stage, companies develop an infrastructure to *collect and store data* from deployed products and that makes data available for analysis. The third stage is concerned with increasing the effectiveness of development teams by *adopting an iterative development approach*. In this approach, features are sliced into smaller parts that can be developed in less than a sprint and for which the team collects data to guide the next steps of development. In the fourth stage, companies seek to further *accelerate the feedback loop*. To achieve this, they develop the shortest possible cycle between development of a feature and deployment in the field. In online companies, the feedback loop ranges from hours to minutes and even seconds and as a result, these companies are able to use data to effectively direct their development efforts. As the final stage, and as the mechanism to ensure alignment between team, system and business level metrics, companies develop a *hierarchical value model* where feature level metrics that are modeled as part of the first stage of the process are connected and aligned with high-level business key performance indicators (KPIs).

3   Research Method

The goal of this study is to explore the challenges that embedded systems companies and companies developing on-premise solutions experience when adopting data driven development. In our study, embedded systems companies are companies that develop larger systems and complete devices including hardware and mechanical parts and in which software is one part [24]. On-premise software is software that is installed and runs on the premises of the organization using the software, rather than at a remote facility such as the cloud [25]. Our study builds on multi-case study research in companies from these two different domains as well as on our previous learnings from the online domain. Case study research focuses on providing a deeper understanding of a particular context and it emphasizes the importance of peoples' experiences [26]. In our study, and as a first step, we reviewed contemporary literature on the adoption of data driven development practices in online companies. In addition, we built on our own experience from working with companies in the online domain and as reported in [1–3, 8, 11, 13, 16, 17, 22, 23]. Based on this, we engaged with nine companies in the embedded systems and on-premise domain to understand the challenges these companies experience when adopting the similar process. The case companies (Table 1) were at different maturity levels in the adoption process of data driven development. At the time of our study, the practices in company E, H and I reflected the initial stages of the process, company C, D, F, G and A were approaching or at the middle stages and company B was aiming for a hierarchical value model. During our study, we engaged in workshop sessions at each company in which we facilitated, as well as documented, their experiences with the different stages in the adoption process. At each company we had developers, product managers, technical specialists, software architects, system engineers, agile coaches and data scientists present. Each workshop session involved between 6–10 people and lasted for 3-5 h. In companies where data driven practices were immature, we had larger groups of 15–20 people as the workshops served the additional purpose of introducing the organization to the concept. Our study involved nine companies (Table 1).

In the continuation of the paper, we provide a summary of the experiences from the case companies in order to establish an understanding for the specific challenges these companies experience when adopting data driven development. For validity of results [24], and to address construct validity, we started each workshop with sharing our definition of the key concepts. This established a common understanding of the topic and we could discuss alternative interpretations already before we ran into potential misunderstandings. With respect to external validity, our contributions provide rich insight in different company domains and we identify implications for research and for practice.

Table 1. The case companies and the domain(s) they operate in.

Case	Description	Embedded systems	On-premise
A	Provider of systems and equipment for network operators	x	x
B	Developer of navigational information and optimization solutions	x	x
C	Developer of network video surveillance solutions	x	x
D	Developer of food packaging and processing systems	x	
E	Provider of systems and solutions for military defense and civil security	x	
F	Developer of automotive technology	x	
G	Engineering and electronics company	x	
H	Manufacturer of vehicles	x	
I	Manufacturer of trucks, buses and construction equipment	x	

4 Findings

Below, we summarize the key findings from our study. When reporting on our findings, we use the five stages of adopting data driven development that we identified in our literature review.

Stage 1: Modeling of Feature Value

To introduce the embedded systems and on-premise software companies to the first stage of adopting data driven development, we initiated a series of workshop sessions in which we met with developers and product managers in order to model the value of a selected feature. As part of the workshops, the teams selected a feature, identified key value factors, prioritized these factors and their relative importance. In the end, a few groups managed to develop a value function to quantitatively express what they optimize for. While the majority of the companies selected existing features to work with we also had companies that used the workshops to model new features that were not yet developed and for which value was not yet proven. In company B, one of the teams succeeded in developing a complete value function for one of their mobile applications. They expressed it as: *0.1*feedback time + 0.2*success rate + 0.2*number of users + 0.2 successful drops – 0.3 cost of ownership* where each value factor was given a relative weight and where the formula indicates whether you look to increase or decrease the value of each factor.

Stage 2: Build Data Collection and Analysis Infrastructure

In the second stage, the companies realized the need for a data collection and analysis infrastructure. As experienced in these companies, the initial focus should be on keeping things simple by collecting data only for the selected feature and only from friendly customers as this allows easier access to data. As the companies had infrastructures for data collection in place already, this stage was mostly concerned with complementing these with metrics that would allow for measuring value according to the new value function. As a common experience, this stage revealed lack of effective analysis tools and often the approach was manual solutions and/or existing web-based solutions.

Stage 3: Adopt Iterative Development Process

As most of the case companies have a hardware and mechatronics background, the adoption of iterative development required a significant change in mind-set. For the companies, the identification of parts of their organizations where these new ways-of-working were feasible was an important step and typically, they selected already agile teams within their software organization. With these teams, we developed hypotheses that could be tested during each sprint and we ran validation workshops to evaluate experiments. Most companies were able to identify 1–4 hypotheses to test during the next 2–3 sprints and with the goal to either (1) increase the number of hypotheses to be tested within their current sprints, or to (2) shorten their current sprints to increase the total number of hypotheses tested.

Stage 4: Accelerate the Feedback Loop

All companies have a tradition in traditional development and they have adopted agile development. To further accelerate the feedback loop, they have started adopting continuous integration and continuous deployment. However, until these practices are fully in place, it is difficult to further accelerate the feedback loop. In all companies, huge efforts were put in place to drive CI and CD initiatives as well as to minimize customer-specific branches of a product and instead strive for a single product branch with configuration opportunities for different customers. In this way, feedback loops were shortened and the companies could benefit from frequent releases.

Stage 5: Build a Hierarchical Value Model

The last stage is to build a hierarchical value model to ensure that team metrics and business metrics align. While online companies have a complete hierarchy of metrics at team – system – business level, the establishment of such a hierarchy proved challenging in the embedded and on-premise companies. While a well-defined set of metrics, such as e.g. customer satisfaction, revenue, sales, customer retention, net promoter score etc., existed at the business level, these did not necessarily translate into executable metrics for teams to optimize for. In the case companies, we noted a willingness to establish a hierarchical value model and we started aligning metrics in a couple of the companies. However, as the previous four stages have to be in place in order to successfully create a value model for the entire business, we did not achieve this within the time span of this study.

5   Key Challenges When Adopting Data Driven Development

The intention with our study was to explore the specific challenges that embedded and on-premise software companies experience when adopting data driven development. Below, we identify the key challenges that these companies experience as they evolve through the process of adopting data driven development.

Stage 1: Modeling of Feature Value

Based on our experiences, the first stage comes with at least four challenges:

Difficulties in agreeing on value factors and the relative priority of these: The workshops revealed that it is very challenging for a team to agree on the relevant factors and the relative priority of these. This stage surfaced deeply held beliefs about the system and its customers that were far from agreed upon among teams. And as the typical development cycles in the companies were long, and with few opportunities for customer feedback, the assumptions that evolve were rarely questioned. This made improvement efforts difficult as there was no shared understanding on what metrics to optimize for.

Painful quantification of value: Especially product managers were reluctant to explain their reasoning behind prioritizing a certain feature and to quantify the expected value of this feature. Instead, value was described in qualitative terms which made prioritizations easier to defend as quantitative metrics did not exist.

Lack of end-to-end understanding of value: Even if a team agreed on the relevant factors and their relative priority, the relationship between the value of the feature and the business impact proved hard to define.

Illusion of alignment: By abstracting topics of contention to a level of vagueness that everyone could agree on, teams in all companies created a false sense of unity. We interpreted this as a way to avoid tension as to get precise might upset the existing illusion of alignment.

Stage 2: Build Data Collection and Analysis Infrastructure

In the second stage, the case companies experienced an increasing organizational resistance against the adoption of data driven development. Often, people used excuses centered around the customer:

"Don't go data driven because customers don't want to": Non-software people raised the concern that customers don't want to share data and that adopting data driven development would be to go against the interests of these customers.

"Don't go data driven because it is risky": Security, safety and reliability issues were brought forward as reasons to not adopt data driven development.

"Don't go data driven because it is expensive and effort-consuming": A common belief was that to iteratively develop a smaller slice of a feature is difficult with the standard argument being: *"You can't deploy something half done…"*, and with many people uncertain about the value of an MVF ('minimal viable feature').

"Don't go data driven because you can't have all customers do this": In the companies with a strong background in traditional development, there was a tendency to think that all customers had to be involved at the same time. This mind-set revealed lack of experience with starting small scale and with only a selected set of friendly customers.

Stage 3: Adopt Iterative Development Process

In the third stage, the case companies faced a number of challenges in relation to the adoption of a more iterative development approach:

Stuck in waterfall development: All case companies struggled with adopting shorter development cycles and more frequent deployment of software. Although both the embedded systems and the on-premise software companies had agile practices in place in parts of their organizations, people failed in realizing that iterative development requires a change of mind-set in relation to communication, coordination and control of teams.

One feature versus several small MVFs: The case companies have a strong engineering background and people who pride themselves based on the completeness of a feature. This made it difficult to break a feature into smaller increments and think in terms of a 'minimal viable feature' (MVF) with only slices being developed at a time.

Surfacing hidden misalignment: The case companies experienced situations in which questions were raised on how to develop and test hypotheses. During this stage, people who thought they agreed on something realized that this was not the case. Also, what sounded as an easy hypothesis to test often turned out to cause the teams major difficulties in actually realizing within the scope of a sprint.

Retrospective reinterpretation of data: The companies experienced situations in which people, whenever data conflicted with their beliefs, sought explanations that would make their beliefs still true. This was evident both in development teams and among product managers and reflected low trustworthiness in data.

Stage 4: Accelerate the Feedback Loop

To accelerate the feedback loop in companies that are used to long development cycles involves a number of challenges:

Shortening of QA cycles: It became evident that in order to align with the shortened time between the end of a development sprint and deployment at customer site, it was critical to shorten feedback cycles for quality assurance (QA) This was experienced as very difficult in all case companies.

Changing practices for QA: The companies realized that the QA teams need to change ways-of-working. Especially, test automation practices were identified as a key practice QA needed to apply. For this to happen, there needs to be the willingness to deploy to customer, test post-deployment and roll back if any issues.

Data-driven versus Requirements-driven: In most companies, situations in which data driven practices will co-exist with situations in which regulations and standards specify requirements. Therefore, the capability to select the most suitable approach is important and this challenge surfaced when aspiring to accelerate the feedback loop.

Stage 5: Build a Hierarchical Value Model

Although the companies that we studied didn't reach the stage of building a hierarchical value model, they reached far enough to have people reflect on why it is critical for data driven development. In these discussions, we noted the following challenges:

Involvement of all company functions: To build a hierarchical value model involves all company functions. While people close to development might be more enthusiastic to data driven development this is not necessarily the case in other parts of the organization.

Alignment of metrics: To agree on low and high-level metrics is difficult as it forces the company to start aligning metrics and to establish relationships between these.

Model maintenance and evolution: As experienced in our work with online companies, metrics need to continuously evolve to not inscribe an inaccurate understanding of value. We foresee this as a relevant challenge also in the embedded and on-premise companies.

Anecdotal prioritization of resources: Senior leaders have to abandon anecdotal prioritization of resources and instead use data to prioritize customer requests. This is important at all stages, but even more so in relation to the creation of a hierarchical value model as this model is intended replace assumptions and encourage data driven decision-making.

5.1   Key Focus Areas

In the above sections, we presented the key challenges that the case companies experience when adopting data driven development. When reflecting on these challenges, we identify three key focus areas that we believe these companies need to address to further evolve their data driven development practices (Table 2).

Table 2. Key focus areas that the case companies need to address to further evolve their data driven development practices.

Key focus areas	Description
Organizational resistance	Due to a tradition in hardware, mechanics and electronics, these companies experience significant *organizational resistance*. Although this might be true for any change initiative, it is especially so when adopting software-based practices that have the power to radically question existing assumptions while at the same time fundamentally change the basis for decision-making in an organization with a non-software background and tradition
Data quality and trustworthiness	*Data quality* is challenging as it involves collection, processing, sharing, storing and management of large and distributed data sets. As a result of the high complexity involved, *trustworthiness* is low and people tend to rather lean back on existing assumptions than trust the accuracy and quality of facts revealed in the data
Development cycle time	To shorten *development cycle time* is problematic. Despite modularized architectures and advice on how to combine and evolve cycle times for mechanics, hardware and software, the concept of iterative development and incremental development of features remains an issue

6   Conclusions

In this paper, and based on multi-case study research, we explore the specific challenges that embedded systems companies and companies developing on-premise solutions experience when adopting data driven development. When reflecting on these challenges, we see that there are three key focus areas that these companies need to address to further evolve their data driven development practices. First, due to a tradition in hardware, mechanics and electronics, these companies experience significant *organizational resistance*. Second, *data quality and trustworthiness* are challenging as it involves collection, processing, sharing, storing and management, as well as trust, in data. Finally, to *shorten development cycle time* is problematic in systems with highly complex architectures and dependencies. In future research, we aim to further explore the challenges the case companies encounter as these provide valuable input for the open research challenges in relation to organizational resistance, data quality and trustworthiness and development cycle time.

References

1. Holmström Olsson, H., Bosch, J.: Towards data-driven product development: a multiple case study on post-deployment data usage in software-intensive embedded systems. In: Fitzgerald, B., Conboy, K., Power, K., Valerdi, R., Morgan, L., Stol, K.-J. (eds.) LESS 2013. LNBIP, vol. 167, pp. 152–164. Springer, Heidelberg (2013). https://doi.org/10.1007/978-3-642-44930-7_10
2. Olsson, H.H., Bosch, J.: From opinions to data-driven software R&D: a multi-case study on how to close the 'open loop' problem. In: Proceedings of EUROMICRO, Software Engineering and Advanced Applications (SEAA), 27–29 August, Verona, Italy (2014)
3. Olsson, H.H., Bosch, J.: Towards evidence-based development: learnings from embedded systems, online games and internet of things. IEEE Softw. **4**(5) (2017)
4. Patil, D.J.: Building Data Science Teams, pp. 1–25. Oreilly, Radar (2011)
5. Bosch, J.: Building products as innovations experiment systems. In: Proceedings of 3rd International Conference on Software Business, 18–20 June, Cambridge, Massachusetts (2012)
6. Kohavi, R., Longbotham, R.: Online controlled experiments and A/B tests. In: Encyclopedia of Machine Learning and Data Mining, no. Ries 2011, pp. 1–11 (2015)
7. Fagerholm, F., Guinea, A.F., Mäenpää, H., Münch, J.: Building blocks for continuous experimentation. In: Proceedings of the 1st International Workshop on Rapid Continuous Software Engineering (RCoSE), pp. 26–35 (2014)
8. Fabijan, A., Dmitriev, P., Olsson, H.H., Bosch J.: The evolution of continuous experimentation in software product development: from data to a data-driven organization at scale. In Proceedings of the 39th International Conference on Software Engineering (ICSE), May 20–28th, Buenos Aires, Argentina (2017)
9. Bosch, J., Eklund, U.: Eternal embedded software: towards innovation experiment systems. In: Margaria, T., Steffen, B. (eds.) ISoLA 2012. LNCS, vol. 7609, pp. 19–31. Springer, Heidelberg (2012). https://doi.org/10.1007/978-3-642-34026-0_3
10. Van Nostrand, R.C.: Design of experiments using the taguchi approach: 16 steps to product and process improvement. Technometrics **44**(3), 289 (2002)

11. Fabijan, A., Dimitriev, P., Vermeer, L., Olsson, H.H., Bosch, J.: Experimentation growth: Evolving trustworthy A/B testing capabilities in oline software companies. J. Softw.: Evol. Process **30**(12), e2113 (2018)
12. Bosch-Sijtsema, P., Bosch, J.: User involvement throughout the innovation process in high-tech industries. J. Prod. Innov. Manag. **32**(5), 793–807 (2015)
13. Olsson, H.H., Alahyari, H., Bosch, J.: Climbing the "stairway to heaven": a multiple-case study exploring barriers in the transition from agile development towards continuous deployment of software. In: Proceedings of the 38th Euromicro Conference on Software Engineering and Advanced Applications, 5–7 September, Cesme, Izmir, Turkey (2012)
14. Ståhl, D., Bosch, J.: Modeling continuous integration practice differences in industry software development. J. Syst. Softw. **87**(1), 48–59 (2014)
15. Humble, J., Farley, D.: Continuous Delivery: Reliable Software Releases through Build, Test, and Deployment Automation. Addison-Wesley, Boston (2010)
16. Fabijan, A., Dmitriev, P., Olsson, H.H., Bosch, J., Vermeer, L., Lewis, D.: Three key checklists and remedies for trustworthy analysis of online controlled experiments at scale. In: Proceedings of 41st International Conference on Software Engineering (ICSE), 25–31 May, Montreal, Canada (2019)
17. Olsson, H.H., Bosch, J.: Make up your mind: towards a comprehensive definition of customer value in large scale software development. CLEI Electron. J. **21**(1) (2018)
18. Pohl, K.: Requirements Engineering: Fundamentals, Principles, and Techniques. Springer, Heidelberg (2010)
19. Ries, E.: The Lean Startup: How Today's Entrepreneurs Use Continuous Innovation to Create Radically Successful Businesses. Crown Business, New York (2011)
20. Dmitriev, P., Frasca, B., Gupta, S., Kohavi, R., Vaz, G.: Pitfalls of long term online controlled experiments. In: Proceedings of IEEE International Conference on Big Data (Big Data), pp. 1367–1376 (2016)
21. Xia, T., Bhardwaj, S., Dmitriev, P., Fabijan, A.: Safe velocity: a practical guide to software deployment at scale using controlled rollout. In Proceedings of the 41st International Conference on Software Engineering (ICSE), 25–31 May, Montreal, Canada (2019)
22. Fabijan, A., Olsson, H.H., Bosch, J.: Customer feedback and data collection techniques in software R&D: a literature review. In: Fernandes, J., Machado, R., Wnuk, K. (eds.) Software Business (ICSOB). LNBIP, vol. 210, pp. 139–153. Springer, Cham (2015). https://doi.org/10.1007/978-3-319-19593-3_12
23. Issa Mattos, D., Dmitriev, P., Fabijan, A., Bosch, J., Holmström Olsson, H.: An activity and metric model for online controlled experiments. In: Kuhrmann, M., et al. (eds.) PROFES 2018. LNCS, vol. 11271, pp. 182–198. Springer, Cham (2018). https://doi.org/10.1007/978-3-030-03673-7_14
24. Heath, S.: Embedded Systems Design. EDN Series for Design Engineers, 2nd edn. Newnes, London (2003)
25. https://www.webopedia.com/TERM/O/on-premises.html. Accessed 20 Sept 2019
26. Maxwell, J.A.: Qualitative Research Design: An Interactive Approach, 2nd edn. SAGE Publications, Thousands Oaks (2005)

Continuous Experimentation for Software Organizations with Low Control of Roadmap and a Large Distance to Users: An Exploratory Case Study

Robin Sveningson[✉] [iD], David Issa Mattos[iD], and Jan Bosch[iD]

Department of Computer Science and Engineering,
Chalmers University of Technology, Hörselgången 11, 412 96 Göteborg, Sweden
robinsv@student.chalmers.se, {davidis,jan.bosch}@chalmers.se

Abstract. With the increasing popularity of A/B testing and other experimentation practices in web systems, companies from a range of different domains are starting to look at continuous experimentation as a way to guide product development and feature prioritization. Research in continuous experimentation traditionally focused on companies that have easy access to user data and that have a high degree of control of the product roadmap. However, little research has been conducted to understand how companies that have a low control of roadmap and have a large distance to the users, such as consultancy companies, can benefit from continuous experimentation practices. To address this problem, we performed an exploratory case study with a software consultancy company combined with a validation procedure with four additional companies. The contribution of this work is three-fold. First, we devised a model to classify a company in the terms of the distance to users and the control of roadmap. Second, we show how control of roadmap and distance to user impacts continuous experimentation. Finally, we present several perceived challenges and benefits of continuous experimentation for companies and directions for future work.

Keywords: Continuous experimentation · A/B testing · Distance to users · Control of roadmap · Benefits · Challenges

1 Introduction

A common problem in a lot of software organizations is that decisions are based on opinions and previous experience of the organization members, rather than collected empirical data and proof [2]. This becomes a problem because humans are bad at making estimations and predicting what will be appreciated and used by software users. This problem is exemplified by for instance Netflix, that according to Moran say that as much as 90% of what they try is wrong [12, p. 240].

© Springer Nature Switzerland AG 2019
X. Franch et al. (Eds.): PROFES 2019, LNCS 11915, pp. 528–544, 2019.
https://doi.org/10.1007/978-3-030-35333-9_37

Continuous experimentation, a general term used for experimentation in the software engineering process [1,6,7,16], is largely advocated by several large software companies (such as Microsoft, Google, Facebook, Netflix, Etsy etc) as a way to support evidence-based decision-making in the development organization [9,11] [12, p. 240]. Continuous experimentation practices include a range of different techniques such as A/B testing, canary releases, gradual rollouts and dark launches [18].

Most of the research on continuous experimentation was conducted in collaboration with large web-faced software companies that operate in a business-to-consumer domain and that own the products they develop [1]. However, continuous experimentation is not restricted to this type of companies. In this work, we investigate the impact of control of roadmap and distance to users on the usage of continuous experimentation. We conducted an exploratory case study with a consultancy company and a validation phase with an additional four companies. The contribution of this paper is three-fold. First, we devised a classification system to evaluate a company in the extent of the distance to users and the control of roadmap. Second, we investigate how control of roadmap and distance to user impacts continuous experimentation. Finally, we present several perceived challenges and benefits of continuous experimentation for the consultancy company, as well as directions for future work.

The rest of this paper is outlined as follows. Section 2 provides background information about continuous experimentation, control of roadmap and distance to users as well as discussion on related work. Section 3 describes the research method and validity considerations. Section 4 presents the main results. Section 5 provides a discussion of the results. Finally Sect. 6 concludes this research and discusses future research directions.

2   Background and Related Work

Continuous Experimentation

Continuous experimentation is a general term that refers to the use of experimentation in the software development process [1,6,7,16]. Continuous experimentation allows the collection of empirical data and evidence in the form of user data and feedback, that can be used to make informed decisions rather than decisions based on opinions and previous experience. Additionally, it can also be used to assure the quality of software deployed to customers. Over the last decade, continuous experimentation has been studied from different perspectives; from the evolution of traditional development to R&D as an Experiment System in the Stairway to Heaven Model [13], building blocks and activities for continuous experimentation [5,8] to the different experimentation practices [18].

Schermann et al. [18] introduces two types of experiments; business-driven experiments and regression-driven experiments. Business-driven experiments are conducted to evaluate what effects features have from a business perspective, mainly with the use of A/B testing. A/B testing is largely used to solve a common issue in software organizations where decision-making is being based on opinions and previous experiences among employees [2]. This is possible since they allow evaluating hypotheses with collected empirical data through a controlled experiment. Regression-driven experiments are used to evaluate the impact that a new deployment has in regards to non-functional requirements in the production environment. The regression-driven experiments can be performed with the aid of canary releases, gradual rollouts and dark launches. This type of experimentation addresses quality issues software organizations might experience in production, by minimizing the exposure of the issues to the users.

Control of Roadmap (COR)

In agile development, the product owner serves an important role and is in charge of managing the requirements, providing a prioritized backlog, communicating with the development team(s) and having partial or full authority over other decisions relating to the product [14]. In the B2B-context, the product owner, who has the authority to plan or prioritize the product's backlog and roadmap, can be either part of the company or the client's company.

In this paper, the authority to plan and prioritize a product's backlog and/or roadmap is referred to as the *control of roadmap*. To the best knowledge of the authors, this is a subject that has not been discussed to any significant extent in other research. We assume that control of roadmap refers to how much control the company, or a team in the company, has over the planning and prioritization of the product's roadmap and backlog. Control of roadmap can refer to the company or to specific product or development teams. A practical example of when control of roadmap becomes relevant is if the product ownership is held by one party and the product development is done by a second party, where the two parties are cooperating with each other in producing the final product.

Distance to Users (DTU)

One recurring challenge in continuous experimentation in the B2B-domain is accessing the end-users of the product for data-collection purposes [10,15,20]. Rissanen and Münch [15] considers the B2B domain and specific challenges and benefits of continuous experimentation for this domain, as well as how continuous experimentation can be introduced. However, the authors focus is on continuous experimentation for the B2B domain in general, and not specifically how accessing data of the users affects the continuous experimentation.

We refer to this challenge of accessing and collecting user data and user feedback as *distance to users*. Since continuous experimentation requires data collected from users it could become more problematic to use continuous experimentation if the organization has a large distance to users.

3   Research Method

This research was conducted in collaboration with a small-scale software consultancy company, with around 20 employees based in Sweden, that works with multiple clients and have a B2B-relationship to these clients. The case study company produces software solutions, in the form of web services to the different clients, who in turn are in charge of the business side of the software products. Although the company have some experience with continuous experimentation its use was not widespread and systematic. An initial hypothesis that motivates this work is that the *low* control of roadmap and *large* distance to users could impact how companies conduct experiments. Given this context, the goal of this research is to explore the impact and relation between control of roadmap and distance to users to the usage of continuous experimentation. For that we formulated the following research questions:

RQ1 "How does control of roadmap and distance to users affect the use of continuous experimentation?"
RQ2 "What are the perceived benefits and challenges of using more continuous experimentation in a company with low control of roadmap and a large distance to users?"

To answer the research questions we conducted an exploratory case study within the case company since it allows the research gap to be further understood by studying a company from the industry in their real environment. By including a company with low control of roadmap and large distance to users it is possible to explore and understand how the low control of roadmap and large distance to their users affects their use of continuous experimentation. Additionally, we investigated the perceived benefits and challenges of using more continuous experimentation for such a company. We conducted validation of the results with an additional four software companies. These companies varied in terms of size, level of control of roadmap and distance to users.

This research was conducted in six phases. The first phase consisted of learning about the case study company and their inner processes, through a first round of interviews. The second phase consisted of assessing the case study company in how well they use continuous experimentation, and several models were considered from external research, such as the Stairway to Heaven model [13], the Experimentation Growth Model [4] and the RIGHT model [5]. In the third phase, we studied the control of roadmap and distance to users in more detail. In the fourth phase, we studied the perceived benefits and challenges of using more continuous experimentation. This was done by conducting a survey in the company, as well as a second round of interviews. In the fifth phase, we conducted the validation by interviewing the four additional software companies. Finally, the last phase consisted of reporting the research, i.e. producing the written results of this paper.

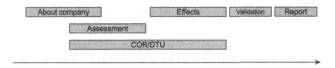

Fig. 1. Different phases of this research

Figure 1 shows the approximate order and duration of the phases for this research. First, we see how the learning about the company phase was executed, and in parallel the phase about the assessment of how well continuous experimentation is used as well as the phase about the control of roadmap and distance to users were started. After the assessment phase the perceived benefits and challenges phase (the effects phase) was started, which was followed by the validation phase and finally the report writing phase.

3.1   Data Collection and Analysis

In the case company, we collected data from internal company documentation, two rounds of interviews and an online survey. For validation purposes we conducted an additional four interviews with external companies that have different control of roadmap and distance to users configurations.

The first round of interviews contained a total of five interviews with five different people in the case study company. The two first interviews were held with the same two people in both interviews, in the form of group interviews, and the additional three interviews were held with one person in each interview. The first round consisted of semi-structured interviews with both closed and open questions. This first round was aimed at understanding the company internal processes and how it used continuous experimentation techniques. In this first round, as a data-triangulation measure, we collected documentation from the company's experimentation system for one of their clients.

The survey conducted was an online survey sent out to the employees of the case study company. The survey consisted of both closed and open questions regarding the advantages, disadvantages and blocking issues that the participants identify that would enable the company to use more experimentation, as well as questions related to control of roadmap and distance to users. The survey had a total of 13 responses, which is a sufficiently high response rate for a company with around 20 employees, and it should be considered high enough to be representative of the entire population. The survey was analyzed with frequency counting.

The second round of interviews consisted of four individual interviews with four people who were selected on an availability basis, i.e. the people who felt that they had the time. The interviews were between 15–20 min long and contained open questions in a semi-structured fashion. The topics discussed were similar to the ones in the survey, and the interviews were conducted to get some elaborated responses on the same topics as the survey.

The interviews and documentations were analysed by first making interview transcripts from recordings. A version of thematic analysis was then used to perform qualitative analysis on these transcripts, which is defined by Braun and Clarke as "a method for identifying, analysing and reporting patterns (themes) within data." [3]. This was done by identifying and highlighting different themes in the interviews, for instance, similar discussion topics, by going through all of the transcripts. Learnings from different interviews on the same themes as well as data collected elsewhere were joined in a combined document, and for each theme, conclusions were drawn based on all of the information on the same theme. Interviewees were sent the transcript and analysis from their interview in order to allow them the possibility to make any corrections.

Finally, the validation was performed by conducting four additional interviews with four other companies than the case study company, i.e. one interview per company. The interviews were about 30 min each, and they contained open questions in a semi-structured fashion. The discussion points were an introduction to their company, how experimentation is used in the company, how they would classify their company or their team in the company when it comes to control of roadmap and distance to users, and if they believe that control of roadmap, distance to users and continuous experimentation are related to each other. These interviews were valuable because they gave the opportunity to learn what other companies think about the topics that are discussed in this research. The validation interviews were analyzed less formally than the initial interviews, and conclusions were drawn directly from the notes and/or the recordings of the interviews. The analysis was made less formally since the discussion topics were few and since the answers clearly mapped to a specific topic. Therefore it still exists a clear trail of evidence. The interview participants were also given the possibility to give feedback on the analysis made, which increased the trust in that the analysis was done correctly.

In this research, some of the interviews were held in Swedish and some in English, and any quotes from the interviews that were originally in Swedish and that are used in this paper were carefully translated to English by the first thesis author. Additional information regarding, for instance, the interviews or survey conducted can be found in the original thesis report that is the foundation of this work [19].

3.2 Validity Considerations

Several measures to prevent threats to validity were made for this research. According to Runeson and Höst [17] there are four key aspects of validity that should be addressed; construct validity, internal validity, external validity and reliability. One measure to achieve construct validity was that the interview and survey participants were provided brief definitions of concept they should know about before participating. Another measure was to try to understand how participants used certain terms, in order to try to find cases where different definitions were used. For internal validity data-triangulation has been used, for instance by looking at the experimentation system data. Given the amount of interviews held related to the size of the company, there is a reason to believe that most or all of the information that was sought after was discovered in the data collection stages. Additionally, external research and feedback from the participants during the research has been used for internal validity purposes. Given that this work is an exploratory case study, external validity and generalizable results were not a main priority. However, the four companies used for validation provided further insights compared to only having worked with the single case study company. Finally, to achieve reliability guidelines on how to conduct a case study provided by Runeson and Höst [17] has been used for a sound research methodology. This was done for instance by keeping detailed case study protocols, working with triangulation and chains of evidence between data collected and conclusions drawn.

The first author of this paper is employed at the case study company which comes with threats to the validity of this research. It was recognized by the author early on that specific measures had to be taken in order to not bias the work. One such measure was to make sure that no data was added to the research based on the author's own experience with the company, and to make sure that conclusions were drawn from an objective point of view. Furthermore, it also helped to follow the case study guidelines by Runeson and Höst [17], as well as cooperating with the second and third author, in order to get a reliable result. Finally, another measure that has been taken is to make sure to objectively observe the company and not try to present information about the company subjectively, for instance, when doing the assessment of how well the company uses experimentation.

4   Results

4.1   Classification

To evaluate the impact of continuous experimentation in the context of this research, we first needed to be able to classify how a company performs in terms of the dimensions control of roadmap and distance to users. To avoid complexity and to achieve a deterministic classification we developed a scale of three stages 0, 1 and 2, to which a company could be assigned. The stages allow for transitioning between them and the implied direction is from stage 0 to stage 2. Below we describe the classification system.

In the classification system, the word "team" is used, which is referring to either the company as a whole or a specific product or feature team inside the company, depending on how the organization structure looks like. The person using the classification system has to set their own context where they decide whether the team should refer to the whole company, or to a single product or feature team. Furthermore, for both the classification models the transitions between stage 0, 1 and 2 are not necessarily equally large. So it can be possible that transitioning between stages 0–1 is not equally difficult as transitioning between stages 1–2.

Control of Roadmap. The classification system for control of roadmap is shown here.

- **Stage 0 or No Control**: The roadmap cannot be controlled by the team. There is no possibility for the team to add desired product changes to the roadmap.

- **Stage 1 or Low Control**: Desired product changes can be added to the roadmap, but there are difficulties. The team does not have full authority to decide on specific changes themselves.
- **Stage 2 or High Control**: Desired product changes can easily be added to the roadmap by the team. The team is allowed to make changes that they evaluate as beneficial for the product. However, decisions that can have a high impact in the product or the company business might still require approval of external stakeholders.

The classification system refers to "product changes" or just "changes", which refers to both short-term product changes such as changes put on the backlog, and long-term product changes such as changes put on the product roadmap.

Distance to Users. The classification system for distance to users is shown here.

- **Stage 0 or Very Large Distance**: Users can not be accessed by the team and there is no possibility of either qualitative or quantitative data-collection.
- **Stage 1 or Large Distance**: Users can be accessed by the team but there are difficulties with accessing them, especially for new types of data.
- **Stage 2 or Short Distance**: Users can be accessed with ease by the team. The decision to collect new data can be done with close to no delay. Decisions on changes in data-collection with a very high impact might still be dependent on external parties.

The classification defines in Stage 1 that for new qualitative and quantitative data it might be difficult to access the users. This means that a company that at this moment already has easy access to specific qualitative and quantitative user data might still have a large distance to users if they have a lot of difficulties in collecting new data. These difficulties would not be technical ones since everyone needs to invest resources into collecting new user data, but rather organizational difficulties.

4.2   Control of Roadmap and Distance to Users for Companies

Based on the empirical data that was collected for this research it was shown that the companies differ in how much control of roadmap and how large distance to users they have. Table 1 shows how the case study company and the four validation companies varies in control of roadmap and distance to users. The fourth validation company has the same control of roadmap and distance to users as the case study company. The other three validation companies differ from the case study company in control of roadmap and/or distance to users.

Table 1. Control of roadmap and distance to users of the five companies

Company	Control of roadmap	Distance to users
Case study company	Low	Large
Validation company 1	High	Short
Validation company 2	Low	Short
Validation company 3	Low	Varied between short - large
Validation company 4	Low	Large

4.3   Relationship Between Control of Roadmap, Distance to Users and Continuous Experimentation

During this work the relationship between control of roadmap, distance to users and continuous experimentation has been studied.

The survey result shows that everyone believes that control of roadmap affects the use of continuous experimentation. The respondents believe that the control of roadmap affects the use of experimentation to different degrees, but no-one believes that there is not a relationship. When it comes to distance to users the same result is shown, and everyone believes that distance to users affects the use of continuous experimentation. Some believe it is more and some believe that it is less, but no-one thinks there is no relationship between the two concepts.

In the second round of interviews, the control of roadmap is also considered to be related to how continuous experimentation is used. Someone points out that in the case study company the low control of roadmap is probably not the biggest thing preventing evolving the experimentation in the company, but that it instead is a lack of knowledge and will to do it. However, other interviewees claim that if they had more control over their own roadmap(s) they would have probably used more experimentation. An interviewee says that since the clients are paying them to do a specific thing they are limited in controlling the roadmap. The interviewee describes the low control of roadmap as a blocking issue for using more experimentation. Finally, one interviewee believes that the control of roadmap is not fixed and that it could perhaps be changed if they wanted to.

When it comes to the distance to users the second round of interviews show that the interviewees from the case study company agree that there is a relationship between distance to users and the use of continuous experimentation. However, not everyone believes that it applies to all types of experimentation or for the company's current circumstances. One interviewee argues that large distance to users is probably not affecting the use of continuous experimentation in the company, because if they wanted to experiment more they could change the distance to users. Another interviewee says that they have good access to a lot of system data, so if they wanted to do experimentation related to for instance infrastructure, it would not be a problem. However, for experimentation like A/B tests the interviewee believes that the large distance to users would be an issue. Another interviewee highlights that a short distance to users makes the experimentation a lot easier to conduct and that user feedback is a precondition for experimentation that should be acquired before the experimentation begins. One interviewee thinks that with a large distance to users experimentation would be possible, but getting results of the experiments would require more time and it would be more difficult to do the actual implementation of the experiments. In one of the interviews, the interviewee says that he/she believes that a large distance to users is a blocking issue to using more experimentation. Finally, more than one interviewee talks about how it perhaps would be possible to reduce the distance to users if they wanted to.

From the validation interviewees with the four different companies, all of the interviewees believe that there is a relationship, or that there probably is a relationship, between control of roadmap and how continuous experimentation is used in their companies or in a company. One interviewee believes that a low control of roadmap would mean that the development team probably views the product differently and not feel the same extent of ownership. This would have probably meant less experimentation. Another interviewee answers the question "Do you believe that control of roadmap is related to how experimentation is used in your company?" with how being a more autonomous team in a company improves the experimentation, and reasons why this is not trivial to achieve.

"Absolutely. It is. [...] The more autonomous you can be, the more control you can have in the team that develops a part of the product, the easier and the better it will become with the experiment. [...] The team defines what the next experiment is, and has a quicker cycle and quicker feedback-loops. That is outermost desirable, but not trivial to achieve. Because of all those reasons that I have mentioned, with organization, culture, process and technology." - Validation interviewee.

Another validation interviewee mentions that he/she believes that having low control of roadmap will make the ambitions of using more experimentation significantly less. If the experimentation was done but the results not used for the roadmap it would make it less desirable to do experimentation.

The validation interviewees are all certain or very certain that there is a relationship between distance to users and the use of continuous experimentation in their companies or in a company. If there would not be any data it would be difficult to experiment. One interviewee points out that with a large distance to users he/she believes that experimentation would be more difficult since it limits what experiments can be run, what conclusions can be made and how well the experiments can be validated. One interviewee reflects on the need to ask why the distance to users in a company with a large distance to users actually is large, and that it is probably often possible to access the users better than initially thought. The interviewee mentions that the distance to users is probably not a fixed thing and that you probably can change it if you want to. He/she describes it as a barrier that you can remove. One interviewee reflects on that they have experienced personally how a large distance to users affects experimentation and gives the example that an experiment that takes three days to execute could require two months for approval of the data collection.

4.4   Perceived Benefits and Challenges

There are several perceived benefits identified by the case study company with using more continuous experimentation. In the second round of interviewees the perceived benefit of having more data to back the arguments the case study company makes towards the clients is mentioned, i.e. more data-driven arguments. The interviewee explains that a benefit of using more experimentation is that they don't have to convince the client(s) to trust them and that they instead can provide evidence for the claims they make. This is also mentioned by another interviewee, who believes a benefit is that less emotional arguments will be used, arguments that instead will be substituted by facts. This would, according to the interviewee, avoid pointless discussions where people have strong personal opinions on specific features. Figure 2 shows the survey responses for the perceived benefits. Almost everyone in the survey identifies the benefit of fewer decisions based on opinions, and many in the survey believe a benefit is the feedback on the decisions made is received faster. One interviewee mentions the benefit of building the right things, or at least to have the feeling of building the right things. Furthermore, an interviewee mentions the perceived benefit of the client making more money, and several respondents of the survey believe that a perceived benefit is that the clients become happier.

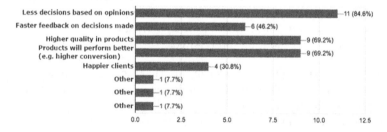

Fig. 2. Perceived benefits of using more continuous experimentation identified in the survey

> *"I think that because there is a lot [specific type of web service] that [case study company name] is doing, it is... Everything that can make the customer earn more money by analyzing how customers [means end users] behave... is a very big advantage."* - Case study company employee.

One perceived benefit that many people in the survey identify is the higher quality in the products, and this is also mentioned by two interviewees as a perceived benefit. One interviewee mentions the ability to identify risks that would perhaps otherwise not have been identified, as well as the benefit of getting new insights from using experimentation. An "other" answer in the survey was that the experimentation could provide a foundation for future decisions that are going to be made. Another "other" answer in the survey revealed that someone perceives the benefit for a better harmony inside the own company since people will not use "vetos". Finally, two interviewees identify the benefit of an improved product, which is also a perceived benefit by many in the survey. However, one interviewee mentions that because the case study company does not own its own products, it is probably not the one benefiting from A/B testing and learning more about how well the products perform, but the employees of the company are happy to do A/B testing for the clients if they desire it.

Several perceived challenges, i.e. disadvantages and blocking issues, with using more continuous experimentation are also identified by the case study company in the second round of interviews.

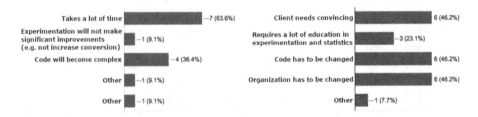

Fig. 3. Perceived disadvantages (left) and blocking issues (right) of using more continuous experimentation identified in the survey. Note: Not all respondents responded to all questions, which is why percentages might differ.

One interviewee mentions the perceived challenge of more complex code, DevOps situation, rollout situation and situation for a new developer. Figure 3 shows the survey response for perceived challenges. To get a more complex code is also something that several people in the survey identify. Furthermore, two interviewees talk about how they have to convince the clients that investments in experimentation are worth it.

"Sometimes the client might not understand the importance of doing these experiments, because they might not be as technical as we are, and then we might need to take a conflict, or what you can call it, with the client to argue for that 'Yes but this is actually worth 120 hours, that you spend on this, you might not immediately now see why, but in the long-term it pays off'." - Case study company employee.

Another perceived disadvantage identified in the interviews is that using more experimentation might require a lot of resources, for instance time, which is also identified in the survey by a large number of respondents. In the survey, an "other" answer is that a perceived disadvantage would be that it would require more of a process in the company. Furthermore, one person in the survey believes that using more experimentation will not make any significant improvements, e.g. not increase the conversion rate. Some general reflections are a survey respondent that says by the "other" answer that using more experimentation takes more time, but that it is almost always worth it. An interviewee also makes a reflection on that the disadvantages that the interviewee perceives are only relevant in the short-term, and that they would not be relevant in a more long-term perspective. Furthermore, that the need for education is a blocking issue, i.e. that there is a knowledge barrier, is also recognized by some of the survey respondents. One interviewee mentions the blocking issue of having to convince the client, for instance, that it is worth it for the client to fund the experimentation, which is similar to a previously described disadvantage. The need to convince clients is also recognized as a blocking issue by several in the survey. Furthermore, one interviewee reflects on that it is not only the client that has to change, and that the case study company also has to change how they are working. That the own organization has to change is also something that several in the survey identify. Furthermore, one interviewee recognizes that limited resources, especially time, are blocking issues to using more experimentation, and an "other" answer to the survey is that experimentation needs to be prioritized when it comes to time can be seen as a blocking issue as well. Finally, several survey respondents also identify the blocking issue of that the code has to change in order to use more experimentation. Table 2 shows a summary of the perceived benefits and challenges of using more continuous experimentation that were identified in this research.

Table 2. Summary of perceived benefits and challenges

Perceived benefit	Perceived challenges
Client trust and evidence for claims	Increased code, devops and rollout complexity for new developers
Building the right things	
Increased client profit	Experimentation training
Increased client satisfaction	Difficulty in convincing some clients to fund experimentation activities
Higher quality products	
Better identification of risks	Need for internal and external organizational changes
Better harmony inside the own company	
	Limited resources, especially time

5   Discussion

Classification Models

During the first phases of this research, we identified the importance of assessing a company on how much control of roadmap and how large or small distance to users they have. However, since no previous research discusses how to evaluate those aspects on a company we created two classification systems, one for control of roadmap and one for distance to users. These systems were useful to be able to correctly classify the companies studied, and to make sure that different people who classify the same company can reach the same conclusion. A problem with the models could be that it is a bit difficult to determine what constitutes as "difficulties", however, it should probably be fairly obvious to most contexts if it is very easy, hard or not at all possible to control the roadmap or access users.

About the Companies

One of the initial theories early in this research was that the case study company could be considered to have a low control of roadmap and a large distance to users. The idea that the company has low control of roadmap and a large distance to users was confirmed by the data collected for this research, which is why the phrasing of the second research question, by specifying low control of roadmap and a large distance to users, still maintains a relevance.

From the interviews with the four validation companies, it was shown that there is a difference between the companies when it comes to control of roadmap and distance to users, and only one of the four companies shares the same classification results as the case study company, i.e. low control of roadmap and a large distance to users. The diversity in control of roadmap and distance to users was a benefit for this research since it allowed other perspectives from companies who were not necessarily all similar to the case study company.

Relationship Between Control of Roadmap, Distance to Users and Continuous Experimentation

It is clear from the interviews and the survey in the case study company that there is a relationship both between control of roadmap and continuous experimentation, as well as the distance to users and continuous experimentation. This was also confirmed by the four validation interviews, who believe the same thing. It is possible to answer research question one (**RQ1**) with that there is indeed a relationship between these concepts, where both control of roadmap and distance to users affects how continuous experimentation is used.

Perceived Benefits and Challenges

Since the case study company was identified to have low control of roadmap and a large distance to users the perceived benefits and challenges that were identified by the case study company, which are shown in the results section, provide an answer to the second research question (**RQ2**). Given that there was only a single case study company considered for this research question, the external validity of the answer might be low. However, given the exploratory nature of this research, the identified perceived benefits and challenges provide an initial answer for this question. It is specifically interesting to consider the perceived benefits and challenges related to this type of company which works with clients, such as the perceived benefit of happier clients and the perceived challenge of having to convince the clients in order to be able to do more experimentation. This perceived benefit and this perceived challenge are very relevant since it would perhaps not be the case if control of roadmap was high and distance to users was short.

Control of Roadmap and Distance to Users as Barriers
There are two additional interesting learnings from this research. First of all it appears by the collected data from interviews with the case study company and the validation interviews that the control of roadmap and distance to users might not be fixed. Several people believe that the control of roadmap and distance to users can be changed if that was desirable. Secondly, the control of roadmap and distance to users are according to some interviewees considered barriers to evolving the experimentation. This means that if a company wanted to evolve their use of experimentation, the control of roadmap and the distance to users could block this evolution. If the control of roadmap and distance could be changed, these barriers could then be overcome for a company who's experimentation suffer as a consequence of low control of roadmap and a large distance to users.

6   Conclusion

The purpose of this research was to explore the impact of and relation between control of roadmap and distance to users and the usage of continuous experimentation. This was done by conducting an exploratory case study with a single company with low control of roadmap and a large distance to users, as well as validation with four additional companies. The contribution of this work is three-fold. First, we devised a classification system to evaluate a company in the extent of the distance to users and the control of roadmap. Second, we investigated how control of roadmap and distance to user impacts continuous experimentation. Finally, we presented several perceived challenges and benefits of continuous experimentation for the case study company.

Future work on this topic should investigate to what extent control of roadmap and distance to users are fixed concepts inside a company and how they relate to internal organization and domain. Additionally, practitioners would value guidelines on how companies can engage in an organizational and business transformation to increase control of roadmap in respect to introduction of experiments and user data collection for experiment evaluation. Finally, it would also be useful to conduct a multi-case study to understand how control of roadmap and distance to users differs between companies in the industry and how it affects their use of continuous experimentation.

Acknowledgments. This work was partially supported by the Wallenberg Artificial Intelligence, Autonomous Systems and Software Program (WASP) funded by the Knut and Alice Wallenberg Foundation.

References

1. Auer, F., Felderer, M.: Current state of research on continuous experimentation: a systematic mapping study. In: Proceedings - 44th Euromicro Conference on Software Engineering and Advanced Applications, SEAA, August 2018, pp. 335–344 (2018)
2. Bosch, J.: Building products as innovation experiment systems. In: Cusumano, M.A., Iyer, B., Venkatraman, N. (eds.) ICSOB 2012. LNBIP, vol. 114, pp. 27–39. Springer, Heidelberg (2012). https://doi.org/10.1007/978-3-642-30746-1_3
3. Braun, V., Clarke, V.: Using thematic analysis in psychology. J. Chem. Inf. Model. **53**(9), 1689–1699 (2013)
4. Fabijan, A., Dmitriev, P., McFarland, C., Vermeer, L., Holmström Olsson, H., Bosch, J.: Experimentation growth: evolving trustworthy A/B testing capabilities in online software companies. J. Softw.: Evol. Process. **30**(12), e2113 (2018)
5. Fagerholm, F., Sanchez Guinea, A., Mäenpää, H., Münch, J.: The RIGHT model for continuous experimentation. J. Syst. Softw. **123**, 292–305 (2017)
6. Fitzgerald, B., Stol, K.J.: Continuous software engineering: a roadmap and agenda. J. Syst. Softw. **123**, 176–189 (2017)
7. Issa Mattos, D., Bosch, J., Olsson, H.H.: Your system gets better every day you use it: towards automated continuous experimentation. In: Proceedings - 43rd Euromicro Conference on Software Engineering and Advanced Applications, SEAA 2017, pp. 256–265 (2017)
8. Issa Mattos, D., Dmitriev, P., Fabijan, A., Bosch, J., Holmström Olsson, H.: An activity and metric model for online controlled experiments. In: Kuhrmann, M., et al. (eds.) PROFES 2018. LNCS, vol. 11271, pp. 182–198. Springer, Cham (2018). https://doi.org/10.1007/978-3-030-03673-7_14
9. Kohavi, R., Henne, R.M., Sommerfield, D.: Practical guide to controlled experiments on the web. In: Proceedings of the 13th ACM SIGKDD International Conference on Knowledge Discovery and Data Mining - KDD 2007, p. 959. ACM Press, New York (2007)
10. Lindgren, E., Münch, J.: Raising the odds of success: the current state of experimentation in product development. Inf. Softw. Technol. **77**, 80–91 (2016)
11. McKinley, D.: Design for continuous experimentation (2012). https://www.youtube.com/watch?v=qCKj_K5RNfY
12. Moran, M.: Do It Wrong Quickly: How the Web Changes the Old Marketing Rules. IBM Press, Indianapolis (2008)
13. Olsson, H.H., Alahyari, H., Bosch, J.: Climbing the "Stairway to heaven" - A mulitiple-case study exploring barriers in the transition from agile development towards continuous deployment of software. In: Proceedings - 38th EUROMICRO Conference on Software Engineering and Advanced Applications, SEAA 2012, pp. 392–399 (2012)
14. Paasivaara, M., Heikkilä, V.T., Lassenius, C.: Experiences in scaling the product owner role in large-scale globally distributed Scrum. In: Proceedings - 2012 IEEE 7th International Conference on Global Software Engineering, ICGSE 2012, pp. 174–178 (2012)
15. Rissanen, O., Munch, J.: Continuous experimentation in the B2B domain: a case study. In: Proceedings - 2nd International Workshop on Rapid Continuous Software Engineering, RCoSE 2015, pp. 12–18 (2015)
16. Ros, R., Runeson, P.: Continuous experimentation and A/B testing. In: Proceedings of the 4th International Workshop on Rapid Continuous Software Engineering - RCoSE 2018, pp. 35–41 (2018)

17. Runeson, P., Höst, M.: Guidelines for conducting and reporting case study research in software engineering. Empir. Softw. Eng. **14**(2), 131–164 (2009)
18. Schermann, G., Cito, J., Leitner, P., Zdun, U., Gall, H.C.: We're doing it live: a multi-method empirical study on continuous experimentation. Inf. Softw. Technol. **99**, 41–57 (2018)
19. Sveningson, R.: Continuous experimentation for software organizations with low control of roadmap and a large distance to users - a case study (2019). https://hdl.handle.net/20.500.12380/300184
20. Yaman, S.G., et al.: Introducing continuous experimentation in large software-intensive product and service organisations. J. Syst. Softw. **133**, 195–211 (2017)

Deep Unsupervised System Log Monitoring

Hubert Nourtel, Christophe Cerisara[✉], and Samuel Cruz-Lara

Université de Lorraine, CNRS, LORIA, 54000 Nancy, France
{hubert.nourtel,cerisara,samuel.cruz-lara}@loria.fr

Abstract. This work proposes a new unsupervised deep generative model for system logs. It is designed to be generic and may be used in various downstream anomaly detection tasks, such as system failure or intrusion detection. It is based on the (reasonable) assumption that most log lines follow rather fixed syntactic structures, which enables us to replace the costly traditional convolutional and recurrent architectures by a much faster component: a deep averaging network. Our model still exploits a standard recurrent model with attention to capture the dependencies between successive log lines. We experimentally validate the proposed generative model on a real dataset obtained from a state-of-the-art High Performance Computing cluster and show the effectiveness of the proposed approach in modeling the "normal" behaviour of the system.

Keywords: Anomaly detection · System log · HPC · Deep learning

1 Introduction

Massive quantity of system logs are produced every second, and analyzing them manually is out of question. However, they contain valuable information related to the status of the system, risks of failures, potential intrusions and attacks, or other types of anomalies that should be detected in advance. A generic approach to predict most of these events is to train a generative model that is able to predict future log lines. When trained on a sufficiently large corpus, the generative model shall capture the "normal" behaviour of the system, and deviations from these predicted logs may be tagged as anomalies. This approach presents several advantages, especially the facts that it does not require any (costly) manual annotation, that it is generic and can be used in various domains and tasks.

We focus in this work on proposing a new deep generative model dedicated to system logs. In a future work, this model will be used to predict system and application failures in advance, by identifying early anomalies that may lead to a process crash. Compared to the state-of-the-art [4], the design of our model is based on two observations: first, system log lines often have a much less variable syntactic structure across words than natural language text; second, massive

Supported by the ITEA 3 PAPUD 16037, the OLKi and CPER LCHN projects.

X. Franch et al. (Eds.): PROFES 2019, LNCS 11915, pp. 545–553, 2019.
https://doi.org/10.1007/978-3-030-35333-9_38

quantities of logs are continuously generated, which can only be treated with fast inference algorithms. Both observations lead us to propose a new deep architecture that replaces the traditional convolutional and recurrent processing within line by a deep averaging component, which is at the same time simpler, faster and powerful, as shown in the recent deep learning literature. Furthermore, we argue that the main drawback of this architecture, which makes the modeling of relative word positions more difficult, is not an issue with this type of data, thanks to the fact that system log lines have much less variability in the structures linking words. We thus reserve the more costly recurrent processing to capture cross-lines dependencies, and simplify the modeling of within-line word sequences.

2   Related Works

The literature about unsupervised deep learning methods mainly focuses on representation learning [24,29] and on deep clustering, with a few additional papers that depart from these mainstream paradigms [9,20,23]. Generative models dominate the field, because of their capability to capture the hidden structures within observations, which constitute the only known information in the purely unsupervised setting.

Deep Belief Networks (DBNs) [14] are one of the first successful deep representation learning models. DBNs are formed by a stack of Restricted Boltzmann machines (RBMs) [13], which learn features one level at a time. This greedy layerwise training is finally used to initialize a deep supervised or a deep generative model like Deep Boltzmann Machines (DBMs) [33]. Nowadays, thanks to recent advances in the field [2], much simpler networks are used to learn good representations of the data, such as the class of Autoencoders (AEs) [22,30,31,38]. Notable models of this class are Variational Autoencoders (VAEs) [21], which are bayesian networks with an autoencoder architecture. These generative models, which try to maximize a lower bound of the data likelihood, can perform efficient inference on large datasets. The hidden layer of these models capture the most salient features of the data [10].

Deep clustering is usually performed on the observations (input space) [25], but- may also be applied on the latent (intermediary) representation space [6, 7,16,18,26,41,42]. The options for the clustering loss are numerous: k-means loss [40], cluster assignment hardening [39], locality-preserving loss [16], cluster classification loss [15] or agglomerative clustering loss [41] to cite a few.

A special type of unsupervised methods, which is of particular interest in our work, concern the training of models on positive examples only, or on a dataset mainly composed of positive examples plus a minority of negative examples, without any label. These methods are often referred to as *anomaly detection* approaches, or *one-class* unsupervised classifiers. Indeed, the positive class is the normal class, i.e., the class of samples that occur when the system is running correctly, or when the observed entities behave normally. Every sample that deviates from this normal behaviour is considered as belonging to the negative class, i.e., an anomaly. By definition, there are many observed positive samples, and only a few negative ones, and we further do not know where these negative samples occur in the training corpus. The methods that handle such a context include the one-class SVM [34], which projects all positive samples into a high-dimensional space and computes an hyperplane that is as close as possible from these samples and separates them from the origin, which is assumed to contain all negative samples. This approach is extended in [36] by replacing the hyperplane with an hyper-sphere, and then in [32] by introducing deep neural architectures in these models. Later on, [5] transposes the original one-class SVM model completely into a deep neural architecture, and [28] projects a similar neural architectures as a supervised model by generating pseudo-labels for negative samples.

Other approaches based on deep neural networks include variational autoencoders [27]. [4] further exploits successfully a recurrent neural network on the difficult LANL dataset for anomaly detection in system logs. Deep architectures are also used on other logs datasets, such as [1,3,37]. Other recent non-deep approaches for anomaly detection in logs include [11,12,19,35]. A review of the field can be found in [8].

3 Proposed Model

We propose a deep generative model, which generates the next log line based on the previously observed log lines. Such a generative model may be used in several applications, such as systems anomaly detection and intrusion detection, but in this work, we focus on the evaluation of the generative model itself, independently of the application.

The proposed model adopts a hierarchical structure, with a lower level dedicated to the modeling of a single line of text, while the upper level captures dependencies across multiple lines. Conversely to most other works [4], we have decided to not use a recurrent neural network at the lower level, but to rather model word sequences through a Deep Averaging Network [17]. This choice is first motivated by complexity considerations: indeed, recurrent networks are among the slowest types of basic neural architectures, which is the main reason why they are nearly never used in unsupervised generative models that have to be trained on very large corpora, such as word embeddings, which either exploit a fast single layer network (Word-to-Vec), or a small convolutional network (Collobert&Weston embeddings), or yet fast transformer networks (BERT, GPT...). Given the amount of system log lines that are generated every second, we have thus decided to base our model on the Deep Averaging Network, which is another type of extremely fast neural architecture that has already proven to be also very powerful in many applications [17].

Figure 1 shows the first step of the model: this step takes as input a log line tokenized into words. Each word is encoded into an embedding, and is then smoothed through a temporal convolution filter, which outputs a sequence of temporal vectors with the same size as the words embeddings. Then, a

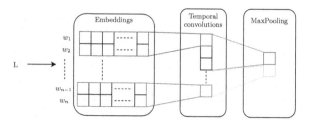

Fig. 1. Predictive model: first step

dimension-wise max-pooling operation is realized to reduce this sequence of vectors into a single vector: this is similar to a Deep Averaging Network, which, despite its name, can be performed either with an averaging or a max operator.

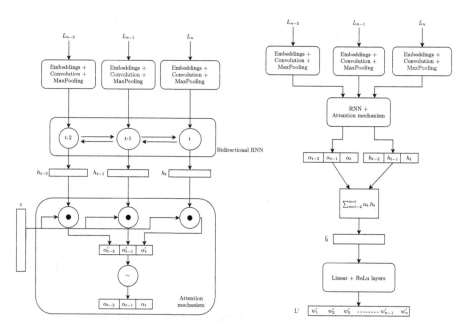

Fig. 2. Predictive model: second and third steps

Figure 2 shows (left) how the line embeddings produced at step 1 are passed to a bidirectional Long-Short Term Memory (LSTM) network with attention: the embeddings of successive lines are passed one after the other into the LSTM, which extracts the most relevant information from these embeddings and cumulates this information into its hidden vector h_t. The LSTM outputs one vector h_t per log line. Then, another parameter vector c is learnt, which role is to weight each h_t through an attention vector α:

$$\alpha_t = \frac{e^{c^T \cdot h_t}}{\sum_\tau e^{c^T \cdot h_\tau}}$$

The right column in Fig. 2 explicits how the hidden states are combined: $\tilde{h} = \sum_t \alpha_t h_t$. The summary embedding $\tilde{h}$ is finally passed to a standard feed-forward neuronal classifier that transforms this vector into a "sequence" of T predicted words: the output dimension of this multi-classification layer is thus $T \times V$ where V is the size of the vocabulary. T softmax operations are applied on this output to obtain word probabilities.

4 Experimental Validation

4.1 Data

We evaluate our model on the Bull-ATOS HPC logs files dataset, which contains anonymized system logs produced by the Deutsches Klimarechenzentrum Supercomputer, ranked #73 in 06/2019 in the TOP500 Supercomputer list. These system logs have been recorded during the execution of real production applications. Every log line contains the following fields: *Timestamp (in seconds)/Node id/User id/Severity/Message*. The training dataset is composed of 318,426 files with 214,379,053 lines; a separate test dataset of 12 files with 5,396 lines is used for validation. An example of sequence of logs is:

```
1527154392 10002 su info pam_unix(su:session): session opened for user b364103 by (uid=0)
1527154392 10002 su info pam_unix(su:session): session closed for user b364103
1527154393 10002 smartd info Device: /dev/sda [SAT], SMART Usage Attribute: 194
Temperature_Celsius changed from 56 to 55
1527154482 10002 pam_slurm info access granted for user root (uid=0)
1527154482 10002 sshd info Accepted publickey for root from 10.50.4.3 port 38260 ssh2
1527154482 10002 sshd info pam_unix(sshd:session): session opened for user root by (uid=0)
```

4.2 Experimental Setup

Every log line is tokenized into a sequence of words, by splitting the line with whitespaces. Then, the length of every words sequence is set to 15 words, after cutting or padding, to make parallel processing easier. All characters are transformed into lower case, and every word that contains one or more digits is replaced by a joker word. Finally, we remove successive lines containing exactly the same words in the same order. The vocabulary contains every word that occurs at least 10 times. Rare words are mapped to the special UNK word. The final vocabulary contains 2,989 words.

Hyper-parameters are set based on reasonable values given in the literature and on a few preliminary experiments: The ADAM optimizer is used with a learning rate of 0.0001 and a batch size of 128. Word embeddings have 100 dimensions. The loss is the cross-entropy between the predicted words and the gold words observed in the following line.

4.3   Results

We compare our generative model in terms of word accuracy, i.e., ratio of predicted words that are correct in all 15-length words sequences, with three baselines in Fig. 3.

Our proposed model outperforms every baseline by a large margin. Furthermore, using two lines of context significantly increases its performances as compared to observing only the previous log line, although using more than two lines does not seem to bring further improvements.

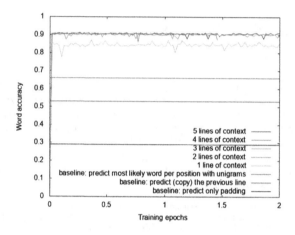

Fig. 3. Prediction accuracy on the Bull dataset over two epochs.

5   Conclusion

We have proposed a deep generative model for predicting system logs. The originality of our model lies in the combination of a fast but powerful component to merge individual word embeddings: the Deep Averaging Network, with a more standard recurrent architecture with attention to model the relation between successive lines. Such a generative model may be used to predict anomalies, system failures or detect intrusions when the proportion of such events is too rare to allow for supervised training. We focus in this work on evaluating the generative capabilities of our proposed model, and experimentally show that it is able to capture correlations both within and across lines to help predict the next log line. In a future work, we plan to exploit attention to build semantically-related chains of events and use the resulting model for anomaly detection.

References

1. An, J., Cho, S.: Variational autoencoder based anomaly detection using reconstruction probability. Spec. Lect. IE **2**, 1–18 (2015)
2. Bengio, Y.: Practical recommendations for gradient-based training of deep architectures. arXiv:1206.5533 (2012)
3. Bontemps, L., Cao, V.L., McDermott, J., Le-Khac, N.-A.: Collective anomaly detection based on long short-term memory recurrent neural networks. In: Dang, T.K., Wagner, R., Küng, J., Thoai, N., Takizawa, M., Neuhold, E. (eds.) FDSE 2016. LNCS, vol. 10018, pp. 141–152. Springer, Cham (2016). https://doi.org/10.1007/978-3-319-48057-2_9
4. Brown, A., Tuor, A., Hutchinson, B., Nichols, N.: Recurrent neural network attention mechanisms for interpretable system log anomaly detection. arXiv:1803.04967 (2018)
5. Chalapathy, R., Menon, A.K., Chawla, S.: Anomaly detection using one-class neural networks. arXiv:1802.06360 (2018)
6. Chang, J., Wang, L., Meng, G., Xiang, S., Pan, C.: Deep adaptive image clustering. In: Proceedings of CVPR, Honolulu, Hawaii, pp. 5879–5887 (2017)
7. Dilokthanakul, N., et al.: Deep unsupervised clustering with Gaussian mixture variational autoencoders. arXiv:1611.02648 (2016)
8. Goldstein, M., Uchida, S.: A comparative evaluation of unsupervised anomaly detection algorithms for multivariate data. PloS One **11**(4), e0152173 (2016)
9. Golts, A., Freedman, D., Elad, M.: Deep energy: Using energy functions for unsupervised training of DNNs. arXiv:1805.12355 (2018)
10. Goodfellow, I., Bengio, Y., Courville, A.: Deep Learning. MIT Press, Cambridge (2016). http://www.deeplearningbook.org
11. Gutflaish, E., Kontorovich, A., Sabato, S., Biller, O., Sofer, O.: Temporal anomaly detection: calibrating the surprise. arXiv:1705.10085 (2017)
12. Harada, Y., Yamagata, Y., Mizuno, O., Choi, E.H.: Log-based anomaly detection of CPS using a statistical method. In: 2017 8th International Workshop on Empirical Software Engineering in Practice (IWESEP), pp. 1–6. IEEE (2017)
13. Hinton, G.E.: A practical guide to training restricted Boltzmann machines. In: Montavon, G., Orr, G.B., Müller, K.-R. (eds.) Neural Networks: Tricks of the Trade. LNCS, vol. 7700, pp. 599–619. Springer, Heidelberg (2012). https://doi.org/10.1007/978-3-642-35289-8_32
14. Hinton, G.E., Osindero, S., Teh, Y.W.: A fast learning algorithm for deep belief nets. Neural Comput. **18**(7), 1527–1554 (2006)
15. Hsu, C.C., Lin, C.W.: CNN-based joint clustering and representation learning with feature drift compensation for large-scale image data. IEEE Trans. Multimedia **20**, 421–429 (2018)
16. Huang, P., Huang, Y., Wang, W., Wang, L.: Deep embedding network for clustering. In: 22nd International Conference on Pattern Recognition, ICPR 2014, 24–28 August 2014, Stockholm, Sweden, pp. 1532–1537 (2014)
17. Iyyer, M., Manjunatha, V., Boyd-Graber, J., Daumé III, H.: Deep unordered composition rivals syntactic methods for text classification. In: Proceedings of the 53rd Annual Meeting of the Association for Computational Linguistics and the 7th International Joint Conference on Natural Language Processing (Volume 1: Long Papers), vol. 1, pp. 1681–1691 (2015)
18. Jiang, Z., Zheng, Y., Tan, H., Tang, B., Zhou, H.: Variational deep embedding: an unsupervised and generative approach to clustering. In: Proceedings of IJCAI, Melbourne, Australia , pp. 1965–1972, August 2017

19. Juan, D.C., Shah, N., Tang, M., Qian, Z., Marculescu, D., Faloutsos, C.: M3a: Model, metamodel, and anomaly detection in web searches. arXiv:1606.05978 (2016)
20. Kilinc, O., Uysal, I.: Learning latent representations in neural networks for clustering through pseudo supervision and graph-based activity regularization. In: Proceedings of ICLR (2018)
21. Kingma, D.P., Welling, M.: Auto-encoding variational Bayes. arXiv:1312.6114 (2013)
22. Lecun, Y.: Modeles connexionnistes de l'apprentissage (connectionist learning models). Ph.D. thesis, Universite P. et M. Curie (Paris 6), Paris, France (1987)
23. Metz, L., Maheswaranathan, N., Cheung, B., Sohl-Dickstein, J.: Learning unsupervised learning rules. arXiv:1804.00222 (2018)
24. Mikolov, T., Sutskever, I., Chen, K., Corrado, G.S., Dean, J.: Distributed representations of words and phrases and their compositionality. In: Proceedings of NIPS, pp. 3111–3119 (2013)
25. Min, E., Guo, X., Liu, Q., Zhang, G., Cui, J., Long, J.: A survey of clustering with deep learning: from the perspective of network architecture. IEEE Access **6**, 39501–39514 (2018)
26. Mukherjee, S., Asnani, H., Lin, E., Kannan, S.: Clustergan: Latent space clustering in generative adversarial networks. arXiv:1809.03627, October 2018
27. Nguyen, Q.P., Lim, K.W., Divakaran, D.M., Low, K.H., Chan, M.C.: Gee: A gradient-based explainable variational autoencoder for network anomaly detection. arXiv:1903.06661 (2019)
28. Oza, P., Patel, V.M.: One-class convolutional neural network. IEEE Sig. Process. Lett. **26**(2), 277–281 (2018)
29. Radford, A., Metz, L., Chintala, S.: Unsupervised representation learning with deep convolutional generative adversarial networks. arXiv:1511.06434 (2015)
30. Ranzato, M.A., Poultney, C., Chopra, S., Cun, Y.L.: Efficient learning of sparse representations with an energy-based model. In: Schölkopf, B., Platt, J.C., Hoffman, T. (eds.) Advances in Neural Information Processing Systems 19, pp. 1137–1144. MIT Press (2007)
31. Rifai, S., Vincent, P., Muller, X., Glorot, X., Bengio, Y.: Contracting auto-encoders: explicit invariance during feature extraction. In: Proceedings of ICML (2011)
32. Ruff, L., et al.: Deep one-class classification. In: International Conference on Machine Learning, pp. 4390–4399 (2018)
33. Salakhutdinov, R., Hinton, G.: Deep Boltzmann machines. In: van Dyk, D., Welling, M. (eds.) Proceedings of the Twelth International Conference on Artificial Intelligence and Statistics, vol. 5, pp. 448–455. Clearwater Beach, Florida, April 2009
34. Schölkopf, B., Platt, J.C., Shawe-Taylor, J., Smola, A.J., Williamson, R.C.: Estimating the support of a high-dimensional distribution. Neural Comput. **13**(7), 1443–1471 (2001)
35. Sun, L., Versteeg, S., Boztas, S., Rao, A.: Detecting anomalous user behavior using an extended isolation forest algorithm: an enterprise case study. arXiv:1609.06676 (2016)
36. Tax, D.M., Duin, R.P.: Support vector data description. Mach. Learn. **54**(1), 45–66 (2004)
37. Tuor, A., Kaplan, S., Hutchinson, B., Nichols, N., Robinson, S.: Deep learning for unsupervised insider threat detection in structured cybersecurity data streams. In: Workshops at the Thirty-First AAAI Conference on Artificial Intelligence (2017)

38. Vincent, P., Larochelle, H., Bengio, Y., Manzagol, P.A.: Extracting and composing robust features with denoising autoencoders. In: Proceedings of ICML, pp. 1096–1103, January 2008
39. Xie, J., Girshick, R., Farhadi, A.: Unsupervised deep embedding for clustering analysis. In: Proceedings of ICML, New York, pp. 478–487 (2016)
40. Yang, B., Fu, X., Sidiropoulos, N.D., Hong, M.: Towards k-means-friendly spaces: simultaneous deep learning and clustering. In: Proceedings of ICML, Sydney, Australia, pp. 3861–3870, August 2017
41. Yang, J., Parikh, D., Batra, D.: Joint unsupervised learning of deep representations and image clusters. In: 2016 IEEE Conference on Computer Vision and Pattern Recognition, CVPR 2016, 27–30 June 2016, Las Vegas, NV, USA, pp. 5147–5156 (2016)
42. Yang, T., Arvanitidis, G., Fu, D., Li, X., Hauberg, S.: Geodesic clustering in deep generative models. arXiv:1809.04747, September 2018

Enablers and Inhibitors of Experimentation in Early-Stage Software Startups

Jorge Melegati[1](✉) ⓘ, Rafael Chanin[2] ⓘ, Xiaofeng Wang[1] ⓘ, Afonso Sales[2] ⓘ, and Rafael Prikladnicki[2] ⓘ

[1] Faculty of Computer Science, Free University of Bozen-Bolzano, Bolzano, Italy
{jmelegatigoncalves,xiaofeng.wang}@unibz.it
[2] School of Technology, PUCRS, Porto Alegre, Brazil
{rafael.chanin,afonso.sales,rafaelp}@pucrs.br

Abstract. Software startups are temporary organizations that develop innovative software-intensive products or services. Despite of numerous successful stories, most startups fail. Several methodologies were proposed both in the scientific and commercial literature to improve their success rate, and a common element among them is the idea of experimentation. This concept was brought to software development as an approach focused on taking critical product assumptions as hypotheses and developing experiments to support or refute them. Although well-known methodologies are based on this idea, the literature shows that software startups still do not follow this approach. The goal of this paper is to identify the enablers and inhibitors of experimentation in early-stage software startups. To achieve the goal, we performed a multiple-case study of four software startups. The results comprise a set of enablers and inhibitors divided into the categories of individual, organizational context, and environment.

Keywords: Software startups · Experimentation · Experiment-driven software development

1 Introduction

Software startups are companies that develop innovative, software-intensive products or services [38]. The software startup context is characterized by a general lack of resources, high reactiveness and flexibility, intense time-pressure, uncertain conditions, and fast growth [29]. This context imposes several challenges to software development activities [29,37]. Although several well-known tech companies were once startups, such as Google, Facebook, and Spotify, more than 90% of startups fail [20]. There are several possible reasons for this result [22]: market conditions, lack of commitment, financial issues or a bad product idea, but "inadequacies in used engineering practices could lead to under or over-engineering the product, wasted resources, and missed market opportunities" [22].

X. Franch et al. (Eds.): PROFES 2019, LNCS 11915, pp. 554–569, 2019.
https://doi.org/10.1007/978-3-030-35333-9_39

Several methodologies were proposed to improve startup success rate, both in the scientific (e.g. [6,40]) and in the commercial (e.g. [4,31]) literature. A common element in these methodologies is the idea of experimentation. Lean Startup [31], the most well-known in the industry [5], is an example of such methodology. Although Lean Startup is based mostly on anecdotal evidence rather than on empirical research [1], this methodology brings elements from established constructs, specially, "heavy use of effectuation logic" and "a clear and explicit emphasis on experimentation" [15]. Therefore, experimentation represents a valuable practice for startups to reach better results.

Even with all these well-known methodologies focusing on experimentation, software startups do not use them as expected. In an initial study to understand how software startups approach experimentation, their challenges, and advantages, Gutbrod et al. [18] concluded that these organizations focus on developing solutions without validating the initial assumptions. Similar results were found by authors investigating the reason for startups failure (e.g. [17]) and the use of Lean Startup practices by software startups (e.g. [27]).

Failing to use experiments is specially detrimental for early-stage startups. At this phase, software startups are looking for a "feasible solution" to a "relevant problem" [22] which is closely related to the idea of experimentation in entrepreneurship. Here, experimentation is related to the idea that an entrepreneurial venture operating under uncertainty should "experiment with a range of business model" represented by several trial and errors along various dimensions [2]. This idea is also present in innovation (e.g. [11]) and entrepreneurship (e.g. [21]) literature. Therefore, better understanding the enablers and inhibitors of experimentation in these early stages could help software startups to thrive. Then, this study will be guided by the following research question:

RQ : What are the enablers and inhibitors of experimentation in early-stage software startups?

To achieve this goal, we performed a multiple-case study in four software startups in two countries. We identified a list of enablers and inhibitors divided into three categories: individual, organizational context, and environment. The remaining of this paper is organized as follows: Sect. 2 presents the background and related work. Section 3 describes the research method used. Section 4 displays the study results and they are discussed in Sect. 5. Finally, Sect. 6 concludes the paper.

2   Background and Related Work

The scientific interest in how software startups perform their engineering tasks is growing. In a systematic mapping study on the topic, Berg et al. [3] identified 74 primary papers in the period of 1994 to 2013 and from those studies 27 were published between 2013–2017. Klotins et al. [22] performed a comprehensive study analyzing 84 startup cases and identified 16 goals, 9 challenges, and 16 common engineering practices among these organizations. To analyze their cases, they used a life-cycle model composed of four stages: inception, stabilization, growth, and maturity. The first stage, inception, happens between the idea and the product first release to the customers. In the stabilization, the startup prepares its product to scale in regard to both technical and operational perspectives. During the growth stage, the startup goal is to gain the desired market share focusing on marketing and sales. Finally, in the maturity stage, the organization transitions into an established company. In summary, in the early stages, that is, inception and stabilization, teams focus on "finding a relevant problem" and "a feasible solution". In the later stages the focus is on marketing and on improving the company's efficiency [22]. It is also important to highlight that a startup may change some critical aspect of the product and, consequently, return to a previous stage.

In the early-stages, software startups should learn about its customers and check if their ideas are valid by using experiment-driven software development processes. This approach is characterized by continuously identifying critical product assumptions, transforming them into hypotheses, prioritizing and testing them with experiments following the scientific method in order to support or refute the hypotheses [23]. It comprises different techniques, such as prototypes, canary flying, gradual rollout, and controlled experiment [12] or even problem and solution interviews [23]. In other words, this process is not restricted by the scientific meaning of experiment, but refers to a broader sense of data-driven decision making instead of opinion-based [23].

In a literature review on customer feedback and data collection techniques, Fabijan et al. [13] grouped practices according to three product development stages: pre-development, development, and post-development. For instance, in pre-development, when "companies aim at identifying market interest in a new product," the authors mention, as used techniques, interviews and observations, in development, prototype testing, and in post-development, A/B tests. Comparing these stages with a startup life-cycle, in early-stages, startups should use techniques such as interviews, observations, surveys, and prototypes as described in Table 1.

Table 1. Software startup early stages, related goals, development stages and experiments that could be used to reach these goals

Startup stage	Goal	Development stage	Experiments
Inception	Release the product first version to the first consumer. Balance customer needs, resources, and time	Pre-development	Problem interviews Solution interviews Observations Questionnaires
Stabilization	Prepare to scale. Product should be easy to maintain and scale, including operations and customer support	Development	Prototype testing Operational data

Several studies investigated inhibitors to experimentation in general software development context. In a mapping study on continuous experimentation, Ros and Runeson [33] found four types of challenges for companies adopting these practices: technical, statistical, management/organizational, and business. In the same vein, based on qualitative survey with 10 companies, Lindgreen and Münch [23] emphasized that: "technology has a supporting role in an experiment system, and that the more significant issues lie elsewhere", and the major obstacles are related to organizational culture, product management and resourcing. Nevertheless, no study focused on early-stage software startups and their specific context.

Some studies focused on to which extent startups perform experimentation or use related techniques. In a large survey based on 1526 software startups, Pantiuchina et al. [27] observed that only 229 (15%) were following Lean Startup according to their criteria. In a grounded theory study on requirements engineering in startups, Melegati et al. [24] observed: "startups very often develop something and then realize that users did not want it. Even though validating assumptions as soon as possible is present in well-known startup development methodologies [...] Unawareness of such methodologies would explain that, but even interviewees aware of them still made these mistakes." Gutbrod and Münch [18] performed, to the best of our knowledge, the most focused study on experimentation in the context of software startups. Through a multiple-case study in four German companies, they concluded that startups spent a lot of time developing their solutions without testing their assumptions. The main reasons are the lack of awareness of the possibility of early testing, and the lack of knowledge and support on identifying, prioritizing and testing hypotheses. Nonetheless, as pointed out by the authors and other papers in the literature [15, 26], Lean Startup is strongly based on the idea of experimentation and is well-known by practitioners. As challenges they identified the following aspects: getting enough subjects for experiments, fear of contacting customers, fear of making cold calls, technical challenges to setup an experimentation infrastructure, lack of skills for conducting customer interviews, lack of resources/staff for experimentation, lack of motivation to conduct experiments, and fear that people steal the startup idea. Nevertheless, a study focused on enablers and inhibitors in early-stage software startups is still missing in the literature.

3   Research Method

Based on what was previously exposed, it is clear that the context where software startups operate is really determinant to the adoption of experimentation. Therefore, a case study is reasonable choice to this study. As Yin [39] highlighted: "a case study is an empirical inquiry that investigates a contemporary phenomenon within its real-life context, specially when the boundaries between phenomenon and context are not clearly evident." Given the plethora of contexts for startups, we performed a multiple-case study.

An important aspect in a multiple-case study is the selection of cases [10]. This is more challenging given the lack of a unique and solid definition of what a software startup is [3]. The most common characteristics given in the literature are innovation and uncertainty [3]. Therefore, in selecting the cases, we decided to take a conservative approach. First of all, we only considered digital startups as a recent paper by Steininger [36] proposes: the value is created through a "completely digitalized product or service, digitally sold and delivered" and IT is diffused in all pillars: infrastructure management, customer interface and value proposition. Besides that, the innovation must be present. As Garcia and Calantone [16] discuss in their seminal work, innovation is seen as a discontinuity in at least one of two dimensions: technological and marketing.

We selected the cases based on convenience through our contacts network having these criteria in mind. Since there are several possible characteristics that could be used to differentiate startups, selecting cases presenting all possible scenarios would not be feasible. However, we selected the cases trying to diversify the characteristics of the studied software startups along the dimensions of startup maturity stage and type of market (B2B or B2C).

The major data source was interviews. Before starting data collection, we developed a case study protocol consisted of different interview guides depending on the interviewee role (non-technical founder, software development manager, and developer), and a set of information about the startup, the market it operates, and its environment. This protocol was used and updated by the researchers throughout data collection. The interviews were performed by at least one author mainly in the startup office to allow the interviewer to observe the company's processes. Interviews were recorded and relevant pieces were transcribed.

Data analysis consisted of thematic analysis. The process of coding followed an integrated approach having deductive and inductive elements [8]. In such a way, a general scheme is created from existent theories or other elements that the research brings to the study that "points to general domains in which codes can be developed inductively," that is, they emerge while reviewing data line-by-line. To create a general scheme, we inspected the Coleman and O'Connor's startup software development process formation framework [7] and came up with a classification of the constructs in three categories (individual, organizational context, and environment). Then, we inductively coded the interviews and researchers' memos, and combined the codes to form themes, increasing the level of abstraction [8].

3.1 Cases Background

We selected four cases from two countries in different continents, as summarized in Table 2. The following subsections describe the cases studied: the product or service, maturity stage, and the level in which experimentation is done and evolved during the team lifetime. In order to preserve the startups identity, we omit some details about the product and the business model.

Startup A designed a software library to be used in software development projects. Through automatic data collection, it would show in a dashboard software runtime problems (e.g. exceptions) and possible solutions from similar issues found on the Internet, along with a list of freelance developers that

Table 2. Case studies description and data collected.

Location	Product or service	Stage	Data collected
A Italy	Software library with intelligent recommendations	Inception	Interview with the founder + meetings with the founder
B Brazil	Mobile app for fitness workout routines	Inception	Group interview with the three founders
C Italy	Two-side web platform Sell of leads to a specific sector	Stabilization	Interview with a founder + interview with software developer
D Italy	Software as a Service targeted to e-commerces	Stabilization	Group interview with the two non-technical founders + interview with the CTO

could help to solve the problem. In some cases, the system would be able to automatically fix some problems. The startup founder is a software development consultant. While working on some projects, he observed that such tool could help him in working more effectively. Besides that, he believed that the technical level of software developers was decreasing. Therefore, it would make sense to develop such a tool. In the current stage, the startup has an initial prototype consisted of a dashboard with some dummy data, and a website that displays the idea. Although tools to collect software runtime data already exist, none of them fix issues automatically, therefore, the proposed innovation is technological. Nevertheless, the display of available freelancers based on the data collected would be a marketing innovation.

The startup is in its initial steps. There are five people working on the project, but none of them are fully dedicated to the startup. A few of them are working on software development, while the others are focused on the business plan and the marketing strategy. The founder appeared to be concerned about the cost related to formally setting up the company. On the other hand, he did not perceive the software development process as a challenge: "it is the easiest part to do", he argues.

Startup B develops an app that enables people to keep track of their workout routines, and to know exactly what they should do in each session to improve results. The project began in 2017, when one of the founders was looking for an app to help him improve his workout routines, but could not find one suitable to his needs. Since he was a computer science student and knew how to develop mobile apps, he started the project along with two other classmates. It is important to point out that all of them had taken entrepreneurship/Lean Startup courses, so they have learned about the process of creating a startup.

Their first strategy was to combine the software development process with some interactions with local gym and fitness centers. The rationale behind this approach was that they could reach several potential users at once. However, they failed in the negotiation process; even though gym owners liked the idea of having an app for their users, none of them wanted to take the risk and pay upfront. Therefore, they decided to move to a B2C (business to consumer) strategy. The goal at first was not to charge for the app, but to deliver a great experience so they could retain customers. The strategy worked and they were able to reach the 30.000 download mark at the beginning of 2019. However, they were facing a big challenge: lack of resources since they failed in monetizing the app. In order to address this issue, they had to invest part of their time to develop software for others in order to survive as a company. At the point this paper is being written, startup B is working on finding a business model. Since they are still looking for a business model, we classified them in the inception stage. Considering the team will use available technologies to develop the app that will focus on a new product to gyms, the innovation is related to marketing.

Startup C develops a web platform that sells software solutions to a specific type of offline business. Revenue is based on possible customers sent to tool publishers (lead generation). Regarding our startup criteria, the service is lead generation and it is completely digitally sold and delivered. It is also innovative since they are the first company focused on this specific segment and they found challenges throughout their history because of this fact.

This project began after one of the founders left a web agency, where he worked for 10 years. This experience made him realize that there are several opportunities to better serve this specific segment. Therefore, he wanted to take advantage of his own background and give this startup a try. Currently there are 3 people working in this organization: two co-founders and one software developer. The company is almost reaching the break-even point, that is, the point where income surpasses expenses. They are now working a new platform that will support their growth.

Startup D develops a software platform to be used in customer interaction and support on websites. The company focus on B2B (business to business), already has some clients, and has also reached the break-even point. The company started back in 2014 when the founder, who does not have a technical background but has an entrepreneurial mindset, was looking at new ways for businesses to interact with one another. Since then, this idea has been also developed by other companies. In spite of it, the founder believes this project can be a business opportunity.

Regarding the criteria, the product is definitely digitally sold and delivered (online), even though there is communication with the customers, for instance, through feature requests. Although the solution is already offered by other companies, we considered it as innovative because, when they started, the idea was new. The project is developed by three founders (two non-technical and one technical), along with two developers that do not work full-time. Currently, they are looking for more developers in order to continue developing the tool.

4   Results

Through data analysis, we identified 12 themes that were grouped into the categories: individual, organizational context, and environmental factors as shown in Fig. 1.

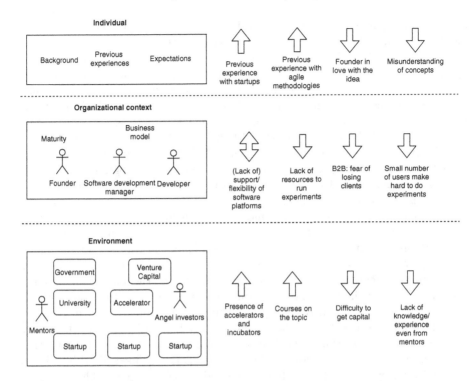

Fig. 1. Enablers and inhibitors of an experimentation in early-stage startups divided in three categories: individual, organizational context, and environment. Each category is represented by the elements that compose it: enablers with up-arrows, inhibitors with down-arrows, and factors that could act as either with two-sided arrows.

4.1 Individual

The first common theme in this category is the **founder in love with the idea** or, in case A founder's words: "an entrepreneur is in love with his idea and then sometimes it takes him to do things that are not rational [...] even before [he knows] there is a market [to the product]." The problem here is investing a lot of time and resources developing the solution without realizing if the user or the customer is willing to pay for it, even though well-known methodologies and practices targeted to this context argue not to do so. This is usually a consequence of the founders' overconfidence on their knowledge about the market. Generally, they are creating their startups to tackle needs they observed in the market they were already working on. This is the main reason case A is not strictly following an experiment-driven approach. Although the founder praises Lean Startup, the focus is clearly on implementing the features imagined for the product rather than checking if the problem is really felt by customers and if the solution would be useful. In the group interview for case B, the founders mentioned: "in the first phase, we ignored Lean Startup because we thought we knew the market since we are users." Similarly, in case C, when asked why he did not use an experimental approach from the beginning, the non-technical founder mentioned: "since I have worked for twelve years in the sector, I thought I knew my clients' problems."

Related to this factor, we observed a clear **misunderstanding of concepts**. A clear example is Case A. Although, as mentioned earlier, the founder said that a common problem is when a founder falls in love with the idea, he is an example of that. We could observe during our meetings that he was concerned about the cost to build the whole solution, although it was not clear if the software would be technologically feasible. He claimed that the development would be the easiest part of the puzzle. In his own words: "at least in programming, everything seems more clear to me in the sense that it works or not [...] my biggest problem is estimate cost." To some extent, we observed in several moments that the interviewees did not fully understand the concept of MVP (Minimum Viable Product). Although Ries [31] described it as a minimum artifact to test a hypothesis (and it does not necessarily mean to develop a piece of software), generally the interviewees take it as an idea of a prototype or a product with a minimum set of features. In case B, during the interview, the founders mentioned that they consider the team passed through three stages considering experimentation. First, they ignored the idea of testing and developed the features they thought would be useful since they assumed they knew the market. Once they realized it was not working, they began to understand the market by visiting gyms and now, once they thought they already had a defined MVP and knew their users, they changed their focus on building the company. Therefore, we could observe some interesting facts. First, initially they considered their idea to be good; they focused on developing it, despite their knowledge about Lean Startup. Once, they realized it was not working, they performed an experimentation cycle: talked to gyms to check whether they would like to have the app, that is, solution interviews. But then, they returned to the previous stage. Therefore, they still do not use the process as a continuous approach; instead, they considered it as an initial first step in building their company. In their own words: "the MVP is already well defined, [and we know] who the users are."

The next factor could be an enabler or inhibitor: the founders' **previous experience with startups**. We could observe this, for instance, in case B, in which the founders mentioned they changed their way from developing to understanding the customer when they realized the first path was not working. The non-technical founder in case C, when asked why they are not doing experiments from the beginning, mentioned that he did not have experience to do so. Therefore, it is reasonable to think that an experienced entrepreneur would think better before developing several features based on her previous experiences. In comparison, as we observed in the cases studied, novice entrepreneurs lack this experience.

In a similar way, **previous experience with agile methodologies** are enabler, since these methods focus on customer feedback. For instance, the founder in case A mentioned that "I was convinced because I already use an agile methodology for software [...] and I thought that it may work as well for business."

4.2   Organizational Context

In this category, we grouped factors related to the startup, its internal and surrounding dynamics, such as its business model, practices and tools used.

Case B interviewees mentioned the problem of **small number of users**. They argued that most of the market test examples are based on quantitative analysis and they cannot support a statistically significant result with a small number of users. For instance, they mentioned the common example of building a landing page to test the customer interest and said that it is hard to "bring traffic to a landing page."

A related problem occurs in a B2B market: **concern of losing clients**. For instance, in Case D, the startup already has some clients, but the non-technical founders mentioned that they cannot make several tests because of the risk of current clients considering tests as problems and decide to abandon the platform. This is more evident in a B2B market because of the possible amount of customer (which is lower when compared to a B2C market) and also because of the customer acquisition cost.

One factor that could have both effects is the **(lack of) support/flexibility from software platforms**. For instance, in Case C, based on the data collected, we considered that the company adheres to an experiment approach to some extent. As the founder mentioned, from the beginning they used "Wordpress with plugins." Wordpress is a content management system (CMS) that allows creating websites without writing code but configuring a set of add-ons among the huge number available, making it easy to customize the website to the user needs [28]. This tool allowed them to create something fast to test; "to verify the business model," which "was the goal [at the time]." Although this choice was also used because of the lack of resources to build it in house. Anyhow, according to the founder and the software developer, sometimes they were not able to do more experiments because the platform was not flexible enough. Because of that, they are considering building their own platform. Nevertheless, the software developer sometimes feels uncomfortable with this idea because "he likes the things well-done and perfect" in a way that "it simply works." However, "now we have the intention to invest a lot in the technological part and we want everything in another framework" because they "have really particular needs," and it became harder to make tests. On case B, the team complained about the Apple App Store, which takes time to make a new version of the product available hindering tests execution.

Finally, the interviewees complained about the **lack of resources to run experiments**. For instance, the case B's founders argue that Lean Startup has "a lack of practicability" since "the first thing a startup has to do is to get money someway." In this case, as already mentioned, they argued that they do not have money to bring traffic to a landing page to test users' interest in their idea. In case C, the non-technical founder said that, because they do not have more employees, "if [we take time to develop something and] I finish the cash flow next month, the company will die."

4.3 Environment

The first observed inhibitor in this category is related to the last in the previous one: **difficulty in getting capital**. We observed in all cases the constant concern about obtaining money to run the company for more time. This fact constraints the team to focus on fast results that allow the company to run further. It is important to point out that an experiment may invalidate a hypothesis. Although this is valuable in regards to the knowledge obtained about customers and the market, it does not represent new income that would allow the team to continue the project.

Finally, a complaint observed in the cases was **lack of knowledge**, specially from mentors. For instance, the non-technical founders in case D mentioned that mentors generally come from a traditional business environment, and are not used to an innovative and disruptive market. Therefore, they are not able to give advice when it comes to experimentation. In case A, the founder admitted that he changed his mind when he went to an incubator: "I arrived here in the [a local incubator] and then they started talking about the need of a business plan." It is surprising to see that some incubators still focus on traditional business plans rather than on startup-related processes and tools.

However, actors and activities in the environment can be enablers. **Accelerators and technology parks** can help software startup founders in applying new practices focused on experimentation, such as Lean Startup. Similarly, the existence of **university courses** on entrepreneurship focusing on these techniques make this content also available to startups. Case A founder mentioned this when talking about the incubator his company is in: "it is really good the fact that they make us aware of these methodologies, for instance, that startups can participate in [a course about Lean Startup taught in the local university]."

5 Discussion

In this section, we present a discussion on the results showing how they are related to previous studies in the literature, and possible ways to increase experimentation in software startups.

First, other studies have already showed the founders' influence on practices selection. While studying the competencies of a software startup initial team, Seppanen et al. [35] concluded that the founder dominates actions and competences related to the business and product innovations of the company. Their knowledge about the market [7] causes their overconfidence on their idea. Founders' overconfidence is a well-known problem in entrepreneurship [19].

This discussion brings us to the concept of cognitive biases. In a recent systematic mapping study, Mohanani et al. [25] argued that "these systematic deviations from optimal reasoning help to explain many common software engineering problems." Using such lenses, we could say that the **founder in love with the idea** is an instance of overconfidence bias, that is, an "inability to question the fundamental way of thinking" [25], and confirmation bias, the tendency to pay more attention to evidence that confirm our beliefs over those that challenge them. The second can be observed when founders guide their experiments (mock-ups, wireframes, etc.) to test if a customer would buy that product, generally asking them. However, this is not even the way Ries proposes the MVP concept [31]. He argues that one should test a hypothesis about the user/customer even without building part of the final product with, for example, a landing page or a video.

Debiasing tasks is a way to tackle this problem since it is easier than debiasing people [25] . For instance, planning poker tackled the anchoring bias when estimating the time to complete a task. Therefore, new socio-technical practices should be developed for software startups to avoid these biases. This is related to Lean Startup lack of a full operationalized framework, making it hard to apply in practice [6].

Besides that, these first two inhibitors could be explained using the cognitive dissonance theory [14]. According to it, individuals seek consistency among their cognitions (beliefs, opinions). Therefore, for instance, if an experiment disproves a founder's belief about the market, the person may look for explanations to it, not abandoning the idea and spending more time and money from the startup, instead of questioning the idea itself and abandoning or modifying it.

Regarding **experience**, several actors in a startup ecosystem could help improve it. This result highlights the importance of accelerators, incubators and technology parks, and which elements they should focus on to improve startup results. Additionally, it shows the importance of university courses in related topics.

Second, the first two inhibitors related to the context are similar: small number of users and B2B startups fearing the customers loss. The first makes hard to perform controlled experiments, the most common examples in the Lean Startup book [31] and in scientific studies (e.g., case studies in big companies [12]). In the case of startups focused on B2B markets, this will always be the case. Therefore, several software startups should collect knowledge through other strategies that may focus on depth instead of quantity. A possible approach to solve this problem may be the use of qualitative research techniques, such as case studies and ethnographies to contrast the use of controlled experiments in a quantitative scenario. These techniques could help to tackle the lack of money since the startup does not need to spend money to bring traffic.

Regarding the similarity to agile methodologies, it refers to the idea of compatibility that is a well-used construct in adoption [30] and diffusion of innovations [32] theory. That is, if the decision taker, in this case, the founder or the software development manager, perceives that the innovation is similar to what she knew before, she will be more inclined to adopt it. This result informs the creation of further practices and techniques for software startups.

Third, the themes related to the environment are discussed in the startup ecosystem literature. In this sense, we can use Cukier and Kon's software startup ecosystem maturity model [9]. The authors classify regions in four different levels: nascent, evolving, mature, and self-sustainable based on a series of metrics regarding financial, market, and knowledge aspects. All identified enablers and inhibitors in our cross-case analysis can be mapped to such metrics. First, the lack of capital is related to access to venture-capital and angel funding. Second, the presence of accelerators, university courses, and the lack of experienced mentors are related to the mentoring quality, accelerators quality, incubators, technology parks, and methodologies knowledge. For instance, regarding mentoring quality, the authors considered "the percentage of mentors that fit one of these criteria: (1) had a successful startup in the past and (2) founded and worked for more than 10 years in one or more startups." From our interviews, this is not the case of the ecosystems, or at least, the accelerators, incubators and technology parks the studied startups are in. Most of the knowledge brought to these startups came from people experienced with traditional businesses that explains their focus on business plans and financial concerns. Clearly, this is a problem of not existing a previous generation of digital entrepreneurs as in more advanced ecosystems, such as Silicon Valley or Israel, a metric called "ecosystem generations" [9].

5.1 Threats to Validity

Runeson and Höst [34] described a common scheme to assess threats to validity when reporting a case study. It is composed by four aspects: construct validity, internal validity, external validity and reliability.

Construct validity reflects "to what extent the operational measures that are studied really represent what the researcher have in mind" [34]. The use of multiple information sources for all four cases reduces this issue [39]. Besides that, through face-to-face semi-structured interviews, it was possible to properly solve any communication misunderstandings between interviewer and interviewee regarding key concepts, such as experimentation. Finally, the interviewees were available to further questions if any doubt occurred during data analysis.

Internal validity is related to causal relationships and represents the possibility of other factors not taken into account are actually causing the observed factor. In order to mitigate this risk, we used triangulation of data from different interviewees within each case study. In addition, the authors inspected the data in order to make sure they all agreed upon the results.

Our case sampling strategy use of 4 cases studies in different scenarios (stage and market) improved **external validity**. Nevertheless, a weakness of this study is the lack of startups present in a more mature ecosystem. This could be an interesting future work.

The **reliability** aims at minimizing errors and biases. In other words, if another researcher performs the same study in the future, she has to reach the same results [39]. In order to mitigate this risk, throughout this study, we described all steps performed in data collection and analysis.

6   Conclusions

Experiment-driven software development could be an important approach to improve software startups success rate. The goal of this paper was to identify enablers and inhibitors for this approach in these early-stage companies where an experimental mindset could bring critical results. We performed a multiple-case study in four startups located in two continents, with distinct products and markets. Our results identified several enablers and inhibitors grouped in three levels: individual, organizational context, and environment. Finally, we compared our results with previous ones found in the literature and presented directions for improvement.

Future work could focus on developing social-technical practices to mitigate human and context inhibitors, and enhance the enablers. An interesting future study could be the replication of this study in more mature startup ecosystems in order to better support our results. Our work could bring important information to practitioners, specially, accelerators or policy makers, for instance, guiding the selection and training of mentors and showing which problems they may face when trying to make the startups they work with use an experiment-driven approach.

Acknowledgments. This work is partially funded by FAPERGS (17/2551-0001/205-4).

References

1. Ahrend, J.M.: Requirements Elicitation in Startup Companies. Research Topics in HCI (2013)
2. Andries, P., Debackere, K., van Looy, B.: Simultaneous experimentation as a learning strategy: business model development under uncertainty. Strateg. Entrep. J. **7**(4), 288–310 (2013)
3. Berg, V., Birkeland, J., Nguyen-Duc, A., Pappas, I.O., Jaccheri, L.: Software startup engineering: a systematic mapping study. J. Syst. Softw. **144**(February), 255–274 (2018)
4. Blank, S.: The Four Steps to the Epiphany: Successful Strategies for Products that Win. Cafepress.com, Louisville (2007)
5. Bortolini, R.F., Nogueira Cortimiglia, M., Danilevicz, A.D.M.F., Ghezzi, A.: Lean Startup: a comprehensive historical review. Manag. Decis. (August) (2018). https://doi.org/10.1108/MD-07-2017-0663
6. Bosch, J., Holmström Olsson, H., Björk, J., Ljungblad, J.: The early stage software startup development model: a framework for operationalizing lean principles in software startups. In: Fitzgerald, B., Conboy, K., Power, K., Valerdi, R., Morgan, L., Stol, K.-J. (eds.) LESS 2013. LNBIP, vol. 167, pp. 1–15. Springer, Heidelberg (2013). https://doi.org/10.1007/978-3-642-44930-7_1
7. Coleman, G., O'Connor, R.V.: An investigation into software development process formation in software start-ups. J. Enterp. Inf. Manag. **21**(6), 633–648 (2008)
8. Cruzes, D.S., Dyba, T.: Recommended steps for thematic synthesis in software engineering. In: 2011 International Symposium on Empirical Software Engineering and Measurement, vol. 7491, pp. 275–284 (2011). https://doi.org/10.1109/ESEM.2011.36
9. Cukier, D., Kon, F.: A maturity model for software startup ecosystems. J. Innov. Entrep. **7**(1), 14 (2018)

10. Eisenhardt, K.M.: Building theories from case study research. Acad. Manag. Rev. **14**(4), 532–550 (1989)
11. Eisenhardt, K.M., Tabrizi, B.N.: Accelerating adaptive processes: product innovation in the global computer industry. Adm. Sci. Q. **40**(1), 84 (1995)
12. Fabijan, A., et al.: Experimentation growth: evolving trustworthy A/B testing capabilities in online software companies. J. Softw. Evol. Process. **30**(12), e2113 (2018). (December 2017)
13. Fabijan, A., Olsson, H.H., Bosch, J.: Customer feedback and data collection techniques in software R&D: a literature review. In: Fernandes, J., Machado, R., Wnuk, K. (eds.) ICSOB. Lecture Notes in Business Information Processing, vol. 210. Springer, Cham (2015). https://doi.org/10.1007/978-3-319-19593-3_12
14. Festinger, L.: A Theory of Cognitive Dissonance, vol. 2. Stanford university press, Redwood City (1957)
15. Frederiksen, D.L., Brem, A.: How do entrepreneurs think they create value? A scientific reflection of Eric Ries' Lean startup approach. Int. Entrep. Manag. J. **13**(1), 169–189 (2017)
16. Garcia, R., Calantone, R.: A critical look at technological innovation typology and innovativeness terminology: a literature review. J. Product Innov. Manag. **19**(2), 110–132 (2002)
17. Giardino, C., Wang, X., Abrahamsson, P.: Why early-stage software startups fail: a behavioral framework. In: Lassenius, C., Smolander, K. (eds.) ICSOB 2014. LNBIP, vol. 182, pp. 27–41. Springer, Cham (2014). https://doi.org/10.1007/978-3-319-08738-2_3
18. Gutbrod, M., Münch, J., Tichy, M.: How do software startups approach experimentation? empirical results from a qualitative interview study. In: Felderer, M., Méndez Fernández, D., Turhan, B., Kalinowski, M., Sarro, F., Winkler, D. (eds.) PROFES 2017. LNCS, vol. 10611, pp. 297–304. Springer, Cham (2017). https://doi.org/10.1007/978-3-319-69926-4_21
19. Hayward, M.L.A., Shepherd, D.A., Griffin, D.: A hubris theory of entrepreneurship. Manag. Sci. **52**(2), 160–172 (2006)
20. Herrmann, B.L., Marmer, M., Dogrultan, E., Holtschke, D.: Startup ecosystem report 2012. In: Telefonica Digital and Startup Genome (2012)
21. Kerr, W.R., Nanda, R., Rhodes-Kropf, M.: Entrepreneurship as experimentation. J. Econ. Perspect. **28**(3), 25–48 (2014)
22. Klotins, E., Unterkalmsteiner, M., Gorschek, T.: Software engineering in startup companies: an analysis of 88 experience reports. Empirical Softw. Eng. **24**(1), 68–102 (2019). https://doi.org/10.1007/s10664-018-9620-y
23. Lindgren, E., Münch, J.: Raising the odds of success: the current state of experimentation in product development. Inf. Softw. Technol. **77**, 80–91 (2016)
24. Melegati, J., Goldman, A., Kon, F., Wang, X.: A model of requirements engineering in software startups. Inf. Softw. Technol. **109**, 92–107 (2019)
25. Mohanani, R., Salman, I., Turhan, B., Rodriguez, P., Ralph, P.: Cognitive Biases in Software Engineering: A Systematic Mapping Study. IEEE Trans. Softw. Eng. **5589**(c), 1–20 (2018). https://doi.org/10.1109/TSE.2018.2877759
26. Olsson, H.H., Bosch, J.: From opinions to data-driven software R&D: a multi-case study on how to close the 'Open Loop' problem. In: 2014 40th EUROMICRO Conference on Software Engineering and Advanced Applications, pp. 9–16. IEEE, August 2014
27. Pantiuchina, J., Mondini, M., Khanna, D., Wang, X., Abrahamsson, P.: Are software startups applying agile practices? the state of the practice from a large survey.

In: Baumeister, H., Lichter, H., Riebisch, M. (eds.) XP 2017. LNBIP, vol. 283, pp. 167–183. Springer, Cham (2017). https://doi.org/10.1007/978-3-319-57633-6_11

28. Patel, S.K., Prof Acharya, A., Patel, M., Rathod, V.R., Prajapati, J.B.: Performance analysis of content management systems-joomla, drupal and wordpress general terms open source content management system. Int. J. Comput. Appl. **21**(4), 39–43 (2011)

29. Paternoster, N., Giardino, C., Unterkalmsteiner, M., Gorschek, T., Abrahamsson, P.: Software development in startup companies: a systematic mapping study. Inf. Softw. Technol. **56**(10), 1200–1218 (2014)

30. Riemenschneider, C.K., Hardgrave, B.C., Davis, F.D.: Explaining software developer acceptance of methodologies: a comparison of five theoretical models. IEEE Trans. Softw. Eng. **28**(12), 1135–1145 (2002)

31. Ries, E.: The Lean Startup: How Today's Entrepreneurs Use Continuous Innovation to Create Radically Successful Businesses. Crown Business, New York City (2011)

32. Rogers, E.M.: Diffusion of Innovations. Simon and Schuster, New York City (2010)

33. Ros, R., Runeson, P.: Continuous experimentation and A/B testing. In: Proceedings of the 4th International Workshop on Rapid Continuous Software Engineering - RCoSE 2018, pp. 35–41. ACM Press, New York (2018)

34. Runeson, P., Höst, M.: Guidelines for conducting and reporting case study research in software engineering. Empir. Softw. Eng. **14**(2), 131–164 (2009)

35. Seppänen, P., Oivo, M., Liukkunen, K.: The initial team of a software startup. In: 2016 International Conference on Engineering, Technology and Innovation (ICE) & IEEE International Technology Management Conference, pp. 57–65 (2016)

36. Steininger, D.M.: Linking information systems and entrepreneurship: a review and agenda for IT-associated and digital entrepreneurship research. Inf. Syst. J. **29**, 363–407 (2019). https://doi.org/10.1111/isj.12206

37. Tanabian, M., ZahirAzami, B.: Building high-performance team through effective job design for an early stage software start-up. In: Proceedings. 2005 IEEE International Engineering Management Conference, 2005, vol. 2, pp. 789–792. IEEE (2005)

38. Unterkalmsteiner, M., et al.: Software startups - a research agenda. e-Informatica Softw. Eng. J. **10**(1), 1–28 (2016)

39. Yin, R.: Case Study Research: Design and Methods. Applied Social Research Methods. SAGE Publications, Thousand Oaks (2003)

40. Zettel, J., Maurer, F., Münch, J., Wong, L.: LIPE: a lightweight process for E-Business startup companies based on extreme programming. In: Product Focused Software Process Improvement, pp. 255–270 (2001)

European Project Space

European Project Space Papers
for the PROFES 2019 - Summary

Alessandra Bagnato[1(✉)] and Davide Fucci[2,3]

[1] Softeam Research & Development Department, Paris, France
alessandra.bagnato@softeam.fr
[2] University of Hamburg, Hamburg, Germany
fucci@informatik.uni-hamburg.de
[3] Blekinge Institute of Technology, Karlskrona, Sweden
davide.fucci@bth.se

Abstract. The European Project Space at PROFES 2019 provides an opportunity for researchers involved in ongoing and recently completed research projects (national, European, and international) related to the topics of the conference to present their projects and disseminate the objectives, deliverables, or outcome.

1 Introduction

Today's collaborative research projects act as a bridge between research (e.g., academia) and practitioners (e.g., industries). Within collaborative projects, the research community can share ideas in real industrial environments while, at the same time, can raise the need for new and different research inspired by the needs of the industry.

The European Project Space at PROFES 2019 provides an opportunity for researchers involved in ongoing and recently completed research projects (national, European, and international), related to the topics of the PROFES conference, to present their results and disseminate their objectives, deliverables, and further endeavors.

The types of projects eligible for presentation in this track were:

- Projects funded by the European Union, by national or local funding organizations, or by individual universities and industries.
- Projects carried out by an international consortium of partners or projects that might involve partners of the same country.

The EPS Workshop will include the presentation of nine different projects, corresponding to the nine accepted papers reviewed by two different reviewers from the selection committee. Projects and projects' representatives who did not submit a paper are also welcome to participate in the workshop to discuss their plans, share ideas, and establish new collaborations.

X. Franch et al. (Eds.): PROFES 2019, LNCS 11915, pp. 573–576, 2019.
https://doi.org/10.1007/978-3-030-35333-9_40

2   Accepted Papers

The PROFES EPS volume contains the proceedings of the European Project Space (EPS'19) held on 27 November 2019 in Barcelona, Spain, in conjunction with PROFES 2019 [1], the International Conference on Product-Focused Software Process Improvement—one among the top recognized software development and process improvement conferences. The 20th edition of PROFES has been held in Barcelona, Spain, from November 27 to 29, 2019 in the North Campus of the Technical University of Barcelona (https://www.upc.edu).

The following papers have been accepted in the proceedings of the workshop:

- Amin Boudeffa, Alessandra Bagnato, Antonin Abherve, Cedric Thomas, Martin Hamant and Assad Montasser. *Application of Computational Linguistics Techniques for Improving Software Quality*: Progress in Artificial Intelligence, Big Data and Computational Linguistics domains offered new way to perform in-depth analysis and evidence-based quality assessments of open source software components. In this CROSSMINER Project paper we have seen how this can be integrated into industrial development to improve the quality of developed software.
- Kaïs Chaabouni, Alessandra Bagnato and Antonio Garcia-Dominguez. *Monitoring ArchiMate models for DataBio project*. The Data-Driven Bio-economy project (DataBio) is a large scale project that aims to develop big data technologies in the domains of agriculture, fishery and forestry. This project applies the standard Enterprise Architecture language: "ArchiMate 3.0" for modelling the pilot case studies and for modelling the software components in order to facilitate comprehension and communication between partners. The models are created with the modelling tool "Modelio" which allows contributors to collaborate on a shared version of the ArchiMate models. These models are monitored continuously by the monitoring tool "Measure Platform" and the model querying tool "Hawk". In this Databio project paper we have seen the monitoring approach and the metrics defined to evaluate the quality level of the models.
- Alessandra Bagnato, Alexandre Beaufays, Etienne Brosse, Kaïs Chaabouni, Uwe Ryssel, Michael Schulze and Andrey Sadovykh. *Showcasing Modelio and pure:- variants integration in REVaMP2 project*. REVaMP2 project is part of the ITEA 3 industry-driven Re-search, Development and Innovation programme in the domain of software innovation. REVaMP2 project aims to develop an automated and comprehensive tool that supports massive customizing of "Software-Intensive Systems and Services" (SIS) Product Lines (PL). This approach requires agile round-trip engineering processes for managing the different configurations in legacy assets, and for more systematic and automated variability management. For this purpose, the project put among its priority the standardization of a variability language called "Variability Exchange Language" (VEL) as a format for describing variability in models. This paper showcases the integration of model-driven engineering (MDE) tool "Modelio" with the variability management tool "pure::variants" using the VEL language as data exchange format. VEL is used to model both the feature model, also referred to as "150% model", with all possible variation

points and all variant configurations coming from the features selection for the variant of a specific product.

- Victoria Torres, Miriam Gil and Vicente Pelechano. *DECODER - DEveloper COmpanion for Documented and annotatEd code Reference.* Software is everywhere and the productivity of Software Engineers has increased radically with the advent of new specification, design and programming paradigms and languages. The main objective of the DECODER project is to introduce radical solutions to increase productivity by increasing the abstraction level, at the specification stage, using requirements engineering techniques to integrate more complete specifications into the development process, and formal methods to reduce the time and efforts for integration testing.

- Juncal Alonso, Leire Orue-Echevarria, Marisa Escalante, Lorenzo Blasi and Kyriakos Stefanidis. *DECIDE: DevOps for Trusted, Portable and Interoperable Multi-Cloud Applications towards the Digital Single Market.* This paper presents a solution implemented in the context of the European project DECIDE which aims to support DevOps teams in the design, pre-deployment, contracting, deployment and operation of multi-cloud native applications with the provisioning of an integrated framework. The project is entering its late phase, in which the DevOps framework is currently being validated and evaluated in various use cases.

- Lidia López and Marc Oriol. *Q-Rapids: Quality-Aware Rapid Software Development – An H2020 Project.* This work reports the objectives and current state of the Q-Rapids H2020 project. Q-Rapids (Quality-Aware Rapid Software Development) proposes a data-driven approach to the production of software following very short development cycles. The focus of Q-Rapids is on quality aspects, represented through quality requirements.

- Wishnu Prasetya, Tanja E. J. Vos, Gordon Fraser, Ivan Martinez-Ortiz, Ivan Perez-Colado, Rui Prada, Jose Rocha and Antonio R. Silva. *IMPRESS: Improving Engagement in Software Engineering Courses through Gamification.* The Eramus+ project IMPRESS seeks to explore the use of gamification in educating software engineering at the university level. When used in the right way, gamification can improve users' engagement and hence their appreciation for the taught subjects. This paper will present the project, its objectives, and its current progress.

- Marcin Wolski and Toby Rodwell. *Software Governance in a large European Project - GEANT case study.* GEANT refers both to the research and innovation community of European NRENs (operators of national networks for science and education), and also a sequence of network-related projects co-funded by the EC and the European NRENs. The latest such project is GN4, sustainable software development is an essential part of GN4, the project co-funded by Europe's NRENs and the EU. This article presents how software governance has been applied in GN4 during its iterations.

- Jose Luis de la Vara, Eugenio Parra, Alejandra Ruiz and Barbara Gallina. *AMASS: A Large-Scale European Project to Improve the Assurance and Certification of Cyber-Physical Systems.* The paper presents the AMASS project and its de-facto European-wide open tool platform, ecosystem, and self-sustainable community for assurance and certification of cyber-physical systems.

Acknowledgement. We would like to thank the people who have contributed to the PROFES EPS 2019 workshop. We wish to thank all authors for their valuable contributions, and we wish them a successful continuation of their work. We wish to thank all the members that served in the international program committee, namely: Danilo Caivano (Università degli Studi di Bari), Ana Cavalli (TELECOM & Management SudParis), Moharram Challenger (University of Antwerp), Marcus Ciolkowski (QAware), Philipp Diebold (Bagilstein), Andreas Jedlitschka (Fraunhofer Institute for Experimental Software Engineering *IESE)*, Lidia López (Universitat Politècnica de Catalunya (*UPC*)), Silverio Martínez (Fraunhofer Institute for Experimental Software Engineering *IESE)*, Markku Oivo (University of Oulu). We then wish to thank all the projects participating in the event namely H2020 Databio [5], H2020 CROSSMINER [2], ITEA 3 *REVaMP2* [6], H2020 DECODER [7], H2020 Decide [8], H2020 *Q-Rapids,* Eramus+ *IMPRESS* [4], ECSEL AMASS [10] *and GEANT* GN4 [3].

References

1. PROFES 2019. https://profes2019.upc.edu/. Accessed 15 Sept 2019
2. CROSSMINER. https://www.crossminer.org/. Accessed 15 Sept 2019
3. GEANT GN4. https://software.geant.org. Accessed 15 Sept 2019
4. IMPRESS project. https://impress-project.eu/. Accessed 15 Sept 2019
5. H2020 Databio. https://www.databio.eu/en/. Accessed 15 Sept 2019
6. Revamp2. http://www.revamp2-project.eu/. Accessed 15 Sept 2019
7. Decoder. https://www.decoder-project.eu/. Accessed 15 Sept 2019
8. Decide. https://www.decide-h2020.eu/. Accessed 15 Sept 2019
9. Q-Rapids. https://www.q-rapids.eu/. Accessed 15 Sept 2019
10. AMASS. https://www.amass-ecsel.eu/. Accessed 15 Sept 2019

Application of Computational Linguistics Techniques for Improving Software Quality

Amin Boudeffa[1(✉)], Antonin Abherve[1], Alessandra Bagnato[1], Cedric Thomas[2], Martin Hamant[2], and Assad Montasser[2]

[1] Softeam, Paris, France
{amin.boudeffa,antonin.abherve,alessandra.bagnato}@softeam.fr
[2] OW2, Paris, France
{cedric.thomas,martin.hamant,assad.montasser}@ow2.org

Abstract. Progress in Artificial Intelligence, Big Data and Computational Linguistics domains offered new way to perform n-depth analysis and evidence-based quality assessments of open source software components. In this paper we will see how this can be integrated into industrial development to improve the quality of developed software.

Keywords: Computational Linguistics · Big Data · Sentiment analysis

1 Project Data

Developing new software systems by reusing existing open source software (OSS) components raises challenges related to the level of quality of different OSS as well as to the level of support that different OSS communities provide to users of the software they produce [2]. The CROSSMINER project aim to address this issue.

- **Acronym:** CROSSMINER
- **Title:** Developer-Centric Knowledge Mining from Large Open-Source Software Repositories
- **Start date:** January 1, 2017
- **Duration:** 36 months
- **Partners:** The Open Group, University of L'Aquila, University of York, Softeam, OW2 Consortium, Edge Hill University, Unparallel Innovation, Eclipse Foundation Europe, Centrum Wiskunde & Informatica, Castalia Solutions, Bitergia, Athens University of Economics & Business.
- **Web site:** https://www.CROSSMINER.org/

Supported by the European Unions Horizon 2020 Research and Innovation Programme.

© Springer Nature Switzerland AG 2019
X. Franch et al. (Eds.): PROFES 2019, LNCS 11915, pp. 577–582, 2019.
https://doi.org/10.1007/978-3-030-35333-9_41

2   CROSSMINER Analysis Platform

2.1   CROSSMINER Project

CROSSMINER is an EU-funded research project which aims to deliver an integrated open-source platform that will support the development of complex software systems by enabling the monitoring, in-depth analysis and evidence-based selection of open source components, and facilitating knowledge extraction from large open-source software repositories. The project leverages multi-disciplinary sub-fields of computer science including Artificial Intelligence, Big Data and Computational Linguistics. The project aimed six main scientific and technology objectives among which the following four were used in the context of this experimentation:

- Development of source code analysis tools to extract and store actionable knowledge from the source code of a collection of open-source projects
- Development of natural language analysis tools to extract quality metrics related to the communication channels, and bug tracking systems of OSS projects by using Natural Language Processing and text mining techniques
- Development of workflow-based knowledge extractors that simplify the development of bespoke analysis and knowledge extraction tools shielding engineers from technological issues to concentrate on core analysis tasks
- Development of advanced integrated development environments that will allow developers to adopt the CROSSMINER knowledge base and analysis tools directly from the development environment will help developers to improve their productivity.

2.2   Natural Language Processing Metrics

Natural language contains vital and potentially hidden information that can be exploited to assist developers in making vital decisions surrounding open source software development [3]. The natural language components developed within the CROSSMINER project used to analyse various source of information of given Open Source software projects. The NLP metrics compute heuristics that summarise the quality of support offered to users over time, and contribute to the CROSSMINER knowledge base by enriching documents with extra information [3].

These metrics process the output classification values or a conversion of texts provided by the main basic metrics associated with various natural language tools integrated into CROSSMINER. We distinguish Sentimental Metric that reveals which sentiments are expressed in a bug tracking system for a project and Emotional Metric that Summarises the emotions expressed in the bug tracking systems of a given project.

The state of the art industrial software development process is based on monitoring the product quality through the use of a low level code-based metrics which are related particularly to the software development implementation phase. In CROSSMINER, the use of NLP tools is of high relevance, as the analysis of the text written by developers and users provides information that would be expensive and laborious to process manually. The extraction of these information about the quality of support offered by the community of an open source software project to be made available the sentiment analysis, classification of emotions, detection of request and replies among messages posted in a communication channel, bug tracker or forum, categorization of messages according to their content type and the classification of threads of messages according to the severity of the issue that they express.

3   Use Case Description

3.1   Softeam Use Case

The first company which perform this experimental integration, Softeam, is a French Company of 1000 employees, which operates in many different domains such as Finance, Banking, Insurance and Service industries. The company led this experiment in the context of the development team of a commercial long live software: Modelio, a modelings tool for developers and architects to support software and system engineering.

Each Modelio release follows a specific development process based on the Agile methodology in order to align Modelio features to market demands and guarantee the product quality. Each developments projects start by an initials specification phases in which the perimeter of the release is defined. At the end of each sprint, the quality issues of delivered components are assessed by the quality team by performing validations activity. Feedback are used to modify and adapt the next sprint plan. The quality assurance process can lead to an update of the project plan and require an adaptation of the architecture of the solution, the specification of the features being implemented or the perimeter of the release.

To develop its solutions, Softeam relies more and more frequently on open source libraries. Due to the critically of open source libraries and framework used as core components of his products, the selection and assessment of the quality of these libraries follow the same level of quality evaluation as Softeam internally developed code source. The selection process and administration of this components are a long and costly process and we expect that CROSSMINER will help us to conduct it.

3.2   OW2 Use Case

OW2 is a global open source software non-profit association, its mission is to foster the development of a portfolio of open source software for information systems and the growth of a business ecosystem around it. OW2 promotes a code base of some 100 open source projects; its global community membership involves some 40 members, including commercial, public and academic organisations, and over 2500 individual members, half of them from Europe.

As the organisation becomes a reference community platform in the open source marketplace, it increasingly stresses the quality and market readiness of its software. OW2 endeavours to integrate solutions helping projects to produce assessment reports on the quality of the code and on the maturity of their governance.

The OW2 use case has two goals. The first one is to provide project leaders and users with cutting edge tools for analysing and measuring accurately their software information sphere. The second goal is to develop a Market Readiness Index that will helps conventional managers select OW2 projects according to criteria spanning from technology quality to business sustainability.

As a result, OW2 will differentiate from comparable organisations, such as the Linux Foundation and the Eclipse Foundation (also a partner in the CROSS-MINER project), which are also working on systems to collect data about their projects.

4   Experimentation

4.1   Increasing Quality of Softeam Product by Including Sentiment Analysis Technics in Development Process

To increase his capacity to evaluate the quality of open source components embeded in his products, Softeam has integrated the provided solution, including the sentiment analysis and classification of emotions techniques, with his standardized development process (Fig. 1).

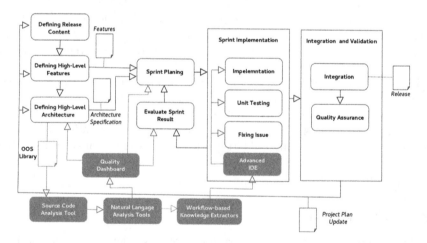

Fig. 1. Softeam standardized development approach with CROSSMINER solution.

In project initiation phase, Softeam evaluates how the source code analysis tool and the natural language analysis tool could be used to assist architects to choose the open sources framework which will be included in project architecture in order to add new services and functionality in Modelio. The result of sentimental analysis of textual data sources related to the component is used to evaluate how the open source community is reacting towards the specific library. In sprint implementation phases, by the intermediary of the IDE, the Computational Linguistics Techniques to identify the more relevant information that must be delivered to the developers.

The first evaluation of the impact of deploying the solution Softeam showed a significant improvement when working with new open source libraries:

- Reduction of 40% of average time needed to evaluate existing open source components used in a Modelio project architecture.
- Reduction of 25% of average time needed to choose open source components to be included in a project architecture.
- Reduction of 10% of average time for development which involved the use of new libraries unknown to our developers.

4.2 OW2 Experimentation with Sentiment Analysis Metrics

The experimentation with sentiments fits with OW2's business need to integrate into its process innovative ways to assess the market readiness of its projects, and to provide project leaders with tools and methods to help them to progress on the path toward greater maturity. The OW2 experimentation concentrates on contributor metrics to provide project leaders with the ability to better monitor and understand the behavior of their contributors.

The first objective is achieved by developing sentiment and emotion analysis based on the application of Natural Language Processing techniques on informal sources such as documentation and code and bug comments. There are three main challenges here. One is to identify metrics that can be collected throughout the whole code base so the method is applicable to all the projects. The second one is to develop data collectors, or readers, that can address the variety of sources. The third challenge is to define how to compute a snapshot indicator from time series covering periods from one quarter to a whole year (Table 1).

Table 1. Sample of the emotions apparition which appear on three projects.

Project	Emotions (count)					
	Surprise	Joy	Love	Sadness	Anger	Fear
XWIKI	326	357	361	364	364	359
Sat4j	0	286	286	184	107	0
asm	5	38	38	37	38	0

The second objective is addressed by setting up visual user interfaces reflecting the metrics that will get computed based on the tools delivered by CROSS-MINER. Such visual interfaces will let the user browse both high level and fine grained information, depending on the type of question. One key challenge here is to produce visual representations that are easily understandable by any reader and operationally meaningful for project leaders (Fig. 2).

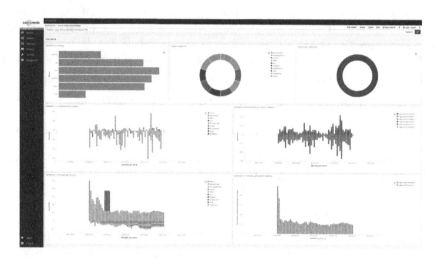

Fig. 2. Dashboard of Sentimental analysis natural language metrics applied so far by OW2 to assess projects

Acknowledgments. The research described has been carried out as part of the CROSSMINER Project, which has received funding from the European Union's Horizon 2020 Research and Innovation Programme under grant agreement No. 732223.

References

1. Boudeffa, A., Bagnato, A., Abherve, A., Di Ruscio, D., Mateus, M., Almeida, B.: Integrating and deploying heterogeneous components by means of a microservice architecture in the CROSSMINER project. STAF-CE **1**(5), 61–66 (2019)
2. Bagnato, A., et al.: Developer-centric knowledge mining from large open-source software repositories (CROSSMINER). In: Seidl, M., Zschaler, S. (eds.) STAF 2017. LNCS, vol. 10748, pp. 375–384. Springer, Cham (2018). https://doi.org/10.1007/978-3-319-74730-9_33
3. Edge Hill University: D3.4 Natural Language Components, 27 December 2017 Final

Monitoring ArchiMate Models for DataBio Project

Kaïs Chaabouni[1]([⊠]), Alessandra Bagnato[1], and Antonio Garcia-Dominguez[2]

[1] Softeam, R&D Department, Paris, France
{kais.chaabouni,alessandra.bagnato}@softeam.fr
[2] School of Engineering and Applied Science, Aston University, Birmingham, UK
a.garcia-dominguez@aston.ac.uk

Abstract. The Data-Driven Bio-economy project (DataBio) is a large scale project that aims to develop a platform that offers access to big data technologies in the domains of agriculture, fishery and forestry. This project applies the standard Enterprise Architecture language: "Archi-Mate 3.0" for modelling the pilot studies and for modelling the software components in order to facilitate comprehension and communication between partners. The models are created with the modelling tool "Modelio" which allows contributors to collaborate on a shared version of the ArchiMate models. These models are monitored continuously by the monitoring tool "Measure Platform" and the model querying tool "Hawk". This paper describes the monitoring approach and specifies the metrics defined to evaluate the quality level of the models.

Keywords: ArchiMate · Enterprise Architecture · Models metrics

Project data

- Acronym: DataBio, Title: Data-Driven Bio-economy
- Start date: January 2017, Duration: 36 months
- Partners: INTRASOFT International S.A. Belgium (project coordinator), VTT Technical Research Centre of Finland LTD, SINTEF and 45 more partners including IT companies and research institutes [1]

1 Introduction

The DataBio project [2] aims to develop a big data platform based on existing partners' solutions and contains 27 pilot studies that fit among one of these categories:

- Improving precision farming and utilizing predictive analysis in agriculture.
- Improving forest monitoring, predicting risks and optimizing tree resources.
- Predicting fishery market and rationalising its environmental impact.

X. Franch et al. (Eds.): PROFES 2019, LNCS 11915, pp. 583–589, 2019.
https://doi.org/10.1007/978-3-030-35333-9_42

Each pilot integrates through its workflow a number of software components that are linked together and act as a data pipeline in which every component has a specific task along the data value chain from data collecting and processing (mostly satellite imagery and IoT sensors data) to analyzing and visualizing [3]. In order to facilitate the comprehension of the pilots requirements and the technological design of the components, there is a need for a common modelling language that allows people to have the same modelling conventions. Therefore we use the standard "Enterprise Architecture" language "ArchiMate 3.0" [4] which proved to be suitable for specifying requirements/strategies and has at the same time a wide range of concepts for modelling IT systems [5]. The modelling environment used for this task is "Modelio" [6] which allows partners to collaborate on synchronized SVN repositories containing the ArchiMate models. In order to maintain the quality level of the models throughout the project we defined new metrics for the models' quality and we monitor continuously the models' repositories with the monitoring tool "Measure Platform" [7] and the model querying tool "Hawk" [8]. This paper is structured as follows: Sect. 2 presents the monitoring of the ArchiMate models, Sect. 3 illustrates the defined model quality metrics and the final section ends with concluding remarks.

2   Monitoring of Modelio ArchiMate Models

The DataBio ArchiMate models are structured in five Modelio projects described as follows:

- Three projects: Project 1, 2 and 3 corresponding to the pilots of the following domains of research: agriculture, fishery and forestry. These projects contain motivation views, strategy views and business process views.
- Project 4 for modelling software and IoT system components.
- Project 5 for modelling "Earth Observation" data services.

These projects are monitored by the monitoring and analysis tool "Measure Platform" designed primarily for monitoring software projects, integrating third party analysis tools and creating a customized dashboard for visualization. Measure Platform collect periodically predefined "measures" that were developed to monitor the ArchiMate Models by interrogating the model indexing tool "Hawk" which allows to query the Modelio repositories [9]. For each metric, we add measures for the five monitored projects where we specify the query expression in **EOL** language (Epsilon Object Language) [11] which is then interpreted and executed by Hawk. Hawk optimizes the querying process by creating a graph database index that contains the different elements of the model and their relationships and thus improving the response time of the queries [10]. The collected measurements are stored in Measure Platform and can be visualized through the platform dashboard. Figure 1 shows an example of the measurements that can be visualized by Measure Platform dashboards.

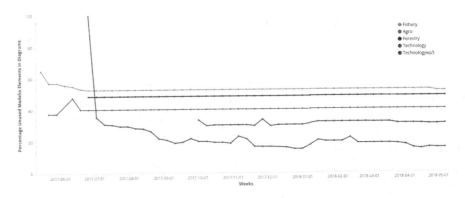

Fig. 1. Percentage of unrepresented elements in monitored Modelio projects

3   Metrics for Evaluating Models Quality

The metrics that we use for evaluating the quality level of the models are inspired in part from literature review such as the "6C quality goals" described by *Mohagheghi et al.* [12] for model driven software development. In addition, these metrics are inspired from our experience with monitoring DataBio models and evaluating their added value regarding to the purpose they serve. Hence, in this context, the models are evaluated by how much they provide understanding and clarity for users while having at the same time an efficient modelling process that makes it well worth the effort.

3.1   Metrics for Optimizing the Modelling Process with Modelio

We present here metrics that reflect how optimal is the usage of Modelio in a manner that guarantees completeness and efficiency in the modelling process. Table 1 gives a summary of the collected measurements by Measure Platform according to the following defined metrics.

Table 1. Metrics for optimizing the modelling process with Modelio

Projects	Proj.1	Proj.2	Proj.3	Proj.4	Proj.5
Percentage of unrepresented elements	40%	52%	49%	15%	31%
Percentage of duplicate elements	49%	54%	44%	12%	10%
Percentage of empty diagrams	13%	6%	15%	29%	16%
Median diagram importance score	0	6	0	16	17.73

Percentage of Unrepresented Elements. Unrepresented elements are elements that have been created in the ArchiMate model and located in the Modelio explorer but are not displayed on any diagram. This is due to the deleting of the element representation instead of the element itself or could be an element created in the model for future use but was never used afterwards. Having a big percentage of unrepresented elements implies having inefficiencies in the modelling process. On one hand these unrepresented elements are considered as a wasted effort because they add no value in the final diagrams. On the other hand, the presence of these unrepresented elements would result in a crowded project explorer which would increase complexity and decrease needlessly the visibility for the modellers. The monitored ArchiMate models for DataBio contain many unrepresented elements, averaging 50% in some projects (see Table 1 and Fig. 1).

Percentage of Duplicate Elements. Duplicate elements are different ArchiMate elements created in the models but represent the same concept. This redundancy can be the result of uncoordinated creation of elements by the different collaborators or a simple misuse of the modelling tool. The presence of duplicate elements add complexity for Modelio users and cause confusion in managing different copies of the same concept. Furthermore, these redundancies prevent Modelio users from identifying shared elements across diagrams and recognizing all relations associated to the same element. The first three DataBio models contain many redundancies (see Table 1) which is explained by the lack of experience of modellers freshly introduced to Modelio who are duplicating shared elements between pilots to use them in different diagrams instead of referencing the same element across different diagrams.

Complete Diagrams. We define two metrics for ensuring the completeness of the ArchiMate diagrams. The first metric is concerned with the percentage of empty diagrams as it is self evident to assume that an empty diagram is a sign of incomplete work. However, when applying this metric in DataBio models we noticed the presence of "almost empty diagrams" that can contain for instance a few not related elements and therefore should also be considered as incomplete or not having a mature enough design. Hence, we introduce the second metric that measures the maturity level or the "importance score" of diagrams. The importance score was introduced by *Singh and van Sinderen* [13] as an attempt to formalize Enterprise Architecture metrics for measuring of the criticality and the impact of an element in an Enterprise Architecture model. The importance score is calculated based on assigned scores to elements and their outgoing relationships and therefore the more the elements inside a diagram are connected together, the more the importance score is bigger. This measure could also be considered as a indication of the maturity level of the diagrams if we assume that any thing of value must be important and should have a certain minimum defined importance score as opposed to "almost empty diagrams" which have very low importance score. In the DataBio monitored projects (see Table 1) we can see that there is still many empty diagrams and that the median importance score for diagrams is still very low especially for the first three projects.

3.2 ArchiMate Comprehensibility Metrics

The comprehensibility metrics evaluate the complexity to read ArchiMate diagrams by distinguishing the different elements and recognizing the connections between them. Moreover, these metrics entail also the ability to understand the concepts represented by ArchiMate diagrams such as the services, the components and their interactions. Table 2 gives a summary of the collected measurements by Measure Platform according to the defined comprehensibility metrics.

Table 2. Comprehensibility metrics for ArchiMate diagrams

Metrics	Proj.1	Proj.2	Proj.3	Proj.4	Proj.5
Number of diagrams	59	36	33	312	141
Number of elements per diagram	13	17	13	7	7
Relations to Elements ratio	0.89	0.80	0.82	0.80	0.86
Percentage of documented elements	15%	19.2%	23.7%	57.9%	61.3%

Number of Diagrams. The number of diagrams reflect the size of the whole model. Having a big sized model increases the complexity for readers. For example, as we can see in the Table 2, the first three projects have reasonable number of diagrams, but project 4 and 5, which represent mostly the technological components in DataBio, have a big number of diagrams which can be disorienting for readers to grasp all the concepts represented by these models.

Number of Elements per Diagram. The number of elements per diagram metric is complementary to the previous metric because it highlights the density of diagrams and thus showing the real size of models in terms of total number of ArchiMate elements. The monitored DataBio models contain a reasonable number of elements per diagram averaging from 7 to 17 elements per diagram (see Table 2) which means that diagrams are not crowded and are easy to read.

Relationships to Elements Ratio. The relationships to elements ratio reflects the congestion of associations between elements and shows the number of different connections associated to the same element. The number of associations per element should be between 1 and 4, so that the resulted diagram would be neither congested too much nor sparse too much.

Percentage of Documented Elements. Modelio allows modellers to attach notes to the ArchiMate elements in order to describe the intended concepts represented in the diagrams. Although most of the elements have self evident names that do not require more explanation, other elements require more explanation for the readers especially if their names contain abbreviations, very technical terms or terms that describe different purpose from the intuitive and most common perception.

4   Conclusion

This paper outlines the adopted approach for monitoring ArchiMate models contained in Modelio repositories and the defined metrics that are used for collecting measurements on the monitored projects. ArchiMate models provided clarity and understanding throughout the DataBio project and therefore we needed to maintain a good quality level for the models. For this purpose, we defined metrics for model quality based on our experience with DataBio and inspired by other literature metrics. This has led to interrogate the models with a model indexing tool "Hawk" and a monitoring tool "Measure Platform" in order to evaluate models quality according to the defined metrics. We defined two sets of metrics: the first type was for optimizing the modelling process with Modelio and the second type for evaluating the ArchiMate diagrams.

For future work, we look forward to experiment with these metrics in other projects and analyse modellers feedback in order to adjust these metrics for ArchiMate modelling or for other modelling languages or methodologies.

Acknowledgements. This work is partially funded by "DataBio project" (No. 732064) under European Commission's Horizon 2020 research and innovative programme and "Measure project" (No. 14009) under the EUREKA ITEA 3 Programme.

References

1. DataBio partners. https://www.databio.eu/en/consortium. Accessed 27 May 2019
2. DataBio homepage. https://www.databio.eu. Accessed 27 May 2019
3. DataBio public deliverable: DataBi_D4.2 Services for Tests
4. Josey, A.: ArchiMate® 3.0 1-A Pocket Guide. Van Haren, 's-Hertogenbosch (2017)
5. Fritscher, B., Pigneur, Y.: Business IT alignment from business model to enterprise architecture. In: Salinesi, C., Pastor, O. (eds.) CAiSE 2011. LNBIP, vol. 83, pp. 4–15. Springer, Heidelberg (2011). https://doi.org/10.1007/978-3-642-22056-2_2
6. Modelio Business Architecture. https://www.modeliosoft.com. Accessed 18 April 2019
7. Measure Platform. http://measure-platform.org. Accessed 21 May 2019
8. Hawk. https://github.com/mondo-project/mondo-hawk. Accessed 21 May 2019
9. Al-Wadeai, O., et al.: Integration of Hawk for model metrics in the MEASURE platform. In: MODELSWARD (2018)
10. Garcia-Dominguez, A., et al.: Integration of a graph-based model indexer in commercial modelling tools. In: Proceedings of the ACM/IEEE 19th International Conference on Model Driven Engineering Languages and Systems. ACM (2016)

11. Epsilon Object Language. https://www.eclipse.org/epsilon/doc/eol/. Accessed 14 June 2019
12. Mohagheghi, P., et al.: Definitions and approaches to model quality in model-based software development-a review of literature. Inf. Softw. Technol. **51**(12), 1646–1669 (2009)
13. Singh, P.M., van Sinderen, M.J.: Lightweight metrics for enterprise architecture analysis. In: Abramowicz, W. (ed.) BIS 2015. LNBIP, vol. 228, pp. 113–125. Springer, Cham (2015). https://doi.org/10.1007/978-3-319-26762-3_11

Showcasing Modelio and pure:variants Integration in REVaMP² Project

Alessandra Bagnato[1(✉)], Alexandre Beaufays[1], Etienne Brosse[1],
Kaïs Chaabouni[1], Uwe Ryssel[2], Michael Schulze[2], and Andrey Sadovykh[1,3]

[1] Softeam, 21 Avenue Victor Hugo, 75116 Paris, France
{alessandra.bagnato,alexandre.beaufays,etienne.brosse,
kais.chaabouni}@softeam.fr
[2] pure-systems GmbH, Otto-von-Guericke-Str. 28, 39104 Magdeburg, Germany
{uwe.ryssel,michael.schulze}@puresystems.com
[3] Innopolis University, Kazan, Russia
a.sadovykh@innopolis.ru

Abstract. REVaMP² project is part of the ITEA 3 industry-driven Research, Development and Innovation programme in the domain of software innovation. REVaMP² project aims to develop automated and comprehensive tools that support massive customizing of "Software-Intensive Systems and Services" (SIS) Product Lines (PL). This approach requires agile round-trip engineering processes for managing the different configurations in legacy assets, and for more systematic and automated variability management. For this purpose, the project puts among its priorities the standardization of a variability language called "Variability Exchange Language" (VEL) as a format for describing variability in models. This paper showcases the integration of the model-driven engineering (MDE) tool "Modelio" with the variability management tool "pure::variants" using the VEL language as data exchange format. VEL is used to model both the feature model, also referred to as "150% model", with all possible variation points and all variant configurations coming from the features selection for the variant of a specific product.

Keywords: Product Lines Engineering · Variability model · Variability

1 Introduction

"**R**ound-trip **E**ngineering and **V**ariability **M**anagement **P**latform and **P**rocess" project, abbreviated to REVaMP², is a research project that started in November 2016 under the ITEA 3 industry-driven Research, Development and Innovation programme and is scheduled for a period of 3 years. The consortium of the project is composed of 30 partners from 5 countries and includes universities, research institutes, IT companies including Softeam (project leader), and industrial giants such as ABB, AVL, Bosch, Siemens, Scania, SAAB and

© Springer Nature Switzerland AG 2019
X. Franch et al. (Eds.): PROFES 2019, LNCS 11915, pp. 590–595, 2019.
https://doi.org/10.1007/978-3-030-35333-9_43

Thales [1]. REVaMP^2 aims to conceive, develop and evaluate the first comprehensive automation tool-chain and associated executable process to support round-trip engineering of "Software-Intensive Systems and Services" (SIS) Product Lines (PL) and thereby helping to profitably engineer mass customized products and services. The Product Lines approach offers significant cost reductions in customization and rapid development of products targeting various market segments. However, Product Lines Engineering (PLE) often requires a complex modelling and a co-evolution of multiple assets. This hinders the proliferation of the PLE approach and constraints its accessibility for small and medium-sized enterprises (SME) and for a large community of system developers [2,3]. In order to tackle this issue, several tools were conceived, during REVaMP^2 project, in an attempt to formalize and automate the variability management process such as the variability management tool named "pure::variants" [4]. "pure::variants" provides a set of features for managing variability in the context of software development. These features can be applied across several development process phases such as specification, design, and implementation independently from the used language. This implies that "pure::variants" can be used in model-driven engineering (MDE) approaches to manage variability in UML models for example. Moreover, "pure::variants" allows variability models to be exported using "Variability Exchange Language" (VEL) [5] serialized as XML files. Thus, these variability models can be exploited for communicating with MDE tools such as Modelio [6]. Modelio is an MDE workbench that provides both model editing, such as UML2 and SysML standards, and round-trip engineering including code generation and reverse engineering. The rest of the paper is structured as follows. Section 2 introduces the different variability concepts as defined in VEL. Section 3 provides a general overview of our proposed approach to express variability in UML/SysML models. Preliminary results of the variability and UML co-modelling are presented in Sect. 4. Finally, Sect. 5 summarizes the paper and presents some future work.

2   Variability

A variability model consists of a set of variation points that can occur in specific parts of the customizable product which in our case is a UML/SysML model. There are four types of variation points, two for structural variations that affect the entirety of the model such as selecting parts of the model, and two for parameter variations that affect only the values of the specific parameter. Hence, the variation points can be categorized as follows:

- Optional structural: No restriction, all structural variation can be selected independently.
- Alternative structural: One and only one structural variation can be selected.
- Alternative parameter: One and only one parameter value can be selected.
- Calculated parameter: Parameter value is calculated by an given expression.

Variability management tool handles several types of variability models across its software product line development workflow. It manages a software product line as a set of integrated "Feature Models" describing the common and variable features and "Variant Models" specifying individual products from the product line. Figure 1 shows an example of feature model (in the left) that contains mandatory features common for all variants of "Car" such as the "Window" and an optional feature such as the "Air Conditionner". Each feature can have a variety of alternatives such as the possibility to have an electric or manual window in the car. Contrary to the feature model that contains all possibilities, the variant model contain a configuration with a selection of alternatives that define a product variant. Figure 1 shows an example of variant model (in the right) where we select a car with two windows, manual gear control and a radio.

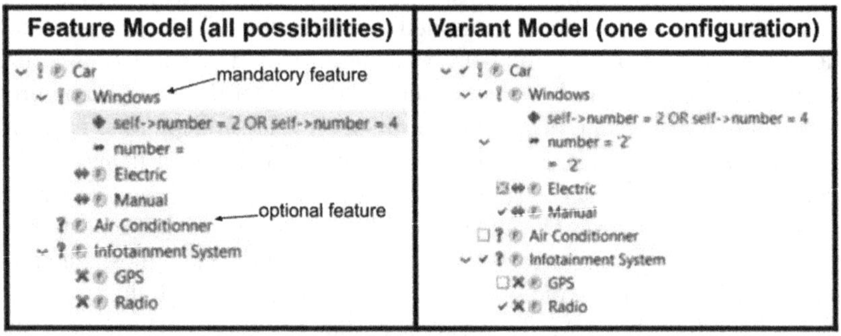

Fig. 1. Feature model vs variant model in pure::variants

3   Variability Integration

Our integration of variability in Model Driven Engineering consists in designing a new UML profile in a Modelio module that includes "Stereotypes" to match the different types of variation points as defined in VEL. The properties of the stereotypes describe a set of information related to variability such as conditions that trigger the variation. In addition, these extensions can be used in UML/SysML diagrams to represent product lines with all possible features (also called 150% model). The "150% models" contain all possible assets of the system and act in a similar way as the feature model in VEL. These constraints can be applied to every asset represented in UML/SysML models such as classes, associations, description notes, attributes, diagrams (e.g. class diagram, sequence diagram), parameters of elements (e.g. "Multiplicity-Max"), etc.

VEL language is used to create two types of files:

1. Description file that represents the global variability model with all possible variation points and associated variations.
2. Configuration file that contains a selection of features for a variant of a product.

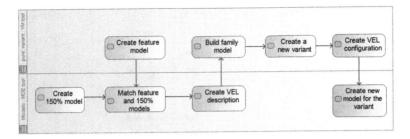

Fig. 2. The modelling process between VM and MDE tools

The global process for creating a model variant with both an MDE tool and a Variability Management (VM) tool (see Fig. 2) can be summarized with the following steps:

- Create a 150% model with MDE tool representing the product line assets with all its variations (see Fig. 3)
- Generate a VEL description file corresponding to the selected 150% Model
- Import the VEL description file with the variability management tool to create a family model
- With the variability management tool couple description file with feature and variant models to create a VEL configuration file
- Import the VEL configuration file within MDE Tool to create the variant of the model which results in duplicating the 150% model all its elements and then removing the elements that are not included in the variant and the variability related constraints. It also changes the value of the elements constrained with parameter variations (see Fig. 4).

4   Results

The integrating of variability in Model Driven Engineering approach resulted in developing a new environment for the modelling process that includes the use of two tools. The first tool is Modelio MDE with its extension "Variability Designer" [7] which provides the variability profile described in the previous section with a set of functionalities (commands, wizards, etc.) that allow users to annotate their UML/SysML elements with stereotyped UML constraints that correspond to the four types of variation points described in Sect. 2. It also provides VEL import/export facilities. The second tool is pure::variant which act as variability management tool that supports VEL language.

These tools have shown promising results in managing variability models and generating variants of the 150% model. Figure 3 depicts 150% system model where the supercharged model is annotated with variability constrains. Then, based on a variant configuration, the variant system model is automatically created containing the selected sub-systems with two windows, manual gear and radio.

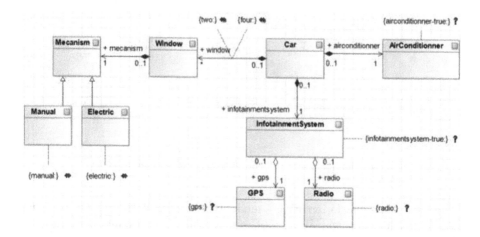

Fig. 3. Annotated 150% system model in Modelio

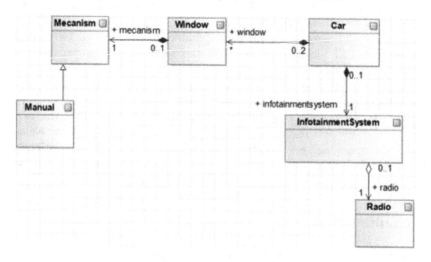

Fig. 4. Variant in Modelio

We note that, as pointed by Dubinsky et al. [8], instead of adopting PLE, many companies clone an existing product and modify it to fit the new customer needs using the clone-and-own approach. Nevertheless, these tools could help companies to adopt PLE in software and information system engineering in order to efficiently managing variability in models.

5   Conclusion and Future Work

At this stage of the development, all the main features are functional, but the user experience and the usability of the tool can still be improved. Additional features are planned for the future such as adding the ability to view and edit the variation points in a more intuitive way, and to add data verification on relevant fields. Moreover, we consider integrating other tools to further automate the process, such as But4Reuse [9] tool helps to automatically create the 150% model from a set of pre-existing variants. Finally, we consider performing several experimentation of this approach with other modelling languages such as ArchiMate in order to expand its field of application.

Acknowledgements. The research leading to these results was partially funded by the ITEA3 project 15010 REVaMP^2, which is funded in part by the national funding agencies in various countries including Fonds Unique Interministériel (FUI), the Ile-de France region and the Banque Publique d'Investissement (BPI) in France.

References

1. REVaMP^2 project homepage. http://www.revamp2-project.eu. Accessed 22 July 2019
2. Sadovykh, A., Bagnato, A., Robin, J., Viehl, A., Ziadi, T., Martinez, J.: REVAMP: challenges and innovation roadmap for variability management in round-trip engineering of software-intensive systems (2017)
3. Martinez, J., Ziadi, T., Bissyandé, T., Klein, J., Le Traon, Y.: Bottom-up adoption of software product lines - a generic and extensible approach. In: SPLC 2015, Nashville, US, 20–24 July (2015)
4. pure::variants. www.pure-systems.com/products/pure-variants-9.html. Accessed 15 Apr 2019
5. Variability-Exchange-Language. variability-exchange-language.org. Accessed 22 July 2019
6. Modeliosoft homepage. https://www.modeliosoft.com/fr/. Accessed 22 July 2019
7. Variability Designer Module. https://forge.modelio.org/projects/variabilitydesigner. Accessed 15 Apr 2019
8. Dubinsky, Y., Rubin, J., Berger, T., Duszynski, S., Becker, M., Czarnecki, K.: An exploratory study of cloning in industrial software product lines. In: 2013 17th European Conference on Software Maintenance and Reengineering, pp. 25–34. IEEE, March 2013
9. BUT4Reuse homepage. https://but4reuse.github.io/. Accessed 24 July 2019

DECODER - DEveloper COmpanion
for Documented and annotatEd code Reference

Victoria Torres⑩, Miriam Gil$^{(\boxtimes)}$ ⑩, and Vicente Pelechano⑩

Universitat Politècnica de València, 46022 València, Spain
{vtorres,mgil,pele}@pros.upv.es

Abstract. Software is everywhere and the productivity of Software Engineers has increased radically with the advent of new specifications, design and programming paradigms and languages. The main objective of the DECODER project is to introduce radical solutions to increase productivity by increasing the abstraction level, at specification stage, using requirements engineering techniques to integrate more complete specifications into the development process, and formal methods to reduce the time and efforts for integration testing. DECODER project will develop a methodology and tools to improve the productivity of the software development process for medium-criticality applications in the domains of IoT, Cloud Computing, and Operating Systems by combining Natural Language Processing techniques, modelling techniques and Formal Methods. A radical improvement is expected from the management and transformation of informal data into material (herein called "knowledge") that can be assimilated by any party involved in a development process. The project expects an average benefit of 20% in terms of efforts on several use cases belonging to the beforehand mentioned domains and will provide recommendations on how to generalize the approach to other medium-critical domains.

Keywords: Requirements analysis · Open source software · Software engineering · Operating systems · Computer languages

1 Project Summary

The DEveloper COmpanion for Documented and annotatEd code Reference (DECODER) project is a H2020 project (H2020-ICT-16-2018 Software Technologies call) that has received funding from the European Union's H2020 research and innovation program under the grant agreement 824231. The project has a duration of 36 months, starting in January 2019 and finishing in December 2021. Currently, the project has already reached the first six months, period in which all work packages have started, and some deliverables have also been submitted. Updated information about the project can be found in the https://www.decoder-project.eu web site. Regarding the project

This work has been developed with the financial support of the European Union's Horizon 2020 research and innovation programme under grant agreement No. 824231 and the Spanish State Research Agency under the project TIN2017-84094-R and co-financed with ERDF.

X. Franch et al. (Eds.): PROFES 2019, LNCS 11915, pp. 596–601, 2019.
https://doi.org/10.1007/978-3-030-35333-9_44

consortium, it is formed by contributors from seven partners from four different European countries (cf. Table 1).

Table 1. List of participating partners and key positions

Partner	Short name	Country	Key positions
Technikon	TEC	Austria	Project Leader and WP8 Leader
CEA Tech	CEA	France	WP1, WP3 Leader
Tree Technology SA	TREE	Spain	WP2 Leader
Capgemini España SL	CAPGEMINI	Spain	WP4 Leader
Universitat Politècnica de València	UPV (PROS)	Spain	WP5 Leader
Sysgo AG	SYSGO	Germany	WP6 Leader
OW2	OW2	France	WP7 Leader

2 Project Motivation

Software drives our modern economy; it is indeed present everywhere, from critical infrastructures supporting our societies, such as energy supply and transportation, down to the smart devices connecting us to the internet (also called IoT). However, too much time is wasted during software development projects due to wrong decisions taken along the whole process. The main reason for taking such decisions is the amount of information stakeholders have to deal with and the lack of proper documentation. To this end, software production is insufficiently supported by effective tools and often, engineers lack a systematic approach for the development and safe reuse of components and their associated knowledge. In addition, a typical development process requires interactions of many stakeholders, at very different abstraction levels, and often over ambiguous and incomplete documents. This makes the integration and even more the maintenance of software systems extremely difficult and costly.

Within this context, support to properly handle project knowledge derived from all the involved artefacts (e.g., source code, specifications, informal documents, etc.) is required; it is software project intelligence that assist developers with an instantaneous access to its documentation, abstract models, verification data and traceability matrix.

3 Detailed Description of the Goals of the Project

The main goal of DECODER is to build a smart environment that could assist and help developers, analysts, testers, etc. to improve the software development process. To achieve this goal, in DECODER we propose to apply and combine techniques from Natural Language Processing, Machine Learning, Process Modeling, Model Transformations, and Verification. Specifically, the detailed objectives are the following:

- Objective 1: High-level abstract models for engineers.
- Objective 2: Significantly increase the software development and maintenance efficiency.
- Objective 3: Drastically improving the use of informal knowledge and artefacts.
- Objective 4: Build collaborative knowledge and smart user interfaces.
- Objective 5: Improve the overall quality of software for medium-criticality domains.

To achieve the aforementioned goals, the project has been designed according to eight work packages as shown in Fig. 1. While the work developed in work packages 1 to 6 are focused mainly on the design and implementation of the technological innovation foreseen in DECODER, in work packages 7 and 8, common activities in such European projects such as dissemination and management activities will be performed.

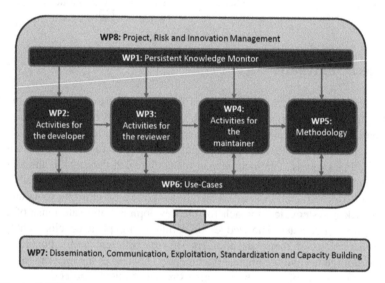

Fig. 1. DECODER work package distribution and the relationships between them

4 Project Expected Achievements and Outcome

The DECODER project addresses objective ICT-16-2018 scope a) and both areas thereof (i.e. code and resources abstraction, and advanced software systems development). The project will support this objective by obtaining the following achievements:

- Improve the productivity of software engineers of medium-criticality applications along the whole lifecycle process by several means: (1) increasing the abstraction level, namely at specification stage, (2) using requirements engineering techniques to integrate more complete specifications into the development process, and

(3) using Formal Methods to reduce the time and efforts for integration testing, replacing it by formal analyses. This achievement is related to objectives 1 and 3.

- Development of novel languages defined from the abstraction of the formalisms used today for requirements analysis and specification: (1) an abstract formal design language, namely ASFM, to navigate between different levels of abstractions, and (2) an abstract graphical specification language, namely GSL, capable of intuitively specifying some code and generating detailed specifications in ACSL/ACSL++ and JML. This achievement is related to objective 1.
- Development of new languages and methods to formalize software requirements that are often informal based on NLP techniques to formalize in a human understandable formalism the informal requirements. These new languages will permit to describe data and processes amenable for specification and refinements. This achievement is related to objectives 1, 3 and 4.
- Demonstrate the applicability and viability of the proposed solution on several use cases from very different categories: (1) IoT/embedded systems, (2) Artificial Intelligence and IoT domains (computer vision), (3) enterprise computing (including Cloud computing/Big Data and Middleware/Cloud computing). This achievement is related to objectives 2 and 5.

Regarding the outcomes, one of the major outcomes of DECODER is the Persistent Knowledge Monitor (PKM) that will be developed in WP1. This PKM will provide a "central" infrastructure to store, access, and trace all the persistent data, information and knowledge related to a given software or ecosystem (notably its source code and related artefacts, and also derived information). As Fig. 1 shows, the PKM will be used in work packages 2, 3, and 4, where activities for developers, reviewers, and maintainers over the PKM are defined. Next, we detail the major outcomes of these work packages.

Regarding WP2 where activities for developers are defined, support for the transformation of informal code related data (e.g., text that captures requirements, informal specifications, internal documentation or even comments in the source code) into formal documentation and also summarize source code will be provided. The generation of formal documentation provides useful information for users who have created that piece of code and have to return to it at some point as well as future maintainers.

Regarding WP3 where activities for reviewers are defined, support for saving in the knowledge database is provided. In particular it will be stored what an external reviewer understands from the code, the comments and how the code intentions are automatically verified. This expert knowledge is usually lost after the code review and the advanced users need to recreate it repeatedly. In this WP, we formalize the results of the review activities into an Abstract Semi-Formal Model. Ideally, such a model would only contain formal properties of the code written in ACSL/ACSL++ and JML and automatically verified by formal deductive verification. However, the definition of such a model requires far too much resources and expertise to build it from scratch. To lower this expertise, we accept definitions coming from different sources: formal description, function calls without any side effect, sequence diagram, formal visualization and abstraction. The ASFM language will contain the functional logic notions of data structure invariant, type states, behaviors based on pre/post-conditions. If the reviewer can write them manually in the ACSL/ACSL++ and JML annotation languages, WP3 proposes many ways to incrementally build and enrich such Abstract Models between the code and the logic specification.

Regarding WP4 where activities for the maintainer are defined, support for controlling the impact of changes through implementation of traceability management will be provided. This means establishing links and maintaining cross-references between artefacts. For this purpose, NLP technologies will be used to build and manage a traceability matrix between requirements, code and documentation. This matrix is a sparse matrix of traces. A trace is made of two anchors (or trace location) with additional semantic attribute (role, level of confidence) and some more technical or management attributes. The anchor references an element in the PKM. The traceability matrix binds high-level requirements with fine-grain specifications of code to help controlling the impact of changes. The traceability matrix binds a piece of code with a piece of documentation to help experienced people to make explicit all implicit knowledge that exists in their mind and will help new staff members to quickly grasp the big picture and the crucial details before doing any change. Traceability management is extended to check consistency with test cases.

Besides these four work packages, in work package 5 methodology support for end-users (C, C++, and Java programmers) along the life cycle will be provided. To ensure that certain software properties are satisfied when applying the proposed methodology, an innovative methodology will be defined based on formal and agile techniques. As a result, the proposed methodology will define the different stages of the complete life cycle development, the different roles involved as well as the intermediate artefacts built, modified or just consumed in the different proposed stages. In addition, the supporting tool will integrate the set of tools proposed in WP1 and WP2 as well as the artefacts consumed and produced by these tools along the life cycle. As a result, the methodology will ensure the generation of better documentation, the construction of critical and medium critical applications ensuring the quality of the obtained artefact as well as the application of the existing standards.

Finally, the framework and tools developed in the previous work packages will be put into practice with real source code, specifically on large use cases provided by partners that are not themselves tool developers but applications developers. This will be performed within the context of WP6, where besides demonstration purposes, feedback on the quality of the maintenance activities in the form of measurements (productivity gains) and recommendations will be also generated. These experimental activities can be considered as a first step towards the later exploitation of the project's tools and framework. In addition to these six work packages DECODER defines two more packages, WP7 and WP8 which are intended mainly for dissemination and management purposes respectively.

5   Existing Collaborations with Other Projects

At the current state, DECODER project maintains collaborations with several projects:

- Project VESSEDIA[1] (Verification Engineering of Safety and Security Critical Dynamic Industrial Applications): Our project will reuse the tools developed by VESSEDIA to develop modular specifications and proofs to render formal specification activities easier to manage.
- Project OpenReq[2] (Intelligent Recommendation & Decision Technologies for Community-Driven Requirements Engineering): Our project will get inspiration from the original requirements specification novelties to enforce its NLP activities and define better languages for expressing semi-formalized requirements. We will assist to the OpenReq week in September 2019 where DECODER project will be presented.

6   Interest in Participating in the EU Project Space at PROFES

DECODER has different reasons to participate in PROFES. First, we would like to announce the project to the PROFES community, a community mainly focused on the software process improvement where DECODER is also putting all its efforts. Secondly, we would like to present all PROFES participants the major research outcomes achieved during the first six months of the project and discuss any potential improvement to them. Thirdly, we would like to learn from the PROFES community the last advances and research developed in this field in order to improve DECODER execution. Finally, we also want to attract DECODER early adopters from practitioners, researchers, and educators interested in the software process improvement. Besides PROFES, in DECODER we have a dissemination plan that has also resulted in the participation of different events during the first six months of execution (see Table 2). However, it is important to continue this task both in industry and in academic contexts. For this reason, the different partners from the consortium are actively working to participate in different types of events, not just to announce the DECODER project but also to discuss the research outcomes with the scientific and industrial communities interested in improving the software development process. In particular, DECODER contributors are working to participate in the next months in the events listed in Table 2.

Table 2. Past and upcoming events where DECODER has participated or will participate

Event	Country	Dates
Testnet Spring event	Nieuwegein, Netherlands	11 May 2019
OW2con'19	Paris, France	12–13 June 2019
OpenReq week	Hamburg, Germany	2–6 September 2019
EclipseCon Europe	Ludwigsburg, Germany	21–24 October 2019
DeVoxx	Antwerp, Belgium	4–8 November 2019
Paris Open Source Summit	Paris, France	10–11 December 2019

---

[1] https://vessedia.eu/.

[2] https://openreq.eu/.

DECIDE: DevOps for Trusted, Portable and Interoperable Multi-cloud Applications Towards the Digital Single Market

Leire Orue-Echevarria[1]([⊠]) [iD], Juncal Alonso[1] [iD],
Marisa Escalante[1] [iD], Kyriakos Stefanidis[2], and Lorenzo Blasi[3] [iD]

[1] TECNALIA, Bizkaia Technology Park, Derio, Spain
{Leire.orue-echevarria, juncal.alonso,
marisa.escalante}@tecnalia.com
[2] Fraunhofer Fokus, Berlin, Germany
kyriakos.stefanidis@fokus.fraunhofer.de
[3] Hewlett Packard Italiana s.r.l., Cernusco sul Naviglio, Italy
lorenzo.blasi@hpe.com

Abstract. The transformation from a product to service economy means that companies need to become software service providers as well as consumers. Cloud enables greater business agility by making IT infrastructure more flexible. The current trends of deploying applications following a hybrid cloud, multi-cloud or cross-cloud architecture, as well as the design, development and operation of multi-cloud native applications based on microservices present several challenges for their developers and operators. This paper presents a solution implemented in the context of the European project DECIDE which aims to support DevOps teams in the design, pre-deployment, contracting, deployment and operation of multi-cloud native applications with the provisioning of an integrated framework. The project is entering its late phase, in which the DevOps framework is currently being validated and evaluated in various use cases.

Keywords: DevOps · Architectural patterns · Optimization · Automatic deployment · Redeployment · Cloud service broker · Multi-cloud Applications · Microservices · Cloud SLA

1 Project Data

DECIDE: DevOps for Trusted, Portable and Interoperable Multi-Cloud Applications towards the Digital Single Market.

The project's website is: https://www.decide-h2020.eu. The duration is 36 months, spanning from December 2016 to November 2019. The project is currently ongoing. The technical developments are being finished and the integrated DECIDE DevOps Framework is planned to be released by August 2019.

The DECIDE consortium is composed by 8 partners from 6 European countries (Spain, United Kingdom, Germany, Belgium, Italy and Switzerland), which are:

© Springer Nature Switzerland AG 2019
X. Franch et al. (Eds.): PROFES 2019, LNCS 11915, pp. 602–607, 2019.
https://doi.org/10.1007/978-3-030-35333-9_45

TECNALIA, EXPERIS IT, ARSYS, AIMES, Fraunhofer FOKUS, Time.lex, HPE and CloudBroker.

This consortium has the right balance between academia and industry in order to achieve cutting-edge research results in the field of Computer Science (Cloud and Software Engineering). It involves internationally recognized research institutes (TECNALIA, Fraunhofer), large companies (HPE, Experis IT), and SMEs (Time.Lex, ARSYS, AIMES, and CloudBroker), with different profiles such as Cloud Service Providers (ARSYS and AIMES), cloud service brokers (CloudBroker), integrators (HPE, Experis IT) and ICT legal companies (Time.lex).

2 Objectives of the Project

The main scientific and technological (ST) objective of DECIDE is to provide a new generation of multi-cloud services-based software framework, enabling techniques, tools and mechanisms to design, develop, operate, and dynamically (re-)deploy multi-cloud aware applications in an ecosystem of reliable, interoperable, and legal compliant cloud services. DECIDE will provide architectural patterns and the needed supporting tools for developers and operators of multi-cloud application providers to develop and operate (following the DevOps approach) multi-cloud native applications that can be dynamically self-adapted and re-deployed using the "best" combination of cloud services in each moment, depending on the existing multi-cloud context considering both the multi-cloud application behavior as well as the behavior of the underlying used cloud offerings. Moreover, DECIDE will enhance the trustworthiness of multi-cloud application providers towards buyers and users of the SaaS applications by setting up a catalog of trusted, interoperable and legally compliant cloud services and the required mechanisms to register, discover, compose, use and assess them.

This main objective has been broken down into smaller scientific and technological objectives, which are explained next.

Objective 1: Set up a development, delivery and operation pipeline covering the stages that a multi-cloud native application goes through, from development to operation, providing the needed mechanisms for continuous architectural design, development, continuous integration, continuous quality control, continuous (re-)deployment and operation. To achieve that, DECIDE will provide a DevOps framework from design and non-functional requirements (NFR) gathering through operation of multi-cloud native applications in compliance with the DevOps paradigm.

Objective 2: Facilitate the continuous architectural design approach by providing a set of architectural patterns along with the supporting tool that will support the design, development, optimization and deployment of multi-cloud native applications. These patterns can be classified as development patterns, optimization patterns and deployment patterns, each covering different phases of the software development lifecycle (SDLC). The developers will be able to define their own set of prioritized NFRs (e.g. Availability, Security, Scalability, Performance, Cost) and, based on them, DECIDE will provide a suggestion of which architectural patterns need to be applied, how they should be applied, to which component and in which order, so as to diminish trade – offs powered by a decision algorithm. These multi-cloud architectural patterns will allow the design and development of distributed applications over heterogeneous cloud resources whose components are prepared to be deployed on different cloud service providers (CSPs) and still, they all work in an integrated way and transparently for the end-user. The main result of this objective is DECIDE ARCHITECT.

Objective 3: Provide mechanisms to analyze alternative cloud deployment scenarios and their impact in the NFRs of the application (e.g. availability, performance), in the multi-cloud application SLA (MCSLA) as well as in the application costs, suggesting the developers and operators the best cloud deployment alternatives - through the simulation of the behavior of the application under stressful conditions - and the cloud resources and cloud nodes communications. The main result of this objective is DECIDE OPTIMUS.

Objective 4: Make available broadly and cross border cloud services, so that enterprises and developers can re-use and combine cloud services, assembling a network of interoperable, legal compliant, quality assessed (against SLAs) single and composite cloud services. This will be achieved through the Advanced Cloud Service (meta-) intermediator (ACSmI), which will provide means to assess continuous real time verification of the cloud services non-functional requirements fulfilment and legislation compliance enforcement. ACSmI will also provide a cloud services store where companies and developers across Europe can easily access centrally negotiated deals of compliant and accredited applications developed by the software sector.

Objective 5: Enable the self-adaptation and (semi-)automatic redeployment of (parts of) the application in real time, in order to comply with the set of predefined NFRs of the application. DECIDE ADAPT will pro-actively adjust the running configuration of the application based on measurements that are derived from the dynamic monitoring activities of both the application and the non-functional properties of the CSPs and cloud offerings where the application is deployed and making use of.

3   Envisioned and Achieved Results of the Project

DECIDE has envisioned the following results, delivered in the form of software components and available for download in the project's public git repository[1]:

- DECIDE DevOps Framework: is the graphical (web-based) entry point to the DECIDE tool suite and it allows multi-cloud native application developers and operators to manage their applications, from dev to ops, following the DevOps philosophy. The DECIDE DevOps Framework integrates the tools that will be presented next as well as additional tools such as:
  - A general form-based editor, which is used to create all the needed information about the application and the corresponding microservices, and to determine the non-functional requirements that are key for that application.

---

[1] https://git.code.tecnalia.com/DECIDE_Public/DECIDE_Components.

- Integration of tools offered in the market for Continuous Integration and Continuous Quality such as Jenkins and SonarQube, in order to cover the complete development lifecycle of an application.
- A Multi-Cloud Service Level Agreements (MCSLA) editor, that allows to create multi-cloud Service Level Objectives (SLO) taking as input the SLOs of the cloud services from the selected CSPs where the application will be deployed initially. These SLOs will be used by ADAPT to verify that these values are kept.
- An application description, which is the way in which all tools communicate with each other for seamless interoperability (Fig. 1).

Fig. 1. DECIDE DevOps framework user interface

- DECIDE ARCHITECT: This tool aims at recommending to the developers, architectural patterns for the design, optimization and deployment of a multi-cloud native application taking into consideration the non-functional requirements (NFRs) as defined by the developer. These patterns are complemented with a set of fundamental patterns, covering basic aspects of multi-cloud native applications. The supported NFRs are performance, scalability, availability, location, cost and legal level. ARCHITECT is offered in two flavors, as an Eclipse plug-in as well as integrated in the DevOps Framework. Both tools have the same functionalities.
- DECIDE OPTIMUS: This tool is composed of two complementary modules, namely a classification tool and a simulation engine. The main objective of OPTIMUS is to provide the best configuration for the deployment of a multi-cloud application on multiple cloud services. In a first step, the developer needs to classify the microservices (e.g. computing, public ip, database, etc.) and their infrastructure requirements while in a second step, taking into consideration the previous data and the defined NFRs, OPTIMUS provides a simulation and optimization of the best combination of cloud services. The algorithm used for this is an adapted version of NGSA II for the problem statement of DECIDE. OPTIMUS is offered also in two flavors, as an eclipse plugin and as part of the UI of the DevOps framework.

- ACSmI (Advanced Cloud Service meta-Intermediator): ACSmI is a tool that allows to discover, benchmark, contract and monitor trusted cloud service offerings. To this end, ACSmI discovery allows to select, manually or through an API to OPTIMUS, the most appropriate set of cloud services, namely virtual machines, databases and storage considering the NFRs specified by the developer. ACSmI contracting allows for an automatic contracting of the cloud services proposed by OPTIMUS. The CSPs currently covered by this functionality are Amazon, Arsys, CloudSigma and Azure. ACSmI monitoring monitors that the CSPs comply with their SLAs, and more specifically, with the SLOs for availability, performance, location and the user entered cost. Finally, ACSmI billing presents the costs attained by each cloud service in a single point.
- ADAPT: It allows the automatic deployment and (semi-)automatic adaptation of the application and redeployment in another multi-cloud configuration when certain conditions are not met. These conditions are, on one hand, the violations of the application's own MCSLA and, on the other hand, the non-fulfilment of the SLOs of the CSPs where the application is deployed (monitored by ACSmI monitoring). These conditions will trigger a violation alert and will cause the OPTIMUS tool to be launched again in order to search for another deployment configuration. Depending on the technological complexity requirement, and the initially prioritized requirements by the user, the application will either be readapted automatically or an alert to the operator will be sent along with a diagnosis of what malfunctioned so that a new optimal configuration can be found.

The aforementioned tools extend the traditional CI/CD pipeline and provide their functionalities throughout the whole application lifecycle. In the design phase, DevOps framework supports the unified definition of the application properties and NFRs while ARCHITECT suggests architectural patterns based on those NFRs. In the testing phase and prior to deployment, OPTIMUS adds the notion of pre-deployment where various deployment schemas are presented based on the application NFRs and the available CSP offerings. ACSmI on the other hand, handles the discovery of the CSP offerings. In the deployment phase, ADAPT provides automatic deployment and configuration management on a multi-cloud environment while ACSmI handles the contracting of the CSP offerings. During operation, ACSmI and ADAPT monitor the application performance against the defined SLA and, in case of SLA violation, ADAPT provides the means for automatic or semi-automatic redeployment of the affected modules in alternative CSPs. The management and orchestration of the tools is done via a unified web-based user interface provided by the DevOps framework.

The evaluation process of the key results against the success criteria defined in the Description of Action of DECIDE project took place in three widely differing use cases, with different requirements. These were a clinical data entry tool (StreamLine), a change-tracking center (CTC), and a block-chain based energy-trading platform.

The project's validation strategy follows an iterative approach where the tools are assessed after the three major release milestones of the project. At the time of writing, the results are limited to qualified, predominantly positive, comments, particularly around usability and function with a positive quantitative result of a 50% reported efficiency improvement on the multi-cloud deployment using the ADAPT module.

More concrete quantitative results are expected after the finalization of the last evaluation at the end of the project.

A market analysis has shown that while there are several DevOps integrated tool suites in the market such as Xebialabs[2] (XL DevOps platform, XL Release and XL deploy), IBM UrbanCode[3], Microfocus[4], AWS Developers Tools[5], and Microsoft Azure DevOps[6], they do not full cover the functionalities presented above for Dev (ARCHITECT, OPTIMUS and ADAPT Deployment), nor the complete Ops lifecycle of monitoring the application and the CSP and re-adapting the application in a (semi-) automatic way.

4   Collaboration with Other Projects

The collaboration in the project has been classified according to three angles or perspectives:

- Types of collaboration: technical, promotional, commercial.
- Levels of collaboration: project organization and interest group
- Degree of collaboration continuous, frequent and punctual.

Technical collaboration has been done with the projects COLA, SHiELD, MUSA, CloudWatch2 and ACROSS, organizations such as OW2 and groups such as the intercloud cluster, software engineering cluster (SE4SA), ERRIN network and Common Dissemination Booster. Promotional collaborations have been performed with projects such as ACTiCLOUD, MELODIC, RESTASSURED, CLOUDPERFECT, MegaMart and TANGO.

5   Interest for the Participation in PROFES 2019

DECIDE would like to demonstrate the results of the project and gather feedback and input from the community of DevOps practitioners, in order to assess the commercial and scientific interest of such a framework and approach. This can result either in commercial opportunities to exploit the results, contributions to the code, which has been released in an open repository in GitLab (link above) and soon in OW2, or in extensions and improvements of the tool chain in new research and commercial projects.

---

[2] https://xebialabs.com/.

[3] https://www.ibm.com/us-en/marketplace/application-release-automation.

[4] https://www.microfocus.com/en-us/services/devops-solutions.

[5] https://aws.amazon.com/en/products/developer-tools/.

[6] https://azure.microsoft.com/us-en/services/devops/.

Q-Rapids: Quality-Aware Rapid Software Development – An H2020 Project

Lidia López and Marc Oriol$^{(\boxtimes)}$

Universitat Politècnica de Catalunya (UPC), Barcelona, Spain
{llopez,moriol}@essi.upc.edu

Abstract. This work reports the objectives, current state, and outcomes of the Q-Rapids H2020 project. Q-Rapids (Quality-Aware Rapid Software Development) proposes a data-driven approach to the production of software following very short development cycles. The focus of Q-Rapids is on quality aspects, represented through quality requirements. The Q-Rapids platform, which is the tangible software asset emerging from the project, mines software repositories and usage logs to identify candidate quality requirements that may ameliorate the values of strategic indicators like product quality, time to market or team productivity. Four companies are providing use cases to evaluate the platform and associated processes.

Keywords: Software quality · Data-driven requirements engineering · Rapid software development · Quality requirements

1 Introduction

The Q-Rapids project (Quality-Aware Rapid Software Development) is a 3-year project funded by the European Union's Horizon 2020 research and innovation programme under grant agreement No 732253. It started in November 2016 and finishes in October 2019. The project website is at https://www.q-rapids.eu/.

The Q-Rapids consortium is composed of serven partners from five European countries, namely three research organisations, one SME, two mid-caps and one corporative:

- Universitat Politècnica de Catalunya, Spain, acting as coordinator.
- University of Oulu, Finland.
- IESE Fraunhofer, Germany.
- Bittium Wireless OY, Finland.
- Softeam, France.
- ITTI SP ZOO, Poland.
- Nokia Solutions and Networks OY, Finland.

As a result, the consortium combines long research tradition in software development and cutting-edge technological knowhow in versatile ICT sectors.

X. Franch et al. (Eds.): PROFES 2019, LNCS 11915, pp. 608–612, 2019.
https://doi.org/10.1007/978-3-030-35333-9_46

2   Project Goals

Figure 1 summarizes the concept of the Q-Rapids project. It shows the full data-driven cycle. Quality requirements (QRs) are incrementally elicited, refined and improved based on data gathered from software repositories, project management tools, system usage and quality of service. This data is analysed and aggregated into quality-related key strategic indicators (e.g., time-to-market delay related to not including the implementation of a given QR in the next development cycle) which are presented to decision makers using a highly informative dashboard. QRs scheduled for the next cycle are integrated with functional requirements for their uniform treatment in the rapid software development life cycle. See [1] for more details.

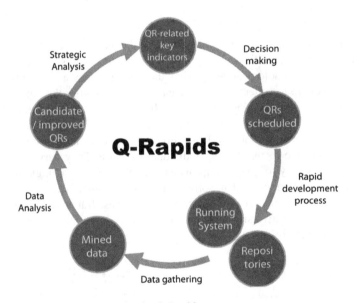

Fig. 1. Q-Rapids concept

The general objectives of the project are:

- *Objective GO1.* Improve the quality levels of software products and services with the support of data-driven IT infrastructure and associated methods and techniques.
- *Objective GO2.* Increase the productivity of the software life cycle with a seamless integration of quality requirements into the development process.
- *Objective GO3.* Reduce the time to market of software products and services by making optimal decisions based on strong evidence and solid experience-based decision-making models.

These general objectives are made actionable through several scientific objectives:

- *Objective SO1.* To provide methods to systematically collect and analyse runtime and development time data to improve software quality.

- *Objective SO2*. To define a rapid software life cycle process that integrates quality requirements and functional requirements into a holistic method.
- *Objective SO3*. To provide quality-related key strategic indicators to support decision makers in managing the development process from a quality-aware perspective.
- *Objective SO4*. To implement adequate tool support to a quality-aware software life cycle.

The outcome of all these objectives will be a validated Q-Rapids framework: a quality-aware rapid software development process supported by advanced tools and methods.

3 Project Use Cases

As usual in H2020 research and innovation actions, the feasibility of Q-Rapids is being demonstrated using a significant portfolio of diverse use cases to demonstrate its potential. From a methodological perspective, the use cases play a two-fold role in this project: (1) They help to collect empirical data needed to solidify the objectives of the project and to create the baseline upon which the methods and tools are defined, and (2) they enable the assessment of the fulfilment of these objectives as the project progresses and thus demonstrate the feasibility and impact of the project results.

Figure 2 shows the focus of every individual use case. They vary in: main focus (e.g., from transparency to quality improvement), setting (from a single product to a product line to multiple independent software products), domain (from highly privacy-aware systems to telecommunication networks) and process framework (from Scrum to ad hoc methods). Their diversity is both an opportunity and a challenge for the solutions provided in the project.

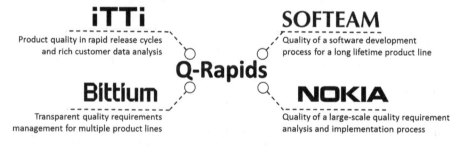

Fig. 2. Q-Rapids use cases

4 Current State

The Q-Rapids project was organized into five phases:

- *Phase 1*: project set-up (months 1–6). Main result: the Q-Rapids platform reference architecture, together with an implementation plan and the use cases specification.
- *Phase 2*: proof of concept (months 7–15). Main result: a first integrated version of the Q-Rapids platform, with simple techniques available.

- *Phase 3*: consolidated framework (months 16–24). Main result: Q-Rapids platform integrating more powerful techniques and methods, with increasing validation from the use cases.
- *Phase 4*: final framework (months 25–33). Main result: final solution offering full functionality and fully-fledged associated processes.
- *Phase 5*: project finalization (months 34–36). Main result: packaging of the final solution.

At the moment of writing this report, Q-Rapids is entering in the final phase. The current framework is completed and the summative evaluation is being reported. A detailed overview of the project is described in [2].

5 Achieved Outcomes

The main outcomes of the Q-Rapids project are the Q-Rapids platform and Q-Rapids process.

The Q-Rapids platform is an advanced data-driven platform to manage quality in Agile and Rapid Software Development. Details on the consolidated version (phase 3) are described in [3]. Q-Rapids platform assists decision makers to make informed decisions by means of:

- Assessing the quality of the software under development at different abstraction levels. The platform relies on a quality model (QM) to define three abstraction levels: key strategic indicators, project and process factors, and metrics [4]. The key strategic indicators can be assessed qualitatively defining a Bayesian Network based on the factors impacting on them [5].
- Predicting future quality levels through multiple predictive methods [6].
- Semiautomatically generating Quality Requirements to improve the quality of the software if such quality goes below some specific thresholds [7].
- Providing what-if analysis simulating the quality levels of the software given a particular scenario (e.g. the addition of a new quality requirement).

The Q-Rapids process is a layered process that relies on the Q-Rapids platform to support the quality management during the development process. The process includes how to use the Q-Rapids platform at the different development activities at three levels: product, release, and sprint. As part of the process development, we defined some process metrics to support the assessment of the development process performance [8].

Q-Rapids platform addresses objective *G01* and Q-Rapids process and process metrics address *G02*. All assets together address objective G03.

6 Why Participating in PROFES 2019 European Project Space?

As mentioned above, Q-Rapids is arriving to its end and in particular, by the time of the PROFES 2019 conference, it will be definitively over. Therefore, the main interest of the consortium is to demonstrate the final platform hoping that some other project, in earlier development stages, may be interested in adopting it. The code is open source and available in GitHub (https://github.com/q-rapids) with permissive licenses, and some of the partners are willing to collaborate in future endeavours. In fact, conversations with the ITEA-3 VISDOM project (https://itea3.org/project/visdom.html) are in place to use Q-Rapids in the context of DevOps processes analysis.

7 Conclusions

In this work, we have presented the objectives and current state of the Q-Rapids H2020 project. More information is available in the project website, www.q-rapids.edu. Components are available at https://github.com/q-rapids.

Acknowledgments. This work is a result of the Q-Rapids project, which has received funding from the European Union's Horizon 2020 research and innovation programme under grant agreement No. 732253.

References

1. Guzmán, L., Oriol, M., Rodríguez, P., Franch, X., Jedlitschka, A., Oivo, M.: How can quality awareness support rapid software development? – a research preview. In: Grünbacher, P., Perini, A. (eds.) REFSQ 2017. LNCS, vol. 10153, pp. 167–173. Springer, Cham (2017). https://doi.org/10.1007/978-3-319-54045-0_12
2. Franch, X., Lopez, L., Martínez-Fernández, S., Oriol, M., Rodríguez, P., Trendowicz, A.: Quality-aware rapid software development: the Q-rapids project. In: Mazzara, M., Bruel, J. M., Meyer, B., Petrenko, A. (eds.) TOOLS 2019. LNCS, vol. 11771, pp. 378–392. Springer, Heidelberg (2019). https://doi.org/10.1007/978-3-030-29852-4_32
3. López, L., et al.: Q-rapids tool prototype: supporting decision-makers in managing quality in rapid software development. In: Mendling, J., Mouratidis, H. (eds.) CAiSE 2018. LNBIP, vol. 317, pp. 200–208. Springer, Cham (2018). https://doi.org/10.1007/978-3-319-92901-9_17
4. Martínez-Fernández, S., et al.: Continuously assessing and improving software quality with software analytics tools: a case study. IEEE Access **7**, 68219–68239 (2019)
5. Manzano, M., Mendes, E., Gómez, C., Ayala, C., Franch, X.: Using Bayesian networks to estimate strategic indicators in the context of rapid software development. In: PROMISE 2018, pp. 52–55 (2018)
6. Manzano, M., Ayala, C., Gomez, C., López, L.: A software service supporting software quality forecasting. In: DSQA 2019 (2019)
7. Oriol, M., et al.: Data-driven elicitation of quality requirements in agile companies. In: Piattini, M., Rupino da Cunha, P., García Rodríguez de Guzmán, I., Pérez-Castillo, R. (eds.) QUATIC 2019. CCIS, vol. 1010, pp. 49–63. Springer, Cham (2019). https://doi.org/10.1007/978-3-030-29238-6_4
8. Ram, P., Rodríguez, P., Oivo, M.: Software process measurement and related challenges in agile software development: a multiple case study. In: Kuhrmann, M., et al. (eds.) PROFES 2018, vol. 11271, pp. 272–287. Springer, Heidelberg (2018). https://doi.org/10.1007/978-3-030-03673-7_20

IMPRESS: Improving Engagement in Software Engineering Courses Through Gamification

Tanja E. J. Vos[1], I. S. W. B. Prasetya[2]([⊠]) [iD], Gordon Fraser[3],
Ivan Martinez-Ortiz[4], Ivan Perez-Colado[4], Rui Prada[5], José Rocha[5],
and António Rito Silva[5] [iD]

[1] Open Univeriteit Nederland, Heerlen, Netherlands
[2] Utrecht University, Utrecht, Netherlands
s.w.b.prasetya@uu.nl
[3] Universität Passau, Passau, Germany
[4] Universidad Complutense de Madrid, Madrid, Spain
[5] INESC-ID and Instituto Superior Técnico, Universidade de Lisboa,
Lisbon, Portugal

Abstract. Software Engineering courses play an important role for preparing students with the right knowledge and attitude for software development in practice. The implication is far reaching, as the quality of the software that we use ultimately depends on the quality of the people that make them. Educating Software Engineering, however, is quite challenging, as the subject is not considered as most exciting by students, while teachers often have to deal with exploding number of students. The EU project IMPRESS seeks to explore the use of gamification in educating software engineering at the university level to improve students' engagement and hence their appreciation for the taught subjects. This paper presents the project, its objectives, and its current progress.

Keywords: Software engineering education · Gamification in education · Gamification in software engineering education

1 Introduction

While our society increasingly depends on software for various aspects of civic, commercial and social life, software engineers struggle to ensure that software achieves the necessary high quality. The increasing complexity of modern software systems and the ever reducing time-to-marked further exacerbate the problem. Although the discipline of Software Engineering offers different techniques

The IMPRESS project https://impress-project.eu/ is funded by EU Erasmus+ Programme, grant nr. 2017-1-NL01-KA203-035259. Duration: 2017–2020. Partners: Open Univ. (NL), Utrecht Univ. (NL), Univ. Complutense Madrid (SP), Univ. Passau (DE), INESC-ID Lisbon (PT). The project is also partially funded by the Fundacão para a Ciência e a Tecnologia (FCT) fund UID/CEC/50021/2019.

© Springer Nature Switzerland AG 2019
X. Franch et al. (Eds.): PROFES 2019, LNCS 11915, pp. 613–619, 2019.
https://doi.org/10.1007/978-3-030-35333-9_47

to ensure quality, programmers in practice are reluctant to engage with them, with detrimental effects on software quality. The root of this situation lies in how software developers are educated. The focus tends to lie on the creative aspects of design and coding, whereas the more laborious and less entertaining necessities to assure the software's quality are neglected. This disengagement carries over to practice. This has to change: tomorrow software engineers need to be raised with appreciation of software quality, and quality assurance techniques need to become a natural aspect of software development, rather than a niche topic. Implementing the change, however, is not easy, as teachers have to motivate students through materials already branded as uninteresting. To help teachers, the IMPRESS project seeks to explore the use of gamification, i.e., the application of game-design elements and game principles in non-gaming contexts, which has seen successful applications in other domains. This paper will present the project objective, the results so far, and a conclusion.

2   IMPRESS Expected Outcomes

Although *gamification* is known to improve users' engagement and appreciation [4], its application to Software Engineering is still limited. IMPRESS seeks to deliver innovations that would help improving students' engagement and enthusiasm on topics traditionally considered boring. It will focus on the following:

(1) Improving *in-class engagement* through gamified quizzes. Quizzes are an effective tool to set a course's pace. A cleverly setup quiz can trigger an engaging discussion, while gamification can stimulate wider engagement through competitive elements. A set of quizzes from selected topics will be developed within the project, along with tools to let others to develop more.
(2) Improving *out-class engagement* through educational games that can be played at home or in unguided lab sessions. We will focus on the subject of quality assurance —a key subject, as pointed out earlier—, in particular in two key competences: formalizing specifications and unit testing.
(3) Enhancing gamification with *story telling AI* for better emotional engagement and *advanced analytics* to provide insight on students' learning progress.

3   IMPRESS Innovations

This section presents the project progress so far.

Keeping Students on the Move with Quizzes. Quizzes have great potential as teaching tools. They can enrich the presentation of a course's content, and foster participation in the class subject. Tools like Kahoot prospered because of this. Quizzes can be used in a class to raise attention to particular issues, e.g. by showing to the students what they do not know, hence, supporting self-awareness of knowledge and make students more receptive to new information. Quizzes can also be used to support revision of knowledge, for example, as a summary in the end of the class, and to evaluate students. Outside the class, quizzes can be a good self assessing tool for students and enhancing their learning process by supporting self-regulation of learning and providing quick feedback about their current state of readiness on their subjects.

We have developed a web-based tool to reduce teachers' effort in preparing quizzes. The tool, available in a GitHub repository: https://github.com/socialsoftware/as-tutor, allows users to search through a repository of questions and quizzes, and create new quizzes by re-using and re-purposing the materials they find. The tool also supports automatic generation of quizzes on students' (or teachers') requests, e.g. classified according to a set of topics. Produced quizzes can then be exported to gamified quiz tools, e.g. ARSnova, https://arsnova.eu/. The repository currently contains over 600 questions and 80 quizzes, mostly on the subject of Software Architecture. A pilot in some of our courses is planned, after which the tool will be deployed open for the community. We plan to extend the tool with automatic classification of questions (for more accurate automatic quizz generation) and generation of post-quiz feedback for both students and teachers on the students' learning progress.

Training Formalization Skill with a Game. Writing formal specifications is a skill that would greatly benefit students. Software with formal specifications can be verified, or at least tested, *automatically*, hence greatly improving its correctness assurance. Unfortunately, this skill is often left underdeveloped. The skill is not easy to master: it is easy to make mistakes, and training it can quickly become boring. In IMPRESS we experiment with a new game called FormalZ [13] to train the basic of writing formal specifications in the form of pre- and post-conditions. Unlike existing Software Engineering themed education games like Pex [15] and Train-Director-B [6], FormalZ takes a deeper gamification approach [1], where 'playing' is given a more central role. After all, what makes games so engaging is not merely the awarded scores and badges, but primarily the experience of playing them. Figure 1 shows a screenshot of FormalZ.

FormalZ also takes a *Constructionism* approach [10]: just typing in formulas, which would be faster, is forbidden. Instead, the user constructs formulas by dragging and connecting blocks of electronic hardware components. The Constructionism theory believes that humans learn by *constructing* knowledge, rather than by simply copying it from the teacher. Framing the knowledge in terms of familiar physical objects, such as electronic components, plays a key role in this process, because the learner already has knowledge on how they work [5], which the learner then uses to construct the new knowledge in his mind. The theory was originally proposed by Papert and Harel [10] and was e.g. used in the programming language LOGO for teaching programming to children.

The initial reaction from our students have been encouraging [13], but more studies are needed to investigate the actual impact on the game's learning goal.

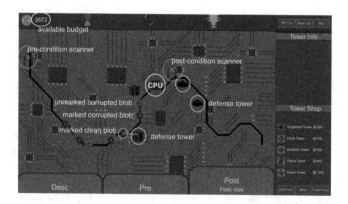

Fig. 1. A screenshot of FormalZ. The game is to defend the CPU in the middle of the circuit board. The small red and blue blobs represent data coming to or leaving the CPU. Some of them might be corrupted. The user builds pre- and post conditions, and defense towers, trying to eliminate corrupted blobs. See also [13]. (Color figure online)

Teaching Software Testing Through a Competitive Game. A further challenging activity in software engineering practice as well as education is testing a program for errors. In IMPRESS we explore improving the education of testing using Code Defenders, a game intended to engage students in the context of a Java object-oriented class under test and its test suite. In the game, *attackers* aim to introduce artificial bugs ("mutants") into the class under test that reveal weaknesses in the test suite, while *defenders* aim to improve the test suite by adding new tests. If a mutant program produces a different output for a test than the original program, then that mutant is detected by the test, and the defender who wrote the test scores points. If a mutant is not detected by any tests, then the attacker scores points. The number of points a mutant is worth depends on the number of tests it "survives", which further encourages players to create as subtle as possible mutants, and as strong as possible tests.

Code Defenders is implemented as a web-based game and is played by teams of students. The players are shown the source code of the Java class under test, with color highlighting to indicate the coverage of the defenders' test suite, and with bug-icons labelling the locations and status of the attackers' mutants. Attackers create mutants by editing the source code of the Java class, and defenders write JUnit tests using a code editor. A scoreboard breaks down the game's current score for each team and player.

We have studied player behavior in detail [14] and shown that players enjoy writing tests in the game more than as a regular developer activity. We have also applied Code Defenders in class and designed a software testing undergrad course around it [3]. Initial evaluation results suggest that Code Defenders supports students in achieving their learning objectives.

3.1 Advanced Analytics

We have extended the analytics platform from the H2020 RAGE project[1] to adequate its functionalities to IMPRESS' needs, in particular to support different types of analytics generating educational activities [7]. These new developments allowed two approaches for analytics integration: *light* and *deep* integration.

Often, educational tools (like Kahoot!) provide a report that summarizes students interaction to some extent. In light integration the underlying educational tool it is not modified at all (e.g. because modification is not possible). RAGE Analytics is simply used on available analytics provided by the educational tool, e.g. to provide better or uniform visualisation across multiple tools.

In deep integration, the developers of the education tool need to integrate a "tracker" [11] into the tool, used to send out the user interaction information. As such, this approach can provide more fine grained analytics and to provide it live and is therefore the recommended integration approach. This was the approach selected for integration of the FormalZ game with RAGE Analytics, allowing us to collect all students interactions and to show them graphically to teachers, near real-time, in a single dashboard (Fig. 2). The analytics can also show how the students evolve their solutions, to give insight on their mental process in constructing the solutions.

Having all analytics in one place allowed us to provide an additional capability for teachers that want to have analytics of multiple heterogeneous activity (e.g. to track student progress during a longer period). This is facilitated through configurator to perform simple operations and weight of activities, so they can build new variables that can be included in class level dashboards [12].

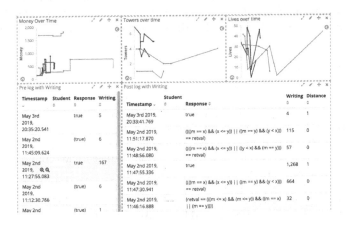

Fig. 2. FormalZ analytics main dashboard.

---

[1] GitHub repository: https://github.com/e-ucm/rage-analytics.

3.2   AI in IMPRESS

One of the use of AI for teaching is the generation and adaptation of learning content [2]. We are currently working on an AI module to create personalization features of the previously mentioned quiz tool we developed. It will work with the data that will be stored by the students performance on the quizzes to define student profiles and choose the best quizzes to enrich their learning experience.

AI can also improve the learning experience by adding a storytelling layer to the content. Stories are common in games and support meaning making and emotional engagement that foster learners motivation and learning [9]. We are developing storytelling components for the Code Defenders and FormalZ games by using the FAtiMA toolkit[2] [8]. Our approach is to put the challenges presented by the games into a narrative, by including a character in the game that will talk to the players contextualizing the challenge that is given to the player(s) and presenting feedback on the performance. The toolkit facilitates the creation of such characters including mechanisms for the generation of personality and emotional responses, an authoring tool for character's behaviour, and integration through a REST API.

4   Conclusion

While the importance of Software Engineering courses is well acknowledged, creating engaging Software Engineering courses is very challenging. Much can be improved through innovative use of modern technology. Along this line, IMPRESS has contributed innovations in gamification, and more can be expected before the project ends in 2020. Ultimately though, energizing Software Engineering education is not a challenge that a single project like IMPRESS can solve on its own. Community, and Industry, should also own the problem and commit to solving it.

References

1. Boyce, A.K.: Deep gamification: combining game-based and play-based methods. Ph.D. thesis, North Carolina State University (2014)
2. Brisson, A., et al.: Artificial intelligence and personalization opportunities for serious games. In: Proceedings of the 8th Artificial Intelligence and Interactive Digital Entertainment Conference (2012)
3. Fraser, G., Gambi, A., Kreis, M., Rojas, J.M.: Gamifying a software testing course with code defenders. In: Proceedings of the 50th ACM Technical Symposium on Computer Science Education, pp. 571–577. ACM (2019)
4. Hamari, J., Koivisto, J., Sarsa, H., et al.: Does gamification work? -a literature review of empirical studies on gamification. In: 47th Hawaii International Conference on System Sciences (2014)
5. Kafai, Y.B.: Constructionism. In: The Cambridge Handbook of the Learning Sciences. Cambridge University Press, Cambridge (2005)

---

[2] https://fatima-toolkit.eu/.

6. Korečko, Š., Sorád, J.: Using simulation games in teaching formal methods for software development. In: Innovative Teaching Strategies and New Learning Paradigms in Computer Programming, pp. 106–130. IGI Global (2015)
7. Martínez-Ortiz, I., Pérez-Colado, I., Rotaru, D.C., Freire, M., Fernández-Manjón, B.: From heterogeneous activities to unified analytics dashboards. In: IEEE Global Engineering Education Conference (EDUCON) (2019)
8. Mascarenhas, S., et al.: A virtual agent toolkit for serious games developers. In: Proceedings of Conference on Computational Intelligence and Games (CIG). IEEE (2018)
9. Ohler, J.B.: Digital Storytelling in the Classroom: New Media Pathways to Literacy, Learning, and Creativity. Corwin Press, Thousand Oaks (2013)
10. Papert, S., Harel, I.: Constructionism. Ablex Publishing, Norwood (1991)
11. Perez-Colado, I., Alonso-Fernandez, C., Freire, M., Martinez-Ortiz, I., Fernandez-Manjon, B.: Game learning analytics is not informagic! In: 2018 IEEE Global Engineering Education Conference (EDUCON) (2018)
12. Perez-Colado, I.J., Rotaru, D.C., Freire-Moran, M., Martinez-Ortiz, I., Fernandez-Manjon, B.: Multi-level game learning analytics for serious games. In: 10th International Conference on Virtual Worlds and Games for Serious Applications (VS-Games) (2018)
13. Prasetya, I.S.W.B., et al.: Having fun in learning formal specifications. In: Proceedings of 41st International Conference on Software Engineering (ICSE). IEEE (2019)
14. Rojas, J.M., White, T.D., Clegg, B.S., Fraser, G.: Code defenders: crowdsourcing effective tests and subtle mutants with a mutation testing game. In: Proceedings of 39th International Conference on Software Engineering. IEEE Press (2017)
15. Tillmann, N., de Halleux, J., Xie, T.: Pex for fun: engineering an automated testing tool for serious games in computer science. Technical report, MSR-TR-2011-41 (2011)

Software Governance in a Large European Project - GÉANT Case Study

Marcin Wolski[1]($\boxtimes$)(iD) and Toby Rodwell[2]

[1] Poznań Supercomputing and Networking Center, Poznań, Poland
marcin.wolski@man.poznan.pl
[2] GÉANT Association, Cambridge, UK
toby.rodwell@geant.org

Abstract. Sustainable software development is an essential part of GN4, the project co-funded by Europe's NRENs and the EU. This article presents how software governance has been applied in GN4 during its iterations.

Keywords: Software governance · Software processes · Software improvements

1 Introduction

GÉANT refers both to the research and innovation community of European NRENs (operators of national networks for science and education), and also a sequence of network-related projects co-funded by the EC and the European NRENs. The latest such project is GN4, a truly pan-European collaboration between 39 partners i.e. 37 European NRENs, NORDUnet (representing the five Nordic countries) and GÉANT Association[1]. The third and final phase of GN4, GN4-3, started in January 2019 and will last 48 months.

The NREN community is involved in collaborative software development activities, focused on delivering software products that provide advanced services. The GÉANT product portfolio contains software with different levels of maturity, size and target domains: starting from prototype solutions (proof of concept), through pilot applications that usually target a closed group of users, to production versions supporting the delivery of operational services. Their users mostly comprise of GÉANT partners and their member institutions, researchers,

---

[1] https://www.geant.org/.

This work is part of a project that has received funding from the European Union's Horizon 2020 research and innovation programme under Grant Agreement No. 856726 (GN4-3).

The scientific/academic work is financed from financial resources for science in the years 2019–2022 granted for the realization of the international project co-financed by Polish Ministry of Science and Higher Education.

X. Franch et al. (Eds.): PROFES 2019, LNCS 11915, pp. 620–625, 2019.
https://doi.org/10.1007/978-3-030-35333-9_48

students and educators, who expect high-quality, reliable services and infrastructure to support their work or studies.

Proper support of the software governance has had significant attention in GÉANT since before GN4 began, and this grew even stronger with the introduction of service transition and operation processes in the first two phases of GN4 (GN4-1 and GN4-2) [6]. This work has been continued and it is currently the responsibility of GN4-3 WP9 Task 2: Software Governance and Support. This task provides comprehensive governance and support for software development within the project, to guarantee a consistent level of software product reliability and resilience, and ensure the overall quality level of the GÉANT services that rely on these products.

The paper is organized as follows. Section 2 describes in more detail the software development effort in GÉANT and presents the main features of the software projects and teams. Section 3 describes the major outcomes of software governance in GÉANT and outlines the future work in GN4-3 WP9 Task 2. Section 4 explains the interest in participation in the Profes 2019 event and the expected collaboration opportunities this will afford.

2 Software Development in GÉANT

Most software teams in GÉANT (SW teams) are distributed and involve engineers from different NRENs and the GÉANT organization. The teams have autonomy in adopting a specific methodology for software development and choosing associated tools [1]. This results in a wide range of processes and approaches to software development [4].

In Table 1 we present selected information for GÉANT software projects:

- Codebase age – time between the first and last commit in the project,
- Codebase size – Source Lines of Code (SLOC),
- Languages – number of languages used in a project,
- Team size – number of GN4-3 contributors for the project in all roles (tester, developer, manager etc.),
- Team size (software developers) – number of GN4-3 software developers contributing to the project,
- Projects per person – a number of projects a single person contributes to.

Currently, there are 29 projects in the GÉANT software portfolio. They are usually developed by the GÉANT and NREN community, but in a few cases they have been inherited from external open source initiatives, and are currently being developed globally (e.g., COTURN[2]).

The GÉANT product portfolio contains software projects with a wide range of sizes (from less than a thousand to nearly one million lines of code) and system age (from 92 days up to more than 17 years), and all of them use more than one language (on average, 9).

---

[2] https://github.com/coturn/coturn/blob/master/README.md.

Table 1. GÉANT software projects and teams as of July, 2019 (source: https://sc. geant.org)

Statistic name	Items	Min	Max	Median
Software projects	29			
Codebase age		92 days	17 years	3 years
Codebase size		858	965989	35864
Languages		4	23	9
Software teams	29			
Team size		1	10	2
Team size (Software developers)		1	6	2
Project per person		1	4	1
Software contributors	63			
Software developers	47			

Moreover, there are 63 GN4-3 software contributors, which is to say someone who commits source codes and/or reports issues. 47 of these people are software developers, who have made at least 1 commit. Notably, GÉANT software teams are usually small, with just two members on average - the largest team has 10 members, of whom 6 are developers. In most cases people contribute to only one project.

3   Outcomes and Planned Work

3.1   Software Catalogue

The GÉANT Software Catalogue (GSC) addresses the recognized need for a unified repository of software teams and projects in GÉANT, which will lead to improvements in software development by facilitating knowledge exchange and fostering opportunities for cooperation. GSC provides a global view of the whole of software development in GÉANT, automatically aggregating and presenting information from different data sources with software artefacts such as source code repositories and issue tracker systems [2]. The tool has successfully accomplished the transition to production phase and it currently holds consistent information on about 30 software projects and over 300 individuals from GÉANT, who have contributed to the software development (i.e. throughout all phases of GN4).

Further development of the GSC is planned for the remaining years of the GN4-3 project. The roadmap includes improvements and new features requested by the software community, for example support for complementary data source with software artefacts (like SonarQube), and extended reporting capabilities.

3.2   Software Maturity Model

The GÉANT Software Maturity Model (SMM) has been designed to achieve two primary goals: to identify and define the key best practices that help to successfully deliver software; and to highlight areas for improvement by teams. Unlike software methodologies, which specify how to undertake certain actions, maturity models propose a framework that simply specifies the goals to be achieved. Therefore it is a good fit for the GÉANT project, where planning and evaluating the implementation of software products within a distributed environment, with only partial and ever changing involvement of team members, remains exceedingly challenging.

The concept of the SMM was presented and evaluated with the help of selected GÉANT software teams [3]. Based on the initial feedback, a revised version of SMM has been prepared. The current effort is concentrated on producing a policy for software best practices in GN4-3 based on the SMM framework [5]. The outcome of this work will be presented in a GÉANT project deliverable.

3.3   Software Developer Training

For almost a decade, the GÉANT project has organised two types of software development training for the project participants, namely Secure Code Training (SCT) and School of Software Engineers (SSE). SCT focuses on secure programming with the aim of minimizing the number of security bugs in the source code. SSE focus on code quality and management. As with SCT, the topics differ from one training to another to address contemporary GÉANT project requirements, and software methodologies and techniques in common current use in the community. Since 2010 SCT and SSE have respectively trained 107 and 73 developers from over 20 NRENs [7].

Both training events are going to be continued and delivered annually to the GÉANT software community.

3.4   Software Code Reviews

Software code reviews are offered as a supporting activity performed by an independent testing team. An independent review is much more likely to detect errors that the code authors are themselves blind to, as the reviewers, being unfamiliar with the code, do not focus on functionality. Typically code reviews are conducted as part of system testing during the transition of a service to production, but they can be requested by any GÉANT software team at any time, even during an early stage of the Software Development Life Cycle.

Currently the reviews are predominantly manual (i.e. an expert developer reads through the code) but it is planned to extend the use of automated tests in the code review process, using the customized and supported SonarQube tool[3].

---

[3] https://ci.geant.net/sonar/.

3.5   Software Tools

GÉANT currently provides a range of services and tools to support software development[4]. These tools are now accessible to the whole GÉANT community through federated authentication and authorisation[5].

Together the tools form a technology stack which supports the full development life-cycle from requirements management via issue/task management to source code repository, and through continuous integration and deployment service to binaries repository and production deployment. Software projects developed with the use of common GÉANT SWD tools set, policies and best practices will benefit from increased transparency and maintainability of the GÉANT projects. Compliance with Intellectual Property Rights (IPR), which is overseen by a different team within the project, can also be facilitated through the GÉANT Software Development Infrastructure.

4   Collaboration

We expect to meeting a variety of different representatives of the software engineering community attending the conference and would be glad to have the opportunity to speak about GÉANT's experience concerning software governance processes. Equally, hearing lessons learned from other projects could provide further refinements to the existing software development practices in GÉANT. Finally, learning about the tools, policies and best practices used by practitioners and researchers will be valuable for influencing the GÉANT software governance roadmap.

The presentation will include the current status and future work in the area of software governance in the GÉANT project. In addition, there may be a demo of the GÉANT Software Catalogue shown to the audience.

References

1. Bilicki, V., Golub, I., Vuletic, P., Wolski, M.: Failure and success - how to move toward successful software development in Networking. In: Terena Networking Conference (2014)
2. Łabędzki, M., Wolski, M.: GÉANT Software Catalogue as a Code Portfolio. GÉANT Connect, p. 58 (2018). https://www.geant.org/News_and_Events/CONNECT/Documents/CONNECT29FINAL(1).pdf
3. Stanisavljevic, Z., Walter, B., Vukasovic, M., Todosijevic, A., Łabędzki, M., Wolski, M.: Géant software maturity model. In: 2018 26th Telecommunications Forum (TELFOR), pp. 420–425, November 2018
4. Stanisavljevic, Z., Wolski, M., Labedzki, M., Kupiński, S., Todosijevic, A., Adomeit, M.: Harmonising the software development process in the Géant community. GÉANT Connect, pp. 50–51 (2018). https://www.geant.org/News_and_Events/CONNECT/Documents/connect_28_web.pdf

---

[4] https://software.geant.org.

[5] https://edugain.org/.

5. Todosijevic, A., et al.: Ensuring best practice For Géant software development. GÉANT Connect, p. 29 (2019). https://www.geant.org/News_and_Events/CONNECT/Documents/CONNECT_31.pdf
6. Wolski, M., et al.: Deliverable D5.3 - analysis of requirements for software management. Technical report (2017). https://www.geant.org/Projects/GEANT_Project_GN4/deliverables/D5-3_Analysis-of-Requirements-for-Software-Management.pdf
7. Wolski, M., Labedzki, M., Frankowski, G., Berus, P., Mazurek, C., Adomeit, M.: Delivering software training to the Géant community. GÉANT Connect, pp. 10–11 (2017). https://www.geant.org/News_and_Events/CONNECT/Documents/CONNECT_24.pdf

AMASS: A Large-Scale European Project to Improve the Assurance and Certification of Cyber-Physical Systems

Jose Luis de la Vara[1](✉), Eugenio Parra[2], Alejandra Ruiz[3], and Barbara Gallina[4]

[1] University of Castilla-La Mancha, Albacete, Spain
joseluis.delavara@uclm.es
[2] Carlos III University of Madrid, Leganes, Spain
eparra@inf.uc3m.es
[3] Tecnalia Research and Innovation, Derio, Spain
alejandra.ruiz@tecnalia.com
[4] Mälardalen University, Västerås, Sweden
barbara.gallina@mdh.se

Abstract. Most safety-critical systems must undergo assurance and certification processes. The associated activities can be complex and labour-intensive, thus practitioners need suitable means to execute them. The activities are further becoming more challenging as a result of the evolution of the systems towards cyber-physical ones, as these systems have new assurance and certification needs. The AMASS project (Architecture-driven, Multi-concern and Seamless Assurance and Certification of Cyber-Physical Systems) tackled these issues by creating and consolidating the de-facto European-wide open tool platform, ecosystem, and self-sustainable community for assurance and certification of cyber-physical systems. The project defined a novel holistic approach for architecture-driven assurance, multi-concern assurance, seamless interoperability, and cross- and intra-domain reuse of assurance assets. AMASS results were applied in 11 industrial case studies to demonstrate the reduction of effort in assurance and certification, the reduction of (re)certification cost, the reduction of assurance and certification risks, and the increase in technology harmonisation and interoperability.

Keywords: AMASS · Cyber-physical system · CPS · Assurance · Certification

1 Introduction

Safety-critical systems are usually subject to rigorous assurance and certification processes to provide confidence that the systems are dependable [18], i.e. acceptably safe, reliable, etc. This is typically performed in compliance with standards, e.g. ISO 26262 in automotive and DO-178C in avionics, and is a requirement so that the systems are allowed to operate. The associated activities are usually complex and labour-intensive because of the large set of compliance criteria to fulfil, the amount of assurance

© Springer Nature Switzerland AG 2019
X. Franch et al. (Eds.): PROFES 2019, LNCS 11915, pp. 626–632, 2019.
https://doi.org/10.1007/978-3-030-35333-9_49

evidence to manage, and the need for providing valid justifications of system dependability, among other issues [18]. Therefore, practitioners need support.

Safety-critical systems have also significantly increased in technical complexity and sophistication toward open, interconnected, networked systems such as "the connected car". This has brought a "cyber-physical" dimension with it, exacerbating the problem of ensuring dependability in the presence of human, environmental, and technological risks. New approaches for assurance and certification are needed so that these activities are cost-effective. The approaches must consider the new system characteristics, e.g. new architectures and the need for guaranteeing several dependability concerns, and provide means that facilitate the collection, management, and reuse of assurance assets.

The AMASS project (Architecture-driven, Multi-concern and Seamless Assurance and Certification of Cyber-Physical Systems; [1]) created and consolidated the de-facto European-wide open tool platform, ecosystem, and self-sustainable community for assurance and certification of Cyber-Physical Systems (CPS) in the largest industrial vertical markets including automotive, railway, aerospace, space, and energy.

The ultimate goal of AMASS was to lower certification costs for CPS in face of rapidly changing features and market needs. This was achieved by establishing a novel holistic approach for architecture-driven assurance (fully compatible with standards such as SysML), multi-concern assurance (for co-analysis and co-assurance of e.g. security and safety aspects), seamless interoperability between assurance and engineering activities along with third-parties (e.g. supplier assurance), and cross- and intra-domain reuse of assurance assets (e.g. of assurance evidence between projects).

The AMASS project started in April 2016 and finished in March 2019. AMASS work built on the results from previous successful EU projects such as OPENCOSS [21], SafeCer [26], CRYSTAL [14], and CHESS [12]. Results from these projects were integrated and further developed in AMASS.

The next sections summarise the AMASS project by presenting its objectives, its organisation, and its main outcomes. Our purpose is to raise the awareness about the project and its results, including its open source community, so that further people and other projects continue researching on and developing solutions for assurance and certification from AMASS outcomes. Prior publications [10] provide further details about the motivation for the project [25], the process for approach application [15], and the Eclipse open source project [16, 17]. Publications on specific research topics are also available, e.g. on quality analysis of system artefacts for assurance [22]. More information about the project and its results are available in AMASS deliverables [2].

2 Project Objectives

The high-level **goals** of AMASS were the demonstration of:

1. G1: A potential gain for design efficiency of complex CPS by reducing their assurance and certification effort by 50%;
2. G2: A potential reuse of assurance results (qualified or certified before), leading to 40% of cost reductions for product (re)certification activities;

3. G3: A potential raise of technology innovation led by 35% reduction of assurance and certification risks of new CPS products, and;
4. G4: A potential sustainable impact in CPS industry by increasing the harmonization and interoperability of assurance and certification tool technologies by 60%.

To achieve the goals, these project **objectives** were specified:

- O1: Define a holistic approach for architecture-driven assurance to leverage the reuse opportunities in assurance and certification by directly and explicitly addressing current technologies and hardware and software architectures needs.
- O2: Define a multi-concern assurance approach to ensure not only safety and security, but also other dependability aspects such as availability and reliability.
- O3: Consolidate a cross-domain and intra-domain assurance reuse approach to improve mutual recognition agreement of compliance approvals and to help assess the return of investment of reuse decisions.
- O4: Develop a fully-fledged open tool platform that allows developers and other assurance stakeholders to guarantee seamless interoperability of the platform with other tools used in the development of CPSs.
- O5: Benchmark the tool infrastructure against real industrial cases in relevant environments.
- O6: Consolidate the AMASS ecosystem and community for:
  - O6.a: Adoption of the AMASS conceptual and methodological approach as a reference tool architecture for CPS assurance and certification.
  - O6.b: Maintenance and further development of the open tool platform as a long-term, API-standardized, and industry-driven assurance and certification environment.

The main envisioned **impact** on the different stakeholders is as follows:

- OEMs (including system integrators) and Component suppliers can use AMASS results to increase CPS design cost-effectiveness, ease innovation, and reduce the costs and risks of CPS assurance and certification.
- Assessors and Certification authorities can provide services that better fit CPS-specific needs.
- Tool vendors can extend their products with new features and integrate them with AMASS tools.
- European society will benefit from the use of CPS with a higher confidence in their dependability.

3 Organisation

The **AMASS consortium** (Table 1) consisted of **29 partners from eight countries** and covered the whole value chain for CPS assurance and certification. The project manager was Alejandra Ruiz (Tecnalia R&I), the technical manager was Barbara

Gallina (Mälardalen University), and the quality manager was Cristina Martínez (Tecnalia R&I). Information about other roles and the implementation plan structure is available online [9]. AMASS also had an **External Advisory Board** [8] that included 14 relevant and influential experts on the topics of the project, including assessors, assurance and certification managers, consultants, engineers, and researchers. This board advised on technical decisions, standardization, and community building.

The industrial application of AMASS was analysed in **11 case studies** [3] from air traffic management, automotive, avionics, industrial automation, railway, and space, e.g. on autonomous driving features and satellite software design. The AMASS partners established **links with related ongoing EU projects** for networking, discussion, and collaboration, such as AQUAS [11], CP-SETIS [13], PDP4E [23], RobMosys [24], and SafeCOP [27]. AMASS also established **links with national projects**. Result **standardisation** was addressed, e.g. through system assurance work at OMG [19].

Table 1. AMASS partners per country and their main role in the value chain: ASR – Assessor, CER – Certification Authority, COS – Component Supplier, OEM – Original Equipment Manufacturer, RES – research, TOV – Tool Vendor

Country	Partner	Role	Country	Partner	Role
AT	AIT	RES	FR	ALL4TEC	TOV
	Virtual Vehicle	RES		Alstom Transport	OEM
CZ	Honeywell	COS		CEA List	RES
	Masaryk Uni.	RES		ClearSy	COS
DE	Ansys medini	TOV	IT	FBK	RES
	Assystem	TOV		Intecs	ASR
	Eclipse Found.	TOV		Rina	CER
	Infineon	COS		Thales	OEM
	Lange Aviation	OEM	SE	Alten	ASR
ES	Carlos III Uni.	RES		Comentor	ASR
	GMV	COS		Mälardalen Uni.	RES
	Schneider Electric	OEM		OHB	COS
	Tecnalia R & I	RES		RISE	RES
	Thales Alenia	COS	UK	Rapita Systems	TOV
	The REUSE Co.	TOV			

4 Main Outcomes

AMASS resulted in three main tangible outcomes.

The **AMASS Reference Tool Architecture** (Fig. 1; [5]) provides a conceptual framework for architecture-driven assurance, multi-concern assurance, seamless interoperability, and cross- and intra-domain reuse of assurance assets. It contains both technological building blocks such as System architecture modelling for assurance and Tool integration management, and the Common Assurance & Certification Metamodel, which provides an information model for CPS assurance and certification, e.g. for Compliance management and for Assurance case specification.

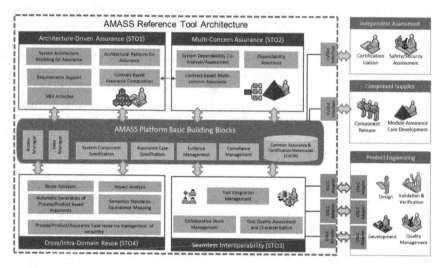

Fig. 1. AMASS Reference Tool Architecture

The **AMASS Tool Platform** (Fig. 2; [6]) is a collaborative tool environment that represents a concrete implementation of the AMASS Reference Tool Architecture with capability for evolution and adaptation. It is released as an open technological solution that integrates and extends different existing open source tools for system modelling and analysis (Papyrus, CHESS, Concerto-FLA), compliance management and argumentation (OpenCert), process engineering (EPF-Composer), variability management (BVR), and traceability (Capra). It is further integrated with over a dozen external tools that provide additional features; usually commercial ones.

The **Open AMASS Community** [7] manages the main project results for maintenance, evolution and industrialization. The Open Community is supported by a governance board and by rules, policies, and quality models. This includes support for AMASS base tools and for extension tools. The OpenCert project of PolarSys/Eclipse [20] hosts the Community.

The achievement of the AMASS goals thanks to these outcomes was demonstrated in the industrial case studies [4]. The achievement varied among the case studies because of their different characteristics (e.g. different base situation) and the different features applied. Videos demonstrating AMASS outcomes are available online [28].

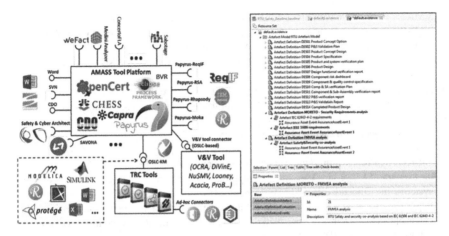

Fig. 2. General view of the AMASS Tool Platform and its ecosystem

5   Conclusion

The AMASS project developed a novel approach for CPS assurance and certification by addressing architecture-driven assurance, multi-concern assurance, seamless interoperability, and cross- and intra-domain reuse of assurance assets. The approach integrated and further developed results from other projects and resulted in three main tangible outcomes: the AMASS Reference Tool Architecture, the AMASS Tool Platform, and the Open AMASS Community. The benefits from using the outcomes were demonstrated in 11 industrial case studies.

We expect that further researchers and practitioners gain interest in AMASS results thanks to the summary presented. They could exploit the results in activities dealing with process or product improvement, mainly for critical systems. New collaborations on assurance and certification could also be created, e.g. around the open community.

We plan to continue working on CPS assurance and certification in the future from the results developed in AMASS. This includes the development of novel solutions for advanced assurance case management and for privacy assurance.

Acknowledgments. The research leading to this paper has received funding from the AMASS project (H2020-ECSEL grant agreement no 692474; Spain's MINECO ref. PCIN-2015-262; Sweden's Vinnova) and the Ramon y Cajal Program (Spain's MICINN ref. RYC-2017-22836; EC's European Social Fund). We are also grateful to all the AMASS partners. Their work and results are summarised in this paper.

References

1. AMASS Project. https://www.amass-ecsel.eu/
2. AMASS Project: Deliverables. https://www.amass-ecsel.eu/content/deliverables
3. AMASS Project: Deliverable 1.6 - AMASS demonstrators (c) (2019)
4. AMASS Project: Deliverable 1.7 - AMASS solution benchmarking (2019)

5. AMASS Project: Deliverable 2.4 - AMASS reference architecture (c) (2018)
6. AMASS Project: Deliverable 2.5 - AMASS user guidance and methodological fwk. (2018)
7. AMASS Project: Deliverable D7.7 - AMASS open source platform (c) (2018)
8. AMASS Project: External Advisory Board. https://www.amass-ecsel.eu/content/external-advisory-board
9. AMASS Project: Organization. https://www.amass-ecsel.eu/content/organization
10. AMASS Project: Publications. https://www.amass-ecsel.eu/content/publications
11. AQUAS Project. https://aquas-project.eu/
12. CHESS Project. http://www.chess-project.org/
13. CP-SETIS Project. https://cp-setis.eu/
14. CRYSTAL Project. http://www.crystal-artemis.eu/
15. de la Vara, J.L., et al.: The AMASS approach for assurance and certification of critical systems. In: Embedded World Conference (2019)
16. Espinoza, H., et al.: Meet the new eclipse-based tools for assurance and certification of cyber-physical systems. Eclipse Newsletter, July 2018. https://www.eclipse.org/community/eclipse_newsletter/2018/july/amass.php
17. Gallina, B., et al.: AMASS: call for users and contributors. Eclipse Newsletter, July 2019. https://www.eclipse.org/community/eclipse_newsletter/2019/july/amass.php
18. Nair, S., et al.: An extended systematic literature review on provision of evidence for safety certification. Inform. Softw. Technol. **56**(7), 689–717 (2014)
19. OMG: System Assurance Task Force. https://www.omg.org/sysa/
20. OpenCert. https://www.polarsys.org/opencert/
21. OPENCOSS Project. http://www.opencoss-project.eu/
22. Parra, E., et al.: Analysis of requirements quality evolution. In: ICSE (2018)
23. PDP4E Project. https://www.pdp4e-project.eu/
24. RobMosys Project. https://robmosys.eu/
25. Ruiz, A., et al.: Architecture-driven, multi-concern, seamless, reuse-oriented assurance and certification of cyber-physical systems. In: SAFECOMP Workshops (2016)
26. SafeCer Project. https://artemis-ia.eu/project/40-nsafecer.html
27. SafeCOP Project. http://www.safecop.eu/
28. YouTube: Opencert. https://youtube.com/channel/UCw_D0l5sDgysEphi6tzzDyw

3rd International Workshop on Managing Quality in Agile and Rapid Software Development Processes (QuASD)

Managing Quality in Agile and Rapid Software Development Processes

Claudia Ayala[1] ⓘ, Pilar Rodríguez[2] ⓘ, and Adam Trendowicz[3] ⓘ

[1] GESSI Group, Universitat Politècnica de Catalunya (UPC) - Barcelona Tech,
Barcelona, Spain
cayala@essi.upc.edu
[2] M3S Group, University of Oulu, Finland
pilar.rodriguez@oulu.fi
[3] Fraunhofer Institute for Experimental Software Engineering IESE,
Kaiserslautern, Germany
adam.trendowicz@iese.fraunhofer.de

Abstract. Optimal management of software quality demands for appropriate integration of quality management activities into the whole software (engineering) life-cycle. However, despite the competitive advantage of ensuring and maintaining high quality levels, software development methodologies still prove to offer little support to the integration and management of quality. This is especially true for, and essential in, agile software development processes and the more recent trends towards rapid and continuous software development. The premise is that faster and more frequent release cycles should not compromise quality. The third edition of the International Workshop on Managing Quality in Agile and Rapid Software Development Processes (QuASD 2019) continues the success of previous editions aiming to exchange challenges, experiences, and solutions among researchers and practitioners to bring agile and rapid software development processes a step further to seamless integrating quality management activities into their practices. In this way, we expect to foster the exchange of ideas between researchers and industry and consolidate a research agenda and collaborations.

Keywords: Quality · Agile Software Development · Rapid and Continuous Software Development

1 Introduction

The fast changing and unpredictability conditions characterizing current software markets have favored methods under the umbrella of Agile Software Development (ASD), which advocate speed, flexibility, and efficiency. These methods have become mainstream in the software industry. Indeed, the current tendency is towards reducing release cycles more and more, in which is known as Rapid Software Development (RSD), i.e. develop, release and learn from software in very short rapid cycles, typically hours, days or very small numbers of weeks. In this highly demanding context, faster and more frequent release cycles should not compromise quality. Thus, a full understanding of the quality of the product is essential in order to ensure that users perceive only improve-ments rather than experience any loss of functionality.

Today, software quality is an essential competitive factor for the success of software companies. For example, recent technological breakthroughs, such as cloud technologies, the emergence of IoT and technologies such as 5G, pose new challenges in software development. These challenges include quality aspects such as availability, reliability, security, performance and scalability, which significantly affect the success of current and future software products and services. Indeed, market studies show a steady increase in the proportion of budged being spent on dealing with software quality. A report by Capgemini states that the average spending on quality management and testing in IT companies has grown from 18% in 2012 to 35% in 2015 and it is estimated that this budged will increase to 40% by 2018. Another example is the automotive industry, in which electronics and software lead over 90% of all innovations, being software quality a critical success factor.

Despite the competitive advantage of ensuring and maintaining high quality levels, software development methodologies still prove to offer little support to the integration and management of quality. This is especially true for, and essential in agile and rapid software development processes. Optimal management of software quality demands for appropriate integration of quality management activities into the whole software (engineering) life-cycle. However, empirical evidence shows challenges when managing quality in agile and rapid software development process. For instance, the high orientation towards customers makes functionality and fast delivery cycles to play a relevant role that may provoke an overlook of quality requirements and quality management activities in general. Further, as the product evolves, software quality may be neglected due to cost and time constraints, which may incur in technical debt. Hence, maintenance costs may rise and the development of functionalities may take longer.

In this context, the QuASD workshop aims at investigating the current challenges that companies using agile software development and rapid release cycles face when integrating quality management activities into their practices. The objective of the workshop is to exchange experiences and solutions to bring agile and rapid software development processes a step further towards seamless integration of quality management activities into their practices. To strengthen this objective, QuASD 2019 is held in the context of one of the top-recognized software development and process improvement conferences: the International Conference on Product-Focused Software Process Improvement (PROFES 2019) on November 27, 2019, in Barcelona, Spain.

2   Contents and Expected Outcomes

The workshop has received a positive response from the community with interesting and valuable contributions. The submissions were peer-reviewed by at least three members of the international program committee in order to evaluate their quality, relevance and potential to foster discussions. Finally three papers were accepted for this edition of the workshop. These works address issues on quality in agile software development from different perspectives.

The first paper: "Do internal software quality tools measure validated metrics?" by Mayra Nilson, Vard Antinyan and Lucas Gren offers an overview of the data and metrics provided by some existing tools and the extent that these metrics have been validated. Their results suggest that a range of metrics do not seem to be validated in the literature and that only a small percentage of metrics are validated by the provided tools.

The second paper "A Unique Value that Synthesizes the Quality Level of a Product Architecture: outcome of a Quality Attributes Requirements Evaluation Method" by Mariana Falco and Gabriela Robiolo presents a five-step architecture evaluation method which defines, analyze and measure the quality characteristics of a product architecture and its implementation. They obtain as a final output, a unique value that represents the quality level of a product. The method is illustrated by an example developed in an agile setting.

The third paper "Comparison of Agile Maturity Models" by Anna Schmitt, Sven Theobald and Philipp Diebold presents a comprehensive comparison of 14 agile maturity models in order to help practitioners to understand the differences among models and to select among them.

With this content, we aim to promote discussions and interchange of ideas among participants from both industry and academia sectors in order to:

- Scope the current state of quality management in agile and rapid software development in both research and practice.
- Compile success and failure experiences.
- Continue on the research agenda from previous editions of the workshop.
- Establish a community to foster long-term collaboration.

We hope that the workshop participants will enjoy the topics presented here and perhaps find the inspiration to push the field a step further, or open the door for new collaborations.

Acknowledgments. We would like to acknowledge all the people who have enabled the organization of QuASD 2019.

The program committee was composed of prominent researchers from several universities and the industrial sector. The effort and dedication of the program committee and the additional reviewers who collaborated in the revision process were outstanding and deserve recognition.

We thank the authors and people that participate in the workshop for being willing to share their experiences on quality and quality requirements in the context of agile and rapid software development; and the organizing committee members, who handled all the complexity of arranging an event such as PROFES 2019 and the associated events.

Do Internal Software Quality Tools Measure Validated Metrics?

Mayra Nilson[2], Vard Antinyan[2], and Lucas Gren[1,2(✉)]

[1] Chalmers, University of Gothenburg, Gothenburg, Sweden
`lucas.gren@cse.gu.se`
[2] Volvo Cars, Gothenburg, Sweden
{`mayra.nilsson,vard.antinyan`}`@volvocars.com`

Abstract. Internal software quality determines the maintainability of the software product and influences the quality in use. There is a plethora of metrics which purport to measure the internal quality of software, and these metrics are offered by static software analysis tools. To date, a number of reports have assessed the validity of these metrics. No data are available, however, on whether metrics offered by the tools are somehow validated in scientific studies. The current study covers this gap by providing data on which tools and how many validated metrics are provided. The results show that a range of metrics that the tools provided do not seem to be validated in the literature and that only a small percentage of metrics are validated in the provided tools.

Keywords: Software metrics tools · Static analysis tools · Metrics · Attributes

1 Introduction

Software quality has been a major concern for as long as software has existed [1]. Billing errors and medical fatalities can be traced to the issue of software quality [2]. The ISO/IEC 9126 standard defines quality as "the totality of characteristics of an entity that bears on its ability to satisfy stated and implied needs" [3]. This standard distinguishes internal and external quality. The former is the quality of pre-release software that determines the ability of a project to be maintained further. Internal quality is observed and experienced by developers. However, it affects the functionality and user experience too [4].

To assess and manage internal quality of software, internal software quality metrics are used. While much research has been conducted on such metrics in forms of empirical studies, mapping studies, and systematic literature reviews [5–7], very little research has been done on the tools that implement these metrics.

One study on software metric tools concluded that there are considerable variations regarding the output from different tools for the same metric on the same software source code [8]. This indicates that the implementation of a given

© Springer Nature Switzerland AG 2019
X. Franch et al. (Eds.): PROFES 2019, LNCS 11915, pp. 637–648, 2019.
https://doi.org/10.1007/978-3-030-35333-9_50

metric varies from tool to tool. We have not found any study that investigates the implemented metrics in the tools and their scientific validity in the research. We, therefore, wanted to investigate whether the metrics provided in the tools are validated in scientific studies: Studies concluding that a given metric can predict an external software quality attribute to an acceptable precision. An external attribute can for example be fault proneness, maintainability, or testability.

The value of validating an internal quality metric in regard to an external quality attributes is to provide solid measures for good predictions of external quality. For example, Santos et al. [5] conducted such a study on eight separate groups of students developing a system based on the same requirements. For each iteration of the software the metrics were studied to see if they could predict the faults that were found by independent testing.

There are many software metric tools but the validity of the metrics they provide is not investigated. Considering that the usefulness of a metric is in its validity we set out to investigate the amount of somehow validated metrics that the current popular tools provide. To the best of our knowledge there is no study which investigates the existing tools in terms of what metrics they provide. To address this research problem the following research questions were formulated:

RQ1 Which internal software quality metrics are validated in scientific studies?

RQ2 Which are the tools that support these metrics?

RQ3 What are the administrative capabilities of these tools to conduct measurements?

2   Related Work

Internal software quality is related to the structure of the software itself as opposed to external software quality which is concerned with the behaviour of the software when it is in use. The structure of the software is not visible to the end user, but is still important since internal attributes (e.g., size, complexity, and cohesion) affect external quality attributes (e.g., maintainability and understandability) [9]. External quality is limited to the final stages of software development, whereas testing for internal quality is possible from the early stages of the development cycle, hence internal quality attributes have an important role to play in the improvement of software quality. The internal quality attributes are measured by means of internal quality metrics [10]. We, of course, recognize that the metric is not the construct in itself, but since it is assumed to be closely connected, we assume the metrics in the empirical studies are close to the construct they aim at measuring.

Metrics can be validated for all programming languages, but some apply only to specific programming paradigms and the majority can be classified as Traditional or Object Oriented Metrics (OO) [11]. Considering the popularity of object oriented metrics it is not surprising that most of the validation studies concentrate on OO [12]. In 2012, Suresh [13] performed a theoretical and empirical evaluation on a subset of the traditional metrics and object oriented metrics used to estimate a systems reliability, testing effort and complexity. The paper explored source code metrics such as cyclomatic complexity, size, comment percentage and CK Metrics (WMC, DIT, NOC, CBO, RFC LCOM). Yeresime's studies concluded that the aforementioned traditional and object oriented metrics provide relevant information to practitioners in regard to fault prediction while at the same time provide a basis for software quality assessment.

Jabangwe et al. [14] in their systematic literature review, which focused mainly on empirical evaluations of measures, used on object oriented programs concluded that the link from metrics to reliability and maintainability across studies is the strongest for: LOC (Lines of Code), WMC McCabe (Weighted Method Count), RFC (Response for a Class) and CBO (Coupling Between Objects). Antinyan et al. [15] proved in their empirical study on complexity that complexity metrics such as McCabe cyclomatic complexity [16], [17] measures, Fan-Out, Fan-In, Coupling Measures of [18], [19] OO measures, Size measure [20] and Readability measures [21,22] correlate strongly with maintenance time. They also suggested that more work is required to understand how software engineers can effectively use existing metrics to reduce maintenance effort.

Another example is a recent study on client-based cohesion metrics for OO classes. The study included a multivariate regression analysis on fourteen cohesion metrics applying the backwards selection process to find the best combination of cohesion metrics that can be used together to predict testing effort, the results revealed that LCOM1 (Lack of Cohesion of Methods 1) LCOM2 (Lack of Cohesion of Methods 2), LCOM3 (Lack of Cohesion of Methods 3) and CCC (Client Class Cohesion) are significant predictors for testing effort in classes [23].

3 Research Method

First, a review of previous work on software metrics validation was done. The main goal was to elicit internal quality measures based on their existence in scientific studies. We only consider empirical validation in this study and therefore exclude theoretical validation without industry, or "real," data. As a second step, we searched and selected tools that support these metrics. Afterwards, relevant data was investigated about the tools which could help with some practicalities when using these tools in software development practice. Finally, consistency of measurement was evaluated between these tools on a set of open source projects.

3.1 Search and Identification of Relevant Papers and Metrics

To identify relevant research papers, the subject area was restricted to Engineering and Computer Science, the string below was built based on keywords as well as synonyms defined for the study. We used the following digital libraries and search engines: Google Scholars[1], IEEE Digital Library[2], Science Direct[3], Springer[4] and Engineering Village[5].

The following search string was used:

(validated OR "verification of internal quality" OR "code quality" OR "software quality") AND (metric OR metrics OR measure OR measuring) AND tools

After the search 567 articles were found (Fig. 1) many of which were irrelevant for the purpose of this paper.

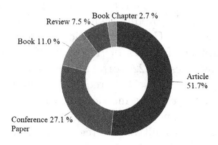

Fig. 1. Pie chart showing types and percentage of papers found

These papers were assessed according the criteria described in Table 1. The output from this step resulted in 292 research papers subjecting 30 internal quality metrics to validation. Afterwards, from these metrics we selected such metrics that were considered somehow validated as results of the papers. If any metric was evaluated inconsistently in different papers we excluded it from our final list. We realize the issue with this type of exclusion criteria, but we wanted an initial assessment of the existence of somehow validated metrics in the available tools. The main criteria of validation was that a metric shall have tangible correlation with an external software quality attribute such as maintainability and defects. However, since the aim of the study was code improvement metrics particularly, we added one more criteria: Besides having tangible correlation, a metric shall also be possible to manipulate for influencing the external quality attributes, see e.g. [24], that is increasing maintainability or decreasing defects. For example, Lines of Code usually has a tangible correlation with defects and maintainability. However, Lines of code is essential for writing code, and therefore cannot be reduced for the purpose of decreasing defects or increasing maintainability. Similarly, McCabe's cyclomatic complexity has tangible correlation with defect and maintainability but cannot be manipulated to a significant degree for code

---

[1] https://scholar.google.se/.
[2] http://ieeexplore.ieee.org.
[3] http://www.sciencedirect.com.
[4] http://www.springer.com.
[5] https://www.engineeringvillage.com.

improvements. It should be clear, however, that if a metric is not supported for quality assessment in a validation study it can be valid for other activities. For example, the same Lines of Code metric can be supported for maintenance effort estimation. Or Cyclomatic complexity can be useful for testability assessment.

Table 1. Criteria

Inclusion criteria	
I1	Papers published in a well-known software engineering journals or conferences
I2	Papers that present studies in empirical validation of internal quality or software metrics
Exclusion criteria	
E1	Papers that are not written in English
E2	Papers that do not have internal metrics context and do not provide scientific validation of internal quality metrics

3.2 Selection of Tools

For the selection of the tools, first, a free search on the Internet was conducted. The main criteria was that the tools should conduct any type of static analysis. As a result 130 tools were found. Because the aim of this paper is to aid practitioners to improve the quality of their code, and because there are several tools that support the same metrics, we set criteria for the selection of the tools. A summary of the criteria is presented in Table 2.

Table 2. Criteria for tool selection

Criteria	
C1	Support automated static analysis
C2	Offer at least one somehow validated metric
C3	Integration to IDEs and version control systems
C4	Be free or at least offer a trial option
C5	Support at least two programming languages
C6	Provide documentation such as user manual and/or installation manual

4 Results

4.1 Selection of Metrics

The first research question was what are the somehow validated metrics according to literature. Based on the inclusion and exclusion criteria described earlier a total number of 292 papers were found which evaluate internal quality metrics. After an in-depth analysis of each of the paper a preliminary table with 30 metrics was created (Table 3). This table presents all metrics that had been subjected to validation in an empirical study.

Table 3. List of metrics subjected to validation in literature and the ones we selected for this study.

#	Metric	No of papers	Selected
1	Lack of Cohesion on Methods	9	X
2	Weight Methods per Class	9	
3	Depth of Inheritance	8	X
4	Response for Classes	8	X
5	Number of Classes	8	
6	Coupling Between Objects	7	X
7	Tight Class Cohesion	6	X
8	Loose Class Cohesion	5	X
9	Lines of Code	4	
10	McCabe Complexity	4	
11	Lack of Cohesion on Methods 2	4	X
12	Lack of Cohesion on Methods 3	3	X
13	Lack of Cohesion on Methods 1	3	X
14	Degree of Cohesion (Direct)	3	
15	Degree of Cohesion (Indirect)	3	
16	Fan-Out Fan-In	2	X
17	Number of Methods	2	
18	Block depth	2	X
19	Weight Methods per Class-McCabe	1	
20	Standard Deviation Method Complexity	1	
21	Average Method Complexity	1	
22	Maximum Cyclomatic Complexity of a single Method of a Class	1	
23	Number of Instance Methods	1	
24	Number of Trivial Methods	1	
25	Number of send Statements defined in a Class	1	
26	Number of ADT Defined in A Class	1	
27	Sensitive Class Cohesion	1	
28	Improved Connection Based on Member Connectivity	1	
29	Lack of Cohesion on Methods 4	1	X
30	Number of Attributes	1	

In the next step all the metrics that were evaluated as somehow validated were selected. After excluding metrics that are invalid for internal quality assessment the final list of 12 validated metrics also presented in Table 3. These are

6   Threats of Validity

There could be errors in the underlying studies, and the validity of the metrics is established in those other papers. The results from those validation studies could be incorrect, which could influence the result of this study. The threat to validity for a specific metric can be assumed to be lower the more independent validation studies have been conducted. This threat was somewhat mitigated by the fact that the selected metrics are supported by 2 or more papers.

Another threat is a potential error in the search process. This kind of limitation is particularly difficult to tackle, we tried to use a not too broad and not to narrow search string to capture relevant papers.

Omission of relevant papers is a third threat we have identified, and as stated in the research method section, during the initial search 567 papers were found but many of these were not relevant to this study as they also included papers about medicine, biochemistry, environmental science, chemistry, agriculture, physics or social science. The reason for these papers being found by the search is presumably that the keywords "metrics," "software" and "validation" are common to many scientific papers. In the second search the subject areas above were excluded and as a result 292 papers were found. There is a chance that there is an unidentified paper conducting metric validation, however, this will not change the general ratio of generally offered and somehow validated metrics.

Naming of metrics is an external threat to validity. Unfortunately each tool can use different names for metrics in scientific papers, which could lead to a mapping problem.

7   Conclusions

This study found 12 somehow validated metrics that can be helpful in practice for code improvements. Popular static code analysis tools capture these metrics partially. But at the same time, they provide overwhelming number of other metrics, the purpose of which are not clear. This may cause confusion for practitioners. Additionally, these tools have capabilities for being integrated to software development environment and helping developers in continuous code improvements, even though they are oriented to specific programming languages.

References

1. Schulmeyer, G.G., McManus, J.I.: Handbook of Software Quality Assurance. Van Nostrand Reinhold Co., New York (1992)
2. Leveson, N.G., Turner, C.S.: An investigation of the Therac-25 accidents. Computer **26**(7), 18–41 (1993)
3. ISO, I.: IEC 9126-1: Software engineering-product quality-part 1: quality model. International Organization for Standardization 21, Geneva (2001)
4. Nicolette, D.: Software development metrics (2015). (Electronic source)

5. Basili, V.R., Briand, L.C., Melo, W.L.: A validation of object-oriented design metrics as quality indicators. IEEE Trans. Softw. Eng. **22**(10), 751–761 (1996)
6. Santos, M., Afonso, P., Bermejo, P.H., Costa, H.: Metrics and statistical techniques used to evaluate internal quality of object-oriented software: a systematic mapping. In: 2016 35th International Conference of the Chilean Computer Science Society (SCCC), pp. 1–11. IEEE (2016)
7. Carrillo, A.B., Mateo, P.R., Monje, M.R.: Metrics to evalute fuctional quality: A sistematic review. In: 7th Iberian Conference on Information Systems and Technologies (CISTI 2012), pp. 1–6. IEEE (2012)
8. Lincke, R., Lundberg, J., Löwe, W.: Comparing software metrics tools. In: Proceedings of the 2008 International Symposium on Software Testing and Analysis, pp. 131–142. ACM (2008)
9. Briand, L.C., Morasca, S., Basili, V.R.: Property-based software engineering measurement. IEEE Trans. Softw. Eng. **22**(1), 68–86 (1996)
10. Ordonez, M.J., Haddad, H.M.: The state of metrics in software industry. In: Fifth International Conference on Information Technology: New Generations (ITNG 2008), pp. 453–458. IEEE (2008)
11. Shepperd, M., Ince, D.: Derivation and Validation of Software Metrics. Clarendon Press, Oxford (1993)
12. de AG Saraiva, J., De França, M.S., Soares, S.C., Fernando Filho, J., de Souza, R.M.: Classifying metrics for assessing object-oriented software maintainability: a family of metrics' catalogs. J. Syst. Softw. **103**, 85–101 (2015)
13. Suresh, Y., Pati, J., Rath, S.K.: Effectiveness of software metrics for object-oriented system. Procedia Technol. **6**, 420–427 (2012)
14. Jabangwe, R., Börstler, J., Šmite, D., Wohlin, C.: Empirical evidence on the link between object-oriented measures and external quality attributes: a systematic literature review. Empirical Softw. Eng. **20**(3), 640–693 (2015)
15. Antinyan, V., Staron, M., Sandberg, A.: Evaluating code complexity triggers, use of complexity measures and the influence of code complexity on maintenance time. Empirical Softw. Eng. **22**(6), 3057–3087 (2017)
16. McCabe, T.J.: A complexity measure. IEEE Trans. Softw. Eng. **4**, 308–320 (1976)
17. Halstead, M.H.: Elements of Software Science. Elsevier Science, New York (1977)
18. Henry, S., Kafura, D.: Software structure metrics based on information flow. IEEE Trans. Softw. Eng. **5**, 510–518 (1981)
19. Chidamber, S.R., Kemerer, C.F.: A metrics suite for object oriented design. IEEE Trans. Softw. Eng. **20**(6), 476–493 (1994)
20. Antinyan, V., et al.: Identifying risky areas of software code in agile/lean software development: an industrial experience report. In: 2014 Software Evolution Week-IEEE Conference on Software Maintenance, Reengineering, and Reverse Engineering (CSMR-WCRE), pp. 154–163. IEEE (2014)
21. Tenny, T.: Program readability: procedures versus comments. IEEE Trans. Softw. Eng. **14**(9), 1271–1279 (1988)
22. Buse, R.P., Weimer, W.R.: Learning a metric for code readability. IEEE Trans. Softw. Eng. **36**(4), 546–558 (2010)
23. Alzahrani, M., Melton, A.: Defining and validating a client-based cohesion metric for object-oriented classes. In: 2017 IEEE 41st Annual Computer Software and Applications Conference (COMPSAC), vol. 1, pp. 91–96. IEEE (2017)
24. Shepperd, M., Ince, D.C.: A critique of three metrics. J. Syst. Softw. **26**(3), 197–210 (1994)
25. Fenton, N.E., Neil, M.: Software metrics: roadmap. In: Proceedings of the Conference on the Future of Software Engineering, pp. 357–370. ACM (2000)

A Unique Value that Synthesizes the Quality Level of a Product Architecture: Outcome of a Quality Attributes Requirements Evaluation Method

Mariana Falco[1](✉) and Gabriela Robiolo[2]

[1] LIDTUA (CIC)/CONICET, Facultad de Ingeniería,
Universidad Austral, Pilar, Buenos Aires, Argentina
mfalco@austral.edu.ar
[2] LIDTUA (CIC), Facultad de Ingeniería,
Universidad Austral, Pilar, Buenos Aires, Argentina
grobiolo@austral.edu.ar

Abstract. The architecture can inhibit or enable the different quality attributes that guide to software product, so it is extremely important to approach the evaluation of the architecture to determine at what level the quality is being achieved. Although there are frameworks and assessment methods for the architecture or quality characteristics in particular, none of them synthesizes in a single value the level of quality of a software product. We address this shortcoming by introducing a new five-step architecture evaluation method which defines, analyze and measure the quality characteristics of a product architecture and its implementation, obtaining as a final output a unique value that represents the quality level. We illustrate the method by analyzing an architecture of a web and mobile application within the healthcare domain, developed in an agile context.

Keywords: Quality attributes · Quality characteristics · Evaluation method

1 Introduction

The quality of a system is extremely necessary to define whether the system satisfies or not the needs of stakeholders, and those needs are precisely what is represented in the quality model; which is characterized by quality characteristics defined by the ISO/IEC 25010 [1]. Different activities can benefit from the use of quality concepts, during product development, like identifying requirements, design and testing objectives, quality control and acceptance criteria, and also establishing measures of quality characteristics.

A quality attribute is a "*measurable feature of a system, which is utilized to stipulate how well the system satisfies stakeholders*" [2]. Bass et al. [3] defines a quality attribute as "*a measurable or testable property of a system that is used to indicate how well the system satisfies the needs of its stakeholders*". Also, the authors say that "*a quality attribute can be thought of as a measuring of the "goodness" of a product*

X. Franch et al. (Eds.): PROFES 2019, LNCS 11915, pp. 649–660, 2019.
https://doi.org/10.1007/978-3-030-35333-9_51

along some dimension of interest to a stakeholder". Likewise, Bass et al. [3] define quality attribute requirements (QARs) as "*qualifications of the functional requirements or of the overall product*". Having these definitions in mind, the research question of the present paper is the following: *Is it possible to define a unique value that synthesize the quality level of a product architecture?* Consequently, the main objective is to introduce the construction, the definition of an architecture evaluation method and its application on a case study, that analyze the quality characteristics of the architecture and their implementation, obtaining a synthesized and unique value that represent the quality level. The evaluation method includes five steps: (1) elicitation of QARs, (2) definition of the acceptance criteria for the expected quality level of the product, (3) measurement of each quality attribute requirements, (4) collect and synthesize the results and finally, (5) the assessment of the product quality level obtained. This method can be applied to every development method that defines iterations, like agile methods.

It is worth mentioning that Step 1 implements the elicitation of QARs through the Goal-Question-Metric method [4, 5], while Step 4 includes the extension of the testing coverage definition [6–8] to analyze each quality characteristic included in the architecture. Later on, a case study was carried out to study the implementation of the evaluation method, conducting the measurement of an architecture embedded in the healthcare domain, for patients in a cardiac rehabilitation program, which it was developed within an agile context. The list of quality characteristics included in the architecture is as follows: Availability, Interoperability, Performance Efficiency, Security, Usability, Modifiability, and Functional Suitability. By calculating the coverage of each quality characteristic, the values evidence the different problems encountered during the implementation of the application. Consequently, through the analysis of the quality characteristic we obtained a feasible representation of the application putting into numeric values how good or how bad each quality characteristic was achieved; leading to a summary value that represent this idea.

The literature describes others architecture evaluation methods like SAAM [9] and ATAM [10] which schematize the procedure in steps approaching the elicitation process with scenarios. The main contributions of the present paper are: (a) we built an architecture evaluation method that includes quality characteristics as defined by ISO 25010 [1], (b) we have extended the use of testing coverage to define QAR coverage, and architecture coverage; (c) we have extended the acceptance criteria for functional and nonfunctional requirements, and (d) we have synthesized the functional and nonfunctional requirements on a number that represents the quality level of an architecture. The present article is structured as follows: in Sect. 2 the related work will be addressed, while Sect. 3 will describe and characterize the method of Elicitation, Measurement and Evaluation of an Architecture. Section 4 will approach the case study, while Sect. 4.2 will address the discussion and threats to validity. Finally, Sect. 5 will describe the conclusions and lines of future work.

2   Related Work

Both the definition of the architecture of a product and the specification of quality characteristics and quality attributes requirements are decisions that should not be taken lightly because they have a high impact on the state of the final product. The literature addresses these issues in different ways, defining models, methodologies, frameworks, and evaluation methods. As far as the quality model is concerned, Ortega, Pérez and Rojas [11] designed a prototype with a systemic approach that contains quality attributes that allows a product to be analyzed, and that when applied, it is possible not only to analyze the weaknesses and strengths, but also discern its compliance with standards. Their goal is to identify the quality characteristics of the product necessary to obtain systemic quality. The biggest beneficiary of this model are the companies, because it serves as a benchmark for their products to evolve and be competitive.

The main difference from our work is that as they built a model, they not only had to identify quality characteristics and measures, but they also created a taxonomy with them. Another difference is within the quality characteristics used: Efficiency, Reliability, Functionality, Maintainability, Portability and Usability. In this line, Bachmann et al. [12] presented a reasoning framework as a means of modularizing the knowledge of quality attributes, where the requirements that the architecture must fulfill are defined as specific quality attribute scenarios; and they also differentiate between an architectural model and a model of quality attributes, and thus achieving the identification of conflicting requirements.

In the same way, some authors have proposed scenarios-based evaluation methods such as SAAM [9], ATAM [10], CBAM [13], ALMA [14], and FAAM [15]. The analysis of an architecture through SAAM (Software Architecture Analysis Method) allows to detect the strengths or weaknesses of it, together with those points where the architecture fails to meet the modifiability requirements. Considering that the steps in a SAAM evaluation session address the management of scenarios, one of the main differences with our evaluation method is that it doesn't include metrics to analyze the quality characteristics.

On the other hand, ATAM (Architecture Tradeoff Analysis Method), based on SAAM, performs an assessment of the following quality attributes: Modifiability, Portability, Extensibility and Integrability; addressing how well the architecture meets quality goals; also through scenarios. Furthermore, it analyzes the interdependencies and trade-offs between quality attributes. A similarity in the steps defined by ATAM with our evaluation method is that they also include the requirements elicitation, and the scenarios they have specified are embedded in the definition of Bass [10] to characterize a quality attribute that includes the following parts: a source of stimulus, stimulus, environment, artifact, response and response measures.

Then, CBAM (Cost-Benefit Analysis Method) is a method that analyzes the costs, benefits and schedule implications of architectural decisions; and positions them with the same level of importance as quality attributes [13]. A partial similarity to our method is that its second step advocates the elicitation of the benefits of quality attributes for managers; in our case, the participation of managers is done in the assessment of the quality of the architecture (step three and six, respectively). The focus of ALMA (Architecture-Level Modifiability Analysis) is modifiability and it's testing in business information systems; and the main difference is that it advocates a set of indicators for the assessment of modifiability: maintenance cost predictions, and risk assessment. With respect to FAAM (Family-Architecture Assessment Method), although our method includes interoperability, we not only advocate interoperability between systems or between families of systems, but we analyze between systems, between systems and sensors, between modules and between services [15].

Later on, the authors in [9] presented the central aspects to achieve an understanding of the structures of an architecture based on quality characteristics, in order to propose a method to find an adequate software architecture structure based on quality requirements of the software product in question. Although it is a generic method, they have presented a case study that addresses the following QAs: Performance, Reliability, Maintainability, and Portability. However, Bass et al. [10] studies the attributes of quality (based on quality attributes requirements) from the definition of scenarios (as also the previous evaluation methods such as SAAM and ATAM do), and definition of tactics, which based on the progress of the technologies currently need to be expanded and completed.

As a summary, some authors approach the study and implementation of specific quality attributes such as interoperability or performance; others include a greater number of quality attributes but none justify the selection of them for any particular reason or by any standard such as ISO 25010 [1]. In the same way, some are domain-specific with a quality attribute. Then, there are several methods of evaluation of architecture, with which the idea of requirement elicitation is shared, but the vast majority of them are based on scenarios, following the idea of Bass [10]. In our case, elicitation is based on the GQM method, to specify the needs of stakeholders in the form of goals, questions, metrics and acceptance criteria for each question. None of the studies proposes any form of synthesis of the analysis, as such, we propose the definition and calculation of coverage values for each selected quality characteristics, and for the entire architecture, which leads to the achievement of a multidimensional number as a summary value of the achieved quality level as final output. Finally, the focus of this method is oriented to the measurement of quality characteristics.

3   Method of Elicitation, Measurement and Evaluation of an Architecture

This section specifies each of the five steps included within the defined evaluation method, which are: (1) elicitation of QARs, (2) define the acceptance criteria for the expected quality level of the product, (3) measure and test each QARs, (4) collect and synthesize results, and finally, (5) assessment of the product quality level.

Step 1: Elicitation of Quality Attributes Requirements

Requirements engineering is the process of eliciting individual stakeholder requirements, and developing them into detailed, agreed requirements documented and specified in such a way that they can serve as the basis for all other system development activities [4]. In our context, this elicitation process approaches the definition of stakeholders needs as a way to specify the quality characteristics of a software product, not only identifying them but also describing for each characteristic what the stakeholder want. This process will be done through the Goal-Question-Metric method [4]. The resulting hierarchical model is composed of three levels that are refined from one level to the other; and consequently, step 1.1 will approach the conceptual level, defining the goals, step 1.2 will embed the operational level, specifying the questions by goal, and finally, step 1.3 will specify the quantitative level, defining the metrics by question. It is worth mentioning that Step 1 should be validated by the stakeholders.

Step 1.1: Select Quality Characteristics and Sub-characteristics. ISO 25010 [1] describes that the quality of a system is the degree to which the system satisfies the stated and implied needs of its various stakeholders; and the quality model categorizes the quality of the product into characteristics and sub-characteristics. The characteristics are Functional Suitability, Performance Efficiency, Compatibility, Usability, Reliability, Security, Maintainability, and Portability; which can be selected by the stakeholders; as each characteristic is mapped with a goal, it is defined by the purpose, issue, object and viewpoint per selected characteristic.

Step 1.2: Specify Quality Attributes Requirements. Bass et al. [3] explain that the requirements of a system originate from different sources and forms (functional, quality attributes and constants). Considering the Step 1.1, the QARs for each of the quality characteristics are now specified by the stakeholder and the development team. These QARs are the questions defined for each of the goals. For example, in the context of Performance Efficiency a QAR can be defined as: *"Does a registry or directory of all personnel who use or access the system is provided?"*.

Step 1.3: Define Metrics and Acceptance Criteria of Each Quality Attribute Requirement. In this sub-step, the metrics that act as a refinement of the questions within the quantitative product measurement process should be defined, will provide the necessary information to answer the questions defined in Step 1.2 [16]. By defining the limits and parameters of a user story or functionality, and determining when a story is complete and functioning as expected, it is possible to specify an acceptance criteria containing conditions that a software product must satisfy in order to be accepted by the user or stakeholder [17]. Acceptance criteria are also discussed when defining what requirements must be met in each incremental version of a software product [3]. In this context, we sought to extend these concepts for each of the metrics defined by goal in order to determine if this measured value was met or not, addressing not only functionalities, but also quality characteristics.

Step 2: Define the Acceptance Criteria for the Expected Quality Level of the Product
This point is key when defining the acceptance criteria of the product expected level that will be subject to measurement, because the value advocates understanding of how well the quality for each goal is achieved, allowing a glimpse of the level of the entire product quality. In this way, the acceptance criteria is a positive number that can take any value between 0 and 1; and is defined by the stakeholders. We must mention that 1 is the best and strictest value of an acceptance criteria: 0 is equal to all QAR are not passed, and 1 is equal to all passed QAR obtaining the same value as TEC which is also

equal to 1. It is important to mention that the acceptance criteria must be defined per each of the expected iterations, which will be different and incremental from the first one to the last one [18]. In the same way, as the stakeholder is the one who defines his needs, he or she also defines the level of quality expected for each iteration.

Step 3: Measure and Test Each Quality Attribute Requirements

Step 3 involves carrying out the measurement of each question, executing the defined metric and describing whether that acceptance criteria was met or not, indicating 1 (passed) or 0 (failed), respectively. In the case of Usability, the measurement binds the responses of the number of users who perform the usability test effective. The final value of each test question will be obtained from the application of Eq. (6), which promotes the unification of the total number of answers per respondent, for each of the defined questions; allowing later to compute the measurement.

Step 4: Collect and Synthesize Results

Within the software process, the coverage testing addresses two uses, where in the first the coverage can be considered as a measure of the quality of the product, and in the second, it is a feedback mechanism for the software engineer. In the context of the evaluation method, we have based on the concept of testing coverage to derive coverage for the different quality characteristics. Based on the foregoing, Eqs. (1) to (5) describe the calculations needed to compute the quality level of an architecture.

$$OCi = \frac{Number\ of\ passed\ QARi}{Number\ of\ QARi} = \frac{NpQARi}{NQARi} \tag{1}$$

$$ECarch(i) = \frac{Number\ of\ QARi}{Total\ number\ of\ QAR} = \frac{NQARi}{TNQAR} \tag{2}$$

$$OCarch(i) = \frac{Number\ of\ passed\ QARi}{Total\ number\ of\ QARi} = \frac{NpQARi}{TNQARi} \tag{3}$$

$$TEC = \sum_{i=1}^{n} ECarch(i) = 1 \tag{4}$$

$$TOC = \sum_{i=1}^{n} OCarch(i) \tag{5}$$

where: i identified each quality characteristic; OC_i is the obtained coverage per quality characteristic, $NpQAR_i$ is the number of passed QARs per quality characteristic, $NQAR_i$ is the number of QARs per quality characteristic; $ECarch_i$ is the expected coverage per quality characteristic within the architecture, $NQAR_i$ is the number of QARs per quality characteristic, $TNQAR$ is the total number of QAR; $OCarch_i$ is the obtained coverage per quality characteristic within the architecture, $NpQAR_i$ is the number of passed QARs per quality characteristic, $TNQAR$ is the total number of passed QAR; TEC is the total expected coverage within the architecture, where n is the number of quality characteristics; and *TOC* is the total obtained coverage of quality attribute requirements within the architecture.

For each QAR corresponding to Usability, z answers will be obtained according to the number of participants that perform the Usability test. With respect to Usability, each QAR is analyze as follows: (1) it is necessary to unify the z answers from the Usability test that were different from 0 and 1 to become 0 or 1, for example those being a qualitative value like low, very low, medium or high can be unified defining a criteria that all those answers with low and very low will be considered as passed (1) and medium and high as failed (0); (2) Then, all the values (0s and 1s) for each QAR are summarized, and it is obtained the value that represents the QARs that passed; (3) Later, the coverage per QAR is calculated as follows (where x is each QAR) with Equation

$$UCx = \frac{Sum\ of\ passed\ answers\ per\ QAR}{Number\ of\ respondents} \tag{6}$$

Where UCx is the Usability coverage per QAR. If the value obtained with Eq. (6) is lower than 0.5 then it is considered as failed, passed otherwise, obtaining the value $NpQAR_i$ for Usability; as the sum of the passed values. (4) Finally, once $NpQAR_i$ is calculated, it is possible to compute the coverage for Usability itself with Eq. (1)-OC_i and (3)-$OCarch_i$; and continue with the calculations in order to obtain the TOC value - Eq. (5).

Step 5: Assessment of the Product Quality Level
It is possible to perform the analysis of the quality level obtained by means of Eq. (5), and the comparison with the acceptance criteria defined by Step 3. If the value obtained in (5) is lower than the criteria, the iteration will not have the expected quality level, and the individual values of each quality feature must be analyzed to determine the points of failure, and continuous working in the iteration.

4   Case Study

4.1   Description

The objective of this case study is to address the application of the proposed evaluation method to a mobile and web app called HeartCare, describing also the results obtained. HeartCare is an application designed and implemented by the authors with engineering students, whose main goal is to ensure that the recovery of cardiac patients can take place in an environment outside hospitals. The layered architecture includes a multi-agent system and a heart-rate sensor (Polar H10) that helps the patient monitor their heart condition while he or she is in rest position, or while performing a physical exercise, through a mobile device with Android. The literature describes similar examples to HeartCare [19–21].

Step 1: Elicitation of Quality Attributes Requirements

Step 1.1: Select quality characteristics and sub-characteristics. Based on the needs of stakeholders, the following characteristics and sub-characteristics have been selected: (a) *Functional Suitability*: Functional Completeness, Functional Correctness; (b) *Performance Efficiency*: Time Behavior, Resource Utilization, Capacity; (c) *Compatibility*: Interoperability; (d) *Usability*; (e) *Reliability*: Availability; (f) *Security*: Confidentiality, Integrity, Authenticity; (g) *Maintainability*: Modifiability, Testability. These QAs were selected based on the requisite of the Cardiology Service of a private hospital, which it was in need of an improvement of their software services quality, in order to provide a better attention for patients with cardiac conditions. In this context, only one goal will be presented to achieve the traceability of the steps, but it is convenient to emphasize that the specific goals of all the quality characteristics have been specified. Instantiating the GQM approach, the goal for Performance Efficiency is specified with a purpose (analyze), an issue (response and processing times), an object (mobile phone, sensor, and web application), and a viewpoint (from the project manager and user viewpoint).

Step 1.2: Specify quality attribute requirements. Considering the goal, one of the questions that arises for performance efficiency is: *Is the user wait-time for the connection of the sensor with the mobile adequate?,* as shown in Fig. 1 row F16. The set of QARs by quality characteristic leads to obtain the set of aspects that are wanted to be analyze in the architecture.

ID	Quality characteristic	Question	Metric	Acceptance criteria	Result
F16	Performance efficiency	Is the user wait time for the connection of the sensor with the mobile adequate?	Number of seconds it takes to make the connection	Less than 10 seconds	1
F17	Performance efficiency	How fast is the measurement interval of the bpm?	Number of seconds of the measurement interval	Less than 5 seconds	1
F18	Performance efficiency	How fast is the task of stop sensing?	Number of seconds it takes to stop sensing	Less han 3 seconds	1
F19	Performance efficiency	How fast is the sensor notification in case of disconection?	Number of seconds it takes to nofity the disconnection	Less than 5 seconds	1
F46	Performance efficiency	How good is the perceived satisfaction of the user of the application?	Apdex score	Closer to 1	1
F47	Performance efficiency	What is the number of web requests that ended up in an error?	Number of web requests	Between 0 and 3	1
F48	Performance efficiency	What is the number of unhandled and logged errors?	Number of unhandled and logged errors	Between 0 and 3	1
F49	Performance efficiency	What is the number of all exceptions that have been thrown?	Number of thrown exceptions	Between 0 and 3	1
F50	Performance efficiency	What is the number of communication exceptions between agents?	Number of communication exceptions between agents	Between 0 and 3	0
F51	Performance efficiency	What is the number of application/service exceptions (persistence, etc)?	Number of application / service exceptions	Between 0 and 3	0

Fig. 1. Performance Efficiency analyzed through GQM, acceptance criteria and result.

Step 1.3: Define metrics and acceptance criteria of each quality attribute requirement. The questions and the quality attributes are stored in a structured spreadsheet as shown in Fig. 1. The ID column allows to identify and quickly group each row by quality characteristic, the header together with columns 3 and 4 address the results of the GQM, identifying the questions (QAR) and each metric. Finally, the *Result* column contains the result of the measurement made per row for all QARs (1 passed, 0 failed). Each QAR was validated by the stakeholder.

Step 2: Define the Acceptance Criteria for the Expected Quality Level of the Product. Following the GQM specification of the previous steps, the stakeholder has defined the acceptance criteria as 0.70. The architecture to be measured outlines the first iteration, so it is feasible to consider a value of 0.70 because at least two more iterations are expected, which will increase the individual value of the acceptance criteria for each of them.

Step 3: Measure and Test Each Quality Attribute Requirements. At this point and to be able to complete the *Result* column of the cell corresponding to the table of Fig. 1, the analysis was made of whether each of those quality attributes requirements were included or not in the measured architecture. For example, the row with ID F16 shown in Fig. 1 ask whether the time the user has to wait for the sensor connection with the mobile is too long or not. Consequently, by measuring this time, a value of 4 s was obtained, so it is considered as "passed" and in the result column, the value "1" was written down. This same procedure was performed for all the QARs.

Step 4: Collect and Synthesize Results. It is necessary to calculate the coverage for each of the defined quality characteristics. Following the example, Eq. (1) allows calculating the coverage value for Performance Efficiency which gives $OC_i = NpQAR_i/NQAR_i = 16/18 = 0.89$. It is worth mentioning that within Usability, each QAR was answered by fourteen respondents, who gave their perspective of the functioning and design of the mobile app. Equation (6) allowed the unification of the Usability answers, obtaining a single value to represent the result per each Usability QAR. Once the results from Eq. (6) and $NpQAR_i$ were obtained, Eqs. (1), (2), (3), and (4) were calculated for all of the characteristics, and therefore completing Table 1, obtaining by means of Eq. (5) a TOC value of 0.775.

Table 1. Summary of results from the application of the proposed evaluation method.

Quality characteristic	$NQAR_i$	$NpQAR_i$	OC_i	$ECarch_i$	$OCarch_i$
Availability	12	12	1	0.086	0.086
Interoperability	31	27	0.870	0.224	0.195
Performance efficiency	18	16	0.888	0.130	0.115
Security	19	9	0.473	0.137	0.065
Usability	27	27	1	0.195	0.195
Modifiability	16	1	0.062	0.115	0.007
Functional suitability	15	15	1	0.108	0.108
Total	**TNQAR = 138**	**TNpQAR = 107**		**TEC = 1**	**TOC = 0.775**

Table 1 shows the list of selected quality characteristics, where i is 7; the second column shows the number of QAR per each quality characteristic where it's sum is TNQAR = 138. Later, the third column includes the values of passed QAR per quality characteristic, achieving a TNpQAR = 107. The fourth column represents the obtained coverage per each quality characteristic, reaching in the fifth column to the expected coverage of each QAR within the architecture; which has a total value of TEC = 1. Finally, the sixth column possess the obtained coverage per QAR within the architecture, which its summarization allows to obtain the TOC value (0.775).

Step 5: Assessment of the Product Quality Level. The assessment itself addresses the analysis of the value obtained by the Eq. (5) based on the previous calculation of the coverage of all quality characteristics. In this case, an acceptance criteria was defined in 0.70; and following Table 1, the quality level (TOC) was 0.775. Consequently, the quality level of the measured architecture reached the expected level of quality. In any case, when analyzing the quality characteristics, it is possible to observe that the characteristics with the lowest level of completeness were security and modifiability; which will be addressed in the first instance of the next architecture iteration.

4.2   Discussion

Based on the literature analysis, some authors have presented different ways of studying the architecture and its quality attributes. Even though there are several frameworks or implementations that address testing coverage [7, 22, 23]; none of them deals with the concept and calculations to understand the quality level obtained for each quality attribute and quality characteristic. For that, we have made an extension to calculate the coverage of each individual quality characteristic and the coverage of all of them as part of the architecture.

The method used to derive the elicitation process within as the step 1 was performed through GQM [4, 5]. Knowing what to measure is a recurrent problem in a data-driven approaches, using GQM for identifying the quality attributes ensures that the assessment of the product is adapted to the organization applying the proposed method. The TOC value, that it was defined to be equal to or exceeds 0.70; was calculated through the coverage of all quality characteristics for the first iteration of the application. In the particular case of the implementation, three iterations are expected, considering that the healthcare quality demand will be high due to the requirements of this particular domain. According to the stakeholder, the first iteration (proof of concept) were set with a 0.70 acceptance criteria, the second (new architecture) with 0.70 as well, and the third one and final (a prototype to attract investors) will have a 0.80 acceptance criteria.

After the application of the proposed evaluation method, it was possible to obtain a coverage of 0.775, from which it can be understood that it can still improve by about 22%, considered as technical debt [24]. The architecture evaluation method presented in this paper positions quality as a multidimensional concept, and whose resulting value (0.775) allow us to demonstrate that one of the greatest achievements of this method is that it has been able to synthesize the multiple dimensions through this number, achieving a complete analysis. Later on, a manager in a business context can use that number as a first means of analyzing the quality of an architecture, because it can determine at a glance if the architecture passes or not the allowed acceptance criteria. If it does not happen, the manager must extract what are the changes that must be made to reach the allowed threshold, and thus achieve the expected product quality.

As threats to validity, it is possible to consider the subjectivity included in the evaluation of the QARs, when we decided to accept or reject them. But it is worth mentioning that all of them were defined in order for them to be easily verifiable, testable or measurable. We must also mention that all the quality characteristics are considered with the same weight, a point that will be improved in the next iteration of the evaluation method. Also, all of those QARs belonging to Usability have a reduced subjectivity due to the number of people involved in the Usability test carried out. It is feasible to mention that we consider that these fourteen respondents were sufficient for this first iteration of the framework measurement. Likewise, it is necessary to ask whether really the quality level represents the quality of the product. In response, it is feasible to mention that the quality level is a percentage measure of the amount of QARs selected, where the selection of each one were validated with stakeholders, so we considered that is not necessary to validate the value obtained per se.

5 Conclusions

The present paper embedded the definition of an architecture evaluation method, and shows a fruitful measurement of a healthcare application. We conclude that it is possible to apply the method within agile methods, achieving a multidimensional value. As future work, the method to include the various iterations of the life cycle of a software product will be generalized, seeking to develop an automated software tool that embodies this evaluation method, including the possibility of specifying a different weight for each of the requirements defined.

References

1. ISO/IEC 25010 (s.f). https://iso25000.com/index.php/en/iso-25000-standards/iso-25010
2. Alenezi, M.: Software architecture quality measurement stability and understandability. Int. J. Adv. Comput. Sci. Appl. (IJACSA) 7(7), 550–559 (2016)
3. Bass, L., Clements, P., Kazman, R.: Software Architecture in Practice, 3rd edn. Addison-Wesley Professional, Boston (2012)
4. Basili, V.R.: Software Modeling and Measurement: The Goal/Question/Metric Paradigm (1992)
5. Caldiera, V., Basili, V.R., Dieter Rombach, H.: The goal question metric approach. In: Encyclopedia of Software Engineering, pp. 528–532 (1994)
6. Yang, Q., Li, J.J., Weiss, D.M.: A survey of coverage-based testing tools. Comput. J. 52(5), 589–597 (2009)
7. Horgan, J.R., London, S., Lyu, M.R.: Achieving software quality with testing coverage measures. Computer 27(9), 60–69 (1994)
8. Parra, P., da Silva, A., Polo, O.R., Sánchez, S.: Agile deployment and code coverage testing metrics of the boot software on-board Solar Orbiter's Energetic Particle Detector. Acta Astronaut. 143, 203–211 (2018)
9. Kazman, R., Bass, L., Abowd, G., Webb, M.: SAAM: a method for analyzing the properties of software architectures. In: Proceedings of 16th International Conference on Software Engineering, pp. 81–90. IEEE (1994)

10. Kazman, R., Klein, M., Clements, P.: ATAM: method for architecture evaluation (No. CMU/SEI-2000-TR-004). Carnegie-Mellon University, Pittsburgh, PA, Software Engineering Institute (2000)
11. Ortega, M., Pérez, M., Rojas, T.: Construction of a systemic quality model for evaluating a software product. Softw. Qual. J. **11**(3), 219–242 (2003)
12. Bachmann, F., Bass, L., Klein, M., Shelton, C.: Designing software architectures to achieve quality attribute requirements. IEE Proc.-Softw. **152**(4), 153–165 (2005)
13. Kazman, R., Nord, R.L., Klein, M.: A life-cycle view of architecture analysis and design methods (No. CMU/SEI-2003-TN-026). Carnegie-Mellon University, Pittsburgh, PA, Software Engineering Institute (2003)
14. Bengtsson, P., Lassing, N., Bosch, J., van Vliet, H.: Architecture-level modifiability analysis (ALMA). J. Syst. Softw. **69**(1–2), 129–147 (2004)
15. Dolan, T.J.: Architecture assessment of information-system families: a practical perspective (2003)
16. Jimenez-Fernandez, S., De Toledo, P., Del Pozo, F.: Usability and interoperability in wireless sensor networks for patient telemonitoring in chronic disease management. IEEE Trans. Biomed. Eng. **60**(12), 3331–3339 (2013)
17. van Solingen, D.R., Berghout, E.W.: The Goal/Question/Metric Method: A Practical Guide for Quality Improvement of Software Development. McGraw-Hill, New York (1999)
18. Segue Technologies: What Characteristics Make Good Agile Acceptance Criteria?, 3 September 2015. https://www.seguetech.com/what-characteristics-make-good-agile-acceptance-criteria/
19. Maia, P., et al.: A web platform for interconnecting body sensors and improving health care. Procedia Comput. Sci. **40**, 135–142 (2014)
20. Vassis, D., Belsis, P., Skourlas, C., Pantziou, G.: A pervasive architectural framework for providing remote medical treatment. In: Proceedings of the 1st International Conference on PErvasive Technologies Related to Assistive Environments, p. 23. ACM (2008)
21. Ray, P.P.: Home Health Hub Internet of Things (H 3 IoT): an architectural framework for monitoring health of elderly people. In: International Conference on Science Engineering and Management Research (ICSEMR), pp. 1–3. IEEE (2014)
22. Sakamoto, K., Washizaki, H., Fukazawa, Y. Open code coverage framework: a consistent and flexible framework for measuring test coverage supporting multiple programming languages. In: 10th International Conference on Quality Software, pp. 262–269. IEEE (2010)
23. Rayadurgam, S., Heimdahl, M.P.E.: Coverage based test-case generation using model checkers. In: Proceedings of Eighth Annual IEEE International Conference and Workshop on the Engineering of Computer-Based Systems (ECBS 2001), pp. 83–91. IEEE (2001)
24. Li, Z., Avgeriou, P., Liang, P.: A systematic mapping study on technical debt and its management. J. Syst. Softw. **101**, 193–220 (2015)

Comparison of Agile Maturity Models

Anna Schmitt[1] , Sven Theobald[1(✉)], and Philipp Diebold[2]

[1] Fraunhofer IESE, Fraunhofer-Platz 1, 67663 Kaiserslautern, Germany
{anna.schmitt,sven.theobald}@iese.fraunhofer.de
[2] Bagilstein GmbH, Mainz, Germany
philipp.diebold@bagilstein.de

Abstract. *Context*: Agile software development is widely used by small teams. Companies want to check their implementation of Agile for different reasons. Many Agile Maturity Models (AMM) exist that support practitioners in assessing and improving their agility. However, practitioners need to be able to make informed decisions on which one to use. *Objective*: The aim of this work is to enable the comparison of existing AMMs. *Method*: We identified 14 AMMs in a non-systematic literature review, considering non-scientific sources as well. We propose criteria for their comparison based on our experience and our understanding of practitioners' needs. *Results*: We present twelve comparison criteria and show how the identified AMMs differ along those criteria. *Conclusion*: Practitioners get an overview of existing models and can select a suitable one with the help of the comparison criteria.

Keywords: Agile Maturity Model · Assessment · Agile software development · Comparison criteria

1 Introduction

Agile is widely used by software development teams [1]. However, many different adaptations to the proposed methods and practices exist [2]. Agile processes are seldomly used in their pure form and often appear as a mix with traditional processes, forming a hybrid process [3].

All teams want to know how well they implemented Agile and how they can improve based on their current status quo. The most common way for process improvement in Agile is continuous process improvement supported by common agile practices like retrospectives. In line with the agile principle of inspection and adaptation, the team regularly inspects its own way of working and looks for improvement possibilities.

This way of improving allows only gradual improvement, but does not allow describing a more objective status quo of the team's agility. Maturity models like CMMI, the Capability Maturity Model Integration [4], define different levels for describing the maturity of existing processes. Similarly, many Agile Maturity Models (AMM) have been constructed to enable teams to assess their agility and determine the quality of their current agile implementation. Also, those maturity models usually describe certain requirements to reach a higher level, which serve as an improvement roadmap.

Thus, a huge number of agile maturity models indicating how well Agile has already been implemented have been developed to measure a team's maturity. This

© Springer Nature Switzerland AG 2019
X. Franch et al. (Eds.): PROFES 2019, LNCS 11915, pp. 661–671, 2019.
https://doi.org/10.1007/978-3-030-35333-9_52

flood of different models provides many opportunities to practitioners. However, practitioners must understand the advantages and disadvantages of each model in order to be able to select the most appropriate AMM for their purpose and context.

The objective of this work is to provide a comparison of existing AMMs based on defined, practical criteria. These criteria are intended to support practitioners in selecting an AMM that fits best to their circumstances and requirements.

2 Related Work

Many Agile Maturity Models (AMM) have been published in the scientific and non-scientific communities. However, not much literature exists comparing existing AMMs in order to understand their commonalities and differences.

In their initial survey, Schweigert et al. [5] compared seven AMMs and mapped their maturity levels to the maturity levels of CMMI [4]. They found that these AMMs even use the maturity level names of CMMI, although their content differs largely from AMM to AMM.

One year later, Schweigert et al. [6] extended their previous survey and compared about 40 different AMMs. Furthermore, they investigated their structure. They grouped the AMMs in two different ways. On the one hand, there are AMMs that use a level structure close to the level structure of CMMI – initial, managed, defined, quantitatively managed, optimizing. On the other hand, there are AMMs that do not use CMMI as a reference, rather using individual names and proposing six maturity levels. Additionally, the considered AMMs were clustered based on the criteria "features", "recommendations", "key questions", "scaling factors", "enablers", "management principles", and "agile improvement procedure".

Özcan-Top and Demirörs [7] chose another way to compare AMMs. They focused on the strengths and weaknesses of five AMMs concerning the aspects of agile process assessment and improvement. Therefore, they applied the considered AMMs in software organizations and assessed the AMMs based on the following quality criteria: fitness for purpose, completeness, definition of agile levels, objectivity, correctness, and consistency. The degree of fulfillment of these criteria was measured with the help of a scale that included "not achieved", "partially achieved", "largely achieved", and "fully achieved".

Leppänen [8] compared eight AMMs on the basis of criteria like purpose, domain, conceptual and theoretical backgrounds, structure, use, and validation.

The main differences to our comparison are that, on the one hand, we regard only those AMMs that offer a detailed description of themselves, especially of their maturity levels. On the other hand, we propose criteria aimed at helping practitioners choose the most appropriate AMM for their circumstances (Sect. 4).

3 Agile Maturity Models

Before we started our search for existing Agile Maturity Models (AMM), we defined the criteria for the selection of appropriate AMMs. Since there is no final definition of what an AMM has to look like or of what purpose an AMM needs to fulfill, we declared our own AMM acceptance criteria. Not at all of these criteria need to be fulfilled together – the considered AMMs only needed to fulfill one of the three defined criteria.

- The first criterion is that an AMM needs to have different maturity levels. On this basis, practitioners can locate themselves at the respective level. They can measure their agility and see what needs to be done to reach the next-higher level. Additionally, the particular maturity levels have to be described in detail. This makes it obvious and easy for experts and non-experts alike to understand how to classify themselves and see what is required for the next level.
- The second criterion is that the AMM needs to provide the possibility to assess a company's or team's own maturity in terms of agility or the attainment of objectives by providing questions that support und guide the assessment activities.
- The third criterion concerns the support of the AMM for providing an improvement roadmap, e.g., by suggesting suitable agile practices for implementation.

After defining the characteristics an AMM needs to have from our point of view, we started our search. We used scientific search databases such as Scopus as well as non-scientific sources on the Internet, e.g., blogs and whitepapers. However, we did not perform a systematic literature review [9]. Instead, we used an unsystematic search approach complemented by a snowballing approach [10].

After browsing our sources, we identified 28 AMMs that seemed to match at least one of our acceptance criteria, as described above. Then we carefully went through every AMM and checked whether it matched one of our criteria. As a result, half of the 28 initial AMMs did not have the characteristics we had previously defined. Finally, there were 14 AMMs that we selected for a more detailed comparison (cf. Table 1).

Table 1. Agile Maturity Models that are compared throughout this paper

Author	Year	Title	Ref.
Ahmed Sidky, James Arthur	2007	The Agile Adoption Framework	[22]
Chetankumar Patel, Muthu Ramachandran	2009	Agile Maturity Model (AMM): A Software Process Improvement framework for Agile Software Development Practices	[16]
Jez Humble, Rolf Russel	2009	The Agile Maturity Model – Applied to Building and Releasing Software	[23]
Mark Seuffert	2009	Agile Karlskrona test	[24]
Robert Benefield	2010	Seven Dimensions of Agile Maturity in the Global Enterprise	[18]
Martin Proulx	2010	Agile Maturity Model (AMM): The 5 Levels of Maturity	[21]
Shirly Ronen-Harel	2010	Agile Testing Maturity Model	[25]
Dan Woods	2011	An Agile BI Maturity Model	[26]
Angela Druckman	2011	Agile Transformation Strategy	[27]
Alexandre Yin, Soraia Figueiredo, Miguel Mira da Silva	2011	Scrum Maturity Model	[19]
Eric Minick, Jeffrey Fredrick	2014	Enterprise Continuous Integration Maturity Model	[20]
Raphael Branger	2016	A Maturity Model for Agile BI	[15]
Programmedevelopment	–	Agile readiness & maturity	[28]
–	2008	Towards an Agile Process Maturity Model	[17]

4   Comparison Criteria

We defined twelve criteria to compare the chosen 14 AMM on a more detailed level (cf. Table 2). These criteria are based on our experiences of what practitioners are looking for and need in their daily work to apply an AMM appropriately. This practical approach is intended to support practitioners in selecting the AMM best suited to their needs. However, the practitioners weight the individual criteria differently, depending on their subjective perception of the importance of the criteria for their needs. For example, startups might focus on other criteria than large, more established companies. They might weight the criteria differently, depending on their own needs. In the following, we will propose those criteria together with a description and motivation for their usage.

Intention: Before choosing an AMM, practitioners should clarify for what purpose they want to choose and apply an AMM. Therefore, it is important to specify what intention the AMM pursues to match their own purpose with the purpose of the AMM. An AMM does not necessarily follow solely one intention, but can also fulfill various intentions that can also depend on each other. The frameworks mention the following intentions: Benchmarking, Self-Assessment, Guide Agile Transition, Improvement, Discover/Remove Bottlenecks, Implementing Practices/Methods, Process Visibility, Goal-Specific Maturity.

Addressing Culture: For a successful agile implementation, two different parts are important: technical agility and cultural agility [11]. Adopting agile methods and practices primarily influences the technical aspects, improving the processes and the organizational work of software engineering in enterprises. The other part, the culture, depends on the mindset of the involved people. They need to internalize the new way of working and collaborating. Thus, the cultural change cannot be seen by looking at the workflow of software engineering, but rather by inspecting the mindset. Since this change of culture is inevitable in order to mature in Agile, it is important that AMMs also support practitioners in assessing and developing their culture. Thus, with these criteria we assess whether culture is addressed or not.

Assessment: Most practitioners use AMMs since they want to measure or check how agile they already are. Therefore, they expect an AMM either to have a structure or levels in which they can classify themselves or to provide questions that help them determine their agile maturity. Therefore, this criterion has two sub-criteria. On the one hand, we compared the AMMs based on the criterion "State Analysis/Assessment", meaning whether they provide an approach with which practitioners can analyze the status quo of their agile maturity. On the other hand, our comparison is based on the criterion "Assessment Questions", meaning whether the AMMs provide questions that support practitioners in their self-evaluation concerning agility.

Improvement Activities: AMMs are known for helping to conduct a state analysis and to show what needs to be done at which maturity level. However, they do not always show how practitioners can reach the next maturity level. Therefore, we wanted

Table 2. Criteria for the comparison of Agile Maturity Models

Criteria	Characteristics
Intention	Benchmarking, Self-Assessment, Guide Agile Transition, Improvement, Discover/Remove Bottlenecks, Implementing Practices/Methods, Process Visibility, Goal-specific
Addressing culture	yes (y)/no (n)
Assessment	
Incl. actual state/state-analysis/assessment	yes (y)/no (n)
Incl. assessment-questions	yes (y)/no (n)
Incl. improvement activities	yes (y)/no (n)
Structure and levels	
Maturity level	yes (y)/no (n)
Capability level	yes (y)/no (n)
Level affiliation	
Team	yes (y)/no (n)
Project	yes (y)/no (n)
Organization	yes (y)/no (n)
Incl. practices	
Technical	yes (y)/no (n)
Managerial	yes (y)/no (n)
Behavioral	yes (y)/no (n)
Documentation (available for Questions/Practices?)	low, middle, high (expresses to what extent functionality, execution, and attributes/components are covered by documentation)
Underlying model	e.g., CMMI, Testing Maturity Model, GQM, OPA.
Scope	agility in general or concrete agile methods/practices like Scrum
Advantages/chances	free text
Disadvantages/challenges	free text

to know whether the considered AMMs provide such improvement activities that help reach a higher level of maturity.

Structure and Levels: Using this criterion, we compared the AMMs regarding their maturity and capability levels. Generally, practitioners anticipate that an AMM has maturity levels – simply because of the name. Practitioners that are more into the matter of maturity models may also expect capability levels (cf. CMMI [4]). So it is interesting to investigate whether the considered AMMs have a maturity or capability level structure. Additionally, we wanted to compare the number of maturity and capability levels, their naming, and their content.

Level Affiliation: Organizations share a common internal hierarchical structure, which can be divided into three different levels: team, project, and organization. Thus, organizations want to apply AMMs at one or more of these levels. The AMM should therefore support assessment of that specific level. This need is reflected in the structure of the AMM, which differs in that different AMMs address different levels – some address only one level, some two, and some even all three.

Including Practices: Since agile maturity is strongly related to the use and implementation of different practices in the software development process, we expect AMMs to provide or suggest certain agile practices that help to reach a specific level of agile maturity. As many different agile practices with different purposes exist, we divided the criterion "Including Practices" into three sub-criteria. We examined whether an AMM contained technical practices, e.g., Pair Programming [12]; managerial practices, e.g., Daily StandUp [13]; and behavioral practices (values/ principles), e.g., self-organization [14].

Documentation: With this criterion, we give practitioners hints on the extent to which they can draw on existing documentation when using the selected AMM. We rated the available information on a scale of "low, medium, high" that expresses to what extent functionality, execution, and attributes/components are covered by documentation.

Underlying Model: Before AMMs came up, there were already other assessments models for the field of software engineering. The most popular assessment model is the CMMI [4], which is not related to Agile at all. Nevertheless, CMMI and other assessment models may provide a good basis for the structured constitution of AMMs. It is interesting to investigate whether the existing AMMs are based on existing assessment models or whether they do not use such a model as a basic framework and instead reassemble themselves from scratch. Additionally, it is helpful for users to know whether an AMM is based on a specific assessment model because if they already have experience with this specific assessment model, it is easier for them to make a decision for or against a model – as they want to build on their existing knowledge.

Scope: Here, the scope of the AMMs regarding the agile methodology is examined. It is interesting for practitioners to know whether an AMM focuses on concrete agile methods or practices or considers Agile in general. Especially practitioners who already use certain agile practices or methods can be supported in their decision regarding which AMM to choose. They can select an AMM that builds on the methods and practices already implemented in order to determine how mature they already are in this field. In addition, they can consciously select an AMM that does not build on the practices already used in order to further collect other improvement ideas.

Advantages/Opportunities: In general, every model has advantages that can be crucial for whether it is used or not. They represent the opportunities for practitioners to decide quickly whether the described advantages map with the advantages they hope to receive by applying a certain AMM.

Disadvantages/Challenges: The opposite of advantages are disadvantages – with the same purpose. They represent challenges practitioners could be faced with when applying a particular AMM.

5   Discussion

In the previous section, we described the criteria chosen for the comparison of Agile Maturity Models (AMM). Now, we will take a closer look at how AMMs differ concerning those criteria. In addition, we will discuss the threats to validity of this work.

5.1   Discussion of Criteria

The first criterion was "**Intention**". This is the criterion where the AMMs differ the most. The most common intention is "improvement", which is the intention of five AMMs. The objective of four AMMs was "Self-Assessment". The intentions "Guide Agile Transition" and "Implementing Practices/Methods" are addressed by three AMMs each. The goal of two AMMs is to "Benchmark" themselves and to achieve a higher maturity by fulfilling defined goals ("Goal-Specific Maturity"). Only one AMM pursued the intention of "Discover/Remove Bottlenecks", another one to make their process visible ("Process Visibility"). However, it is not the case that every AMM only pursues one intention. We discovered AMMs that have two or three intentions. So in total, 9 AMMs have one concrete intention, three AMMs have two intentions (Improvement & Discover/Remove Bottlenecks; Self-Assessment & Improvement; Improvement & Goal-specific Maturity), and two AMM pursue three intentions, namely "Improvement & Implementing Practices and Methods & Process Visibility" and "Benchmarking & Improvement & Implementing Practices/Methods".

Concerning the criterion "**Addressing Culture**", we found that although culture is so important for applying agile methodology [14], only five of the 14 AMMs address this issue. One example is the AMM "A Maturity Model for Agile BI" [15]. The issue of culture is addressed by starting with the teaching and implementation of the agile mindset and basics in the first step of this AMM – in fact, in the whole organization. Another example is the AMM "Agile Maturity Model (AMM): A Software Process Improvement Framework for Agile Software Development Practices" [16], which tries to identify improvement areas by defining one's own assessment questionnaire, which is mainly based on the agile mindset.

As mentioned above, we divided the criterion "**Assessment**" into two sub-categories, State Analysis and Assessment Questions. We found that 11 AMMs provide a State Analysis. "Towards an Agile Process Maturity Model" [17], for example, furnishes two axes, the technical and the managerial, each consisting of three maturity levels. At each maturity level, it is described in detail when practitioners can classify themselves at these levels and what practices they need to implement to this end. However, three AMMs do not provide any sub-category, neither a State Analysis nor Assessment Questions, and no AMM provides solely Assessment Questions. Indeed, three AMMs developed both a State Analysis and Assessment Questions.

A logical step after providing a State Analysis and/or Assessment Questions would be to allocate "**Improvement Activities**" as well. However, only five AMMs provide support regarding activities for improving a team's own agile maturity. It is interesting to see that out of these five AMMs, only three match the AMMs fulfilling the criterion "Assessment". This means that only three of the 11 AMMs that offer "Assessment" also offer "Improvement Activities". Benefield [19] describes seven dimensions, where each dimension provides benefits that might help with delivery and that improve the quality of work and the speed of the team.

One interesting observation regarding the next criterion "**Structure and Level**" is that none of the 14 AMMs developed capability levels, as CMMI did. Only maturity levels were developed. There are similarities concerning the used maturity levels, but also differences. Most (10) have five maturity levels. Two AMMs present four, one AMM presents presents two axes (managerial, technical) with three levels at a time. Another AMM presents six levels. Here are some examples to show the differences in the naming of AMMs that have five levels:

- Patel and Ramachandran [16]: 1-Initial, 2-Explored, 3-Defined, 4-Improved, 5-Sustained
- Yin et al. [19]: 1-Initial, 2-Managed, 3-Defined, 4-Quantitatively Managed, 5-Optimizing
- Minick and Fredrick [20]: 1-Base, 2-Beginner, 3-Intermediate, 4-Advanced, 5-Extreme
- Benefield [18]: 1-Emergent Engineering Best Practices, 2-Continuous Practices at Component Level, 3-Cross Component Continuous Integration, 4-Cross Journey Continuous Integration, 5-On Demand Just in Time Releases

Another example are the six maturity levels of the "Agile Maturity Model (AMM)" from [21]: 1-Team Level Maturity, 2-Department Level Maturity, Business Level Maturity, 4-Project Management Level Maturity, 5-Management Level Maturity, 6-Corporate-wide Level Maturity.

Another important criterion was the "**Level Affiliation**", which helps practitioners to understand at which level of the organization they can use which AMM. Four AMMs solely deal with the team level, three solely with the organizational level. One AMM deals with the team and project level, two with the team and organization level, one with the project and organization level, and three with all three levels.

Another fact that is important when talking about Agile is the use and implementation of agile practices. Therefore, we also examined the AMMs in terms of the criterion "**Including Practices**". Since there are many practices with different purposes, we divided this issue into three areas: technical practices, managerial practices, and behavioral practices. Four AMMs do not consider agile practices at all. Three AMMs focus on the use and implementation of technical practices only, e.g., Continuous Deployment, Test Automation [21], Code Quality Metrics, Test Driven Development, Automated Builds and Configuration [19]. Technical and managerial practices were used by five AMMs, where, e.g., Daily StandUp, Sprint Planning [20], or User Stories [16] represent managerial practices. Two AMMs also deal with behavioral practices, meaning that the values and principles of Agile are considered. Example practices used include co-location, self-organization [15], and collaboration [23].

Concerning "**Documentation**", most AMMs provide a good documentation basis so that practitioners can try to apply those AMMs even if they have no relevant experience. However, three models offer only little information.

What is obvious when comparing the maturity levels of AMMs is that there is a strong connection with the criterion "**Underlying Model**". Six AMMs, especially those with five maturity levels, are based on the CMMI assessment model [4], e.g.,

[16]. However, AMMs with fewer levels are also oriented towards CMMI, e.g., the "Agile Process Maturity Model (APMM)" [17]. Other underlying models include: GQM and OPA (one AMM, 1–5 levels), Agile Engineering Fluency and Agile Data Warehouse Design (one AMM; 1–4 levels), Testing Maturity Model and Traditional Process Maturity Model (one AMM, 1–5 levels). Five AMMs stated that they had not used any other model as a basis.

With the help of the criterion "**Scope**" we wanted to examine on which agile methods or practices the AMMs build on, or whether they just generally build on Agile. We found that seven AMMs are not related to any special practices or methods. One AMM explicitly refers to the values and principles of the Agile Manifesto [14]. Another two AMMs build on Extreme programming [12], and two build on Scrum [13]. A more famous scope is the testing field – three AMMs refer to this. Additionally, one AMM uses automation as its base. What can be seen here is that there are some models that rely on more than one scope, e.g., "Agile Maturity Model (AMM): The 5 Levels of Maturity" (Scrum, FDD, TDD, XP) [22] or "Maturing Agile Processes to Deliver Better Value" (generally agile, but little focus on TDD und CI) [18].

We do not discuss the criteria "**Advantages/Opportunities**" and "**Disadvantages/ Challenges**" in this paper. Every AMM mentions its individual advantages and disadvantages that are too specific to discuss.

5.2   Threats to Validity

No systematic literature review (SLR) was conducted to identify the models for comparison. However, only conducting an SLR in a scientific database would not have brought the same number of sources, since we also considered models not published in the scientific literature. The definition of three acceptance criteria for the inclusion of appropriate AMMs is based on our subjective opinion of what an AMM should entail. The same applies to the twelve criteria used for the comparison of the 18 considered AMMs. Their selection is based solely on our experience concerning the needs, challenges, and daily work of practitioners concerning the maturing their own agility. External researchers or practitioners did not evaluate these criteria. This fact also extends to the assessment of the AMMs. It is a subjective assessment based on our expertise and on the clarity of the criteria. Hence, the set of criteria as well as the assessment of the AMMs based on these criteria could be subject to some bias.

6   Conclusion

Many teams have applied agile development approaches and are now looking for maturity models to support them in assessing and improving their agility. Many Agile Maturity Models (AMM) have been proposed, but practitioners do not know which one to choose. Using a broad but unsystematic literature search, we identified 28 agile maturity models, of which 18 satisfied our self-declared criteria for an AMM. We propose twelve criteria on which AMMs can be rated and compared based on our experiences and insights regarding what practitioners need to select the best-fitting model. We discussed each criterion based on the analysis of the identified AMMs to provide an overview of the differences of the existing models.

As a result, one AMM can be recommended, as it is the one that meets most of the criteria. The AMM of [16] has a specific Intention (improvement, goal-specific), addresses Culture, supports Assessment by providing a State Analysis and Assessment Questions, and includes Improvement Activities. Additionally, it supplies maturity levels from one to five (Structure and Levels), is usable at the team, project, and organization level (Level Affiliation), provides technical and managerial practices (Including Practices), has a high level of Documentation, uses CMMI as the underlying model, and has a wide scope, including agile values, principles, and practices. However, it is not complete. It does not provide capability levels (Structure and Level) nor behavioral practices (Including Practices).

In general, the comparison was made to help practitioners select an appropriate AMM for their circumstances. This means that the criteria can be weighted individually, depending on the needs and subjective perception of the importance of the criteria. We do not specify which criteria must be considered first or which are most important, since every company has different needs and circumstances. In future work, we will present the details of our model comparison. Although they did not fulfill our definition for an AMM, the ten excluded models should also be analyzed to identify their benefit for practitioners.

Acknowledgements. This research is funded by the German Ministry of Education and Research (BMBF) as part of a Software Campus project (01IS17047). We also thank Sonnhild Namingha for proof reading this paper.

References

1. Version One: 12th Annual State of Agile TM Report (2018). https://www.versionone.com/
2. Diebold, P., Ostberg, J.-P., Wagner, S., Zendler, U.: What do practitioners vary in using scrum? In: Lassenius, C., Dingsøyr, T., Paasivaara, M. (eds.) XP 2015. LNBIP, vol. 212, pp. 40–51. Springer, Cham (2015). https://doi.org/10.1007/978-3-319-18612-2_4
3. Kuhrmann, M., et al.: Hybrid software and system development in practice: waterfall, scrum, and beyond. In: Proceedings of the 2017 International Conference on Software and System Process, pp. 30–39 (2017)
4. Software Engineering Institute: CMMI for Development, Version 1.3 – Improving processes for developing better products and services (2010). http://www.sei.cmu.edu
5. Schweigert, T., Nevalainen, R., Vohwinkel, D., Korsaa, M., Biro, M.: Agile maturity model: oxymoron or the next level of understanding. In: Mas, A., Mesquida, A., Rout, T., O'Connor, R.V., Dorling, A. (eds.) SPICE 2012. CCIS, vol. 290, pp. 289–294. Springer, Heidelberg (2012). https://doi.org/10.1007/978-3-642-30439-2_34
6. Schweigert, T., Vohwinkel, D., Korsaa, M., Nevalainen, R., Biro, M.: Agile maturity model: a synopsis as a first step to synthesis. In: McCaffery, F., O'Connor, R.V., Messnarz, R. (eds.) EuroSPI 2013. CCIS, vol. 364, pp. 214–227. Springer, Heidelberg (2013). https://doi.org/10.1007/978-3-642-39179-8_19
7. Ozcan-Top, O., Demirörs, O.: Assessment of agile maturity models: a multiple case study. In: Woronowicz, T., Rout, T., O'Connor, Rory V., Dorling, A. (eds.) SPICE 2013. CCIS, vol. 349, pp. 130–141. Springer, Heidelberg (2013). https://doi.org/10.1007/978-3-642-38833-0_12

8. Leppänen, M.: A comparative analysis of agile maturity models. In: Pooley, R., Coady, J., Schneider, C., Linger, H., Barry, C., Lang, M. (eds.) Information Systems Development, pp. 329–343. Springer, Heidelberg (2013). https://doi.org/10.1007/978-1-4614-4951-5_27

9. Kitchenham, B.A., Charters, S.: Guidelines for performing systematic literature reviews in software engineering. Technical report EBSE-2007-01, School of Computer Science and Mathematics, Keele University (2007)

10. Wohlin, C.: Guidelines for snowballing in systematic literature studies and a replication in software engineering. In: Proceedings of the 18th International Conference on Evaluation and Assessment in Software Engineering (EASE 2014), no. 38 (2014)

11. Diebold, P., Küpper, S., Zehler, T.: Nachhaltige Agile Transition: Symbiose von technischer und kultureller Agilität. In: Engstler, M., et al. (Hrsg.) Projektmanagement und Vorgehensmodelle, pp. 121–126 (2015)

12. Wells, D.: Extreme Programming: A Gentle Introduction (2013). http://www.extreme programming.org/

13. Sutherland, J., Schwaber, K.: The Scrum Guide (2016). http://www.scrumguides.org

14. Beck, K., et al.: Manifesto for Agile Software Development (2001). http://agilemanifesto. org/

15. Branger, R.: A Maturity Model for Agile BI (2015). https://rbranger.files.wordpress.com/ 2016/01/a-maturity-model-for-agile-bi_en_v1_1.pdf

16. Patel, C., Ramachandran, M.: Agile maturity model (AMM): a software process improvement framework for agile software development practices. Int. J. Softw. Eng. 2(1), 1–26 (2009)

17. Towards an Agile Process Maturity Model (2008). https://pdfs.semanticscholar.org/2a99/ 3ed7c2ab66700f54f19809a7617c7b9949fc.pdf

18. Benefield, R.: Seven dimensions of agile maturity in the global enterprise: a case study. In: Proceedings of the 43rd Hawaii International Conference on System Sciences (2010)

19. Yin, A., Figueiredo, S., Da Silva, M.M.: Scrum maturity model. In: The Sixth International Conference on Software Engineering Advances (2011)

20. Minick, E., Fredrick, J.: Enterprise Continuous Integration Maturity Model (2014). https:// developer.ibm.com/urbancode/docs/continuous-delivery-maturity-model/

21. Proulx, M.: Yet Another Agile Maturity Model (AMM) – The 5 Levels of Maturity (2010). https://danossia.wordpress.com/2010/07/12/yet-another-agile-maturity-model-the-5-levels-of-maturity/

22. Sidky, A., Arthur, J., Bohner, S.: A disciplined approach to adopting agile practices: the agile adoption framework. Innov. Syst. Softw. Eng. 3(3), 203–216 (2007)

23. Humble, J., Russel, R.: The agile maturity model – applied to building and releasing software (2011). ThoughtWorks STUDIOS. https://info.thoughtworks.com/rs/thoughtworks2/images/ agile_maturity_model.pdf

24. Seuffert, M.: Agile Karlskrona Test (2009). https://mayberg.se/media/downloads/karlskrona-test.pdf

25. Ronen-Harel, S.: ATMM - Agile Testing Maturity Model: Practical View (2010). https://de. slideshare.net/AgileSparks/atmm-practical-view

26. Woods, D.: An Agile BI Maturity Model (2011). https://www.forbes.com/sites/danwoods/ 2011/10/26/an-agile-bi-maturity-model/#5bb8247b5960

27. Druckman, A.: Agile Transformation Strategy (2011). Whitepaper. https://www.collab.net/

28. Programmedevelopment: Agile Readiness & Maturity. Programmedevelopment.com/agile-readiness-maturity.htm (website not available anymore)

4th International Workshop on Human Factors in Software Development Processes (HuFo)

Human Factors in Software Processes

Silvia Abrahao[1], Maria Teresa Baldassarre[2], Fabio Q. B. da Silva[3],
and Simone Romano[2]

[1] Universidad Politecnica de Valencia (UPV), Spain
sabrahao@dsic.upv.es
[2] Università degli Studi di Bari Aldo Moro, Italy
{mariateresa.baldassarre, simone.romano}@uniba.it
[3] Federal University of Pernambuco, Recife, Brazil
fabio@cin.ufpe.br

Abstract. Software Engineering and Human-Computer Interaction look at software processes from different perspectives. They apparently use very different approaches, are inspired by different principles and address different needs. But, they definitely have the same goal: develop high quality software in the most effective way. The fourth edition of the workshop continues the success of previous editions placing particular attention on efforts of the two communities with respect to software processes.

Keywords: Human Computer Interaction · Software Engineering · Human factors · Software process

1 Introduction and Motivation

Software development is a human intensive activity whatever the underlying production process it is based on. Though both software engineering (SE) and human-computer interaction (HCI) communities aim towards creating better software products, the two communities are still far from being synergic while they could both gain from a better integration. Recent efforts have contributed to increase the synergy between SE and HCI. Nevertheless, this has not led to expected results and impacts with respect to software processes. Software product industry emphasizes the importance of contact with users and customers in order to understand requirements both regarding the functionality and the usability of software products. At the same time, multi layered software architectures are pursued in order to have robust and evolvable software products, according to the customers' needs, even if they were not properly taken in to account at the beginning of the development process.

One might expect that such issues would lead to emphasize the core importance of human factors in software. Unfortunately, this has not been the case. Indeed, recent literature has pointed out how in most empirical evaluations only a small number of works include human participants. Moreover, there is still little experience in conducting empirical studies with human participants.

The overall goal of this interdisciplinary workshop that has come to its fourth edition has been to raise the level of engagement and discussion about human factors in software product engineering and processes in order to identify opportunities to improve the quality of scientific results and improvements on human aspects of software product development. A further goal of the workshop has also been to identify opportunities to improve the quality of scientific discourse and progress on human aspects within software processes, as well as to identify opportunities able to educate researchers about how to conduct sound human-centered evaluations in the context of software engineering.

The submissions received have addressed the following research questions:

- What are the key methods that allow the integration of human factors in software processes?
- What methods do current software development teams use to engage users in software processes?
- How can the level of human factor involvement be objectively verified during and after software development?
- How to educate researchers on performing human-centered evaluations in software engineering processes?

Researchers and practitioners who face the problem of integrating human factors in software quality evaluation should have a place to discuss their experiences, lessons learned and future intentions to reach a common understanding on evaluation topics.

2   Audience and Expected Outcomes

Although researchers and practitioners from the two communities share the same goal of developing high quality systems, the methodologies, methods and metrics they use to evaluate such quality are very different due to their background and expertise.

The fourth edition of the workshop on Human Factors in Software Processes aims at providing a forum for discussing measuring system quality from both perspectives. The workshop has received a positive response from both HCI and SE communities with several interesting and valuable contributions. The submissions were peer-reviewed by international committee members for their quality, topic relevance, innovation, and potentials to foster discussion. Finally, five papers were accepted.

In the first paper "Dealing with Comprehension and Bugs in Native and Cross-Platform Apps: A Controlled Experiment", authors present the results of a controlled experiment conducted with developers, aimed to investigate whether there is a difference when comprehending apps implemented with either cross-platform (Ionic-Cordova-Angular) and native (Android) technologies.

The second paper "Understanding how and when human factors are used in the software process: a text-mining based literature review", aims at indicating the state of the art of the literature on human factors in the software development process, assessed through a literature review using text mining techniques.

In the third paper "Working Conditions for Software Developers in Colombia: An Effort-Reward-Imbalance-based Study", authors focus on diagnosing the working conditions of employees in the area of software development, based on existing models that measure their satisfaction with the current positions in the area of software construction in Colombia.

The fourth paper "Towards a better Understanding of Team-driven Dynamics in Agile Software Projects", describes a study with 15 software projects and a total of 130 undergraduate students where authors developed a plugin that enables the assessment of team behavior in combination with exploratory analyses for JIRA. The study reveals a set of team-related sprint dynamics.

Finally, in the fifth paper "A Case Study for Validating the Usability Model for Software Development Process and Practice", researchers define a Usability Model for Software development Process and Practice (UMP), consisting of characteristics and metrics, in the quest to improve the work experience of software development practitioners and the effectiveness of process and practice adoption initiatives.

Acknowledgment. We would like to thank the organizers of PROFES 2019 for giving us the opportunity to organize this workshop. We are also grateful to our international program committee of experts in the field for their reviews and collaboration.

Dealing with Comprehension and Bugs in Native and Cross-Platform Apps: A Controlled Experiment

Maria Caulo[1]([envelope]), Rita Francese[2], Giuseppe Scanniello[1], and Antonio Spera[2]

[1] University of Basilicata, Potenza, Italy
{maria.caulo,giuseppe.scanniello}@unibas.it
[2] University of Salerno, Fisciano, SA, Italy
francese@unisa.it, a.spera18@studenti.unisa.it

Abstract. In this paper, we present the results of a controlled experiment aimed to investigate whether there is a difference when comprehending apps implemented with either cross-platform (Ionic-Cordova-Angular) and native (Android) technologies. We divided participants into two groups. The participants in each group were asked to comprehend the source code of either the app implemented using Ionic-Cordova-Angular technology or its Android version. We also asked the participants to identify and fix faults in the source code. The goal was to verify if the technology might play a role in the execution of these two kinds of tasks. We also investigated the affective reactions of participants and the difficulty they perceived when accomplishing the tasks mentioned before. The most important take-away result is: there is not a statistically significant difference in the comprehension and in the identification and fixing of bugs when dealing with either native or cross-platform apps.

Keywords: Android · Cross-platform · Ionic · Sentiment analysis

1 Introduction

All the software organizations have to afford the problem of developing the same mobile application several times for different mobile operating systems (*i.e.,* Android and iOS) and running on many target devices, while preserving the performances and the user interface interaction of the native approaches. It is not possible to share code among the various implementations, which have to be separately developed. As a result, the development process might take a longer time. Also, maintenance is very expensive because all the maintenance activities have to be simultaneously conducted on all the software variants.

To try to reduce the development and maintenance costs and time-to-market many mobile cross-platform development approaches have been proposed, some of them are still in development phase [7]. Their main advantage is that the apps for several mobile platforms are developed and maintained one time. In addition, many cross-platform tools are based on web technologies and this avoids

© Springer Nature Switzerland AG 2019
X. Franch et al. (Eds.): PROFES 2019, LNCS 11915, pp. 677–693, 2019.
https://doi.org/10.1007/978-3-030-35333-9_53

web developers to be forced to learn many new languages and development environments. Another reason for choosing cross-platform frameworks is that they can be adopted for rapid prototyping of apps to be run in various hardware/software platforms. It is also a quick way to be operative in the market and to reach the maximum number of users with the plan of re-implementing or migrating them towards native platforms. Research work is focused on the comparison of the performances of cross-platform apps and the native ones by evaluating the performances of the apps on different platforms and their User Experience [19,25]. In the recent past these results where still in favor of native platforms, especially in case of applications stressing the user interface or massively exploiting the hardware resources, such as games. For this kind of applications cross-platform technology could be lagging and/or producing a worst User Experience. At present, the adoption of cross-development technologies is increasing due to the higher performances of top-level devices and we can expect they will overcome their limitations.

In this paper, we present the results of a controlled experiment aimed to investigate whether there is a difference when comprehending apps implemented with either cross-platform (Ionic-Cordova-Angular) and native (Android) technologies. Source-code comprehension is vital to deal with many software engineering tasks concerning existing code, *e.g.*, testing [3]. For example, before testing source code a developer should first comprehend it and then identify the bug described in a bug report. On this respect, we decided to study also if there is an effect of cross-platform and native technologies on bug identification and fixing. To complete our study, we investigate the affective reactions of participants and the difficulty they perceived when accomplishing source-code comprehension and bug identification and fixing.

This paper is organized as follows: Sect. 2 discusses related work; Sect. 3 presents the planning of the controlled experiment, while Sect. 4 summarizes the experiment results. Final remarks conclude the paper in Sect. 6.

2   Related Work

The greater part of the empirical research in the context of cross-platform apps is either on the perspective of the end-user while using this kind of apps or on the analysis of their performances. As an example, the authors in [25] and [19] compared the application performances of native and cross-platform apps, such as disk space and battery usage. Results that are negative for cross-platform solutions at the beginning improve for them in the years because the mobile device resources increased. Corral *et al.* [5] evaluated app performances by considering: hardware access, access to native features such as accelerometer and Network access. The study was focused on PhoneGap and Android apps. Results revealed that generally, Android performs better, but that the difference may be not relevant for general-purpose business applications.

Heitkotter *et al.* [9] provided a set of criteria for comparing cross-platform and native apps, *e.g.*, license and cost, supported platforms, application speed, and scalability. The criteria were founded on the authors' and professional developers' opinions. On the other hand, Dalmasso et al. [6] provided several decision criteria for selecting the appropriate cross-platform technology, including quality of the User Experience, the potential users, the security of the app, supportability, easiness of updating and time to market. Performances have been evaluated by developing Android test applications using four different cross-platform tools. Differently, Malavolta et al. [17] analyzed hybrid mobile apps from the end-users perspective by mining reviews from the Google Play Store. Results suggested that hybrid development is more suitable for data-intensive mobile apps, whereas it got poor performances when the app exploits platform-specific features.

Differently from the research highlighted before, Que et al. [19] approached cross-platform development from the developer's point of view. The authors considered aspects related to the easiness of coding, debugging and testing. Easiness of use is discussed together with performances. This paper represents the closest to ours. One of the most important differences concerns the method to investigate the defined research questions. In particular, the authors did not founded their research on users' study.

Our research improves the body of knowledge in the context of cross-platform development because we empirically investigated—through a controlled experiment and quantitative data gathered during this experiment—the developers' performances in source-code comprehension and bug identification and fixing. Another remarkable difference concerns the study of the affective reactions of participants while accomplishing these tasks.

3   Controlled Experiment

We followed the guidelines by Wohlin et al. [26] and Juristo and Moreno [12] to conduct our controlled experiment. The planning of this experiment follows the template suggested by Jedlitschka et al. [11].

3.1   Goals

We investigated the following main Research Question (RQ):

RQ1. *Is there any difference when dealing with source code of native and cross-platform apps?*

We detailed RQ1 as follows:

> *RQ1.1. Is there any difference when dealing with native and cross-platform apps in terms of source code comprehension?*
> *RQ1.2. Is there any difference when dealing with native and cross-platform apps in terms of bug identification?*
> *RQ1.3. Is there any difference when dealing with native and cross-platform apps in terms of bug fixing?*

We also studied the affective reactions of the participants when dealing with source-code comprehension and bug identification and fixing. To this end, we defined the following RQs:

RQ2. Is there an effect on pleasure, arousal, dominance, and liking?

A positive (or negative) effect of a technology with respect to these four dimensions might imply that a developer is more (or less) effective when performing the considered tasks. We deepened our investigation by focusing on the difficulty the participants perceived when accomplishing experiment tasks. Accordingly, we defined and studied also the following RQ:

RQ3. Is there an effect on the difficulty the participants perceived when accomplishing source code comprehension tasks and bug identification and fixing?

3.2   Experimental Units

Initially, 40 people accepted to take part in the experiment, but 39 actually participated. The participants were students of the "Enterprise Mobile Applications Development" course at the University of Salerno (Italy). This course focuses on the study of Ionic-Cordova-Angular technologies. A few days before the experiment, we asked the participants to fill in a pre-questionnaire. The goal was to gather demographic information on the participants and their perspectives with respect to points in favor and against cross-platform development.

The average age of participants was 24. At the time of the experiment, participants were 39 months (on average) experienced with programming and 10 months (on average) experienced with mobile programming, in particular. They passed the programming exams with a rating of 27.4/30 on average. Most of them attained the Mobile Development course focused on Android, in particular 35/39, and were rated 27/30, on average.

The results of the pre-questionnaire also indicated that the participants were in favor of cross-platform development for the following reasons: *(i)* simplicity of development, *(ii)* complete abstraction of native programming languages, *(iii)* "reusability" of the code, in the sense that they have to write it only once and then they can deploy the app for the operative system(s) they need, *(iv)* development speed, *(v)* wider number of reachable users, *(vi)* ease of maintenance, *(vii)* big support in the development of graphical interfaces. The participants declared the following points against the cross-platform development: *(i)* hard management of native functionality (low control), *(ii)* big effort in finding a single best possible solution valid for all operating systems, *(iii)* low performance (and lags), *(iv)* wide occupation of resources, and *(v)* poor customization and no possible use of specific features of a platform.

3.3   Experimental Material

As experimental objects, we used the source code of two versions of Movies-app:[1] the original one—implemented by Ionic-Cordova-Angular technologies—and the

---

[1] https://github.com/okode/movies-app.

one migrated towards Android. Movies-app allows searching movies information, then it is possible to filter the movies. Once selected a movie, it is possible to have details on it and on its actors. We opted for this real-world app because *(i)* it is not very complex (although not obvious), *(ii)* its problem domain can be considered familiar with the participants, and *(iii)* it is small enough to allow a good control over the participants that accomplished the tasks.

We migrated the original version of Movies-app to Android using an approach based on the most followed and well known one, named "chicken little" [2]:

- *Reverse Engineering,* to analyze the project structure and identify the Ionic pages that could be grouped to implement a given functionality.
- *Migration planning,* to define a migration order of the functionality and services. For each Ionic page, we performed three steps: *(i)* Pre-processing, *(ii)* GUI-Reengineering, and *(iii)* Single page and component code reengineering.
- *Data Reengineering,* to store key/value pairs, files and SQLite data on the device file system.
- *Provider Reengineering,* to map Ionic providers (*i.e.,*, services) into Java classes in Android.
- *Incremental integration and testing,* to integrate each page with those of the same group. Starting from the Ionic app, test cases can be derived and used to exercise the developed apps and find eventual differences in the behavior.

To gather affective reactions, we used the SAM [1] questionnaire, which consists of a nine-point rating scale to evaluate pleasure, arousal, and dominance. The pleasure scale ranges from "unhappiness/sadness" to "happiness/joyfulness". The arousal scale ranges from "calm/bored" to "stimulated/excited". Finally, the dominance scale varies from "without control" to "with control". We also included the liking dimension. It consists of a nine-point rating scale: from "dislike" to "like". This further dimension is inspired by Koelstra *et al.* [16].

We also asked participants to rate the level of difficulty (from one to five) when comprehending source code and accomplishing a bug identification fixing tasks. We used an approach similar to that by Scanniello *et al.* [20] in their family of controlled experiments.

3.4   Tasks

We asked the participants to perform three tasks in the following order:

1. *Comprehension Task.* We defined a comprehension questionnaire composed of six questions that admit open answers. We formulated these questions on the basis of the study by Sillito et al. [23]. In particular, we picked the most asked by developers during change tasks and adapted them to our experimental material (*i.e.,* the two apps). Sillito [23] organized such questions in four groups:
   - Finding Focus Point (FFP) aiming at finding points in the source code that were relevant to a given task.

- Expanding Focus Point (EFP) aiming at expanding a given entity in the source code believed to be relevant often by exploring relationships among entities (*e.g.*, classes and methods).
- Understanding a Subgraph (UAS) aiming at building an understanding of concepts in the code that involved multiple relationships and entities.
- Questions over a Group of Subgraphs (QGS) aiming at understanding the relationships between multiple subgraphs or understanding the interaction between a subgraph and the rest of the application.

The questions of the comprehension questionnaire are shown in Table 1. This questionnaire was the same for both the groups of participants; those working with the Android version of the app and those working with the Ionic-Cordova-Angular version. We collected answers by a Google Form. For each question, we also asked the participants to provide the time when they start to work on a given question and the time when they believed to have correctly provided the answer. We did not force participants to provide answers to the questions.

2. *Bug Identification.* Similar to Scanniello *et al.* [21], we seeded (four) bugs in the source code of the two apps. We asked the participants to fix these bugs providing them with a bug report for each seeded one. The bug report was the same independently from the app version. The bug seeding was based on the mutation operators[2] by Kim *et al.* [15]. We used the following operators:
    - Language Operator Replacement (LOR), that replaces a language operator (*e.g.*, $<, >, <=, >=$) with other legal alternatives.
    - Variable Replacement Operator (VRO), that replaces a variable name with other names of the same or compatible type(s).
    - Statements Swap Operator (SSO), that swaps contents of compatible blocks.

A few details on the seeded bugs are shown in Table 2. An example of bug report for a seeded bug is shown in Table 3.

We asked the participants to document where they believed each bug was in the source code. To this end, the participants had to write two lines of comment one before and another one after the statement/s containing the bug. The first line had to indicate the bug id as reported in the bug report. It is worth mentioning that we seeded the same bugs in both the versions of the apps. We show in Fig. 1 how the same bug (*i.e., Search by Name of Authors not working*) appears in the source code of the cross-platform version of the experimental object and its Android version.

3. *Bug Fixing.* Participants had to fix the bugs they identified. We asked the participants to work with a bug at time. Bugs do not interfere one another.

4. *Post questionnaire.* Participants had to fill in a post questionnaire. It includes a SAM questionnaire for each kind of task the participants accomplished (*i.e.*, source-code comprehension, bug identification and bug fixing). We also asked the participants to assess the difficulty they perceived to execute these tasks.

---

[2] Mutation operators are *predefined program modification rules* [14].

Table 1. Comprehension questions.

ID	Questions	Category
1	Where in the code is the text of the error message concerning the absence of popular movies?	FFP
2	Where is there any code involved in the implementation of HTTP request to get the list of upcoming movies?	FFP
3	Where is called the method that shows the description of a movie?	EFP
4	What are the arguments to be given to the function that loads the detail of a movie?	EFP
5	How does the list of movies resulting from the search by title look at runtime? (Indicate the code block responsible to display it)	UAS
6	How can we know that the Persona data type (concerning the actor of a movie) has been created and initialized correctly in all its fields?	QGS

Table 2. Seeded bugs

Title in the bug reports	Mutation operator type
Search by Name of Authors not working	LOR
Incorrect Value of the Duration of a movie	VRO
No Actor's Picture	LOR
Second Star for movie Ratings wrongly Displayed	SSO

Table 3. A bug report used in the experiment

Bug ID:	10348095
Title:	"Search by Name of Authors not working"
Description:	"The search field should return real-time clickable results, related to the name of the typed actor. For example, if I type the string 'Angelina', the screen should display all the actresses with that name in the results; if I complete with 'Jolie', the screen should display a single result, which refers to the actress detail. Instead, when searching for an actor by name, the list of results is ALWAYS empty"
Submit date:	02/20/2019
Author:	meryk90

3.5   Variables and Hypotheses

We considered one independent variable: Technology. It indicates the technology used to implement the app. It is a categorical (or nominal) variable that can assume the values of *Android* or *Ionic*.

```
<!-- Person results -->
<div class="results-flex" *ngIf="searchType == 'persons' && results && results.length > 0">
  <div class="result" *ngFor="let person of results" (click)="onPersonDetail(person.id)">
    <div class="poster">
      <img *ngIf="person.profile_path" class="poster" [src]="'https://image.tmdb.org/t/p/w185' + person.profile_path">
      <img *ngIf="person.profile_path" class="poster-effect" [src]="'https://image.tmdb.org/t/p/w185' + person.profile_path">
    </div>
    <div class="data">
      <ion-icon class="arrow" name="arrow-forward"></ion-icon>
      <div class="title">{{ person.name }}</div>
      <div class="subtitle" *ngIf="person?.known_for?.length > 0">
        <small>Películas destacadas:</small><br>
        <span *ngFor="let m of person.known_for; let last = last">
          <span *ngIf="m.title">{{ m.title }}<span *ngIf="!last">, </span></span> <!-- ignore tv shows -->
        </span>
      </div>
    </div>
  </div>
</div>
```

(a)

```
if(personList != null && personList.size() < 0){
    text_error_search.setVisibility(View.INVISIBLE);

    personSearchAdapter = new PersonSearchAdapter(getActivity().getApplicationContext(),personList);
    recyclerView.setAdapter(personSearchAdapter);

}else{
    text_error_search.setVisibility(View.VISIBLE);
}
```

(b)

Fig. 1. Bug 10348095 in the (a) cross-platform and (b) Android versions of the app.

As far as source-code comprehension, we used the dependent variable *Comprehension*. It measures the correctness of understanding of a participant given a version of Movies-app by analyzing the answers provided to the comprehension questionnaire. We used an approach based on that by Kamsties *et al.* [13] that computes the number of correct responses to the questions of the comprehension questionnaire. We consider a response to a question to be correct if the participant selected all the correct alternatives and no incorrect alternatives were selected. The correct alternatives were defined before the experiment took place. *Comprehension* assumes values between zero and six. A value close to six means that a participant comprehended source code very well. A value close to zero means that a participant obtained a low comprehension.

A bug is successfully identified if the participant marks the source code where the bug was seeded. We named the variable counting the bugs correctly identified as *Correctness of Bug Identification*. This variable assumes values between zero and four. The higher the value the better it is.

As for bug fixing, we considered the variable: *Correctness of Bug Fixing*. It counts the number of bugs the participants correctly fixed. A bug is correctly fixed if the participant replaced the source code as it was before the application of the mutation operator. In other words, the participants did the "undo" of a given mutation operator we executed on the source code. In such a way we assumed that there was only a way to fix each bug. *Correctness of Bug Fixing* assumes values between zero and four. The higher the value the better it is.

As for affective reactions, we considered four dependent variables (one for each dimension of SAM plus the liking one) for each kind of task the participants performed: comprehension, bug identification, and bug fixing. Therefore, the dependent variables are: PLS_K, ARS_K, DOM_K, and LIK_K, where K indicates the kind of task and assumes one of the following values: *Comp* (source code comprehension), *Ident* (bug identification), and *Fix* (bug fixing). Each of the twelve introduced dependent variables assumes values between zero and nine. The best value is nine, while zero is the worst.

We defined a dependent variable to measure the perceived difficulty for each kind of task. As for the comprehension task, we defined $Diff_{Comp}$. Similarly, we defined $Diff_{Ident}$ and $Diff_{Fix}$ for the tasks bug identification and fixing, respectively. All these three variables assume values between zero and five. The higher the value, the better it is.

To answer RQs, we tested the following parametrized null hypothesis.

$H0_X$: *There is no statistically significant difference between the participants who were administered with the cross-platform and the native versions of Movies-app with respect to X.*

X indicates one of the dependent variable described just before and then assumes one of the following possible values: *Comprehension (RQ1.1)*, *Correctness of Bug Identification* (RQ1.2), *Correctness of Bug Fixing* (RQ1.3), PLS_{Comp} (RQ2), ARS_{Comp} (RQ2), DOM_{Comp} (RQ2), LIK_{Comp} (RQ2), PLS_{Ident} (RQ2), ARS_{Ident} (RQ2), DOM_{Ident} (RQ2), LIK_{Ident} (RQ2), PLS_{Fix} (RQ2), ARS_{Fix} (RQ2), DOM_{Fix} (RQ2), LIK_{Fix} (RQ2), $Diff_{Comp}$ (RQ3), $Diff_{Ident}$ (RQ3), and $Diff_{Fix}$ (RQ3).

3.6 Experiment Design

We used the one factor with two treatments design [26]. We randomly divided the participants into two groups: Ionic and Android. The participants in the first group were asked to accomplish the experiment tasks on the app implemented by using the cross-platform technology, while those in the second group to on the app implemented in the native technology. The participants in the Ionic group were 20, while those in the Android one were 19.

3.7 Procedure

The experimental procedure included the following sequential steps.

1. We invited all the students of the "Enterprise Mobile Applications Development" course at the University of Salerno. They filled in a pre-questionnaire.
2. We randomly split the participants into: Ionic and Android.
3. The experiment session took place under controlled conditions in a laboratory at the University of Salerno. The participants accomplished the tasks under the supervision of the authors to avoid any kind of interaction. All the used PCs had the same (Hardware/Software) configuration.
4. The participant performed the comprehension task by answering the questions of the comprehension questionnaire.

5. We asked the participants to deal with each bug at time. The participants could pass to the next bug only when they either fixed the previous bug or were aware that they could not identify/fix it. Given a bug, participants first had to identify and mark the bug (as described before) and then they could pass to fix it.
6. Participants filled in the post-questionnaire by rating affective reactions and perceived difficulty.
7. Participants compressed and archived their version of the app with the source-code they modified. We then collected all those versions.

Participants in the Android group could run the app either on the emulator of Android Studio or on their own smartphone. Similarly, participants in the Ionic group could run the app either on a web browser or on their own smartphone.

3.8   Analysis Procedure

To perform data analysis, we used the R environment[3] for statistical computing and we carried out the following steps:

- We undertook the descriptive statistics of the dependent variables.
- To test the hull hypotheses concerned to RQ1 we planned to use either an unpaired t-test or the Mann-Whitney U test [18]. Unlike the t-test, the Mann-Whitney U test does not require the assumption of normal distributions. This is to say that if data are normally distributed we will apply the unpaired t-test, the Mann-Whitney U test otherwise. To study the normality of data, we use the Shapiro-Wilk W test [22]. In the case of a statistically significant effect of Technology, we plan to compute effect size to measure the magnitude of such a difference. If data are normally distributed we will opt for Cohen's d, while Cliff's δ otherwise. As for RQ2 and RQ3, we consider ordinal scales. Therefore, we could only apply a non-parametric statistical inferences. The Mann-Whitney U test [18] is the most appropriate.
- To summarize and analyze raw data and to support their discussion, we exploited different graphical representations: boxplots and clustered bar charts.

To verify if an effect is statistically significant, we fixed α to 0.05. That is, we admit 5% chance of a Type-I-error occurring [26]. If a p-value is less than 0.05, we deemed the effect is statistically significant.

4   Results and Discussion

In this subsection, we present and discuss the results according to our RQs.

---

[3] www.r-project.org.

4.1   RQ1: Native Vs Cross-Platform Apps Concerning Source-Code Comprehension and Bug Identification and Fixing

In Table 4, we report the descriptive statistics for the dependent variables: Comprehension, Correctness of Bug Identification, and Correctness of Bug Fixing. In this table, we also show the results of the statistical tests performed. To summarize the distribution of these variables we used the boxplots shown in Fig. 2.

As for *Comprehension*, descriptive statistics and boxplots do not show a huge difference in the source-code comprehension the participants achieved in the Ionic and Android groups. Descriptive statistics indicate that the participants in the Ionic group better answered the questions of the comprehension questionnaire: the mean and median values are 0.625 and 0.667, respectively. On the other hand, the mean and median values for the Android group are both 0.5. The results of the Shapiro-Wilk W test[4] indicate that data are not normally distributed in the Ionic group (p-value = 0.007). For such a reason, we performed the Mann-Whitney U test. As shown in Table 4, the p-value this test returned is 0.109. That is, there is no statistically significant difference between the comprehension that the participants in the two groups achieved.

Concerning *Correctness of Bug Identification*, descriptive statistics (Table 4) and boxplots (Fig. 2) indicate that the participants in the groups (Android and Ionic) achieved a high correctness in the identification of the bugs (*e.g.,*, the mean value for Correctness of Bug Identification is 0.882 for Android and 0.9 for Ionic) in both the versions of Movies-app. The data are also similarly distributed and do not follow a normal distribution as the results of the Shapiro-Wilk W test

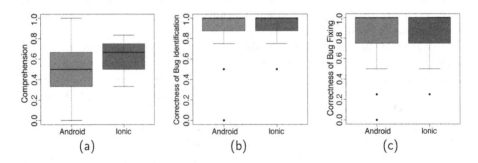

Fig. 2. Boxplots for *Comprehension, Correctness of Identification* and *Fixing*.

Table 4. Descriptive statistics for *Comprehension, Correctness of Bug Identification* and *Correctness of Bug Fixing* dependent variables with respect to Technology.

Technology	Comprehension				Correctness of bug identification				Correctness of bug fixing			
	Mean	Std. Dev.	Median	p-value	Mean	Std. Dev.	Median	p-value	Mean	Std. Dev.	Median	p-value
Android	0.5	0.266	0.5	0.109	0.882	0.255	1	0.971	0.829	0.289	1	0.935
Ionic	0.625	0.152	0.667		0.9	0.189	1		0.850	0.235	1	

---

[4] A p-value less than *alpha* (*i.e.,* 0.05) indicates that data are not normally distributed.

show (p-values are 1.294e-06 for Android and 1.422e-06 for Ionic). The results of the Mann-Whitney U test do not (Table 4) indicate any statistically significant difference between the data in the two groups since the p-value is 0.971.

Finally, we observed a pattern similar to *Correctness of Bug Identification* for *Correctness of Bug Fixing*. The participants in the groups achieved a high correctness in the fixing of the bugs in both the versions of Movies-app. For example, the mean value is 0.829 for Android, while 0.85 for Ionic. Data are still not normally distributed. The Shapiro-Wilk W test returned the following p-values for the groups Android and Ionic: 2.04e-05 and 2.656e-05. Therefore, we applied the Mann-Whitney U test and we obtained 0.935 as the p-value.

4.2 RQ2: Native Vs Cross-Platform Apps Concerning Pleasure, Arousal, Dominance, and Liking

As Sullivan and Artino [24] suggest, we used median values and frequencies as descriptive statistics of the dependent variables PLS_K, ARS_K, DOM_K, and LIK_K (where K is the kind of task). In Table 5, we report the median values and the p-values of the statistical test performed, while we used the clustered bar charts (Fig. 3) to show the frequencies.

As for the Comprehension task, medians and clustered bar charts do not show a wide difference between the dependent variables measured on the two groups. However, medians of dependent variables for the Ionic group were always higher than the Android group ones (*e.g.*, median of DOM_{Comp} is 8 for Android and 9 for Ionic), except for ARS_{Comp} (7 for Android and 6.5 for Ionic). The Mann-Whitney U test returned p-values higher than 0.05 for all the dependent variables, hence there is no statistically significant difference between the affective reactions of both the groups of participants.

Also for the Bug Identification task, median values and clustered bar charts do not show a huge difference between the two groups. However, in this case, medians of dependent variables of the Ionic group were always greater or equal to the Android group ones (*e.g.*, median of DOM_{Comp} is 8 for Android and 9 for Ionic). Also, the Mann-Whitney U test returned p-values higher than 0.05 for all the dependent variables signifying that there is no statistically significant difference between the affective reactions of both the groups.

The analysis of the Bug Fixing task follows the same pattern of the Bug Identification task.

Table 5. Median values for affective reactions and statistical test results.

Technology	PLS_{Comp}	ARS_{Comp}	DOM_{Comp}	LIK_{Comp}	PLS_{Ident}	ARS_{Ident}	DOM_{Ident}	LIK_{Ident}	PLS_{Fix}	ARS_{Fix}	DOM_{Fix}	LIK_{Fix}
Android	7	7	8	7	8	7	8	8	8	7	8	8
Ionic	7.5	6.5	9	8	8	7.5	9	8	8	7.5	8	8.5
p-value	0.988	0.503	0.106	0.326	0.352	0.626	0.206	0.912	0.538	0.966	0.768	0.59

4.3 RQ3: Native Vs Cross-Platform Concerning the Difficulty

In Table 6, we report the median values for $Diff_{Comp}$, $Diff_{Ident}$, and $Diff_{Fix}$. The p-values of the performed statistical tests are shown as well. The clustered barcharts in Fig. 4 summarize the frequencies of the answers for task difficulty.

Concerning all the three tasks, descriptive statistics do not show a difference between the difficulty perceived by the participants of the two groups. Furthermore, medians are the same in the two groups for both $Diff_{Comp}$ and $Diff_{Fix}$ (4 and 5, respectively), while $Diff_{Ident}$ has a slightly lower median for the Ionic group (*i.e.*, 4.5, while it is 5 for Android). The Mann-Whitney U test returned

Table 6. Median values for difficulty with respect to Technology.

Technology	$Diff_{Comp}$		$Diff_{Ident}$		$Diff_{Fix}$	
	Median	p-value	Median	p-value	Median	p-value
Android	4	0.159	5	0.876	5	0.789
Ionic	4		4.5		5	

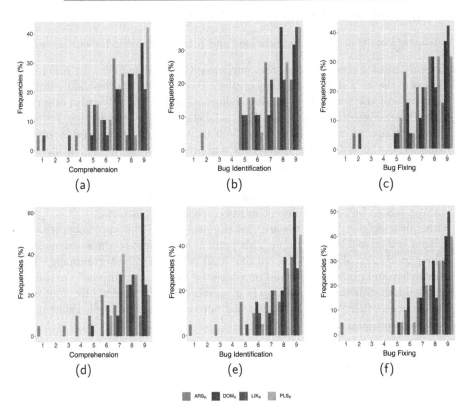

Fig. 3. Frequencies of the affective reactions for Android (a), (b), and (c) and Ionic (d), (e), and (f) groups.

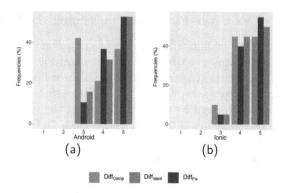

Fig. 4. Frequencies of the difficulty for Android (a) and Ionic (b) groups.

p-values always higher than 0.05, hence there is no statistically significant difference between the difficulty perceived by the participants of both the groups.

4.4 Implications and Future Extensions

We delineate main practical implications and future extension for our research.

- Overall results suggest that the participants did not find any difference between the two studied technologies with respect to source-code comprehension and the correctness in identifying and fixing bugs. We also observed that also the affective reactions might not be affected by technology. In addition, participants administered with the two treatments perceived difficulty in completing the tasks (*i.e.,* source-code comprehension and bug identification and fixing) similarly. This outcome might be relevant to the practitioner. In particular, our study seems to support one of the main results from an industrial survey [8] that states that cross-platform development is valuable when an app has to be run in different hardware/software platforms.
- Outcomes suggest future research on the design and the implementation of native and cross-platform apps. This point is of interest to the researcher.
- The experiment object is of a specific kind of app, *i.e.,* entertainment. The researcher and practitioner could be interested in studying whether our results also hold for different kinds of app (*e.g.,* games). Finally, it could be of interest for the researcher to study whether our outcomes scale to applications more complex and larger.

5   Threats to Validity

We report threats to validity from the most to the least sensible. Since we were more interested in studying cause-effect relationships, the most sensible kind of threat is Internal Validity.

Internal Validity. A possible threat to Internal Validity is voluntary participation in the study (*selection threat*). However, we limited this threat by embedding the experiment in a course at the University of Salerno and we did not consider its outcome when grading the students. To deal with *threat of diffusion or treatments imitations*, we monitored participants and asked back material to prevent them from exchanging information. Another threat might be *resentful demoralization*—participants assigned to a less desirable treatment might not perform as good as they normally would.

Construct Validity. Each of the investigated constructs was quantified by means of one assessment at the end of the task, which might affect the results (*i.e., mono-method bias threat*). The participants were not informed about RQs. However, they might guess them and change their behavior accordingly (*i.e., threat of hypotheses guessing*). To deal with this kind of threat (*i.e., evaluation apprehension threat*), we did not evaluate the participants on the basis of their performances. We also acknowledge the presence of a *restricted generalizability across constructs*. That is, the technology can affect other relevant constructs which we did not observe (cognitive load).

Conclusion Validity. To mitigate a *threat of random heterogeneity of participants*, our sample included students with a similar background. In particular, the participants followed the same course at the same university, underwent similar training, and had similar background, skills, and experience. *Reliability of measures* is another threat to conclusion validity. To deal with this kind of threat, we used well known and widely used measures.

External Validity. The participants in our study were graduate students. This could pose some threats to the generalizability of the results to the population of professional developers (*threat of interaction of selection and treatment*). However, the use of students has the advantage that they have a homogeneous background and are particularly suitable to obtain preliminary evidence [4]. Therefore, the use of students could be considered appropriate, as suggested in the literature [4,10]. In addition, the studied cross-platform technology is relatively novel and then we can speculate that the participants are not so far from many professional developers. The used experimental object might pose a *threat of interaction of setting and treatment*.

6 Conclusion and Final Remarks

We presented the results of an experiment to investigate source-code comprehension of apps implemented either with native or cross-platform technologies. We also investigated if these kinds of technology might play a role in the identification and fixing of bugs in the source code. Furthermore, we studied the affective reactions of participants and the difficulty they perceived when accomplishing the tasks before mentioned. The data-analysis results suggested that there is not a statistically significant difference in the comprehension and in the identification and fixing of bugs. This outcome holds also with respect to affective reactions and the difficulty the participants perceived when accomplishing the tasks.

References

1. Bradley, M.M., Lang, P.J.: Measuring emotion: the self-assessment manikin and the semantic differential. J. Behav. Therapy Exper. Psychiatry **25**(1), 49–59 (1994)
2. Brodie, M.L., Stonebraker, M.: Legacy Information Systems Migration: Gateways, Interfaces, and the Incremental Approach. Morgan Kaufmann Publishers Inc., San Francisco (1995)
3. Canfora, G., Di Penta, M.: New frontiers of reverse engineering. In: Proceedings of Workshop on the Future of Software Engineering, pp. 326–341. IEEE (2007)
4. Carver, J., Jaccheri, L., Morasca, S., Shull, F.: Issues in using students in empirical studies in software engineering education. In: Proceedings of International Symposium on Software Metrics, pp. 239–251 (2003)
5. Corral, L., Sillitti, A., Succi, G.: Mobile multiplatform development: an experiment for performance analysis. Procedia Comput. Sci. **10**, 736–743 (2012)
6. Dalmasso, I., Datta, S.K., Bonnet, C., Nikaein, N.: Survey, comparison and evaluation of cross platform mobile application development tools. In: Proceedings of International Wireless Communications and Mobile Computing Conference, pp. 323–328 (2013)
7. El-Kassas, W.S., Abdullah, B.A., Yousef, A.H., Wahba, A.M.: Taxonomy of cross-platform mobile applications development approaches. Ain Shams Eng. J. **8**(2), 163–190 (2017)
8. Francese, R., Gravino, C., Risi, M., Scanniello, G., Tortora, G.: Mobile app development and management: Results from a qualitative investigation. In: Proc. of Intl. Conference on Mobile Software Engineering and Systems. pp. 133–143 (2017)
9. Heitkötter, H., Hanschke, S., Majchrzak, T.A.: Evaluating cross-platform development approaches for mobile applications. In: Cordeiro, J., Krempels, K.-H. (eds.) WEBIST 2012. LNBIP, vol. 140, pp. 120–138. Springer, Heidelberg (2013). https://doi.org/10.1007/978-3-642-36608-6_8
10. Höst, M., Regnell, B., Wohlin, C.: Using students as subjects-a comparative study of students and professionals in lead-time impact assessment. Empirical Softw. Eng. **5**(3), 201–214 (2000)
11. Jedlitschka, A., Ciolkowski, M., Pfahl, D.: Reporting experiments in software engineering. In: Shull, F., Singer, J., Sjøberg, D.I.K. (eds.) Guide to Advanced Empirical Software Engineering, pp. 201–228. Springer, Heidelberg (2008). https://doi.org/10.1007/978-1-84800-044-5_8
12. Juristo, N., Moreno, A.: Basics of Software Engineering Experimentation. Kluwer Academic Publishers, Dordrecht (2001)
13. Kamsties, E., von Knethen, A., Reussner, R.: A controlled experiment to evaluate how styles affect the understandability of requirements specifications. Inf. Softw. Technol. **45**(14), 955–965 (2003)
14. Kim, S., Clark, J.A., Mcdermid, J.: Class mutation: mutation testing for object-oriented programs (2000)
15. Kim, S., Clark, J.A., McDermid, J.A.: The rigorous generation of Java mutation operators using HAZOP. Technical report (1999)

16. Koelstra, S., et al.: Deap: a database for emotion analysis using physiological signals. IEEE Trans. Affect. Comput. **3**(1), 18–31 (2012)
17. Malavolta, I., Ruberto, S., Soru, T., Terragni, V.: End users' perception of hybrid mobile apps in the Google play store. In: Proceedings of International Conference on Mobile Services, pp. 25–32 (2015)
18. Mann, H.B., Whitney, D.R.: On a test of whether one of two random variables is stochastically larger than the other. Ann. Math. Statist. **18**(1), 50–60 (1947)
19. Que, P., Guo, X., Zhu, M.: A comprehensive comparison between hybrid and native app paradigms. In: Proceedings of International Conference on Computational Intelligence and Communication Networks, pp. 611–614, December 2016
20. Scanniello, G., Gravino, C., Risi, M., Tortora, G., Dodero, G.: Documenting design-pattern instances: a family of experiments on source-code comprehensibility. ACM Trans. Softw. Eng. Methodol. **24**(3), 14:1–14:35 (2015)
21. Scanniello, G., Risi, M., Tramontana, P., Romano, S.: Fixing faults in C and Java source code: abbreviated vs. full-word identifier names. ACM Trans. Softw. Eng. Methodol. **26**(2), 6:1–6:43 (2017)
22. Shapiro, S., Wilk, M.: An analysis of variance test for normality. Biometrika **52**(3–4), 591–611 (1965)
23. Sillito, J., Murphy, G.C., De Volder, K.: Asking and answering questions during a programming change task. IEEE Trans. Softw. Eng. **34**(4), 434–451 (2008)
24. Sullivan, G.M., Artino, A.R.: Analyzing and interpreting data from likert-type scales. J. Graduate Med. Educ. **5**(4), 541–2 (2013)
25. Willocx, M., Vossaert, J., Naessens, V.: Comparing performance parameters of mobile app development strategies. In: Proceedings of International Conference on Mobile Software Engineering and Systems, pp. 38–47, May 2016
26. Wohlin, C., Runeson, P., Höst, M., Ohlsson, M., Regnell, B., Wesslén, A.: Experimentation in Software Engineering. Springer, Heidelberg (2012). https://doi.org/10.1007/978-3-642-29044-2

Understanding How and When Human Factors Are Used in the Software Process: A Text-Mining Based Literature Review

Mercedes Ruiz[1](✉) and Davide Salanitri[2]

[1] University of Cadiz, Avda. de la Universidad de Cadiz, 10,
11519 Puerto Real, Cádiz, Spain
`mercedes.ruiz@uca.es`
[2] University of Nottingham, Nottingham, Nottinghamshire, UK
`Davide.Salanitri@nottingham.ac.uk`

Abstract. Human Factors (HF) is the study of the interaction between users and technology with the aim of improving the user's experience of a product and avoid unwanted issues in the usage of the system. HF is largely applied in several fields such as industrial processes, education, training, and design. In software development, HF plays a crucial role in the efficient and effective development of a software product and the success of the final product. This paper aims at indicating the state of the art of the literature on HF in software, in general and in the software development process in particular. To do so, a preliminary literature review using text mining has been performed. This work gathered papers using the terms "human factors" and "software" from four of the most used scientific digital databases (ACM DL, Scopus, Science Direct and IEEE Xplore). A total of 2192 papers were selected and automatically gathered into three clusters by using the X-means algorithm, which automatically recommended that number of clusters. The results show that there are three main areas where HF have been researched within software development: (1) the field of product evaluation (user experience) (2) the field of software development process, especially in the project management processes (3) the field of education. The results are an initial indication of the evolution of research in this area and where and how HF is applied in software engineering.

Keywords: Human factors · Software process · Literature review · Text mining

1 Introduction

In this paper, we address the aim of providing a structured overview of the landscape of research on the topic of human factors in software. To reach this objective, we use text-mining techniques in order to automate as much as possible the analysis of the research literature, characterized by a high number of non-structured text documents.

Text mining can be defined as the automated or semi-automated processing of usually unstructured text. When applied to the field of literature review, text mining

X. Franch et al. (Eds.): PROFES 2019, LNCS 11915, pp. 694–708, 2019.
https://doi.org/10.1007/978-3-030-35333-9_54

helps to consider the works published and identify reasonable and significant groups of papers that follow objectively justifiable patterns [1].

In recent years, some authors have been applying text mining to broadly review the scientific literature in different areas [2–4]. In this work, we provide the results of applying a similar process to analyze the research published in the last 20 years on the domain of human factors and software.

The paper is structured as follows: Sect. 2 provides a summary of conventional literature reviews conducted in the area of human factors in software. Section 3 describes the aims and procedures of each step of the method we have applied in this study. The results obtained are presented and discussed in Sects. 4 and 5, respectively. Section 6 describes the issues affecting the validity of our study. Finally, Sect. 7 summarizes our paper and draws our conclusions and future work.

2 Related Work

We searched for literature reviews in the area of human factors in software by using the search string "human factors" AND software AND "literature review" in the title + abstract + keywords in several search engines such as Science Direct, Web of Science and Scopus. The searches helped us retrieve eight systematic literature reviews or mapping studies directly related to the search string.

The influence of human factors on the role of the software developer has been the topic that has attracted more attention in the reviews located by our searches. Cruz et al. aimed at summarizing the different ways of measuring and assessing the personality of the software developers [5, 6]. Soomro et al. [7] analyzed the impact of personality on different aspects of the software production, such as the team climate, and the individual and the team performance. A broader analysis of the factors impacting on software productivity was conducted by Oliveira et al. [8]. In their tertiary study, they collect the influential factors identified in the secondary studies they analyzed. The factors are grouped into organizational and human-related factors, being cohesion and team communication the two most influential human factors identified. In this study, motivation of software developers was identified as the fifth most influential factor. In their review, Beecham et al. [9], go deeper in the analysis of the main motivators and demotivators for the software developers, the models of motivation commonly used in software development staff and the outcomes of motivation.

The relation of human factors and the software development approach has also been a subject of study in some of the reviews found. In her work, Askarinejadamiri [10] identifies which personality factors of software developers are most crucial for requirement engineering in web development. She concluded that the technical knowledge that the software developer has, their communication skills and their abilities for customer interaction were the human factors most frequently mentioned in the studies she analyzed. Likewise, Sánchez-Gordon and Colomo-Palacios [11] focused on the role of culture of the DevOps software development approach [12] by synthetizing the main attributes of the DevOps culture and analyzing the emotional phenomenon implied in this way of producing software.

Finally, Pocius studied the relation between human personality and human computer interaction [13]. In her work, the author provides an analysis of the studies and reports on: (a) non-concluding relation between the programmer personality and their programming aptitude and achievement, and (b) the relationships reported about the personality traits and the performance in computer-assisted instruction.

After analyzing the literature reviews retrieved by our search, we can conclude that even though the topic seems to be attracting the interest of the research community, the reviews available are mainly focused on categorizing particular approaches such as how to measure the impact of personality traits of the developers on the software production. In this work, we propose a broader and more holistic approach to our review, by addressing the works published in the last twenty years describing any type of relation between human factors and software, so that the predominant themes discussed can be identified and their time evolution tracked.

3   Method

3.1   The Research Questions

To address the main aim of this work, we set the following research questions:

RQ1: How much research has been published in the area of human factors and software in the last twenty years?
RQ2: What have the broad topics of research in that area been?
RQ3: What is the relation between human factors and software process studied in the works published?
RQ4: What is the trend of research in this area?

3.2   Search Process

In order to retrieve as many works as possible that could be related with human factors in all aspects of software, we conducted automated searches in four of the most widely used digital libraries and search engines: ACM Digital Library, Science Direct, Scopus and IEEE Xplore. The search string used was "human factors" AND "software". All queries were based on Title + Abstract + Keywords within the scopes of journal or conference papers published in English between 2000 and 2019. Table 1 shows the number of papers retrieved from each digital library after removing the 34 duplicated papers. It is noticeable that almost 83% of the papers were located by IEEE Xplore, whereas ACM Digital Library and Science Direct helped retrieved only 0.3% and 2.7%, respectively. All the works retrieved by the searches were imported to the Mendeley[1] reference manager to save all the relevant data about each work.

---

[1] https://www.mendeley.com/.

Table 1. Number of papers retrieved from each digital library.

Digital library	Number of papers retrieved
ACM Digital Library	6
Science Direct	59
Scopus	315
IEEE Xplore	1812
Total	*2192*

3.3 Data Extraction Process

In this step of the process, we selected the required data items for the analysis. As in previous similar works [2–4], we decided to use only the abstract as the source of information extraction and to leave out of our analysis the list of keywords. The reasons that prevent us from adding them are that the keywords normally take also part in the abstract of the paper and, therefore, including them in the analysis would add repetition, raising their numerical weight and potentially leading to wrong conclusions. Additionally, the key words of a paper are chosen by the authors to set the key terms they intend their work to be associated with. Since this is meant to facilitate the location of the works associated with some particular key terms and does not add any extra meaning to the abstract, including them in the analysis would have also led to unnecessary repetition of terms.

3.4 Text Mining Approach

Most of research papers come in the form of text data files, which is a form of unstructured information. They constitute an immense source of information and knowledge that can be mined using text mining and knowledge discovery approaches [1]. In this work, we make use of the following text-mining components:

- Preprocessing and feature extraction. The main aim in this step is to identify the relevant terms that represent each abstract by removing unnecessary data.
  - Tokenization: To split the text of the abstract into a sequence of tokens.
  - Filtering and transforming: To remove unwanted words, such as stop-words, and to transform all characters to lowercase.
  - Stemming: To find the stem or root of derived words.
- Vector Space Model (VSM): The main of this step is to build a representation of each abstract as a numeric vector for efficient analysis of the large collection of abstracts. Each abstract is represented by its VSM that has as many positions as terms remain after the previous step and that holds a number in each position. Depending on the study carried out, the number may be:
  - Occurrence: The number of times the term appears in the abstract.
  - TF-IDF: The term frequency-inverse document frequency, which weighs how important a term is to an abstract in the collection.
- Clustering: The aim of this step is to find groups of similar abstracts in our collection.

- X-Means: We used X-Means as the clustering algorithm, since it determines the correct number of centroids based on a heuristic and does not require the user to input the number of clusters beforehand.

4   Results

4.1   RQ1: How Much Research Has Been Published in the Area of Human Factors and Software in the Last Twenty Years?

The conference paper is the most frequent type of paper, with 70% of the papers of that type in our collection. Figure 1 shows the number of papers published per year and reveals that the amount of research published on the topic has increased notably in the last years. If during the three first five-year periods (2000–2004, 2005–2009, and 2010–2014) the average number of papers published is 481, this same metric grows to 749 for the period 2015–2019. This represents an increment of 1.6 over the previous periods. However, there seems to be a positive trend in the first three years of the last period analyzed, reaching its maximum value in 2017 with 217 papers published, followed by what looks like a negative trend in the remaining two years. It is important to note that at the time of writing this paper, the last year of the period, 2019, is halfway only, but the trend shows a clear reduction of the number of papers published on the topic.

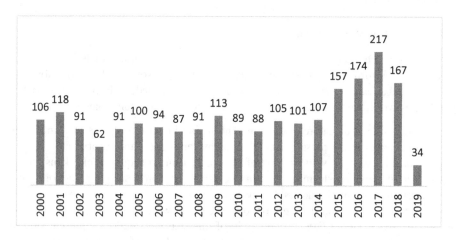

Fig. 1.   Number of papers published per year.

As shown in Table 2, three IEEE journals are among the top five journals publishing papers on human factors and software, being IEEE Software the leading journal. Table 3 shows the equivalent list for conferences publishing papers in this topic. The list is headed by two highly reputed conferences such as the International Conference on Software Engineering (ICSE) and the Hawaii International Conference on System Sciences (HICSS) followed by the CHASE workshop.

Table 2. Top five journals publishing papers on the topic of human factors and software.

Journal	Number of papers
IEEE Software	43
IEEE Transactions on Software Engineering	37
Information and Software Technology	19
IEEE Access	12
Empirical Software Engineering	10

Table 3. Top five conferences publishing papers on the topic of human factors and software.

Conference acronym	Conference full name	Number of papers
ICSE	International Conference on Software Engineering	97
HICSS	Hawaii International Conference on System Sciences	63
CHASE	International Workshop on Cooperative and Human Aspects of Software Engineering	21
CISTI	Iberian Conference on Information Systems and Technologies	18
EDUCON	IEEE Global Engineering Education Conference	17

4.2   RQ2: What Have the Broad Topics of Research in that Area Been?

To perform this analysis, we used the text-mining capabilities of RapidMiner's[2] text analytics extension. The key element in this process is the X-means operator, which implements the x-means algorithm published by Pelleg and Moore [14]. The *x-means* algorithm is considered to overcome some of the limitations of the *k-means* clustering algorithm [15], since it does not require the user to give the number of clusters as an input, among other improvements. This algorithm was suitable for our case, since our intention was to find groups of related papers that can then be allocated to different topics of research in the area of human factors and software.

The x-means operator found three main clusters on the preprocessed abstracts retrieved by our search. As Table 4 shows, the clusters did not have a uniform number of papers. The first cluster, cluster 0, grouped together more than half of the papers retrieved (66%). Cluster 1 has the smallest number of papers, only 10%.

Table 4. Clusters quantitative data.

Cluster	Number of items	Ratio of total
Cluster 0	1449	66%
Cluster 1	519	24%
Cluster 2	224	10%

---

[2] https://rapidminer.com/.

In order to find the topics of the papers pertaining to each cluster, we performed, for each of them, an analysis of the most frequent terms appearing in the abstracts of the papers in that cluster. For each cluster list obtained, we selected the 20 most frequent terms. Table 5 shows the number of occurrences of each of the terms *(# ocurr)* and the number of abstracts in which such term was used *(#docs)* for the top 10 most frequent terms.

Table 5. Top 10 most frequent terms per cluster.

Cluster 0			Cluster 1			Cluster 2		
Term	# ocurr	# docs	Term	# ocurr	# docs	Term	# ocurr	# docs
System	2119	951	Software	1534	446	Student	632	245
User	1887	866	Development	567	276	Learning	516	162
Human	1325	655	Project	525	273	Software	203	110
Software	1045	658	Human	470	242	Study	159	101
Design	865	425	Factors	454	224	Computer	156	76
Model	691	334	Engineering	416	202	Results	124	95
Information	643	339	Process	401	191	Programming	120	42
Data	631	317	Developers	330	134	Motivation	119	60
Study	606	402	Research	327	193	Teaching	115	64
Use	579	390	Study	316	205	Education	112	77

A word cloud representation of the 20 most frequent terms in each cluster helps to identify more clearly the topic of research of each one. As it can be seen in Fig. 2, Cluster 0 seems to be more focused on the area of user research on the software development products. This type of human factors methods has the product as target. The words "human", "system", "user" and "software" define the possible subject of the cluster while the words "design", "model", "study" and "research" could suggest the method used. Example of this could be the usability evaluation of a system. For example, some of the titles which enter in this cluster are: *"From users involvement to users' needs understanding: A case study"* [16], *"Implementation of end-user development success factors in mashup development environments"* [17] and *"Information system design for a hospital emergency department: A usability analysis of software prototypes"* [18]. As it can be seen, these papers focus on either the development of new software products or the evaluation of existing ones to verify human factors issues.

Cluster 1 seems to be more focused on the software development process as the words "software", "development", "engineering" "team", "projects" and "process" seem to suggest. For instance, *"The impact of human factors on the participation decision of reviewers in modern code review"* [19], *"The effect of software engineers' personality traits on team climate and performance: A Systematic Literature Review"* [7], *"QUASE - A quantitative approach to analyze the human aspects of software development projects"* [20]. Contrary to Cluster 0, these papers do not have the software product as their target, but the professional figures who develop software and how the improvements of human factors aspects and, consequently, the improvement of team performance, could increase software quality and productivity.

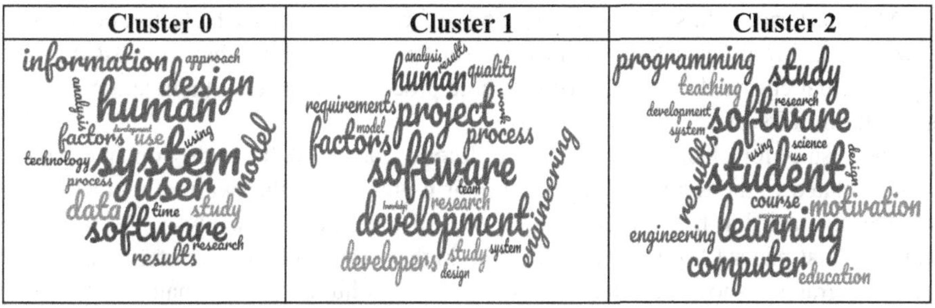

Fig. 2. Word clouds of the 20 most frequent terms in each cluster.

In Cluster 2, the words "student", "teaching", "learning" and "education" suggest that this group is focused on the process of educating new computer science experts and how human factors can improve their knowledge. Example of this are mostly on how to increase the interest in coding and programming and how to improve the quality of teaching. Another part of this cluster focuses on teaching Human Factors techniques to computer science students and a small number of papers approaches the human factors evaluation of educational systems and software. This last topic may be also related to cluster 0, as they essentially regard the evaluations of software products. However, since they concern education, they were included in cluster 2 by the algorithm. Examples of papers included in this cluster are: *"A Gamification Technique for Motivating Students to Learn Code Readability in Software Engineering"* [21], *"Software Engineering: Research-Led Education with Human Values"* [22] and *"Reflection and abstraction in learning software engineering's human aspects"* [23].

To make a more complete analysis of the results, the number of papers for each cluster has to be taken into consideration. Indeed, not all the three groups have the same amount of interest in the academic community. Cluster 0 is the most populated with 1449 papers, while Cluster 1 includes 518 and Cluster 2 is composed by 224 papers. This data suggests that while human factors have been applied to education and the process of development, it seems that the focus has been on the evaluation of the software systems.

4.3 RQ3: What Is the Relation Between Human Factors and Software Process Studied in the Works Published?

To find the papers with the strongest relation with the topic of human factors and software process, we performed another individual analysis on each cluster. This analysis consisted in obtaining a series of consecutive tokens where the term "process" is present. We made use of the n-Grams operator to create n-grams of maximum three-token length used in the abstracts of each cluster. Then we selected the ones in which the terms "process" and "human factors" were present and finally ordered the results to find the top five papers of each cluster according to the frequency of appearance of the n-grams. By doing so, we not only get the papers whose abstracts include the term "process" more frequently, but the tokens to which the term "process" is frequently associated.

After performing this analysis, we found different results in each cluster. For cluster 0, we did not find any n-gram with the term "process", which may suggest that the papers in that cluster do not deal with specific processes or parts of them and make use of the term in its most general meaning.

The results for cluster 1 were very different. Table 6 collects the top five papers mostly related to the term "process" and their n-grams, together with an extract of the original abstract that helps validate the result of the automatic analysis. As it can be seen, the first paper [24] is the one with the highest frequency of such term and it has three n-grams showing the chain: "involves-human", "human-perspective", "perspective-development" and "software-development". For the second paper [25], the topic predicted is the person-to-role allocation in the software process, as it can be easily deduced from its n-grams. In the case of the third paper [26], the topic seems to be related to software quality control process, the fourth paper [27] deals with software process improvement initiatives and the last one [28] with software process assessment.

Surprisingly, the term "process" was not considered relevant by the operator in any of the abstracts of the cluster 2.

Finally, when mapping the former top five works found in Cluster 1 to the knowledge areas of Software Engineering Body of Knowledge (SEWBOK), it can be found that three of them are related with the *Software Engineering Management* area [25–27]. The areas of *Software Requirements and Software Design* [24] and *Software Engineering Process* [28] follow with one work each.

Table 6. Top papers showing relation of human factors with the "process" in Cluster 1

Ref	Title	"Process" n-grams	Aim of the paper (*as in abstract*)
[24]	*"Impact of Human-Centered Design Process (HCDP) on Software Development Process"*	involves_human human_perspective perspective_development software_development	*"This paper encompasses the impact of applying human-centered design process (HCDP) to the software development process (SDP)"*
[25]	*"Human capacities in the software process: empiric validation"*	person_role role_allocation allocation_process software_process	*"In this paper, an empirical validation of a person-to-role allocation process is presented"*

(*continued*)

Table 6. (*continued*)

Ref	Title	"Process" n-grams	Aim of the paper (*as in abstract*)
[26]	*"A model and system for applying Lean Six sigma to agile software development using hybrid simulation"*	software_quality quality_control quality_control_process	*"The model and system introduced in this paper applies Six Sigma methodologies to software processes using hybrid simulation .... The System collects empirical data on process actors and uses them in simulation to provide estimations that incorporate the human factor that has substantial role in software processes"*
[27]	*"Designing Software Project Management Models Based on Supply Chain Quality Assurance Practices"*	approach_software software_process software_process_improvement	*"In short, this is a snapshot of how a process improvement model can be designed which has a productivity analysis capability for a self-feedback. This paper also describes the human factors such as reluctance to change and the overhead for the project members"*
[28]	*"The need of a person oriented approach to software process assessment"*	critique_software software_process software_process_assessment	*"This paper represents a coherent critique of software process assessment, focusing on the concerns and perceived shortcomings present. A call is made to re-direct attention and resources toward understanding the true nature of people in software process assessment"*

4.4   RQ4: What Is the Time Trend of Research in This Area?

After identifying the topic of research of each cluster, we analyzed the evolution of the number of publications in each cluster in the last 20 years to find if there had been a particular tendency that could reveal different research interests at different moments of time.

The results represented in Fig. 3 show that for all the clusters there is an increasing tendency in the past 5 years (2015–2018)[3]. However, while cluster 0 has a softer increase (average 2000–2014 = 63.2, average 2015–2018 = 105.25), cluster 1 and cluster 2 have a much higher increase, with cluster 1 having more than double the average in the past 5 years (Average 2000–2014 = 20.26, average 2015–2018 = 50.5) and cluster 2 past five-year average being almost three times higher than the average of the previous 15 years (average 2000–2014 = 8.4, average 2015–2018 = 23). Figure 3 shows the time evolution for the tendency of publication in each cluster.

In order to find specific research interests along time within each cluster, we divided the period of analysis into four five-year periods and, for each cluster and time period, we analyzed the most frequent terms used in the abstracts of the papers pertaining to such period. However, this study did not offer any conclusive results that could help us identify research trends within each cluster. The same analysis applied to the complete collection of abstracts did not offer any conclusive results either.

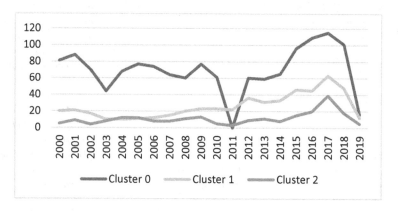

Fig. 3. Distribution of papers per cluster and year.

5   Discussion

In this work, we set four research questions aimed at finding and categorizing the work published as conference papers and journal papers during the last twenty years on the topic of human factors and software in general by applying text-mining techniques.

---

[3] In this analysis, 2019 was not considered, as at the moment this review is being written, several papers could still be under review or in press.

As for RQ1, we found 2192 papers related to our topic of interest. The majority of the works conducted on the topic of human factors and software were published as a conference paper (70%). ICSE and HCISS proceedings, together with IEEE Software are the preferred places to publish works on the aforementioned topic. The highest number of works has been published in the last five years, especially during 2017.

Using text mining algorithms in this review, the papers were clustered automatically intro three groups. After an analysis of the most frequent terms in the abstracts of the papers in each group, we found three main areas of research: a) user research and product evaluation, mostly grouping papers describing new approaches to evaluate the software product including human factors, or analyzing the role of the user in the software development, b) human factors in the software development process, which groups papers dealing with how personality factors and other human factors of the development team impact on aspects such as the teamwork and their productivity, and c) software development education, grouping papers dealing with the education of software engineers in human factors and also how human factors, such as motivation and engagement impact on the education of future software engineers (RQ2).

A further analysis of the works which were closely related to the software development process enabled us to find that the processes of software project management are the ones that have attracted more research relating human factors and the software process. Having into consideration how human factors impact on the productivity and teamwork effectiveness of software developers is crucial for project planning and cost estimation, and, therefore a high number of the papers focused on the impact of human factors on software development describes this relation within the scope of the project management processes (RQ3).

Finally, our analysis of the research trends in the area revealed that in the last five years, there are two topics that have attracted a significant interest from the research community in software-related human factors. The number of papers describing experiences considering human factors such as motivation and engagement in the computer science education has been three times higher in the last five-year period than ever before, being gamification and serious games frequent topics of discussion in those papers. Likewise, the effect of human factors, such as personality of software developers, in the software development process is another topic that has duplicated the number of publications in the last years (RQ4).

6   Threats to Validity

One important issue of a literature review is not missing any relevant study. We used four of the most frequently used digital libraries of research literature and searched for conference and journal papers written in English and published in the last 20 years. In the case that a relevant work has not been indexed in the four digital libraries used or has been published in a different language or as a different type of paper, that work has not been included in this study.

Additionally, the findings of our work are necessarily influenced by the text-mining process followed on the papers abstracts and the algorithms applied. As a relatively recent approach, text-mining has also its disadvantages. One of them is the presence of overlapping when analyzing words that take part in two-words expressions, as in "user" and "user experience". In this work, the automatic process was done based on single terms, although we manually analyzed the relevance of the two-word expressions making use of the n-grams algorithm. Another issue is the effect of the stemming algorithm that can lead to missing relevant results. For example, the algorithm can identify terms such as "use" and "user" by their common stem. Since in this particular area, the term "user" has a significant and distinctive meaning, to avoid this issue, we manually excluded this term 'user' from the stemming process. Additionally, splitting a set of papers into a number of clusters, requires the use of a clustering algorithm, such as k-means. However, this algorithm requires the number of clusters as an input. Since providing the number of broad topics of research to cluster the paper set would have added the authors' biases to the process, we opted for the x-means algorithm which automatically identified three groups of papers. Consequently, we did not applied any further method to determine the optimal value of the number of clusters (k), as in k-means application.

7 Conclusions

In this work, we preliminary revised and categorized the research literature published in the last twenty years on the topic of human factors and software using a text-mining approach. This review helped identify the trends of research and the three broad topics of research interest together with their time evolution. It also helped identify the predominant research interest of human factors in software project management.

As our future works, it is our intention to further develop this analysis by completing the search of literature by using other digital libraries, exploring the results offered by other text-mining techniques, comparing the results obtained when feeding the operators with particular sections of the papers texts and correlating the results with the bibliometric data and network that can be obtained from this collection of works.

Acknowledgements. This research was partly supported by the Spanish Ministry of Science and Innovation and the ERDF funds under project BadgePeople (TIN2016-76956-C3-3-R and the Andalusian Plan for Research, Development and Innovation (TIC-195).

References

1. Allahyari, M., et al.: A brief survey of text mining: classification, clustering and extraction techniques. In: KDD 2017 (2017)
2. Rekik, R., Kallel, I., Casillas, J., Alimi, A.M.: Assessing web sites quality: a systematic literature review by text and association rules mining. Int. J. Inf. Manag. 38(1), 201–216 (2018)
3. Galati, F., Bigliardi, B.: Industry 4.0: emerging themes and future research avenues using a text mining approach. Comput. Ind. **109**, 100–113 (2019)
4. Delen, D., Crossland, M.D.: Seeding the survey and analysis of research literature with text mining. Expert Syst. Appl. **34**(3), 1707–1720 (2008)

5. Cruz, S.S.J.O., da Silva, F.Q.B., Monteiro, C.V.F., Santos, C.F., dos Santos, M.T.: Personality in software engineering: preliminary findings from a systematic literature review. In: 15th Annual Conference on Evaluation & Assessment in Software Engineering (EASE 2011), pp. 1–10 (2011)

6. Cruz, S., da Silva, F.Q.B., Capretz, L.F.: Forty years of research on personality in software engineering: a mapping study. Comput. Hum. Behav. **46**, 94–113 (2015)

7. Soomro, A.B., Salleh, N., Mendes, E., Grundy, J., Burch, G., Nordin, A.: The effect of software engineers' personality traits on team climate and performance: a Systematic Literature Review. Inf. Softw. Technol. **73**, 52–65 (2016)

8. Oliveira, E., Conte, T., Cristo, M., Valentim, N.: Influence factors in software productivity—a tertiary literature review. Int. J. Softw. Eng. Knowl. Eng. **28**(11n12), 1795–1810 (2018)

9. Beecham, S., Baddoo, N., Hall, T., Robinson, H., Sharp, H.: Motivation in Software Engineering: a systematic literature review. Inf. Softw. Technol. **50**(9–10), 860–878 (2008)

10. Askarinejadamiri, Z.: Personality requirements in requirement engineering of web development: a systematic literature review. In: 2016 Second International Conference on Web Research (ICWR), pp. 183–188 (2016)

11. Sánchez-Gordón, M., Colomo-Palacios, R.: Characterizing DevOps culture: a systematic literature review. In: Stamelos, I., O'Connor, R.V., Rout, T., Dorling, A. (eds.) SPICE 2018. CCIS, vol. 918, pp. 3–15. Springer, Cham (2018). https://doi.org/10.1007/978-3-030-00623-5_1

12. Debois, P.: DevOps: a software revolution in the making? J. Inf. Technol. Manag. **24**(8), 3–5 (2011)

13. Pocius, K.E.: Personality factors in human-computer interaction: a review of the literature. Comput. Hum. Behav. **7**(3), 103–135 (1991)

14. Pelleg, D., Moore, A.: X-means: extending K-means with efficient estimation of the number of clusters. In: Proceedings of the 17th International Conference on Machine Learning, pp. 727–734 (2000)

15. Bishop, C.M.: Neural Networks for Pattern Recognition. Clarendon Press, Oxford (1995)

16. Niès, J., Pelayo, S.: From users involvement to users' needs understanding: a case study. Int. J. Med. Inform. **79**(4), e76–e82 (2010)

17. Lizcano, D., López, G., Soriano, J., Lloret, J.: Implementation of end-user 'development success factors in mashup development environments. Comput. Stand. Interfaces **47**, 1–18 (2016)

18. Karahoca, A., Bayraktar, E., Tatoglu, E., Karahoca, D.: Information system design for a hospital emergency department: a usability analysis of software prototypes. J. Biomed. Inform. **43**(2), 224–232 (2010)

19. Ruangwan, S., Thongtanunam, P., Ihara, A., Matsumoto, K.: The impact of human factors on the participation decision of reviewers in modern code review. Empir. Softw. Eng. **24**(2), 973–1016 (2019)

20. Prikladnicki, R.: QUASE - a quantitative approach to analyze the human aspects of software development projects. In: 2009 ICSE Workshop on Cooperative and Human Aspects on Software Engineering, p. 78 (2009)

21. Mi, Q., Keung, J., Mei, X., Xiao, Y., Chan, W.K.: A gamification technique for motivating students to learn code readability in software engineering. In: 2018 International Symposium on Educational Technology (ISET), pp. 250–254 (2018)

22. Sangal, R.: Software engineering: research-led education with human values. In: 2009 22nd Conference on Software Engineering Education and Training, p. 1 (2009)

23. Hazzan, O., Tomayko, J.E.: Reflection and abstraction in learning software engineering's human aspects. Computer (Long. Beach. Calif) **38**(6), 39–45 (2005)

24. Farooqui, T., Rana, T., Jafari, F.: Impact of human-centered design process (HCDP) on software development process. In: 2019 2nd International Conference on Communication, Computing and Digital systems (C-CODE), pp. 110–114 (2019)
25. Acuna, S.T., Lasserre, C.M., Quincoces, V.E.: Human capacities in the software process: empiric validation. In: Proceedings of the 24th International Conference on Software Engineering, ICSE 2002, p. 715 (2002)
26. Ghane, K.: A model and system for applying Lean Six sigma to agile software development using hybrid simulation. In: 2014 IEEE International Technology Management Conference, pp. 1–4 (2014)
27. Reddy, G.: Designing software project management models based on supply chain quality assurance practices. In: 2009 WRI World Congress on Computer Science and Information Engineering, pp. 659–663 (2009)
28. Sampaio, A., Sampaio, I.B., Gray, E.: The need of a person oriented approach to software process assessment. In: 2013 6th International Workshop on Cooperative and Human Aspects of Software Engineering (CHASE), pp. 145–148 (2013)

Working Conditions for Software Developers in Colombia: An Effort-Reward-Imbalance-Based Study

Judy Moreno[1]([✉]), Jairo Aponte[2], and Mario Linares-Vásquez[3]

[1] Unipanamericana Fundación Universitaria, Bogotá, Colombia
jmmorenoo@unipanamericana.edu.co
[2] Universidad Nacional de Colombia, Bogotá, Colombia
jhapontem@unal.edu.co
[3] Universidad de los Andes, Bogotá, Colombia
m.linaresv@uniandes.edu.co

Abstract. The peopleware concept, although introduced in the field of computer science since the seventies, is still in the process of consolidation given that the vast majority of previous studies have mostly focused on theoretical and technical aspects of software construction. Nowadays, companies recognize that human assets are a key component of any strategy that seeks to increase their productivity, since identifying and dealing with psychosocial factors in its personnel often allows project managers to maintain a working team at ease and, therefore, productive. This research focuses on diagnosing the working conditions of employees in the area of software development, based on existing models that measure their satisfaction with their current positions. The main contribution of the study is an initial characterization of the working conditions in the area of software construction in Colombia. It may serve as a starting point for future research aiming at improving existing development models and organizational structures in such a way that the welfare of employees is of greater significance, and consequently, more productive and happy work teams are consolidated.

Keywords: Peopleware · Occupational stress · Psychosocial factors · ERI

1 Introduction

The software industry, like other ones in the productive sector, is continuously looking for efficiency and increased productivity [27]. In the particular case of software companies, they have been designing and implementing environments and strategies aimed at improving developers' performance. Examples of this are the transition to agile methods that are more centered in the team members than in the process [3], the design of spaces that improve working conditions and team's integration [25], and the introduction of a wide variety of tools that reduce the time required to build and release a software product.

© Springer Nature Switzerland AG 2019
X. Franch et al. (Eds.): PROFES 2019, LNCS 11915, pp. 709–724, 2019.
https://doi.org/10.1007/978-3-030-35333-9_55

However, aspects related to developer welfare and how it motivates their productivity is still an area that requires more empirical studies. Welfare is a subject that has transcended to the software industry, with the existence of different tools and guidelines that have been implemented to guarantee the well-being of software developers. Concepts such as *occupational health* or *worker's mental health* have been introduced recently into the software engineering community [10], and have motivated the design of healthy work environments and stress reduction programs [12,14]. With increasing interest, from both researchers and practitioners, software companies have begun to recognize that the psychosocial aspects of developers are as important as their technical skills and background.

Previous studies involving people working at different organizations, have focused on emotions and their impact on productivity [9,13,35]. This is also the case of studies about social and human aspects of software engineering that have indicated that the wide range of emotions that developers experience in their daily activities, might affect their individual performance and team productivity. However, a potential issue in some of previous studies, is the intrusiveness, in the sense that the type of study (e.g., ethnography) might have an impact on the results. Thus, it is desirable to use less-intrusive methods to avoid biases introduced by intrusive methods.

One widely used non-intrusive method is the Effort-Reward Imbalance (ERI) model [28], which has been extensively applied since its introduction in 1986 to analyze the working conditions of employees across a broad range of occupations, in several countries [4,5,30,33]; however, the context of software companies has not been analyzed yet using this model in Colombia.

In this paper, we report the results of an empirical study, aimed at evaluating the working conditions and developers' perceptions at software development companies in Bogotá (Colombia), applying the ERI model. The results of the analysis suggest that the participants perceive a high level of stress and there is no reciprocity in their work in terms of effort versus reward, i.e., the participants perceive their labor activity as a high-effort with moderate rewards.

The rest of this paper is organized as follows. Section 2 describes the related work, with emphasis on previous studies using the ERI model. Section 3 describes the study and the procedures for data collection and analysis. In Sect. 4 we report the results and discuss the limitations of the study. Finally, Sect. 5 reports the conclusions and future work.

2   Related Work

Based on a number of studies, since 1984 the International Labor Organization and the World Health Organization have recognized that the psychosocial factors at work contribute to a wide range of workers' health disorders [18]. These stressful psychosocial factors include personal aspects of the worker (e.g., the employee's skills, needs, expectations, and culture), as well as characteristics of the environment (e.g., conditions of the organization, way of working, and management style). The ongoing or progressing stress an employee experiences due to all these factors is commonly named *occupational stress* [20].

In the eighties and nineties, the first studies on occupational stress among information systems personnel were conducted. Self-reports, surveys, and interviews have been the typical instruments used to identify job factors that are perceived as stressful and examine their relationships with psychological disorders [19, 23]. For instance, a study with software engineers in Japan reported lack of job control, lack of intrinsic rewards, and ambiguity of career development as the main predictors of depressive symptoms [17].

By the year 2000, advances in communications technologies and the consolidation of the cooperative software engineering (e.g., mobile devices, video chat systems, version-control systems) had made work an on-going concern and an omnipresent activity, and in particular, they brought the office home. As a result, the causes and effects of occupational stress are becoming a serious concern, not only for researchers and IT companies, but also for national and global labor and health organizations. Tong and Yap [32] reviewed 12 existing occupational stress models and suggested 9 critical aspects to take into account for the definition of an occupational stress model for IS professionals. Rajeswari and Ananthara-man [26] designed a survey and measures to study sources of pressure among software professionals. They carried out a study with software professionals in India and identified 10 causes of negative pressure on software developers, being fear of obsolescence and individual team interaction the most influential factors. Chilton et al. [8] highlight the mismatch between the preferred cognitive style of a software developer and her perception of the cognitive style required by the job environment as a factor that impacts stress/strain and performance. The results show that the stress level is higher and productivity decreases as this mismatch becomes greater.

More recent studies have focused on examining in more detail the consequences of occupational stress in system and software professionals. Love et al. [24], confirmed the predictive capabilities of the job stain model (JSM) by investigating whether perceived work demands, job control and social support are suitable predictors of UK information systems employee's health and job satisfaction. Tominaga et al. [31], designed a survey-based study to investigate the effects of occupational stress (micro and macro stressors) on the subjective health status and productive behavior of Japanese computer engineers. They identified relevant predictors such as quantitative and qualitative work overload, career and future ambiguity, insufficient evaluation systems and poor supervisor's support. Anantharaman et al. [1], examined the relationships between occupational stress and demographic characteristics in Indian software development professionals. They found that men and women professionals experience similar levels of stress; those over 30 years old have stress due to work family interface; those who work less than 10 hours a day are more stressed due to fear of obsolescence, individual interactions, work culture, family support, and technical risk propensity.

On the other hand, the ERI model, used in this study, has been empirically validated [33] and widely used to understand and predict the effects of working conditions on the well-being of workers, in multiple occupations and countries [30]. In the particular case of Latin America, a study in Chile addressed the association between the dimensions of the ERI model and the mental health model (General Health Questionnaire, GHQ-28). The data collected from health service workers show positive associations between poor mental health status (e.g., symptoms of depression, anxiety, and insomnia) and the presence of occupational stress (e.g., job insecurity) [6]. Another Chilean study focuses on exploring and describing the prevalence of job stress in gendarmerie officials of the preventive detention center CDP, through the application of the ERI model. The findings indicate that 28.3% of the workers had low prevalence of job stress. Likewise, the study determined that the job stress is associated mainly with some sociodemographic characteristics and the workplace [34].

Work stress in Colombian workers has been studied using the ERI model and other empirically validated models. For example, a combination of the Job-Demand Control (JDC) [11] and ERI models was used to predict the bus operators' blood pressure (BP) and psychological strain. It was found that the JDC and ERI models combined explain 10% of systolic BP variance, and 34% of psychological strain variance [7].

Another Colombian study was performed with high school teachers in Bogotá with the aim of identifying the prevalence of psychological job factors, measured with the JCQ (Job Content Questionnaire) and the ERI models [16]. The authors evaluated the relationship between psychological factors, mental health and blood pressure. The results showed significant relation between job tension and the effort-reward imbalance with the mental health, but not with the blood pressure in the complete group. The study findings confirmed that there is a high risk of job stress when teachers work in adverse psychosocial conditions, which are related to negative health indicators.

3   The Empirical Study

The goal of this study is to assess the working conditions of software developers in Colombia by using a non-intrusive analysis method that links features of the work environment with well-being and related behavior, for the purpose of providing some insight into psychosocial stressors that may impact people's health.

3.1   The Sample

The target population is software developers working in Bogotá (Colombia). We include all roles that are directly involved in software construction: analysts, designers, programmers, project leaders, testers, etc. We exclude administrative and commercial roles because their main daily work is not part of the activities of the software process model. About 21,000 software developers work in the Colombian center region. We sent the questionnaire to 378 developers and obtained valid answers from 169 of them. This is a representative sample with a 95% confidence level, and 7.5% confidence interval.

3.2   The ERI Model

Although there are several models that relate the working conditions of employees with their physical and mental health [22,28], the ERI model has characteristics that make it suitable for our purposes. First of all, it is a non-intrusive model in which employees anonymously self-report their experiences and perceptions of their current working conditions. Secondly, the data can be acquired through standardized questionnaires that can be easily distributed through web-based surveys. In third place, the ERI model has been already tested and validated in Colombia within studies that involved various occupations [2,16,21]. In fact, in 2010 Gómez-Ortiz validated the reliability of the numerical scales used in the model [15]. Lastly, and most importantly, a strong body of scientific evidence is now available demonstrating that the ERI model effectively uncovers associations of adverse psychosocial working conditions with a variety of stress-related disorders.

Specifically, the ERI model establishes that when there is a notorious imbalance between employees' perceptions of the effort made at work and their perceptions of the rewards received for that work, sustained stress reactions are created. Moreover, this model indicates that a high level of over commitment may further increase the risk of strong negative emotions, stress reactions, and adverse effects on health. In this context, the rewards refer not only to the salary, but also to esteem (recognition, adequate support, and fair treatment at work), job stability, and promotion opportunities [28].

With respect to the survey, we used the short version of the ERI questionnaire, consisting of 16 questions [29]. Table 1 shows the questionnaire which consists of 3 questions to evaluate the effort (ERI1 to ERI3), 7 questions to assess the reward perceived for respondents (ERI4 to ERI10), and 6 overcommitment questions (OC1 to OC6). We decided to use the short version with the intention of having a better acceptance rate among the respondents.

Each question is an assertion about the conditions of the participant's current work (See Table 1). In each response, the participant indicates how much the respective statement reflects their typical condition in current work. The rating procedure is a 4-point Likert scale where the respondent expresses her perception choosing (1) strongly disagree, (2) disagree, (3) agree, or (4) strongly agree. Thus, scales and scoring ranges for each of the dimensions of the ERI model are constructed as shown by Table 2. In particular, the last column shows the maximum and minimum values in each scale and subscale of the model.

3.3   Data Collection

In addition to the ERI questionnaire, we formulated demographic questions to better characterize the population, so that the results of other studies can be compared with ours, or future replications or extensions can be performed precisely. Tables 3 and 4 show the variables used for demographic information, which includes gender, age, education level, work experience, salary, and characteristics of the current job.

Table 1. Short questionnaire of the ERI model

Label	Question
ERI1	I have constant time pressure due to a heavy work load
ERI2	I have many interruptions and disturbances while performing my job
ERI3	Over the past few years, my job has become more a more demanding
ERI4	I receive the respect I deserve from my superior or a respective relevant person
ERI5	My job promotion prospects are poor (Reverse coding)
ERI6	I have experienced or I expect to experience an undesirable change in my work situation (Reverse coding)
ERI7	My job security is poor (Reverse coding)
ERI8	Considering all my efforts and achievements, I receive the respect and prestige I deserve at work
ERI9	Considering all my efforts and achievements, my job promotion prospects are adequate
ERI10	Considering all my efforts and achievements, my salary/income is adequate
OC1	I get easily overhelmed by time pressures at work
OC2	As soon as I get in the morning I start thinking about work problems
OC3	When I get home, I can easily relax and 'switch off' work (Reverse coding)
OC4	People close to me say I sacrifice too much for my job
OC5	Work rarely lets me go, it is still on my mind when I go to bed
OC6	If I postpone something that I was supposed to do today I'll have trouble sleeping at night

Table 2. Construction of scales and scores

Scales	Questions	Range
Effort scale	ERI1 to ERI3	3 to 12
Reward scale	ERI4 to ERI10	7 to 28
Overcommitment	OC1 to OC6	6 to 24
Subscales of the reward scale		
Esteem	ERI4, ERI8	2 to 8
Promotion	ERI5, ERI9, ERI10	3 to 12
Security	ERI6, ERI7	2 to 8

The ERI questions, as well as the demographic questions, were distributed from April to October 2017, through the web-based survey tool Survio[1]. Initially, it was distributed freely via convenience sampling to developers in the contacts network of the authors. In a second stage, we contacted developers from the same

---

[1] https://www.survio.com/en/.

companies where the first stage respondents work. In a third stage, we asked the Colombian Federation of Software and IT Industry (Fedesoft[2]) to distribute the survey among its associates. At the end, we obtained 169 complete questionnaires with valid answers.

4 Analysis and Results

4.1 Demographics

The details of the demographic characteristics of the sample are summarized in Table 3. 43 respondents are women and 126 men. The majority of respondents are under 30 (62%) and only 5.6% of them are over 40 years, which indicates that the population working in software development is young. As for the educational level, most of the participants have at least one bachelor degree (64%), but it is interesting that more than a third of them (36%) are undergraduate students or have only technical studies. In relation to work experience, most of them (54%) already have more than three years of work experience, but many of them (74%) have already worked for two or more different companies.

Table 4 lists the participants (169), differentiated by gender, and the distribution with respect to the sample of each variable measured. The respondents work in different companies having their headquarters in Bogotá. With respect to their occupational profile, a high diversity can be observed in the sample, as follows: 54% are developers/programmers; 12% corresponds to project leaders; 11% are software analysts; 23% is distributed in other profiles such as testers, process managers, functional consultants, architects, and project managers; and 1% indicate the "other" option without specifying their position. Note that, although the headquarters of the companies are located in Bogotá, only 78% of the respondents carry out their work in Bogotá, followed by 18% working in Cali and 4% in cities outside Colombia (e.g., Lima).

We found that 53% of the respondents work in national companies, while the rest work for multinationals. Besides, 44% of them are in companies with more than 200 workers, followed by 33% who work for companies that have between 51 and 200 employees, 15% are in companies with between 11 and 50 employees, and only 8% are in companies with a staff less than 11. These numbers indicate that the surveyed people work mostly in large companies.

Regarding the duration of their current jobs, we found that almost 44% of them have been working in the current company for less than one year, while 43% report between 1 and 3 years of work in the present company. Only 13% of the respondents have been working for more than 3 years in their current companies. These percentages suggest that in the Colombian software industry, the employee turnover rate is high.

Each year the Colombian government establishes the legal monthly minimum wage (SMMLV, for its acronym in Spanish). For this reason, the question of the survey that refers to salary, asks the respondent to say if her current salary is

---

[2] https://fedesoft.org/.

Table 3. Demographic characteristics of the 169 respondents

	Women n = 43	Men n = 126	Frequency	Percentage
Age (years)				
Under 20	1	1	2	1%
20–30	22	83	105	62%
31–40	16	30	46	27%
Over 40	4	12	16	9%
Education level				
Technician	7	44	51	30%
Undergrad	0	10	10	6%
Professional	27	59	86	51%
Grad	9	13	22	13%
Number of companies you have worked for				
1	12	31	43	25%
2–4	28	77	105	62%
5 or more	3	18	21	12%
Experience (years)				
Less than 1	6	18	24	14%
1–3	15	38	53	31%
more than 3	22	70	92	54%

less than 2 SMMLV, is between 2 and 4 SMMLV, is between 4 and 6, or if it is greater than 6 SMMLV. For 2017, one SMMLV was equivalent to approximately 250 USD. Thus, we found that 11% of the respondents earn less than 2 SMMLV (less than 500 USD), 50% earn between 2 and 4 SMMLV (between 500 and 1000 USD), 16% between 4 and 6 SMMLV (between 1000 and 1500 USD), and 23% earn more than 6 SMMLV (more than 1500 USD). These data may indicate that the majority of people working in the software industry in Colombia do not earn high salaries. Although a deeper study is required, this salary issue could explain why the employee turnover rate is high.

We also inquire about the schedule and the workplace. Regarding the place, 6% are remote workers, 71% work always at their offices, and 23% use a mixed modality, in which some days they go to the office, and in others, they work from home. Regarding the working hours, 67% indicate having a fixed schedule and 33% have a flexible one. These results indicate that about one-third of employees benefit from the possibility of working from wherever they choose and/or with a flexible schedule while maintaining full-time employment.

Table 4. Job characteristics

	Women n = 43	Men n = 126	Frequency	Percentage
Professional profile				
Analyst	6	12	18	11%
Architect	3	5	8	5%
Consultant	1	2	3	2%
Developer	14	78	92	54%
Process Manager	6	5	11	7%
Tester	5	4	9	5%
Project Leader	7	13	20	12%
Other	1	6	7	4%
City				
Bogotá	27	104	131	78%
Cali	15	15	30	18%
Chilpancingo	0	1	1	1%
Lima	0	2	2	1%
Santiago	1	4	5	3%
Number of employees in the company				
1–10	1	12	13	8%
11–50	6	20	26	15%
51–200	10	46	56	33%
Over 200	26	48	74	33%
Time in the current company (years)				
Less than 1	18	57	75	44%
1–3	21	51	72	43%
more than 3	4	18	22	13%
Salary (SMMLV)				
Less than 2	2	16	18	11%
2-4	23	62	85	50%
4-6	7	20	27	16%
Over 6	11	28	39	23%
Work modality				
In person	25	95	120	71%
Mixed	17	22	39	23%
Remote	1	9	10	6%
Work schedule				
Fixed	30	83	113	67%
Flexible	13	43	56	33%

4.2 The ERI Model Results

Table 5 shows the mean, the standard deviation, and the minimum and maximum values obtained in each dimension of the ERI model. According to the means of the scores obtained in each one of the dimensions, it can be seen that the participants perceive moderate efforts to carry out their work, as well as moderate rewards. In the case of esteem, job security, job promotion and overcommitment, their perception is average, while the effort-reward ratio is perceived as high.

Table 5. Variables in the ERI model (N = 169)

DIMENSION	Mean	S.D.	Min.	Max.	Range
Effort	8.61	1.74	3	12	3 to 12
Reward	18.12	2.96	8	25	7 to 28
Effort-Reward ratio	1.16	0.40	0.35	2.92	
Esteem	5.26	1.22	2	8	2 to 8
Job Security	5.62	1.28	2	8	2 to 8
Promotion	7.24	1.54	3	12	3 to 12
Overcommitment	14.8	3.83	6	24	6 to 24

ER Ratio. The Effort-Reward ratio (See Table 5) shows whether there is an imbalance between a developer's effort and the reward earned for her work when the value is not equal to one. A ratio greater than one is a signal of work stress. Table 6 lists the cases of stress at work, according to the Effort-Reward ratio and surprisingly, 63.31% of the respondents suffer some degree of stress at work due to an effort-reward imbalance.

Table 6. Stress prevalence by ERI

Effort-reward imbalance	N	%
Without work stress	62	36.69
With work stress	107	63.31
Total	169	100

According to the age, 66% of the participants between 20 and 30 years are suffering stress due to effort-reward imbalance, while 63% of the respondents in the range between 31 and 40 years are in similar condition. Furthermore, the level of studies shows that stress is more prone in levels equal to or higher than the level of professional studies (more than 67%), compared to workers that are still students. According to gender, the analysis shows similar work stress in both men and women. However, women have significantly less participation in positions in the area of software development as it was reported above. With regard to experience, the stress is greater in those who have been in the same work position for more than 1 year or similar positions, in contrast to those who have been working for less than one year in the current position.

Hypothesis Tests. In addition to the descriptive statistics-based analysis we used hypotheses testing to identify whether there are significant differences in the data. The inference analysis was carried out using the T-Student test, since it allows to estimate if the averages of effort, reward, promotion and estimation are the same regardless of the gender. To reject or not a hypothesis we used $\alpha = 0.05$. The results for the test are depicted in Table 7. On the one hand, statistically significant differences were found between effort ($p = 0.04378$) and reward ($p = 0.01233$); therefore, it is inferred that there are significant differences by gender in these categories. On the other hand, there are no significant differences with respect to promotion ($p = 0.06399$) and esteem ($p = 0.166$). Thus, it can be assumed that the perceptions of esteem and promotion are the same in both men and women.

Table 7. Bivariate analysis among effort, reward, promotion and esteem according to gender

Dimension	Gender				T-Student	p-value
	Men		Women			
	Mean	S.D.	Mean	S.D.		
Effort	13.56	10.25	5.11	4.20	2.288	0.04378
Reward	7.18	6.0	2.71	3.48	2.657	0.01233
Promotion	13.56	11.03	5.11	5.69	2.041	0.06399
Esteem	17.43	17.25	5.88	6.73	1.665	0.1366

According to the tests, men who work in the area of software development (mean $= 13.56$), report greater effort at work than women (mean $= 5.11$), with statistically significant difference ($p = 0.04378$). Unlike women (mean $= 2.71$), men also have a greater perception of reward (mean $= 7.18$), with statistically significant difference ($p = 0.01233$). Men perceive the same financial status or job promotion and salary ($x = 13.56$) that women ($x = 5.11$) since there is no statistically significant difference between the means ($p = 0.06399$).

In relation to the dimension of esteem, men perceive the same esteem at work ($x = 17.43$) that women ($x = 5.88$). The difference is not statistically significant between the means of these groups ($p = 0.166$).

Lastly, the results suggest that the workers in the software development area who have been working in their current company for less than 3 years ($x = 7.74$) are more overwhelmed and overloaded at work, compared to workers who have been working for 3 or more years in the same company. There is a statistically significant difference of the means between both groups ($p = 0.0064$).

4.3 Discussion

The application of the ERI model allowed us to analyze in a non-intrusive way, characteristics such as: esteem, job security (job stability), promotion in employment, as well as overcommitment. The results suggest that the practitioners in the analyzed sample perceive a moderate esteem (5.26/8), also average job security (5.62/8), as well as a not very high promotion (7.24/12) and a moderate/high over-commitment (14.8/24). As a result, it is estimated that developers are barely satisfied with their present working conditions.

The influence of the psychosocial state on the activities carried out by the practitioners was determined by taking into account that the ERI model has as premises the work effort, the rewards obtained and the overcommitment that the workers perceive of their work. In our study, a high prevalence (mean = 1,160, s.d. = 0.40) of work stress was found, since it occurred in 63.31% of the sample. This means that these workers perceive their labor activity as a high-effort (mean = 8.61/12, s.d. = 1.74), with moderate rewards (mean = 18.12/28, s.d. = 2.960). Consequently, the results suggest that the respondents perceive a considerable level of stress and there is no reciprocity in their work. Specifically, according to the ERI model, 63% of the respondents experience work stress.

A summary of other relevant findings and recommendations are the following:

- **Economic compensation**: lower levels of work stress occur when the economic remuneration of employees is higher;
- **Home office working day**: those developers who reported Home-Office benefits experience lower levels of work stress;
- **Stability**: the average is 5.62/8, which suggests to look for strategies to improve the perception of job stability among software developers;
- **Esteem**: The average is 5.26/8, so that recognition and support at work are aspects to be improved by generating non-monetary incentives for the work carried out by developers;
- **Promotion**: it relates to the possibilities of personal and professional growth in the company. It is another aspect to be taken into account since the average is 7.24/12.
- The other variables analyzed in the correlations, such as age, level of studies, gender, experience and working hours, do not seem to be relevant enough to drive specific initiatives of developers well being.

Previous Studies. Compared with [9], there are many reasons that coincide in the characterization they performed, such as: perceived workload (overload), lack of rewards, uncertain progress and insecurity (safety at work) and effort-reward imbalance. According to our results, in Colombia there is currently a greater turnover of personnel than in Spain. With regard to job stability, the Spanish study showed that it is one of the most notorious causes of job abandonment, while for our study the variable measured as moderate. In [9] the salary was identified as a variable perceived as low with respect to the effort devoted. This result was consistent with ours, which also shows a non-conformity with respect to salary remuneration as depicted in Table 8.

Table 8. ERI distribution according to salary

Salary (SMMLV)	Effort-reward imbalance			
	Without work stress		With work stress	
	N	%	N	%
Less than 3	9	21	34	79
3–5	32	37	55	63
5–8	21	54	18	46
Total	62	37	107	63

4.4 Limitations of the Study

This study has some methodological limitations. Getting a large sample of developers is often a frustrating and time-consuming task. Aware of this drawback, we made several rounds of participants' recruitment, starting with our direct contacts, and ending with companies and business associations. Despite this, replications of the study are needed to reach a diagnosis at the country level, and increase the reliability of the results. However, the study has benefited from a representative sample calculated with a 5% expected accuracy and a 7.5% confidence level.

In addition, some researchers in the area of social sciences recommend conducting studies using the ERI Questionnaire in combination with the Job Content Questionnaire since they have found that they are complementary, and therefore, allow broader and more solid conclusions. Thus, studies applying both models are recommended and desired.

5 Conclusions and Future Work

On the one hand, this study characterized the population of software developers in Bogotá, in terms of gender, age, education level, salary, experience, and career mobility, as well as, the type of companies where they work and the kind of jobs they do. On the other hand, it evaluated the working conditions of this population by using three standardized psychometric scales of the ERI model, i.e., effort, reward and overcommitment, after collecting and measuring perceptions and experiences of developers. We consider it essential to carry out replications of this study in other areas of the country to reach a more complete diagnosis of the working conditions of developers in Colombia. Thus, we plan to extend the scope of this diagnosis by replicating this initial study.

References

1. Anantharaman, R., Rajeswari, K.S., Ajitha, A., Jayanty, K.: Occupational stress and demographic characteristics among information technology professionals. Int. J. Bus. Manag. **13**, 140 (2018). https://doi.org/10.5539/ijbm.v13n12p140

2. Balcázar, A., Rubio, M.: Análisis de las Propiedades Psicométricas del Cuestionario Desbalance-Esfuerzo-Recompensa ERI en Conductores Colombianos. Thesis, Universidad de los Andes, Bogotá, Colombia (2006)
3. Beck, K., et al.: Manifesto for agile software development (2001)
4. Calnan, M., Wainwright, D., Almond, S.: Job strain, effort-reward imbalance and mental distress: a study of occupations in general medical practice. Work Stress 14(4), 297–311 (2000). https://doi.org/10.1080/02678370110040920
5. Calnan, M., Wadsworth, E., May, M., Smith, A., Wainwright, D.: Job strain, effort - reward imbalance, and stress at work: competing or complementary models? Scand. J. Public Health 32(2), 84–93 (2004). https://doi.org/10.1080/14034940310001668. pMID: 15255497
6. Canepa, C., Briones, J., Pérez, C., Vera Calzaretta, A., Juárez García, A.: Desequilibro esfuerzo-recompensa y estado de malestar en trabajadores de servicios de salud en chile. Ciencia & Trabajo, ISSN 0718–2449, N°. 30, 2008, pp. 157–160 (2008)
7. Cendales, B., Useche, S., Gómez, V.: Psychosocial work factors, blood pressure and psychological strain in male bus operators. Ind. Health 52(4), 279–288 (2014). https://doi.org/10.2486/indhealth.2013-0156
8. Chilton, M.A., Hardgrave, B.C., Armstrong, D.J.: Person-job cognitive style fit for software developers: the effect on strain and performance. J. Manage. Inf. Syst. 22(2), 193–226 (2005). https://doi.org/10.1080/07421222.2005.11045849
9. Colomo-Palacios, R., Casado-Lumbreras, C., Misra, S., Soto-Acosta, P.: Career abandonment intentions among software workers. Hum. Factor. Ergon. Manuf. 24(6), 641–655 (2014). https://doi.org/10.1002/hfm.20509
10. Cullen, K.L., et al.: Effectiveness of workplace interventions in return-to-work for musculoskeletal, pain-related and mental health conditions: an update of the evidence and messages for practitioners. J. Occup. Rehabil. 28(1), 1–15 (2018). https://doi.org/10.1007/s10926-016-9690-x
11. der Doef, M.V., Maes, S.: The job demand-control (-support) model and psychological well-being: a review of 20 years of empirical research. Work Stress 13(2), 87–114 (1999). https://doi.org/10.1080/026783799296084
12. Graziotin, D., Fagerholm, F., Wang, X., Abrahamsson, P.: What happens when software developers are (un)happy. J. Syst. Softw. 140, 32–47 (2018). https://doi.org/10.1016/j.jss.2018.02.041
13. Graziotin, D., Wang, X., Abrahamsson, P.: Are happy developers more productive? In: Heidrich, J., Oivo, M., Jedlitschka, A., Baldassarre, M.T. (eds.) PROFES 2013. LNCS, vol. 7983, pp. 50–64. Springer, Heidelberg (2013). https://doi.org/10.1007/978-3-642-39259-7_7
14. Graziotin, D., Wang, X., Abrahamsson, P.: Do feelings matter? On the correlation of affects and the self-assessed productivity in software engineering. J. Softw. Evol. Process 27(7), 467–487 (2015). https://doi.org/10.1002/smr.1673
15. Gómez-Ortiz, V.: Assessment of psychosocial stressors at work: psychometric properties of the Spanish version of the ERI (effort-reward imbalance) questionnaire in Colombian workers. Revista de Psicología del Trabajo y de las Organizaciones 26(2), 147–156 (2010)
16. Gómez-Ortiz, V., Moreno, L.: Factores psicosociales del trabajo (demanda-control y desbalance esfuerzo-recompensa), salud mental y tensión arterial: un estudio con maestros escolares en Bogotá, Colombia. Universitas Psychologica 9(2), 393–407 (2009)

17. Haratani, T., Fujigaki, Y., Asakura, T.: Job stressors and depressive symptoms in Japanese computer software engineers and managers. In: Anzai, Y., Ogawa, K., Mori, H. (eds.) Symbiosis of Human and Artifact. Advances in Human Factors/Ergonomics, vol. 20, pp. 699–704. Elsevier (1995). https://doi.org/10.1016/S0921-2647(06)80297-2

18. International Labour Organisation: PSYCHOSOCIAL FACTORS AT WORK: Recognition and control. Technical report, Report of the Joint ILO/WHO Committee on Occupational Health (1984)

19. Ivancevich, J.M., Napier, H.A., Wetherbe, J.C.: Occupational stress, attitudes, and health problems in the information systems professional. Commun. ACM **26**(10), 800–806 (1983). https://doi.org/10.1145/358413.358432

20. Jex, S.M.: Stress and Job Performance: Theory, Research, and Implications for Managerial Practice. Advanced Topics in Organizational Behavior. SAGE Publications Ltd, Thousand Oaks (1998)

21. Jiménez, L.: Ampliación de la validación del JCQ y del ERI en Colombia. Thesis, Universidad de los Andes, Bogota, Colombia (2014)

22. Karasek, R., Brisson, C., Kawakami, N., Houtman, I., Bongers, P., Amick, B.: The job content questionnaire (JCQ): an instrument for internationally comparative assessments of psychosocial job characteristics. J. Occup. Health Psychol. **3**, 322–355 (1998). https://doi.org/10.1037/1076-8998.3.4.322

23. Lo, M.W.: Occupational stress in the information systems profession. ACM SIGCHI Bull. **18**, 25–29 (1987). https://doi.org/10.1145/25281.1044286

24. Love, P., Irani, Z., Standing, C., Themistocleous, M.: Influence of job demands, job control and social support on information systems professionals' psychological well-being. Int. J. Manpower (2007). https://doi.org/10.1108/01437720710820026

25. McBreen, P.: Questioning Extreme Programming. Addison-Wesley Longman Publishing Co., Inc., Boston (2002)

26. Rajeswari, K.S., Anantharaman, R.N.: Development of an instrument to measure stress among software professionals: factor analytic study. In: Proceedings of the 2003 SIGMIS Conference on Computer Personnel Research: Freedom in Philadelphia-leveraging Differences and Diversity in the IT Workforce, SIGMIS CPR 2003, pp. 34–43. ACM, New York (2003). https://doi.org/10.1145/761849.761855

27. Sadowski, C., Zimmermann, T. (eds.): Rethinking Productivity in Software Engineering. Apress, Mountain View (2019)

28. Siegrist, J.: The Effort-Reward Imbalance Model, Chap. 2, pp. 24–35. Wiley, Hoboken (2017). https://doi.org/10.1002/9781118993811.ch2

29. Siegrist, J., Li, J., Montano, D.: Psychometric Properties of the Effort-Reward Imbalance Questionnaire. Technical report, Duesseldorf University, Germany (2014)

30. Siegrist, J., et al.: The measurement of effort-reward imbalance at work: European comparisons. Soc. Sci. Med. **58**(8), 1483–1499 (2004). https://doi.org/10.1016/S0277-9536(03)00351-4. Health inequalities and the psychosocial environment

31. Tei-Tominaga, M., Asakura, T., Akiyama, T.: The effect of micro and macro stressors in the work environment on computer professionals' subjective health status and productive behavior in Japan. Ind. Health **45**, 474–486 (2007). https://doi.org/10.2486/indhealth.45.474

32. Thong, J.Y., Yap, C.S.: Information systems and occupational stress: a theoretical framework. Omega **28**(6), 681–692 (2000). https://doi.org/10.1016/S0305-0483(00)00020-7

33. van Vegchel, N., de Jonge, J., Bosma, H., Schaufeli, W.: Reviewing the effort-reward imbalance model: drawing up the balance of 45 empirical studies. Soc. Sci. Med. **60**(5), 1117–1131 (2005). https://doi.org/10.1016/j.socscimed.2004.06.043
34. Cardenas Villar, P.A.: Estres laboral: modelo desequilibrio esfuerzo-recompensa en funcionarios de gendarmeria del centro de detencion preventiva (CDP), Santiago sur. Thesis, Facultad de Medicina, Universidad de Chile, September 2016. http://bibliodigital.saludpublica.uchile.cl:8080/dspace/handle/123456789/457
35. Yilmaz, M., OConnor, R.V., Colomo-Palacios, R., Clarke, P.: An examination of personality traits and how they impact on software development teams. Inf. Softw. Technol. **86**(C), 101–122 (2017). https://doi.org/10.1016/j.infsof.2017.01.005

Towards a Better Understanding of Team-Driven Dynamics in Agile Software Projects
A Characterization and Visualization Support in JIRA

Fabian Kortum$^{(\boxtimes)}$, Oliver Karras, Jil Klünder, and Kurt Schneider

Software Engineering Group, Leibniz University Hannover,
Welfengarten 1, 30167 Hannover, Germany
{fabian.kortum,oliver.karras,jil.kluender,
kurt.schneider}@inf.uni-hannover.de

Abstract. In agile software development, proper team structures and sprint estimations are crucial aspects to reach high-performance outcomes. Performance can vary due to the influence of social-driven team factors. Resulting in team dynamics with the focus on human factors are usually difficult to capture and thus often not monitored. However, their impact can impede the planning and fulfillment of sprints.

Data on team behavior should be simplified to track, analyze, and interpret as sprint influences are important to understand. We provide a centralized solution that extends JIRA functionally and continuously captures sprint characteristics in the daily working environment of teams.

In this paper, we describe a JIRA plugin that enables the assessment of team behavior in combination with exploratory analyses. The tool became approached with six software projects and a total of 53 undergraduate students. Characterizations made with the plugin can reveal sprint and team dynamics over time, involving development performance and team-related measures. The feature comes with a feedback mechanism for teams that visualize and implicates the sprint dependencies.

The approach reveals a set of team-related sprint dynamics, its systematically capturing, and characterization. With the achieved solution, team leader and developer can be supported to understand the ongoing sprint and team-driven dynamics better. Thus, they can keep track of their habits for future sprint planning and team adjustment impacts.

Keywords: Team behavior · Human factors · Agile · Exploratory analyses · Interdependency graph · Sprint characterization

1 Introduction

In agile software development, team- and process-related factors have increasing importance for sprint estimations and executions [16,19]. Both elements are often reflected in the performance outcome of sprints, usually measured by the comparison of scheduled versus completed story points per sprint.

© Springer Nature Switzerland AG 2019
X. Franch et al. (Eds.): PROFES 2019, LNCS 11915, pp. 725–740, 2019.
https://doi.org/10.1007/978-3-030-35333-9_56

However, the estimation and prioritization of development tasks can be a sophisticated and experience-based challenge for teams and stakeholders [15]. An extensive international survey in the industry revealed that sprint retrospectives of post-mortem experiences and knowledge are applied in three out of four projects [11]. In retrospectives, teams share, discuss, and interpret negative as well as positive aspects according to past sprint conditions and occurrences, e.g., neglected tasks due to insufficient estimations or workloads [16]. Awareness of the team, as well as an understanding of influences and interdependencies during sprints, is the first step towards improvement opportunities that lead to the planning of adjustments for follow-up sprints.

The team-driven factors in sprints are not trivial to characterize due to lacking information sources [9]. Human factors are challenging to capture or often not adequately taken into account [1]. As a consequence, interpretation gaps of performance changes often remain uncovered or insufficiently questioned. Nevertheless, human factors and the social-driven nature of agile teams have been found by many studies to present key-directing impacts for the success in software projects [3,24]. In particular, the social aspects in organizations commonly involve, i.a., proper communication structures, meeting manner, group spirit, and emotional constitution [20,21].

Recent studies have shown that regular retrospectives that combine data analytics with past sprint records provide more comprehensive insights and explanations of sprint dynamics for teams [10,22]. As a result, pro-active feedback mechanisms from an analytical perspective provide comprehensive and simplified summaries of past sprint conditions, even with trend implications for teams [3]. The additional knowledge helps teams and leaders to estimate sprints more accurately based on features that grant an increased awareness of highlighted behavior habits. However, along with the pre-processing and visualization of retrospective sprint feedback, we assume a further problem concerning the clarity and transparency of team-driven dynamics over time. Some dependencies and behavioral patterns are more prevalent than others, which in some cases create more sustainable relevance to the teams. If particular positive or negative behavior patterns persist over time, the teams should be aware of these patterns to track them.

In this paper, we introduce an approach that applies exploratory analyses [17] to provide pro-active feedback about sprint-wise characterizations and visualizations of team-driven sprint dynamics in agile software projects. We strive towards investigating sustainable interdependencies with long-term relevance for individual teams and across projects. This approach is part of a series of previous publications on team feedback described by Kortum et al. [8,10]. The authors focus on pro-active feedback using retrospective sprint visualizations and future trend highlighting. We developed a JIRA plugin called *ProDynamics*. Based on this plugin, we collected sprint data of six software projects with a total of 53 undergraduate students using controlled self-assessments on the social-driven team factors and productivity measures [8,10].

Considering team characteristics and statistical implications of sprint influences, as well as dynamic performance changes over time, are of particular relevance. The research goals of this approach are expressed in RG-1 and RG-2.

> RG-1: Resolve a combined solution covering exploratory analyses and statistical implications of sprint interdependencies with concern for the social-driven team and sprint-performances in JIRA.

> RG-2: Resolve a proper visualization concept covering sprint-interdependencies in JIRA that achieves a higher cognitive perception and awareness of long-term sprint-affects in teams.

In this approach, we resolve interdependency interpretations of sprint performances and psychological team measures of teams through maximal information coefficient analyses (MIC) [17] and force-directed network graphs. Previous work indicated that the characterization and visualization of dependencies allow teams and leaders to review and understand sprint effects better, especially in case of significant and long-term sprint habits [6]. The use of exploratory analyses revealed team-related sprint influences with direct relevance across the projects, while a specific behavior pattern becomes more recognizable and transparent.

The paper is structured as follows: In Sect. 2, we outline previous results and related work with relevance for this approach. Section 3 covers the methodology, highlights the considered dataset and the exploratory analyses, as well the visualizing strategy applied in *ProDynamics*. We interpret the findings on sprint-interdependencies in Sect. 4, followed by the threats to validity in Sect. 5. We conclude our work and outline some future work in Sect. 6.

2   Related Work

This approach is based on previous work with the focus on pro-active knowledge and awareness enhancement on social-driven team factors in the agile context. Advanced data analysis and visualization methods are used to provide a characterization of information and feedback support for teams.

Cockburn et al. [3,25] describe the relevance of human factors in agile software projects. The authors highlight the central impact of team communication and organizational structures in agile teams. They appraise that iterative feedback enables the opportunity to adjust the process and behavior of a team due to increased awareness and expertise for dysfunctional conditions.

Feedback is crucial because it can trigger process and behavior changes within projects [25]. Nonetheless, only a few publications focus on the effect of team feedback involving human behavior aspects. Current studies usually refer to sole self-management and productivity measures in combination with the performance outcome of a team [16,22].

In recent years, investigations on human factors became intensified due to an increased interest towards the team-driven effects and feedback influence on development performances [16,19]. Missing awarenesses for ongoing habits, especially in younger teams, often come along with improper sprint estimations or problems in self-organization. This can harm the performance of teams, and consequently, the success of projects [5].

In previous studies, Klünder et al. [6] and Kortum et al. [10] conducted studies in industry and student software projects to observe and characterize the appearances of particular behavior patterns in software development teams. The authors studied how exploratory analyses, together with proper visualization technologies, can enhance the interpretation of human factors and reduce estimation gaps for the development process [9]. The approach results revealed social-driven dependencies, for instance, between social conflicts, communication, and organizational structures [7,21] as well as the impact of interactions during team-meetings on positive mood afterward [20].

In this approach, we address the pro-active feedback support for JIRA covering visualizations and statistical implication of sprint interdependencies. The derived effects are results of exploratory analyses introduced by Reshef et al. [17]. They manifested a novel measure called *Maximal Information Coefficient* to capture and characterize dependencies with linear and non-linear associations. Thus, mutual information can be expressed through advanced statistical properties, whereby even sophisticated or not distinct dependencies are characterizable.

A team can increase its awareness for particular conditions of problem causes by enabling advanced cognitive perception besides solely textual feedback. As Lehtonen et al. [13] describe in their study that the key for improvements in the agile context strongly depends on information and its adequate visualization.

In a related Jermakovics et al. [4] studied the benefits of analyzing and visualizing developer networks. The authors characterize the interactions of different team members based on data from repositories to identify and highlight the workloads and internal development structures. The authors' strategy is a central aspect of this approach leading for interdependency visualizations expressed through force-directed network graphs [2].

3   Methodology

In this methodology, we describe how team-driven dynamics can be systematically characterized and visualized across multiple sprints, e.g., in JIRA.

The *ProDynamics* plugin architecture enables the JIRA system to assess repeatedly, and analyze sprint-wise development performances as well as team-behavior features. Implication results become reflected through force-directed network graphs and textual statements. We conducted an approach involving six academic software projects that enabled us to capture team-related dynamics.

Customers from industry, government, and public institutions founded the projects and accompanied as stakeholders in weekly meetings. All project teams used Scrum as the development framework. Atlassian JIRA [14] and Gitlab were applied to manage their projects. The JIRA system helped the teams to self-organize, trace, and update daily activities during the sprints. Each project took 15 weeks, involved 8–9 team members, and had an estimated workload of 2,000 person-hours. The software project is mandatory for students in the 5th semester but does not include gradings. The primary goal is to provide students with a realistic software project, to use theoretical knowledge from their studies and apply it practically as a team. In the following, we describe the team-driven information and productivity measures [10] that we captured and analyzed within JIRA.

Sprint and Team-Driven Data: Sprint performances can involve multiple information aspects, e.g., a subjective team atmosphere and objective productivity metrics. The success of projects depends on functional communication and efficient team performances [3,15], while dysfunctional structures often lead to more conflicts and failure potentials [7]. The interdependency characterizations consider the subjective and objective features shown in Fig. 1.

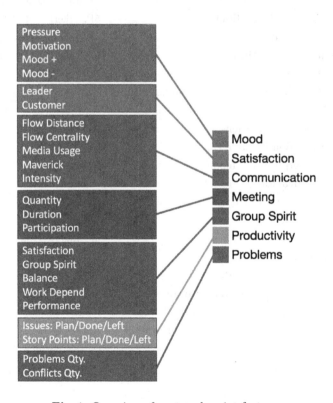

Fig. 1. Overview of captured sprint features

The listed categories with their sole features are based on previous work [21] and related studies with established metrics from human-centered software engineering [1,16] as well as organizational psychology [5,23]. Understanding influential factors, in particular, the behavior-driven interdependencies during sprints allows the teams to react on habit, by adjusting processes or organization. Interdependencies are derived, e.g., from sprint retrospective and future trends within a known system boundary [10]. The exploratory analyses in this approach take part since they provide advanced characterization support of dynamics compared to conventional linear statistics [24]. Therefore, the system can even interpret social-driven factors of agile teams at a broader functional scope. The details of each feature are listed in Table 1.

Table 1. Overview of sprint characteristics consider by ProDynamics

Sprint and team factors	Measurement	Ref.
Perceived project **pressure**	5P. Likert scales	[9]
Perceived team **motivation**	5P. Likert scales	[9]
Perceived **positive affects**	5P. Likert scales	[23]
Perceived **negative affects**	5P. Likert scales	[23]
Team leader **satisfaction**	5P. Likert scales	[10]
Customer **satisfaction**	5P. Likert scales	[10]
Flow Distance: Decentralized communication	Ratio [%]	[7]
Flow Centrality Centralized communication	Ratio [%]	[7]
Perceived communication **media usage**	Ratio [%]	[21]
Maverick manifestations in team	Ratio [%]	[21]
Communication **intensity**	5P. Likert scale	[21]
Meeting **frequency** (amount)	$\emptyset$ per Sprint	[5]
Meeting **duration** (minutes)	$\emptyset$ per Sprint	[5]
Meeting **participation**	Ratio [%]	[5]
Team **satisfaction**	5P Likert scale	[10]
Group spirit and solidarity	5P. Likert scale	[9]
Workload **balance**	Ratio [%]	[10]
Perceived **work dependencies**	5P. Likert scale	[10]
Perceived development **performance**	5P. Likert scale	[10]
Planned, completed vs. left **Sprint-Issues**	Ratio [%]	[6]
Planned, completed vs. left **Story Points**	Ratio [%]	[6]
Development **Problems**	$|x|$ per Sprint	[7]
Social **Conflicts**	$|x|$ per Sprint	[7]

Self-assessments in JIRA: *ProDynamics* is designed for teams with open mindsets for self-reflection in exchange for sustainable feedback. It was introduced to all groups at the project start, mentioning its feedback opportunities for a broader understanding of the ongoing sprint dynamics [10].

Six groups approached the plugin to receive pro-active feedback on their team performances and behavioral dynamics in exchange for sharing their individually collected sprint experiences. Each developer's reflection [3, 21] was autonomously captured and processed through our JIRA plugin using weekly self-assessments. The additional response effort required 1–2 min on average for each student, which is a proper outcome based on the integrated elicitation within their project managing environment [12]. The assessment design and question set are based on previous studies, also related work [18, 21].

The self-assessments primarily capture the social- and organization aspects in teams, e.g., who-to-whom communication and media channel usage, meeting quantity and average duration, the atmosphere in groups, also personal mood, satisfaction, and the perceived development performances during the last week. Some questions can be directly analyzed, while others, e.g., whom-to-whom communication requires additional computations to derive the maverick scores and similar. The question types are limited to the measures listed in Table 1. Most questions are based on Likert scales determining the interviewees' level of agreement on an asymmetric disagree-agree scale with predefined sprint or team statements. A sample of the customer satisfaction assessment is shown in Fig. 2.

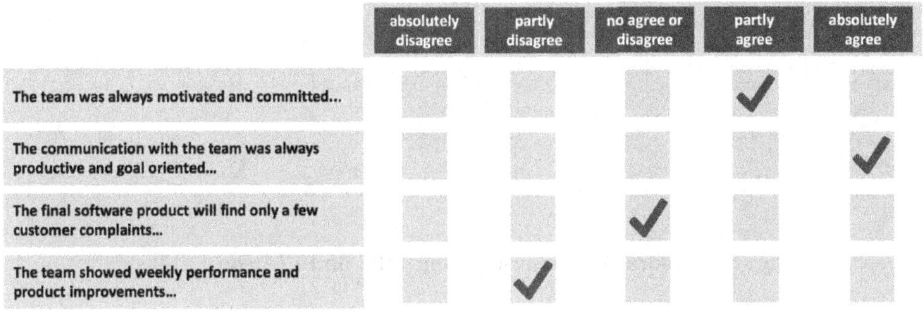

	absolutely disagree	partly disagree	no agree or disagree	partly agree	absolutely agree
The team was always motivated and committed...				✓	
The communication with the team was always productive and goal oriented...					✓
The final software product will find only a few customer complaints...			✓		
The team showed weekly performance and product improvements...		✓			

Fig. 2. Assessment excerpt with 5-points Likert scale

Next, in line with the subjective self-assessments features are the objective system measures, e.g., workloads, development velocities, and estimation gaps. Such information is directly accessed from project records natively tracked within JIRA and is of equal importance for the sprint characterizations. Considering both subjective and objective features allow a broader characterization of interdependencies, thus more awareness and understanding of the reason for particular sprint performance outcomes.

3.1   Characterization of Sprint-Dependencies

Software development effects related to human factors can have a sophisticated origin and are not always explainable through sole linear statistics. As a consequence, it is highly desirable to consider more adequate methods that can characterize and interpret team-driven dynamics during sprints [6, 10]. Automated exploratory analyses as introduced by Reshef et al. [17] can support analysts to detect and understand effects, e.g., during sprints more extensively [9]. Without such advanced analyses, inadequate interpretations often remain as a result of analyzes gaps through sole linear measures. In the following, we describe the exploratory analyses of sprint dynamics using MIC [17].

Exploratory Analyses: The team-driven phenomena in agile development are often interpreted intuitively or experience-based, e.g., using empirical studies that disclose valuable insights [1,16]. Unfortunately, many studies explain human factors only through simple linear correlations [9,17]. Reshef et al.'s MIC-algorithm [17] considers complex types of relationships, allowing to autonomously identify, e.g., the dependency abstractions shown in Fig. 3.

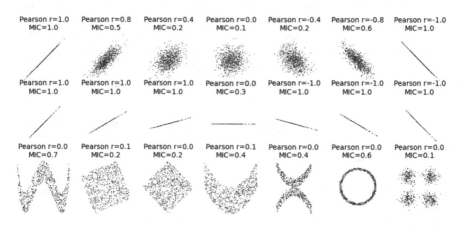

Fig. 3. Exploratory analyses using MIC and Pearson r [17]

Figure 3 shows three rows, each with seven data example characterizations that cover the interpretation gaps as mentioned above, i.e., between conventional Pearson correlations (linear) and the MIC. A direct comparison of both analyzing strategies for the first 14 data examples within the first and second row shows complementary coefficients measures.

However, for the case of more sophisticated dependencies as in the third row, the MIC reveals its strengths against sole linear analyses. The first example of the third row has sinusoid characteristics, barely recognized when solely considering Pearson r. The extensive functional property analysis of the MIC algorithm can find and characterize the dependency adequately. But especially when interpreting recurring behavior patterns, these characteristics should be taken into account [9]. The applied MIC algorithm in this approach is optimized to inter-work within the JIRA architecture.

3.2   Visualization of Sprint-Dependencies

In agile software development, adequate summaries, visualization of rapidly changing sprint condition, and progress information are essential [4,13]. Retrospective reports and futurespective implications enable overall conclusive insights about sprint performances and functional manners, thus support teams in the next sprint planning [8,10]. This part of the research extends the existing visual concepts in *ProDynamics* with force-directed network graphs for enhanced transparency and understanding of team-driven dependencies during sprints.

The Force-Directed Network Graph: The visualization in JIRA provides a fully interactive concept that empowers teams to access sprint-insights over time from 2-factor up to multi-factor dependencies. The graph is a D3-adaptation [2] and operates as front-end visualization for the sprint-wise dependency interpretation by the exploratory analyses. The graph settings are predefined and visualize only relevant sprint-dependency findings, i.e., interdependencies with very strong coefficients r or $MIC \geq .9$ and significances $p\text{-}value \leq .05$. The color of each node corresponds to one of the seven above categories. The sizes of nodes depend on the impact of each factor, measured by the number and strength of in- and outgoing forces. The forces are directed by the strengths and effect polarity between two nodes. Figure 4 shows an example for a particular sprint selection in JIRA. Visualizations across all yet completed sprints work in the same way and only require to be selected.

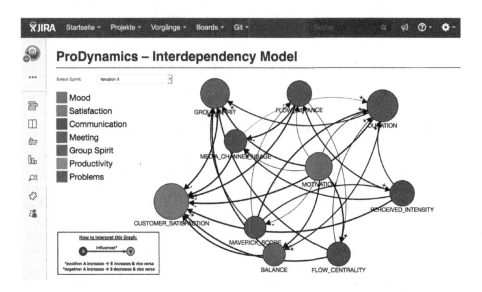

Fig. 4. Example of Force-directed network graph for sprint-dependencies in JIRA

Tool-tips support the graphs with additional background information on selected nodes, e.g., description of factor, impact score within sprints, infor-

mation type, and more. In case that the user is interested in a particular interdependency, a single force can be select as well, highlighted in the close-up view
in Fig. 5. The manual dependency selection enables to review the detailed relationship characteristics. The example selections show that with increasing team
motivation, the tendencies for more mavericks in the team will decrease.

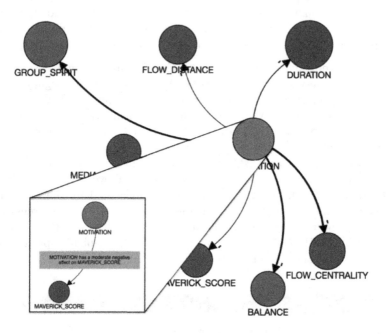

Fig. 5. Interdependency graph for an explicit factor selection

4   Interpretation Support of Sprint Dynamics

In the previous chapter, we described the methodology enabling software development teams to access and gain sprint-insights about their individually social-
driven dynamics during projects. With this, the theoretical and practical aims
towards *RG*-1 could be entirely fulfilled. However, with *RG*-2, we wanted to
investigate the applicability towards better information transparency and higher
cognitive understanding for significant team dynamics in agile projects. We ret-
rospectively explored six software projects from a previous study using the *Pro-
Dynamics* plugin [8]. The six projects covered complete data sets from four
sprints on both social-related team records and objective development performance measures. In the following, we show the sprint-wise characterizations on
the most relevant sprint-dynamics across all six projects.

The **Sprint "Exploration"** targeted project-specific tasks, e.g., framework
configurations, testing development environments, but also forming communication and work-flows. In Fig. 6, four relevant clusters of sprint-dynamics were

identified. All projects emphasized a team satisfaction increase with higher participation rates in meetings. Also, task-oriented pressure seemed to enforce for more loners with the result that more work was done as the number of tasks increased. The most relevant finding is that decentralized communications, e.g., through digital channels, caused perceiving on lacking information exchanges.

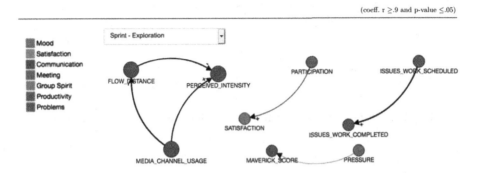

Fig. 6. Identified team-driven dynamics during Sprint-Exploration (1 of 4)

The **Sprint "Iteration I"** addressed development-tasks, e.g., fulfilling the sprint-backlog, scrum-meetings, and realize a $\alpha - version$ of the intended software product. Compared with the previous sprint, more significant activities and team-driven dynamics came upfront in a total of five clusters, as Fig. 7 shows. Unchanged, the decentralized communications still caused perceiving of lacking information exchanges with adverse effects for work dependencies. Team satisfaction in all projects changed not significantly due to higher participation rates in meetings. Instead, it decreased whenever an additionally scheduled team meeting occurred. The group spirit changed positively with centralized team communications, also when the workload balance was equally distributed and less maverick activities. Besides, the team meeting durations often shortened when the backlog issues became completed within the estimated times.

The **Sprint "Iteration II"** continued on the development outcome from the previous sprint. The overall sprint goal across the projects was to realize a $\beta - version$ of the intended software product. Four dynamics cluster with strong significances were determined, shown in Fig. 8. As for the previous sprints did a decentralized communication structure cause a decreased perception of lacking information transfers. Also, the teams increased the number of scheduled issues, while the estimated story points were optimized. This shows an optimal adjustment effect in sprint planning. Besides, due to the additional development issues, the teams also perceived a slightly higher pressure, while the completion of all tasks resulted in self-satisfaction. The most significant changes relate to the development performances, which tend to increase due to a stronger consideration of the scrum master's reflections on the product and team performances.

The **Sprint "Polishing"** goal was to finalize the $\beta - version$ from the previous sprint, optimize existing features, and release the final software product

(coeff. r ≥ .9 and p-value ≤ .05)

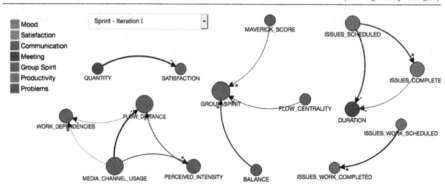

Fig. 7. Identified team-driven dynamics during Sprint-Iteration I (2 of 4)

(coeff. r ≥ .9 and p-value ≤ .05)

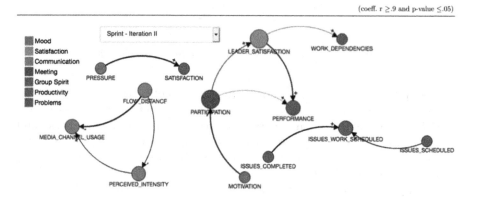

Fig. 8. Identified team-driven dynamics during Sprint-Iteration II (3 of 4)

to the customers. Figure 9 reveals, that the team-driven dynamics in the last sprint were intense, as often the case in other agile projects. The most critical impact presented the customer reflection on the current product and perceived team performances. This involved software demonstrations, usability tests, and so on. It seems that the teams across all projects, especially channelized their focus to enhance customer satisfaction in this last sprint, not before. Reduced decentralized communications prevailed to hold longer face to face meetings. The latter was recognized by the teams and increased the perceived information transfer with all participants. Positively activated mood triggers resulted in stronger team motivations with effect for increased group spirits. The visualized scope of all sprint dependencies only showed findings with very strong coefficients $r \geq .9$ and significance level $p \leq .05$. Moreover, several other significant dynamics with strong or moderate relationships were found but would exceed the interpretable outcome in this paper.

(coeff. r ≥ .9 and p-value ≤ .05)

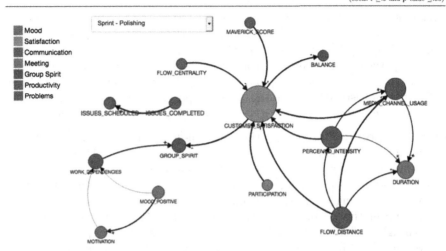

Fig. 9. Identified team-driven dynamics during Sprint - Polishing (4 of 4)

Table 2. TOP 10: captured team-driven dynamics from four sprints

Sprint feature	Abs. relevance	Sprint 1	Sprint 2	Sprint 3	Sprint 4
Flow Distance	16%	16%	12%	9%	11%
Media Channel Usage	16%	16%	12%	9%	11%
Communication Intensity	14%	16%	8%	9%	10%
Customer Satisfaction	12%	–%	–%	–%	21%
Work Dependencies	8%	–%	7%	4%	8%
Meeting Durations	7%	–%	8%	–%	8%
Group Spirit	7%	–%	11%	–%	5%
Meeting Participation	7%	7%	–%	13%	3%
Team Satisfaction	6%	16%	4%	5%	–%
Issue Workload Schedule	6%	8%	4%	9%	–%

Table 2 lists the interpreted sprint factors in teams, sorted by their sole relevance during the sprints. The results show that the communication and information flow in teams, expressed through the Flow Distance had a strong meaning in the projects. For example, the teams seemingly started their projects with a strong focus on information exchanges but neglected this manner over the time.

5   Threats to Validity

By Wohlin et al. [26], studies consist of threats limiting the conclusion, construct, internal, and external validity. Results might not be overgeneralized.

Construct Validity: We characterize team-driven dynamics in sprints solely through statistics. Team performance changes could also occur due to latent independent variables, e.g., weather influences, which cannot be considered. The teams were equally formed based on self-rated development skills, also previous project experiences. The characterizations and visualization of sprint dynamics only show significant (p-$value \leq .05$) factors with very strong coefficients (r or $MIC \geq .9$). Statistical implications in the graphs are limited to human factors identified from previous work [6,10] and are not equal to improvement advice.

Internal Validity: The interpretations of team-driven dynamics depend on self-assessed team reflections and individual team performances. All team assessments were voluntary activities in exchange for receiving pro-active feedback through the *ProDynamics* plugin. For managing the projects, JIRA was mandatory. When assessing team information, we believe that the students and customers were motivated to reply truthfully, mostly in exchange for supportive project insights. The software projects did not involve gradings or parallel classes. However, no bias within the responses can be expected. Feedback included personalized information, such as the sprint-wise moods, and other emotion-related factors, but was implicated as aggregated team values for anonymity.

External Validity: The interpretation of team-driven dynamics during the student software projects might not be overgeneralized [18]. However, each project was founded from public institutions, government, or industrial partners. Nevertheless, results cannot be necessarily transferred entirely to other software projects. Sprint reflections from other customers or developer teams may result in different dynamics interpretations when reconstructing the approach. Besides, whenever considering team-driven dynamics, explanations are limited.

Conclusion Validity: The exploratory analyses and all interpreted dynamics during the software projects are reliable and statistically valid. The textual and visual feedback aspects within *ProDynamics* might not be comparable with oral concepts. The methods are generalizable and applicable to other agile development teams that use JIRA or similar project managing software.

6   Conclusion and Future Work

We described an approach using a JIRA plugin called *ProDynamics* to support agile development teams with sprint-feedback and insights on team-driven dynamics. We aimed to enable a better understanding and awareness of the effects and influencing factors in socio-technical systems, without extraordinary efforts for developers. We applied exploratory analyses [17] with force-directed network visualizations [2] in an enclosed JIRA-plugin. The exploratory analyses allow sprint-dynamics interpretation considering subjective records on team-driven factors as well as objective development metrics in sprints [8].

The sprint characterization detects even sophisticated dependencies in project data. Statistic results became abstracted in force-directed graphs for a simplified and applicable knowledge gain on the captured team-dynamics. We addressed two research goals that covered the realizations of a *ProDynamics* plugin feature for automated interpretations and visualizations of team-driven dynamics. We also targeted an applicability approach of the tool with six student software projects. We could identify several sprint dynamics with very strong (Pearson r or MIC $\geq .9$) and significant ($p \leq .05$) dependencies across the teams. Especially the last sprint revealed a broad set of dynamics with the primary objective in fulfilling the essential customer expectations. Compared with the previous sprints, customer satisfaction seemed to be of relevance for the teams only near the end of a project, but never before. This presents more or less a trivial situation in agile projects, and it also reflects the applicability of this work.

We can conclude that the *ProDynamics* sprint-dynamics feature provides a supportive feedback mechanism on team-driven dynamics with its integrated complex analyses and visualization strategies. It provides a simplified and automated information source for agile development teams, scrum masters, and managers. In future work, we plan to perform a transfer from academia to industry projects considering the practicability of team-dynamics characterizations using ProDynamics. We also plan to extend the so far sole statistical implications with an automated sprint-adviser for improvements of ongoing team dynamics.

Acknowledgment. This work was funded by the German Research Society (DFG) under the project name Team Dynamics (2018–2020). Grant number 263807701.

References

1. Basili, V.R., Reiter Jr., R.W.: An investigation of human factors in software development. Computer **12**, 21–38 (1979)
2. Bostock, M., Ogievetsky, V., Heer, J.: D^3 data-driven documents. IEEE Trans. Visual Comput. Graph. **17**(12), 2301–2309 (2011)
3. Cockburn, A., Highsmith, J.: Agile software development, the people factor. Computer **34**(11), 131–133 (2001)
4. Jermakovics, A., Sillitti, A., Succi, G.: Mining and visualizing developer networks from version control systems. In: Proceedings of the 4th International Workshop on Cooperative and Human Aspects of Software Engineering, pp. 24–31. ACM (2011)
5. Kauffeld, S., Lehmann-Willenbrock, N.: Meetings matter: effects of team meetings on team and organizational success. Small Group Res. **43**(2), 130–158 (2012)
6. Klünder, J., Kortum, F., Ziehm, T., Schneider, K.: Helping teams to help themselves: an industrial case study on interdependencies during sprints. In: Bogdan, C., Kuusinen, K., Lárusdóttir, M.K., Palanque, P., Winckler, M. (eds.) HCSE 2018. LNCS, vol. 11262, pp. 31–50. Springer, Cham (2019). https://doi.org/10.1007/978-3-030-05909-5_3
7. Klünder, J., Schneider, K., Kortum, F., Straube, J., Handke, L., Kauffeld, S.: Communication in teams - an expression of social conflicts. In: Bogdan, C., et al. (eds.) HCSE/HESSD -2016. LNCS, vol. 9856, pp. 111–129. Springer, Cham (2016). https://doi.org/10.1007/978-3-319-44902-9_8
8. Kortum, F., Klünder, J., Brunotte, W., Schneider, K.: Sprint performance forecasts in agile software development - the effect of futurespectives on team-driven dynamics. In: 31st International Conference on Software Engineering and Knowledge Engineering. KSI Research Inc. (2019)

9. Kortum, F., Klünder, J., Schneider, K.: Don't underestimate the human factors! Exploring team communication effects. In: Felderer, M., Méndez Fernández, D., Turhan, B., Kalinowski, M., Sarro, F., Winkler, D. (eds.) PROFES 2017. LNCS, vol. 10611, pp. 457–469. Springer, Cham (2017). https://doi.org/10.1007/978-3-319-69926-4_36

10. Kortum, F., Klünder, J., Schneider, K.: Behavior-driven dynamics in agile development: the effect of fast feedback on teams. In: 2019 IEEE/ACM International Conference on Software and System Processes (ICSSP). IEEE (2019)

11. Kuhrmann, M., Tell, P., Klünder, J., Hebig, R., Licorish, S., MacDonell, S. (eds.): HELENA Stage 2 Results. ResearchGate (2018)

12. Lee, G., Xia, W.: Toward agile: an integrated analysis of quantitative and qualitative field data on software development agility. MIS Q. **34**(1), 87–114 (2010)

13. Lehtonen, T., Eloranta, V.P., Leppanen, M., Isohanni, E.: Visualizations as a basis for agile software process improvement. In: 2013 20th Asia-Pacific Software Engineering Conference (APSEC), vol. 1, pp. 495–502. IEEE (2013)

14. Li, P.: JIRA Essentials. Packt Publishing Ltd., Birmingham (2015)

15. Martin, R.C.: Agile Software Development: Principles, Patterns, and Practices. Prentice Hall, Upper Saddle River (2002)

16. Moe, N.B., Dingsøyr, T., Dybå, T.: A teamwork model for understanding an agile team: a case study of a scrum project. Inf. Softw. Technol. **52**(5), 480–491 (2010)

17. Reshef, D.N., et al.: Detecting novel associations in large data sets. Science **334**(6062), 1518–1524 (2011)

18. Ross, J.A.: The reliability, validity, and utility of self-assessment (2006)

19. Salo, O., Abrahamsson, P.: Empirical evaluation of agile software development: the controlled case study approach. In: Bomarius, F., Iida, H. (eds.) PROFES 2004. LNCS, vol. 3009, pp. 408–423. Springer, Heidelberg (2004). https://doi.org/10.1007/978-3-540-24659-6_29

20. Schneider, K., Klünder, J., Kortum, F., Handke, L., Straube, J., Kauffeld, S.: Positive affect through interactions in meetings: the role of proactive and supportive statements. J. Syst. Softw. **143**, 59–70 (2018)

21. Schneider, K., Liskin, O., Paulsen, H., Kauffeld, S.: Media, mood, and meetings: related to project success? ACM Trans. Comput. Educ. (TOCE) **15**(4), 21 (2015)

22. Vetro, A., Dürre, R., Conoscenti, M., Fernández, D.M., Jørgensen, M.: Combining data analytics with team feedback to improve the estimation process in agile software development. Found. Comput. Decis. Sci. **43**(4), 305–334 (2018)

23. Watson, D., Clark, L.A., Tellegen, A.: Development and validation of brief measures of positive and negative affect: the PANAS scales. J. Pers. Soc. Psychol. **54**(6), 1063 (1988)

24. Whitworth, E., Biddle, R.: The social nature of agile teams. In: Agile (AGILE 2007), pp. 26–36. IEEE (2007)

25. Williams, L.A., Cockburn, A.: Agile software development: it's about feedback and change. Computer **36**, 39–43 (2003)

26. Wohlin, C., Runeson, P., Höst, M., Ohlsson, M.C., Regnell, B., Wesslén, A.: Experimentation in Software Engineering. Springer, Heidelberg (2012). https://doi.org/10.1007/978-3-642-29044-2

Evaluating the Utility of the Usability Model for Software Development Process and Practice

Diego Fontdevila[1]($\boxtimes$) ⓘ, Marcela Genero[2] ⓘ, Alejandro Oliveros[1] ⓘ, and Nicolás Paez[1] ⓘ

[1] Universidad Nacional de Tres de Febrero, Caseros, Argentina
{dfontdevila, aoliveros}@untref.edu.ar,
nicopaez@computer.org
[2] Department of Technologies and Information Systems,
University of Castilla-La Mancha, Ciudad Real, Spain
marcela.genero@uclm.es

Abstract. Processes and practices are tools that organizations use to improve their capabilities. Agile transformations are very popular, as are process and practice improvement and adoption initiatives, but they face many challenges, including low adoption rates. Improving process and practice usability might increase adoption rates and effective use. This idea led us to define a Usability Model for Software development Process and Practice (UMP), consisting of characteristics and metrics, in the quest to improve the work experience of software development practitioners and the effectiveness of process and practice adoption initiatives. The goal of this paper is two-fold: (1) to present the refined version of the UMP and (2) to describe a study on the application of the UMP to the Visual Milestone Planning (VMP) method in order to evaluate UMP's utility, specifically its ability to produce useful feedback in a real-life scenario. The study produced preliminary confirmation that the UMP is applicable to the VMP, along with specific feedback on improvement opportunities for the VMP. An interview with the VMP creator confirmed that the UMP model and the evaluation feedback were valuable for enhancing VMP adoption. In summary, we can conclude that the empirical results obtained show that UMP can be useful. Nonetheless, more studies are needed to provide further confirmation in different scenarios.

Keywords: Usability · Process and practice · Improvement · Interview · Design Science Research

1 Introduction

Improvement in software engineering increasingly takes the form of initiatives to adopt pre-existing processes, practices, methods, frameworks, etc. As used to be the case with generic "best practices", agile methods have become a focus of popular interest in the software development community (and beyond), and many organizations are attempting agile and digital transformations [1]. Agile methods, like other related trends such as DevOps, tend to be very attractive to newcomers, but sometimes seem deceptively simple and easy to implement [2]. Research on actual agile projects shows

© Springer Nature Switzerland AG 2019
X. Franch et al. (Eds.): PROFES 2019, LNCS 11915, pp. 741–757, 2019.
https://doi.org/10.1007/978-3-030-35333-9_57

significant differences between method definitions and actual implementations [3], including lack of implementation of many of the practices defined by those same methods [4, 5]. This affects the ability of these initiatives to produce their intended results. For example, agile engineering practices like Frequent Delivery have been shown to be key success factors in agile projects [6, 7].

There is also growing evidence that human factors, emotions in particular, affect software development productivity, turnover and job satisfaction [8]. Furthermore, developer acceptance of new ways of working is a cornerstone of success for improvement initiatives [9, 10]. Overall, the quality of interactions between practitioners and their processes and practices affects the chances of success of improvement initiatives and their effectiveness.

Although there are several process quality models [11, 12], none of them focuses specifically on process usability. In its effort to improve both the overall experience of practitioners and their effectiveness, the UMP provides support for the improvement of the design of processes and practices, as well as their adoption plans. In particular, the UMP should help practitioners to:

- Have a better understanding of usability issues related to processes and practices.
- Evaluate the fitness of potential processes or practices to specific contexts (for example, mature teams might be better suited to hard-to-learn but potentially beneficial practices).
- Adapt processes or practices by highlighting specific concerns (e.g. particular characteristics), in an attempt to enhance the adoption process.
- Support planning of improvement initiatives by providing specifics on usability related risks.
- Provide explanation for obstacles found in the adoption process.

In this context we have defined the long-term goal of our research as:

Define and validate a usability model for software development process and practice (UMP) to support the enhancement of usability aspects of process and practice, in order to improve the work experience of software development practitioners and the overall effectiveness of process and practice adoption initiatives.

To achieve this main goal, a Design Science approach was followed. Design Science proposes creating artifacts to solve a practical problem, together with knowledge that is of general interest [13]. The research methodology shown in Fig. 1 was followed. For each step the figure shows the associated Design Science activity [13] and the research sub-activities performed:

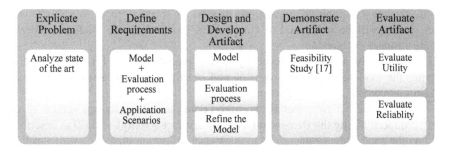

Fig. 1. Design Science Research methodology overview

To allow readers to understand the complete investigation process to which the current paper belongs, the main aspects of the research methodology are introduced briefly as follows:

Explicate Problem: The initial analysis of the state of the art was conducted, in which the relevant literature was identified. Expert interviews were conducted to help identify appropriate sources for the model, given the very limited search results that matched process and practice usability research.

Define Requirements: The artifacts to be produced would be a quality model and an evaluation process. Moreover, real life UMP application scenarios were defined (see Appendix) to describe in detail the intended scope of applicability, including who would use the model, what they would use it for, and which model elements (e.g. empty model or model evaluation results) would be used.

Design and Develop Artifact: The UMP model was defined from the following sources: the ISO 25010 international standard [14], the process quality model by Kroeger et al. [11], and classic usability literature [15, 16].

To facilitate the application of the UMP, an evaluation process was defined by adapting the reference model for software product evaluation proposed in the ISO 25040 international standard [17].

To refine the model, a focus group [19] with expert practitioners was conducted to obtain feedback related to the clarity, understandability, precision, and relevance of model characteristics and metrics (see Appendix for the detailed data collected). Finally, the UMP was modified to address the improvement opportunities identified in the focus group.

Demonstrate Artifact: An initial feasibility study was conducted by applying the model to Scrum (this was the initial publication of the model [18]). Although Fig. 1 might seem like a sequence, the Design Science method framework is iterative; as an example, the feasibility study [18] was performed before the refinement presented here.

Evaluate Artifact: A preliminary study was conducted through the evaluation of the Visual Milestone Planning (VMP) method [20]. This was at the request of the method creator, who was interested in an external evaluation. The objective of this study was to evaluate UMP utility, i.e. its ability to produce actionable feedback that can be used in real-life scenarios to improve the adoption process for specific processes and practices. Other studies will be conducted to complement this preliminary study, in order to provide stronger evaluation.

UMP reliability will be evaluated by asking practitioners to fill in a survey on applying the model to specific processes and practices, and by assessing the inter-evaluator agreement on the evaluations.

The goal of the current paper is two-fold: (1) to present the refined version of the UMP (produced during the Design and Develop Artifact activity), and (2) to describe a study on the application of the model to the Visual Milestone Planning (VMP) method to evaluate UMP's utility, i.e. its ability to produce actionable feedback that is useful in a real-life scenario (first step of the Evaluate Artifact activity).

The rest of this paper is structured as follows: Sect. 2 presents work related to Process and Practice Usability; Sect. 3 describes the UMP model in detail, including its characteristics and metrics; Sect. 4 provides a description of the study on applying UMP to the evaluation of VMP; Sect. 5 reviews the threats to validity, and Sect. 6 outlines the conclusions and future lines of work.

2 Related Work

In this section, we present literature related to process and practice usability:

- Feiler and Humphrey describe the challenges of improving process usability due to long feedback loops, but do not include it in their list of process quality attributes [12].
- Culver-Lozo limits the analysis to process documentation usability [21].
- Cockburn has reflected on the concept of high-discipline methodologies, which he describes as those hard to sustain, and requiring a specific mechanism to keep them in place [22]. This distinction touches on one aspect of the relationship between methodologies and their users, through the associated risk of abandonment.
- Riemenschnaider et al. have found that practitioner acceptance of methodologies can be strongly influenced by subjective norm, i.e., acceptance by close members of the same organization. This highlights the importance of context and the social aspect of usability beyond individual interactions [9].
- Kroeger et al. [11] built their process quality model through a sound grounded theory research. The emergent process quality attributes were organized into 4 groups: Suitability, Usability, Manageability and Evolvability. Usability emerged as a grouping of: Learnability, Understandability, Accessibility and Adaptability. Though their process quality model emerged from interviews with practitioners, its sub-attributes have little relationship with actual process performance by users.
- The ISO 25010 Standard on Systems and software quality models is a product-oriented international standard that includes usability aspects. The process as software analogy [12] supports the inclusion of software usability, given there is no software development process quality standard. This standard was the only source that provided specific metrics for the UMP.

- The works of Norman [15] and Nielsen [16] provided deep product usability concepts and rich terminology.

To our knowledge, research on process and practice usability is very limited, since most existing work does not consider people as users of their processes and practices. We propose the UMP as a means of filling this gap, to help improve the experience of practitioners and the overall effectiveness of adoption initiatives.

3   The UMP Usability Model for Process and Practice

We defined the UMP [18] to help consultants, researchers, teachers and practitioners to enhance the usability aspects of software development processes and practices in order to improve the adoption experience for newcomers and practitioners of software development processes, practices and methods. The UMP consists of several artifacts: The UMP itself (characteristics and metrics definitions), the UMP Evaluation Process, and the Usability Profile (metric values and evaluation comments with improvement recommendations) resulting from the evaluation of a specific process and practice.

The UMP can be used in several modes:

- **Evaluation:** the UMP is used to evaluate a specific process or practice and thus produce a usability profile with improvement recommendations. In this mode, the goal of the model user is to get systematic feedback on the process/practice under evaluation. The UMP itself and the evaluation process are used to produce the usability profile with improvement recommendations.
- **Profile:** the UMP was previously used by a third-party to perform an evaluation and now the user applies the results of that evaluation to a specific context (e.g. team considering adopting a specific practice, as in Scenario #4, see Appendix). In this mode, the usability profile is the only artifact used.
- **Framework:** the UMP is used as a usability framework for process and practice improvement, acting as a checklist that provides potential risks/root causes that can assist in planning and assessing adoption/improvement initiatives. In this mode it also provides metrics that can be used to assess the improvement initiative.

Given that the model is rather complex (its 10 characteristics aimed at being complete), and that it tends to require significant experience with process for someone to be able to perform effective evaluations, these modes allow practitioners to eventually benefit from third-party (and even reusable) expert evaluation results (in the Profile mode) or to use only parts of the model in the Framework mode.

This section presents the refined version of the UMP. The model characteristics modified from the original version of the model [18] during the refinement process are marked with an asterisk in Table 1.

The construction of the UMP consisted of defining the 10 usability characteristics and 24 metrics that the model is composed of. The construction process was based on an adaptation of the top-down methodology for building structured quality models [23], which proposes starting with the top-level elements (i.e. characteristics) and proceeding to the lower level elements (i.e. metrics). More details on the model development process are available in [18].

Table 1 presents the model characteristics, which apply to several aspects of the process and practice adoption lifecycle. For example, for process and practice adoption planning: Self-evident Purpose, Understandability, Learnability, Attractiveness; for process and practice performance: Visibility, because it characterizes how transparent the status and intermediate products of a process are to its stakeholders; Controllability, because it describes how easy it is for different stakeholders to control a process or practice during execution; and User satisfaction, which is a by-product of the experience of using the process or practice. This does not mean that other characteristics might not support those activities as well, but it highlights the fact that in different contexts different sets of characteristics might prove more significant.

Table 1. UMP characteristics

Characteristic	Definition
Self-evident purpose*	Ease with which users can recognize what a process or practice is for by its name
Learnability*	Ease with which a process or practice user is able to learn how to perform its activities at a novice level of ability [24]
Understandability*	Ease with which a process or practice user is able to apprehend how the underlying principles, structure and dynamics make it work to achieve the desired results
Safety*	Degree to which a process or practice is safe for its users, preventing errors, including using the practice or process incorrectly, or limiting the impact of such errors
Feedback*	Degree to which use of a process or practice produces or promotes reactions or responses to actions performed
Visibility*	Degree to which a process or practice helps make activities, status, obstacles and information inputs and outputs visible to people
Controllability*	Degree to which a process or practice allows its users to check status and make decisions that affect the outcomes during process or practice execution
Adaptability	Ease with which a process or practice user is able to adapt the process or practice for use in different contexts
Attractiveness	Degree to which users of the process or practice find it attractive or appealing because of its form, structure or reported results
User satisfaction	Degree to which user needs are satisfied when using a process or practice

The Goal Question Metric (GQM) [25, 26] paradigm was used for the definition of the metrics for each characteristic. For each metric, several meta-data were defined: description, measurement method, type of scale (e.g. nominal), scale (e.g. yes/no), unit of measurement and most favorable value. The meta-data fields were selected based on the ISO 15939 Systems and Software Engineering – Measurement process Standard

[27]. Care was taken to keep the model as simple as possible and to improve ease of use of the metrics. Overall, metrics were changed significantly during model refinement and were simplified to enhance the experience of model users, based on feedback from the focus group (see Appendix for details).

Table 2 shows the definition of the metrics for each characteristic:

Table 2. Overview of UMP metrics for each characteristic

Characteristic	Metric	Definition	Values
Self-evident purpose	Appropriateness of name	Measures how appropriate the name is for describing the purpose of the process or practice (consider, for example, whether names are translations or are in a foreign language)	Deceiving, Ambiguous, Partial, Appropriate, Accurate
Self-evident purpose	Recognized purpose	Measures whether new adopters usually recognize the purpose of the process or practice	Yes/No
Learnability	Time required to learn to perform	Measures the time required to learn to perform process or practice activities on tasks of average complexity independently, at a novice level of ability	Number of hours
Learnability	Standard introductory course duration	Measures standard course duration in hours, as defined by authoritative sources	Number of hours
Understandability	# Of specific conceptual definitions	Measures how many specific (new) definitions make up the conceptual model of the process or practice (evaluators must specify the concepts considered)	Number of specific conceptual definitions
Understandability	Conceptual model correspondence	Measures the correspondence between the conceptual model of the process or practice and the user's own conceptual model for the same activity	Low, Medium, High
Understandability	Conceptual model complexity index	Measures the subjective complexity of the conceptual model of the process or practice	Low, Medium, High
Safety	Cost of incorrect adoption	Measures the cost of adopting the process or practice incorrectly as overall impact. Errors include applying the process or practice inappropriately; failing to understand its purpose or dynamics, failure to perform its activities and to evaluate results correctly. For example, incorrect adoption might produce burnout, a high cost, or local inefficiencies, a medium cost	Low, Medium, High

(continued)

Table 2. (*continued*)

Characteristic	Metric	Definition	Values
Safety	Reduction in cost of error	Measures how applying the process or practice correctly reduces the overall cost of errors made in the work system. For example, iterative processes are designed to reduce the cost of errors by checking early on, through intermediate results	Low, Medium, High
Safety	Safety perception	Measures how the users perceive the process or practice in terms of safety for themselves and others. For example, if the by-products of executing the process or practice can be used against them, the safety perception might be low	Low, Medium, High
Safety	Use of restraining functions	Measures whether the process or practice provides hard restrictions to prevent the materialization of significant risks	Yes/No
Feedback	Timeliness of feedback	Measures the timeliness of the feedback as perceived by the actor with respect to the action performed and the consequent actions that need to be performed	Immediate, Prompt, Delayed, Non existent
Feedback	Feedback richness	Measures the value of the information received in terms of significance, breadth, depth or nuance	Low, Medium, High
Feedback	People feedback	Measures if the process or practice promotes feedback from people interactions	Yes/No
Feedback	Automatic feedback	Measures if the process or practice provides automatic feedback	Yes/No
Visibility	Defines indicators	Measures if the process or practice defines standard indicators	Yes/No
Visibility	Information tailored to audience	Measures whether information is tailored to better suit different audiences	Yes/No
Controllability	Defines checkpoints	Measures whether the process or practice defines specific checkpoints where users can make decisions that control the outcomes of the process or practice. For example, Scrum Reviews are specific points to evaluate the product and eventually decide whether to accept, reject, or refine a product increment	Yes/No

(*continued*)

Table 2. (*continued*)

Characteristic	Metric	Definition	Values
Controllability	Explicit outcomes	Measures if the process or practice defines outcomes explicitly	Yes/No
Controllability	Level of autonomy	Measures the level of autonomy users have in making decisions related to the execution of the process or practice. Examples include handling unexpected results or deciding whether to proceed or not at specific checkpoints	Low, Medium, High
Adaptability	Defines adaptation points	Measures whether the process or practice defines adaptation points or not. Adaptation points are specific opportunities for variation described by the process or practice. For example, in Scrum the Retrospective is focused on process adaptation	Yes/No
Adaptability	Ratio of roles allowed to adapt	Measures how many roles, from among the process or practice users, are allowed to modify the process or practice, out of the total number of roles (evaluators must specify the roles considered; if no roles are distinguishable, value should be 1)	0 to 1
Attractiveness	User attractiveness rating	Measures how attractive the process or practice is to prospective users (i.e. those lacking experience)	1 to 5
User satisfaction	User experience rating	Measures the subjective experience of using the process or practice	1 to 5

To define a usability profile for a specific process or practice the UMP Evaluation process shown in Table 3 is applied by performing the four activities described.

Table 3. UMP evaluation process.

Activity	Description
Evaluation design	Define the objectives, characteristic and metric exclusions, reference sources and evaluators
Evaluator training	Introduce the usability model and evaluation process to evaluators
Evaluation execution	Perform the evaluation process by analyzing the process or practices according to each sub-characteristic. Determine values for all included metrics according to the analysis performed
Evaluation process review	Complete the evaluation process questionnaire. Review the evaluation results

4   The VMP Study

The study was conducted as preliminary evaluation of UMP utility. The study selected is a naturalistic evaluation according to the classification by Johannesson et al. [13]. A naturalistic evaluation "assesses the artefact in the real world" [13]. The research method selected was the Interview, which "are effective instruments for gathering stakeholder opinions and perceptions about the use and value of an artifact" [13].

The study goal was to evaluate UMP utility in a real-life scenario, specifically whether the evaluation results were valuable to the user.

The VMP method is a participatory approach to milestone planning [20], created to improve the experience of development teams and students who are planning software development projects.

In the Define Requirements activity of the Research Methodology (see Fig. 1) ten potential real-life model application scenarios were defined to help determine applicability (see Appendix). The VMP study was selected because it was an example of one of them, specifically Scenario #8, "Researcher evaluates method, process or practice". This scenario corresponds to an academic context in which a researcher wishes to assess the usability of a process, practice or method. In this case the researcher is the creator of the VMP method. The opportunity for conducting the study arose when the researcher asked the first author to perform an external usability evaluation on the VMP. In this specific situation, given that the researcher required an external evaluation to further his own research activities, the UMP usage by the researcher was restricted to the Profile mode, that is, the researcher used only the evaluation results, and he did not perform the evaluation himself, which was performed by the first author.

The rest of this section is organized as follows: Sect. 4.1 provides an overview of the VMP, while Sect. 4.2 provides details on how the study was conducted.

4.1   VMP Overview

The VMP method is built on top of two existing planning processes, namely Milestone Planning and Participatory Planning [20]. The main VMP contributions are: "The integration of the milestone planning and participatory planning approaches through a visual planning process. A novel construct called the milestone planning matrix, that systematically and visually captures: (1) temporal dependencies between milestones and (2) the allocation of work elements to the milestones they help realize. The reification of work packages by means of sticky notes which must be physically accommodated on a resource and time-scaled milestone scheduling canvas to derive the milestones due dates" [20].

As revealed in [20], student teams in the Master of Software Engineering Program at Carnegie Mellon University have successfully used the VMP for planning their capstone projects, and it has also been taught in several industrial and governmental organizations.

4.2 VMP Study Description

In order to reach the goals of the study, three research questions were posed:

- *RQ1: Is the UMP applicable to the evaluation of the VMP method?*
- *RQ2: Are the UMP model evaluation results helpful in assessing the usability of the VMP method?*
- *RQ3: Is the feedback produced from the UMP evaluation valuable and applicable from the point of view of the VMP creator?*

RQ1 was answered by the feedback from the execution of the UMP Evaluation process by the first author of this paper. An affirmative answer to RQ1 would arise from an effective execution of the UMP evaluation process. RQ2 and RQ3 were answered via a short questionnaire used during the final interview with the VMP creator. Affirmative answers to the questions in the questionnaire would confirm RQ2 and RQ3, as described below.

The VMP study had two roles, researcher (the VMP creator, actor using the evaluation results as described in scenario #8 in Appendix) and evaluator (the first author of this paper who applied the UMP for evaluating the VMP).

The study activities were: (1) Initial definition of expectations of both parties; (2) evaluator (first author) performed VMP evaluation taking as input VMP documentation [20] and information provided by the VMP creator; (3) Evaluator provided feedback to the researcher (an early version of Table 4) who in turn provided minor comments; (4) Final interview where researcher responded to questionnaire; (5) Data analysis and reporting.

The initial interactions were aimed at setting expectations on both parties. Specifically, it was validated with the researcher that the evaluation feedback (VMP usability profile) would take the form of a table with metric values and comments, and that the documentation and interview time from the researcher would be available.

After the initial interactions, the evaluator studied the VMP documentation [20], planned and executed the UMP Evaluation Process on the VMP. Given that the evaluator was the first author of the UMP, the evaluator training activity was not necessary. In the evaluation design all characteristics and metrics were included, although during evaluation some metric values were deemed non-applicable. The execution of the evaluation produced a usability profile with evaluation metrics and comments, presented as feedback to the researcher (as recommended by [28]), who in turn provided confirmation and minor comments. These results are shown in Table 4.

Table 4. VMP usability profile

Metric	Comments	Value
Appropriateness of name	The name describes the essential aspects of the method, that it is visual (and reified), that it is milestone-based and that its purpose is planning	Appropriate
Recognized purpose	From the experiences described by the VMP creator	Yes
Time required to learn to perform	From the experiences described by the VMP creator	4 h
Standard introductory course duration	Informed by the VMP creator	8 h
# Of specific conceptual definitions	Outcomes, Dependencies, Milestone Planning Matrix, Milestone Sequence Diagram, Milestone Effort, Cross-cutting Effort, Milestone Dates, Soft Milestone, Hard Milestone. Milestone work package, Effort unit of time, Milestone scheduling canvas, Milestone list	13
Conceptual model correspondence	It is a participatory planning activity, where the team is responsible for carrying out the plan. The meaning of milestones and due dates is fairly straightforward, as is the rest of the conceptual model	High
Conceptual model complexity index	In general, the data model has low complexity, but specific elements like the pair-wise dependency matrix "roof", the existence of two types of milestones and two types of effort make the overall data model less simple	Medium
Cost of incorrect adoption	It seems hard to use the method so badly that it would produce serious damage	Low
Reduction in cost of error	The focus on milestone planning makes plans "much more stable and practical" than task or activity-oriented plans [20]. The cost of modifying milestones is lower than that of modifying tasks. Making the plan and its elements visual also makes it easier to detect issues and gauge the impact of modifications	High
Safety perception	The team participates in planning its own work. That provides a safer environment for establishing commitments, since these are not imposed from the outside. Depending on the culture of the organization around the team, and the level of autonomy that the team has in planning and executing the plan, the cost of error may vary	High
Use of restraining functions	Matching the scheduling canvas scale to the sticky notes size offers visible hard restrictions on milestone planning to avoid resource over-allocation and help validate milestone viability	Yes

(continued)

Table 4. (*continued*)

Metric	Comments	Value
Timeliness of feedback	Creating the Milestones Planning Matrix and the Scheduling Canvas provides early feedback on the soundness of the plan	Prompt
Feedback richness	The feedback confirms that the plan is sound, but does not provide more details	Medium
People feedback	The method does not describe a specific stage to request feedback from others	No
Automatic feedback	Not applicable	No
Defines indicators	The Scheduling Canvas	Yes
Information tailored to audience	Not necessary, the information seems fairly general and without much detail	No
Defines checkpoints	The method describes explicitly several checkpoints during planning	Yes
Explicit outcomes	The Milestone Planning Matrix and the Scheduling Canvas	Yes
Level of autonomy	Teams have a say and are involved, but are not necessarily self-organized	Medium
Defines adaptation points	Milestone sequence diagram is optional	Yes
Ratio of roles allowed to adapt	No roles are defined	Non-applicable
User attractiveness rating	Evaluator opinion after reading the documentation	4
User experience rating	The VMP creator reports anecdotal positive initial responses encountered in both classroom and industry settings. A more precise measurement of satisfaction might provide interesting insights	Not available

The effective evaluation confirmed applicability of the UMP (RQ1) and produced feedback that was presented to the VMP creator.

The questionnaire used during the final interview is shown below, with the corresponding answers:

- Q1: Was the feedback from the evaluation clear and understandable? Yes.
- Q2: Is it useful and applicable in practice? Yes. It was also valuable that the UMP model was already published, and that the UMP first author could act as an external evaluator.
- Q3: Is it coherent with the adoption potential perceived in interactions with method users? Yes.
- Q4: Are you satisfied with the results? Yes.
- Q5: Why? The evaluation touched upon all the main features of the method, and highlighted its contributions.

The analysis of data was very straightforward, given that there was a single data point and the information was aimed directly at evaluating the UMP model. No coding techniques were considered necessary.

The questionnaire answers confirmed that the feedback in the form of the evaluation results was useful and applicable (Q2 for RQ2 and the rest for RQ3). This, together with the manifest initial interest of the VMP creator to have the UMP evaluation performed, provides preliminary confirmation that the UMP was useful in Profile mode; that is, the VMP creator deemed the evaluation results valuable. The VMP creator also valued that the UMP was already published, allowing the UMP to be referenced. It must also be noted that the VMP creator highlighted that the UMP evaluation results touched upon all of the main features of the VMP, hinting that the UMP sensitivity to the VMP was appropriate. In terms of the evaluation results, it is interesting that several salient aspects of the VMP design, such as the reification of work packages as post-it notes and the use of the scheduling canvas as a time-scaled restrictive function, match classical usability principles like affordance and forcing functions and are thus positively highlighted in the evaluation.

The main recommendations provided to the VMP creator were to consider a simplified version of the model for simpler projects and to include some form of satisfaction evaluation in VMP trainings, in order to obtain more systematic feedback.

5   Threats to Validity

In this section the threats to validity of empirical studies are presented, following the categorization provided in [29]:

- Threats to construct validity: for the final interview, this validity may have been affected by the questionnaire design. Care was taken to make answering easy for the respondent, and two authors reviewed and refined the questionnaire.
- Threats to internal validity: In the study, only the VMP creator was interviewed; information about the actual experience of VMP method users is thus not directly available. Future work might include direct measures of the user experience of the VMP, as recommended to the VMP creator. Both the VMP creator and the authors had interests at stake in the study, but the study was carefully designed to reduce bias. For the VMP researcher, the interest at stake was having an external review of the VMP (and possibly a positive evaluation), thus, it did not introduce bias but rather suggests that the UMP evaluation results were applicable. Regarding RQ1 in the study, about UMP applicability to the VMP, the bias of the first author is consistent with the stated interests and typical of Design Science research; evaluation of the UMP by third-parties has been studied in [18] and will be further studied during reliability evaluation.
- Threats to external validity: the bias introduced by limited access to study subjects can have a significant impact on the research. To limit the bias towards accepting any available subjects, the application scenarios for the UMP were defined beforehand. In addition, the ability to generalize from a single preliminary study is very limited, so future studies should encompass other scenarios to improve

generalizability. In particular, the study is an example of the Profile mode, in which only the evaluation results are used; other studies that might assess the Evaluation and Framework modes are needed to further evaluate UMP utility.

- Threats to conclusion validity: the number of observations limits the conclusion validity in this study; further studies for other application scenarios will strengthen the significance of the results. That is why we present this as a preliminary evaluation study, and will expand on it in future work.

6 Conclusions and Future Work

This paper presents a refined version of the Usability Model for Software development Process and Practice (UMP) and a preliminary study for evaluating model utility i.e., its ability to produce valuable results that are useful in a real-life scenario.

The preliminary study results show that the UMP assessment of the usability of the Visual Milestone Planning (VMP) was valued by the VMP creator as an assessment of the VMP contributions and a source of opportunities for improvement. This study was focused on the Profile mode, in which the UMP evaluation performed by the first author provided a usability profile that was used by the VMP creator. In this mode, using the UMP is simpler since evaluations performed by a third-party can be reused, thus reducing the need to perform evaluations, which can be time consuming and require more experience. The VMP creator's interest in having the evaluation also strengthens this preliminary confirmation.

Future research activities include further utility evaluation through other studies that include different scenarios and modes of use (see Appendix) and performing reliability evaluation. For reliability evaluation practitioners will be asked to fill in a survey on applying the model to specific processes and practices, and the inter-evaluator agreement will be assessed on the evaluations, to gauge metric consistency.

Acknowledgements. The research work presented in this paper has been developed within the following projects: the GEMA project ("Consejería de Educación, Cultura y Deporte de la Dirección General de Universidades, Investigación e Innovación de la JCCM", SBPLY/17/180501/000293), the ECLIPSE project ("Ministerio de Ciencia, Innovación y Universidades, y FEDER", RTI2018-094283-B-C31) and the Software Development Process Research Project at the Universidad Nacional de Tres de Febrero (Project lines: Usability of Process and Practice, Agile Practices and Techniques and Requirements Engineering Processes).

Appendix

Supplementary data available at https://doi.org/10.6084/m9.figshare.8292314.

References

1. Conboy, K., Carroll, N.: Implementing large-scale Agile frameworks: challenges and recommendations. IEEE Softw. **36**(2), 44–50 (2019)
2. Kchwaber, K., Sutherland, J.: Scrum Guide. http://www.scrumguides.org/scrum-guide.html. Accessed 08 June 2019
3. Paez, N., Fontdevila, D., Gainey, F., Oliveros, A.: Technical and organizational Agile practices: A Latin-American survey. In: Garbajosa, J., Wang, X., Aguiar, A. (eds.) XP 2018. LNBIP, vol. 314, pp. 146–159. Springer, Cham (2018). https://doi.org/10.1007/978-3-319-91602-6_10
4. Kuhrman, M, et al.: Hybrid software development approaches in practice: a European perspective. IEEE Softw. (2018)
5. Ambler, S.: Agile practices survey results, July 2009. http://www.ambysoft.com/surveys/practices2009.html. Accessed 08 June 2019
6. Chow, T., Cao, D.B.: A survey study of critical success factors in agile software projects. J. Syst. Softw. **81**(6), 961–971 (2008)
7. Forsgren, N., Humble, J., Kim, G.: Accelerate: The Science of Lean Software and DevOps: Building and Scaling High Performing Technology Organizations. IT Revolution Press, Portland (2018)
8. Graziotin, D., Wang, X., Abrahamsson, P.: Software developers, moods, emotions, and performance. IEEE Softw. **31**(4), 24–27 (2014)
9. Riemenschneider, C.K., Hardgrave, B.C., Davis, F.D.: Explaining software developer acceptance of methodologies: a comparison of five theoretical models. IEEE Trans. Softw. Eng. **28**(12), 1135–1145 (2002)
10. Overhage, S., Schlauderer, S., Birkmeier, D., Miller, J.: What makes IT personnel adopt scrum? A framework of drivers and inhibitors to developer acceptance. In: The Proceedings of the Annual Hawaii International Conference on System Sciences (2011)
11. Kroeger, T.A., Davidson, N.J., Cook, S.C.: Understanding the characteristics of quality for software engineering processes: a Grounded Theory investigation. Inf. Softw. Technol. **56**, 252–271 (2014)
12. Feiler, P., Humphrey, W.: Software process development and enactment: concepts and definitions. Software Engineering Institute, CMU/SEI-92-TR-004 (1992)
13. Johannesson, P., Perjons, E.: An Introduction to Design Science. Springer, Heidelberg (2014). https://doi.org/10.1007/978-3-319-10632-8
14. International Organization for Standardization, ISO/IEC 25010 Systems and Software Engineering - Systems and Software Quality Requirements and Evaluation (SQuaRE) - System and Software Quality Models, Geneva, Switzerland (2011)
15. Norman, D.A.: The Design of Everyday Things. Basic Books, New York (1988)
16. Nielsen, J.: Usability Engineering. Elsevier, Amsterdam (1994)
17. International Organization for Standardization: ISO/IEC 25040 Systems and Software Engineering – System and software Quality Requirements and Evaluation (SQuaRE) – Evaluation process, Geneva, Switzerland (2011)
18. Fontdevila, D., Genero, M., Oliveros, A.: Towards a usability model for software development process and practice. In: Felderer, M., Méndez Fernández, D., Turhan, B., Kalinowski, M., Sarro, F., Winkler, D. (eds.) PROFES 2017. LNCS, vol. 10611, pp. 137–145. Springer, Cham (2017). https://doi.org/10.1007/978-3-319-69926-4_11
19. Kontio, J., Bragge, J., Lehtola, L.: The focus group method as an empirical tool in software engineering. In: Shull, F., Singer, J., Sjøberg, D.I.K. (eds.) Guide to Advanced Empirical Software Engineering, pp. 93–116. Springer, London (2008). https://doi.org/10.1007/978-1-84800-044-5_4

20. Miranda, E.: Milestone Planning: A Participatory and Visual Approach (2018). https://www. researchgate.net/publication/328918275_A_Participative_Visual_Approach_to_Milestone_ Planning, https://doi.org/10.13140/rg.2.2.18969.06241. Accepted to be published in The Journal of Modern Project Management

21. Culver-Lozo, K.: The software process from the developer's perspective: a case study on improving process usability. In: Proceedings of the Ninth International Software Process Workshop, Airlie, VA, pp. 67–69 (1994)

22. Cockburn, A.: Agile Software Development: The Cooperative Game. Pearson Education, London (2006)

23. Franch, X., Carvallo, J.P.: Using quality models in software package selection. IEEE Softw. 20(1), 34–41 (2003)

24. Dreyfus, S.E., Dreyfus, H.L.: A five-stage model of the mental activities involved in directed skill acquisition. University of California/Berkeley Operations Research Center. DTIC ADA084551 (1980)

25. Basili, V, Caldiera, G., Rombach, H.D.: The goal question metric approach. In: Encyclopedia of Software Engineering. Wiley (1994)

26. Fenton, N.E., Pfleeger, S.L.: Software Metrics: A Rigorous and Practical Approach. CRC Press, Boca Raton (1997)

27. International Organization for Standardization: ISO/IEC 15939 Systems and Software Engineering – Measurement process, Geneva, Switzerland (2017)

28. Runeson, P., Höst, M.: Guidelines for conducting and reporting case study research in software engineering. Empirical Softw. Eng. 14, 131 (2009)

29. Wohlin, C., Runeson, P., Höst, M., Ohlsson, M.C., Regnell, B., Wesslén, A.: Experimentation in Software Engineering. Springer, Heidelberg (2012). https://doi.org/10.1007/978-3-642-29044-2

Short Tutorials

PROFES 2019: Tutorial Summary

Matthias Galster[1]([⊠]) [iD] and Dietmar Pfahl[2] [iD]

[1] University of Canterbury, Christchurch, New Zealand
mgalster@ieee.org
[2] University of Tartu, Tartu, Estonia
dietmar.pfahl@ut.ee

Abstract. The 20th International Conference on Product-Focused Software Process Improvement (PROFES 2019) was held in Barcelona, Spain. As part of PROFES 2019, four tutorials were held. Tutorials complemented the main conference program, offering participants hands-on experiences on topics related to product-focused software process improvement. In the following, a brief summary of these tutorials is given.

Keywords: PROFES 2019 · Tutorials · DevOps · Conformance checking · Grey literature · Data preparation

1 Tutorials at PROFES 2019

The 20th International Conference on Product-Focused Software Process Improvement (PROFES 2019) was held in Barcelona, Spain. Tutorials at PROFES 2019 covered a wide range of topics related to product-focused software process improvement from theoretical foundations to practical applications. Tutorials provided a valuable opportunity for conference participants to expand their knowledge and skills in specific topics under the umbrella of product-focused software process improvement. The tutorials aimed at participants from both industry and academia. PROFES 2019 included four half-day tutorials on November 27, 2019, the day before the main conference: (1) DevOps in Practice; (2) Conformance Checking: Relating Processes and Models; (3) Benefitting from Grey Literature in Software Engineering Research; (4) Hands-on Data Preparation.

2 Tutorial 1 – DevOps Practices

DevOps is currently one of the most popular topics in the software industry. Most big software vendors implement some kind of DevOps. This tutorial presented the foundations of DevOps and core practices. It offered a mix of theory and practice following a hands-on approach. The two main topics covered in this tutorial were: Infrastructure as Code and Continuous Delivery. These topics include other topics: immutable infrastructure, monitoring and observability, database versioning and evolution, feature toggles and canary releases. DevOps practices like Infrastructure as Code, Database

© Springer Nature Switzerland AG 2019
X. Franch et al. (Eds.): PROFES 2019, LNCS 11915, pp. 761–763, 2019.
https://doi.org/10.1007/978-3-030-35333-9

Versioning, Immutable Infrastructure and Continuous Delivery were presented using tools like Docker, Kubernetes, Vagrant, Jenkins, FlywayDB and Ansible.

Presenter: Nicolas Paez (Universidad de Buenos Aires and Universidad Nacional de Tres de Febrero, Argentina).

3 Tutorial 2 – Conformance Checking: Relating Processes and Models

This tutorial aimed at providing a concise introduction to conformance checking. Conformance checking defines models and methods to analyze the relation between the behavior of a process as captured by a process model and the behavior of it as captured by event data that is recorded by an information system during process execution. The goal was to introduce the essential ideas of how to relate modelled and recorded behavior on an intuitive level, and outline applications that may benefit from conformance checking.

Presenter: Josep Carmona (Universitat Politeecnica de Catalunya, Spain).

4 Tutorial 3 – Benefitting from Grey Literature in Software Engineering Research

Grey literature is becoming more and more important as a source of knowledge because software engineering practitioners write and share information in different forms of grey literature (GL) like blogs, videos or white papers. The overall goal of this tutorial was to present how software engineering research can benefit from the vast amount of information covered by GL. The participants of this tutorial learned how GL can be used for various aspects of software engineering research, e.g., shaping new directions of research, or using knowledge and evidence from grey literature in empirical studies in software engineering. First, the concept of GL in general and from the perspective of different disciplines, like health sciences or social sciences, was presented. Second, the concept of GL in software engineering and types of GL were presented. Third, ways how GL can be used in primary studies and secondary studies in software engineering were presented. In secondary studies, GL can be incorporated into multi-vocal literature reviews and grey literature reviews. The instructors presented their guidelines for these reviews. Finally, challenges and benefits of using GL in software engineering were discussed.

Presenters: Michael Felderer (University of Innsbruck, Austria), Vahid Garousi (Queens University, UK), Mika Mäntylä (University of Oulu, Finland), Austen Rainer (Queens University, UK).

5   Tutorial 4 – Hands-on Data Preparation

From a process point of view, CRoss-Industry Standard Process for Data Mining (CRISP-DM) describes six major steps for any data analysis project. After gaining business understanding, required data need to be identified and semantically understood, which requires domain knowledge, data engineering skills and data analysis knowledge. In this phase, it is essential to assess the quality of the data. Data understanding is the starting point for data integration and preparation. For the integration, various technologies are available. The goal of the analysis and the planned analysis approach influence the technology stack as well as an existing infrastructure. The analysis also poses concrete requirements on the data. The task of data preparation step is to extract the required data from their sources through transformation, cleaning, filtering, missing value treatment, etc. The explorative character of data analyses as well as the strong influence of the data preparation on the results of the analysis require that data preparation is performed repeatedly while parameters are changed based on evaluation results. In addition, due to the exploratory nature of an analysis it is often seen only in the course of the project, which data is actually important, how data needs to be prepared, and which data lead to better results. Consequently, data scientists spend a lot of time solely on data preparation. Within this hands-on tutorial, participants learned, based on concrete examples, how to kick-start a data analysis project (i.e., data integration, data preparation). Based on their experience from many projects, the presenters highlighted what the caveats are and how to avoid them. The tutorial used different examples from process improvement in Jupyter Notebooks.

Presenters: Andreas Jedlitschka (Fraunhofer Institute for Experimental Software Engineering, Germany) and Julien Siebert (Fraunhofer Institute of Experimental Software Engineering at Fraunhofer, Germany).

DevOps Practices Tutorial

Nicolás Paez[✉][iD]

Universidad Nacional de Tres de Febrero, Caseros, Argentina
nicopaez@computer.org

Abstract. DevOps is currently one of the most popular topics in the software industry. All the important software vendors have some kind of DevOps offering today. This popularity brings some confusion and for many people it is not completely clear yet what DevOps is. This article presents a summary of a DevOps tutorial that covers DevOps foundations and its core practices. The tutorial offers a mix of theory and practice with a hands-on approach. DevOps core practices like Infrastructure as Code and Continuous Delivery are presented using tools like Ansible, Docker, Kubernetes, FlywayDB and Jenkins.

Keywords: DevOps · Continuous delivery · Infrastructure as code

1 Introduction

DevOps is currently one of the most popular topics in the software industry [1]. The term DevOps comes from the union of Development and Operations but as noticed by Jabbari et al. [2] there is no unified definition of what it really is. Len Bass [3] defines DevOps as a set of practices that tend to reduce the time between the moment a change is generated in the source code of a system and the moment that change is effectively applied in the production environment, ensuring the quality of the whole process. Even when there are other definitions of DevOps, most of them translate into a specific set of practices and that is why Bass's definition is so appropriate. Depending on the author the list of DevOps practices varies but there is a core set of practices in which all authors agree. This tutorial is focused on 2 of those key practices: Infrastructure as Code and Continuous Delivery.

The learning objectives of the tutorial are

- Understand the set practices involved in the DevOps mindset.
- Experiment DevOps practices by using some popular tools usually used to implement those practices.

The tutorial is composed of 3 kinds of activities: short-lectures, hands-on exercises and facilitated discussions. Each topic is presented in a short-lecture and then the participants do some hands-on exercises with the guidance of the instructor. After analyzing practices in isolation a discussion is facilitated to debrief and contextualize each practice in the software delivery process.

© Springer Nature Switzerland AG 2019
X. Franch et al. (Eds.): PROFES 2019, LNCS 11915, pp. 764–765, 2019.
https://doi.org/10.1007/978-3-030-35333-9

2   Infrastructure as Code

According to Kief Morris [4] Infrastructure as Code is an approach to infrastructure automation based on software development practices. Infrastructure as Code emphasizes consistent and repeatable procedures for creating and updating infrastructure and configuration by representing in it plain text files that act as source code for an infrastructure as code tools. Any change required in the system is made in source code, and then rolled out to the system through automated processes that include validation and ensure repeatably and traceability. During the tutorial a map of tools is analyzed. A set of hands-on activities are performed using Ansible, Docker and Kubernetes.

3   Continuous Delivery

Continuous Delivery is set of capabilities that enable to get changes of all types (new features, fixes, configuration, etc.) into production or into the hands of the users in a quickly, safety and sustainable way [5]. During the tutorial the key principles and practices of Continuous Delivery are analyzed. Also some hands-on activities are performed using FlywayDB and Jenkins.

4   Take-Away Message

DevOps is not a methodology. DevOps is a mindset that involves a set of key practices and those practices require some tools. The tutorial allow the participants to meet and experiment with some of those tools. But tools are changing all the time. So beyond the tools, the important concerns are the practices the tools help to implement. Each organization and team has to think how to fit these practices in their specific context and processes and should also define which tools to use in order to implement these practices.

References

1. Version One.: 13th annual State of Agile Report. Version One (2018)
2. Jabbari, R., Ali, N.B., Petersen, K., Tanveer, B.: What is DevOps? A systematic mapping study on definitions and practices. In: ACM International Conference Proceeding Series (2016)
3. Bass, L., Weber, I., Zhu, L.: DevOps, A Software Architect's Perspective, 1st edn. Addison-Wesley Professional (2015)
4. Morris, K.: Infrastructure as Code, Managing Servers in the Cloud, 1st edn. O'Reilly Media (2016)
5. Forsgren, N., Humble, J., Kim, G.: Accelerate, Building and Scaling High Performing Technology Organizations, 1 edn. IT Revolution Press (2018)

Conformance Checking:
Relating Processes and Models

A Tutorial for Researchers and Practitioners

Josep Carmona[✉]

Computer Science Department, Universitat Politècnica de Catalunya,
Barcelona, Spain
jcarmona@cs.upc.edu

Abstract. The tutorial aims at giving participants a concise introduction to the field of conformance checking. Conformance checking defines models and methods to analyze the relation between the behavior of a process as captured by a process model and the behavior of it as captured by event data that is recorded by an information system during process execution. Our goal is to introduce the essential ideas of how to relate modelled and recorded behavior on an intuitive level, and outline the space of applications that may benefit from conformance checking.

1 Motivation

Process mining bridges the gap between process modelling on the one hand and data science on the other [3]. In many practical process mining applications, relating recorded event data and a process model is an important starting point for further discussion and analysis. Conformance checking, one of the main dimensions in process mining, provides the models and methods to analyze the relation between modeled and recorded behavior [1].

In the course of the last decade, manifold approaches to conformance checking have been developed in academia. With the respective models and methods become more mature, the field of conformance checking is subject to consolidation. That includes convergence on essential properties of conformance checking (e.g., in terms of axioms on how to quantify aspects of the relation between event data and process models), significant improvements of conformance checking efficiency that enables analysis of large, real-world processes, and, most prominently, an increasing interest and take-up in industry (e.g., by companies such as SAP and Celonis).

While a large number of scientific results on conformance checking have been published in recent years, there is a lack of a concise introduction to the essential concepts underlying it. With this tutorial, we intend to contribute to making these results more broadly accessible, for practitioners and researchers with, so far, little exposure to approaches for data-driven analysis of information systems in general, and process mining in particular.

© Springer Nature Switzerland AG 2019
X. Franch et al. (Eds.): PROFES 2019, LNCS 11915, pp. 766–767, 2019.
https://doi.org/10.1007/978-3-030-35333-9

2 Content

The PROFES community has already shown interest in the field of process mining [2]. This tutorial can be seen as a continuation of the aforementioned tutorial, where now the focus is narrowed-down to the dimension of conformance checking.

More concretely, we focus on three concepts: Processes, Process Models, and Event Logs, along with their relations. The tutorial starts with a short introduction to the concepts of event logs and process models. We then introduce fitness as a metric to compare event logs and models on an intuitive level, i.e. we use BPMN models and animations to explain the main ideas behind token-based replay and alignments without presenting any formal definition or algorithmic details.

In the second part of the tutorial, we introduce the notion of a 'process' or 'system' next to the event log and the model. Again, the above example will be used to make these concepts easily interpretable by a large audience. In this part, we will raise the awareness for the impact of the abstractions applied when obtaining event logs and modeling a process.

We will overview in an accessible way concepts such as precision, generalization, exceptions, illegal activities, fraud, etc., to outline the spectrum of relations between possible, recorded, and modelled behavior. We then discuss what actions can be taken to identify classes of deviations and how to deal with them in the context of conformance checking. We provide an intuitive overview of techniques for model-repair, log-repair, whitelisting, and blacklisting, as they have been recently adopted by respective solutions in industry. As part of that, we reflect on limitations and risks related to the use of conformance checking, as imposed, for instance, by event data that is not trust-worthy.

References

1. Carmona, J., van Dongen, B.F., Solti, A., Weidlich, M.: Conformance Checking - Relating Processes and Models. Springer, Cham (2018). https://doi.org/10.1007/978-3-319-99414-7
2. Janes, A., Maggi, F.M., Marrella, A., Montali, M.: From zero to hero: a process mining tutorial. In: Felderer, M., Méndez Fernández, D., Turhan, B., Kalinowski, M., Sarro, F., Winkler, D. (eds.) PROFES 2017. LNCS, vol. 10611, pp. 625–629. Springer, Cham (2017). https://doi.org/10.1007/978-3-319-69926-4_55
3. van der Aalst, W.M.P.: Process Mining - Data Science in Action, 2nd edn. Springer, Cham (2016). https://doi.org/10.1007/978-3-662-49851-4

Benefitting from Grey Literature in Software Engineering Research (Tutorial Summary)

Michael Felderer[1]([⊠]), Vahid Garousi[2], Mika Mäntylä[3],
and Austen Rainer[2]

[1] University of Innsbruck, Innsbruck, Austria
michael.felderer@uibk.ac.at
[2] Queen University Belfast, Belfast, UK
{v.garousi,a.rainer}@qub.ac.uk
[3] University of Oulu, Oulu, Finland
mika.mantyla@oulu.fi

Abstract. Grey literature is becoming more and more important as a source of knowledge because software engineering practitioners write and share information in different forms of grey literature like blogs, videos or white papers. The overall goal of this tutorial is to present ways in which software engineering research can benefit from the vast amount of information covered by grey literature. The participants of this tutorial will learn how grey literature can be used for various aspects of software engineering research, e.g., shaping new directions of research, or using knowledge and evidence from grey literature in empirical studies of software engineering.

Keywords: Grey literature · Multivocal literature reviews · Software processes · Evidence-based software engineering · Empirical software engineering

1 Introduction

Grey literature, which is typically neither formally published nor peer-reviewed literature, is becoming more important as a source of knowledge because software engineering practitioners write and share information in different forms of grey literature like blogs, videos or white papers [1]. Software engineering researchers who work in close collaboration with industry, have started to incorporate grey literature in their research. The instructors of this tutorial have therefore started to systematically investigate the role of grey literature in software engineering [2, 3] and they share their findings and experiences in this tutorial.

© Springer Nature Switzerland AG 2019
X. Franch et al. (Eds.): PROFES 2019, LNCS 11915, pp. 768–769, 2019.
https://doi.org/10.1007/978-3-030-35333-9

2 Description of the Tutorial

The overall goal of the tutorial is to define what grey literature is for software engineering and consider how it can be used in studies of software engineering. The tutorial does not have specific entrance requirements. It will be structured as follows and cover the following topics:

- **Motivation.** The need for integration of grey literature, and of specific analysis methods of grey literature is motivated by examples including study results from the authors [1, 3].
- **The general concept of Grey Literature.** The definition of the concept of grey literature is discussed from a general perspective. Definitions and applications are considered from other disciplines like health sciences, social sciences, natural sciences, and humanities.
- **Grey Literature in Software Engineering.** The concept of grey literature in software engineering and types of grey literature (like videos, blogs, white papers, etc.) are presented and discussed with the participants. Also, ways to classify grey literature and a model of the generation of grey literature content is presented.
- **Usage Scenarios and Analysis of Grey Literature in Software Engineering.** Ways in which grey literature can be used in primary studies and secondary studies in software engineering are presented, in particular.
  - *Application in primary studies*: The discussed application scenarios in primary studies comprise three scenarios, i.e., (1) analysis of grey literature materials with a qualitative approach, (2) analysis of grey literature with a quantitative approach and (3) reference of grey literature sources as related work or examples
  - *Application in secondary studies*: Different types of systematic literature studies including grey literature, i.e., multivocal literature reviews and grey literature reviews will be discussed. Then, the steps when performing such a review are presented based on the guidelines developed by the instructors [2]. The presented guidelines are explored by the participants.
- **Reflection.** Challenges and benefits of using grey literature in software engineering are presented and discussed together with the participants. Finally, the tutorial is closed.

The tutorial includes lectures on the covered topics, discussions with the participants, and hands-on exercises, where the participants explore the steps of a grey literature review in software engineering

References

1. Garousi, V., Felderer, M., Mäntylä, M.: The need for multivocal literature reviews in software engineering: complementing systematic literature reviews with grey literature. In: EASE 2016, pp. 1–6. ACM (2016)
2. Garousi, V., Felderer, M., Mäntylä, M.: Guidelines for including grey literature and conducting multivocal literature reviews in software engineering. Inf. Softw. Technol. **106**, 101–121 (2019)
3. Rainer, A., Williams, A.: Heuristics for improving the rigour and relevance of grey literature searches for software engineering research. Inf. Softw. Technol. **106**, 231–233 (2019)

Tutorial: Data Preparation – Tackle the Most Effort-Prone Phase in Data Projects

Adam Trendowicz, Julien Siebert[(⊠)], and Andreas Jedlitschka

Fraunhofer-Institut Für Experimentelles Software Engineering IESE,
Fraunhofer-Platz 1, 67663 Kaiserslautern, Germany
{adam.trendowicz,julien.siebert,andreas.jedlitschka}
@iese.fraunhofer.de

Abstract. From a process point of view, CRoss-Industry Standard Process for Data Mining (CRISP-DM) describes six major steps for any data analysis project. Having gained business understanding, required data need to be identified and semantically understood. In this phase, it is essential to assess the quality of the data. The analysis' goal and planned analysis approach influence the technology stack as well as an existing infrastructure. The analysis also poses concrete requirements on the data. The task of the data preparation step is to extract the required data from their sources through transformation, cleaning, filtering, missing value treatment, etc. The explorative character of data analyses as well as the strong influence of the data preparation on the results of the analysis require that data preparation is performed repeatedly while parameters are changed based on evaluation results. In addition, due to the exploratory nature of an analysis it is often seen only in the course of the project, which data is actually important, how data needs to be prepared, and which data lead to better results. Consequently, data scientist spends a lot of time solely with data preparation (up to 70% of the project effort). Within this tutorial, you will learn, based on concrete examples, how you kick-start your data analysis projects (i.e., data integration, data preparation). We will show, based on our experience from many projects, where the caveats lie and how you safely ship around them. During the tutorial, we will use different examples and will work together to implement data preparation steps in Jupyter Notebooks.

Keywords: Big data analytics · Data preparation · Data quality

1 Motivation

The most effort-consuming phase in data science projects is data preparation. No standard procedure that covers all potential data preparation issues exist. In this tutorial, you learn how to increase the efficiency of data preparation in order to gain faster insights into your data using data analytics. From a process point of view, the CRoss-Industry Standard Process for Data Mining (CRISP-DM) describes six major steps for any data analysis project [1]. After having gained *Business Understanding*, we need to identify and semantically understand required data (*Data Understanding*). This requires domain knowledge as well as data engineering and data analysis knowledge.

© Springer Nature Switzerland AG 2019
X. Franch et al. (Eds.): PROFES 2019, LNCS 11915, pp. 770–771, 2019.
https://doi.org/10.1007/978-3-030-35333-9

Therefore, data understanding is the starting point for data ingestion and data preparation.

The task of the *Data Preparation* step is to extract and prepare required data from their sources through transformation, cleaning, filtering, missing value treatment, etc. Each analysis technique states concrete requirements on the data. During the course of a project experts iteratively adjust which data is important, how data needs to be prepared and which data lead to better results. In addition, it is essential to assess the quality of the data. It is among the most critical steps of any data-driven project, be it about classical data analytics or artificial intelligence ("garbage in, garbage out"). Data analysts repeatedly perform the Data Preparation phase due to the explorative character of data analyses as well as to the strong influence of the Data Preparation on the results of the analysis. The analysis' goal, the planned analysis approach as well as technical aspects influence the technology stack used for data ingestion and Data Preparation. Data scientist spend a lot of time solely with Data Preparation (up to 70% of the project effort [2]).

2 Tutorial

Within this tutorial, you will learn basic approaches to prepare the data for your data analysis projects. Based on concrete examples and on our experience from various data analysis projects, we show typical data quality deficits and possible solutions to use during data preparation. You learn how to perform data preparation steps using the Jupyter Notebooks platform, Python and R programming languages. You will get an understanding of the necessity of the data preparation phase in CRISP-DM and get to know the methods and tools to assess data quality and learn how to mitigate commonly available issues. The tutorial covers the following topics: *Data Preparation*: Why is it important? What are the basic tasks of data preparation? *Data quality*: What is data quality? What are relevant aspects of it? What are the challenges of data quality management, e.g., in the context of big data? *Data Quality assessment and improvement*: How to analyze and visualize data quality? How to detect and handle potential data quality deficits? How to prepare data for specific analyses?

2.1 Target Group

Data Engineers and Data Scientists working with data in industrial context to develop or maintain data-driven business solutions.

References

1. Shearer, C.: The CRISP-DM model: the new blueprint for data mining. J. Data Warehous. **5**(4), 14–22 (2000)
2. Alegion: What data scientists tell us about AI model training today, checked on 24 June 2019

Author Index